Mexico at the World's Fairs

THE NEW HISTORICISM: STUDIES IN CULTURAL POETICS

Stephen Greenblatt, General Editor

1. *Holy Feast and Holy Fast: The Religious Significance of Food to Medieval Women,* by Caroline Walker Bynum
2. *The Gold Standard and the Logic of Naturalism: American Literature at the Turn of the Century,* by Walter Benn Michaels
3. *Nationalism and Minor Literature: James Clarence Mangan and the Emergence of Irish Cultural Nationalism,* by David Lloyd
4. *Shakespearean Negotiations: The Circulation of Social Energy in Renaissance England,* by Stephen Greenblatt
5. *The Mirror of Herodotus: The Representation of the Other in the Writing of History,* by François Hartog, translated by Janet Lloyd
6. *Puzzling Shakespeare: Local Reading and Its Discontents,* by Leah S. Marcus
7. *The Rites of Knighthood: The Literature and Politics of Elizabethan Chivalry,* by Richard C. McCoy
8. *Literary Practice and Social Change in Britain, 1380–1530,* edited by Lee Patterson
9. *Trials of Authorship: Anterior Forms and Poetic Reconstruction from Wyatt to Shakespeare,* by Jonathan Crewe
10. *Rabelais's Carnival: Text, Context, Metatext,* by Samuel Kinser
11. *Behind the Scenes: Yeats, Horniman, and the Struggle for the Abbey Theatre,* by Adrian Frazier
12. *Literature, Politics, and Culture in Postwar Britain,* by Alan Sinfield
13. *Habits of Thought in the English Renaissance: Religion, Politics, and the Dominant Culture,* by Debora Kuller Shuger
14. *Domestic Individualism: Imagining Self in Nineteenth-Century America,* by Gillian Brown
15. *The Widening Gate: Bristol and the Atlantic Economy, 1450–1700,* by David Harris Sacks
16. *An Empire Nowhere: England, America, and Literature from "Utopia" to "The Tempest,"* by Jeffrey Knapp
17. *Mexican Ballads, Chicano Poems: History and Influence in Mexican-American Social Poetics,* by José E. Limón
18. *The Eloquence of Color: Rhetoric and Painting in the French Classical Age,* by Jacqueline Lichtenstein, translated by Emily McVarish
19. *Arts of Power: Three Halls of State in Italy, 1300–1600,* by Randolph Starn and Loren Partridge
20. *Expositions: Literature and Architecture in Nineteenth-Century France,* by Philippe Hamon, translated by Katia Sainson-Frank and Lisa Maguire
21. *The Imaginary Puritan: Literature, Intellectual Labor, and the Origins of Personal Life,* by Nancy Armstrong and Leonard Tennenhouse

22. *Fifteen Jugglers, Five Believers: Literary Politics and the Poetics of American Social Movements,* by T. V. Reed

23. *Romancing the Past: The Rise of Vernacular Prose Historiography in Thirteenth-Century France,* by Gabrielle M. Spiegel

24. *Dearest Beloved: The Hawthornes and the Making of the Middle-Class Family,* by T. Walter Herbert

25. *Carnal Israel: Reading Sex in Talmudic Culture,* by Daniel Boyarin

26. *Dilemmas of Enlightenment: Studies in the Rhetoric and Logic of Ideology,* by Oscar Kenshur

27. *Writing and Rebellion: England in 1381,* by Steven Justice

28. *Roads to Rome: The Antebellum Protestant Encounter with Catholicism,* by Jenny Franchot

29. *The Renaissance Bible: Scholarship, Sacrifice, and Subjectivity,* by Debora Kuller Shuger

30. *Another Kind of Love: Male Homosexual Desire in English Discourse, 1850–1920,* by Christopher Craft

31. *Nobody's Story: The Vanishing Acts of Women Writers in the Marketplace, 1670–1820,* by Catherine Gallagher

32. *Mapping the Renaissance World: The Geographical Imagination in the Age of Discovery,* by Frank Lestringant, translated by David Fausett, with a Foreword by Stephen Greenblatt

33. *Inscribing the Time: Shakespeare and the End of Elizabethan England,* by Eric S. Mallin

34. *Resistant Structures: Particularity, Radicalism, and Renaissance Texts,* by Richard Strier

35. *Mexico at the World's Fairs: Crafting a Modern Nation,* by Mauricio Tenorio-Trillo

Mexico at the World's Fairs

Crafting a Modern Nation

Mauricio Tenorio-Trillo

UNIVERSITY OF CALIFORNIA PRESS
Berkeley   Los Angeles   London

The preparation of this work was made possible in part by a grant
from the National Endowment for the Humanities, an independent
federal agency

University of California Press
Berkeley and Los Angeles, California

University of California Press, Ltd.
London, England

© 1996 by
The Regents of the University of California

Library of Congress Cataloging-in-Publication Data

Tenorio-Trillo, Mauricio, 1962–
    Mexico at the world's fairs : crafting a modern nation / Mauricio Tenorio-Trillo.
    p.   cm. — (The new historicism ; 35)
    Includes bibliographical references and index.
    ISBN 978-0-520-30107-8 (pbk. : alk. paper)
    1. Trade shows—Mexico—History—20th century.   2. Trade shows—Mexico—
    History—19th century.   I. Title.   II. Series.

CONTENTS

LIST OF ILLUSTRATIONS / *ix*
PREFACE / *xi*
INTRODUCTION / *1*

PART I · PORFIRIAN MEXICO AND WORLD'S FAIRS

1. France and Her Followers / *15*
2. The Imperatives of Mexican Progress / *28*
3. Mexico and the World at Large / *38*
4. The Wizards of Progress: Paris 1889 / *48*
5. The Aztec Palace and the History of Mexico / *64*
6. Mexican Anthropology and Ethnography at the Paris Exposition / *81*
7. Mexican Art and Architecture in Paris / *96*
8. Mexican Statistics, Maps, Patents, and Governance / *125*
9. Natural History and Sanitation in the Modern Nation / *142*
10. Irony / *158*

PART II · WORLD'S FAIRS AND MEXICO AFTER THE REVOLUTION OF 1910

11. Toward Revolutionary Mexico / *181*

12. The 1922 Rio de Janeiro Fair / *200*

13. The 1929 Seville Fair / *220*

EPILOGUE / *241*
APPENDIX 1. THE PORFIRIAN WIZARDS OF PROGRESS / *255*
APPENDIX 2. THE ECONOMIC COST OF WORLD'S FAIRS / *262*
NOTES / *267*
BIBLIOGRAPHY / *331*
INDEX / *357*

ILLUSTRATIONS

1. The Mexican Alhambra, New Orleans 1884 / *42*
2. Building to house an international exhibition in Mexico / *46*
3. Covers of *México a través de los siglos* / *72*
4. Plans for two facades of the Mexican palace, Paris 1889 / *74*
5. Entrance to the Aztec Palace, Paris 1889 / *76*
6. Design for interior of the Aztec Palace, Paris 1889 / *79*
7. Interior of the Aztec Palace, Paris 1889 / *83*
8. Aztec-Inca dwelling in the "History of Habitation" exhibit, Paris 1889 / *86*
9. "Aztecs and Their Industries," Saint Louis 1904 / *87*
10. Jesús Contreras's sculpture *Tlaloc* / *106*
11. Contreras's *Centeotl* / *107*
12. Contreras's *Xochiquetzal* / *109*
13. Contreras's *Cuauhtémoc* / *110*
14. Contreras with his sculpture *Malgré-tout* / *111*
15. Poster for Contreras's company, Fundición Artística Mexicana / *113*
16. José María Velasco, *Valle de México desde el cerro de Santa Isabel* / *116*
17. Velasco, *La Cañada de Metlac* / *117*
18. Rodrigo Gutiérrez, *El Senado de Tlaxcala* / *119*
19. José Obregón, *El descubrimiento del pulque* / *120*
20. Sketch for a geological map of Mexico / *132*
21. Miguel Saldaña's henequen-processing machine / *135*
22. Maximino Río de la Loza's machine to avoid railroad accidents / *136*
23. Newspaper cartoon: "Doña Paz Trancazo, Ice Sculpture" / *163*
24. Newspaper cartoon: "Springtime in Tuxtepec" / *164*
25. Newspaper cartoon: "Niobe and Her Sons" / *165*
26. Facade of the Aztec Palace, Paris 1889 / *171*
27. Newspaper cartoon: "Our Facade in Paris" / *172*
28. Newspaper cartoon: "Escape-If-You-Can Street" / *174*
29. Tobacco advertisement depicting the Aztec Palace / *177*
30. Contreras's sculpture *Totoquihuatzin* / *183*

31. Maya ruins in Chicago / *186*
32. Mexican pavilion, Buffalo 1901 / *187*
33. Mexican pavilion, Saint Louis 1904 / *188*
34. Mexican pavilion, Paris 1900 / *192*
35. Contreras's model of the Mexican palace, Paris 1900 / *193*
36. Construction of the Mexican pavilion, Paris 1900 / *195*
37. Mexican pavilion, Rio de Janeiro 1922 / *207*
38. Indigenous motifs in tobacco advertising / *210*
39. Cuauhtémoc replica, Rio de Janeiro 1922 / *213*
40. Mexican pavilion, Seville 1929 / *226*
41. Sculpture and fountain of the Mexican pavilion, Seville 1929 / *229*
42. Victor Reyes and his mural in the Mexican pavilion, Seville 1929 / *230*
43. Mexican pavilion, Paris 1937 / *238*

PREFACE

Think for a moment of *The Book of Thousand and One Nights* as a model of historiographical narrative. History, it would be contested, cannot be so chaotic, inclusive, and unprofessional. Yet there is a logic, a crystalline sequence of argumentation, between and within the stories told in *The Book of Thousand and One Nights* that is, I believe, akin to the chaos that is history. But the writing of history has suffered what a learned seventeenth-century New Spanish poetess called *"hidropesía de mucha ciencia"*: *"Para todo se halla prueba / y razón en que fundarlo; / y no hay razón para nada de haber razón para tanto."*[1] In effect, through the constant work of our imagination and research, we have furnished history with an accessible profile. But if we were to be fair with history when writing it, our narratives would approximate more that of *The Book of Thousand and One Nights* without abandoning our linear monographs. This study is a monograph that, nonetheless, resembles the polyphony of a chronological history telling, for here an effort is made to respect the varied interactions and simultaneity of historical occurrence. Accordingly, the reader might find himself or herself shifting from account to account, detecting concepts, characters, or arguments that gradually become familiar. This familiarity constitutes the narrative plot of this work.

    The book is limited, however, both by our current way of arranging knowledge and by the author's ignorance. Throughout, I had to face these limitations in trying to tell a story. The repercussions of these limitations may be found in the constant interaction between a general, provocative, abstract, and speculative realm and a concrete, empirical, and temporally and spatially confined domain. Consequently, this study moves back and forth between general and abstract topics, such as nationalism and modernity, and the concreteness of Porfirian Mexico as represented at late-nineteenth-century world's fairs. In short, this study examines Mexican exhibits at world's fairs with the larger objective of evaluating how these exhibits reflected the emerging concept of an ideal modern Mexican nation as formulated during those decades. It is a history of Mexico set within the context of the origins of Western nationalism, cosmopolitanism, and modernism.

As a history of Mexico, this study suggests that cultural and political phenomena must be seen in a larger context from the second part of the nineteenth century to the 1920s. The historiographical gap created by the overwhelming preference of historians to study the Mexican Revolution of 1910 needs revision. Periodization is always an arm of our imagination, but if we are to mark the origins of modern Mexico, the Porfirian era (1877–1910) constituted the first period of relative social peace, political stability, and dynamic economic development since independence had been won in 1821, and it was during these years that the notion of a modern nation took hold.

As a study of modernity, this work attempts both to redefine the common dichotomy between tradition and modernity and to show how the global phenomena of nationalism occurred in the specific locale of Mexico. In this sense, the book seeks to recapture for Mexican history that subtle, fleeting, and quintessential nineteenth-century transitional moment between the emergence of modern, industrial, and capitalist progress and its acceptance as an ahistorical and natural scenario of humankind.

This work has benefited enormously from various academic and nonacademic studies. To call the approach of this book a theory would be both pretentious and ambitious; on the other hand, to fully enumerate the inspirations of this study would be a lengthy and redundant task because they are evident in every chapter. But empirical research guides this study, almost in the same way that a writer with no inventiveness looks for inspiration in a personal adventure or in history; this work is empirical research and all eclecticism implied therein.

The study consists of two parts, following an introductory chapter which develops a general scheme of the components of world's fairs and the elements of them that are emphasized in this study. The first part focuses on Porfirian Mexico's presence in world's fairs, especially in the Paris Universal Exhibition of 1889 as a paradigmatic example of the national drive toward modernity. Mexico's presence in Paris 1889 was the largest and most expensive display Mexico had ever put on at a world's fair. Although Mexico participated in numerous American expositions, throughout the nineteenth century France was the cultural point of reference for Latin American elites, and this in part explains the Mexican effort in 1889. But Mexico also had pragmatic goals in Paris 1889: to show the progress of Mexico and to change the common impression of a violent, uncivilized, insecure, and wild country and present instead the picture of Mexico as "the promised land." These efforts, it was believed, would eventually attract foreign investment and Northern European immigration. To produce this image, the Porfirian elite undertook to present in impressive fashion both the economic and the human resources of the nation for the world to see. Indeed, they consciously produced an ideal of what modern and progressive Mexico was supposed to look like.

Mexico's involvement in world's fairs paralleled the process of political and economic consolidation of the Porfirian elite. Moreover, the accumulated experience, common interests, and international links of this elite made possible the emergence of a group of professional world's fair experts that I call the "wizards of progress," who were able to construct the image of the modern nation at all levels.

Through analysis of the Mexican pavilion in Paris—the Aztec Palace— part 1 also undertakes journeys of inquiry into deep-rooted components of the Porfirian notion of a modern nation: history writing, science, arts, and irony.

Part 2 contrasts the 1889 exhibition with an overview of Mexico's presence at two postrevolutionary fairs, Rio de Janeiro (1922) and Seville (1929). This examination depicts the enduring nature of Mexico's national image from the 1880s to the 1920s. The Mexican Revolution occurred in a context of global political, social, and cultural transformation. The nineteenth-century model of world's fairs was radically transformed from the prototype of the Crystal Palace and the Eiffel Tower to a Disneyland model. Mexico's presence at world's fairs after 1910 displayed the adjustments of a changing and dynamic national elite to both its national circumstances and the international situation. Hence, part 2 shows that the changes and continuities in the postrevolutionary modern image of Mexico cannot be understood without consideration of nationalism and modernism as global phenomena.

The epilogue both advances tentative general conclusions and clarifies the use of concepts throughout the book. It is therefore presented in propositional essay-like terms, seeking to foster further research and to modestly challenge political and historiographical premises of the history of both Mexico and the modern world. Together, the introduction and the epilogue work as a brief historiographical and conceptual glossary of the book—though at different levels of abstraction.

This is, in sum, an account of histories that collided. Urged to incorporate the nation into the international circuits of capital, the Porfirian elite did not—could not—aim to modernize a nation of nearly ten million people spread out over a vast territory. But it did create an ideal type of modern Mexico, constantly updated for its national and international acceptance. Pursued for so long, and with such intensity, this model eventually came to be the nation, the sole entity that not only the elites but also the growing middle class and urban sector could recognize as their own. Thus the image of the modern nation went from abstract, propagandistic form to quasi-essence; an essence which was adapted and redefined by the post-1910 revolutionary governments. There was no other choice, because indeed there was no paradise of pristine and absolute modernity, and it was impossible to stop the transformation, re-creation, and invention of traditions, either for Mexico or for Paris itself. This is, therefore, a history of Mexico and yet, at the same time, a report on Western modernity.

Frederick P. Bowser made this work possible in all sorts of ways. I thank him for both his kindness and his critical respect for my work. To him go my profound gratitude and esteem. Helena María Bousquet Bomeny, David Brading, John Cowens, Jeff Fear, Stephen Haber, Charles R. Hale, Ramón González Ponciano, Alan Knight, John Lear, C. López Beltrán, Seth Meisel, Jean Meyer, Sonia Moss, Paolo Riguzzi, Carmen Ruiz, Peter Stansky, William Summerhill, William Tobin, and Josefina Vázquez generously contributed their advice and comments. Professors Charles A. Hale and Richard Warren were especially helpful in the last stages of this manuscript, when their intelligence and patience were most appreciated. I value the support of all of these persons, and I am flattered by their friendship. I also wish to thank the Department of History and the Center for Latin American Studies at Stanford University for their invaluable support, as well as the Centro de Investigación y Docencia Económicas A.C. in Mexico City for granting me the time to make this manuscript into a real book. Finally, I thank both the anonymous readers of the University of California Press for their important critiques and suggestions and Sarah K. Myers for her invaluable help in the editing of my tropical use of the English language.

Unless there is indication to the contrary, quotations are presented in my translation, though Lucía Rayas, José Gabriel Martínez, Cindy Avitia, Gregory Greenway, and Dale Yeatts assisted in the translation.

This book is for Apen, Lilia, Leonor, and Arcelia, from whose wisdom I have not been able to flee.

Introduction

On the Universe of Fairs

In the modern world, progress is the standard by which the age prefers to measure itself. The history of modern progress is the history of the self-awareness of progress and modernity; that is, of how modern times produced a comprehensive picture of itself. This transformation was conceivable only by the modern view of history as a totality that progresses—both as a matter of fact and as a form of knowledge—but that is never completed because the future always remains unidentified. The consciousness of this totality in a particular span of time has formed what historians have habitually called an era, an epoch. Certainly, and however post-this-and-that we may feel, we must modestly realize that the growing secularization, rationalization, and technologization brought about by the modern era, together with our inability to escape our own present, have made "the modern" our inescapable frame of reference. As if we are all partners in crime, we have modernity as our common code: to it we constantly refer; on it we depend. But to what extent? This study of world's fairs seeks to recount a history that belongs to the fleeting realm between the emergence of modern, industrial, and capitalist progress and its duration as a seemingly ahistorical and natural stage of humankind, between what is already history, albeit of yet-unclear meaning, and what is difficult to observe before us because it molds the consciousness of our own times.[1]

World's fairs are excellent vantage points from which to examine these phenomena. Indeed, nineteenth-century world's fairs were the quintessence of modern times almost as much as were the cities that hosted them—London, Paris, and Chicago—because metropolitan centers that were truly bubbles of universal modernity arose in the Western world during this period. These cities were cosmopolitan, financial, and cultural nuclei that concentrated and combined both national and international trends. Powerful European and American cities offered both a culture and an order that were believed to be ecumenical and atemporal yet were in fact full of incongruities and, above all, unmanageable. Late-nineteenth-century cosmopolitan cities combined canonized fashions, habits, and aesthetic forms with the uncontrollable chaos of inequality, marginality, and practices of survival and protest adopted in desperation by large segments of their inhabitants. By contrast, world's fairs were the controlled portrayals of these cosmopolitan cores, as much as they were the cities' greatest spectacles.

World exhibitions were conscious universal representations of what was thought to be progress and modernity, and they were thus both the métier and the ideal rendition of the modern city. Such exhibitions aimed to be object lessons about those beliefs, and often, indeed, their vestiges became the symbols of modern cities. But a late-nineteenth-century world's fair was also invariably a magnificent show, an "oasis of fantasy and fable at a time of crisis and impending violence."[2]

To investigate the nineteenth-century world's fairs is to grasp the internal composition of the awareness of modernity. The fairs embodied and fostered primary components of nineteenth-century modern existence: the belief in positive, universal, and homogeneous truth; the presumption of freedom achieved and the inherent contradictions of this idea; the concept of ending history by recapitulating the past and controlling the future (that is, the potential for considering the present as the best of all possible times, which has already revealed the essential course of the future); and the creed of nationalism as an intrinsic part of both international cosmopolitanism and economic imperialism. These ideas guide this study, leading it both to the nineteenth and the twentieth centuries.

UNIVERSAL TRUTHS

In the last part of the nineteenth century, the ultimate foundations of progress were held to be science and industry. Both were paranational, natural, objective, and unstoppable forms of human production and knowledge. The world's order and self-confidence were set accordingly. The era of progress assembled an ideal picture of itself, and this picture became the optimal model of how the world ought to be. Only modern times were capable of delimiting a comprehensive view of how all that belonged to them looked. Once this modern world picture emerged, cosmopolitanism was made possible in all spheres: science, art, costumes, and technology.

As a common experience of accelerated time and simultaneity, since its inception the modern world picture was composed of various and often contradictory versions. And yet, as a more or less harmonious abstraction, the picture was by necessity articulated and developed independently of views and facts of the world. After all, what has been regarded as modern has never referred to the real world; it has conformed to notions about the most advanced and optimal world as made publicly intelligible by economic, political, and intellectual elites.

Nineteenth-century universal exhibitions were consciously erected to satisfy the requirements of this comprehensive picture; in turn, they reinforced the authenticity of such a picture. They were conceived to be a miniature but complete version of modern totality. And in the quest for universalism and completeness, world's fairs reincarnated the principle that had fostered late-eighteenth-century encyclopedias: they reinforced the possibility of conceiving a general picture of the world. They epitomized what Ortega called "the disquieting birth of a new reliance based on mathematical reasoning."[3] They could never be more than an attempt, however, because the modern world was too multifarious and complex to be homogeneously and harmoniously represented. Therefore, the idea of modern became an unobtainable and supreme metaphor, one which nonetheless was included in each thing that was thought to be modern.

World's fairs were thus selective versions of the picture they aimed to represent. They were moments when industry and science could exist with all of their virtues and none of their imperfections. They were natural residences of industrial innovation, as well as of scientific and commercial development. Therefore, nineteenth-century world's fairs were indeed petite cosmos of modernity formed, observed, and copied for all modern nations—extravagant spectacles for the confirmation of universal truths.

For today's historians, it is not clear whether the exhibits at world's fairs aimed to confirm belief in scientific and industrial progress by making the beliefs come true or aspired to be celebrations that honored those universal truths in a quasi-religious way with countless symbolic appeals: the challenge of the weight and strength of a steel building, the numerous industrial, commercial, and social statistics, the bright reality of electric lights, and the very altitude of the Eiffel Tower.

This study examines how Mexico joined the world's fair circuit in order to learn, imitate, and publicize its own possession of the universal truths of progress, science, and industry. It shows how the Mexican elite, in doing so, had to confront an ideal reality that was difficult to understand in its full scope and simultaneity. Yet it was easy to imitate. Consequently, Mexico had to undertake an additional selection in the already selective nature of world's fairs, in order to make the idea of the modern world even more suitable for the Mexican elites' own circumstances and interests. That additional selection is what came to be known as Mexican: Mexican sciences, Mexican art, Mexican nationhood. . . .

In participating in world's fairs, however, the Mexican elites learned the universal truths in order to consolidate their national and international integrity. In fact, they mastered what was fundamental in those universal truths: form, style, and facade. This mastery was especially visible in three aspects of Mexico's presence at late-nineteenth-century fairs: the scientific exhibits, the statistical demonstrations, and the constant use of a scientific discourse to express everything from an understanding of public administration to the effects of pulque on the Indian population; from the measurement of skulls to the calculation of the resistance of the hymens of Mexican women. These tools were used to emphasize the necessary components of a modern nation: a well-defined and well-integrated territory, a cosmopolitan culture, good sanitation conditions, and a racial homogeneity that squared with Western notions of white supremacy.

THE IDEA OF FREEDOM

World's fairs promoted the idea of freedom as it has been understood in the political, economic, and social thought of the West since the late eighteenth century. Rousseau, for example, believed that history was the unfolding of human freedom to achieve self-consciousness in order to be even more free. In turn, belief in free economic decisions governed by invisible rules overthrew the meaning of moral economy, thus marking the beginning of neoclassical economic thought. Reason, in enlightened thought, had liberated humankind; history was only the development of reason. This modern freedom was what world's fairs acclaimed. Universal exhibitions were neither carnivals of collective or individual passions nor mere rituals of harvest. Their festival character was, above all, the celebration of the human accomplishment of productive liberty that was epitomized in the veneration of free commerce. In the report of the 1889 Paris exposition, Alfred Picard traced the history of world's fairs back to the proclamation of freedom of commerce and industry in 1791, when, he argued, "public administrators, learned and worried about the country's future, understood the vices and dangers of an ominous regime which kills initiative, suffocates progress, and places national production in the most humiliating situation of inferiority."[4] Indeed, "the idea of trade was transformed from the relatively simple exchange of goods for profit, to a concept having metaphysical dimensions."[5] Freedom to profit, to purchase, to sell, to exhibit, and to advertise, it was assumed, would not only naturally develop but would also ultimately serve to equalize humankind with the immense wealth produced therefrom. World's fairs, then, were above all expressions of belief in the civilizing capabilities of the free market and a laissez-faire economy. They strived to be the visible and tangible attestations to the modern promises of freedom and equality. Hence a description of London's 1851 world's fair claimed that "[a]s the wind carries winged seeds over the earth, so commerce carries arts, and civilization, and humanity as a consequence."[6]

Like the terms *republic* and *nation*, the word *democracy* was, of course, fundamental to the concept of modern freedom. The connotation of democracy had often changed, however. At times it tended to have a social connotation (equality); at other times it favored political aspects (popular representation). Modern republican freedom—understood as the political and social rights granted by the French Revolution—was to democracy what in fact democracy was to late-nineteenth-century political regimes: a fundamental philosophical principle, not an indispensable practice. Thus democracy, without a fixed meaning, was conceived by special, and often nondemocratic, adjectives—authoritarian, conservative, socialist, liberal, caesarean. The need for an economically or militarily strong state and the heavily nationalistic environment made democracy and its inherently ambivalent liberty dispensable though valuable components of the model modern nation. Economic and productive laissez-faire was at the core of the late-nineteenth-century's pride in freedom.

In the great world's fairs of the nineteenth century, Mexico aspired to participate in the economic advantages and civilizing effects of commerce. The Porfirian elite created commercial commissions to promote Mexico's traditional and yet-to-be-discovered raw materials. They expected those products to give Mexico a place in the international economy.

In turn, freedom as a political virtue was understood as peace. Mexican intellectuals followed the legal and philosophical discussions of the French Third Republic and proposed constitutional limitations to a strong government. Peace, however, was Mexico's greatest achievement and also the supreme achieved liberty that became freedom from violence and uncertainty. In Mexico, as in the French Second Empire, the term *democracy* became synonymous with *republic*. The concept of a Mexican republic already included as much democracy as was possible in a country that could not even attempt to hide its internal inequality and racial differences, let alone afford the luxury of effective suffrage. Therefore, the Porfirian elite decided to exhibit in universal expositions the advantages of a strong government. And Mexico's authoritarian and enlightened government stood in good stead at world's fairs hosted by countries like France, which, however modern, were both constantly facing the ungovernability of democracy and maneuvering its meanings.

THE GREAT ENDS

World's fairs would have not been conceivable if the concept of universal progress had not offered a chance to experience contemporaneity as a sort of culminating moment. Within the sense of progressive, linear time, all present tense became unmistakably paradise, and the various exhibited phenomena of the modern world were perceived most of the time with admiration—but some of the time with terror or nostalgia.

Technology and progress made it possible to appreciate present time as the best of all feasible worlds, and universal expositions were the vivid confirmations of the greatness of the present tense. The understanding of the present was composed of a specific recapitulation of the past and exceptional previews of the future. In the 1900 Paris universal exposition, for instance, a pamphlet argued that "the expositions are not only days of leisure and gaiety in the midst of the toils of the people. They appear, at long intervals, as the summits from which to measure the course we have traveled. Mankind goes out from them comforted, full of courage and animated with profound faith in the future."[7] Along similar lines, a commentator on the 1904 Saint Louis world's fair observed that "expositions accentuate the deficiencies of the past, give us a realization of our present advantages, predict the developments of the near future, and equip the arm and brain alike of the mechanic, the engineer and the philosopher for further and immediate advances into the realms of the possible."[8]

Although the notion of progress had achieved visible manifestations and an extensive theoretical corpus by the 1880s, to sense that the final stage of history had been achieved was not necessarily to share in the optimistic industrial view of the world. The feeling was also expressed in what world expositions overlooked in their enthusiasm and pomposity—the sensation of decadence, a weakening of the moral and intellectual strength of the times; the sense that the "events experienced during a lifetime" could seem to be not in the present but in the past.[9] In fact, for some late-nineteenth-century modernists, all that seemed familiar and secure was disappearing, and there was neither an assurance of future progress nor anything by which to teach individuals how to live in what appeared to be a weightless present. As Baudelaire said in commenting on the 1855 Paris world's fair, "but where is, I ask you, future's guarantee of progress? . . . Within the realm of imagination, the idea of progress . . . appears to be a gigantic absurdity, something so grotesque it reaches the horrendous."[10] Thus, in their affirmation of a Panglossian world of progress, late-nineteenth-century world's fairs were bright lights that did not enable one to see the shadows beyond.

Hence world's fairs encompassed and confronted two contradictory connotations of modernism. Expositions were capitals of modernism informed by industrial optimism. But they were also unintended stages on which to view the achievements of the age while deploring the accompanying degeneration of the spirit. In this sense, world's fairs furnished images and pretexts for quintessential modernists such as the young Eliot, whose early work, "The Man Who Was King," was inspired by his observations of the Philippine village displayed at the 1904 Saint Louis world's fair;[11] Dostoyevsky, who was sarcastic in the face of the "halcyon days" of the 1851 Crystal Palace, which covered everything with calculated reasoning but also (in his view) with boredom and desperation;[12] that cunning observer, Henry Adams, who saw the 1893 Chicago Columbian Exposition and, full of amazement, said, "After this vigorous impulse, nothing remained for a historian but to ask—how long and how far?"[13]

From the great openings to the colossal closings, world's fairs epitomized a full cycle of the linear and progressive realization of time. And yet they were ephemeral, passing moments of self-congratulation and self-deceit. Each exhibition was like a succinct epilogue for history, because the life span of a fair was as evanescent as it was complete: modernity's "eternity in an hour." They were, as a U.S. senator noted in 1889, "the flash photograph[s] of civilization on the run."[14] Their short existence certified the infinite power of their creators: technology, industry, and capital. Therefore, on one hand, it was possible for them to become moments of reconciliation—all nations together despite past troubles and advancing increasingly paranational interests. On the other hand, rather than mere futurist theaters, they were able to amalgamate past and present promises. They included the future, but only insofar as it was an inevitable outcome of present greatness.

Consequently, the concept of great ends constituted the historical consciousness of modern progress and the control of the discernible future. Thus the fairs were occasions for reviewing the Western past and its contrasts and for evaluating the antique and the different, by rewriting the past and by gaining and governing the exotic. In this sense the colonial exhibits in French world's fairs were the archetypical expressions of a blend of exoticist, economic, and imperialist desires. These displays lasted until the 1940s, when colonies were neither politically nor economically profitable, as if a nation could not be modern or cosmopolitan without its beloved colonies.

Confidence in the superiority of the Western present—and thus of the inferiority of any other past, present, or future—was achieved through sciences—anthropology, scientific history, ethnology, criminology, archaeology, economics, sociology, medicine, architecture, engineering, and so forth. Furthermore, the goal of world's fairs was to assure that only one future could be derived from their revision and reinvention of the past: that of inevitable progress.

Mexico's presence at world's fairs shows how Mexicans were capable of enjoying the grand finales while presenting themselves as part of them. But it also shows how Mexicans' self-positioning in the last stage of evolutionary time made them the most fit to exercise the power they already had domestically. In fact, Mexico in nineteenth-century world's fairs shared Europe's orientalist and exoticist concerns and in turn undertook an "autoethnography." It fed the hunger of these exhibitions for exotic objects and people. Mexico thus offered indigenous food and drink, dresses, and *tipos populares* (popular characters) at the fairs; in the same way, it exhibited the head of the Indian Juan Antonio in Paris 1889 and Indian people in the so-called Street of Mexico exhibited at the 1901 Buffalo world's fair. In turn, what the fairs epitomized in their rewriting of the past and conquest of the exotic, the Porfirian elite did with their own country's history and reality.

In sum, "the normal organization of humanity"[15] that world's fairs aimed to enact achieved its ephemeral grand finales in the nineteenth century when they were, as the great French critic of modern bourgeois life, Flaubert, described them, *"sujet de délire du XIXe siècle"* (a cause of the delirium of the nineteenth century).[16] Neither before nor since has the self-consciousness of an era obtained such a visible, comprehensive, and astonishing materialization.

NATIONALISM

World's fairs emerged out of—and embodied—nationalistic interests in an international cosmopolitanism.[17] For the nation-empires of the late nineteenth century, universal exhibitions were both settings for the display of power and expansionist interests and part of the paraphernalia of presumed racial and cultural superiority. Impressive military exhibits thus contrasted with the spectacles of flags, national anthems, and national culinary and literary traditions. In fact, nineteenth-century fairs were often the zenith of particular patriotic calendars.

For impoverished nations, in contrast, world's fairs were opportunities for being part, albeit briefly, of the cosmopolitan concert of nations, to be one with the modern community of values, beliefs, and concerns. Simultaneously, world's fairs were showcases for the exhibition of whatever was demanded by the international market of commodities and ideas, a stage on which poor nations could exhibit everything from their raw materials to their native peoples and customs.

As nationalistic commemorative events, world's fairs included all modern forms of expression—from art to science, from commercial propaganda to statistics, from landscape canvases to architectural structures.[18] In this way, through universal exhibitions and their assembled belief in universal truths, freedom, and ideas of great ends, nations were imbued simultaneously with a recognizable and acceptable national uniqueness and an approved cosmopolitanism and modernity.

But world's fairs were also sites for the encounter of antagonistic views. Nationalistic, cultural, and racial prejudices battled in the images, symbols, and commentaries of visitors to world's fairs. For instance, remarking on the 1893 Chicago Columbian Exhibition, the American artist W. Hamilton Gibson claimed that the exposition was the realization of the "Heavenly City," or the "New Jerusalem"—and to him its creators were almost gods. At the same exposition, the Franco-Argentine historian Paul Groussac saw in

Chicago a mammothlike expression of American primitivism, a display of a "young nation, newly arrived at the historical scene," a sad effort of a naive people. "Pobre ¡White City!" he concluded.[19]

Late-nineteenth-century world's fairs were thus the most comprehensive and outrageous attempts to portray in miniature a modern picture of the world. Indeed, because the rise of modern industrial societies made possible both the universal language of progress and the world extension of fairs, to analyze fairs is both to make a checklist of modernity's components and to dissect the craftiness of nationalism as a global phenomenon.

World's fairs, albeit scientifically managed, contained the contradictions inherent in the very attempt to reproduce the modern world in miniature. As a picture of the modern world itself, a world exposition was the simulacrum of something that never had a concrete existence. Nevertheless, the modernity of the times resided in the conscious endeavor to isolate a coherent, optimistic, and promising representation of the world. Ironies and conflicts were inevitable in such an attempt.

For instance, cultural, economic, and political nationalism was at odds with both cultural and political cosmopolitanism. Cosmopolitanism was a model of modernity that simultaneously required the homogenization of all human characteristics and desires and recognized and appreciated the exotic and bizarre. That was an insurmountable existential irony: an organized model of the world, and a fascination with what was not part of the model but which ought to be part of the picture of the modern world. In addition, the very national need to be cosmopolitan seemed to be in conflict with the requirement of being culturally and racially unique and, presumably, superior.

Furthermore, whereas world's fairs did not reflect the contradictions of the modern world, they displayed so-called progress in the well-being of the masses, as if that progress came solely from technological advancement and philanthropy and was not prompted by fear of the growing discontent of peasants and workers. However, nineteenth-century world's exhibitions gradually started to display new concerns that had to do with the growing problems of modern times. For example, by 1900 social economy exhibitions and women's pavilions were part of the ideal conception of the world.

What was more ironic about the values epitomized by world expositions was their momentariness. For the astute observer, the short life of world's fairs was less a testimony to technological and industrial improvement than a caution about the universality and reliability of the pledges symbolized by world's fairs, a warning that all good things could not last forever. Implicit doubts abounded. Why were not modern times a perennial fair of progress?

Both questions inquire into the sincerity of what world's fairs exhibited and what they ignored. Both questions certainly address the same predicament, namely, the dichotomy between the real—that mutating and historically created reality we strive to grasp—and the fictional—that imagined actuality we assign to human beings in history. World's fairs are valuable for historians not to establish the falsity of modern capitalist ideologies but to situate the parameters and changing characteristics of the disparity between a presumed reality and its perception both by contemporaries and by historians. Therein, I believe, lies a clue for understanding the history of modernity as more than a purely economic phenomenon.

By the 1930s the Western world as conceived and defined during the nineteenth century seemed to be undergoing serious political, social, and cultural transformation. The Baudelairean critics of modern times were becoming the prophets of modernist disenchanted thought. Around 1910, it was asserted, even human character changed radically. That assertion was made not by a Mexican revolutionary in reference to the Mexican Revolution but by Virginia Woolf, commenting on the aesthetic, cultural, and social transformation that Europe underwent between 1910 and 1914.[20] The nineteenth century finally concluded in 1914, historian Eric Hobsbawm has argued.[21] Consequently, the monumental nineteenth-century world's fairs became unrepeatable. The picture of the modern world changed, and its comprehensive pocket portraits, the world's fairs, acquired a new nature.

The survival of world's fairs throughout the twentieth century illustrates how durable belief in progress has been. However, whereas late-nineteenth-century expositions (from the 1860s to the 1910s) were the paradise of modern optimism, world's fairs during the 1920s and 1930s became the epitome of modernist ambivalence. Ironically enough, it was progress itself and its avatars that made obsolete expositions like those that created the Crystal Palace, the Eiffel Tower, or the White City. Modernity is ungrateful: it devours its own portraits, thus making its identity even more ambiguous. This is so because, first, the universal expositions, as miniature ideals of the virtues of progress, had to confront the growing intellectual and artistic criticism of progress in the first decade of the twentieth century. World's fairs lost their technical optimism and innocence. In turn, the philanthropic, Saint-Simonian type of optimism that gave French fairs their concern with social economy in the nineteenth century was dimmed by growing socialist and anarchist discontent. Second, industrial and technological progress itself made it impossible to comprise all human production in a single space-time location. It was not only difficult but useless to try to encompass and classify the entire production of modern industry, agriculture, mining, and sciences. Instead, countless specialized fairs began to take place all over the world: displays of machinery, art, agricultural products, and so forth. Finally, although the nationalist and imperialist aspects that propelled international expositions in the last part of the nineteenth century did not significantly decrease during the first decades of the twentieth century, the more or less stable crystallization of European national identities transformed the general symbolic displays. Museums, scientific exhibits, sporting events, and, especially, the emergence of radical nationalism and massively destructive wars fulfilled the symbolic functions that had been entrusted to fairs. Ironically enough, the nationalistic ideologies that had emerged during the second half of the nineteenth century radicalized in the 1910s and 1920s, thus making partially obsolete the nationalistic uses of world's fairs.

Moreover, by the beginning of the twentieth century modern capitalism had produced what thereafter would become the mainstays of world's fairs: great corporations, tourism, and mass consumption with its inherent propaganda. Throughout nearly a century of world expositions, the liberty they epitomized gradually conquered unimaginable economic and ideological frontiers. International corporations started to emerge. With them came sophisticated advertisements disseminated by the latest technology and a massive appropriation of popular taste and consciousness.

Still, today's or tomorrow's universal exhibitions will follow their nineteenth-century counterparts because, as William McKinley, the U.S. president who was assassinated during the 1901 Buffalo fair, noted, "Expositions are the time-keepers of progress."[22] In the late twentieth century, world exhibitions seek to continue this role because the belief in universal truths, in productive freedom, in progress, and in national symbols, however dispersed and weak, remains alive. Yet the modern world picture has suffered numerous cracks. What would the paradise of modernity look like if we were to delineate it in these overwhelmingly disenchanted times? The great future imagined by past visionaries is not in the present but in the past, in the great late-nineteenth-century universal expositions. They were the "futures of the past," and today, because of their very attempt at totality and progressivism, they appear to be part of modern capitalism's nostalgia for a golden age. Late-twentieth-century world's fairs are themselves less an endeavor to continue to portray the modern world than an effort to duplicate previous attempts: the nineteenth-century universal expositions that have become modernity's archetype.[23]

In effect, Disneyland has become the model of twentieth-century world's fairs, a "degenerated utopia" that was a particular ideology materialized in the form of a myth.[24] As such, late-twentieth-century world's fairs reflect the era's supports (international capital and mass consumption) and enduring obsession (nostalgic faith in progress). They are as modern as the Quixote who finally realized he was insane; but they are Quixotic efforts to continue the delirium, as if Alonso Quijano would decide, once aware of his madness, to play again the role of Knight for the sole sake of nostalgia. Nonetheless, because of their extremely futurist emphasis—which always becomes a record of past promised futures—the fairs are the headquarters of the twentieth century: echoes of Disneyland or Hollywood.

To examine the role of powerless and peripheral nations such as Mexico in the fairs of the nineteenth and early twentieth centuries is to write the history of what modernity and progress have meant for them: a continual, tiresome, expensive, hopeless, and yet unavoidable attempt. World exhibitions were, in the words of Mexican Minister Manuel Fernández Leal, the opportunity for Mexico to become a "part of the admirable group of countries that, sharing ideals, ambitions, and trends, advance together, led by progress."[25]

In 1889, for instance, Mexico was in Paris with the expressed goal of learning from and duplicating the French example. This was so because Paris was indeed the "capital of the nineteenth century." Despite France's economic weakness vis-à-vis England, by the late nineteenth century French culture was believed to be the natural and universal conclusion of the evolution of modern Western thought. This belief was given substance by the predominance of French culture throughout the Western world and by France's notorious patriotism based on the idea of France as the center of the universe. Jules de Michelet, one of the great creators of the epic of universal France, modestly but confidently argued that "France imports and exports new ideas enthusiastically and builds on them with a wonderful strength. It is the legislating country of modern times, just as Rome was for antiquity."[26]

Indeed, for Mexico, Paris was the arbiter of progress, as it was for all of the nineteenth century Western world. Elisée Reclus, the insightful French geographer, clearly saw this at the beginning of the twentieth century: "Paris is the city Mexicans consider the center of the world. . . . It is to Paris that they turn to find out what is good or bad, to ask about science, art, poetry, novel ideas or the futility of fashion, the nonsense of false spirits, the perversity of vice."[27] Accordingly, it is only natural to take as my focus of analysis a Parisian fair. Ironically, the ambitions of Mexico and Paris were the same—the attempt at modernity proved to be what modernity consisted of. The supreme and complete modernity that Mexicans aimed to reach had never existed. Mexico began its entrance into the modern world during the late nineteenth century, and thereafter its development and problems would fundamentally be those of the modern world. To learn the cultural or intellectual lessons of the late-nineteenth-century modern world was relatively easy, because, after all, cosmopolitanism was nothing more than a set of parochial figures made universal. What was difficult was to be powerful, because power was, and is, a matter of competition, exploitation, and comparative advantage. There was no fixed paradise of modernity, and it was impossible for either Mexico or Paris to stop the transformation, invention, and re-creation of traditions.[28]

ONE

Porfirian Mexico and World's Fairs

ONE

France and Her Followers

Paris and its fairs were long the laboratory and the school in which statesmen, scientists, and artists tested and learned about the modern world. The meaning of Mexico's presence in Parisian fairs can be grasped by asking two questions: What did universal expositions mean to France? What did France mean to Mexico's Porfirian elite? This chapter deals with these questions in order to place Mexico's concept of a modern nation in its historical and ideological context and to trace the wellsprings of what Mexico aspired to be during and after the Porfiriato—from the 1870s to the 1910s, in fact the first thirty years of relative political and social stability for independent Mexico.

THE PARIS 1889 FAIR AND ITS PARTICIPANTS

The first issue of the *Bulletin de l'Exposition Universelle de Paris 1889* asserted that "the law of progress is immortal, as progress itself is infinite."[1] Armed with this faith in progress, the 1889 world's fair celebrated what the modern world considered the triumph of modern democratic, liberal, and republican values. Despite both domestic and foreign resistance, the explicit purpose of the exposition was to honor the centennial of the French Revolution of 1789.[2] It was a universal as well as an international fair because it proposed to include all of humankind's knowledge and production in natural, hierarchical order.[3] This intention was expressed in a specific classification of products into groups that corresponded to a particular view of the division of labor and harmony of things.[4] The exposition was also international because it was meant to be attended by all important nations of the world. The idea of internationalism in the late nineteenth century embraced colonialism, and international expositions were thus attended by both nation-states and their colonies, which were an intrinsic component of national power and pride.

Indeed, the 1889 Paris Universal Exposition was—as several previous fairs had been—an ephemeral and diminutive portrait of what was then considered the modern world. It attempted to be an exact scale model of modern reality. The official commission in charge of the exposition maintained that the exhibition was the outcome of the order and logic of the years. That is, eleven years had been the interval between the 1855 fair and that of 1867, and between this last and that of 1878. Accordingly, the year 1889 was set to have a world exhibition. These cycles seemed to follow what a German thinker later labeled a ritualistic "pilgrimage of the commodity fetish."[5]

Should the fair be a national event? Should it emphasize the commemoration of the French Revolution as a great national leap forward? Should the revolution be considered a universal patrimony? These and other questions were discussed within the framework of the unstable French Third Republic.[6] After long debates, in 1884 the French President Jules Ferry issued the decree for the organization of an international fair to be held between 5 May and 31 October 1889.[7] This was only one of many acts that were designed to secure a place for the revolution in the national consciousness. In fact, French modern nationalism owes to the Third Republic the taming and epic mystification of the French Revolution.[8] For late-nineteenth-century Parisians, to arrange a universal exposition was almost a habit—after all, Paris's history and urban planning were replete with the remains of previous fairs. But once the world's fair project started to become reality, public and private concordance emerged on one issue: the Paris exhibition of 1889 was to be the greatest fair in the universe, in order to celebrate the most important revolution in modern times, and the principal source of France's universalism.

The 1889 Paris universal exposition was indeed the greatest fair of the nineteenth century, echoed only by the world's fair of 1900, also staged in the French capital. The cost of the fair, about 46 million francs, was covered by an arrangement between the state, the city council, and a group of private investors organized as an Association de Garantie. For France, this figure shows how prized world's fairs had become in the late nineteenth century, largely as a result of belief in their efficacy in promoting industrial development and national pride. In turn, this belief justified the huge expenditures involved. Had the cost of the fair been fully met by the French state alone, it would have consumed 15 percent of all French revenues for the year 1889.

The way in which world's fairs were financed shows the specific conception of the role of the state in the construction of the national image. The financing system of the 1889 Paris fair became characteristic of the French method. The first universal expositions arranged by France were financed totally with public money. However, due to the enormous losses of the Paris fair of 1878, in 1889 the system was divided into three financial components—state, city council, and private. By contrast, the British system relied less on state intervention. British world's fairs were also controlled by a state agency, but the British Royal Commission was in charge of soliciting the necessary funding from private interests. The U.S. strategy for the economic management of world's fairs was even more dependent on private organization and funding.[9]

As for Mexico, it was up to the state to finance Mexican participation at world's fairs as part of promoting national industrialization. As historians of Mexico's industrialization have argued, the state—directly formed by private interests—was the fundamental agent of industrialization.[10] Thus the Mexican exhibit at the Philadelphia fair of 1876 was fully sponsored by the government of Sebastián Lerdo de Tejada. The Mexican displays in Paris 1889, Paris 1900, and Chicago 1893 were also fully funded by the Mexican government. The same was true of Mexico's presence in the New Orleans exhibition of 1884. Government expenditures to sponsor these exhibitions consumed a significant percentage of the national budget, particularly if we consider that these were only ephemeral events.

The role of the Mexican state included public participation and sponsorship of private exhibitors.[11] In fact, the French media acknowledged the remarkable industrial patronage of the Díaz regime. In 1891 *Tout-d'Union*, commenting on Mexico's performance at Paris, argued that expositions were not schools of imitation but modern showcases for new industrial and commercial needs. The sole role of government should be to facilitate private initiative, and Mexico was held up as an example of how this might be accomplished.[12]

Mexico's presence at the 1889 Paris fair took place within the context of an intricate international environment. After long debates, the Paris world's fair of 1889 finally commemorated the republican values of the French Revolution. Therefore, in addition to the traditional French enemies, several European monarchies were unwilling to celebrate the murderers of kings.[13] Ultimately, a monarchical boycott of the exposition occurred, and in a show of solidarity, Germany, Austria-Hungary, Belgium, Spain, England, Italy, the Low Countries, Portugal, Russia, and Sweden decided to have no official participation. However, thanks to French diplomatic efforts, private attendance was allowed by most of these monarchies.[14]

England, the reigning industrial power, was not willing to sanction with its presence either the French industrial and military displays or the rhetorical republican nationalism of France. French patriotism adjusted quickly to the circumstances. French nationalism ideologically overcame the boycott through references to the modern consensus on universal truths and values. For France, what was important was that private scientific and industrial progress was exhibited in Paris. Although the assumption was that science and industry had no citizenship, their universal presence in Paris effectively reinforced French modern nationalism. The French republic was hence viewed as the monarchy of science, and the attendance of a scientist such as Thomas Alva Edison was therefore itself a great royal approbation: "If the kings of war have refused to visit the 1889 exposition, who cares? We have the king of science [Edison]."[15]

Although the French fair did not succeed in attracting the participation of all Europe, it was proclaimed as a great moment for the imperial and colonial pursuits of France. The French colonies had an enormous display on the Esplanade des Invalides. Various pavilions represented Cochin-China, Cambodia, Algeria, and the "villages" of Senegal, Gabon-Congo, New Caledonia, and Tonkin. The products and people from these regions were brought to Paris to round out the material and human circus of the exposition.[16] Indeed, France's geopolitical concerns were part of the whole event. The official and nonofficial invitations to African, Asian, and Latin American countries were imbued with French imperialist longing that dated back to the two Napoleons.

From the French perspective of the time, the interests of France in Latin America were being seriously threatened by Germany, England, and the United States. In 1886, in *La Revue Diplomatique,* Auguste Meulemans candidly verbalized France's ambitions in Latin America on the eve of the international fair. For him, Hispanic American attendance at the fair would be rather *sympathique* (curious and entertaining). Such a presence would also be advantageous for France because, first, it could assure France's supremacy in a market of "forty million men who have our *gustos* [tastes], traditions, and aptitudes." Second, it could help France promote the collection of needed statistical data and the establishment of French chambers of commerce in Latin America. Both were important considerations in view of the proposed opening of the Panama Canal.[17]

In truth, in the late nineteenth century all worldwide events took place within the economic and political context established by imperialist expansions and rivalries.[18] This was especially true for Latin American countries, which had acquired the very concept of Latinness from the imperialist ambitions of Napoleon III and which had been economically, and especially intellectually, tied to France.[19] French efforts to encourage Latin American participation had particular import in Porfirian Mexico.

Taking advantage of the European boycott to more prominently display their own advantages and promise, Latin American countries undertook costly exhibits at the 1889 Paris fair. After all, for non-European countries such as Mexico, the language of modern culture and politics was largely animated by the French Revolution and its consequent developments. Beyond a doubt, if modernity was the goal, France was the place to be in 1889.[20] Hence, among the countries that officially accepted the French invitation were Argentina, Bolivia, Costa Rica, Chile, the Dominican Republic, Ecuador, Guatemala, Haiti, Honduras, Nicaragua, Paraguay, El Salvador, Uruguay,

Venezuela, and Mexico. Nevertheless, there were even more distinguished guests from the New World. The United States was among the "noble" guests. French media were less captivated by Latin America's products than by Edison's phonograph, Tiffany's glass, and the "Buffalo Bill Wild West Show."[21] They were impressed by both the prosperity and the industrialism of Americans, who were, in the words of a French art critic, "*enfants prodiges*" who "undertake the conquest of science with a constant fever."[22]

For all countries of the New World, the pragmatic goal in joining international exhibitions was basically the same—to offer raw materials and to publicize a modern image of the nation in order to attract immigrants and investment. However, for the United States—the *enfants prodiges*—European world's fairs were occasions to certify already achieved strength, advertising, as an American historian candidly argued, "American power and greatness to the world."[23] In essence, whereas Mexico and other Latin American countries had to produce—industrially, commercially, artistically, and scientifically—the image of a modern nation from zero, countries like the United States had to reproduce and redefine the American image as a military and industrial power and to work hard to gain acknowledgment as a modern nation in culture, the arts, and education. Mexico, Brazil, or Argentina could never equal the success of the United States in international fairs or match its theatrical capacity, of which the best example was Chicago's 1893 Columbian fair, a rough copy of the 1889 Paris exposition.

While the United States was already the promised land, countries such as Mexico and Brazil were at least promising nations. Hence Mexican rhetoric made constant reference to unexploited resources and a benign climate that made Mexico "a country picturesque beyond description and beautiful beyond belief . . . with that indefinable charm which those indolent, lotus-eating lands exercise always over the sterner and colder nature of the northman."[24] Throughout the Porfirian period this image of an unexploited and rich land was fostered nationally and reproduced internationally. Equally, Brazil was always portrayed as a "promising tropical country."[25] Bolivia, in turn, aimed to lure European investors with its abundant mineral resources. Therefore, a tunnel of silver, which functioned as the entrance to Bolivia's pavilion, constituted both an exact copy of the entrance to the mine at Pulacayo and a Midas-like experience for visitors. In contrast, Argentina employed French sculptors, designers, and engineers to build the likeness of the "whitest" and richest of the Latin American nations. It constructed a monumental French-style pavilion, inside which Argentina introduced itself as a young woman reclining on a cow, having at her feet three male figures, denoting industry, commerce, and livestock.[26]

In Mexico, therefore, in an effort to construct a cosmopolitan and modern image of the nation, the Porfirian elite began a portrait of both their country and themselves. This, they believed, would have several useful functions. It would serve as Mexico's passport to modernity's paradise, as their own sense of identity and unity, and as a source of domestic legitimacy.

THE MEXICAN PARADOX OF *AFRANCESAMIENTO*

Despite the abortive and resented French-supported empire of Maximilian in Mexico (1864–1867), by the 1880s France was the foremost cultural and intellectual model for the Porfirian elite. Whereas Mexican liberals after the 1860s were ambivalent toward Europe as a whole, most shared a nationalistic republicanism which responded sympathetically to the reestablishment of the republic in France. And once positivist ideas—which were unmistakably French—were widely accepted, the concept of scientific politics embraced by Mexican elites could not be dissociated from the French milieu. In fact, cultural and intellectual analyses of the period often have been written as the history of Mexico's *afrancesamiento* (Francophilia). It is important to bear in mind, however, that Mexican elites were not seeking to be French specifically, merely to be modern. Thus Mexican emulations were an echo of a wider process that included many other nations and, even within France, the Paris-like modernization of rural areas.[27] France, as arbiter of late-nineteenth-century culture and politics, was a process of colonization and homogenization of which the ostensible center was Paris but which in fact had no center. Ideas, products, and people circulated throughout the world in an uncontrollable fashion. Mexican and French elites, as well as those of other Western nations, were simultaneously colonizers and colonized in this process.

For Mexico, this process of cultural and political colonization was composed of a twofold perspective: on one hand, Mexico's somewhat idealized view of France; and on the other, France's own striving to be the ideal picture of progress and cosmopolitanism, of which the world's fairs, and Mexico's presence in them, were the main expressions.

The events of the French Third Republic were followed closely by the emerging Porfirian elite. The new French republic paralleled the consolidation of a stable political status quo in Mexico.[28] As historian Charles Hale has shown, the consolidation of the opportunistic French republic was very well received by intellectuals like Justo Sierra, Santiago Sierra, and Francisco Cosmes. Indeed, in achieving a peaceful political balance marked by conservatism, France became again an unparalleled model. According to the newspaper of the Porfirian avant-garde liberal group, *La Libertad*, the French Third Republic was an example of a liberal party that, in turning into a party of government, had also somehow become conservative.[29]

Throughout the 1880s the emerging Porfirian elite—more urban and cosmopolitan than ever before—readily absorbed and idealized French thought. For the elite of Mexico at this time, Hippolyte Taine's scientific determinism was the model for the construction of scientific politics, even though Taine's ideas were being seriously challenged in France at the same time. These challenges eventually were raised in Mexico as well, especially in the 1910s with the intellectual group of El Ateneo de la Juventud (see chapter 12), but in the 1880s Mexicans still saw France as an unstoppable economic, intellectual, and political wave of progress. Mexico's presence at the 1889 Paris fair, therefore, represented more than the achievement of economic advantages. It also symbolized Mexico's quest to be recognized as a nation that formed part of the cosmopolitan world. It was to be part of Zola's France, from which, as Justo Sierra later argued, Mexicans learned "the brutal and sinister poem of matter."[30] It was a dream come true, epitomized in a poem composed by Rafael de Zayas Enríquez for the awards ceremony to honor Mexican exhibitors in Paris 1889:

> Thanks my God! It came true,
> the dream I conceive in my delirium,
> patriotic and poetic,
> Juárez and Porfirio's Anáhuac
> I have seen honored
> by the France of Thiers and Gambetta.[31]

However, in honoring and making use of French culture and history, Mexicans had to make them fit the epic structure of their own intellectual landscape. In 1899 Francisco Bulnes observed that France had hypnotized Mexico and the rest of the "Latin" countries.[32] In the same way, in his poem entitled "Le Mexique, a la France," Auguste Genin, a Franco-Mexican writer and entrepreneur resident in Mexico and a long-time freelance writer for the Mexican government, paid poetic tribute to France on behalf of Mexico in verses that simultaneously and candidly expressed the Mexican idealization of France and Mexico's intellectual self-conformation to that idealization:

> O France! It is from thee that books come,
> it is from thy lucid spirit that my spirit becomes intoxicated,
> my voice is the echo of your voice;
> my sons love thy sons; thy festivities are my festivities
> and it is through thy singing that today my poets
> fascinate their lyres in Mexico.
> Their accents touched upon thy heart
> because their genius
> is born under the sun of thy infinite glory
> from a spark inspired by the vision of thee,
> Alarcón and Corneille have walked together,
> Ignacio Ramírez resembles Voltaire,
> as Juárez resembles Gambetta.
> France, I have Juan de Dios Peza, my sweet François Coppée;
> Guillermo Prieto sings my epic poem,

A Béranger close to my national symbols,
Gorostiza, for me, is Collin d'Harleville;
Sierra is Saint-Beuve and Casasus, Delille;
Altamirano, Mirabeau!³³

In turn, the French media considered almost all aspects of Mexico's presence in Paris not so much a self-serving Mexican extravaganza as a "great manifestation in honor of France."³⁴

The idealized France emulated by Latin American republics in fact existed in, and only in, the terrain of the world's fair, and indeed the 1889 exhibition helped France persuade itself of its greatness. Beyond the fairgrounds, however, and beyond the apparent political and social consensus they epitomized, France was still recovering from the aftermath of its disastrous defeat at the hands of Prussia: Alsace and Lorraine had been lost. In addition, the consequences of the French commune could still be felt in the Paris of the Third Republic. Nonetheless, for France the 1880s were an era of striking economic growth and resurgent nationalism. Just as the debt to Germany was paid early, "La Marseillaise" was made the French national anthem in 1879, and July 14th was proclaimed the national holiday. It was the era of debates regarding patriotic monuments, especially to honor the French Revolution, an era that combined republicanism with nationalism and both with positivism.³⁵ Yet political instability was such that arrangements for the celebration of the centenary of the 1789 revolution were only finalized at the last moment.³⁶

In truth, the year 1889 may be analytically viewed as a small fragment of the rapid process of transformation of late-nineteenth-century French society. In the late 1880s France underwent simultaneous and accelerated changes, including the growth of the working class in both size and importance. Political protests by socialists and anarchists were common and frequently violent, eventually resulting in the assassination of President Sadi Carnot in 1894.³⁷

The perception of contemporaries about the fragility of the social balance of their era was expressed in the Paris exposition of 1889. Great emphasis was placed on the well-being of the working class—a sign of modernism. To be socially and politically enlightened within a modern idealized world meant, hence, to be committed to an intricate combination of sanitary, anthropological, criminological, industrial, Saint-Simonian, and educational concerns about the lower classes, or at least to advertise such concerns. The utopian picture of a world rationally ordered and guided both by the entrepreneurial spirit and by science was not at odds with the frank economic, imperialist, and racist aspects of the French world's fair. Indeed, the socialism of French fairs ought to be understood as a part of the attempt to produce an idealized portrait of the modern world; that is, it furnished the utopian ingredients indispensable for a worldview that could remain an alluring hope despite all odds.

Through its churches and philanthropism, Saint-Simonian thought generated a sort of socialist education that was the ideological point of reference for numerous middle-class professionals, and not merely in France. They, in turn, started to play an important role in the growing technocratic states of the late nineteenth century. The international fairs were, as historian Pascal Ory argues, the common experience of these professionals.[38] Economists such as Le Play, a Catholic monarchist who had a great concern for the situation of workers and who institutionalized sociological inquiry to measure the true situation of the lower classes, fulfilled the state's technocratic tasks during the middle of the nineteenth century. Le Play himself organized the imperial French exhibition of 1855, and his follower, Jean-Baptiste Krantz, directed France's first republican fair. Alfred Picard, the force in the organization and architectural works of the 1889 fair, together with George Berger, director-general of operations, was inspired by Le Play's legacy. In 1889 Picard helped include a class in hygiene and public charity in the fair as well as a special exhibit on social economy.[39]

In addition, the social recruitment of political elites in late-nineteenth-century France was changing. The old military men and politicians began to share power with a bureaucracy of technocrats, and French world's fairs echoed this social change. Civil engineering influenced and in turn gained strength from world's fairs and their industrialist and Saint-Simonian inspirations. Engineers, as well as doctors, architects, and other professionals, obtained a well-defined political place more or less linked to their particular expertise. Thus the growth of technocracy created an illusion of non-ideological politicians—neutral and scientifically objective experts—who reinforced the idea of "scientific politics" as nothing more than management of the state.[40]

For late-nineteenth-century France (or Mexico) to achieve modern government organization, it was necessary to develop the ideology of scientific politics. To do so, a technocracy was required. However, universal scientific politics proved to be a selective ideological discourse that depended on both the circumstances of each specific country and the interests of its national elite. In fact, Mexico's attendance at Parisian fairs also illustrates the emergence of a Mexican technocratic elite. By the late 1880s the political group known as the Científicos was emerging as the elite that claimed to rule the country scientifically. Economists (including Joaquín Casasus, José Yves Limantour, and Emiliano Busto), engineers (such as Gilberto Crespo, Antonio de Anza, and Luis Salazar), and doctors (for example, Domingo Orvañanos, Eduardo Liceaga, and José Ramírez) were in attendance at the Mexican exhibit in Paris and very much a part of Mexican politics.

The social concerns of Mexican technocrats, however, did not echo those of the France they aspired to imitate in 1889. In fact, in 1888 Manuel Flores, a member of the Mexican exhibition team, was commissioned to evaluate the French plans for an exhibition of social economy. After reviewing the plans, he argued: "As can be seen, the Exposition on Social Economy is . . . a vast statistical work about the present and real conditions of the working class." For Flores, Mexico had no cooperative societies or any sort of workers' organization that could be exhibited in a social economy display, and Mexico especially lacked fabricated hygienic housing for workers. Social economy, understood as an elaborate French combination of Saint-Simonianism, socialism, and social Catholicism, was not a Mexican preoccupation.[41] Flores's advice was, in the last analysis, to exhibit the benefits that came from having no social concerns at all: "Mexico cannot join the exposition of social economy. . . . The statistical data that Mexico is able to submit in this regard . . . should only appear in the official section of the Mexican exposition, as a way of making the world learn about the conditions of our workers from the point of view of their meager salaries, their austerity, resistance, and working capacity; these are qualities that distinguish them from European workers."[42]

Porfirio Díaz himself was aware of workers' protests in Europe—he was informed by Mexican diplomats and travelers. He expressed concerns regarding the workers' discontent, but he wished his country to remain exempt from these problems. In 1891 he wrote to Vicente Riva Palacio, "Of course I am aware of labor protests in Europe" and—no matter that Mexicans' daily workload exceeded eleven hours—added, "I believe that European governments ought to give workers the eight-hour day they request." His ambivalence was such that he acknowledged the prudence of workers in their protests but believed it to be the consequence of official repression. Díaz, like the wizards of progress, thought that this type of bourgeois European concern did not apply to Mexican workers. In the last analysis, he said to Riva Palacio, the workers' victory over the bourgeoisie would mean that "they [will] all become bourgeoisie."[43]

Mexican indifference to French social concerns can also be observed in Mexico's participation in the congresses affiliated with the 1889 exposition. Of the thirteen congresses that dealt with social issues, Mexico attended only five, whereas Mexican representatives were present at nearly all of the artistic and scientific congresses, including those dealing with pigeon breeding and with colonial questions.[44]

The condition of women was another concern that Mexican Científicos did not seriously consider. French world's fairs gradually included concern with the condition of women in the social economy exhibits, whereas U.S. fairs contained women's pavilions and buildings. At these, in addition to the traditional domain assigned to women, suffrage and social issues were addressed by women themselves. Mexico's displays at the women's exhibitions in Philadelphia (1876), New Orleans (1884), and Chicago (1893) illustrate the growth of a female Porfirian aristocracy. Whereas in Philadelphia and in Paris 1889, numerous women individually sent samples of their woven or embroidered textiles, in Chicago a Ladies' Board (Junta de Señoras) was created and was headed by no less than Carmen Romero Rubio, Porfirio Díaz's wife. But these Mexican exhibits only reinforced traditional female roles.[45] The social implications of modernity, then, were at the bottom of the modernization agenda of Porfirian Mexico.

The year 1889 can also be viewed as an especially meaningful time in the political transformation of the French Third Republic. The stable and scientific French republic that was featured in Mexican accounts was at odds with both the perceptions of the French people and the European view of France. By the 1880s republicanism had lost its utopian appeal for some sectors of French society. The republic—reduced to political bargaining among numerous factions—faced economic and military failure. In addition, the republican spirit was seriously threatened by waves of scandals that began in 1887 and continued through the Dreyfus affair in 1894. Illegal traffic in Legions of Honor brought about a government crisis that concluded with the dismissal of President Grevy in 1887. In turn, the Panama Canal Company started to collapse in 1889, exposing a Pandora's box of corruption in the French government.

Political discontent and what might be called revenge nationalism finally threatened to disrupt the political status quo of the 1880s French republic. The traditional opposition between radicals and opportunists was seriously endangered by the emergence of Gen. Ernest Jean Marie Boulanger.[46] By January 1889 the fragile French republic seemed about to succumb to the peculiar Boulanger, whose party knew how to appeal to popular nationalistic sentiments, to the appetite for revenge against Bismarck's Germany, and to the exposure of republican corruption. Despite Boulanger's political strength, his expected coup d'état never occurred. Instead, after being exiled, he died in the arms of his lover, an ending worthy of the French belle epoque.

Hence it was Sadi Carnot—the obscure president who emerged in 1889 as a compromise among the republican factions and the victor over Boulanger—who inaugurated the 1889 world's fair. Carnot undoubtedly gained public confidence and political strength as a result of the fair's pomp and glitter, a fact that was not lost on William Henry Bishop, a U.S. journalist at the Paris exposition: "If the Exposition can serve as a bond for keeping the peace for even six months, its promoters will have built better than they knew."[47]

In addition, in the late 1880s French nationalism drew strength from France's expanding colonial empire. The isolationist nationalism of the conservatives was overcome, and colonialism began to be seen as part of the nation's strength. This was especially true after the resignation of Bismarck in

1890 and the signing of the Russo-French pact that established a new European balance of power which permitted France to embark on more colonial adventures.

By 1889 the French economy showed signs of slow recovery, and controversy began regarding the merits of the different projects for national economic development. There were good reasons for this debate: in the early 1880s France had been second only to Britain as an industrial power, but by the end of the nineteenth century it had declined to fourteenth place.[48] In addition to increasing anxiety about industrial weakness vis-à-vis Germany, England, and the United States, there were also worries about the constant decline in France's birthrate.[49] Small wonder that a well-established rhetorical faith in the free market came to be challenged by protectionist policies designed to encourage national development.

French precariousness in the 1880s is best demonstrated in the cultural and intellectual realm. In French intellectual circles the 1880s saw the questioning of the belief in science and progress. The positivist consensus, which the world's fair epitomized, started to be attacked by an "antipositivist reaction in science."[50] By the early 1890s French intellectuals started to talk about the bankruptcy of science.[51] Nationalism nevertheless remained a strong, though ambiguous, component of French cultural life. It included, on one hand, the universalist tradition rooted in the French Revolution—that is, a belief in rationalistic, democratic, and liberal values—and, on the other hand, a more parochial nationalism based on local interests and on racial arguments. Nonetheless, throughout the Third Republic universalist tendencies seemed to dominate the political and intellectual life of Paris.[52] Victor Hugo's funeral ceremonies in 1885 were a grandiose extravaganza of French national pride understood as a universal patrimony; they honored a national poet but indeed celebrated a universal man.[53] However, nationalism started to be influenced by certain social concerns which in turn were saturated by new scientific theories. This was especially noticeable in literature—for instance, in Émile Zola's naturalistic fiction. Yet by the late 1880s naturalism came under attack in French intellectual circles, and the love-hate relationship with naturalism eventually became the important underlying factor of the intellectual life of fin-de-siècle France. Then symbolism—as pioneered by Verlaine and Mallarmé—emerged as the new intellectual vogue, at the same time as Baudelaire was canonized. In art, although impressionists and their existential anguish for the temporariness of modern life had been visible since 1874, high culture was formed by the approved bourgeois taste of the salons' dogmatic style, neoclassical sculpture and architecture, and the imitation of Henry II's decorative style. The 1880s brought the consolidation of a noncanonical culture: in 1889, while the exposition's art gallery exhibited Roman-like marble sculptures, the Moulin Rouge opened its doors, and the Chat Noir and Le Mirliton cabarets offered a new kind of Bohemia for the bourgeoisie escaping modern life.[54]

For outsiders, French culture was often understood as a high cultural production which readily became a universal canon, making it difficult to distinguish between what was merely an expression of French nationalism and what were actually universal values. In history, Michelet had solved this distinction by making France equivalent to the universe. In literature, Victor Hugo had resolved this confusion by making France the world in his panegyric to the 1855 Paris exposition: "O France, adieu! You are too great to be merely a country.... You are so great that you soon will no longer be. You will cease to be France, you will be Humanity.... Resign yourself to your immensity... O my country, and, as Athens became Greece, as Rome became Christendom, you, France, become the world."[55]

The 1889 fair combined both universalist (French) conservative art and progressive industry and science. Technology in 1889 was already more than mere machine making. It included its social appreciation, experience, and suffering.[56] For France, as for industrialized Europe, technology was a generous, albeit awe-inspiring, promise. This was expressed, for instance, by an ironic prayer directed to the Eiffel Tower by Émile Goudeau: "Oh iron lady, pray for us, you who are in heaven, *Turris ferrea, ora pronobis, peccatoribus* [iron tower, pray for us sinners]."[57]

In short, beyond the fairgrounds, beyond the Boulevards Pigalle, Montmarte, and Saint Germain, beyond the cafés, a France of insurmountable economic difficulties, political instability, and cultural uncertainty lay hidden from visitors such as the Latin American elites who went to Paris to learn the majestic lesson represented by the exposition. At the time, France was experimenting with unorthodox doctrines to catch up with industrialization, improvising political alliances to maintain stability, undertaking social reforms in fear of revolution, and questioning the positivist and neoclassical intellectual and cultural canon. Latin American elites did not see this France—it was beyond their view of the modern world picture as learned through the extravagant fairs of Paris. As for instability, poverty, and chaos, Latin Americans must have thought that such weaknesses were exclusively theirs, along with marginality. The world's fair of 1889 was an illusory lesson in progress, but nonetheless a great lesson in comparison with which everything else seemed to be secondary.

TWO

The Imperatives of Mexican Progress

Mexico began its great performances at world's fairs in the 1880s. The same decade saw the end of the turbulence that had characterized the country since independence and the beginning of the modern Mexican nation-state.[1] Progress thereafter was a bizarre amalgamation of the collective hopes of the elite, actual industrial and social changes, rhetorical consensus, and constant accommodation between modern and traditional patterns. To trace the modern connotations of progress in Mexico, I analyze the political and economic centralization of power in the 1880s as an inherent component of the formation of those who created the image of the modern Mexican nation. What characteristics of late-nineteenth-century Mexican political life made possible the conscious and sophisticated attempts to summarize the idea of the nation in Paris 1889, Chicago 1893, or Paris 1900? What economic interests and conditions permitted and benefited from these Mexican displays? Were these exhibits mere facades orchestrated with Machiavellian cleverness to support the economic interests of the elites, or did they indeed constitute the only substance from which nationhood could have been made? To answer these questions it is necessary, first, to abandon the idea of establishing a clear cause-and-effect relationship between the Mexican extravaganzas in Paris and the political and economic condition of the country. Let us instead look for the common ground that simultaneously supported and was promoted by events like Mexico's presence in Paris 1889, Porfirio Díaz's third election, the emergence of the Científicos, and the promotion of foreign investment and immigration as part of an elite plan for economic development. In search of this common ground, we must examine what I term the political, intellectual, and social commonplaces and the *dineros* (economics) of those times.

COMMONPLACES

On 1 December 1888 Díaz began his third presidential term, the second in a row after the Manuel González interim. Díaz was in power, as Justo Sierra cynically argued, "less by the vote than by the national will."² By this date, the caudillos of the first years of the Porfirian regime had become less caudillo-like. Through military, political, and economic means the revolutionary group had established a relatively homogenous power base. As different political groups, especially those headed by Sebastián Lerdo de Tejada and José María Iglesias, were reconciled and absorbed into the Liberal Party, shared interests gave rise to a relatively cohesive elite. Furthermore, the old economic oligarchies were gradually becoming as one with the new political and economic groups.³ The tone this elite gave to urban life created the impression that Mexico was enjoying a belle epoque.⁴ With political opposition either dissipated or mastered, with increasing international recognition, and—after 1885—with relative economic stability, Porfirian Mexico was indeed embarked on the creation of a modern (that is, nineteenth-century) national economy, society, and image.

By 1889 this elite was so linked by mutual interests as to make any attempt at a quarrel treacherous for them all. They had begun to consolidate their wealth with that of the northern and central mining interests, of the railroad magnates, and of the speculators in central Mexico. Most of them, in addition, played a role as intermediaries with foreign interests. Increasingly, this elite started to look to the world outside. They were, as one German commissioner called them, the cosmopolitans.⁵

The 1880s were the years in which the Porfiriato started to exhibit itself as the inevitable, necessary, and optimal political solution. Although the Científicos did not become consolidated until the middle of the 1890s, by 1889 technocrats were already replacing the old caudillos, and the battle cry of the decade was more administration, less politics.⁶ Díaz himself, having married Manuel Romero Rubio's aristocratic daughter, resembled a statesman more than a caudillo. Underscoring this transformation, Díaz, a mestizo from Oaxaca, began to be portrayed as whiter and whiter on the countless canvases that were painted of him at this time.⁷

In addition, a new generation of intellectuals and politicians began to influence the direction of this elite. The early ideas of Mariano Otero and Gabino Barreda were echoed by the group called La Libertad, headed by the brothers Santiago and Justo Sierra.⁸ Justo characterized this period as one of "diplomatic discipline, of order, of peace." These qualities were necessary for the achievement of the "only supreme goals"—freedom and *patria* (country). But colonization, an ample labor force, abundant capital, and efficient means of communication were also needed to achieve those goals in Mexico.⁹ Therefore, the legal equality of all citizens (including Indians), strong government, and liberalism's harmony of proprietors were considered natural ingredients in the emergence of a scientific management of politics.[10] For Mexico this era was, as Alan Knight has argued, "the end of ideology."[11]

The centralization of power and administration achieved during the 1880s, though more comprehensive than before, still could not encompass the diversity and distances of the country. Vast sectors of the population remained cut off. Even so, the 1880s saw unprecedented efforts to achieve a centralized and coherent administration, a more or less consolidated political elite, a unified internal market, and a well-defined and well-promoted national culture.

A rhetorical piece may serve to recapitulate the commonplaces of late 1880s Mexican polity. In May 1889 Alfredo Chavero, a long-time member of the Porfirian exhibition team, addressed a panegyric to ex-president Lerdo de Tejada, Díaz's former enemy, who had died in exile in April:

> Lerdo may rest at ease in this land which is his own; Juárez the indomitable, Ocampo the inflexible, Zaragoza who taught the world with how much glory one can be defeated, they all rest within it. This land of Mexico is worthy of the distinguished *maestro* [Lerdo de Tejada], accustomed as it is to guarding the purest silver and dazzling gold in its entrails. In closing this grave, an altar is erected, watched in silence under the shadows of the night, by science, freedom, and *la patria*.[12]

In this sermon, as in countless political speeches, all of the political components of the late-nineteenth-century Porfirian formula for a modern nation were included. First, an official requiem for Lerdo de Tejada, leader of the Lerdista group, adversary of Díaz's group, epitomizes the idea of reconciliation, which was understood as national maturity. The nation had grown up; previous conflicts were part of its unstable adolescence. This belief was constantly repeated regarding not only politics but economic and social issues as well. The truth, especially the new truth in a recently built nation-state, was a matter of repetition.

Reconciliation, in fact, meant the achievement of an internal political balance after the defeat of the Lerdista liberals. Although the Díaz regime did not overcome what some authors have termed political and economic atomization,[13] it did institute a central authority, a central command based, above all, on solid, common material interests. It was an order founded on mutual elite convenience, and their *solidarités*, whether modern or traditional, were rooted in the inherent pragmatism, amodern and atraditional, demanded by the exercise of power.[14]

Second, Chavero's discourse alluded to the crystallization of an Olympus of heroes for a modern nation: Juárez and Ocampo as national idols of pristine liberal justice, Zaragoza as military hero of a nation that, with no victories in war to venerate, had to create the national epic out of losses, an epic of triumphant capitulations to consummate the greatest victory—peace and stability. This national epic—as we will see in the examination of the Mexican Aztec Palace in Paris 1889—was crucial in the creation of a symbolic horizon where regional and ideological differences could be surmounted. But in fact one of the mandatory roles of the national state—and perhaps its ontological raison d'être—was theatrical: to invent, re-create, and manage the national mythology.

Third, Chavero raised the idea of a nationalism constituted by both the economic potential and the beauty of the Mexican territory. As Francisco Xavier Clavijero or Alexander von Humboldt or Bernardo de Balbuena had in earlier times, by the 1880s the Porfirian elite had come to regard the country as immensely rich, unexploited, and naturally splendorous.[15] By this date the great economic potential and scenic grandeur of the nation had become even more well known with the development of charts of all sorts, statistics, paintings, photographs, and exhibitions of products. Immigrants would surely come, Mexicans believed, if only they heard about Mexico's beauty and wealth.

Fourth, Chavero incorporated the unifying ideas and myths that had composed the Porfirian liberal consensus of the 1880s—that is, science, patriotism, and freedom. Together, these three safeguarded Lerdo's grave in the same way they protected the nation as a whole. This conception of science included a complex network of collective certainties that explained and enforced educational, political, and daily-life decisions—a view related to the emergence of positivism and of a particular Mexican Darwinism, both of which have been widely studied.[16] But this conception of science went beyond a mere consumption of foreign ideas; it included attempts to be a part of and to understand the comprehensive and dominant world-view of modern times. No nation was modern if it did not follow the natural—that is, scientific—order of things and possess a scientific organization.

By the late nineteenth century the notion of *patria* was directly linked to a weighty generational historical experience that included both the old criollo patriotism and the liberal nationalism fortified by two painful wars of intervention.[17] The Porfirian elite, however, added to the old understanding of *patria* a more intelligible historical, political, and geographical content: the first comprehensive synthesis of patriotic history, the reorganization of bureaucracy at all levels, and the increasing scientific study of Mexico's territory. Freedom, in contrast, was the most ethereal of the rhetorical resources of the Porfirian elite. They assigned to the Western idea of freedom only a few narrow connotations: political (freedom from violence), international (freedom from the oppression of other nations), and economic (freedom of the market).

Finally, Chavero's oration was expressed in the eloquent style of the period, which, far from being merely an accessory of late-nineteenth-century culture, was an intrinsic component of the ideals mentioned above—political reconciliation, nationalism, and scientism. For the idea of a modern nation could hardly be conceived without its rhetorical style. In constructing a nationalist ideology, the distinctions between form and content vanished. The so-called imagined communities of the late nineteenth century were, as was cultural modernity itself, a matter of form; that is, a question of style. Thus the Mexican exhibits in world's fairs fought for the form they believed to be the closest synonym of the modern form. And this effort was managed by politicians and technocrats who simultaneously were poets, writers, and historians[18]—at best, truly men of letters; at worst, *picos de oro* (silver tongues), as historian Luis González characterized them.[19]

The national project articulated by the Porfirian elite for such fairs as the 1889 Paris exhibition was but a miniature version of the above-mentioned features. When Chavero honored Lerdo, and when the exhibitions team prepared Mexico to join the Paris world's fair of 1889, the country had attained a political and economic stability unknown throughout the nineteenth century. Peace seemed to be the most significant achievement of those years.

Peace meant political and economic reconciliation after decades of political unrest and economic chaos. But once achieved, peace also constituted the first substantial political consensus since independence, and to maintain it and protect it became a collective goal. An Argentine observer of Mexico's display at the 1900 Paris exposition clearly saw this in commenting on Díaz's regime: "The need for repose is a social sensation that precedes the emergence of these arbitrary regimes; when peoples are tired of civil unrest, such a caudillo-like regime is the consequence of the search for peace at all costs."[20]

For a long time, peace was considered a primary requirement for the consolidation of a governing elite. Oddly enough, once peace was visible it became the reason for this elite's unity and relative cohesion. Yet peace alone was not enough; it had to be transformed into productive and manageable tranquility. Thus, above all peace was the sine qua non for economic progress. Because foreign capital, Northern European immigration, and improved communications were considered economic necessities, domestic peace was viewed as an indispensable component of the economy. Hence the enjoyment of peace became the construction of a modern nation. In essence, peace meant the nation, as shown by the spirit of the 1889 exposition:[21] only in the aftermath of war, Mexicans believed, could the nation develop its natural attributes.

In sum, in the late 1880s the Porfirian elite achieved a clear awareness of the coherence and unity of its interests and, therefore, a collective expression of its ambitions. It must have seemed as though the past had been overcome and as though, for the first time in independent Mexico, the present and the future had an articulate and palpable affinity.

DINEROS

For Mexico, the last two decades of the nineteenth century were a time of unique economic transformation that, despite its failures and problems, can be depicted as a profound process of modernization in the contemporary sense of the term. In fact, twentieth-century Mexican industrial development is inconceivable without its nineteenth-century origins, especially without Porfirian industrial development.[22] While so-called traditional economic structures merged with modern patterns, the characteristic problems of nineteenth-century world economies started to appear in Mexico. What historian Stephen Haber has called "obstacles to industrialization"—insecure property rights, low per capita income growth, precapitalist agricultural organization, lack of a national market—were recognized and addressed at the end of the 1880s.[23]

In the 1880s the Mexican economy seemed to have entered a period of sustained growth; the first part of the decade saw substantial investment in railroads and overall economic growth. The economy experienced a severe financial crisis in 1884,[24] but within the whole Porfirian era—from the 1870s to the 1910s—the period between 1885 and 1891 can be seen as a time of relatively healthy economic growth. In contrast, a combination of factors—among them the decline of international silver prices and a series of bad years for agriculture—led to a profound economic crisis in the 1890s, which, among many other things, prevented Mexico from repeating at the 1893 Chicago exposition the lavish expenditure for the 1889 fair.

Thus when Mexican politicians, scientists, and writers arrived in Paris 1889, they had left in Mexico what seemed to be a promising economic situation. For them, railroads, mining output, certain industries (textiles, cigarettes, and alcoholic beverages), and export crops (henequen, coffee, and cacao) were leading economic sectors. Railroad construction went from 640 kilometers in 1876 to 12,172 kilometers in 1898. Foreign investment was expanding within the framework of an increasingly interrelated world economy whose main actors were Great Britain and the United States.[25] The textile industry, cigarette manufacturing, and beer production all enjoyed high rates of growth.[26] Overall, from 1884 to 1900 the average annual rate of economic growth approached 8 percent.

The 1880s were also a period of transition for the economic-administrative concerns and approaches of the Porfirian elite. The circle led by Romero Rubio had acquired expertise and sophistication, and it attempted to diversify Mexico's foreign investment. New laws were passed to favor foreign ownership of land and mining, as well as possibilities for incorporation. A technocratic class was growing in size and complexity.[27]

In this sense, for Mexico the world's fairs were laboratories in which to test at an international level the national administrative achievements as well as to learn of new worldwide trends and methods for managing the economy and the government. Thus advertisements heralding the country's progress not only included material advancement but also stressed social, administrative, and political progress. Mexico's publicists often spoke of the accomplishment of scientific politics. For example, Rafael de Zayas Enríquez, in his book especially written in French for Mexico's presence at the 1889 Paris world's fair, argued that administration through the study of sociology and economics was helping Mexico solve all of its problems with "tact, honesty, and good faith, with a clear direction, with no political factions, only one national, scientifically ruled party."[28]

As has been the case throughout the history of independent Mexico, a main goal of the Díaz administration was to attract foreign investment, not only for its economic and "civilizing" benefits but also because such sums indirectly represented Mexico's main source of income, through customs duties on the goods that were imported and taxes on the precious metals that were exported. Mexico's presence at world's fairs like that of Paris 1889 was, in this sense, part of a commercial attempt to diversify Mexico's international links. The growing importance of U.S. capital challenged European interests in Mexico. English and French yearly economic almanacs reported with concern the growing superiority of the United States as a source of imports and capital for Mexico, as well as a customer for Mexican exports.[29] British investment, more indirect than its American and French counterparts, found ways to coexist with American investment, but English entrepreneurs were nevertheless concerned with their loss of influence in Mexico.[30] In 1890 a British observer believed that Mexico was rich and stable and "only need[ed] English capital and English energy to reap one of the richest harvests which history can show."[31]

French interests—in the amount of some 165 million francs[32]—also felt seriously challenged by American and German investments. The French community in Mexico, composed of large-scale industrialists and others who were an important part of the commercial sector, was prosperous and influential.[33] Cautiously, the French invested largely in wholly owned types of businesses. Their investment in state funds, concentrated in banks, railroads, and, in the 1880s, mining, was relatively low compared to that of other countries.[34]

After 1890 this investment started to expand, in part due to the publicity efforts by the Porfirian elite at events such as the international fairs. In a book distributed in Mexico's pavilion in Paris 1889, F. Bianconi discussed the growing commercial weakness of France in Mexico. He believed this weakness was the result of a "stupid colonial policy" that was "a very serious mistake" in a country like France. The French government, he argued, ought to oppose the colonial ventures of competing countries and should not undertake more colonial ventures itself. What France needed instead, he claimed, was a commercial policy; in it, Mexico deserved special attention.[35]

Mexico's presence in world's fairs was also part of a Porfirian import-substitution policy under which emerging Mexican industry received tariff protection and government subsidies.[36] Ricardo de Maria y Campos, in charge of the Mexican commerce commission in Paris 1889 and Paris 1900, distributed many *Renseignements commerciaux* about Mexico. De Maria y Campos's commercial books were devoted mainly to an explanation of import tariffs and the costs of transportation, manufactures, and raw materials in Mexico. High tariffs were imposed on cigarettes, paper, cotton and woolen textiles, some live animals, manufactures of precious metals, diamonds, emeralds, and certain chemicals, while technological apparatus were exempted.[37]

The other main socioeconomic goal of the Díaz regime—especially stressed in world's fairs—was the inducement of Northern European immigration. Although Mexico's population increased from 9.3 million in 1877 to 15.1 million in 1919, the figure masks the ups and downs of an endemic demographic stagnation. Mexican physicians and journalists complained of the high level of infant mortality, unsanitary conditions, and poor medical services.[38] Foreign immigration never was significant enough to have an important impact on the entire economy and culture of the country.

This was not through lack of trying. Beginning in the 1880s, the Mexican government made an intense effort to attract foreign immigrants, offering land and tax exemptions as the main incentives. Toward that end, vast stretches of public land were surveyed by private companies to be sold to foreign colonizers.[39] But fiscal and military exemptions were not enough to attract foreigners, or at least not sufficient to lure the type of foreigners desired by the Porfirian elite.

By and large, the relatively few immigrants attracted to Mexico came from Spain, Italy, the United States, and China.[40] American immigrants, albeit "racially correct" by the racist standards of the Porfirian elite, were nevertheless feared as part of U.S. expansionism. Historical memory played a role in this phobia. Spanish colonists were all too common for the comfort of some Mexicans and, though officially welcomed, were not numerous enough or culturally capable of Europeanizing Mexico. Chinese and black immigrants have long been neglected in Mexico's bizarre melting pot. Overall, not even American, Spaniard, and Chinese immigrants were numerous, and the long-desired massive wave of Northern European colonists never arrived.[41]

Mexican presence in world's fairs pointed up the strenuous effort made during this period to attract immigrants. Special books and pamphlets were written to explain Mexican immigration facilities and procedures. Those books aimed to overcome Mexico's long-standing reputation as an inhospitable, savage nation.[42] In a book produced especially for distribution at the Paris fair of 1889, Antonio García Cubas, the well-known Mexican geographer, argued that Mexico offered colonists franchises and land for sale at a "very low price." Immigrants were also "exonerated from military service and from the payment of all taxes for ten years."[43]

Countless propaganda books that explained Mexico's advantages for immigrants were printed or sponsored by the Mexican government. For example, in 1886 a French journalist traveling in Mexico remarked that Díaz wanted him to say that the economic crisis of González's time was over. He stated that Díaz was especially committed to French immigration.[44] Other books, such as Archibald Dunn's, which was dedicated to President Díaz for his "honesty of purpose," argued that Mexico wanted immigrants with capital to invest, small farmers who were willing to work, and agricultural workers who were willing to be guided by capitalists.[45] Other books contained information about prevailing land prices and detailed explanations of the tax policies of the Mexican government.[46]

As the Porfirian elite saw it, Mexico's failure to attract immigration stemmed in part from the nation's bad reputation as an unstable and unsanitary region, a legacy of previous political and economic chaos. According to the perception of Mexican authorities, immigrants did not come simply because they were unaware of the advantages Mexico offered in terms of vast lands, cheap labor, and plentiful natural resources. Mexico's presence at world's fairs was a unique way of overcoming its bad reputation.[47]

By 1889, however, a new generation of politicians and intellectuals was articulating other ideas about immigration. *La Libertad* pointed out that much of Mexico's unsettled territory, far from being an immensely rich land, was in fact inhospitable. Immigration, according to this group, was of course needed, but in order to procure it several issues had to be addressed—land tenure, religious freedom, sanitation, allocation of the labor force, and, especially, the so-called Indian problem.[48]

The Porfirian elite thus discussed unused lands, campaigns against vagrancy, methods for recruiting workers, and ways of civilizing Indians. There was a consensus about the scarcity and low productivity of mestizo and Indian workers and about the cultural and physical superiority of white immigrants. These last, it was believed, would eventually produce the economic, cultural, and racial modernization of the country.

With white immigrants slow to arrive, however, throughout the second part of the nineteenth century Chinese and black immigration was considered by the Mexican government. Nonetheless, it was abandoned as a project in the first part of the Porfirian period. In 1879 the prolific philologist and writer Francisco Pimentel responded to a request of the Mexican minister of foreign affairs regarding the convenience of black immigration: "The presence of Blacks in Mexico would increase all the problems we already face due to the heterogeneity of races. . . . Because our country needs industrialists rather than farmers, Blacks are not useful because they do not belong to the class of industrialists."[49] In 1889 the possibility of bringing in black workers was again rumored, but opposition, headed by Justo Sierra and E. M. de los Ríos, was promptly voiced.[50] Nevertheless, Chinese immigrants did begin to arrive in the late nineteenth century. They became part of a cheap labor force that, in addition to exploitation, had to face constant discrimination.[51]

At the 1889 Paris world's fair, Mexican officials witnessed one of the main causes of Mexico's failure to attract foreign immigrants, namely, competition from democratic countries. Because of Mexico's low wage structure, throughout the 1880s and 1890s Argentina and the United States were better destinations for would-be immigrants. Mexican officials were aware of this, but instead of marketing an attractive image of a country of good salaries for low-income European workers, the Mexican elite emphasized the advantages of a country of vast land and low wages, aiming to captivate middle- and high-range investors (who very rarely migrate). Unlike Mexico's, Argentina's propaganda at the 1889 exposition emphasized good salaries, democratic rights, and the overall coexistence of various European nationalities. Argentina estimated that nearly 200,000 immigrants would arrive in 1889, and these immigrants, it was argued, would obtain, in addition to goods and property, all the guarantees of a liberal democratic nation as granted by the Argentine constitution.[52]

In Mexico, therefore, foreign investment did indeed arrive, but not the rush of immigrants that would have translated into population growth and cultural learning. If only for this blindness about the reasons why people migrate, which reflected a lack of democratic discussion of national and international realities and options, the Porfirian elite was to be blamed, as José Vasconcelos noted in the 1930s.[53]

The imperatives of progress were as much a part of Mexico's displays at world's fairs as was their nationalistic symbolism. The pragmatic goal of attracting foreign investment and immigrants was not at all at odds with the allegorical role played by world's fairs for Mexican nationalism. In fact, they were complementary: the economic goals would have been inconceivable without the unifying myths of the nation and its nationality, while the theatrical duties of the state could not have been understood without its economic imperatives.

THREE

Mexico and the World at Large

Mexicans believed that "in the world at large, a community yet exists for us."[1] By 1889 Mexico had acquired some experience as a participant in world expositions, especially during the Porfirian peace. In fact, Mexico's involvement in world's fairs paralleled the process of political and economic consolidation of the Porfirian elite. The accumulated experience, common interests, and international links of this elite made possible the emergence of a group of professional world's fair experts who were able to construct the image of the modern nation at all levels (see Appendix 1). These wizards of progress staged their first major performance at the New Orleans exposition of 1884. Nonetheless, their long history of trial and error included not only Mexico's participation in American and European expositions but also the idea of a Mexico City world's fair.

MEXICO AT THE PHILADELPHIA AND NEW ORLEANS FAIRS

Many Mexicans viewed participation in world's fairs as one of the best ways of changing the widespread perception that Mexico was violent and uncivilized. During the first years of the Porfiriato the Ministry of Economic Development maintained that "[Mexico has been] splendidly endorsed by nature. . . . To show such riches and thereby open a wide road for the development of industry and commerce is a patriotic deed that we can achieve only by means of world's fairs."[2]

Although the belief that progress would be encouraged by participation in fairs appeared in the 1850s, not until the Philadelphia world's fair of 1876 did Mexico begin its official participation in international exhibitions. And not until the New Orleans world's fair of 1884 did Mexico undertake a major effort to postulate the ideal type of a modern Mexican nation.[3]

In 1875 Gabriel Mancera, special commissioner of the Mexican Board of Expositions in the United States, wrote two long letters in which he analyzed the possibilities and potential advantages of Mexico's participation in Philadelphia 1876 and thus convinced the Mexican government to participate. According to Mancera, economic and social problems in the United States would eventually result in migration to Mexico. In particular, he believed that workers' discontent in American cities was producing more repression than social reform and that some of the more disaffected laborers would eventually opt for migration to Mexico.[4]

Mexico occupied a small area of the 11,644-square-foot building prepared to hold products from various countries in the 256 acres of Philadelphia's Fairmount Park.[5] Mexico's stand was formed by a structure of arches with showcases. A New York newspaper described it as a stand "almost exclusively built with plaster casts which show all the notable features of Aztec architecture during Moctezuma's rule."[6] In fact, the style of the stand was not pure Aztec but, rather, neoclassical with some Aztec adornments. But Western eyes saw what they expected to see. To a British newspaper the Mexican stand was semi-Gothic.[7] In addition to this display, Mexico was represented in an annex of the Art Gallery, together with artwork from Chile and Argentina.[8] A Mexican newspaper announced that altogether, 300,000 pesos had been allocated from the national budget for Mexico's display in Philadelphia (see Appendix 2).[9]

In agreeing to participate in Philadelphia's exposition, despite Mexico's political and economic problems, President Sebastián Lerdo de Tejada aimed to acquire international recognition for his regime. The Mexican government argued that "to have declined the invitation would have amounted to being defeated. A defeat all the more appalling since it would have meant deserting the struggle, confessing impotence, recognizing Mexico as unworthy of participating among the learned peoples."[10] The government had good reason to be concerned by its lack of international credibility. In the United States a general anti-Mexican feeling arose as a result of the Mexican-American War, and the belief that Mexico was unstable and barbaric was widespread. For instance, the *New York Times*, commenting on the arrival of boxes containing the Mexican exhibit for the Philadelphia fair, observed: "It is universally understood that the staple production of these republics is their frequent and regular political revolutions. To box up a revolution and send it to Philadelphia is impossible."[11]

The image of Mexico created for the Philadelphia exposition, and the individuals involved, formed the bedrock for many future exhibitions. In 1876, however, the group of organizers still lacked cohesion and experience. Moreover, the group had been formed before the Tuxtepec rebellion that brought Porfirio Díaz to power, so several political readjustments, conciliations, and conflicts were yet to occur. In addition, the unstable economic situation of

Lerdo's regime limited the actions of the group at Philadelphia; the more ample budget of the Porfiriato gave wizards of progress greater range and ambition.

After Philadelphia, Mexico did not resume its attendance at international expositions until the World's Industrial and Cotton Centennial Exposition that was held in New Orleans between 1884 and 1885.[12] This fair commemorated the first shipment of cotton from America to England, as well as the emergence of the post-civil-war American New South. It included a women's building and "the Exhibit of the Colored Races."[13] It was at this world's fair that the wizards of progress acquired a more or less clear configuration. In tracing back Mexico's presence in international fairs, Sebastián B. de Mier, the Mexican commissioner for the 1900 Paris world's fair, argued that Mexico's progress began to be internationally appreciated at the 1884 New Orleans fair.[14]

Gen. Díaz himself, at the time "on leave" from the presidency during Manuel González's tenure, briefly headed the Mexican Commission for the New Orleans world's fair. The commission included many of the wizards of progress and ranged from politicians like Mariano Bárcena to famous publicists like José Francisco Godoy, who was to become a diplomat and a polyglot freelance writer often hired by the Mexican government in its publicity enterprises (see Appendix 1).[15] In addition, the engineer Santiago Ramírez was asked to write a "special report on the occasion of the New Orleans Industrial and Cotton Exhibition" on Mexico's mining resources.[16]

Like its French counterparts, the New Orleans fair was a showcase for U.S. imperial aspirations, and Mexico, of course, was within the scope of those ambitions. Again like the French, the American fair organizers encouraged Latin American countries to participate and thereby lend credence to a U.S. commercial "protectorate," an unofficial support for the Monroe Doctrine. In 1884 Isaac W. Avery, who was responsible for encouraging Latin American countries to take part in the New Orleans fair, traveled around Latin America for nine months, publicizing not only the fair but also the Nicaraguan Canal project—which aimed to supplant the Panama Canal project of the French.[17]

Certainly Mexico's presence at New Orleans reflected both its domestic hopes and its international ambitions to find an outlet for its raw materials in the modern world economy. Thus, in New Orleans Mexico occupied a display of nearly 50,000 square feet within the main building of the fair, in addition to 200,000 square feet inside the gardens near the horticulture building. Without question, Mexico's attendance at New Orleans constituted the first major effort to portray itself as a modern nation on the world stage.

The Mexican presence in New Orleans was an expensive enterprise, though the U.S.$200,000 spent by the Mexican government would eventually pale before outlays at later world's fairs.[18] Díaz was informed of all financial procedures, and following the Lerdo regime's lead, the government paid the total expense, although numerous private interests, from railroad companies to a Freemason lodge in Mexico City, which gave 400 pesos, made generous donations.

In this patronage, the Mexican state approximated the French model: the state ought to manage the economy and, through expositions, seek international prestige for the ultimate economic benefit of the nation. This pattern eventually led to total governmental sponsorship, including the cost of products exhibited and both local and international transportation expenses, as in the case of Mexico's attendance at Paris in 1900.[19]

In the exhibits, the wizards of progress chose not to exploit the Indian exoticism of Mexico but, rather, to emphasize an exoticism more familiar to European eyes: Moorish architecture. Ramón Ibarrola, in charge of the architectural and engineering works for the exposition, designed the Mexican pavilion (see Fig. 1). Known as the Mexican Alhambra, it was a multicolored steel-and-iron Moorish-style construction that housed Mexican minerals, including half a ton of silver displayed as a mountain.[20] The pavilion was in fact inspired not so much by Mexico's Moorish-Spanish legacy as by the popular Moorish horticulture hall of Philadelphia 1876, in which exotic and tropical products had been exhibited.[21] Ibarrola's pavilion of 1884 was built by the Keystone Bridge Company of Pittsburgh as a structure that could be assembled and dismantled.[22] In addition to the Mexican Alhambra, a wooden building was constructed to house both a Mexican martial band and a cavalry squadron. Indeed, according to those who commented on the fair, Mexico and Japan staged the two most impressive foreign exhibits at New Orleans.[23]

The Mexican exhibit was notable for its impressive displays of minerals and agricultural products, especially tropical fruits and vegetable fibers such as henequen. For balance, a Mexican steamship, built in English dockyards, was also exhibited to exemplify Mexican progressivism.[24] In the middle of the exhibition's main corridor was a model of the "ship railroad planned by Captain Eads for the Tehuantepec Isthmus."[25]

Mexican art was an important part of the nation's international image on display at New Orleans, as it had been in Philadelphia. In the arts section, Mexico's School of Fine Arts displayed paintings by such artists as José Obregón, Santiago Rebull, Gonzalo Carrasco, and José María Velasco. As I will later show, these artists were important contributors to Mexico's modern national image. In addition, the New Orleans fair, in common with that in Philadelphia, included a women's pavilion, in which the presidential canopy made by the girls of the National Secondary School and other works by Mexican women were on display.[26]

The New Orleans fair was followed by many less important international fairs held in the southern United States. But even New Orleans eventually paled in comparison with the greatest American world's fair: the Chicago Columbian Exposition of 1893, which crowned the inclusion of the American

1. The Mexican Alhambra, as Mexico's pavilion at the 1884 New Orleans world's fair was dubbed. The structure is now on the Alameda in Santa María la Ribera, Mexico City. (Photograph by the author)

West into the great industrial development of the United States. In the meantime, those who constructed Mexico's national image moved their equipment and interests to the great European fairs—that is, to Paris.

MEXICO AT EARLY LONDON AND PARIS FAIRS

Mexico's participation in European world expositions began in the 1860s, but its presence became significant only at the Paris fair of 1889. In fact, Paris 1889 was to be the largest and most expensive of Mexico's international performances. Even Mexico's presence at the 1900 Paris fair, though less costly than that of 1889, was impressively expensive in relation to the national budget for that year.

Few traces remain of Mexico's participation in London's Crystal Palace fair of 1851. Though some products and private exhibitors came from Mexico, apparently no official Mexican commission attended.[27] Mexican antiquities, natural products, and exotic peoples had been exhibited especially in London, where the naturalist and entrepreneur William Bullock organized an inclusive Mexican display in 1824.[28]

In the 1855 imperial exposition of Paris some Mexican products were exhibited, although Mexico's economic and political chaos did not permit a significant undertaking. The Mexican government did, however, appoint a commission to represent the nation in the 1855 exposition.[29] Pedro de Escandón, head of the commission, claimed that Mexico's greatness ought to be admired, not only for the "tropical nature" which was one of its "most powerful industrial agents" but also for the potential the country would develop if it "were able to calmly devote itself to progress and development."[30]

Mexico had 107 exhibitors in 1855, in contrast with the 130 from the United States, 7 from Guatemala, 6 from Argentina, and 4 from the Brazilian Empire. The Mexican displays were largely samples of mineral and agricultural products. In addition, five cigarette-manufacturing machines were displayed, as were plans for "a musical machine that simultaneously [produced] sound and [transcribed] musical notes," a device that, Escandón claimed, could not be finished in time.[31] All of the machines were inventions by Juan Nepomuceno Adorno, a peculiar Mexican inventor who kept submitting all sorts of inventions to Mexican authorities throughout the 1860s and 1870s—from armament, accounting devices, and hydraulic plans for Mexico City, to a "kaleidoscopic machine" to avoid falsification of official documents.[32] Mexico also exhibited the saddle that had been given to Prince Albert of England by Mariano Arista.[33] All in all, Mexico's presence in Paris 1855, though somewhat weak and insignificant, launched the symbolic and propagandistic display of what were to become the main aspects of Mexico's presence in later international fairs: mining, agriculture, and native peoples and products.

Evidence of Mexican participation in European world's fairs between 1855 and 1867 is scattered, so it is difficult to draw a clear picture of the nature of its involvement.[34] We do know that a pre-Hispanic Mexican-style building was exhibited at the Paris universal exhibition of 1867. Just as Napoleon the Great had sent an archaeological commission with the army that invaded Egypt, Napoleon III sent a French scientific commission to Mexico during the intervention. This scientific group delineated and copied, among other pre-Hispanic ruins, the temple of Xochicalco.[35] The resulting model, constructed by French private interests, was exhibited at Paris in 1867 to demonstrate that "there exists thus a social life and an art in Mexico, over which Europeans have put their foot."[36] Few other traces of Mexico's participation in this world's fair remain.

Eleven years later, Paris hosted another universal exhibition. Despite French efforts to encourage Mexico's participation, Ignacio L. Vallarta, then minister of foreign affairs, strongly opposed attendance because of the continuing strain on Franco-Mexican relations in the wake of the French intervention of the 1860s.[37] Diplomatic complications made it impossible for France to officially invite Mexico to attend the Paris world's fair of 1878.[38]

Mexico took some part in various later European and American world's fairs, notably the Hispanic fair of 1883 in Buenos Aires and Berlin's fair of the same year.[39] Along similar lines, temporary and permanent Mexican exhibitions of this sort in European and American cities became quite common during the last two decades of the nineteenth century.[40] Mexico's exhibits were often forced to compete with other Latin American exhibits, so much so that Mexican official Mariano Bárcena complained in 1889 that "for Mexico, it is inconvenient to confuse its products with those of other countries, and to establish competition in such a limited ground as the one presently being offered."[41]

A MEXICO CITY FAIR?

The staging of a world's fair in Mexico City was much discussed throughout the Porfirian period, for the project was supported by various political and economic interests. To many people, a fair in Mexico City was a contradiction in itself: Mexico needed to approach the world; the world was not going to come to Mexico. But others, who thought that Mexico needed to organize its own universal exhibition, made their case by voicing a common economic concern of the time: Mexico's economic difficulties derived not from lack of production but mainly from the weak and traditional patterns of consumption. A world's fair in Mexico City, they believed, would be influential in transforming Mexican consumption habits. The project never materialized, however. The high cost of the enterprise, coupled with the main goal assigned to world's fairs—to serve as a backdrop for Mexico's display of its optimal image, not simply of itself—made the realization of a universal exposition in Mexico City impossible. Creating a picture of Mexico to be exhibited at fairs attended by all the world was one thing; making the world come to an old city full of problems was quite another. Nevertheless, brief mention of these projects will highlight the importance that Mexican elites gave to these events.

During the first years of the Porfirian period, world's fairs were used to demonstrate national stability and progress, both of which were indispensable for international recognition. Therefore, in March 1878, a month before the United States formally recognized the Díaz regime, Manuel María de Zamacona came up with the notion of a "Mexican-American" fair.[42] Because Zamacona was the main architect of American recognition,[43] a key member of the exhibition team, and an astute political actor, a fair along these lines would have further enhanced his personal prestige. Although Zamacona's idea was initially approved, it was later rejected, much to his disappointment.

In what seems to be a sequel to Zamacona's project, in 1879 the engineer Ramón Rodríguez y Arangoity, together with the American firm Edge Moor Iron Company, conceived the idea of an international exposition in Mexico City for the year 1880 (see Fig. 2). They proposed that the exposition be situated in the area surrounding the monument to Columbus on Mexico City's most elegant avenue, the Paseo de la Reforma.[44] This fair, however, never amounted to more than another unsuccessful promotional scheme, perhaps linked to real-estate interests in Mexico City.

Another project for a world's fair in Mexico City emerged in 1889, when Antonio A. de Medina y Ormaechea, founder of the Sociedad Mexicana de Consumo (Mexican Society for Consumption), proposed a universal exhibition for the year 1910.[45] Medina y Ormaechea argued that not only would a Mexican world's fair take advantage of Mexico's national and international experience, but an exposition on native soil would have fruitful educational results. For whereas Mexico's displays in American or European cities demonstrated the progressivism of the Mexican elite to the world, a universal exhibition in Mexico itself would help to educate and modernize Indians who were "satisfied with a shirt and a *calzón de manta* [cheap cotton trousers] to cover their flesh, with a pair of sandals for their feet . . . with a bowl of chiles, beans, and tortillas and a ration of pulque."[46]

In the 1890s the growth of companies—often funded by American capital—that specialized in the management and organization of world's fairs, together with Mexican and international private interests in Mexico City's profitable urban development, came together to envision a Mexican fair. René de Cornely interested a group of Mexican politicians and industrialists (including some members of the Porfirian exhibition team) in staging an international exhibition from September 1895 to April 1896 in Mexico City.

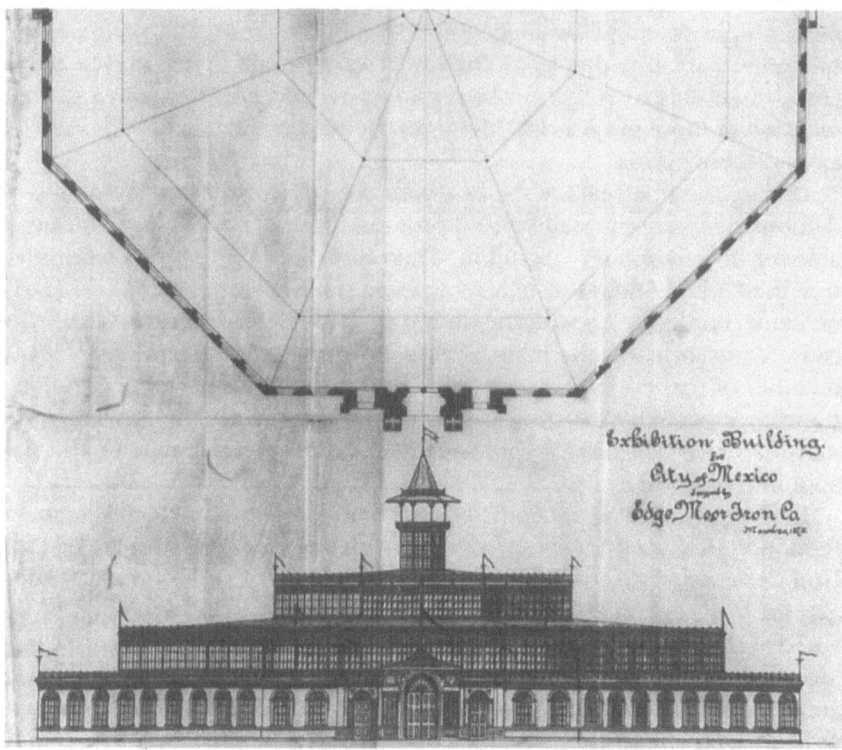

2. Drawing by the Edge Moor Iron Company of a building to house an international exhibition in Mexico. Source: EXP, Box 31, Exp. 9; reproduced courtesy of the Archivo General de la Nación, Mexico City. (Photograph by the Archivo General de la Nación)

This exhibition was publicized and, indeed, arranged down to almost the last detail.[47] The former hacienda of Anzures, near the Paseo de la Reforma and Chapultepec Park and owned by Salvador Malo, was the proposed location of the fair. Malo was a wealthy, well-known aristocrat of Porfirian Mexico. Perhaps the group was using the fair as an opportunity to rapidly urbanize the Anzures area of Mexico City in order to profit from real-estate speculation, but their plans evaporated.

PREPARATIONS FOR THE PARIS FAIR OF 1889

From 1884 to 1888 the Mexican embassy in Paris acted as a clearinghouse for information regarding the impending universal exhibition. It seems clear that Mexican bureaucrats were aware of the fact that prominent European nations were planning to boycott the French event, but they were also conscious of the major economic interests that supported the idea of a fair in Paris. Despite this realization, Mexico hesitated to officially announce its participation because of the prospect of being compelled to exhibit collectively with the other Hispanic nations, as had been the case for the Latin American countries that had taken part in the Paris exhibition of 1878.[48] Mexico's dilemma was resolved when, as a result of diplomatic pressure by Ramón Fernández, Mexican minister in Paris, the French minister of commerce assured Mexico of its right to a separate exhibit, together with all requisite facilities.[49] Thus, in August 1887 the Mexican government appointed Manuel Díaz Mimiaga, the *oficial mayor* (chief officer) of the Mexican Ministry of Foreign Affairs and a former Mexican minister to Guatemala, as its delegate to the French exhibition.[50]

This diplomatic process can be considered an expression of willingness on both sides to end the long years of tension that had characterized Franco-Mexican relations after the French intervention. Even after Maximilian's death, Mexico could not even attempt to reestablish diplomatic relations with France until Napoleon III died in 1870. Not until the Porfirian regime achieved a certain domestic political balance did the international arena regain importance for the Mexican government and did Emilio Velasco successfully negotiate the reestablishment of Mexican diplomatic relations with France.[51] Mexico's attendance at the Paris world's fair of 1889 thus appeared to be a way of promoting internationally both Mexico's republicanism and its socioeconomic maturity. It also meant the final symbolic act of reconciliation with the ever-admired French nation.

Díaz put the Ministry of Economic Development in charge of all matters relating to Mexico in Paris 1889.[52] The ministry was then headed by Gen. Carlos Pacheco, one of the few surviving old friends of Díaz, and thereafter all dispatches, products, and suggestions related to the fair were directed to Pacheco.[53]

From 1887 to 1891 the Díaz regime made a major effort to produce an image of modern Mexico. Every pamphlet, book, building, statistic, and speech displayed was meant to be part of this image. Diverse metaphors and allegories echoed a rather meager set of shared values (that is, progress, science, a cosmopolitan style, a search for uniqueness); a modern Mexican savoir faire was in the making.

FOUR

The Wizards of Progress
Paris 1889

Creating a bureaucratic class proved to be anything but natural or harmonious in Mexico. The new class emerged only through continual trial-and-error, which included learning technical processes as well as the art of political bargaining. The development of the Porfirian exhibition team—the wizards of progress—showed how growing technical and administrative expertise could be harmonized with the autocratic, centralized organization of caudillo rule. Technical skills were needed to create and maintain the modern Mexican nation. The wizards were quick to realize that modernity—understood as the maximizing of power advantages—was, on one hand, a diverse and comprehensive set of techniques to be mastered and, on the other, a means of showing that their interests coincided both with those of the nation and those of the modern civilized world.[1]

The wizards' job included the setting in motion of an intricate set of relationships that extended from the local level to the municipal, state, and national levels. They had to promote private participation from remote parts of Mexico, to collect statistical data, and to gather images of people and places for the graphic construction of an acceptable national past. At times personal relations made this task simple. For instance, it was easy for the minister of economic development to ask for photographs of and data about railroads because he was involved in their construction. However, on other occasions questionnaires were sent to the entire country to acquire necessary demographic, agricultural, educational, and sanitary information.

The Mexican exhibition team was both extremely competent and inefficient. It could produce a complete, comprehensive, accurate, and up-to-date image of the modern Mexican nation in a matter of a few months. Yet it was often disorganized and expensive. Recruitment of the wizards was based on familial, personal, and political connections, as well as on particular professional expertise. As an organization, the team functioned in an extremely centralized and hierarchical fashion, but the various components enjoyed a certain autonomy, again depending on personal and political connections and the field of expertise. Because the team was so small, each individual on it could have direct access to the top without going through many intermediaries. Its effectiveness was based on fidelity to a set of shared interests and to the values of modern cosmopolitan nationalism, as well as on loyalty to the authority of the president.

This chapter analyzes the structure and functioning of the wizards of progress, taking as its focus of analysis the 1889 Paris fair. Information on individual wizards is included in Appendix 1.

THE 1889 WIZARDS OF PROGRESS

As preparations for Paris 1889 began in earnest, numerous tasks were distributed among old and new wizards of progress.[2] A central organizing committee was approved: Alfredo Bablot of the Ministry of Justice; Emiliano Busto of the Treasury; Rodrigo Valdés and Joaquín Beltrán of the War Ministry;[3] Manuel Zapata Vera of the Foreign Affairs Ministry; José Yves Limantour, first, and later Ramón Rodríguez Rivera of the Ministry of the Interior;[4] and, finally, Manuel Díaz Mimiaga as delegate of the Mexican government in Paris.[5] The central committee began to meet in February 1888. During that year and the next, it named numerous individuals to various positions of responsibility, including directors for the nine groups at the Paris exhibition, delegates to congresses, architects, artists, draftsmen, servants, and clerks. Before the exhibition team departed for Paris, this committee discussed and decided all aspects of the Mexican display, in direct consultation with Porfirio Díaz. The Mexican display was governed by a general regulation, by which the second section of the Ministry of Economic Development was in charge of all Mexican affairs at Paris 1889 and of all other Mexican presences at international fairs for the rest of the century.

In February 1888 a provisional budget for Mexico's exhibit in Paris was offered. The projected total of 398,000 pesos[6] served as the point of reference during the first year of preparations for the Paris display.[7] But even before the budget was proposed, the Mexican government had authorized the central committee to make monthly expenditures of 10,000 francs (about 3,500 pesos) toward Mexico's participation in the fair. In fact, Mexico's actual expenditures far exceeded the estimates made by the wizards of progress, because the official figures do not reflect numerous expenses that an examination of the available archival material brings to light.[8] Sebastián B. de Mier, director of Mexico's display at the 1900 Paris fair, estimated that approximately 605,318 pesos had been spent in 1889 (see Appendix 2), but even this sum seems too modest. The official French report of the fair, written by

Alfred Picard, maintained that Mexico agreed to a government subsidy of 5 million francs (almost 1.5 million pesos), the largest sum spent by any foreign country on the 1889 exposition.[9] Whatever the precise figure, this fair was an extremely expensive event for Mexico, as it was for France.

In addition to submitting the budget, the central committee, following the French classification, appointed the directors of the various groups of displays. Leandro Fernández was put in charge of the arts (Group 1); Fernando Ferrari Pérez, of education (Group 2); Manuel Flores, of furniture (Group 3); Eduardo Zárate, of textiles (Group 4); Gilberto Crespo, of raw and manufactured products (Group 5); José María Velázquez, of general mechanics and electricity (Group 6); Antonio Peñafiel, of food products (Group 7); Pedro Sentíes, of agriculture (Group 8); and Mariano Bárcena, of horticulture (Group 9).[10] In addition, there was a large and capricious number of honorary members.[11]

Between 1888 and 1889 three significant changes in the original configuration of the team occurred. In January 1889 Leandro Fernández resigned as chief of Group 1 (works of art). Fernández argued that, though he had collected the artistic works, an artist should judge their qualities, and José María Velasco was appointed in his stead.[12] Another significant change occurred when the Mexican consul in Paris, Díaz Covarrubias, died in May of 1889. His place was filled in September by the writer Manuel Payno, then consul in Barcelona and Santander.[13] A final change occurred when José María Velázquez was replaced by Rodrigo Valdés as chief of Group 6. There is no evidence about the political or technical reasons for this last modification.[14] Minister of Economic Development Carlos Pacheco and President Díaz frequently asked Díaz Mimiaga to employ Mexican citizens who were living in Paris. In fact, on several occasions Díaz Mimiaga was compelled to accept new members as auxiliaries to the central committee due to the patronage of high-ranking Mexican personalities. For instance, Bernardo Reyes, then governor of the state of Nuevo León, recommended Abraham P. de la Garza, a Mexican engineering graduate from a Paris university, who was included as an honorary member in March 1888.[15] Similar pressure was exerted on many occasions, especially by President Díaz's wife, Carmen Romero Rubio, and by José Yves Limantour, who in 1889 was living in France, reportedly for reasons of health.[16] In addition, although not every Mexican state sent a special emissary, virtually every state appointed a member of the exhibition team or a Mexican citizen resident in Paris as its delegate. For instance, Julio Limantour was appointed representative of the Federal District (Mexico City).[17]

There were also some individuals who, though not officially listed, were nevertheless part of the Mexican team in Paris. Among them was Auguste Genin, the Franco-Mexican writer and entrepreneur mentioned in chapter 1.[18] He was the prototype of the entrepreneur of propaganda and images among the wizards of progress.[19] By September 1889, in addition to the Mexican central committee, numerous Mexican exhibitors and officials were in Paris, including the powerful northern landowners Evaristo and Francisco Madero—of the family that initiated the revolution of 1910—and the influential economist José Yves Limantour (and his wife).[20]

The central committee included, among other commissions, a press commission, an essential part of the propaganda network of the team. Its members were in charge of "writing or requesting and publishing articles, magazines, studies, etc. about the Mexican exhibition."[21] Later in this chapter I will address this type of commission.

Almost all of the wizards of progress were distinguished personalities of Porfirian Mexico. For this reason, salaries were high, especially for the directors of groups and for the persons in charge of special commissions. Most group chiefs and commissioners secured more than one income. One salary might be paid for employment in the public administration, another for being part of the exhibition team—and thus as an employee of the Ministry of Economic Development—and still another from service as deputy or in some other official post. To be part of the exhibition team was to enjoy a lucrative position,[22] in addition to the status and cachet derived from having experienced the Parisian belle epoque firsthand.

Within Mexico, an intricate network for the location and collection of products and data was organized, and all states and districts were asked to encourage local participation. Local fairs took place in the states of Jalisco, Morelos, and Nuevo León in order to preselect the products to be sent to Paris.[23] In addition, special commissioners traveled around the country looking for specific commodities—minerals, medicinal plants, raw materials, and exotic products and people. To stimulate participants, the Mexican government offered a medal to all those who took part, as well as a grant of 100 pesos.[24]

During the collection process, each group's chief was in direct contact with Gen. Carlos Pacheco and Manuel Fernández Leal, minister and vice-minister of economic development, who made most of the final decisions, often in consultation with Porfirio Díaz. Through a rather disorganized and complicated bureaucratic process at the Paris end of this chain of location and collection, products were somewhat arbitrarily secured by the directors of the various groups. All exhibitors had to fulfill some requirements, and most of them had to do with the Mexican government's main goal of promoting immigration and foreign investment.[25] One requirement was for each group to distribute all published materials to the main European libraries and museums, as well as to the other countries' committees at the exhibition.[26]

Although private participation was strongly encouraged, it was clear to the Mexican government that only the state was able to provide an accurate and complete view of the modern nation.[27] The coherent and homogeneous representation of the nation could only be a task for the state to fulfill. But what aspects ought to be emphasized in this representation? How should they be displayed in order to put forward the idea of a nation simultaneously cosmopolitan and unique? In responding to these questions, the Mexican exhibition team frequently adjusted its already pragmatic goals to its cultural and ideological objectives, especially to the changing requisites for entrance into the select club of modern nations.

THE WIZARDS' GOALS

Originally, the Mexican government designed a profile of what the Mexican exhibit ought to include. This general plan clearly expressed the Mexican elite's concept of a modern nation as well as their particular interest in world's fairs. In the end, this plan was carried out only in part, and each group, in a rather chaotic fashion, organized its own exhibit.

What the government wanted to emphasize were Mexican crafts and raw materials that would fill European needs or appeal to European tastes. In 1888 Minister Pacheco sent a memorandum to the Porfirian cabinet and to the exhibition team, arguing that "various industries in Mexico, as in all new countries, are still too primitive." However, he continued, "the modest conditions of the product say nothing against its quality." Therefore, Mexican small producers were to follow the example of the sombrero makers at the New Orleans exhibition, where "our modest palm-sombrero manufacturers found . . . a market that was as important as it was unexpected." Toward that end, Pacheco asked the state governments to finance the efforts of small producers who could not themselves afford to join the Mexican exhibit in Paris.[28] In fact, in 1889, 1893, and 1900 the Ministry of Economic Development received numerous requests for assistance from small producers.[29]

The orientation and tone of the Mexican exhibit, however, necessarily had to be provided by the various agencies of the Mexican government. Thus, overlapping and crossing the French classification and beyond the private displays of railroad companies, agricultural entrepreneurs, tobacco companies, and textile industrialists, the Mexican government targeted those aspects of the nation that were to be stressed. The idea was to create an image of Mexico that could be easily grasped by both nationals and foreigners. This goal required that the physical, economic, and social diversity of the country be reduced to an analytical reality through the massive production and ordering of maps, photographs, albums, almanacs, artistic canvases, and especially statistics, which included the "inflexible logic of numbers."[30]

In addition, those who created this image had to rearrange the stubborn national characteristics to fit the criteria of a cosmopolitan modern nation.

Therefore, on one hand, the Indian past was selectively interpreted and utilized to construct a modern secular, liberal, and republican epic for Mexico. The Mexican wizards of progress intended the uniqueness of the country, interpreted in a universal fashion, to be sufficient for admission into the cosmopolitan modern world. On the other hand, the strategic aspects—tropical fertility, good sanitation, and overall civilized development—were emphasized in order to overcome foreign prejudices.

A fundamental part of the official participation of Mexico was thus composed of samples and collections of "the most promising products already being exploited,"[31] namely, gold, silver, henequen, coffee, cacao, tobacco, cedar, and so forth. Regarding manufacturing, the Porfirian team had a pragmatic approach: first, it acknowledged and protected small-scale industry; second, it recognized the general backwardness of Mexican industry vis-à-vis France, Germany, and the United States, not to mention England. These factors combined to create a sort of official disinterest in Mexican industrial development. Thus, from the beginning the attempt was to show Mexico's "imperfect and expensive industrial products" and the facilities offered by Mexico for improvement and investment in those areas.[32]

For the Mexican team, however, the most important component of Mexico's image were public works, of which the Porfirian elite was so proud, for railroads, bridges, and factories were clear signs of progress and civilization. Consequently, numerous photographs of railroads and bridges were requested of railroad companies. Textile and other industrial manufacturing plants were also asked to send pictures of their buildings and technology. The Mexican government also aimed to give proof of its consolidation as a national republic by exhibiting pictures of national monuments and buildings, both actual and projected.

At the Paris exposition it was necessary to manipulate not only the Indian past but also the reality of a country with a large Indian population. The Mexican exhibit was therefore designed to show Europeans at one and the same time the exoticism, the nobility, and the hygienic characteristics of the Mexican Indian people. The goal was to show the good faith of Indians, which often implied the Indians' willingness to be mastered. Accordingly, the Mexican government thought to display at Paris a study of the way of life of Mexico's inhabitants, especially of the "moral and material conditions of the Mexican proletariat and peasantry." This task was originally assigned to one of the few Indians who had achieved recognition within the Porfirian elite—Ignacio Manuel Altamirano, perhaps the most important literary figure of the second half of the nineteenth century. Finally, the Mexican exhibit in Paris had to invent Mexico's cosmopolitanism. Hence, there were plans to offer a "summary of the current stage of modern Mexican culture."[33]

This very ambitious original plan was only partially fulfilled. What took place was a rather rapid collection of objects by each ministry. Each ministry had its own special program to assist the general exhibition project, with an individual in charge of the works collected under its auspices. These delegates were invariably already part of the exhibition team and occupied other posts within it.

The Ministry of Finance, represented by Emiliano Busto, was in charge of exhibiting Mexico's advancement in the scientific management of both the government and its finances. Accordingly, in addition to the official bulletin and general publications, this ministry collected photographs of the machines used to print tax stamps, descriptions and designs of the fiscal offices throughout the country, and two general volumes of statistics—*Cuadro estadístico,* by Bodo von Glümer,[34] and a compilation of agricultural, mining, and industrial statistics under the direction of Busto himself.

In order to collect these statistics, Busto suggested conducting a commercial and economic census. Toward this end, a questionnaire was to be sent to all commercial agents by way of local fiscal authorities, customs administrators, and post office employees. In addition, as part of the original plan, Busto proposed what eventually became the major display of the Ministry of Finance's in Paris 1889: a comprehensive comparative study of the public administration of France and Mexico (see chapter 8).[35]

The War Ministry, represented by Rodrigo Valdés, who was also chief of Group 6, exhibited arms, uniforms, and tools. The Museo del Hospital Militar also contributed in a major way to the exhibit on education, science, hygiene, and medicine. Included were several human organs infected by various diseases and, especially striking, the head of the Apache Indian Juan Antonio, a trophy gained by the Porfirian army during its repression of northern Indian tribes.[36]

In addition to the displays of the ministries, a commercial commission was created by initiative of Ricardo de Maria y Campos. This commission was in charge of making available and displaying a wide range of data of interest to potential immigrants and investors. Data on political organization, economic and social statistics, commercial tariffs, and legal issues in migration were widely distributed.[37]

Not all of Mexico's elaborate plans were successfully carried out, however, largely because they were too ambitious and because implementation was hampered by time pressure, inefficiency, and bad organization. Indeed, the Mexican exhibit was finished so late in mid-1889 that it could not be included in the general French catalogue of the exposition.[38] To trace the extent to which the integrity of the original master plan survived we would have to analyze its piecemeal implementation by the various groups—a long and detailed task. A review of the essential content and key personalities of Mexico's exhibit at the 1889 Paris fair will suffice to make my points.

MEXICO ON DISPLAY

The core of Mexico's display in the 1889 Paris fair was found in the exhibits of arts, education, textiles, and extractive arts (Groups 1, 2, 4, and 5). Group 1, works of art, was directed by the well-known artist Jose María Velasco, a distinguished landscape painter whose work had been greatly admired at the Philadelphia and New Orleans fairs.[39] Indeed, Velasco, rivaled only by the sculptor Jesús Contreras, was the most prominent plastic artist of late-nineteenth-century Mexico.[40] Because of his expertise as a painter and his links with intellectual circles—which dated from the middle of the nineteenth century—Velasco occupied a high position in the cultural bureaucracy and in the exhibition team, despite his humble origins.[41]

In March 1888, several well-known personalities were assigned to Velasco's group. Among them were Cayetano Ocampo, a medal engraver; Santiago Rebull, a classical painter who had been Emperor Maximilian's official painter; and Gabriel Guerra, a distinguished sculptor. All were professors at the Academia de San Carlos.[42] In addition, in September 1889, Antonio Rivas Mercado was nominated as member of this group. He was a French-trained architect and eventually became the official Porfirian architect of many buildings and monuments—among them the Columna de la Independencia, inaugurated in 1910 for the centennial celebration of independence, which still stands on Mexico City's Paseo de la Reforma. On this occasion, Rivas Mercado was commissioned to study European architectural improvements.[43] Later, in May 1889, Díaz Mimiaga suggested that Contreras be appointed auxiliary to this group for his valuable services as sculptor in charge of statuary for the Mexican pavilion.[44]

The French descriptions of the Mexican art exhibit reveal a fascination with the numerous paintings by Velasco and with the canvas entitled *El Senado de Tlaxcala*. They represented, French critics argued, a real Mexican style. In truth, in the 1889 Paris fair the core of the display of Group 1 was formed by sixty-eight Velasco paintings, five canvases by Cleofas Almanza (Velasco's student), and other works by Alberto Bibriesca, José Obregón, Adolfo Tenorio, Juan Ortega, Alberto Herrera's design of Cuauhtémoc's monument, and Contreras's busts of Porfirio Díaz and Manuel Díaz Mimiaga. In architecture, the project for a legislative palace by Anzorena y Agreda, as well as Luis G. Molina's project for a national theater, were ostentatiously exhibited.[45]

Group 2, education, was directed by Fernando Ferrari Pérez, a teacher in various Mexico City schools and a distinguished naturalist. The well-known Mexican geographer Antonio García Cubas and the historian, archeologist, and writer Alfredo Chavero were also assigned to this group.[46] In addition, in April 1888, Justo Sierra, then aged forty and a prominent educator, intellectual, and politician, became an active member,[47] though there is no evidence that he traveled to Paris in 1889 (he was present at the 1900 Paris fair).[48]

The main part of the education exhibit consisted of educational statistics, issues of major Mexican newspapers and journals, and numerous copies of works from countless schools. The exhibit as a whole was designed to portray the image of a free, liberal, well-funded, and positivist national educational system. Indeed, various French newspapers took this image more or less at face value.[49] The statistics had been prepared through a general questionnaire, supposedly sent to all educational institutions in Mexico, that was designed to elicit information on endowment, government subsidies, expenses, study programs, demographic composition, schedules, sanitary conditions, support for students, and library size. Another part of this group's exhibit dealt with natural history and included paintings of native animals, many of which were by Velasco. But what most amazed visitors was the collection of dissected small Mexican birds.

Mexico exhibited a total of 1,763 articles in this group, according to the French report. Many were grouped in Class 8—organization, methods, and appliances for higher instruction—because of the important role played by professional schools and scientific societies. However, education was of such importance for nineteenth-century Mexican liberals that, in the number of objects exhibited, Mexico was second only to France itself.

Another important exhibit was that of Group 4, textile fabrics. It was directed by Eduardo Zárate, a lawyer and professor at the Escuela de Artesanos, who had been a member of Philadelphia and New Orleans commissions as well. One of the first persons assigned to this group was Emiliano Busto, as representative of the Ministry of Finance.[50] In Mexico, the textile industry had been well established since the colonial period, and to exhibit its products in Paris was of major significance for the Mexican government. Eduardo Zárate prepared a detailed description of products for eventual exhibition, together with an inventory of textile producers, both of which were compiled by research teams that traveled to the important textile centers of the country. Eventually this research led to the compilation of a general handbook of textile statistics for the Chicago world's fair of 1893.

Zárate believed that three aspects of the textile industry should be stressed by the Mexican exhibit. First, samples of textile production of all kinds and from all regions of the country should be gathered for display. Second, the statistical compilation should be displayed for maximum impact in what Zárate envisioned as "a great statistical table of the textile industry, artistically laced at the center of the display of this branch's products in such a way that the industry's situation in our Republic will be made evident at a glance."[51] Finally, in his view, the exhibit should highlight popular Mexican clothes and costumes.[52]

On this last point, Zárate wished to harmonize the industrial and economic interests that spurred the Paris fair with the great cultural and ethnographic concerns of the late nineteenth century, likewise so evident at the exposition. Thus he proposed that dresses made of Mexican textiles be displayed on mannequins that were faithful representations of the size and physical characteristics of the inhabitants of the different regions of Mexico (that is, *tipos populares*).[53] In all, Mexico exhibited 403 objects in this group—also second only to the great French textile exhibit.

Group 5, extractive arts, was directed by Gilberto Crespo, an engineer and a former member of the New Orleans commission. The most important part of this group's exhibit was formed by various samples of mining products, statistics, photographs of mines, and specimens of all kinds of wood. The mining aspects of this exhibit were highlighted in the French catalogue over all other Mexican products.[54] This group contained specimens provided by various public figures, including Porfirio Díaz himself, who sent various samples of minerals from mines in which he had some interest, including silver and gold.[55] Other mineral products on exhibit were copper and onyx.[56]

The Mexican government was anxious that tobacco be prominently featured in this group's exhibit, because Mexico's tobacco producers, domestically protected, asked for official help to promote their product in Paris for possible use in the European market. Therefore, Ignacio Mariscal visited the Gros Caillou tobacco factory to investigate what type of tobacco the management of the French tobacco monopoly was looking for. He reported that Mexican tobacco, especially that produced by the El Valle Nacional company, was of sufficient quality to compete with Brazilian and U.S. tobacco. Acting on this report, Mexican tobacco producers named Auguste Genin as their commercial representative in Paris.

Obstacles had to be overcome in Paris, however: American, Brazilian, and Cuban competition. Even worse, La Régie (the state-owned French tobacco company) attempted to prohibit trade in tobacco at the fair. Responding to pressure by Mexico, La Régie proposed a solution: all countries would be allowed to sell tobacco in their respective pavilions, but "*La Régie* will set up a large deposit where all tobacco for the exposition will be placed."[57]

According to Genin's final report, Mexican tobaccos enjoyed great success in Paris. "Our tobacco has been remarkably welcome by the cosmopolitan public of the Exposition," he claimed, adding that better packages and publicity were needed to surmount Cuban dominance in this realm in the future.[58] In fact, E. Gabarrot and Cía., proprietor of El Valle Nacional, won two gold medals for its cigars, and M. Rivero and E. Pugibet were awarded silver medals for their cigarettes.

A total of 358 different products in Group 5 were exhibited. The larger part of the Mexican exhibit was concentrated in Classes 41 and 44—products of mining and metallurgy, and agricultural products not used for food. Mexico exhibited many other items at the various displaying groups, for a total of 3,206 different products, according to the French count. After France and its colony Algeria, Mexico's display was the largest, though not the most successful one, as the number of prizes received reveals—of its 953 prizes, only 14 were grand prizes.[59]

PROPAGANDA AND THE NATIONAL IMAGE

The functions of the wizards of progress were capped by a large propaganda network. The Porfirian regime realized the importance of propaganda to obtain international recognition and capital.[60] Porfirian officials were prompt to recognize that in modern European and American cities, everything and everybody had a price. Therefore, they reasoned, Mexico's image could look as modern and attractive as that of any other nation provided the appropriate prices were paid. Toward this end numerous writers and lobbyists, both foreign and national, became freelance writers for the Mexican government, and in the United States and Europe many books, pamphlets, and articles were directly or indirectly subsidized by the Porfirian authorities.[61]

Although Mexico's total propaganda expenses at the 1889 expositions cannot be calculated with precision, from available evidence we have to assume that the sum was significant. For example, José Francisco Godoy, the Mexican journalist who wrote various propaganda books about Mexico for distribution at international fairs,[62] received 2,500 pesos to write his *México en París*.[63] The Mexican writer Ireneo Paz, editor and director of Mexico City's newspaper *La Patria*, received 2,500 pesos to write *Los hombres prominentes de México*, which included texts in Spanish, French, and English.[64] It supported not only Mexico's international image but also the reelection of Díaz. The book consisted of biographies of Mexican entrepreneurs, politicians, artists, writers, and scientists, among them almost all of the members of the Mexican exhibition team. Those who wished to appear in this propaganda book had to pay 50 pesos. The handsome edition of this book won a silver medal in Paris.[65]

In addition, to advertise the scientific image of Mexico, the Mexican writer Manuel de Olaguíbel received 2,000 pesos to compile a bibliography of Mexican science in the nineteenth century.[66] Moreover, to have a better international impact in Paris, it was agreed that a bulletin on scientific activity in Mexico was to be published from 1888 to 1890, with no more than four issues per month.[67]

In France, F. Bianconi, author of *Le Mexique a la portée des industriels, des capitalistes, des négociants importateurs et exportateurs et des travailleurs avec une carte du Mexique commerciale, boutière, minière et agricole*, was the principal writer to publicize Mexico. Bianconi received at least 4,000 francs for his work.[68] In addition, Felipe Cazeneuve was paid 100 pesos a month to write *Le Mexique, son passé, son présent, son avenir*.[69] These efforts to exalt Mexico did not match the extravagant standards of the book published in connection with

Mexico's display at the 1900 Paris fair, for which E. Levasseur, a well-known French publicist and economist, edited the expensive two-volume work *Le Mexique au début du XXe siècle*.[70] In it, prestigious writers, politicians, and scientists were paid to write wonderful things about Mexico. The general commissioner for the 1900 Paris exposition, Alfred Picard, wrote about Mexico's industry, commerce, and transportation; the greatest of the nineteenth-century French geographers, Elisée Reclus, wrote a geographical description of Mexico; Prince Roland Bonaparte, a distinguished traveler, ethnographer, and collector, dealt with population and colonization; the ideologue of *solidarité*, Louis Bourgeoisie, wrote about Mexico's institutions; and the French senator and former minister of agriculture, Hippolyte Gomot, wrote on agriculture. This anthology aimed to portray the new Mexico for the new century, and although it is impossible to calculate the total cost, one can assume it was not cheap to collect papers from those personalities, although most of them seem only to have lent their names and signatures to what was otherwise customary propaganda, with the brilliant exception of Reclus, who included a section on Mexico in his geography of the world.[71]

By far the most important part of the propaganda network had to do with newspapers. In Paris 1889, and again in Paris 1900, the Mexican government hired the French-Polish-Mexican publicist Gustave Gostkowski as a media agent.[72] In July 1889 Gostkowski signed a contract with Díaz Mimiaga to publish articles in Parisian newspapers. These articles, it was agreed, would not only praise Mexico's exhibit but also provide data of interest to capitalists, industrialists, and businessmen. Gostkowski agreed to pay numerous writers to publish articles in such newspapers as *La Liberté, Petite République, Le National, Paris, Justice, Échos de Paris, La Nation, Le XIXe Siècle,* and *L'Événement Petit National*. In return, Gostkowski received 3,500 francs for his services.[73] Throughout 1889 he sent newspaper clippings from Paris containing very favorable articles about Mexico.[74]

At American expositions, the wizards of progress preferred the services of José F. Godoy, but in France Gostkowski and, to a certain extent, the Mexican-French entrepreneur Auguste Genin, were the main organizers of Mexican propaganda. In 1900 Gostkowski was again hired, and he produced another propaganda book, one that included a new target: tourism. The book's title suggested the new emphasis: *Au Mexique: Études, notes et renseignements utiles au capitalistes, a l'immigrant, e au touriste*.[75] Overall, the propaganda network was expensive and ineffective.[76]

The wizards of progress complemented this propaganda function with their own lobbying for Mexico in different instances. Nothing illustrates this better than the bargaining for awards at the 1889 Paris exposition. French honors had to be ardently and painfully negotiated. As soon as Díaz Mimiaga obtained the official list of awards to be granted by the French organizers, he began to lobby for many more prizes than those originally announced.[77]

In the same way he negotiated honors for various wizards of progress, obtaining a total of 94 recognitions and 37 diplomas.[78] Thus the Legion of Honor and similar awards began to be distributed for Mexicans.[79]

In sum, judged by the results obtained in immigration and foreign investment, the exhibition team was modestly successful. But judged by the speed, efficiency, and accomplishments in term of propaganda and lobbying, one could argue that Mexico did not assemble a team of similar quality until the 1990s, when the Mexican government undertook a successful and expensive campaign for an international free trade agreement.

THE RHETORIC OF CONFLICT AND THE CONFLICT OF RHETORIC

The wizards of progress, though a well-articulated and organized team, were divided by internal conflicts. Most members had direct personal economic and political reasons for safeguarding the world's fair. Those with interests in mining, agriculture, or manufacturing tried to earn the favor of international capitalists and to promote their own companies. Bureaucrats and scientists were prompt to foster their own political or scientific areas of influence within the Mexican government. All personal interests operated within a small and tightly linked framework of relationships. Conflicts were often incited by personality differences or by the all-too-common attempts to bypass the hierarchical order. Because all of the members were so closely related, it was easy for almost anyone to gain the ear of Minister Pacheco or even President Díaz—a frequent occurrence in the many years during which the group labored for the success of Mexico's presence at world's fairs.

Devotion to Díaz's authority was what ultimately unified the group. Nationalism and professionalism were understood as loyalty to a set of principles and ideas. In the application of their ideas and in their loyalty to authority, they were quite a complex and disciplined team; that is, one could say that, though full of conflicts, they formed a modern team.

The wizards of progress weathered many personal difficulties during the course of their service. Except for the serious economic problems they experienced in preparing for the 1893 Chicago exhibition, the greatest conflicts among the members of the exhibition team had to do with the 1889 world's fair. Most of the problems were caused by the very structure of the team, and the fashion in which those conflicts were expressed is fundamental to understanding the nature of the Porfirian political organization. No conflict was openly discussed until all avenues of reconciliation were exhausted. Once a conflict became public, the first priority of all factions was to express loyalty to Díaz and/or Pacheco, which meant—through bizarre rhetorical twistings and turnings—loyalty to the country they represented. Finally, whenever friction rose, language was both the weapon and the battlefield, and, as with the whole Porfirian political culture, an eloquent style was indispensable because, as argued before, style was far from a mere rhetorical accessory, it was what late-nineteenth-century culture was all about.

Countless frictions emanated from Díaz Mimiaga's difficult personality. He seems to have been pretentious and authoritarian, and, although Porfirio Díaz trusted him, he never achieved a position higher than that of *oficial mayor* in the Ministry of Foreign Affairs. His status within the Porfirian hierarchy can be judged by the fact that his biography appears in only one of the many biographical dictionaries of the epoch: Ireneo Paz's *Hombres prominentes de México*, for which, as mentioned above, those who wished to be included had to pay 50 pesos.[80] Díaz Mimiaga died in Italy in 1891, while serving as Mexican minister to that country.[81]

Díaz Mimiaga's angular personality impeded the work of the exhibition team on more than one occasion. Quarrels with various team members prompted Alfredo Bablot, general secretary of the Mexican commission in Paris, to write a letter to the minister of economic development in April 1890 in which he blamed Díaz Mimiaga for much of the delay in the inauguration of the Mexican pavilion. Bablot characterized Díaz Mimiaga as "a real disaster."[82] Another scandal erupted among the wizards of progress when Ramón Fernández accepted a Bolivian invitation to attend what was billed as a dialogue to foster scientific discussion among the Latin American nations. Fernández informed the Mexican minister of foreign affairs of his plans in order to guard himself against the wrath of Díaz Mimiaga, who had forbidden his colleagues to attend meetings at which he could not also be present. Díaz Mimiaga tried to censor all memoranda directed to Pacheco and Porfirio Díaz.[83] He considered Fernández's action an affront to his authority. The subsequent debate among the commission members was resolved only when Fernández, ordered by Pacheco, apologized, even though the wizards of progress present at Paris declared themselves unable to achieve a final verdict.[84]

In all conflicts the final decision was made after consultation with President Díaz himself. So it was in the case of Jesús Contreras, the famous Mexican sculptor who tried to have a hand in the construction of the Mexican pavilions at both the 1889 and the 1900 Paris world's fairs.[85] Not until Díaz ordered that Luis Salazar and Antonio de Anza were to be in total control of the construction did Contreras cease all artistic and entrepreneurial efforts, including plans prepared with the assistance of a French engineer.[86]

One other conflict illustrates both the issue of loyalty and the significance of language. In November 1889, according to the session's minutes, a great debate took place among the members of the commission regarding the feasibility of fulfilling all of the conditions established by the *Reglamento económico* for the Mexican display in Paris. Zárate verbalized his interpretation of the *Reglamento*, making clear that it was impossible to complete what had originally been mandated. He acknowledged Bablot's good intentions in preparing this document and praised him highly. But at the same time he called

Bablot and his *Reglamento* an "extremely compassionate father of a brutal son,"[87] and in an eloquent speech he assailed various aspects of the *Reglamento* as infeasible. Bablot, no less well spoken, said of Zárate's criticism that "it is a pity that so much beauty is not true." He maintained that Zárate and those who agreed with him aimed to "innocently cast me, expiatory victim, into eternal flames." However, in his defense Bablot pointed to his loyalty to President Díaz and Minister Pacheco and said he would go to the "dark Avernus in good company" because both Díaz and Pacheco had approved the *Reglamento*.

Bablot then argued that labeling his *Reglamento* a *monstrum horrendum* had been unfair, and in rebuttal he reviewed the *Reglamento* item by item. For instance, regarding article 16, which mandated that group chiefs keep themselves up-to-date concerning the different aspects of the production of their particular products, Bablot responded to Zárate's criticism by arguing that indeed group chiefs were constantly comparing Mexican products with their foreign counterparts. Thus, he ironically asserted, "not even remotely could it be assumed that Mr. Zárate thinks that his colleagues are so unconscious as to comply with Article 16 the same way Mr. Jourdain in Molière's drama spoke in prose without being aware of that fact." To Zárate's complaint regarding the impossibility of having each chief write a report on the development of his disciplines, Bablot replied that the travel impressions of each were sufficient. Sarcastically, Bablot commented: "And surely we needed Mr. Zárate to tell us his story to know that today it is an insufferable sacrifice to travel through Europe in a sleeping car, with toilet, shower, dining room, boudoir, salon, smoking room, and all those unbearable discomforts invented by that cannibal Pullman." Bablot concluded the defense of his *Reglamento* by accusing Zárate of stigmatizing, "through the annihilating rays of his eloquence," the *Reglamento* with "touches of rhetorical flowers called exaggeration."

In fact, Bablot was, as poet Manuel Gutiérrez Najera characterized him, the prototype of the orator who "distracts the enemy with fast moves, zigzagging, making the enemy feel drowsy, and, at precisely the right moment, opens the joints of the armor and calculates and nails the rapier from there."[88] The rhetoric with which this conflict was expressed caricatured the role of style in a courtlike bureaucratic structure. Zárate's speech and Bablot's response not only made references to but also created the common reality over whose details the two men quarreled. Thus both proclaimed their loyalty to Pacheco, to Díaz, and to the idea of progress. Moreover, this conflict demonstrated how, in an openly eloquent era, the human pecking order worked through rites of intimidation expressed with pure and penetrating selection of words.

By 1889 Mexico's exhibition team was more or less consolidated. The wizards of progress constituted a group that eventually included a large portion of the elite: from Porfirio Díaz to such literary and artistic heroes as José María Velasco or Amado Nervo; from prominent economists and financiers like José Yves Limantour to official historians and archaeologists like Antonio Peñafiel. Most of Mexico's regional and national elites were at some point involved with Mexico's presence at world's fairs—from Francisco Madero (the father), who was a distinguished personality at Paris in 1889, to Justo Sierra in Atlanta's exhibition of 1895 and Paris 1900.[89] By the end of the Porfirian era this team was so specialized and so capable of producing a complete image of the nation in a very short period of time that—as I will show in chapter 11—even the first revolutionary government requested its help when attempting to join San Francisco's Pan-American world's fair of 1915.

FIVE

The Aztec Palace and the History of Mexico

The French diplomas awarded at the 1889 world's fair pictured the chariot of peace and progress, pulled by two lions that were, in turn, led by two short human figures carrying giant drums. Just as the diplomas represented an attempt to allegorize what was considered modern, the 1889 Aztec Palace allegorized the entire world's fair. The palace was meant to highlight the great, though atypical, lineage of the nation it represented: a national entity with a glorious past but ready to adjust to the dictates of cosmopolitan nationalism and eager to be linked to the international economy. As the Cuban poet José Martí explained to Latin American children: "This steel Aztec temple was erected at the foot of the Eiffel Tower by Mexicans, so that their history, which is like the mother of their country, would not be touched by those who do not see themselves as sons of Mexico—such is the way one ought to love the land in which one is born! with such fearlessness, with such tenderness."[1]

The exoticism of the Aztec Palace, as well as its combination of archaeology, history, architecture, and technology, was seen by Mexicans and Europeans alike as no more than an essay, an attempt. If all material things were ephemeral in world's fairs, then the ideas they symbolized were expressed as an essay. They formed a coherent, incomplete, and experimental proposal that sought to persuade spectators of the reality of its propositions. The Aztec Palace thus constituted a trial in several ways. It was an attempt to recapitulate and incorporate diverse interpretations of the domestic past; it was an experimental synthesis of Mexican perceptions of the European commercial, industrial, and exotic appetite for the non-European; it was an effort to achieve the proper combination of particularism and universalism; and it was an overall essay on the modernity of the Mexican nation.

In another respect, the Mexican pavilion in the 1889 Paris world's fair was not an essay but a conclusive statement. The Aztec Palace ratified the value, importance, and truth not only of the modern creed itself but also, and especially, of the very import of continuing the attempt to follow the creed, to reproduce it, to copy it. Consequently, the Aztec Palace faithfully re-created the Panglossian sense of the end of history that the whole fair epitomized. It was a categorical petition to enter the modern world.

From the historian's point of view, the Aztec Palace can be seen as a frozen portion of time and space that fossilized an emblematic moment—of conclusiveness and experimentation—in the attempt by the Mexican elite to formulate a vision of its past, present, and future. This chapter and the next two are devoted to understanding this frozen evidence. But because the historian's practice is inescapably a sequential task—that is, one must retain the chronological order of events—the principal themes in the history of the Aztec Palace must be explored concurrently. Especially relevant for the Aztec Palace is the unfolding of two stories: the record of the various ways in which the nation's history was conceived, which I tell in the remainder of this chapter; and the chronicle of the scientific (that is, archaeological and anthropological) ideas about Mexico and Mexicans that were articulated both domestically and internationally, covered in chapter 6. A third historical track converged with and included these two histories: the history of the material (more or less artistic) depictions of the nation, the subject of chapter 7. Although these chapters focus on the Aztec Palace, in fact they take the palace as the pivot for the examination of a larger cultural contour that encompasses the period between the 1870s and the 1910s.

The Aztec Palace was ostensibly nothing more than the Mexican pavilion at the 1889 Paris fair, but it also represented a moment in the writing of the history of Mexico. Tracing the evolution of the conception of the palace involves the appraisal of what it synthesized in the late 1880s: the long political and intellectual dispute over the Indian past; the historiographical infrastructure developed throughout the nineteenth century (both by Mexicans and foreigners); and the latest theoretical, rhetorical, and graphic tools for developing a comprehensive national identity that could be taught and enacted.

When the Mexican authorities announced the construction of a Mexican pavilion for the 1889 Paris world's fair, they declared that it ought to be "a building which at its sides and angles would characterize the architecture of the most civilized races of Mexico, but which would distance itself from the dimensions of ancient monuments that opposed modern necessities and taste."[2] The effort to be authentically Mexican was combined with that of being modern. To be genuinely Mexican implied a particular view of the Mexican past, especially of the Indian past that had been, throughout Mexican history, vital for the definition of a self-assured national identity.

As a specific view of Mexican history, the Aztec Palace responded both to domestic and to international political and cultural impulses. Nationally, it was as eloquent as, and even more vivid than, the first great general and comprehensive compendium of Mexican history, *México a través de los siglos*, which was also completed in 1889. In a sense the whole nation was crystallized in a book at the same time as it was being exemplified in a building, overriding internal political, racial, and regional disparities. Internationally, as following chapters will illustrate, it constituted an ad hoc complement for late-nineteenth-century Western orientalism.[3] The concurrences between the Aztec Palace and *México a través de los siglos* best characterize the boundaries within which those elements of Mexican history that were national, homogeneous, logical, and learnable were discussed during the Porfiriato. Previous nineteenth-century historical reconstructions of the nation's past had not reconciled themselves into a single comprehensive history in chronological, geographical, or ideological terms. Porfirian intellectuals finally achieved the desired synthesis, which put special emphasis on two central issues: on one hand, the creation of a civic religion with a well-delineated chronology and hierarchy of events and a demarcated set of heroes; on the other, the reconstitution of the Indian past as an inherent component of Mexican nationhood. The latter issue was in turn the late-nineteenth-century solution to the long-standing dilemma of Mexico's criollo identity—that is, the conflict between the Spanish heritage and the Indian present and past.

The process of designing the Aztec Palace was the physical resolution of the intricate debate over how to make a modern country in the late nineteenth century. The resolution came after long bureaucratic and intellectual negotiation. Two commissions were assigned to submit proposals for the Mexican pavilion in Paris. The engineer Luis Salazar and the architects Vicente Reyes and José María Alva formed the first team; the second comprised the historian and statistician Antonio Peñafiel and the engineer Antonio de Anza. Both proposals were only syntheses of the national history in visual, monumental form, and both sought architectural inspiration in histories that had preceded them while reinforcing a new patriotic history.[4]

In the early 1880s the beatification of the Indian president, Benito Juárez, and of the last Indian emperor, Cuauhtémoc, were emblematic of the attempts to create a civic religion around well-established—and graphically perceivable—deities. By the early twentieth century it was commonplace for Mexicans to praise three great national heroes and their individual contributions to the nation's evolution: Hidalgo for independence, Juárez for liberty, and Díaz for peace.

In reviving the Indian past, late-nineteenth-century historians, writers, and politicians were not working in a vacuum. From Bernardino de Sahagún to Francisco Xavier Clavijero, from Carlos María de Bustamante to Manuel Orozco y Berra, the Indian past had gained a more or less distinct form and content. Foreign observers such as Alexander von Humboldt, Guillerme Dupaix, Edward King (Viscount Kingsborough), William H. Prescott, and Desiré de Charnay, among many others, were also influential in the historical reconstruction of Mexico's Indian past.

For Mexican criollo patriots since colonial times, the Indian past was an invaluable source of pride and legitimation, a means of seeking equality with and recognition from Europeans. Attachment to the beauty and resources of Mexico, as well as fidelity to religious values and figures, also played a part in the criollo patriotism, which, it can be argued, had never actually disappeared from the debates over Mexican historiography and nationalism.[5] By the late nineteenth century, the long-standing appreciation of the Indian past was incorporated into modern liberal conceptions.

Thus criollo patriotism and liberal nationalism contained an indigenist element. However, this indigenism was not accompanied by a substantial general and total reinterpretation of the Mexican past or by a general idea of the nation's future shape. The early criollo indigenism—of, for instance, Carlos María de Bustamante or Fray Servando Teresa de Mier—was too radical to serve as a guideline for writing the general history of an Indian nation ruled by a white minority.[6]

The conservative Lucas Alamán, on the other hand, composed the first extensive historical account of Mexico's past and, with it, a more or less articulate program for the modern nation. In *Historia de Méjico* he attempted an unbiased analysis of the Indian past, acknowledging the technological advancements of the natives but stressing their barbaric religion.[7] But for him the origins of the Mexican nation were in the Spanish Conquest, which had made a tabula rasa of all prior histories. However comprehensive and well constructed, Alamán's history became prey for the tumultuous political life of Mexico during the nineteenth century. Alamán's links with conservative and monarchist circles in contentious times and the final ruin of the conservative cause brought about by the French intervention made his type of national project politically suspect and difficult to propose. Yet Alamán condensed a historical view of Mexico that remained in the background of Mexico's nationalistic discourses as late as the 1920s.[8]

The liberals of the first half of the nineteenth century simply did not count on a Lucas Alamán to assemble a comprehensive liberal history of Mexico. But factionalism and endemic wars did not help the liberals compose a comprehensive liberal account of the nation's history, and their creolism and tamed indigenism (if indigenism at all) prevented them from following the example of reformist groups like the young Ottomans who, in the 1860s, used Islamic ideas to legitimize the need to modernize (Westernize) the Ottoman

Empire along European lines. The Ottoman reformers came to equate progress with "a return to the true spirit of Islam."[9] Mexican liberals, in contrast, were too Europeanized to even conceive of a modern milieu that would be Indian or to use the concept of Indianness in the cause of modernity (not, at least, until the 1910s).

After the overthrow of Maximilian's empire and the definitive establishment of the Reform laws in the 1860s, liberal factions began to rewrite Mexico's past and map out its future. This was a process of ideological and historiographical negotiation, for liberals did not have a golden age—as Alamán had found in the Hispanic colonial era—to look back on, at least until the crystallization of the Reform as an epic moment. In the middle of the nineteenth century, liberal romantics—such as Manuel Payno, a great synthesizer whose history textbook became quite influential in the 1870s—could not look to the colonial period as their paradise lost, especially because the independence movement was too close to them, both chronologically and emotionally. Instead, they turned to the Spanish Conquest and portrayed Indians as brave and noble warriors.[10]

By the 1880s, once various regional and political factions had established a relative status quo, Porfirian liberals realized that a comprehensive nationalistic history was a sine qua non both for the consolidation of the nation and as a proof of stability and civilization.[11] They were especially aware that such a history had to be taught and disseminated if a national consciousness was to form.[12] For them, if history was not a lesson—in both an exemplary and an educational sense—it was not history. The nation, it was claimed by the Porfirian government, would be consolidated in the classrooms. However, the liberals soon learned to be unfaithful to their goal, restricting themselves to making the nation not by teaching it to a dispersed and illiterate population but, rather, by exhibiting it both domestically and internationally. In any event, not until the 1880s did concise liberal histories of the nation start to materialize.[13] Then came the first general and comprehensive synthesis of Mexico's past: *México a través de los siglos,* a collective, reconciliatory, and conclusive enterprise that included authors from different liberal factions.

The Aztec Palace in Paris was the steel version of *México a través de los siglos.* In its walls, as well as in the displays they sheltered, the story told by the new history text was echoed. The book was a five-volume compendium written by the victorious liberals, headed by Vicente Riva Palacio and including Alfredo Chavero, Julio Zárate, Juan de Dios Arias, Enrique de Olavarría y Ferrari, and José María Vigil. It was published by Santiago Ballesca, then a well-known Catalan publisher who lived in Mexico and published many important books in the late nineteenth century.[14] Although it is not clear how the book was originally conceived, it seems to have been fostered by a conscious will to reorder and put together the whole Mexican history in one book according to the views of the liberals in power.[15] But Riva Palacio's historiographical endeavor especially echoed the goals of the Aztec Palace in the sense that, from its original conception, the book was meant to introduce Mexico to the civilized world as a modern nation: "a first class book . . . to be known throughout the enlightened world."[16]

Riva Palacio wrote the second volume—*El virreinato*—of *México a través de los siglos*. Above all, he was a writer, truly a man of letters,[17] and his treatment of the colonial period can be viewed as that of a liberal who had come to terms with the Spanish past, a period that had long been the patrimony of conservative historians. Accordingly, the conquest was the painful and inevitable defeat of a great nation at the hands of a still more advanced civilization. The encounter was, in Riva Palacio's view, the first step in the emergence of the new nation. Hence, following the then-in-vogue French writer Ernest Renan and his question, *Qu'est-ce qu'une nation?*, he maintained that the nation needed a unified territory, language, culture, and that "all attempts at independence will be in vain until the crossbreeding of race produces a new people, exclusively Mexican."[18]

In effect, what Riva Palacio argued was that, beginning with the Spanish Conquest, a mestizo nation had emerged as a natural fusion, and this fact gave new value to both of its inherent components: Indians and Spaniards. Riva Palacio fashioned a cunning argument through an intricate amalgamation of Renan's type of nationalist thought, Darwin's transformism, and classical criollo patriotism. That is, cultural (linguistic and racial) nationalism and social Darwinism combined with the old patriotism of Mexican criollos that went back to the 1780s and these liberals' common nationalist education during foreign interventions (1840s and 1860s).[19] Therefore, Riva Palacio could justify the very task of writing a national history as something beyond the mere recounting of the past for its own sake. For Riva Palacio, and unlike Lucas Alamán fifty years earlier, the consolidation of nationhood was beyond the capacity of mere antiquarians and above narrow considerations of objectivity. And thus his literary capacities gained importance, because in writing about the nation, the form became the essence. Riva Palacio thought that empirical historical facts made sense only as expressions of something more essential (divine). The nation therefore seemed to occupy the place of God in Riva Palacio's writing.

Ironically, Riva Palacio combined this romantic nationalism with a description of the racial characteristics of Indians that followed Darwinian parameters filtered through French translations.[20] In common with the criollo patriots of the independence period, he even praised, albeit in Darwinian terms, the superiority of the Indian race vis-à-vis the European races, because Indians "[have] lost beard and bodily hair, lost the wisdom teeth, and acquired a new molar, substituting the canines which in Europe's most advanced races still exist in a rudimentary state." Nonetheless, as I have mentioned, Riva Palacio thought that mestizos would eventually become a new race that incorporated the best features of its two constituents and formed the real Mexico.[21] In fact, Riva Palacio's transformation of traditional criollo patriotism advanced what would eventually become, without the heavy racial component, the official twentieth-century mestizo definition of Mexican nationhood.[22]

The Aztec Palace echoed *México a través de los siglos* most noticeably when it came to the liberal reconstruction of the pre-Hispanic past. The volume that Alfredo Chavero wrote for *México a través de los siglos* dealt with pre-Hispanic times.[23] Like Riva Palacio, Chavero was a man of letters: an archaeologist and historian of pre-Hispanic Mexico as well as a writer of dramas that—by the 1870s—often had Aztec motifs.[24] He was the prototype of the late-nineteenth-century Mexican indigenist.[25]

Chavero's prose, like that of Riva Palacio, was especially well suited to the construction of a liberal past for Mexico. His writings, as Riva Palacio himself argued, were motivated by a patriotic spirit, "striving to bring to the stage characters such as queen Xochitl and Meconetzin, but with these characters nobody can make a name for himself in Mexico, because it multiplies insurmountable problems."[26] In fact, Chavero's and Riva Palacio's rhetorical abilities included the intersection of old and new means of expression: the neoclassical liberal rhetoric—a legacy of late colonial times and liberal republicanism—and the emerging professional languages fostered by various sciences.[27] Thus while the engineers of the Aztec Palace debated whether to use steel and marble in neoclassical or purely Aztec fashion, the writers of Mexican liberal history experimented with baroque Greco-Roman metaphors versus organicist, biological, and technical ones.

In *México a través de los siglos* Chavero emphasized the strength and significance of the Nahua culture over other cultures, as well as his conviction about the degeneration of races: "It would be a mistake to judge the greatness of the ancient Mexican empire by our present-day Indians."[28] He concluded with an evolutionist view of the growth of Aztec preeminence: "Thus started gestating the three [Otomi, Nahua, and Maya] civilizations that would develop in the course of several centuries, until the Nahua, the most perfect and powerful of the three, would expand and dominate the entire territory."[29] This epitomized the late-nineteenth-century liberal appropriation of the Aztecs as the only past of the modern nation.

Together, all the authors of *México a través de los siglos* achieved what the country had never before had: a comprehensive and articulated picture of its entire history. But it was not a purely Mexican perspective. The work was a synthesis directed at domestic readers, but it also served as a point of reference for readers from abroad. On one hand, the book was paid for in part by private subscribers who received it in periodical deliveries. According to Ballesca, the number of subscribers reached 7,000 in 1882 but declined to

3,000 by 1889.[30] On the other hand, the book was meant to be, like the Aztec Palace, a modern monument, as Riva Palacio put it, "a monument worthy of the advancement that typography has achieved in our century."[31] The picture of the country the book presented sought to resolve internal disparities and to foster nationalism, but it also aimed to fit together the parameters of the political, social, and economic ideas, many of them foreign, that inspired the multivolume book. And it did so in a beautiful and colorful Catalan edition, subsidized by the Mexican government, that made use of all of the representational resources then available to the printing arts. Lithographs and pictures were as much part of the late-nineteenth-century literature as were romantic novels and travel descriptions, and the lithographs by F. Fuste and R. Canto in *México a través de los siglos* produced a vivid, animated, and pedagogic impression.[32] In addition, photographs and lithographs from national and international expeditions, as well as descriptions and reproductions from foreign historians and archaeologists, were included and so became part of the national symbolism.[33] *México a través de los siglos* was thus an object lesson on the importance of books to the modern world (see Figs. 3a and 3b).[34]

The nationalism that *México a través de los siglos* synthesized and that the Aztec Palace expressed was simultaneously paralleled by international political and cultural trends that in some way fostered this reargumentation of the Mexican past. Oddly enough, this growing radical nationalism coincided with the growth of cultural cosmopolitanism, because an international common model of values and fashions had emerged among the middle classes. On one hand, cosmopolitanism was considered an attribute of the adventurous and tolerant, the conquest and appreciation of the exotic. In this sense, cosmopolitanism meant open-minded European acknowledgment of other values, things, and peoples. As Baudelaire himself claimed when he commented on the 1855 Paris world's fair, "That divine grace of cosmopolitanism" meant that "beauty is always bizarre."[35] On the other hand, cosmopolitanism was a set of European values, things, and attitudes that had to be adopted if one was to be modern.

Mexico's elite was linked to the transformation of nationalism as well as to both notions of cosmopolitanism. Accordingly, they racially—scientifically—redefined Mexican nationhood by supplying Mexico with an acceptable national uniqueness and a degree of exoticism.

The two proposals for a 1889 Mexican pavilion that were submitted sought to represent the Indian past faithfully and to make it coincide with modern progress, and both were historically supported and inspired by the historical synthesis introduced by *México a través de los siglos*. Both proposals attempted to satisfy the cosmopolitan and exotic appetites of the modern

3. Covers of *México a través de los siglos,* vols. 1 (top) and 4 (bottom). Sources: Vicente Riva Palacio, ed., *México a través de los siglos,* vols. 1, 4 (Barcelona, 1887–1889).

world; both shared the conviction of having arrived at the final stage of progress and the idea of reconciliation. Yet they varied in the extent and weight they gave to the different components of the nationhood they sought to mirror.

The building design submitted by Luis Salazar, Vicente Reyes, and José María Alva was a bizarre architectural synthesis of pre-Hispanic architectural styles based on a collection of antiquities assembled by Lord Kingsborough, *Antiquities of México*.[36] Jean Fréderic Waldeck's lithographs of the pre-Hispanic architecture of the Maya region were also used by Salazar.[37] In addition, Salazar was influenced by the pioneering work of Capt. Guillerme M. Dupaix, who had been commissioned by the king of Spain to study the Maya ruins during the first decades of the nineteenth century, as well as that of the photographer and archaeologist Desiré de Charnay, who was part of the 1857 French scientific commission that photographed and studied pre-Hispanic ruins in Mexico.[38] In fact, Salazar above all used Chavero's synthesis of all the above-mentioned works that had been included in *México a través de los siglos*.[39]

Salazar Reyes and Alva conceived a pavilion that merged features of ancient Indian buildings with those of modern architecture, especially with steel and wood construction (see Figs. 4a and 4b). The structure was meant to be dismantled and later reassembled to serve as a government building in Mexico. Salazar thus imagined a complex combination of Indian architectural styles with ornamentation inspired by pre-Hispanic mythology. As historian Fausto Ramírez observed, the combination was in tune with the fusionist policies of the Díaz regime.[40] In the Salazar palace, all pre-Hispanic styles and histories were synthesized into one single architectural past, which in turn was the stylistic antecedent of the modern nation. The building was 70 meters long, 30 meters wide, and 17.20 meters tall. The shape of the base was a copy of Xochicalco's temple, combined with motifs taken from Mitla's ruins. The monolith of Tenango was used as a model for the columns, and the lateral windows were copied from Palenque's forms as described by Dupaix and Charnay and reinterpreted by Chavero.[41]

The second proposal for a Mexican pavilion, that of Peñafiel and de Anza, was the project finally accepted. According to Peñafiel, their building epitomized the essential features of the Mexican pre-Hispanic monuments and the Mexican national history. Unlike Salazar, Peñafiel aimed not to develop a national architectonic style but to be faithful to the real pre-Hispanic past of the Mexican nation and to the natural organic evolution of Mexico. Thus his project was a reproduction of a *teocalli* (an Aztec temple), because in his view Aztecs conformed to the authentic past of Mexico. He guaranteed that in his project "there is no detail, symbol, or allegorical figure that has not been drawn from the true Mexican archaeology and with the only intent of bringing back to life a genuine national civilization."[42]

4. Plans for facades of the Mexican palace at the 1889 Paris Universal Exhibition, by Luis Salazar (top) and J. M. de Alva (bottom). Source: México, Secretaría de Fomento, *Proyectos de edificio para la Exposición Internacional de París 1889* (Mexico City, 1888).

In formulating his proposal, Peñafiel followed the official historiography, especially Chavero's account in *México a través de lo siglos,* and his own research. In addition, he incorporated into his project the investigations of the Prussian scholar Edward Seler in European archives.[43] In the end, Peñafiel considered only the Aztec people as being worthy of pride and celebration, the true antecedent of the Mexican modern nation.[44] In the official pamphlet that explained the Mexican pavilion, Peñafiel contended that the building was constructed in the "purest Aztec style," as described in his own book, *Monumentos del arte mexicano antiguo.*[45] He maintained that it was to be constructed in steel for easy disassembly and reconstruction in Mexico, "should the government deem it appropriate,"[46] for an archaeological museum. This pavilion was 70 meters long, 30 meters wide, and 14.50 meters tall, with a glass ceiling and no internal walls except the steel skeleton and the glass showcases.

Peñafiel's goal was to allegorically depict the vigor of the Aztec religion, agriculture, and arts, all understood within an evolutionary line from the beginning of the Aztec civilization to its end, the starting point of Mexican nationhood. Therefore, the building comprised three sections: "The building's central part stands for the capital ideas of religion; the sides stand for agriculture and the arts, principal elements of its progress, and in the middle figures representing the beginning and the end of the ancient Mexican civilization" (see Fig. 5).[47]

What Peñafiel did was to select, from what he knew of Aztec architecture, the elements that would meet the requirements of modern nineteenth-century allegorical architecture. Therefore, he looked for Mexican-style columns to substitute for the Greco-Roman columns so common in the neoclassical constructions of his own day. In the portico of the building were "two caryatids, whose shape I took from an archaeological study I did recently in Tula, state of Hidalgo, with the purpose of finding columns that could be used in [modern] Mexican architecture."[48]

The official guide to the building, unlike Salazar's description, did not explain the aesthetic origins of each section of the building; rather, it was a narrative of the heroics of the Aztec people. In the guide, Peñafiel explained that his design was a "mythological representation akin to the exposition's ends."[49] By the goals of the exposition he meant the French exhortation to the builders of foreign pavilions to show their native styles. However, in picturing Aztec gods and heroes Peñafiel was doing something more than satisfying the French requirements. He was continuing a long ideological and cultural Mexican tendency to selectively reevaluate the Indian past as part of the national identity.

Following this rendering of a national epic, the Aztec heroes were cautiously depicted and arranged in a symbolic order, so as to clearly present the epic of the Mexican nation. Therefore, the facade of the Aztec Palace was divided

5. Entrance to the Aztec Palace at the 1889 Paris Universal Exhibition. Source: William Walton, *Chefs-d'oeuvre de l'Exposition Universelle de Paris, 1889* (Philadelphia and Paris, 1889).

into two sets of bronze sculptures, all designed by the Mexican sculptor Jesús Contreras, who was then studying in Paris. One set was located at each side of the facade; the other decorated its central part. In the first set, on the right side of the palace, were Centeotl (goddess protector of agriculture), Tlaloc (god of rain), and Chalchiutlicue (goddess of water). On the left side were Xochiquetzal (god of arts), Camaxtli (god of hunting), and Yacatecuhtli (god of commerce). In the central facade were six representations of Aztec heroes: on the right, Itzcoatl, Nezahualcoyotl, and Totoquihuatzin; on the left, Cacama, Cuitlahuac, and Cuauhtémoc. I will examine these representations later.

Although Peñafiel was considered both an archaeologist and a statistician, his language was even more rhetorically neoclassical than was that of Riva Palacio or Chavero. Peñafiel's official description of the building was a romantic narrative, full of classical references that highlighted the heroism and high degree of civilization of the Aztec world. The Aztecs, he maintained, were superior to the Greeks in their arts "because they managed to do with the straight line, the most ingrate of the lines, what the Greeks did with the curve, which has always easily brought with it beauty at its best."[50] His classicism was also expressed in his metaphors of the heroes Cacama, Cuitlahuac, and Cuauhtémoc, who stood for what he called "the end of the Mexican monarchy" and whose lives, he claimed, were like a "chant by Homer.... Plutarch would have painted those three towering heroic figures of Mexico with the colors of Scipio and Graco."[51]

Although Peñafiel emphasized the greatness of the Indian past and thus talked about the brutality of the Spanish Conquest, his stance was far from rigidly anti-Spanish. Like Chavero and Riva Palacio, Peñafiel depended heavily on Orozco y Berra's description of the conquest, and he established a distinction between sixteenth-century Spain and modern, progressive Spain.[52]

In the end, both Peñafiel's and Salazar's proposals were submitted to the Mexican Central Committee for the 1889 Paris fair and to Porfirio Díaz himself, and in May 1888 the central committee discussed both projects. Chavero favored the Salazar-Reyes-Alva project, arguing that it was "the perfect creation of a new and splendid style taken from the ancient monuments of Mexican art";[53] that is, a reconciliation both of the various Indian pasts and of these pasts and the present. However, frictions were obvious among committee members regarding the proper degree of indigenism to incorporate into the building. To minimize these, Zárate and Flores proposed that the committee's choice be considered only a recommendation and that the final decision be left to Porfirio Díaz and Carlos Pacheco. They also proposed that a plaster scale model of the losing design be constructed and shown as part of the Mexican exhibit in Paris. A special session of the commission was set for 2 June in Pacheco's residence. The committee voted nine to five in favor of Peñafiel's project.⁵⁴ As a partial consolation, both de Anza and Salazar were put in charge of constructing the Mexican pavilion.

Salazar's eclectic, Maya-oriented building did not materialize, though it was reproduced in miniature—also by Jesús Contreras. As we will see, however, Salazar's experiment acquired new life forty years later in the 1929 Seville world's fair, ironically to celebrate the remnants of Spanish imperialism (see part 2). In that year an eclectic Maya building depicted a different regime and nation.

Once the project for the Mexican pavilion was approved, its construction became a constant process of negotiation between and within the Mexican and French governments over economic interests and varied strategies of representation. The main compromises concerned the size and location of the area assigned to the Mexican Aztec Palace, the cost of the building and its decoration, the timing of construction, and the appropriateness of the building's style.⁵⁵ The first problem the commission faced was the size and characteristics of the site assigned to the pavilion. Mexico's request for a larger location had more to do with the impact of its exhibition than with the size of the area assigned to it. As Díaz Mimiaga noted, the small area assigned to the Hispanic American countries would have to be shared with the exhibits of some European countries, and perhaps the Hispanic Americans would come off second best in comparison.⁵⁶ Indeed, for Mexico, careful placement of the exhibition area became very important. In the end, as a result of a long negotiation, Mexico gained what it requested: a rectangular area 70 meters long and 30 meters wide. It was 15 meters away from Argentina's exhibit but far from the great European displays.⁵⁷

Once the design of the pavilion had been chosen, the committee began to consider construction details. After considering various proposals, in November 1888 Díaz Mimiaga signed a contract with the Société Cail, which did not include the artistic works.⁵⁸ The artistic tasks were assigned, as mentioned above, to the Mexican sculptor Jesús Contreras, who had been given a grant in 1887 to study bronze working in France. In 1889, still in Paris, he had to work arduously on (and was poorly paid for) all of the artistic needs of the building. Yet, as we will see, he eventually became the master and manufacturer of Mexico's late-nineteenth-century craze for statuary, with great fame and profit.⁵⁹ The estimate of total cost submitted by the Cail firm was 385,000 francs, or about 40,600 pesos.⁶⁰

The interior designs were let to the French designer E. Rousseau at a cost of 280,000 francs. According to Díaz Mimiaga, Rousseau spent two months researching samples of indigenous Mexican adornments in the ethnographic collections of the Trocadero Museum.⁶¹ Although little graphic evidence of

6. Design for the interior of the Aztec Palace. Source: José Francisco Godoy, *México en París* (Mexico City, 1891).

the interior of the building has survived,[62] it seems that the resulting interior decoration was all too French (see Fig. 6). Rousseau apparently designed curtains and internal ornamentation with pre-Hispanic motifs, but the total effect was as modern and cosmopolitan as was that of all of the other palaces in Paris 1889, with curtains and shades recalling haremlike scenarios of oriental exoticism rather than Aztec decor.

Although the Aztec Palace was scheduled to open in March 1889, it was actually inaugurated on 22 June 1889. At 9:00 A.M. "La Marseillaise" and the Mexican national anthem were played by the Mexican 101st battalion orchestra while French President Sadi Carnot, joined by the directors of the exhibition and by Ramón Fernández and Gustavo Baz, climbed the steps of the Aztec Palace. "At that very moment, the Eiffel Tower began to be lit up by fireworks, and the light fountains began to function."[63]

The inauguration was covered in various French newspapers. For some of them the Aztec Palace was "one of the most original [pavilions] of the Exposition."[64] For others it was "the exact reproduction of the Aztec temple known as the "Fire Temple"; a temple in which were performed "torture and human sacrifice." The stairs were bizarre, "straight like an arrow, virtually insurmountable. . . . They are called the stairs of torture [*supplice*], being one of the notable variety of tortures that the Mexicans of long ago had invented."[65] For still others the Aztec Palace was a bizarre pastiche that was at odds with the general cosmopolitanism of the fair.[66]

Put in a larger perspective, the Aztec Palace was only a brief episode in a long story. It was complete, in common with the entire fair, and yet as such it was also ephemeral, as was the image of the homeland itself. Mexican liberals were keenly aware of this. Although the nation in 1889 was in an Aztec mood and had attained a conclusive general liberal history, some Mexican intellectuals knew that the situation was only temporary. The Aztec Palace was eventually disassembled, and *México a través de los siglos* was surpassed by yet another liberal, though more positivist, general history, *México: Su evolución social.* In fact, the great synthesizer of Mexican history, Riva Palacio, wrote from prison of his ambivalence about the winterlike nature of his *patria:*

> When I was young, your rumor spoke
> of phrases my thought had guessed;
> and later, while crossing the campsite,
> *patria,* your bass voice said.
> Today I feel you striking
> the strong bars of my cell
> amidst my dark nights;
> but my misfortunes have taught me
> that you are but wind, and no more, when you moan,
> you are wind if you roar or if you murmur,
> wind if you come, wind if you leave.[67]

SIX

Mexican Anthropology and Ethnography at the Paris Exposition

The Aztec Palace was, above all, a statement about Mexico's Indian legacy in an era of science and nationalism. In this chapter I explain how the issue of exoticism, race, and nationalism came to be part of the image of a modern nation and thus of world's fairs and how this fact marked Mexico's efforts to display itself in Paris. Next I describe the anthropological, archaeological, and exoticist exhibits, both of Mexico and of the fair in general, as being mutually supportive. Third, I deal with the particular way in which Mexicans viewed race in the second part of the nineteenth century. This excursion is indispensable to an understanding of the way in which Mexico was presented as a modern and universal nation by its elite, despite its mixed-race configuration. Hence, fourth, making use of what the fair displayed, I review Western theories on race and nationalism in order to show where Mexicans found the arguments with which to fit their country into the concepts.

THE HISTORICAL CRISIS OF AN ECUMENICAL WORLD

"The exotic Exposition makes us reflect on the new duties that we assume in the world," observed Eugène-Melchior de Vogüé, commenting on the ethnological exhibits at the 1889 Paris world's fair. He added that in the "ecumenical city of Invalides . . . everything proclaims the rupture of the ancient equilibrium," because of "the reciprocal penetration of [peoples]." This, he added, constituted "the fusion of men . . . , a crisis of history."[1] Because the alien was at last in the familiar, such a shock, as de Vogüé's anguish exemplifies, both was inevitable and would have unknown future consequences. History was in a quandary because for the first time the exotic needed the cosmopolitan as much as the reverse. For "exotic" Latin American intellectuals, like the Cuban poet José Martí, the fair represented the beginning of a harmonious, all-inclusive world.[2] But what was civilized and what was not? What was primitive and what was modern? The fair tried to answer these questions conclusively, but in doing so it made them all the more sonorous and unsolved.

In 1889 the Aztec Palace was only one of the many exotic aspects of the fair. For example, various peoples were brought to Paris and used as subjects of anthropometrical research. Racial hypernationalism required this sort of show, composed not only of the exoticism of others but also of the European nations' own folk peoples.[3] In this sense modern nationalism constituted— regardless of each country's particularities—a twofold mandate: to create one's own self by reviewing geographical, cultural, and temporal others; and to make one's self at home in modern nationalism by recounting and inventing one's own traditions. The nationalism of the late-nineteenth-century industrialized nations was also embraced by the modernizing elites of so-called exotic and backward countries. That is, the mandate was followed by both the modern observers of the "precipices of time" that were world's fairs and the observed exotic Others.[4] If what was modern was the mandate, then both the fair and the Mexican pavilion were countenances of modernity.

The French organizers suggested that Mexico and other exotic countries display their national styles in the architecture of their pavilions. For France an Aztec Palace was a complement, albeit minor, to its fin-de-siècle orientalism —a combination of anthropological, archaeological, aesthetic, and nationalistic concerns that conformed to a graphical ethnology.[5] In Paris 1889 the "Rue du Caire" and the exhibit on the "History of Habitation" were the foremost examples of this orientalism. Visitors walked through a replica of an historical street in Cairo that was so perfect it caused Eugène-Melchior de Vogüé to exclaim: "Here are our slaves."[6] In contrast, Gypsy and Javanese dances and music were performed all around the fair.

All of that was just a facade, however, a scenario that displayed European architectural, ethnological, and artistic concerns and done in a way that could easily become daily fare for late-nineteenth-century Parisians.[7] Behind the facade rested the belief in, and the will to try, another expression—harmonious progress. In effect, late-nineteenth-century world's fairs displayed not only modern nationalism but also modernity's unavoidable component: the self-defeating awareness of its stylistic experimental nature. This irony permeated the entire fair.

The facade of the Aztec Palace simultaneously satisfied French orientalism and reconstructed Mexican national history. In contrast, its interior was more a statement about the present and the future than it was an assertion about the past. If one overlooked the overall French style in decoration, the interior of the Mexican pavilion contained an impressive anthropological, archaeological, and natural history display (see Fig. 7). In effect, in the interior of the Aztec Palace the issue of race was treated in the same fashion

MEXICAN ANTHROPOLOGY AND ETHNOGRAPHY 83

7. Interior of the Aztec Palace. Source: José Francisco Godoy, *México en París* (Mexico City, 1891).

as in the whole fair: within a scientific paradigm, with a nationalistic concern, and with a pragmatic (that is, a commercial and quasi-touristic) approach.

The Aztec Palace also shows how modern Western understanding of nationalism and progress was created both from the outside and from the inside. The understanding was constructed by the elite of a country that was incompletely Western. The elite had created its own conception of modern nationalism and progress in accordance with what they believed to be a universal outside, even though they were, in fact, secretly contributing to the construction of that universal.[8]

PARALLEL EXHIBITS

At the 1889 exhibition, "the New World [appeared] rich in exotic realities," C. de Varigny observed. But "in the interior everything is made of steel, everything is modern, and has been classified according to methodic and wise skills. There, everything talks about a young, active, and vigorous race.... For the first time, the New World affirms itself in its cosmopolitan diversity and in its individual originality."[9] That is, the nations of the New World had achieved the perfect combination of particularism and universalism. Therefore, for Varigny, the Aztec Palace was a great example of the superiority of modern times that could reconcile the architectural exoticism of other civilizations with modern cosmopolitanism—all the more remarkable since the palace was the creation of a country largely populated by Indians.

Another visitor, Charles Possonnier—in a pamphlet that was part of the propaganda package distributed by the Mexican exhibition—argued that Mexico was marching under the guidance of modern progress and liberty.[10] A reporter was especially impressed by the painting *El Senado de Tlaxcala*, which portrayed Indians conferring in a Roman-style parliament, while dining-room furniture in Aztec style also caught his eye. He reported, with emotion but without surprise, seeing "the head of an Apache chief admirably conserved."[11]

In addition to the Aztec Palace itself, Mexico's exhibit included books on antiques, studies of Indian customs, and scientific treatises. Leopoldo Batres, chief of the office of Inspección y Conservación de Monumentos Arqueológicos de la República (whose very foundation in 1885 exemplifies the era's archaeo-anthropological concerns) exhibited his book *Monografías de arquelogía mexicana: Teotihuacán; o, la ciudad sagrada de los Toltecas*, published in English and Spanish.[12] In it, Batres developed an anthropological theory on the degeneration of the Mexican races. Alfredo Chavero, in addition to the handsome edition of his volume on Mexico's pre-Hispanic history, *México a través de los siglos*, exhibited novels and dramas with indigenous themes. Antonio Peñafiel displayed the attractive edition of his *Monumentos del arte mexicano antiguo*, published in Berlin, and countless copies of his *Explication de l'edifice mexicaine*.[13]

Mexico was also represented at the "History of Habitation" display, though with a structure not made by Mexicans. "The architectural representation of cultures at the world's fairs," architecture historian Z. Çelik observes, "was double-sided, making a claim to scientific authority and accuracy while nourishing fantasy and illusion."[14] The architect of the Paris Opera, Charles Garnier, conceived the idea of displaying a history of human habitation at the foot of the Eiffel Tower. The exhibit included forty-four different buildings illustrating the "march of humanity through the ages." It was a main attraction, popular for the contrast with the Eiffel Tower that it offered. The dwellings exhibited claimed to be "truer than the truth."[15] For some, the display was scientific proof of the evolution of humanity from barbarism to civilization; for others, like José Martí, what was remarkable about the exhibit was not the progressive evolution, which demonstrated innovation in materials and styles, but the fact that modernity meant that "in each city there are Moorish, Greek, Gothic, Byzantine, and Japanese dwellings, marking the beginning of the happy times in which men treat each other as friends."[16]

In November 1888 Mexico had been requested both to design a dwelling in Aztec style and to send a group of people distinctively Mexican in look and dress to inhabit the so-called Aztec dwelling. Mexico's government asked the distinguished historian Francisco del Paso y Troncoso to evaluate the French proposal.[17] He advised against joining the habitation exhibit, arguing that it would be impossible to reproduce genuine Aztec interior decoration and furniture. The truth was that, in terms of exoticism, for Mexico one Aztec Palace was enough, and the government was reluctant to disperse its theatrical effect in various palaces. Nevertheless, Garnier constructed an Aztec dwelling following the descriptions of the French ethnographer and traveler Desiré de Charnay and of the architect and philosopher Viollet-le-Duc.[18] With the help of archaeology, the Aztec dwelling was depicted as belonging to a civilization that, according to Garnier's classification, remained outside the development of modern architecture, though with some Egyptian influences (see Fig. 8).[19]

A world's fair was not only an architectural circus but also a human one. Native peoples from Africa, America, and Asia were brought and exhibited with the same principles, techniques, and interests as those of a zoo.[20] In fact, if Mexico fulfilled in Paris the standards of the plastic orientalism of the West, then in Buffalo's 1901 Pan American Exhibition, the "Rue du Caire" exhibit of 1889 was replaced by a "Streets of Mexico," a supposedly realistic reproduction of the architecture of a Mexican village, with entertainment provided by live Mexicans dressed in traditional costumes and performing the routines of daily life in Mexico. Porfirio Díaz himself agreed to send Mexican Indians for this display on the condition that they were not to be ridiculed.[21]

It should be noted that precedent existed for the Buffalo display. At the Atlanta (1895) and Nashville (1896) fairs, Mexicans (along with Asians and Afro-Americans) were put "on view in villages on the entertainment avenues of the fairs that were also the areas of the exposition set aside for cheap thrills and monkey houses."[22] Even earlier, in the 1850s, in the aftermath of the London Crystal Palace exhibition, an exhibit of Aztec Lilliputians was applauded not only by thousands of visitors but also by the English Ethnological Society and by the royal family itself.[23] Along similar lines, if in 1889 people and products were brought from the French colonies to reproduce villages of exoticism in Paris, in 1895 the Atlanta Cotton States International Exhibition displayed a "Mexican Village." This village was formed with people from Tehuantepec, brought to Atlanta by the Mexican Village Company.[24] Once again, at the 1904 Saint Louis exposition an exhibit of "Aztecs and Their Industries" was staged (see Fig. 9 and chapter 11).

The Aztec Palace and all of Mexico's ethnographic and anthropological displays ought not to be considered apart from the anthropological focus of world's fairs. For instance, the 1889 fair featured a retrospective exposition of anthropological research and science.[25] The entrance gallery of this exhibit demonstrated the progress and orientation of anthropology (which at the time included ethnography and archaeology) as a field of knowledge.

8. The Aztec-Inca dwelling in the "History of Habitation" exhibit in Paris, 1889. Source: William Walton, *Chefs-d'oeuvre de l'Exposition Universelle de Paris, 1889* (Philadelphia and Paris, 1889).

9. "Aztecs and Their Industries" at the 1904 Saint Louis world's fair. Source: David R. Francis, *The Universal Exposition of 1904*, vol. 2 (Saint Louis, 1913), 119.

To the left of the entrance there stood an image of a naked woman of huge physical proportions—a sort of Amazon—while on the right, there was a representation of a half-naked Indian man. Crowning the entrance was a frieze containing the great names in the history of anthropology: Buffon, Blaumenbach, Lamarck, Cuvier, Hilaire, Retzius, Broca, and Darwin.[26] This set of heroes was established by a disciplinary infrastructure that included research institutions, journals, congresses, and government agencies. But the exhibition consisted of more than thought: a hundred masks and full-sized models of individuals of various races, "77 pieces or molds . . . of the brain, fifteen of the hand, 234 molds of human skulls, of which 48 are prehistorical or ancient."[27]

Anthropology was then considered at the root of human labor, a discipline concerned with the historicization of labor itself, while ethnography was considered the history of progress in material things.[28] The focus of anthropology was in the essence of human labor: the brain. Therefore, all sorts of anthropometric instruments were displayed at world's fairs, as was the case with the arrays of the British biologist Francis Galton.[29] Thus Mexico also exhibited Indian skulls, measurements, and statistics. This was a Mexico anthropologized by itself, demonstrating the existence of a common set of references between Mexico's exhibits and world's fairs: science, progress, race, skulls, primitive, civilized oriental, Aztec. . . .

MEXICAN UNDERSTANDING OF RACE

Before explaining the interaction between Mexico and the universal exhibitions as a whole, let us briefly examine the apparently conclusive view held by Mexican intellectuals concerning the Indian component of Mexican nationhood, a view that was epitomized by the 1889 Mexican exhibit. By 1889 this view constituted an intellectual, pragmatic, but, above all, ambivalent perspective. The Aztec Palace reflected this pragmatism and ambivalence. Whereas the facade of the Aztec Palace praised Mexico's pre-Hispanic past, the interior hinted at the inferiority of the majority of Mexico's population (that is, the Indians and the hybrid races). On one hand, this view pointed out the "scientific" inferiority of both Indian and mixed-blood people; on the other, it explained how such an inferiority was in fact an advantage for the development of a modern nation.

The ambivalence led to different ways of dealing with the issue of race. First, Porfirians presented a racist social hierarchy as a modern class structure. Second, they consolidated an anthropological scientific perspective. And finally, they introduced education, combined with biological natural selection, as the final solution for their own ambivalence toward the so-called Indian problem.

By 1889 it was unfashionable to accuse American-born Europeans of intrinsic inferiority by virtue of the climatic or geographical imperatives of their development—as Buffon and Gobineau had at the end of the eighteenth century. However, Mexican criollos felt the necessity to prove, through the scientific language furnished by Europe, the particular advantages of a good racial mixture. To do so, Mexican anthropologists, physicians, and philosophers had to carefully read their European lessons in search of the in-betweens to make their own country square with white cosmopolitanism. In 1889, therefore, the most prominent Mexican archaeologists, anthropologists, naturalists, and publicists of race found themselves at the Paris fair—Alfredo Chavero, Antonio Peñafiel, José Ramírez, Auguste Genin, Rafael de Zayas Enríques, and Leopoldo Batres.

As the 1889 fair illustrated, a cosmopolitan modern nation inevitably included a racial core. The superiority of the white European race was so forcefully promoted by the late-nineteenth-century scientific perspective that no nation seeking to be considered modern and cosmopolitan would even attempt to propose the superiority or equality of other races. For Mexico it was a lost cause to try to prove the pure and unmixed white nature of the modern Mexican population. But all of the Mexican propaganda in Paris emphasized that the Mexican upper classes were unmistakably white and, hence, that Mexico fit modernity according to one criterion established by modern societies—namely, through a well-defined class structure.

Consequently, in a Mexican study prepared for and displayed in Paris, the distinguished Mexican geographer Antonio García Cubas included an ethnographic section in which he argued that 19 percent of the Mexican population was European, 43 percent mestizo, and 38 percent Indian. Nonetheless, he argued, Europeans commanded the country. He stated that Europeans and significant numbers of mestizos were the most noteworthy and dynamic factor in Mexico's progressive development. García Cubas explained that despite the large Indian population, Spanish was the official language and that French, English, and Italian were spoken by the high society. The European population, he stated, resided in Mexico City and directed agriculture, mining, and industry. Mestizos were distributed throughout the country and made up the entire working class. Not only did mestizos represent a good and reliable labor force, they were also, contrary to common prejudice, very capable imitators—thus the excellent quality of their products. On the other hand, García Cubas described Indians as leading a quasi-bucolic, healthy existence in the countryside and mountains, but as becoming a degenerate race when transplanted to the cities. All were brave and resistant workers, save the northern tribes of Comanches, who were "perfidious, traitorous, and cruel."[30]

In order to equip this modern class structure with a scientific corpus, Mexicans had to construct a native anthropological, archaeological, and ethnographic tradition. This they began to do in the 1860s.[31] According to the eminent physician Nicolás León, however, anthropology and archaeology attained a definitive impulse in 1887, with the creation of an archaeological section in the National Museum. Two years earlier, the office of Inspection and Conservation of Monuments had been created with Leopoldo Batres as permanent chief. By 1889 this agency of the government was consolidated and publicized abroad.[32] Nonetheless, it was not easy to establish the necessary infrastructure for anthropological research in a poor country.[33]

A Mexican anthropological, ethnographic, and archaeological perspective was fairly well established by 1889.[34] In fact, since 1884 the Mexican scientific journal *La Naturaleza* had echoed the anthropological focus of world's fairs by arguing that whereas "old anthropology took charge of moral man," modern anthropology dealt with "the anatomical man" and thus was "the accessory part of comparative osteology that is concerned with the state of variations of the skull in diverse human races."[35] Indeed, though neither Indians nor the concept of race were novel for Mexicans, the way these problems were discussed in the late nineteenth century meant a radical change from the previous three centuries.

The most visible aspect of ambivalent domestic views of indigenous traditions was the belief in the educability of Indians. In the last three decades of the nineteenth century, education became a fundamental topic of discussion when it came to what Mexican liberals considered the Indian problem. This, to a certain extent, was a direct consequence of the liberal belief in equal citizenship as the formula for national development. But it also represented an ad hoc adaptation of liberal and scientific ideas to the Mexican context. A consensus prevailed about the educability of Indians that extended to an acceptance of the eventual fusion of the two races.[36] However naive this position might seem, it represented a determined and skillful, if somehow tricky, intellectual withdrawal from the mainstream racial theories of the 1880s, which had endorsed the idea of the degeneration of races and the degenerative consequences of miscegenation.[37]

In sharp contrast to the belief in the educability of Indians, the consideration of live Indians included an important anthropological theory on the inferiority of Indians. This consideration had to be constantly transformed and rephrased according to the increasingly "scientific" parameters set by European and American ideas. The scientific foundation of the understanding of Indians was made not through simple imitation of European theories but through a laborious process of continual modern learning in which Western thought was included both as master and as apprentice. To fully understand this, it is necessary to briefly consider the way in which race was debated in the West during the last part of the nineteenth century.

DEBATING RACE

In the 1880s anthropology had three main concerns that were relevant to understanding race in Mexico. One was the reactivation of the old debate between those who believed that humankind had multiple origins and those who supported the idea of a unified origin (that is, polygenism versus monogenism). The debate seemed to have been solved by the 1840s in favor of polygenism, but it was reactivated by the emergence of Darwinian evolutionism, which linked all human races to a single line of evolution, and by the reinforcement of anthropometrical and anatomical studies of races (especially in France). This last phenomenon gave new strength to polygenism and to the rigidity of racial definitions. Therefore, throughout the last decades of the nineteenth century what best characterized anthropology was the conflict between ethnographers and hard-core physical anthropologists.[38]

As a result, anthropology developed an emphasis on the temporal dimension of human races. That is, instead of the study of geographical places, the focus was on the position of races in the evolutionary chain. As an historian of anthropology observed, because the archaeological and biological discoveries of the 1860s, "anthropological inquiry, which for decades had focused on the problem of human unity, was now refocused on the problem of the origin of human civilization."[39]

Finally, by the 1880s modern anthropology and archaeology reinforced their links with the strong nationalistic tendencies of the late nineteenth century. They furnished a professional language for talking about race. Race, in turn, was the key to the fundamental change from the romantic nationalism of the earlier nineteenth century to the state-oriented nationalism of the late decades. Race became a fixed characteristic of a permanent ethnic matrix in which degeneration followed from miscegenation. Once nations became so attached to the idea of race, there was no way to talk about race without making nationalistic statements. Thus the scientists' goal was to dehistoricize the issue of the nation and make it a terrain of anthropology. Only anthropology could provide genuine scientific generalities about peoples, so the historian must become an anatomist and a linguist.[40] This is not to say that the identification of nation with race was a smooth and easily accepted process. Indeed, ideas about race had to be constantly adjusted to fit new criteria and knowledge about both race itself and nationalism, which in turn were shaped by political and economic circumstances.

These concerns of Western anthropology had been applied to—and in—Mexico throughout the nineteenth century. European ethnographical, anthropometrical, and archaeological studies of Mexico were abundant sources of scientific discussion for both Mexicans and Europeans. By the 1880s a well-established French anthropological interest existed in Mexico. As E. T. Hamy argued, in the 1860s "Mexico gained ... its range within the history of humanity's past."[41] J. M. A. Aubin, Brasseur de Bourbourg, Desiré de Charnay, G. d'Eichtal,[42] and, later, the Scientific Commission of Mexico[43] provided European minds with a clear ethnographic, anthropological, and archaeological picture of Mexico, which often was adapted by Mexican scholars to study their own country.

In fact, as a part of European orientalism, French and European Americanism emerged simultaneously. Within the well-established field of Americanism, and by virtue of its archaeological and anthropological abundance, Mexico sought to be recognized. Therefore, in 1895 an Americanists congress —the eleventh—for the first time took place on the American continent, in Mexico City, the "Egypt of America."[44] In common with the orientalism of the period, Americanism reinforced European nationalism by identifying a racial and cultural Other to contrast with the attributes of civilization.

But what was especially relevant for the relationship between race, civilization, and nation was the debate between hard-core physical anthropology and the ethnographic approaches that included race, but not such purely physical aspects as skull measurements. This was especially true in the French context of the 1880s, in which the anatomical trend of anthropology was particularly strong and in which radical nationalism was flourishing.[45] On one hand, for physical anthropologists, to educate a race was a chimera because racial characteristics were fixed and unchanging. Thus colonialism and/or genocide could be justified by using the idea of racial superiority. On the other hand, within the ethnographic terrain—where French orientalists and Americanists found themselves—the role of political, social, and moral factors in reshaping racial characteristics was acknowledged. Of course, it would be difficult to argue that ethnologists were outside the racist paradigm of the period, but they also believed that political and moral factors were influential in the configuration of human characters. However, anthropology (that is, physical anthropology) was the dominant school in France until the beginning of the twentieth century.[46]

French interest in ethnology went back to the late eighteenth century and was directly linked to natural history. Ethnography sought to study the particular histories of races, their intellectual and moral development, their language and behavior, and their role in civilization. In contrast, since the late eighteenth century, anatomy had developed various studies of the human body, while geology advanced in the study of the evolution of the earth. A. de Quatrefages, following Cuvier and the German scholar Blumenbach, believed in the unified origin of humankind through the physiological definition of the species. With the appearance of Darwin's *On the Origin of Species by Means of Natural Selection* in 1859, the emphasis was on the study of humankind as a natural inhabitant of earth and on the superiority of humans over other species. Darwinian evolutionism was used and abused by both ethnographers who aimed to emphasize a common origin of humankind and by physical anthropologists who sought to study human beings as part of their analysis of the animal world, thus focusing on what made humans different from other animals; that is, the brain and its surroundings. Accordingly, in 1859 the physician Paul Broca founded the Société d'Anthropologie de Paris. With it, French anthropology clearly defined its object of study and method, for the rest of the century subsuming ethnology and all other studies to it.

Race, language, and natural conditions were all important factors in the creation of a modern cosmopolitan world culture of so-called superior nations. And late-nineteenth-century anthropology (that is, anthropometrics) furnished much of the scientific authority for each of these factors.

MEXICO SEARCHES FOR AN ENTRANCE INTO THE MODERN DEBATE

Mexicans who followed these debates became very proficient in anthropometric techniques and very cognizant of the terms of discussion. After all, they were searching for an interstice where the idea of a modern but explicitly hybrid country might fit. Throughout the Porfirian period, Mexican anthropologists moved within European tendencies. Not until the final triumph of culturalism within Western anthropology and archaeology did Mexican thinkers find a spacious intellectual framework for their ideas. Within this context Mexico's prerevolutionary and postrevolutionary support of the culturalism of Franz Boas must be understood.[47] Porfirio Díaz's official support of the International School of Anthropology—established in Mexico City in 1910, with Boas as first president—and later of Manuel Gamio's (Boas's student) official postrevolutionary indigenism, exemplified the fruitful and useful ground Mexicans found in international cultural anthropology.[48]

But in the 1880s the ways in which Mexican intellectuals located themselves in the intersection of the pure ethnographic and physiological explanations constituted intricate attempts to achieve an acceptable modern national image. One example of this was Riva Palacio's account of the physical evolution of the Indian, designed to support the idea that Indians were physically more advanced than were some European races (see chapter 5). Riva Palacio relied on Darwin's ideas, as historians Moreno and Hale have demonstrated. Nonetheless, in making his assertion Riva Palacio did not step outside the French milieu, for he read Darwin in French and placed Darwinian thought within the logic of French debates. In the same way as the Aztec Palace, Riva Palacio's understanding of race appeared nonconflictive. But unlike Riva Palacio, the Mexican scientists who were seriously dealing with mainstream anthropological sciences were aware of complexities and contradictions in the discussion of race. These scientists were acquiring the cosmopolitan expertise and language to speak about race.

Riva Palacio, thus, personally consulted such Mexican experts as the physician Nicolás León and the biologist Alfonso Herrera. León, as he himself explained, was searching for the "Indian of pure race," just as Broca, in France, looked for the pure French type. Riva Palacio asked León whether, in Tarascan Indians, "the canine tooth is replaced by a molar in both jawbones," and whether "Indians of pure race lack down or hair in the meeting of the limbs at the trunk, armpit and pubis?" León had argued that among Tarascan Indians there was a "replacement of the canines by small molars" and no "wisdom tooth." These observations were used by Riva Palacio to prove the superior place of the Indians in the evolutionary chain. Later, however, León pursued his research and discovered that dental mutilation, a practice common among pre-Columbian and nineteenth-century Indians, and not evolution accounted for his earlier findings about teeth.[49] Nonetheless, Riva Palacio trickily utilized the expertise of Mexican anthropologists and presented Mexican Indians in the terms of physical anthropology, concluding the fitness of Mexican Indians for modern civilization.

In the same way, the famous Mexican archaeologist and anthropologist Leopoldo Batres tried to prove (in Paris and in front of Hamy and Quatrefages) that Mexican Indians did not belong to an inferior race: "On the contrary, [the indigenous race] is endowed with conditions superior to many European races." He bolstered his argument with skull measurements and with ethnographic knowledge he acquired while studying in Paris with Hamy in 1887, observing that "despite the wretchedness in which it [the indigenous race] lived for so many years, it is the true producer of the republic. . . . One could argue that how is it that being the most vigorous race of the republic, [the Indian race] has endured the Iberian yoke for three centuries. It is because it is not one, but many varied races, each one of them with different types." Thus, though the Mexican Indian race was well fitted for evolution, the promiscuity of various racial types brought about the weakness of the Mexican race as a whole. In such a way, Batres affirmed the validity of phrenology and of the degenerationist antimiscegenation thesis, while supporting the idea of a strong and superior Mexican race that was able to match European races.[50]

In an 1889 article, Batres gave another example of how Mexicans were locating themselves in the in-betweens of the European scientific discussion. Following the classificatory obsession of European anthropology, Batres developed a method for identifying "the physiognomic type of the principal inhabiting tribes of Mexico." He was on risky scientific ground: "I will not enter into the difficult question of polygenesis and monogenesis because, in dealing with America, it would be very hazardous to give an opinion in whichever of the two senses." Batres then measured the skulls of Indians from various regions of the country in order to "compare the type of living Indian with that of the sculptures of his predecessors, and in this way to establish the type from that which can be called ancient tribes." He combined ethnography, phrenology, and archaeology, as well as the well-accepted Indian past with the difficult issue of the Indian present. And in this way the Indian past acquired greater veneration, and the live Indians a clear classificatory structure; that is, a scientific definition that directly linked live Indians both to the great Indian past—overlooking but not neglecting degeneration—and to a modern anthropological specificity that provided Mexican Indians with a secure spot in modern ethnography.[51]

In the same way, Peñafiel's historico-ethnographic design for the facade of the Aztec Palace tried to merge the anthropological, historical, and ethnographic aspects of the Mexican Indian. He did not face too many problems because he dealt with the legacy of pre-Columbian Indians—commonly accepted as a technically elevated, albeit barbaric, civilization. Peñafiel's Aztec Palace combined the long-established study of archaeological structures with the ethnographic ideas of late-nineteenth-century Europe. The facade was not at all at odds with the obvious inferiority of Indian race, because only the Western reconstruction of the Indian past was exhibited. But ethnographic knowledge was at the core of the very idea of having an Aztec Palace in Paris, and it determined the items Mexico displayed inside the palace. Therefore, the Aztec Palace was indeed a way for Mexico to be in those interstices of the French anthropological debate.

The international scientific community did not view the Aztec Palace in the way Peñafiel wished, however. He had no qualms about introducing the

Mexican pavilion to the international anthropological community, as an incorporation of ancient ruins into modern architecture.[52] But for the European scholarly community, not all archaeological ruins were interpreted in the same way. If ruins were considered part of the general evolution of humankind (as Garnier assumed with the Greco-Roman dwellings in his "History of Habitation") they were seen as mythic ancestors of all European culture, removed from the present by mythical time. However, if ruins were considered merely exotic, they were distanced from the European present by a "cultural space."[53] Hence, although written in the same terminology, Peñafiel's archaeology could not overcome the cultural space. However scientific his archaeology, his palace belonged to the realm of the exotic. Thus for Europeans, the exhibit of Mexican ruins attested to the veracity of evolution; for Mexicans, to furnish European sciences with elements to affirm Europe's superior evolution was at least a first step in entering into the mainstream flow of evolution.

To sum up, in the 1880s a long historiographical labor had at last produced a consensual liberal reconstruction of the Mexican past. At the same time, an anthropological focus had been laboriously developed to account for the past, present, and future of Mexico in a scientific fashion. Through national histories, Mexico consolidated its civic religion and uniqueness, though using the international lexicon of liberal republicanism. Mexico's past thereby obtained a distinctively Mexican coherence and logic, but with a modern, progressive, and evolutionist structure that was easily recognized and understood by modern European standards. In turn, through the anthropological scientific focus Mexicans sought to join modern civilized times in a twofold manner: by catching up with European concerns and prejudices; and by conducting an intricate explanation—made possible by the constant catching up—of their own potential and fitness for joining civilization. Through the kind of understanding of race displayed in Paris, the Mexican elite appealed for European recognition, but it also worked to prove (to itself and to others) that it was on the right track. One has to concede not only that Porfirians displayed all of these ideas but also that they truly believed them.

SEVEN

Mexican Art and Architecture in Paris

Patriotic history and the scientific claims of an anthropological nationalism became a single formula in graphic arts. The art scholar Fausto Ramírez has lucidly shown the chief dilemma that permeated Mexican art during the late nineteenth century: the dichotomy between nationalism and cosmopolitanism.[1] What follows explains how this dichotomy was an inherent component of late-nineteenth-century culture. In being modern there was no way to opt for either pure nationalism or pure cosmopolitanism, only—and inevitably—to be part of the continuing dichotomy.

This inquiry into the artistic aspects of the emblematic Aztec Palace in Paris comprises several stages. First, I will examine the architectural foundations of the palace, which reveal much about the political and artistic negotiations behind the construction of a modern nation. Second, I consider the facade of the palace, because in it the summary of history and art acquired its best expression. Lastly, I analyze the many paintings and photographs that made the nation look both modern and truly colorful. These examinations show that there was an art to the art involved in assembling a tangible representation of a modern nation.

THE ARCHITECTURAL FOUNDATIONS

In 1889 a question much pondered by Mexicans was how to show any meaningful art in Paris, "the capital of France, at present the world's most artistic nation," as it was described by the Mexican painter and director of the Mexican art exhibit in Paris, José María Velasco.[2] This was a problem not only for Mexico but also for all Latin American, African, and Asian countries. They all confronted the dichotomy between national motifs, tendencies, and schools and cosmopolitan techniques and canons.[3] Their solutions varied. Whereas Mexico decided to experiment with a particular combination of national figures in a cosmopolitan fashion, Argentina hired the French architect A. Ballu and various French sculptors to construct its pavilion and the sculptures that adorned it.[4] Chile also hired a French architect —Picq, the creator of the Gas Industry Pavilion. Other Latin American countries decided to play it safe by using the Spanish artistic synthesis that was more or less well recognized by the rest of Europe. Thus Bolivia constructed a Spanish Renaissance building. Still others decided, as Mexico had, to exploit their exoticism. Accordingly, Ecuador constructed a representation of the Inca Temple of the Sun, even though the project was not only designed by French architects but also conceived by the French anthropologist E. T. Hamy, who donated some authentic figures to give the building a more genuine flavor.[5] That is, it was a ready-made exotic ruin, conceived by French architects and anthropologists, to satisfy French orientalism. Mexico, in contrast, did not hire French engineers, architects, or anthropologists. The expenses were already too high, and, besides, there was no need to hire them, because Mexico already had confident, French-trained technocrats and architects.

As I have argued in chapters 5 and 6, the Aztec Palace, never reconstructed, constituted an experimental architectural form, which was to be constantly referred to in the continuing discussion over how to represent the nation. Although Mexico participated in the Madrid historical exhibition of 1892 and the 1893 Chicago world's fair, it was not until the 1900 Paris fair that the exhibition team designed another pavilion. By then, the 1889 Aztec Palace was regarded as a total failure, a judgment applied not only to the building itself but also to the entire effort to achieve a true national architectural style through the use of pre-Hispanic models. Sebastián de Mier, in charge of Mexican efforts at the 1900 Paris fair, concluded that a real Mexican architectural style did not exist. In his view, to imitate pre-Hispanic styles was as artificial and useless as trying to copy colonial Spanish structures. Both tendencies were simply inadequate for modern standards of comfort, hygiene, and aesthetics. More importantly, neither one fully represented what nineteenth-century Mexico was like. De Mier believed that until a real Mexican style was developed, Mexico's best option was to adopt a proven style. Thus Mexico opted for a neoclassical palace for the 1900 Paris fair.[6]

Undoubtedly, this decision was motivated more by changing European taste than by the long-lasting nationalistic debates.[7] Nonetheless, it does illustrate relative agreement among the Porfirian elite on the issue of how to represent the Mexican nation artistically. Open debate over this issue began in the 1860s in literature, painting, and architecture, and the point in question was how to develop a real national style—or, better yet, paraphrasing Ignacio Manuel Altamirano, how to achieve a relative originality for Mexico's artistic forms,[8] relative because the style had to be Mexican while following the universal patterns of beauty. Intellectual circles, from the Academia de Letrán (1830s) to the romantic Renacimiento group (1860s), to the more "scientific" *La Libertad* group (1870s), all dealt with this issue, summarized by one literary critic as "the on-going fights and transitory weddings of banana and marble."[9]

To bring about a national style might be considered commonplace in the literary and artistic history of any nation. From this perspective, the Aztec Palace could be seen as just one example of the various architectural styles employed in the nineteenth century.[10] Yet, from the perspective of a history of modern nationalism, these attempts epitomized by the Aztec Palace acquire a different configuration. In fact, the accomplishment of a modern nation was a matter of experimenting with forms; that is, styles. Thus, to achieve a national style (architectural, literary, artistic) was a redundancy, because the nation was style itself. A national style was, at bottom, a question of incorporating styles into a homogeneous and relatively harmonious form recognized as being that of the nation. This incorporation was a manner of constant negotiation among and within political and cultural elites. Accordingly, the 1889 Aztec Palace made use of pre-Hispanic features to portray the nation in the same way that the 1900 neoclassical building also symbolized the nation; each represented a different moment in the negotiation of national representations (that is, the set of styles identified as national at certain historical moments). Both buildings were simultaneously, on one hand, domestic and international experiments and, on the other, statements regarding modernity and nationalism. Let me explore this negotiation through the example of the Aztec Palace.[11]

The 1889 Mexican pavilion did not receive universal applause. Both Mexicans and foreigners criticized it, but it generated more commentary than any other Mexican building, however great, ever had. The international decline of classicism in architecture, together with the emergence of innovative modern styles, as exemplified by the Eiffel Tower and the Machines Gallery, formed a peculiar and somewhat auspicious setting for the Aztec Palace to be appreciated and accepted. People who favored conservative classical tendencies did not seriously consider the Mexican pavilion; those who supported innovative tendencies were too amazed by such technological experiments as the Eiffel Tower to be very impressed by the Mexican effort.[12] Even so, late-nineteenth-century ethnographic and orientalist tendencies had provided a special place for exotic architecture, as architectural historian Z. Çelik argued in the case of the Arab pavilions.[13]

Despite the many official and semiofficial reports that applauded the Mexican pavilion, important architects—for example, the French designer of the Paris Opera House, Charles Garnier—could scarcely conceal their dislike of it.[14] Albert Ballu, the French architect who designed the 1889 Argentine pavilion and who was also hired by Argentina to report on the advancement of architecture in Paris 1889, informed his employers that the Mexican building was not to his taste. He asserted that the Aztec Palace looked "somewhat heavy" and that its sculpture was "quite weak." He criticized Mexico for having the audacity to exhibit such sculpture in Paris.[15] Similarly, in Mexico Alfredo Bablot deplored the contrast between the palace's facade and its modern interior. He claimed that the building presented an antiartistic monotony, "without any of the notoriety, appeal, or optical diversity found in the building's interior, whose forms and lines had nothing of the Aztec."[16] In addition, and despite the fact that most Mexican media did not print either national or international criticism of the building, *El Hijo de Ahuizote* often caricatured the indigenist architectural and ideological claims of the Porfirian elite. It especially satirized the irony of the members of a very pro-French elite wearing pre-Hispanic outfits and functioning as idol-shaped columns for a palace of Aztec authoritarianism, which echoed Porfirio Díaz's dictatorship (see chapter 10). Mexican Catholic opinion very much resented the building (which had a *teocalli* form) for its pagan connotations. For example, in 1890 *El Nacional* published an article which supported the idea that universal criteria of beauty were derived from God and which, therefore, observed that both the Eiffel Tower and the Aztec Palace were vain efforts at "genuine creations."[17] Later on, between 1898 and 1900, when an open discussion about a national architectural style took place among architects, the Catholic architect Manuel Francisco Álvarez sarcastically described the Aztec Palace as a structure that "is reduced to mimicking a *teocalli*, which is to say a truncated pyramid with a rectangular base, in whose top platform human sacrifice took place."[18] In effect, there was no way to portray the nation in an Indian-like fashion without causing controversies.

The search for a style for the nation was coming to a critical juncture in the 1880s, as a result not only of the previous long-lasting ideological discussions but also of the artistic and economic framework that the Porfirian regime furnished for the debate. For the construction of national architectural symbols there were an old tendency and two new trends. First, there were those who planned a lasting trust in Mexico as a continuation of Spanish colonial times, with colonial architecture as the natural national style. Second, there were those who sought to use the pre-Hispanic past to construct a real national architecture. Third, there were those who favored the imitation of European schools, with its implicit attempt to keep up-to-date on European architectural stylistic developments. All these schools of thought shared a belief in the need to follow advances in modern construction and standards of comfort and hygiene.

French discussions of how to architecturally represent the nation were neither consensual nor definitive. Technological advances were promptly accepted and used by all styles, though they were not unanimously considered art. French architects were trying to bring about a new synthesis, one that could overcome stale classicism, passé romanticism, and the national historicism of the sort proposed by Eugène Viollet-le-Duc.[19] Since the 1850s, some architects had favored synthesizing advances in engineering construction with architectural aesthetics, and others affirmed the purely artistic character of architecture. The 1889 Paris fair meant the momentary triumph of the former, with the Eiffel Tower and the Machines Gallery as their major symbols. But at the 1900 fair, the artistic architects took revenge.[20]

Indeed, the entire "nineteenth century [was] the period *par excellence* of architectural revivals,"[21] because modernity had produced progress but also disharmony, "without the power to create and ... constrained to borrow."[22] After 1855 a general eclecticism prevailed: in this era of revivals it seemed that no new architectural styles could be created, only technical capabilities to better reproduce and combine old styles. "The relics of the past have been restored with a perfection that was unknown in the epochs of their creation," Eugène-Melchior de Vogüé observed in his commentaries on the 1889 fair.[23] In such a wide discussion there was a huge spectrum of principles and ideas for Mexican architects to copy.

In discovering the Mexican architectural past, Mexican architects had to face a technical-aesthetic problem that had to do both with the specificities of European eclecticism and with the development of the architectural profession in Mexico. In 1889 Antonio Peñafiel and Antonio de Anza, as well as Luis Salazar, believed that the spatial usage and construction techniques of pre-Hispanic cultures were adaptable to modern building construction. This had already been demonstrated in the Egyptian pavilion for the 1867 Paris world's fair—"a living lesson in archaeology," which summarized Egypt's history in a modern and useful structure—so it was not surprising that the Aztec Palace had a peculiar similarity to its Egyptian precursor.[24]

But the pre-Hispanic Mexican style was considered, as Garnier's *Histoire de l'habitation* illustrated, outside the development of modern architecture. Nonetheless, world's fairs were unique stages for using pre-Hispanic (that is, exotic) styles to create a feasible and acceptable form of architectural modernity—or at least such was the belief echoed by Mexican officials and intellectuals. After all, the renowned Crystal Palace of 1851, constructed by Owen Jones, was inspired by exotic archaeological sources—Greek, Egyptian, and Moorish.

Of course, the Mexican pavilion and the Aztec dwelling in the French habitation exhibit appealed to an already established European interest in pre-Hispanic architectural forms.[25] French classicist architectural studies hardly dealt with Mexican pre-Hispanic architectural forms, although history and archaeology, through the obsession with Egyptian and oriental styles, were fundamental parts of late-nineteenth-century French architecture.[26] Nonetheless, influential and revolutionary architects like Viollet-le-Duc had written about pre-Hispanic American architectural styles. Both in his exhibit and in his prologue to Charnay's book, Viollet-le-Duc had praised pre-Hispanic techniques and environmental adaptability.[27] For him there was only one style—"the manifestation of an ideal based on a principle"—the rest were various forms that helped to distinguish schools and epochs. Style was a rational human process of appreciation and creation, not an attribute of objects.[28] Hence pre-Hispanic Mexican architecture was less a style than a form: one that was known in Europe but that was not considered an authentic style. Although European archaeologists praised pre-Hispanic architectural forms, architectural historians often referred to their backward use of space and to their general barbarism. Mexican builders were thus caught between European archaeological and architectonic appetites.

Aesthetically, the Mexican revival of pre-Hispanic forms was indeed at odds with the European revivals, but not with the very important fact of reviving. The Aztec Palace appealed to the ethnographic, archaeological, and anthropological concerns of Europeans, but as an artistic depiction it aimed to be approved within the European decline of classicism. Simultaneously, it sought to finally attain what a Mexican architect of the 1910s called the *directriz* (main guidance) from which to develop a genuine national architectural style.[29]

Technically, the search for a national architecture had to confront the problems of technology transfer as much as the cross-cultural techno-aesthetic difficulties. Since the 1870s Mexican architecture had kept relatively well abreast of European and American developments in the field. Mexican architects like Antonio Rivas Mercado, who had studied in Europe, played an important role in bringing technical innovation to the country. But more significant in this regard were the various foreign architects who were privately and officially hired to construct buildings in Mexico. Along with technological innovation, however, came conservative resistance to innovative styles.

In Mexico engineering and architecture had been separated as disciplines as early as 1867.[30] Engineering acquired its own spot in the Colegio de Minería; architecture remained part of the Bellas Artes school of San Carlos. Conflicts between the two professions were common throughout the last two decades of the nineteenth century, when engineers began to construct houses and public buildings.[31] Until the beginning of the twentieth century, Mexican architects fought back by seeking to control the architectural forms of the Porfirian regime. Beyond a concern with protecting the economic and political interests of each guild, this struggle was also an echo of international tendencies. Conflicts among European architects and engineers were also common. At the 1889 Paris world's fair, for instance, the Eiffel Tower and the Machines Gallery, the most noteworthy structures in the exhibition, were planned by engineers. French architects complained on the same grounds their Mexican counterparts used: architecture was an art and belonged to artists (that is, to architects).[32]

In Mexico, architects were technically trained in new construction methods, but they resented the engineers who constructed the buildings. But in Mexico's presence at world's fairs, engineers were the executors of the ideas of artists and architects. De Anza belonged to the generation that had experienced the separation between engineering and architecture; he himself was both an architect and an engineer.[33] Luis Salazar graduated in 1873, and although he belonged to the first generation to have been fully trained in engineering, he also studied at the Academia de San Carlos.[34] The technical influence of both de Anza and Salazar meant that the 1889 pavilion combined architectural eclecticism with the then high-tech exhibitions architecture based on metal structures.[35]

At the 1889 Paris fair, France's longing for exoticism and its own endeavor to achieve new eclectic architectural forms constituted a mandate to a Mexican government that was eager to link itself to international culture and markets. But the discussion that underpinned the 1889 Aztec Palace was postponed until the last years of the nineteenth century, when a debate about pre-Hispanic style in architecture acquired importance. In such a debate, the Spanish legacy was revived yet again to serve as the matrix for a national architectural representation of the nation. In this exchange the Aztec Palace was commonly cited either as the example to be followed or, more often, as a mistake to be avoided (about this debate, see chapter 11).

It is important to explain why such a discussion achieved a full and vivid expression only in the late 1890s and not in 1889. In the first place, an international—mostly French—decline of aesthetic exotic eclecticism occurred, as signaled by both the classicist revival and the art nouveau tone of the 1900 Paris fair.[36] Second, by the late 1890s Mexican architecture achieved a hitherto unknown level of professionalization and technical expertise, becoming both an important subject of study and a significant industry. This was made possible in large part by urbanization and a growing demand for both public and private buildings.[37] Finally, in the 1890s the discussion was also influenced by the emergence of a historical perspective in architecture, fostered by the traditional Mexican architectural training and by nationalism. This historicization of architecture made it possible to see that what had previously been regarded as only trial-and-error episodes in Mexico's architecture, with no apparent history, could in fact be organized in a progressive line of architectural development.

In 1899, in an article discussing the upcoming 1900 Paris world's fair,[38] Nicolás Mariscal argued that whereas in 1889 the star attraction of the exhibition had been the Eiffel Tower, in 1900 the Palace of Electricity was to be the core of things. To prove his point that France itself had retreated from its extravagant mechanistic demonstrations of 1889, Mariscal noted that the Eiffel Tower was being painted blue to reduce its visibility, a clear sign that the architectural excesses of the preceding decade were now being camouflaged by the French themselves. Mariscal seemed to suggest that Mexico also ought to abandon its architectural radicalism of 1889. But this occurred in the context of a debate about what building would depict Mexico in the 1900 fair. In this connection, between 1895 and 1899 Luis Salazar published and republished various works on archaeology and architecture to support his idea of a national architecture inspired by the pre-Hispanic tradition.[39] (It will be remembered that he had proposed a pre-Hispanic design in 1889 and had helped to construct the winning Peñafiel and de Anza design.) The Aztec Palace of 1889, together with the Cuauhtémoc monument and the monuments to the Aztec kings Ahuizotl and Itzcoatl on the Paseo de la Reforma, were the most significant examples of this sort of architecture, and Salazar continued to approve of it. For him, race and civilization were fundamental concepts, whose development should be reflected in architecture. However, Salazar also believed that it was impossible to create a genuinely new style; all attempts were in essence revivals and reconstructions of past models. What he proposed was an eclectic and selective search through the past for useful and needed elements for present usage, just as the Europeans were doing. Indeed, this eclectic selectiveness echoed the entire Porfirian treatment of Mexico's Indian past and present.

Salazar maintained that "paying no attention to pagan constructions . . . and the ancients' needs which do not fit today's [needs], it is feasible to *ensayar* [attempt] the creation, if not of a complete new style, at least of an architecture that is characteristically national." Consequently, in searching for useful pre-Hispanic forms, Salazar referred to Garnier's reconstruction of an Aztec dwelling. With regard to the Aztec Palace, he noted that it was not really an incorporation of archeological styles into modern architecture. Instead, he proposed to adapt pre-Hispanic styles to modern architecture, in order to achieve an "improved imitation" and a "fruitful appropriation."[40]

Salazar's architectural proposal received an immediate and sarcastic response from one Tepoztecaconetzin Calquetzani, who seems to have been either Nicolás Mariscal, director of *El Arte y la Ciencia*, or the architect Francisco Rodríguez. The author believed that although the pre-Hispanic style was proper for Cuauhtémoc's monument—a monument to an Indian—other uses of the style were a "chimeric and useless undertaking." He also believed that the eclectic selectiveness and combinations of the various pre-Hispanic styles were at odds with modern techniques and uses of space. In particular, he deplored the Aztec Palace of the 1889 Paris world's fair as a structure in which all styles had been fragmented and made into pure fantasy. "Was there ever a sound reason for a rebirth of aboriginal architecture?" he wondered. No. World's fair pavilions "should bear contemporary society's aesthetic feeling, and reflect as truly as possible the host country's arts and architecture." An Aztec Palace would not serve, because it portrayed a Mexico before the Spanish Conquest (that is, a non-Mexico), and the author hoped that the failure of the structure would serve as a lesson to avoid future mistakes. For him, archaeological ruins ought to be preserved in museums as the remains of a civilization and a race "lost forever in eternity."[41]

Both Salazar and Mariscal, albeit in very different fashions, were trying to be cosmopolitan. The designs of both men were used in international fairs or in public buildings according to the decisions of their elite clientele who had to take into consideration the domestic debate as well as international fashion.[42] In fact, their attempts to construct a cosmopolitan style were not determined solely by artistic tendencies, but by the intersection of many tendencies that had to do with race, economics, cultural progress, and nationalism.

In our eyes, the architects of late-nineteenth-century Mexico may seem to have been particularly penetrating in their understanding of the relationship between nationalism and modernity. Both those who favored European classical styles and those who endorsed pre-Hispanic models showed signs of being aware of their own eventuality. Buildings are erected with an inevitable hope that they are permanent, but also with an awareness of the ephemeral character of their stylistic conception.[43] Some of the Mexican architects involved in the discussion of national architecture understood this and stated their different proposals accordingly. Mexican architects believed that they were living in a time when modern forms and contents were being negotiated. They sought only a provisional solution: to *ensayar* and to find *directrices*.

Ensayar meant that it was worthwhile to experiment, not with a new style but with a variant of late-nineteenth-century eclecticism. In the 1880s architects had no alternative but to keep trying to come up with the proper combination of national and international tendencies in order to define the nation architecturally.[44] Even later architects, promoters of the revival of the colonial style, were uncertain about the real form of a national architecture. Jesús T. Acevedo, an architect trained in the last decade of the Porfirian period, also criticized the Aztec Palace, because he believed that the pre-Hispanic structures could "only be the result of archaeological lucubrations." Making use of a biological metaphor, he claimed that colonial architecture was the *directriz* of evolution from which a real national architecture could emerge.[45] Also in 1913, Federico E. Mariscal criticized the attempts to recreate pre-Hispanic architecture and pointed out that it was in the colonial period that the elements of Mexican nationhood were combined. Yet these pro-colonial architects only indicated where the roots of a possible transformation could be; they did not elaborate a clear image of what a national style should look like.[46] They too were experimenting.

In sum, Mexican architecture displayed a great deal of ambivalence and disenchantment about the possibilities of a national architectural style. In their confusion, however, Mexican architects were more modern than they often realized.

FACADES

The Aztec Palace was also a showcase for various forms of artistic expression that echoed domestic interpretations of universal principles. On the facade of the building, twelve figures of Aztecs gods and kings were represented. Inside, countless sculptures, canvases, and photographs were displayed.

In order to acquire a bronze existence, the gods and goddesses Centeotl, Tlaloc, Chalchiutlicue, Camaxtli, Xochiquetzal, and Yacatecuhtli and the kings and heroes Itzcoatl, Nezahualcoyotl, Totoquihuatzin, Cacama, Cuitlahuac, and Cuauhtémoc had to have a historical existence demonstrated by historiographical endeavors (see chapter 5). But to actually acquire specific physiognomical characteristics, positions, and overall image, they needed to be artistically conceived. The archaeologist and historian Antonio Peñafiel, in collaboration with the young sculptor Jesús Contreras, undertook this task.[47]

Tlaloc was described by Peñafiel as a man carrying thunder in his right hand and "a hieroglyph in the face." As represented by Contreras, Tlaloc appeared with a snake in his left hand and wearing Roman-style clothing (see Fig. 10). In fact, in the Aztec mythology Tlaloc was often represented carrying a snake. The historian Francisco del Paso y Troncoso had interpreted this snake as meaning "tempestuous cloud." What Peñafiel described as a hieroglyph was indeed a mask that covered the god's face, as was the case with all deities in Nahuatl mythology. Contreras, however, interpreted the mask as being the crown of a Western monarch.[48]

Centeotl, according to Peñafiel, was the deity of maize, who carried in her hands "a distinctive sign of her functions." She was represented by Contreras in a Greek dress, her hands by her waist, with ears of maize in each (see Fig. 11). Peñafiel chose to highlight the productive aspects of the Aztec past, so Centeotl stood in her role as a goddess linked to maize and agriculture. Moreover, just as the French Republic was customarily represented as a neutral female national symbol, Centeotl was represented as a woman in spite of the fact that Centeotl was often portrayed in Nahuatl mythology indistinctly either as a man or woman.[49] Chalchiutlicue, in turn, was interpreted by Peñafiel as "the provider of water's benefits" and was represented in vaguely Greek or Persian clothing.[50]

These three deities—Tlaloc, Centeotl, and Chalchiutlicue—represented, Peñafiel argued, "the protectors of agriculture and soil fertility."[51] They stood on the right side of the building, representing not only pre-Hispanic religious thought but also national agricultural production and prosperity.

In the left corner of the facade three deities were represented: Xochiquetzal, Camaxtli, and Yacatecuhtli. For Peñafiel, Xochiquetzal represented the goddess of art, Camaxtli the god of hunting, and Yacatecuhtli the god of commerce. Contreras's depictions were frontal female and male figures,

10. Jesús Contreras, *Tlaloc,* designed for the 1889 Aztec Palace. Source: Jesús Contreras's personal papers, reproduced courtesy of Carlos Contreras. (Photograph by Carlos Contreras)

11. Jesús Contreras, *Centeotl*, designed for the 1889 Aztec Palace. Source: Jesús Contreras's personal papers, reproduced courtesy of Carlos Contreras. (Photograph by Carlos Contreras)

with Grecian-style dress and physiognomy. Yacatecuhtli was described by Bernardino de Sahagún with his *viatl*—a sort of cane—and as the god Indians believed "started this people's trade and commerce."[52] In Camaxtli is the ironic spectacle of a god who was not genuinely Aztec placed together with Tlaloc and the rest of the Aztec pantheon in a supposedly pure Aztec Palace. That is, Camaxtli had been interpreted in different fashions—for example, as the god of fire by Chavero, as Jesus Christ on the Cross by Teresa de Mier. Camaxtli was generally venerated as the god of fairs, though in Tlaxcala and Huegotzingo as the god of hunting, but emphatically, Chavero argued, he was a god who, in common with Tlaxcalan Indians, was never captured by the Aztecs.[53] Nonetheless, Peñafiel needed a deity of productive activities to complement his composition, so he used Camaxtli despite the mythological inconsistency. He interpreted Xochiquetzal as a Grecian-style muse or goddess of art, even though she was more often considered the goddess of sexual pleasure (see Fig. 12).[54]

In visually reconstructing the nation's noble origins, commerce, hunting, and the arts seemed an accurate trio. But it was a careful selection of characters and emphases, for the trio could have easily been that of barter (having nothing to do with modern capitalist commerce), fire, and erotic love.[55]

The heroes were located in the central part of the building's facade, on either side of the main entrance. To the right were the beginnings of the Aztec nation: Itzcoatl, Nezahualcoyotl, and Totoquihuatzin, who together formed, according to Peñafiel, "the triple alliance of the monarchies of Mexico, Texcoco, and Tlacopan." To the left was the end of the Aztec monarchy: Cacama, Cuitlahuac, and Cuauhtémoc. Although Itzcoatl was, Peñafiel claimed, "the true founder of the nation and the monarchy," Nezahualcoyotl was epitomized as the poet king and Totoquihuatzin as the representative of the triple alliance that began the hegemony of the Aztecs. Cacama was considered a martyr in the defense of Mexico during the Spanish Conquest; Cuitlahuac, as the vanquisher of Cortés on La Noche Triste. Cuauhtémoc, according to Peñafiel, was "the greatest figure of national heroism" as well as the last Aztec emperor (see Fig. 13).[56]

All of these figures were copied from the narrative and graphic descriptions in books that had been studied, made available, or produced by the liberal intellectuals who were rewriting Mexico's ancient past (see chapter 5). Chavero's works and those by the older historian Orozco y Berra[57] apparently were fundamental for the modern depiction of these figures, which were then reinterpreted by Contreras in an eclectic fashion that combined the resources of Western classical sculpture with what were believed to be pre-Hispanic motifs.[58] The last three rulers of the Aztecs, following Orozco y Berra's history and Chavero's account, were depicted as heroic figures, dressed for battle,

12. Jesús Contreras, *Xochiquetzal*, designed for the 1889 Aztec Palace. Source: Jesús Contreras's personal papers, reproduced courtesy of Carlos Contreras. (Photograph by Carlos Contreras)

13. Jesús Contreras, *Cuauhtémoc*, designed for the 1889 Aztec Palace. Source: Jesús Contreras's personal papers, reproduced courtesy of Carlos Contreras. (Photograph by Carlos Contreras)

with furious gazes. The whole made a clever composition: on one hand, the noble beginning; on the other, the epic ending; in the middle, the entrance to the Mexican pavilion and modern Mexico. In the same fashion that nineteenth-century museums depicted the evolution of men and civilization, or in similar fashion to the portico of the retrospective exposition of anthropological research and science, the Aztec Palace depicted the nation's evolution and introduced visitors to Mexico's version of modernity.

The author of this composition, Jesús Contreras, went on to become a prominent personality in the plastic arts of Porfirian Mexico, as well as a permanent member of the Mexican exhibition team. His grand prize at the 1900 Paris fair for his sculpture *Malgré-tout* became one of the Porfiriato's "greatest hits" (see Fig. 14). He was also a personal beneficiary of the official effort to modernize the national image. Contreras was granted an official scholarship to study in Europe, as were many other artists during this period.[59] With his focus on bronze, he was only following international trends that, after the decline of neoclassicism and with the growth of bronze sculpture as the material of nationalist symbols, made France, not Italy, the place to be in the 1880s.[60]

As he eventually did for the 1900 world's fair, in 1888, together with E. Colibert, Contreras presented a proposal for a Mexican pavilion in Paris (see

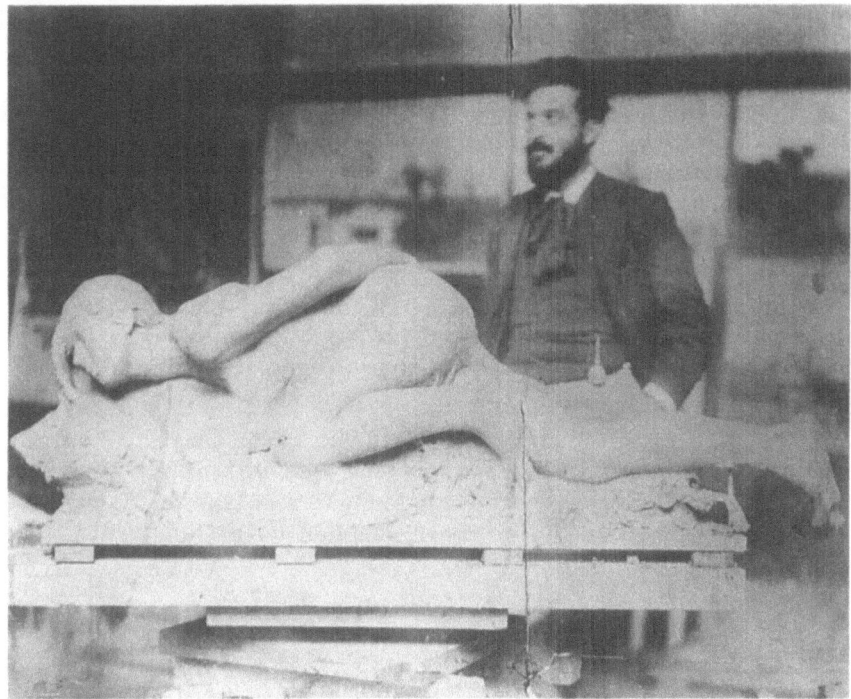

14. Jesús Contreras and *Malgré-tout*, which won a grand prize in the 1900 Paris exhibition. Source: Jesús Contreras's personal papers, reproduced courtesy of Carlos Contreras. (Photograph by Carlos Contreras)

chapter 11). Among the designs, Contreras and Colibert proposed a copy of El Templo de la Merced, a stand for musical performances to be constructed in Mitla style, and a reproduction of buildings from Palenque. Throughout 1888 Contreras lobbied hard for his proposal, and not until Porfirio Díaz himself gave orders to Díaz Mimiaga to put de Anza in charge of all architectural works did Contreras cease his insistent petitions.[61]

Nonetheless, in 1889 Díaz Mimiaga was a great protector of Contreras, who was only twenty-three at the time. Through this sponsorship, Contreras obtained great favors from the government. With Díaz Mimiaga as intermediary, Contreras was put in charge of the sculpture for the exhibit, a task that included not only the works for the facade of the Aztec Palace but also the reproduction in miniature of Salazar's pavilion and some of the interior sculptures—that is, two huge, sculptured candelabra. In tribute to his patron, Contreras also exhibited a bust of Díaz Mimiaga in Paris. He returned to Mexico in 1890, with warm recommendations from Díaz Mimiaga and with great plans to establish a profitable business catering to the mania for statuary that swept modern nationalist Porfirian Mexico.[62] With this enterprise in mind, he returned to Europe a year later to purchase the necessary machinery to establish the Fundición Artística Mexicana, a corporation to produce images in stone, bronze, or marble for the state and for private customers. The chairman of the Fundición's board of directors was Porfirio Díaz, and Contreras was the technical director (see Fig. 15). The Fundición was supposed to be dedicated "especially to monumental statues, candelabra, bronze salon statues, and imitation of French, Belgian, and Japanese works."[63] This corporation was an uncommon example of a combination of artistic concerns with capitalist and patriotic goals.

In his twelve sculptures, Contreras fulfilled both the historic-anthropological-archaeological plan conceived by Peñafiel and the technical and stylistic characteristics given to the building by the engineer de Anza. In addition, he furnished the cosmopolitan Parisian public with visible images of the strange characters of Mexico's exotic story. These characters were not at all at odds with the rest of the fair, and their pre-Hispanic inspiration only made more attractive what otherwise might have been regarded as ordinary sculptures.[64] Domestically, Contreras represented the first fully secular Mexican entrepreneurial artist.[65]

INTERIOR ARTWORK

Contreras's sculptures were requested and paid for by the Mexican government as official efforts to portray the nation. However, inside the Mexican pavilion were other paintings, sculptures, and images that, though not officially sponsored, were also linked directly or indirectly—either by location or by theme—with the national values that the government promoted. Among the various Mexican artistic objects exhibited in Paris, two items were especially welcomed by the French media: Velasco's landscape-painting school, and some canvases with pre-Hispanic motifs. However, it is difficult to believe that late-nineteenth-century foreign art critics would have bothered to look at Mexican paintings so closely had it not been for the convincing inducement of money paid by the Mexican government.

According to art critic Léon Cahun, Mexico, unlike the rest of America, had an original artistic school that depicted both its natural beauty and its heroic history. He especially liked the scene from national history in which "a Mexican orator is seen speaking, before the Senate of Tlaxcala, against the alliance with Cortés." He was also impressed by Velasco's works: "Yes, there is a landscape-painting school in Mexico, and a school that does not owe anything to anyone, that does not imitate anyone, that has been formed by itself, by looking at the marvelous vegetation of the [Mexican] valleys." According to Cahun, Velasco's works differed from those of Corot or Rousseau—who were then in the vanguard of French landscape painting—in the same way

15. Poster for Jesús Contreras's company, Fundición Artística Mexicana. Source: Jesús Contreras's personal papers, reproduced courtesy of Carlos Contreras. (Photograph by Carlos Contreras)

that "Mexico differs from the countryside of the Seine valley."[66] Cahun believed that in Velasco's painting Mexico achieved what modern art was all about: a unique but universal style.

The Mexican art exhibit was composed mainly of paintings by Velasco, which combined various emphases: tropical or exotic natural beauty, historical allegories of the official historiography, and modernism through technological advances (especially railroads, the epitome of late-nineteenth-century modernism). As representations of natural beauty, these canvases reflect the naturalist scientific concerns of the era. As art historian Juan de la Encina argued in the 1940s, Velasco's work represents the national achievement of a preimpressionist but postromantic positivist naturalism. This process began with official efforts in the midnineteenth century to hire experts to teach aspiring Mexicans how to render representations of the national territory and history (for which purpose the Italian landscape painter Eugenio Landesio was employed). The process was accelerated by the flowering of natural history, geology, anthropology, and archaeology as scientific and objective views of nature.

As portraits of Mexican modernity Velasco's paintings were postcards that served both for the popularization of technology and as international propaganda for the coexistence in Mexico of tropical backwardness and modernity. In particular, the depiction of bridges and railways served as striking contrasts to the wildness of the landscapes. The canvases were thus genuine advertisements for the industrial transformation of Mexico, however slight. They also responded to pragmatic economic interests; that is, before the appearance of photography, and even with the advent of the camera, railroad companies and industries paid to have artistic vistas of their roads and buildings created.[67]

No one rivaled Velasco's expertise in the various aspects of landscape painting. Velasco managed to make himself indispensable as a masterful depicter of a scientific, nationalist, and modern era. His technical expertise allowed him to achieve the objectivity and accuracy that realism and scientism required,[68] and his pragmatic and nationalistic imagination allowed him to satisfy different representational needs, both his own and those of his clients.

Undoubtedly, by the early 1890s Velasco's type of landscape naturalist painting had already seen its best moments, at least by European standards. However, it continued to be produced and appreciated.[69] More importantly, for the industrialized world, landscape painting was a sharp ideal contrast with life in many industrial cities and towns. Canvases such as Velasco's were bucolic visions of a paradise lost. For Mexico's modern national image Velasco's landscape painting constituted also a twofold exercise. First, it was precisely that: a bucolic scenario with a tropical mixture that could furnish a contrast with the newly industrialized world. But it was also a symbolic, flashlike, and easily learnable report on the state of the nation expressed in a common cosmopolitan language. It wooed emigration, investment, and international confidence through the depiction of nature, progress, and history.[70]

Among the paintings Velasco exhibited in Paris were two general views of the valley of Mexico, a view of Guelatao (Oaxaca), various waterfall scenes from Orizaba (Veracruz), two views of the *Cañada de Metlac,* and *Ahuhuétes* from Chapultepec. In all of these paintings the natural, pure, fertile, or tropical aspects of Mexico were emphasized. Also included were the national symbols and icons of the official nationalist ideology, presented as part of an overall realist impression. For, as Cahun argued, "Velasco knows how to make the trees and the mountains live and speak in his own country of Mexico, that is clear: I do not know what he would do in France. . . . No one is a real writer except in his own language. . . . M. Velasco is a genuine painter, and his painting is the robust and healthy child of his native soil."[71] Thus one of the paintings of the valley of Mexico included some scenes of manners and customs, and the other featured an eagle and a nopal cactus. Guelatao was not only part of Oaxaca, Díaz's beloved state, but also the birthplace of Benito Juárez, the Porfirian-sponsored member of the Mexican pantheon. The painting of the bridge of Metlac pictured a railroad crossing the Mexican tropics, thus placing an emphasis on Mexican progress.[72] Velasco painted various views of railroads in Metlac, which he exhibited in Paris 1889 and 1900—such as *Cañada de Metlac* (1897), *Puente curvo del Ferrocarril Mexicano en la Cañada de Metlac* (1881), and *Cañada de Metlac* (1881).

Velasco was not the first to paint the valley of Mexico, but he was the first to combine realism in painting with scientific accuracy, a combination that echoed the interaction of national and international trends. He was a naturalist who had studied zoology and botany in the national school of medicine, from which resulted various paintings reproduced in *La Naturaleza,* the journal of the Sociedad Mexicana de Historia Natural. His realist view thus harmonized easily with the scientific objectivity of a positivist era. In addition, Velasco's scientific objectivism went beyond the realm of nature to gain inspiration from historical and anthropological accounts. As Ramírez argues, whereas Velasco used scenes of manners and customs in his romantic beginnings, he gradually moved toward greater proficiency in realistic representations and drew his inspiration from historical themes.[73] Comparing the view of the valley of Mexico exhibited by Velasco at the 1876 Philadelphia fair with the one presented at the 1878 Paris world's fair (both of which were also displayed in 1889), Ramírez has shown how the genre scenes of the former gave way in the latter to a grandiose panorama in which an eagle flies, with prey in its fangs, toward a nopal. This change made of Velasco's landscape painting a real national emblem: the city, surrounded by unpolluted wilderness, and the national symbol flying (see Fig. 16).

Velasco began to paint railroads in 1869, and in Paris 1889 he exhibited

16. José María Velasco, *Valle de México desde el cerro de Santa Isabel* (1877). Source: Museo Nacional de Arte, Mexico City; reproduction authorized by the Consejo Nacional para la Cultura y las Artes, Instituto Nacional de Bellas Artes, Museo Nacional de Arte, Mexico. (Photograph by the Museo Nacional de Arte)

two views of the Metlac barranca (see Fig. 17). Since the late 1870s, railroads in landscape paintings had been all too common, for a steel track over wild and untamed nature was unequaled as a symbol of progress. However, by the 1880s Velasco's vistas were echoed by numerous photographic images. At the 1889 Paris fair the Ferrocarril Nacional Mexicano exhibited thirty-four photographic views, and the Ministry of Economic Development displayed photographs of the Mexico–Veracruz railroad.[74] When the Mexican government promoted the national image of progress, it requested that private companies send photographs of their latest projects, and the requests were answered with the efforts of some of the best photographers available. Nonetheless, most of the landscape photographs were taken by foreigners.[75] Among the most renowned photographers of Mexican railroads was the American William Henry Jackson. He was hired by the Compañía del Ferrocarril Central and came to México to work in 1882, 1891, and 1893. Jackson was one of the most prestigious photographers of the American West, an important personality among those who fashioned symbolic images of American nationalism. In Mexico he had the same motivations that inspired

17. José María Velasco, *La Cañada de Metlac* (Citlaltepec) (1897). Source: Museo Nacional de Arte, Mexico City; reproduction authorized by the Consejo Nacional para la Cultura y las Artes, Instituto Nacional de Bellas Artes, Museo Nacional de Arte, Mexico. (Photograph by the Museo Nacional de Arte)

his pictures of the American West: "to celebrate the technologization of wilderness" and to show "its availability to tourists."[76] He photographed railroads in exactly the same way that Velasco painted them.[77]

However great the effort to mirror reality, naturalist and realist paintings were inescapably ideal and subjective. The camera, in contrast, seemed to be "a near magical device for defeating time, for endowing the past with a present it had previously had only in memory."[78] However, in the late nineteenth century, although photographs put past and present together in instant flashes easily and cheaply available, they were considered mere testimonies, not art.[79] In 1889 the objectivity of the photographic image, though powerful, did not possess the authority of an artistic-scientific representation. A Velasco painting included what photography was able to produce, together with the subtleties of color and perspective that inspired his renderings (that is, aesthetic, nationalistic, and moral elements).[80]

Photography itself was used at this time to depict much more than railroads. The sculptures of the facade of the Aztec Palace contrasted with the numerous photographs of Mexican Indians that were displayed within the structure. For instance, the government of Colima sent various photographs of Indians from Colima; the photography studio of Valleto sent numerous portraits of *cartas de presentación* (calling cards); the state of Morelos sent twenty-two photographs of Tlahuica idols; and Yucatán, twenty-six photographs of antiquities. The Mexico City collection included portraits of *tipos populares* made by the photographic establishment Cruces y Compañía (also known as Cruces y Campa), pictures that had had a great reception at the 1876 Philadelphia fair.[81] This type of view helped to create a portable image of the exotic for both national and international consumption.[82]

Photography was considered "The Pencil of Nature," and its objectivity was believed to be beyond style.[83] The existence of photography was itself proof of modernity, whether it portrayed a railroad or a *tipo popular*. Paintings, in contrast, had to construct the modern forms through their style and content. That is, whereas photographs could serve as objective reports to prove that Mexico was capable of receiving immigrants and foreign investment, they were not evidence of Mexico's cosmopolitan culture. Once again, to be modern and nationalist was above all a matter of style, and only such painters as Velasco succeeded in this difficult task. Therefore, until the beginning of the twentieth century, his works were indispensable components of both Mexico's presence at world's fairs and the construction of the image of a modern nation as a whole. For, as art historian Justino Fernández has argued, very few artists could make Mexico look the way Velasco did: in his works Mexico was itself being like Europe.[84]

The Contreras sculptures and the entire facade of the Mexican building were echoed by numerous paintings with pre-Hispanic motifs: *El Senado de Tlaxcala* by Rodrigo Gutiérrez, *Xochitl presenta al rey Tépancalzin el pulque* by José Obregón, *Funerales de un Indígena* by José Jara, together with a replica of the Cuauhtémoc monument. Although pre-Hispanic-oriented paintings had been rendered previously, after 1870 works in this vein acquired ideological value for the Porfirian regime as well as some national and international artistic recognition.

One of the most noted of these paintings was *El Senado de Tlaxcala* (see Fig. 18). The author, Rodrigo Gutiérrez, had exhibited a painting in the classical style at the 1884 New Orleans fair,[85] but he had changed his source of inspiration by treating pre-Hispanic motifs, though in identical classicist fashion. *El Senado de Tlaxcala* was in fact painted at the request of the wealthy lawyer and historian Felipe Sánchez Solis, who needed the image for his general collection of pre-Hispanic antiquities.[86] The painting depicted a Roman-style senate with Tlaxcalan Indians discussing whether to join Cortés's venture against the Aztecs. Likewise, a canvas by José Obregón, known as *El descubrimiento del pulque* (originally painted in 1869), was also commissioned by Sánchez Solis, and it depicted the Tula's ruler, Tecpancaltzin, in the act of receiving from Xochitl the pulque beverage extracted from maguey (see Fig. 19). Obregón had a classical academic training, generally devoted to biblical topics. His incursion into pre-Hispanic motifs was especially wel-

18. Rodrigo Gutiérrez, *El Senado de Tlaxcala* (1875). Source: Museo Nacional de Arte, Mexico City; reproduction authorized by the Consejo Nacional para la Cultura y las Artes, Instituto Nacional de Bellas Artes, Museo Nacional de Arte. (Photograph by the Museo Nacional de Arte)

comed in the 1880s, when both *El Senado de Tlaxcala* and *El descubrimiento del pulque* were purchased by the Mexican government for exhibition at world's fairs and on other special occasions.[87]

These two paintings were emblematic of an official sanction of the Indian past. As with the facade of the Aztec Palace, the paintings sought to order, classify, and civilize knowledge of the Indian past in such a way as to make it accessible and worthy of respect. Reproductions were included in numerous textbooks, including *México a través de los siglos*. However, in the relationship between artistic-historical depiction of this sort and history and archaeology, the aim was not historical accuracy but rather a mimetic mutual convenience: patriotic history and archaeology procured with these paintings useful representations to reinforce their stories; and these paintings obtained from history and archaeology the inspiration for every detail.

El descubrimiento del pulque echoed the clamor that surrounded the fashioning of a national culture, whose most important speaker was Ignacio

19. José Obregón, *El descubrimiento del pulque* (1869). Source: Fomento Cultural Banamex, from the collection of the Banco Nacional de México. (Photograph by Rafael Doniz)

Manuel Altamirano. According to Fernando de Alva Ixtlilxochitl, Xochitl was a virgin who, accompanied by her father Papantzin, presented "the honey of the maguey" to Tecpancaltzin, then ruler of the Toltecs.[88] Xochitl was so beautiful that Tecpancoltzin seduced her, procreating a son who eventually became a ruler. But in the painting, as art historian Justino Fernández observed, Tecpancoltzin was portrayed as a Hellenic Apollo, and Xochitl as a Greek princess. This story of love, beauty, and power could not be better suited to the Western romantic spirit of the second half of the nineteenth century. The Indian past was thus civilized through a classical romantic filter.

Contemporaries were aware of the fact that this type of artistic representation took excessive liberties with historical data. Graphic artistic representations of history, because they were considered art, were not criticized for maneuvering reality in order to display not truer and more accurate versions but the most effective visual impressions of historical events. Objectivity was less important than were didactic and artistic effectiveness. Thus, whereas French critics considered *El descubrimiento del pulque* as an authentic and vivid representation of the Aztec past, Altamirano acknowledged that the painting was a bit conventional. He pointed out that the Xochitl of Obregón's canvas was not an Indian woman at all: the artist took as his model "for the graceful Xochitl not a bronze-skinned Indian mistress, but a beautiful mestiza whose light swarthy complexion revealed the mixing of European blood." For Altamirano, the image of old Indians in the canvases were too modern, but he believed that *El descubrimiento del pulque*, "as an *ensayo* in national painting . . . deserves the best compliment."[89] That is, in developing a national image, every single effort was an *ensayo* and that was what was expected.

However, the paradox between accuracy and effectiveness echoed a larger incongruity: the Mexican elite's contradictory consideration of the Indian past and present. Ironically enough, what Xochitl offered the Toltec ruler was pulque, an Indian alcoholic beverage that Mexican criollos considered an important cause of Indian degeneration. In this regard, *El descubrimiento del pulque* embodied the Porfirian elite's ambivalence toward Mexican Indians: on one hand, the epic past in which a princess presents a king with a respectable alcoholic beverage; on the other, the repugnant present situation of the Indians' addiction to pulque. This last factor was noticeable not only in the disapproval of pulque displayed by the urban elite but also in scientific treatises. Medical studies of the effects of pulque on the so-called popular classes discovered a particular sort of "Mexican pathology" that was distinct from cirrhosis. Some of these studies—for example, the one by Francisco Altamirano—were exhibited in Paris in 1889. A natural proclivity to alcoholism was believed to be present among Indians.[90]

Despite these scientific reservations, since the 1884 New Orleans fairs, pulque was depicted (and also distributed) as an exotic beverage. In the same way that in 1884 a pamphlet on pulque was prepared,[91] in Paris 1889, in Obregón's painting, pulque was romanticized into a benevolent and acceptable beverage, not only through its depiction as part of a "past past" but also through the subtle inclusion of a common nineteenth-century erotic motif: the myth of the sexually desirable Amazon-like woman.[92]

THE ART OF ART

Mexico's artistic display was admired by Europeans especially for its exotic aspects, and thus the landscape paintings and canvases with pre-Hispanic subjects won recognition in France. Velasco's work (and also a bust of Díaz sculpted by Gabriel Guerra) obtained silver medals, the highest award given to Mexican artistic objects. In addition, Velasco was named a member of the Legion of Honor.[93] Aside from Guerra's bust of Díaz, only two other artists who shunned the pre-Hispanic received awards: Antonio Bibriesca and Andrés Belmont. The former exhibited a portrait of the French consul in Guanajuato; the latter, a portrait of Porfirio Díaz![94]

As with the entire Aztec Palace, the Mexican paintings were seen as laudable and valid, though not necessarily successful, attempts to emulate French models. Nonetheless, Mexico's exotic artistic display was also seen by some European eyes—like Van Gogh or Gauguin who saw in 1889 the architecture and culture of a primitive people—as a potential source of renewal and spontaneity for Western art. But this last perspective was yet to be fully developed in 1889,[95] and Mexico had to wait for European tastes to change and for its French-trained Diego Riveras to emerge.

Velasco himself, as chief of the arts group, wrote a report on Mexico's performance at Paris.[96] He believed that the reason Mexico won so few awards in this category was that its art was not exhibited in the art palace, unlike the United States and other countries. Velasco's silver medal was put into perspective by Velasco himself, when he explained that grand prizes were conferred only on exceptional artists, such as Leopold Flameng. Mexico's awards were in the same category as such distinguished painters as Moreno Carbonero.[97]

In 1889 French painting was experiencing—as we can acknowledge a posteriori—the last moments of the preeminence of neoclassical and romantic styles, which were widely displayed in official salons. These tendencies were embodied in J. L. Ernest Meissonier, who in 1889 was the president of the great art jury. He was a salon painter of famous historic portraits of France's greatest collective unspoken self-esteem: Napoleon.[98] Although impressionist painters were represented, they would not obtain official recognition until the 1900 Paris fair. In effect, the germs of so-called modern art were present at Paris 1889—for example, Monet and Degas—as they had been in the 1860s' Salon des Refusés, but the 1889 fair was dominated by academic classicist tendencies.

Velasco himself viewed those seeds of modern art with distaste. He admired the museum and the canonic exhibitions more than the streets of Bohemian Paris,[99] but he did report favorably on some paintings he had seen in the French exhibition.[100] Among the exhibits of other countries he especially liked the Spanish painter Francisco Pradilla (*La rendición de Granada*), but he pointed out the overall weakness of the Latin American exhibits. For him, very few Latin American artists were worthy of mention.

The Mexican artists who came to Paris, Velasco explicitly agreed, were there to learn and copy the art of the city—the artistic capital of the world. But how did the models who were being copied react to this mimetic Mexican exercise? Mexican newspapers reproduced numerous favorable reports from the French media. Indeed, French art critics were officially invited to write about Mexico, and they interpreted Mexican art as functioning within an evolutionary line and thus as still rather childlike and immature. Those epithets, of course, served then (and now) to disqualify artistic works.[101] In this connection, Velasco reported to the Mexican commission on his personal journey through the Mexican art exhibit accompanied by various European artists and art critics, and he described the impressions of the British art critic George A. H. Sala and those of the French artists Meissonier, Pierre Fritel, and François Pierre Guillon.[102]

If, as has been so often argued, Mexican artists were merely imitating French artistic fashions, they were doing so mostly for domestic consumption. Velasco believed that despite the fact that European art and artistic influence was dominant in Mexico, there existed some autonomy in Mexican paintings of figures and landscape scenes—especially in the latter, because since Landecio's arrival there had been little importation of artistic tendencies to Mexico. Velasco argued that all countries followed France—save England, he believed; and yet, all European countries had an original style. All of those styles were in contact, unlike Mexican art, which remained apart from mainstream artistic tendencies. But Velasco was certain that art was "essential to every country regardless of its development," because "men in particular and societies in general show a tendency toward beauty."[103] Therefore, there was no option for Mexico but to continue the efforts to develop a national art, though those efforts had to be conscious of their own weaknesses and tentative nature. Therefore, he believed, there was no art in America in part because of the underdevelopment of both art and industry.

In sum, Velasco's was perhaps the most acute Mexican artistic eye to appraise fin-de-siècle Paris. But he left no images of it; he was as parochial and as universal as his paintings, which, according to Manuel Payno, were considered by Meissonier *croûtes* (bad paintings).[104] The ideal image of the homogeneous classical French art that he had learned in Mexico was threatened by the rather heterogenous, chaotic, and contradictory images of fin-de-siècle Paris, and he opted to defend the ideal image of France, even if in so doing he seemed to be defending France from itself: "In spite of the great liberty for artists that prevails in France, there are a number among them who maintain good principles, and do not let art just rush in. . . . Today's situation would be very appropriate for despairing, for arriving at a complete baroquism, at the most untasteful extravaganza, if not for a certain number of maestros with great talent who sustain high art."[105]

To sum up the analyses of the Aztec Palace presented in the last three chapters, some general aspects can be highlighted. First, since reconciliation was the key term in Mexican politics, the whole cultural panorama had to do with joining pieces, with eclecticism, with pragmatic selection from whatever was available to bring about the impression of homogeneity and harmony. Thus, while the architectural facade of the Aztec Palace had to reconcile pre-Hispanic styles with modern forms, it also had to join various understandings of the pre-Hispanic past.

Second, this variety of eclecticism was especially characteristic of modern times because it was consciously ephemeral yet comprehensive and universal. Whereas there were no doubts about progress—for either French or Mexican officials—they were all too aware that whatever they did was only a trial, however scientific and complex it might be. Mexican architects were well aware that an Aztec Palace constituted the strongest chance of having an important impact in France, yet they knew that it was only an attempt whose contribution to a stable national style was yet to be seen. The essaylike nature of their ventures was especially evident in late-nineteenth-century world's fairs that were themselves the greatest state-of-the-art *ensayos* on modernity in the Western world.

Finally, if experimental eclecticism characterized modern times in 1889, it was because what was in play was forms. Thus classificatory and hierarchical arrangements were inevitably artificial; that is, contingent and eclectic. Late-nineteenth-century nationalism and progress were a matter of facades. The facades were not hypocritical accidental forms, but indeed the only essence available in modern times to constitute collective and individual identities. Consequently, the Aztec Palace manipulated different styles to form a universal nationhood, recognizable to the Western world, and acceptable and learnable for the inhabitants of Mexico.

Whatever appellation the Aztec Palace earned—exotic, uniquely Mexican, traditional, antique, non-Western—it incarnated a specific hierarchical classification set by unequal economic and cultural relations. Of course, the Aztec Palace and its exhibit were less advanced—technologically and industrially—than the rest of the fair was. And yet, formally it was less modern only because it was less powerful: it was the symbol of a poorer nation. It was included in classifications, but it did not participate in classifying. The entire fair, including its Aztec Palace, was forging the terms modern, progressive, and national. Dichotomous hierarchical classification—barbaric-civilized, modern-traditional, exotic-cosmopolitan—would endure, mutating to adjust to changing power relations. But as far as the idea of a modern nation was conceived, and as far as a Westernizing Mexican elite was concerned, to be modern constituted a multifaceted and painful collective outgrowth; in this modern way of being, it was difficult to point out insides and outsides.

EIGHT

Mexican Statistics, Maps, Patents, and Governance

Above all, nineteenth-century great exhibitions were about science. Science was both the midwife and the firstborn child of modern times, and it would be hopeless to attempt to present a modern appearance without a scientific outfit. The Enlightenment had brought about the possibility of uniting, as Condorcet proclaimed in 1793, all sciences and arts to achieve "an equilibrium of knowledge, industry, and reason necessary for the progress and the happiness of the human species."[1] Science was considered universal—a form of knowledge that knew no national context. Nonetheless, science was produced in different and competing national settings,[2] with a paranational consensus about the effectiveness of scientific knowledge. That modern consensus was tightly linked to nationalism. What in modern times was essentially new was not the existence of nationalist sciences but the insurmountable requirement of conceiving nations through science.

French universal exhibitions were an extravaganza of science that proved not only France's modernity but also its national existence. They proved that France was more than the abstract land of freedom and fraternity; it was also the concrete reality of a national entity captured in maps, statistics, and numerous socioeconomic reports. As historian Claude Nicolet has demonstrated, in order for the republican ideology to be reported to other republics (that is, Germany, England, and the United States), it had to "provide something more: the confirmed conviction of being a form of political organization that not only favor[ed] but, to a great extent, depend[ed] on science."[3]

Mexico's displays in world's fairs echoed to the last detail the dictates of the era of science and nationalism. Accordingly, in 1889 the Aztec Palace housed countless statistics and studies on medicine, administration, chemistry, physics, criminology, electricity, mineralogy, and so forth. Several scientific societies (including the Sociedad Antonio Alzate, the Sociedad de

Geografía y Estadística, the Sociedad Mexicana de Historia Natural, the Sociedad de Ingenieros y Arquitectos, the Observatorio Astronómico Central, the Museo Nacional, the Escuela de Bellas Artes, the Escuela Nacional de Ingenieros, the Escuela Nacional de Medicina, and the Escuela Nacional de Jurisprudencia) exhibited their works in 1889, as they did in Chicago 1893 or Paris 1900.

By 1889 Mexico's political and cultural life had experienced a scientific turn,[4] which echoed the international Western trend of framing all knowledge in a scientific format. That Mexicans shared that format is evident. What is important to determine is how the demanding and intricate construction of scientific explanations (in all realms of the national life) occurred. Here lies a clue for understanding both Mexico's particular version of modern times and modernity's own coming into being.

During the Porfiriato, Mexico's urban elites created a scientific milieu that included the concept of scientific politics, the terminology of which was endlessly repeated in specialized writings, in political speeches, and in literary pieces. With the consolidation of power in the hands of the Científico group, the country's development could only be dealt with through scientific explanations. Accordingly, in 1901 José Yves Limantour, the Científico par excellence, observed: "Science has just put at our disposal the driving force which we were so lacking." The nation could now be completed.[5]

For Mexico's technocrats, therefore, to have a presence in world's fairs constituted a great opportunity both to display the progress the country had achieved and to learn about advancements in the unstoppable course of Western progress. For the wizards of progress science was indeed a two-way street: Mexico had to look scientific, and it had to look for science. Consequently, "to make Mexico known in Europe" and "to make Europe known in Mexico"[6] were the explicit goals of the Mexican team in the 1889 Paris fair: more specifically, to "make our political and social organization known in all its principal forms and with all the unique circumstances that could interest especially immigrants, be they capitalist or worker, permitting them to judge the rights that they can enjoy in this country, the franchise and guarantees granted to them, the public health and security, the criminality, etc."[7] To accomplish such a goal, the exhibition team arranged its Parisian performance simultaneously as a demonstration of Mexico's modernity and natural abundance and as a call for immigration and investment. What was created, thus, was both a show of symbols and a socioeconomic report.[8]

For the latter, the goal was crystal clear: to convince Europeans of Mexico's possibilities for investment and advantages for migration. Nonetheless, the goals of the scientists who undertook this task went beyond the pragmatic objectives of the Mexican government. They had their own scientific agenda—to develop their areas of expertise.

In world's fairs, therefore, it is possible to see how Mexicans commanded the language of science in what were the most important scientific events of the century. The significance of world's fairs in the development of science in Mexico, if evident, is still to be historically pondered. Indeed, Mexico's presence at world's fairs accelerated the processes that had been taking place quietly in Mexican laboratories, scientific associations, and universities. Mexican attendance fostered publications, created new institutions, and sponsored scholarship and scholarly congresses. For instance, in 1889, thanks to the suggestion of a Mexican chemist who was sent to Paris to study laboratories and to participate in international congresses, the laboratory of the Instituto Médico Nacional was conceived. The first general medical geography of the country was published for display in 1889. The first sketch of a national map was synthesized to be sent to Paris. Textile statistics were gathered and exhibited at the 1893 Chicago Columbian exhibition, and general agricultural statistics were prepared for the 1900 Paris fair.

Mexico's scientific image in world's fairs tells us a great deal. In the first place, through these displays the specific status of Mexican science is disclosed at a particular moment in time. Science was difficult to improvise, so scientific formality required a background of laborious and long hours of thinking, researching, and writing throughout Mexico's history. Second, in world's fairs we are able to observe how the profile of Mexican science was reshaped by the inherently trendy nature of professional modern science. That is, in universal exhibitions the particular stage of science in Mexico was remodeled in order to suit particular scientific criteria and developments, thus allowing the historian to see both the new profile of Mexican science and the way in which it was reshaped. Finally, in Mexico's scientific image in world fairs we are able to ponder the width of the scientific gap between Mexico and the mainstream Western nations.

With this in mind, in this chapter and the next one I examine Mexico's scientific exhibition at world's fairs, once again taking as the pivot of analysis the 1889 Paris fair. The larger objective is to analyze Mexico's proficiency in the lingua franca of late-nineteenth-century Europe: science in its diverse forms.

NUMBERING AND MAPPING

In Mexico, as in any other modern state, concrete notions of society and state came into being through numbers. Statistics became the technology of ruling and the foundation of late-nineteenth-century scientific politics.[9] The Paris exposition of 1889 was, of course, a fiesta of numbers, because since the London Crystal Palace exhibition of 1851 statistics had been a fundamental part of the picture of the modern world.[10] In the 1889 fair, every area of display included statistics: hygiene, criminology, agricultural production, industrial production, anthropology, social economy, geography, sanitation, and so forth. Even the exposition itself had a statistical account in the ninth volume of Alfred Picard's report.[11]

From the 1770s to the 1840s the science of statistics experienced its golden age, from the statistics produced by the early postrevolutionary regimes to the massive production of numbers by the Napoleonic empire.[12] Deriving first from astronomy and geodesy and later from biology and physics, statistics had been a common ground of scientific expression that gradually was applied to the social realm, despite, for instance, the influential opposition of Comte's positivism.[13] By 1889 the idea of mere descriptive social physics based in numbers was already transformed into the deterministic notion of scientific statistics. That is, by the 1880s statistics were defined in French as "the profound knowledge of the specific and comparative situation of states," or better yet, "statistics is history resting, history is statistics in motion."[14]

In Mexico, as in France, statistics were first associated with the geodesical and geographical sciences but gradually became the expression of the state's actuality and actions. As was the case in France, Mexican statistics were not an inherent component of positivistic science. On the contrary, statistics in Mexico also suffered a transformation from mere descriptive reports to deterministic law; and, as in France, Mexican orthodox positivists rejected statistics as an accurate form of scientific knowledge. For instance, in 1857 Jesús Hermosa observed in one of the first statistical guidebooks of Mexico that statistics was not an exact science but was one "of the fundamentals of politics."[15] However, by 1880 Emiliano Busto, a statistician and a member of the wizards of progress, defined statistics as "the profound understanding of society"; a science that had "figures as its language," which "gives [society] a precise and assured character, as with the exact sciences."[16]

Busto's conviction epitomized the Científico consensus that had equipped statistics with a deterministic twist. This determinism was not a natural and harmonious result but an intellectual outcome determined by international and domestic needs. In fact, the orthodox Comtian positivists were inclined to repudiate statistical determinism as a form of positivist explanation of social phenomena. Therefore, as late as 1902 the prominent positivist Agustín Aragón considered that those who used statistics without philosophy were merely ignorant.[17]

According to Antonio Peñafiel, who in addition to being an archaeologist and historian was one of the main producers of statistics in the second part of the nineteenth century, Mexico's statistics went back to pre-Hispanic times. Following his indigenist bias, Peñafiel believed that statistics in Mexico began with the Chichimeca ruler Nepaltzin, who ordered that the members of his tribe be counted when the valley of Mexico had been reached. He was, Peñafiel claimed, "the first statistician, if by this word one means a ruler who makes good use, like him, of numbers, for the benefit of his subjects and well-being of those he ruled."[18] Nonetheless, Peñafiel affirmed that modern statistics in fact began in Mexico with the works of Alexander von Humboldt. These efforts were later developed by the Instituto Geográfico (1833–1838), and by the Sociedad Mexicana de Geografía y Estadística.[19] However, as late as 1893 the Mexican economist Carlos Díaz Dufoo affirmed (in a book published for the 1893 Chicago world's fair) that the science of statistics was still only beginning in Mexico.[20]

Following the construction of a social physics based on statistical laws, as affirmed by the most famous statistician of the first part of the nineteenth century, Adolphe Quetelet,[21] various statisticians emerged in Mexico, such as Antonio Peñafiel, and flourished during the Porfirian peace.[22] By 1882, thanks to the influence of Antonio García Cubas and Emiliano Busto, Minister Carlos Pacheco created the Dirección General de Estadística, which was administered by Peñafiel.[23] By the 1890s the demographic, criminal, sanitary, geodesical, geographical, and administrative aspects of Mexico were all addressed statistically. For the 1889 Paris fair, statistics on education, crime, and health, as well as graphic explanations of the Mexican political and administrative legal framework, were prepared.[24] Therefore, as part of the exhibit of the agriculture group, its director, Pedro J. Senties, undertook an intricate and massive research project. He requested data from the state governments regarding climates, altitudes, directions and speeds of winds, rainfall totals, and other technical information. He also inquired about the characteristics of soils as well as the various types of agricultural products.

Clearly this investigation aspired to present a comprehensive view of the state of Mexican agriculture. Toward that end, statistics were also compiled on salaries for machinery workers and day laborers and on prices of the haciendas and ranchos, together with pictures or photographs of the rural buildings, livestock, tools and feeding equipment. Much of this information was concentrated in tables that contained data on name, price, size, and location of ranchos and haciendas; salaries paid to men, women, and children; machinery used; amount of land under irrigation; and types of fertilizers utilized. However, the task of compiling these statistics was not finished until the 1900 Paris world's fair. The result was a rich source of information that deserves to be included in studies of Mexican agriculture, although it is important to keep in mind its main purpose: to attract foreign investment and immigration by creating an image of a promising modern nation. Thus salaries seem exaggeratedly low in the complete compilation of 1900, and the good conditions on haciendas are perhaps exaggerated.[25] The demand for this type of statistics grew constantly, making it necessary for the Mexican government to undertake more statistical works for future displays.[26]

International investors and observers assessed Mexican potential through agricultural statistics and maps, which constituted universal forms of presentation for modern nations. Argentina presented two comprehensive statistical studies whose only difference from those of Mexico was that instead of referring to races, the Argentine study talked about nationalities (that is, Spaniards, Italians, Chinese, and so forth).[27] The Franco-Brazilian commission hired a well-known French economist, E. Levasseur (who, as we saw in chapter 3, was hired by Mexico in 1900), to produce Brazil's statistical image.[28] El Salvador also efficiently, if modestly, assembled a statistical image.[29]

For Mexico, and for other Latin American countries, the numerous statistics reported at the 1889 exhibition had a mutually reinforcing international and national use. For France, these statistics were not only arguments expressed in a familiar language, but also a sine qua non for its own statistical existence. For Mexico, statistics were an important part of a larger social, cultural, and physical topography of the nation which included, in addition to statistics, maps, photographs, and natural history studies.

By definition, statistics were comparative, and only through comparison could what was then called the law of large numbers be uncovered.[30] As historian of statistics Ian Hacking has explained, "that statistics should be comparative is part of their original mandate to measure the power and wealth of the state, as compared with other states."[31] Thus in an increasingly numerical world, statistics were always welcome, as was shown by the numerous European comparative statistical studies on crime, industrial production, races, and hygiene. In essence, more than one set of statistics was needed in such comparisons, and thus all components being compared acquired equal importance in creating statistical images. In fact, Mexicans compared their statistics with French statistics. In turn, some specific Mexican statistics were used and shown to prove France's progress or backwardness. Indeed, whether Mexican statistics were actually used by French or European statisticians to make a comprehensive comparison (such as that of France and England) was only secondarily important. What was essential for both France and Mexico was that statistics be universally available. Only in a sea of numbers provided by all nations could the statistical picture of the ideal modern nation have emerged.

This could be exemplified even in the revolutionary transformation that statistics underwent with the works of the British biologist Francis Galton. At the 1889 Paris fair Galton measured heads of Parisians, and in the same year he published in London his celebrated *Natural Inheritance*.[32] At the same time, the Mexican exhibit at Paris displayed collections of skulls and statistics on the facial angles of Mexicans. In fact, it would be difficult to imagine the type of transformation introduced by Galton in statistics, if not for the availability of statistics collected in many countries. One can argue that in the realm of statistics, the global creation of the picture of the modern world becomes historically noticeable.

Cartography was another tool in the self-creation of a national image. As late as 1880, Manuel Orozco y Berra affirmed that "as of yet, exact knowledge of the vast extent of our country is not possible."[33] But by 1889 Mexican scientists had already advanced in this regard, mainly because of the efforts of the Sociedad Mexicana de Geografía y Estadística and the Comisión Geográfico-Exploradora (created in 1878).

Thus in 1889 the Mexican exhibition team decided to exhibit a *Carta geográfica* of Mexico that was to be prepared by the cartography section of the Ministry of Economic Development (which in fact consisted of the Comisión Geográfico-Exploradora) (see Fig. 20).[34] The plan for this map summarized all the factors that the Porfirian elite wished to emphasize: the Mexican climate, which offered advantages for agriculture; Mexico City, which proved Mexico's modernity; the political and social organization of Mexico, which demonstrated that order existed and explained the bureaucratic and financial facilities offered by the state to investors and immigrants; the extent and quality of Mexico's communication system, especially telegraphs and railroads; the quantity and quality of civic buildings and monuments, which exemplified Mexico's republican and aesthetic advancements; the condition of public health and hygiene, which were sine qua non ingredients of modern development; the state of Mexican culture, which could be understood as modern nineteenth-century high culture (a review of the most French of the Mexican artists and intellectuals); and the ingredient of exoticism, which made Mexico simultaneously European and modern, yet unique.[35] This plan was not fully carried out, but it constituted an ideal description of what the map ought to include.

The history of late-nineteenth-century Mexican cartography is closely connected with displays at world's fairs. In 1884 a *Carta general geográfica* had been prepared for exhibit at the New Orleans fair. A larger and more comprehensive one was displayed in Paris 1889, and it became the basis for the general map of Mexico, which was not finished until 1906.[36] For the Chicago fair of 1893 another map was made, this time a hydrologic one.

In addition, in 1889 there was an important scientific-cartographic display: the exhibit of the Comisión Geográfico-Exploradora, which was highly praised by the French scientific community.[37] The director of this commission was the Mexican military cartographer Agustín Díaz.[38] He had worked in the Comisión de Límites, which had been established after the Mexican-American war, and was appointed by Porfirio Díaz to undertake a map of Puebla in 1877. As Agustín Díaz himself explained in the catalogue of the commission's display in Paris, the commission was made possible by "the urgent need for drawing and designing better maps than those that had been conceived to that date."[39]

The French scientific community singled out for praise Mexico's geodesical, topographical, and geographical maps and calculations, as well as twenty issues of *La Carte générale de la République contruite à la cent-millionèsime partie, par le système horizontal*. In addition, topography and technology were combined in a map of Mexico's telegraph system that was especially prepared

20. Sketch for a geological map of Mexico, made for the 1889 Paris exhibition. (Photograph by the author)

for the Paris exposition. Antonio García Cubas, the most prominent geographer of nineteenth-century Mexico, was also represented in Mexico's cartographic display.[40] He exhibited his "Statistics and History of the Mexican Republic Comprised by Thirty-one Maps of the States, Territories, and a Map of Railroads with Texts in Spanish, French, and English," a revision of his work for the 1884 New Orleans world's fair.[41]

The general topography of the nation included more than maps and statistics; geology was also important in descriptions of the national territory. Therefore, another topographic effort was the *Carta general geológica*, undertaken by the Ministry of Economic Development for exhibition in Paris. Antonio del Castillo, with the technical expertise of the geologist José G. Aguilera, was in charge of this task.[42] This map encompassed various strategic concerns of the Porfirian government. The study of earth science was tightly related to productive activities such as mining and agriculture.[43] It was also associated with international anthropological and archaeological concerns about the origins of humankind in America, which in turn formed part of the national discussion of Darwinist theories and racist speculation about the backwardness of Mexican Indians. Thus, among the maps were the *Plano geológico del Peñón de los Baños donde se encontró el hombre fósil prehistórico* and the *Carta general minera de la República Mexicana.*[44]

One hundred copies of the geological and mining maps were distributed in France and Europe to, among others, the director of the French geological map, the director and professors of Paris's Mining École Supérieur, and the professors of geology of the Musée National d'Histoire Naturelle. In Austria they were given to the Geologische Reichsanstalt of Vienna and to professors of mineralogy and geology at the Naturhistorisches Museum, also in Vienna.[45] In truth, promotion was as important in the sciences as it was in commerce.

To advance geology in the nation, Antonio del Castillo was sent to Paris with the commission to travel in Europe and study all of the advancements and geological institutions.[46] Therefore, he simultaneously directed the exhibition of Mexican maps and studied French scientific concerns and Mexico's possibilities for being included in those concerns. Consequently, in January 1889 he reported that meteorites in the Musée National d'Histoire Naturelle were well appreciated and that for Mexico "it would be beneficial to exhibit them in Paris," because "it would make Mexico known worldwide as the country where the largest number of meteorites have fallen." In effect, natural randomness worked in favor of Mexico's national pride,[47] and models of Mexican meteorites were in fact displayed in Paris. At least two meteorites, weighing approximately 14 tons, were brought from Chihuahua to Mexico City, copied, and exhibited in replica.[48]

Together, statistics, maps, and geological studies created a clear picture of the nation's topography. The ideal image of the modern nation could observe its full likeness in such a mirror.

PATENTING

Universal expositions were the capitals of invention because they epitomized the marriage of science and technology that accelerated the Industrial Revolution.[49] Not surprisingly, on these occasions European laws and customs placed great emphasis on property rights and patents. Hence English, French, and American legislation on property rights was tightly linked to world's fairs.[50]

In Mexico some laws in this regard were derived from the Spanish decree of October 1820, and in newly independent Mexico Lucas Alamán conferred the first patent license.[51] However, not until the Ministry of Economic Development was created in 1853 did patent rights obtain a clear legal status.[52] In 1890 a final law was passed that accelerated the process and established better guarantees for the registration of patents. This was not essentially a policy to develop domestic technology, but rather part of the general objective of attracting foreign investment and immigration by protecting the technology of foreigners in Mexico. Therefore, after 1890 the majority of the registered patents in Mexico were foreign. By the 1900s Mexico took care at world's fairs, especially American ones, to emphasize that a legal framework for protecting patent rights existed in Mexico, again with the hope of inducing American companies to establish factories there.[53]

In 1889, when the industry group of the Mexican exhibition was collecting Mexican inventions, the tediously bureaucratic registration process meant that most of the items that came to be exhibited in Paris were not properly registered in the Ministry of Economic Development.[54] In fact, it seems that Mexican regulations were not especially concerned with the protection of patents on items displayed at Paris, though efforts were made to assure the authenticity of some products.

The French government, however, although authorizing certain exceptions to property rights on products exhibited at Paris, also required that the appropriate royalties be paid by those who made use of any invention or product.[55] Therefore, in the case of inventions or manufactures, Mexican exhibitors were required by the government to obtain a certificate signed by the respective Mexican local authorities of the authenticity of their work.[56] In this way the legislation on Mexican intellectual and scientific property rights was simplified but not strongly enforced by the central legal and bureaucratic structure.

In part, the government's casual attitude toward patent protection may have derived from the fact that the Mexican exhibit was not especially oriented toward technology. Most displays of native technological advancements focused on those areas in which Mexican industry had been especially successful, namely, textile, vegetable fibers, grain mills, and cigarette production (see Fig. 21).[57] For example, the Franco-Mexican entrepreneur Ernesto Pugibet displayed his machine to fabricate cigars, while the government of Yucatán and the private inventor Isaac Esparza exhibited various examples of Mexican technology, machines for scraping henequen.[58] In addition, Maximino Río de la Loza exhibited a device to avoid railroad accidents (see Fig. 22), Angel Acedo exhibited a dynamo, and José María César exhibited a steam engine. F. Paez, the Acedo Brothers, and Rivera exhibited mills for grinding tortilla corn, and Leandro Ramírez displayed a sewing machine.[59]

In 1889 Paris also attracted flamboyant Mexican inventors, who followed in the footsteps of Juan N. Adorno at Paris 1855 (see chapter 3). One of these was Antonio García Chávez, an auxiliary of the industry group, who requested 1,500 pesos at the beginning of 1889 to construct an engine for exhibition at Paris. García Chávez claimed he could produce an electric engine that would be "the definitive solution in the use of electricity as a driving force." The project was studied by the official commission, which rejected the request. But a few months later García Chávez presented another project, this time for the construction of an airplane. Once again his project was rejected.[60] Antonio Carbajal, a physician who often wrote scientific articles for the *Gaceta Médica de México*, was more successful. He received 500 pesos to

STATISTICS, MAPS, PATENTS, AND GOVERNANCE   135

21. Miguel Saldaña's henequen-processing machine, an example of Mexican technology. Source: Patentes y Marcas, Box 34, Exp. 1435, reproduced courtesy of the Archivo General de la Nación, Mexico City. (Photograph by the Archivo General de la Nación)

design a mask to protect against infection, which was actually exhibited as part of Mexico's display in the hygiene and sanitation class.[61]

Despite some legislation on technology and the machine, the emphasis of Mexico's display of products at Paris was clearly on agriculture. By 1889 the Porfirian plan for national economic development was oriented toward strengthening Mexico's participation in the Industrial Revolution as a supplier of raw materials and as a consumer of international technology. To foster industrialization through native technological inventions was a rhetorical commonplace, but in fact the Mexican elite had already abandoned the idea of catching up with the rapid pace of industrial technology and aimed only to be a cosmopolitan and wealthy supplier of raw materials. In sharp contrast, Thomas Edison's inventions were of the greatest interest in Paris, and his concerns with patent rights were epitomized by the registration of his patents not only in Paris but in Mexico even before 1889.[62] Of the new nations, the United States was definitely the technological master. By 1862 Jules Verne had already imagined that technology would develop until "[men are] swallowed up by their own inventions. . . . I bet the Yankees will have a hand in it."[63] Realists that they were, Mexican authorities were well aware of the impossibility of finding a Mexican Edison.

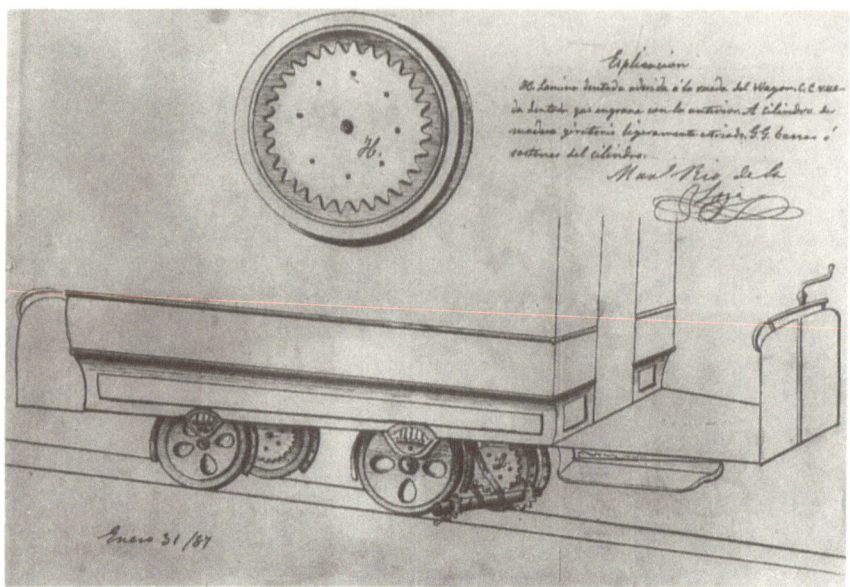

22. Maximino Río de la Loza's machine to avoid railroad accidents. Source: Patentes y Marcas, Box 33, Exp. 1384, reproduced courtesy of the Archivo General de la Nación, Mexico City. (Photograph by the Archivo General de la Nación)

GOVERNING

Statistics, together with economics, eventually became the fundamental support for administrative knowledge, a major component of modern nations.[64] Public administration was created to meet the needs brought about by modern society: increasing complexity, division of labor, demographic growth, urban expansion, professionalization, and rationalization of time and resources. By the late nineteenth century it was a mixture of organizational skills, written laws, accounting methods, and division of labor supported on two pillars: the liberal political philosophy and the scientific consensus of the late nineteenth century. Through the first, public administration was part of a long-standing philosophical and political definition of the role of the state.[65] As such, public administration was linked to the particular ways in which each nation constituted a centralized power made into a state and to specific legal traditions that controlled power relationships. By being part of a scientific consensus, public administration became an arrangement of methods, techniques, and laws; that is, the science of modern administration.[66]

The politico-philosophical and scientific bases of public administration were threatened by three related ghosts: state intervention (fear of socialism), social control (fear of revolution), and corruption. In the French Third

Republic, as we saw in chapter 1, these ghosts were alive and present in the French government.[67]

Economic liberalism and radical political liberalism opposed state intervention. But the fear of social unrest, the need for social control, and the urge to promote public welfare made state intervention necessary. More importantly, the need for state sponsorship in economic development was recognized and exercised, especially by countries like France, which were trying to catch up with industrialization. Therefore, in the late nineteenth century the political formula employed by various European countries was conservative liberalism, which added to the traditional areas of state intervention, such as national security and tax collection, new areas such as sanitation, housing, and industrial promotion. The role of the state as a universal referee expanded, and consequently the need for reliable professional civil servants grew. A well-organized and scientifically trained bureaucracy became an important facet of a modern state and perhaps its very essence, as Max Weber noted at the beginning of the twentieth century.[68]

Although the idea of public administration was part of the general conception of the role of the state, it possessed its own logic and functioning based on the technicalities of decision making and the geographical and physical organization of government.[69] In this realm, administrative knowledge was gradually developing relatively fixed forms for routine functions. In time these new developments crystallized and became proofs of modernity and efficiency in the handling of state affairs. Accordingly, regardless of the actual efficiency and honesty of bureaucrats, in modern states it became necessary for each agency to display crisp administrative formalities: trained personnel, an organizational scheme defined according to the fashionable style, and a well-defined division of labor and use of time and space. These formalities became fundamental in the general picture of the modern world.

Hence, for a nation to prove itself modern, it had to show that it was ruled by modern public administration, and at world's fairs Mexico aimed to show its recent advancements in government administration, to establish that Mexico had a theoretical awareness of how to govern a modern nation scientifically. Of course, the countless propaganda books distributed by the government invariably contained a section on administration (that is, territory, ministries, division of power, and so forth), and the organization of the wizards of progress was an attempt to prove the modernity of Mexican public administration. In addition, for the 1889 Paris fair Emiliano Busto suggested that he write a comparative analysis of the Mexican and French public administration systems, which would include "all the diverse services that compose [the Mexican government,] accompanied by statistical charts and tables."[70] Busto was the *oficial mayor* of the Mexican Ministry of Finance, a member of the Mexican commission in Paris, and a bureaucrat with long involvement in financial affairs both in the state of Guanajuato and in the federal government.[71] The study was published in French and Spanish, in a handsome edition,[72] and completed in no more than six months.[73] Busto himself kept Porfirio Díaz informed of the progress of his work.[74]

Busto's book was part propaganda, of course, and its goals were harmonious with the general objectives of Mexico's display in Paris. Hence, once Busto's initiative was approved, the Ministry of Economic Development asked that his study provide immigrants, capitalists, and workers with the needed information about "the rights they enjoy in this country, the franchise and guarantees."[75] But it was also assumed that Busto's book was to be a scientific study, and therefore the Mexican government arranged for it to be distributed to European newspaper editors and publicists, as well as to such distinguished scientists as Louis Pasteur and Dr. Jean-Martin Charcot.[76]

The book was a detailed description of the division of powers and of the organization of the six Mexican ministries vis-à-vis the ten French ministries. For each Mexican ministry, a complete organizational chart was prepared and compared with its French counterpart. Administration was, according to Busto—who literally translated the definition from a French study—"the conjunction of public services meant to assist, under government direction, the execution of laws, decrees, and rules that have as their objective the benefit of the state, the protection of its interests, or the maintenance, within just limits, of the exercise of public liberties."[77] Indeed, the role of the state was explicitly delineated in the concept of public administration: on one hand, the promotion of both private and state economic interests and, on the other, social control. Busto explained that the backwardness of Mexico's economy and society meant that the Mexican government had a larger role to play than did that of the French state. Along these lines, he maintained that taxes in Mexico served not only, "as with the French government," to provide national security, education, and communication services but to protect "railroad business in order to obtain speedy and reliable lines of communication." Accordingly, Busto affirmed, the Mexican government presented "the attributes that Josat finds in the universal tutor."[78]

In fact, Busto's book was based largely on a recently published study of the organization of the French Ministry of Finance, written by a rather obscure bureaucrat named Jules Josat, deputy bureau chief at the French Finance Ministry, who has left almost no historical record.[79] For Josat, scientific administration was the natural component of modern states: "If, within a state, the government is the soul that inspires, the administration is the body that acts."[80] Busto followed Josat's study in detail, even imitating the format and analytical schemes of his books.[81] Meticulously, Busto examined every agency of the various ministries, explaining its function and organizational structure and then comparing each with its French counterpart. Overall, Busto's work constituted a comparative proof of Mexico's administrative advancement, a confirmation of Mexico's disciplined society in which, as he observed in explaining the goal of financial administration, "the entire lives of citizens . . . seem to have been enveloped in the ingenious net woven by the men of the treasury division."[82]

Busto's book was by no means an innovative or landmark study of Mexican administration, although it was indeed the first comparative study in this area.[83] However, it is quite revealing from the point of view of the construction of a modern national image. The very fact of its rapid, improvised, superficial, but elegant production says a great deal about the state of so-called scientific administration in Mexico. And it is precisely because of its comparative character that Busto's book acquired historical significance.

Doubtless Busto's work was rapidly executed following the latest studies—which proved to be ephemeral—of French administrative techniques. Busto must have believed that Josat's study of the reorganization of the French Ministry of Finance would have a significant influence on French thinking about public administration. In addition, Josat's study facilitated Busto's work because its organizational focus and charts invited comparison even in purely visual terms (for example, chart to chart). However, Josat had no major effect on the history of French public administration. Indeed, unlike the medical sciences, hygiene, and natural history (see chapter 9), in the domain of public administration, Mexican officials tended to be much more naive and generally unaware of the terms of the discussion. Mexican theoreticians of bureaucracy pale before Mexican physicians, hygienists, or naturalists.

In no small measure, this was the result of the particular history of Mexico's administrative structure, which by the 1880s had found a new form of centralized authority with which to solve the nineteenth-century enigma of how to rule the country. This solution, of course, favored pragmatic authoritarian rule through violence, coercion, cooptation, and bargaining, devices that had little to do with innovative technical or theoretical administration. Further, in Mexico the philosophical, political, and scientific implications of administration were debated not in the rather confined and precisely limited realm of administration but in a wider ideological arena: within Mexico's liberal constitutionalist tradition.

Whatever its virtues or flaws, Busto's book achieved its immediate objective: to show Mexico, through comparison with France itself, as a well-structured, disciplined modern nation. Through comparison, Mexico's governing style was diffused into the structure, forms, and entire fashion of what was then understood as scientific administration. Mexico's administration could be read by the modern world as epitomized by the fair, in French and in a familiar conceptual structure. In addition, as with statistics, within a comparison the elements being compared acquired equal import and mutual relevance. In any comparison, similarities and differences acquire meaning only insofar as they make reference to a common ground of understanding, which the elements being compared mutually create. Busto's book attempted to prove that Mexico's administration belonged to that common modern ground of public administration. Mexico's administrative structure, thus, was presented as a particular version of a universal form, and Mexico appeared to be not only echoing it but also contributing something to it through Mexican particularities. By doing so, and regardless of its actual impact on French officials, Busto's book gained for the Porfirian regime what nationally could be presented as a seal of approval. Mexico's administrative similarities with France could be internationally, but above all nationally, introduced as proof that Mexico was moving on the right track. And Mexico's administrative differences with France were presented by Busto as merely ad hoc additions required by the country's uniqueness. By attaining this seal of approval, Mexico could presumably claim to have the right to reap the fruits of a modern administration: investment, development, security, and political rights.

In addition, through comparisons the very idea of universal truths of general applicability in administration was reinforced. For France and for Mexico, the fact that an obscure Mexican official in a newly politically stabilized country could demonstrate that the formalities of modern scientific administration were being observed proved the universalism of modern administration. Through this mechanism, such works as Busto's aimed to take the historical particularities of Mexico's governing style and fashion them in the form of a common (with all modern nations) universal present of modernity.

It was in liberal constitutionalist discussions that the philosophical, political, and scientific aspects of administration had been debated in Mexico since the 1860s. The very idea of scientific administration as the solution to such problems as the role of the state and social control was deliberated in constitutional and political terms.[84] The new conservative scientific liberals of the late 1880s favored strong government and order. Conservative liberalism (epitomized in a statist administration charged, as Busto maintained, with more functions than the traditional notion of universal referee) was believed to be an organic result of both Mexico's violent history and economic backwardness. As Busto implied, in a recently pacified new country, only a strong state could create a real nation and lead it to the standards of international progress—hence the doggedly repeated battle cry of "less politics, more administration," in which administration was not at issue but rather seen as an assortment of scientific techniques, methods, and theories that needed to be applied in the daily exercise of governance.

In effect, Busto was not concerned with the actual creation of a professional group of employees or civil servants but with learning the technical and methodological formalities to clothe the new ideology that was presented as the end of ideologies, as the completion of politics itself: administration. Thus the ethical aspects (such as corruption) of public administration, which were often talked about by professional bureaucrats in Mexico,[85] and which were a regular issue in the debate over public administration in England or France,[86] were not considered in Busto's work on administration. Busto was less interested in explaining the training, recruitment, honesty, and functioning of bureaucracy in Mexico than in showing the parallels between the formal structures of ministries in France and Mexico.

In sum, in world's fairs the Mexican elite utilized all the formalities of public administration as the attire of a nation that was aiming to catch up with modernity. During the 1880s and 1890s, for countries like Mexico, the apparatus of public administration was only a formal framework, a technically useful overlay for the habits, legal forms, and particular arrangements of the Mexican elite. Such a framework became both a learning process for new administrative methods and techniques and a normative criterion only applicable at specific moments and for particular sectors of the population. Within these limits, Porfirian bureaucracy doubtless worked rather well. Public administration was thus the black-tie attire indispensable for attendance at the reception of modern nations, the idea being that pragmatic rule clothed as modern public administration would gradually function in a modern manner . . . as if in the old tale, had the mendicant persisted in dressing like a prince, a king he would have become.

NINE

Natural History and Sanitation in the Modern Nation

NATURAL HISTORY

In promoting modern Mexico, the efforts of the Porfirian elite to develop the nation's natural resources went beyond reports on mining and agriculture; studies of the flora and fauna of Mexico were also part of this concern. Natural history had been part of the Spanish process of colonization since the eighteenth century. By the end of the nineteenth century the study of nature was reinforced by the development of scientific chemistry, biology, and medicine within an evolutionist paradigm.

Mexico had a well-established natural history tradition,[1] and naturalists persisted in their work during the second half of the nineteenth century, albeit within serious economic limitations. By the 1870s this tradition began to have large and impressive displays in Mexico's presence at world's fairs.[2] At the 1889 fair Mexican naturalists had one of their best performances. In 1888 the newly created National Medical Institute had undertaken the task of studying and classifying Mexico's flora and fauna, as well as many other natural history studies that often were published in the institute's journal *El Estudio* (which in 1890 became *Anales del Instituto Médico Nacional*). In fact, the distinguished Mexican naturalist Francisco Altamirano, a member of the institute, was appointed by the Mexican government to classify all botanical collections sent to Paris.[3] He presented a catalogue of 300 different plants with their botanical classifications according to the French scheme, which enabled him to point out various promising scientific or curative plants.[4] He was the first to translate into Spanish Francisco Hernández's study of New Spain's natural history (the twenty volumes of which he sent to Paris).

As early as 1884 the Comisión Geográfico-Exploradora had secured a place for natural history in Mexico's displays at world's fairs. For the New Orleans exposition of 1884 the modern classification of Mexican species began again, but just after the New Orleans fair, this collection had a tragic end—important scientific material was lost when the steamship *City of Mérida* sank in Havana on 29 August 1884.[5] The commission began a new collection, and in 1889 a carefully selected grouping of fossils, plants, insects, and animals was sent to Paris.[6]

On a different front, the natural history exhibit mounted by the Comisión Geográfico-Exploradora was such a great success in New Orleans that the Mexican government decided to found a Natural History Museum administered by the commission.[7] Following the example of the New Orleans exhibit, this museum included sections on geology, paleontology, botany, and zoology.

In the second part of the nineteenth century, natural history in Mexico was especially active in a reexamination of the old faith in curative or economically productive discoveries of new products.[8] It had long been common in Western scientific "mythology" to hope for miraculous cures from exotic plants. Mexican native medicine and botany had been studied as early as Francisco Hernández's *De historia plantarum Novae Hispanae* (1570–1577), commissioned by Philip II.[9] In the nineteenth century, the creation in 1868 of the Sociedad Mexicana de Historia Natural was a landmark in such studies. Numerous studies of Mexican flora and fauna were published in *La Naturaleza* —the society's remarkable periodical—and in the *Boletín de la Sociedad Mexicana de Geografía y Estadística* throughout the second part of the nineteenth century.

At the 1889 Paris fair, in addition to various volumes of these publications, numerous collections of indigenous medicinal plants were exhibited, with the explicit goal of "enriching Mexican therapeutic sciences and fostering exports of useful Mexican flora."[10] With this type of natural history exhibit, Mexican officials had a twofold intention: to satisfy the exoticist desires of Europeans, and to provide scientific data to foster both scientific interchange and economic investment.

In the latter sense, Francisco and Maximino Río de la Loza were important chemists and botanists who were envoys of Mexico at world's fairs. Maximino, considered a Mexican inventor,[11] exhibited in Paris, according to the Mexican catalogue, various "scientific works written for the exposition," including the description of a device to avoid railroad accidents and some pills to cure epilepsy.[12] Francisco's work was of more importance, and in it he followed in the steps of his father, Leopoldo Río de la Loza, the greatest chemist of nineteenth-century Mexico.

Thus in April 1889 Francisco Río de la Loza was commissioned to study laboratories for chemical analysis in Paris and in other European countries.[13] As with all Mexican scientific envoys, he was concerned both with the promotion of Mexico in Europe and with the development of his own profession in Mexico. He therefore proposed to Minister Carlos Pacheco that Mexico's vast botanical diversity could be of great interest to Mexican and foreign scientists because of its industrial and medical potential.[14] Francisco Río de la Loza's trip to Paris was fundamental for the final design of the laboratory of the National Medical Institute. In 1889 he exhibited many documents and plans for the creation of the institute and sent back his analysis of European institutions. In 1891 the institute's laboratory was inaugurated with the objective of "[studying] the national flora, fauna, climatology, and medical geography."[15] The institute was part of the Ministry of Economic Development, and one of its specific objectives was to recover the Mexican Indian medical tradition.[16]

Also included in the display of natural history were various paintings of native animals, many of them by José María Velasco. What most amazed visitors was the collection of dissected diminutive Mexican birds. In the enthusiastic words of *La Laterne* of Paris, that diminutive world of birds "would have overburdened Buffon himself."[17]

The beauty and utility of nature's gifts to Mexico were thus exhibited to satisfy both the economic interests of the nation's elite and the economic needs and cultural desires of Europe. This meant the appropriation of native beauty and productivity and thus the recuperation of a long-standing natural history tradition in Mexico, which was redirected according to the scientific trends of late-nineteenth-century European sciences.

SANITATION, HYGIENE, AND PUBLIC HEALTH

A truly modern Mexico had to be necessarily a sanitary Mexico. To understand the sanitary aspects of Mexico's modern image, a brief examination of nineteenth-century European (especially French) hygienic thinking is indispensable.

If Paris was a stage of industrial growth, miasma, unemployment, epidemics, and worker discontent, then its fairs had to present the utopian and scientific solutions to those problems. Therefore, the Parisian fairs became idealized shows of the latest developments in social economy. For example, in the 1860s Frederic Le Play founded the *Société des Études Pratiques d'Économie Sociale*, the ideas of which he applied to the organization of Group 10 (material and moral improvement of workers) at the 1867 Paris imperial exposition.[18] By the 1900 Paris fair, Charles Gide and Alfred Picard had made social economy a domain apart from either liberal or socialist cooperativism. Social economy was part of progress, and as such it was considered a scientific enterprise.[19]

Since the beginning of the nineteenth century, the proponents of hygienic reforms and assistance discussed whether the state should be in charge of hygiene and sanitation. For the liberal paradigm, the state possessed well-defined areas of intervention (such as national security and public administration), but assistance and hygiene were not fully legitimized as areas of state jurisdiction. By the 1880s social economy (with its Saint-Simonian overtones) and the idea of assistance had to deal with whether to sanction or oppose state intervention in the private sphere in the name of hygiene and sanitation.[20] In fact, the role of the state in assistance and hygiene remained a controversial issue until the beginning of the twentieth century.[21]

Another realm of debate was hygiene itself. World's fairs often displayed the scientific progress of hygiene and, above all, the emergence of a public hygienic consciousness. Jules Rochard, a distinguished hygienist and author of *Traité d'hygiène sociale* (1888),[22] described the status of hygiene in Paris 1889.[23] He delimited three main concerns in the 7,600-square-meter Parisian exhibit on hygiene: food, sanitation of cities and houses, and the water supply and sewer system. The fountain of the Greek goddess of health, Hygie, crowned this exhibit.[24]

Indeed, by the late 1880s hygiene in Europe was acquiring a scientific configuration, surpassing its utopian quasi-philanthropic emphasis in favor of a more clearly defined scientific and political role.[25] The early-nineteenth-century utopian hygienists became the professional technocrats of the late nineteenth century, with complex and ambivalent relationships with the government.[26] In turn, the medical profession passed from a corporate guild to an entity with clear connections and power within the state, owing to their scientific expertise.[27]

By the beginning of the 1880s, in the context of uncertainty about the way in which diseases were transmitted, such scientific tools as sanitation questionnaires were developed;[28] these tools—again, in a context marked by scientific uncertainty—served as a way to incorporate statistics, geography, socioeconomic explanations, and microbiological Pasteurian theories in the understanding of the origins and transmission of diseases. The development of this type of technique eventually furnished the state with a scientific basis for justifying intervention in the private realm in the interest of improved sanitation.[29]

From the historian's point of view, however, one can argue that by 1889 the scientific transformation of hygiene was stalled. For hygiene to acquire its new political and scientific status, various related phenomena needed to come together, and this process was not yet complete in 1889. For their part, Mexican scientists were reading these debates on sanitation and hygiene.

In the scientific realm, the development of statistical data and innovative scientific techniques was rapid (most especially the Pasteurian bacteriological revolution in hygiene that began in the 1880s). These factors eventually transformed both the scientific standing and the social role of hygiene. By 1889 hygiene had acquired a scientific status but had not yet fully gained the scientific authority and the political status that would eventually come by virtue of the Pasteurian discoveries—and also by the hygienists' own influential articulation of their scientific expertise as an essential component of national security and nationalism.[30] In 1889 public hygiene in Europe, concerning most of the important diseases, was still being debated in a rather eclectic, pragmatic fashion that included not only Pasteurian microbiology but many others forms of explanation as well. The origin and transmission of diseases were studied by those who variously favored the contagionism, anticontagionism, and germ-theory approaches.[31] In the end, from those who believed that the advancement of civilization would eventually bring about the end of diseases to those who used statistics to establish the relationship between misery and illness, almost all approaches had something to contribute to the explanation of diseases in a context of uncertainty.[32]

In the sociopolitical domestic realm there were two interrelated phenomena. First, European governments came to be dominated by a centralized bureaucratic technocracy that was eager to discover new areas for state intervention, among the most fundamental of which were public sanitation and health. Here hygienists finally found authority and power for their particular expertise. Second, as a consequence of these trends, by the 1880s in France and other European countries feeling was growing that a direct relationship existed between poor hygiene and national decline. If France lost markets and wars, it was because its population was sick and poor, whereas countries like England and the United States had improved the health of their peoples.[33] Indeed, despite scientific maturity, what had been a matter of fact since the midnineteenth century was that civilization, good sanitation, and hygiene came together in the educated mind. A modern nation had to be a spotless and white nation.[34]

Regardless of the actual sanitary conditions of the country, Mexico's display at the world expositions echoed the modern basic concerns with hygiene and, to some extent, social economy. Representing a country and a capital city with grievous sanitation problems, the Mexican exhibit on hygiene attempted, first, to show and learn the methods and advances that European scientific hygienism had achieved. Second, Mexico's hygienists in world's fairs depicted not only the state of Mexico's hygiene and sanitation but also their own standing as a new technocracy of experts. Thus they showed the French experts and public, and also the Mexican authorities, the importance of their task. Finally, regarding the tension between statism and liberalism on the issue of hygiene, the Mexican exhibit at fairs underlined the nation's unmistakable statism, which reflected both the domestic power base of the elite and the need to modernize the nation, an undertaking in which the state was fundamental. In effect, through Mexico's presence at Paris 1889 we can see how the need for sanitation reforms became an important component of economic and political development and also of Mexico's particular nationalism.

Mexico's official participation in world's fairs attempted to change the country's long-standing image as an unhygienic and unsanitary place. During the first part of the nineteenth century the sanitary problems associated with endemic national strife had to be faced, and in 1841 the Consejo Superior de Salubridad (Superior Sanitation Council) was created to deal with the issue. The role of this agency was to advise the government on sanitation concerns and to regulate the practice of medicine by establishing examinations and licenses and by monitoring medical activities in Mexico City.[35] In this way the growth of hygienism was clearly related to the professionalization and consolidation of the modern medical profession in Mexico. In 1872 the council was reformed to give more emphasis to the issue of public sanitation, and in 1879 it was reorganized into a federal consultative group, with a federal budget, becoming a genuine scientific agency and also a modern sanitation police force.[36] Until 1885 Dr. Idelfonso Velasco headed this medical corporation, and with his death Dr. Eduardo Liceaga became the director of the council, a position he held until the end of the Porfirian regime.

Hygiene in Mexico was more than a mere scientifically determined necessity, however. Scientific hygiene emerged in Mexico as part of the politico-cultural transformation called modernization that the country underwent during the years of Porfirian stability. Scientific hygiene was of major importance for the betterment of the sanitary conditions of the nation, and it was also indispensable to achieving a modern urban culture.

But the path to proclaiming these goals had not been a smooth one: hygiene as a scientific endeavor and as public knowledge was a difficult task to undertake in Mexico during the troubled years that preceded the Porfiriato. Before appropriate measures could be taken, Mexican physicians had to convince authorities and the general public of the utility of hygiene in the face of the manifold political and economic problems that beset the country. Public hygiene, as the director of the council observed in 1867, possessed an importance that was "barely known to the common people, but of high administrative interest in civilized nations even when its brilliance is not enough to dazzle the multitudes."[37] By the 1880s, however, the significance of sanitation and hygiene were well recognized and fostered, both by the state and by private associations—that is, the church, scientific associations, and social clubs. By 1889 the Mexican hygiene experts, headed by Dr. Eduardo Liceaga, the most distinguished hygienist of late-nineteenth-century Mexico, were just beginning to decipher the scientific and political implications of hygiene and sanitation in a modern fashion. It was precisely in 1889 that Liceaga headed a team of hygienists who proposed to the Ministry of the Interior that a modern sanitary code be proclaimed for Mexico. This code was in fact publicized at the International Congress of Hygiene at the Paris fair.[38] In it, hygiene in Mexico acquired its modern scientific connotations, and it included a real inventory of the concerns of modern hygiene: air, water, dwellings, physical education, epidemics, management of residuals, food, and so forth.[39]

Drainage in Mexico City became the main sanitary project of the Porfirian regime. For the 1889 exposition numerous sketches and maps of the Mexican drainage works were prepared by the two main sanitary engineers of late-nineteenth-century Mexico: Roberto Gayol and Miguel Angel de Quevedo.[40] Quevedo wrote a report on the state of the works for distribution in Paris.[41]

In this fashion, Mexico demonstrated in Paris that sanitary engineering was also part of Mexico's modern image. As in Europe, in Mexico it was believed that the miasma of the valley of Mexico was the cause of several diseases (such as typhus, tuberculosis, and cholera). Potable water and a sewer system for such a valley as Mexico City's (surrounded by lakes and mountains) was the great solution. Hence throughout the Porfiriato the drainage of Mexico City became the most salient evidence of Mexico's modern hygiene, one that was continually exhibited on many international stages.

The sanitation concerns of Mexico went beyond the miasma approach and its concomitant engineering concerns. In constructing a hygienic picture of Mexico in 1889, Rodrigo Valdés arranged a description of the army, the regular police force, and the rural police force. The description included photographs of soldiers and their uniforms, which were in tune with the general tendency to portray *tipos populares*. This worked to attract Europeans who longed for the exotic and to depict the physical, nutritional, and civic advancement of those social classes that were often considered savage. In addition, in the hygiene and assistance class, Mexico's exhibit included various mineral waters from different regions of the country and a hygienic and antiseptic mask designed by Dr. Antonio Carbajal, as well as various plans for the construction of hospitals, mental institutions, and penitentiaries in Puebla and Mexico City.[42] But Mexico's main display in this regard was in the professional education class. There, documents related to the creation of the National Medical Institute were exhibited, together with the memoir of the sanitary works of Mexico City, Dr. Flores's history of medicine, and the first medical geography of Mexico (by Dr. Domingo Orvañanos), as well as various other medical studies.[43] In the medicine class, the military hospital of Mexico City exhibited anatomical models and replicas of infected arms and legs, together with the head of an Apache Indian.

In addition, Mexico sent envoys to congresses on public assistance, dermatology and syphilology, mental medicine, and hygiene and demography.[44] Antonio Peñafiel (a medical doctor), José Ramírez, Angel Gaviño, and Manuel Flores attended the hygiene congress.[45] In regard to hygiene, Mexico was especially cosmopolitan: not only were representatives sent to Paris, they were also asked to travel around Europe distributing Mexican scientific works and learning new methods and theories. While Peñafiel, Gaviño, and

Ramírez were in Paris in 1889, another distinguished hygienist, Ignacio Alvarado, was in New York sending reports for the preparation of Liceaga's sanitary code.[46]

With all of this, Mexico displayed its strong interest in the methods of modern hygiene, which in turn was harmonious with the positivist bent of the Mexican elite in the late 1880s. Mexican hygienists also participated in the international debate on hygiene. For instance, while French and European hygienists were deliberating the causes of yellow fever and its means of transmission, Dr. Manuel María Carmona y Valle exhibited in Paris his *Leçons sur l'étiologie et la prophylaxie de la fièvre jaune*, with a preface by Eduardo Liceaga, published in 1885. In fact, the etiological microorganism that causes yellow fever was discovered by Carlos Finlay in Havana in 1881, but eight years later, the means by which it is transmitted were not yet clear, and Carmona y Valle's study contributed the vast Mexican experience to the international study of the disease and quoted Pasteur and Koch before the bacteriological revolution in hygiene was completely accepted.[47] In essence, while Finlay isolated the microorganism *micrococcus tetragenous febris flavae*, Carmona y Valle isolated what he called a mold *peronospora lutea*, for which he claimed to have found a form of vaccine. However accurate the discoveries of Carmona y Valle may have been, the fact is that they were part of international debate on yellow fever.[48]

Leprosy was another disease the treatment for which attracted the efforts of Mexican medical men. In 1851 Dr. Rafael Lucio published his *Opúsculo sobre el mal de San Lázaro o elefantiásis de los griegos* which was republished by the Ministry of Economic Development in 1889 for exhibition at Paris. In it, Lucio for the first time described a particular kind of leprosy called *manchada*, which he found in Mexico.[49] In the same way, Mexico exhibited in Paris a collection of articles in French taken from one of the most important medical journals of late-nineteenth-century Mexico, *El Estudio*, published by the National Medical Institute. In it the advances of Mexican hygiene, surgery, biology, and criminology were reported.[50] In these articles, as in other short studies and books, Mexico's physicians and hygienists demonstrated that they shared the concerns of international science and that they were keeping abreast of its progress. These studies emphasized advancements in the etiology of diseases, in anthropology, and in an area of concern that dealt with the relationship between women and hygienico-medical science.

This concern took various forms. At the same time that Rafael Lavista detailed in *El Estudio* his diagnosis of a clitoral tumor of eleven centimeters found in a syphilitic woman patient, in Paris Francisco Flores was displaying an impressive expertise in statistics and legal medicine in his book *El himen en México*. This was a study of the hymens of 181 women, classified according to complex formulas, demonstrating that the ring-shaped hymen was the most common among Mexican women. Flores believed that this discovery would help forensic medicine to protect female virginity because, he affirmed, "today virginity is one of the jewels sought so much by men.... What is more beautiful than that white flower of virginity still unaccosted by the vicious zephyr."[51] This was scientific study at its best, but it was conceived in the language and moral axioms of late-nineteenth-century Mexico. And it was yet another example of the type of comparative-statistical anatomical and anthropological work that sought to scientifically establish the particular anatomical characteristics of the Mexican people within universal science. In the same way, in 1881 Dr. Florencio Flores wrote a comparative analysis of the pelvises of Mexican and European women which concluded that "if the European pelvis as described in books should be held as the normal type, [then] the Mexican pelvis, in relation to it, should be considered as a physical defect." However, for Mexico, he argued, such a pelvis was normal.[52]

By the same token, *La Gaceta Médica de México* of the Academia Mexicana de Medicina, three volumes of which were exhibited at Paris, reported in 1889 a new *reglamento* for prostitution in Mexico City, drawn up by Domingo Orvañanos, Manuel S. Soriano, and Luis E. Ruiz. In it, the regulation of prostitution was considered important both from the sanitary point of view (that is, fewer men infected) and from the fiscal point of view (that is, more taxes collected). This meant, as historian Alain Corbin argued for the case of France, the triumph of regulationism over the political, medical, and economic aspects of female prostitution.[53]

Thus the particular Mexican version of the modern regulatory paternalistic treatment of women was displayed by Mexican officials at Paris through many medical, anthropological, and legal studies. These studies, in turn, echoed certain fundamental ideas found also in Federico Gamboa's famous novel, *Santa* (1903), in which it is said that Santa belonged as much to the police as to sanitation, or in the poem of the then renowned suicidal poet Manuel Acuña, *La Ramera:* "Poor woman, who abandoned and alone . . . instead of a hand to save her, finds a hand that pushes her to the abysm."[54]

Along similar lines, Mexican women were barred from the discussions of the very publicized (nationally and internationally) Congreso Pedagógico Higiénico that took place seven years before the 1889 fair. All of the hygienists who were in Paris in 1889 attended the 1882 congress, but no woman was present at either event. Thus, an Orvañanos or a Ramírez might speak at the Paris fair on the statistical control of prostitution and the sanitary police on the domestic role of women, but the congress itself had resolutely opposed the participation of women. Because hygiene in education involved the discussion of personal hygiene and sexual conduct, Mexican scientists, however advanced their scientific knowledge, did not want to break from *las buenas costumbres* (good manners) and speak to female teachers about these subjects. There were a few dissenters. Carlos de Olaguíbel y Aristas, for example, supported the idea of female participation, not only because of the all-important role women played, especially in the education of girls, but also because of their need to emancipate women from domesticity. But the majority argued that because the congress was about science and not sentiment, women were not needed, despite general agreement that men and women possessed the same brain capacity. A vote was taken, and women were not allowed to attend the session. The doctors preferred that the subject of their discussions—women—remain at home.[55] The same rule was maintained within the medical establishment, which made it almost impossible for women to obtain medical degrees.[56]

Mexican doctors also took advantage of world's fairs to study these kinds of concerns. In August 1889 Dr. Alberto Aizpurul was appointed to travel to the exposition to study advancements in the treatment of female diseases and syphilis. He was asked to travel not only to Paris but also to London and New York.[57]

What best condensed the stage and concerns of Mexico's hygienists in the 1889 exposition, however, was Domingo Orvañanos's *Ensayo de geografía médica y climatología de la República Mexicana*, specifically published for the exhibition in two volumes with a prologue by Eduardo Liceaga.[58] This was one of the main scientific displays of Mexico in Paris, and although it was not originally intended to be exhibited there, the exposition accelerated the research and the completion of the book. With the fair booming, in 1888 Orvañanos was tapped to undertake a detailed study of the nation's climates and diseases as part of the creation of the National Medical Institute and of Mexico's display in Paris 1889.[59] Orvañanos quickly sent letters to the various states requesting detailed information in questionnaire form on climate and diseases.[60] These were in fact the Mexican versions of the French *enquêtes* (questionnaires). Gustavo Ruiz Sandoval and Ramón Rodríguez Rivera designed a questionnaire to be distributed to local authorities and physicians. Among many other items, this questionnaire requested data on rainfall, climate, water conditions, general occupation of the population, home conditions, most common diseases (epidemic and endemic), race, and the existence of leprosy, yellow fever, and goiter.

In 1886 José Ramírez and Rodríguez Rivera published *Noticias climatológicas de la República, recopiladas por la Secretaría de Fomento, para la formación de la Geografía Médica Mexicana*. It was a preliminary study, which Orvañanos continued for the Paris exposition and published as an *ensayo* (a first-draft attempt) because it was indeed incomplete. In effect, the 1889 fair fostered this study as part of Mexico's construction of a national image because the work combined (as did the French questionnaires of the 1880s in the context of general uncertainty as to how diseases were transmitted) three forms of knowledge, which were, in turn, three ways of describing the nation: social and geographical mapping, statistics, and various explanations of the origins of diseases (Pasteurian and non-Pasteurian).

The book consisted of two volumes: the first contained Orvañanos's studies; the second, forty-six maps. Orvañanos's study was divided into three parts: a geographical sketch of Mexico's climates, a description of the main diseases in Mexico, and an appendix.[61] The appendix compared mortality rates in Mexico City with those for the entire country. Following a geographical textbook published in 1889 by Alberto Correa, Orvañanos estimated Mexico's population at 11.25 million.[62] He divided the population into four races: Indians, Europeans, Blacks, and mestizos.[63] Then he analyzed the atmospheric pressures and altitudes of Mexico in order to specify what he termed the air diet of the inhabitants of the various regions. He concluded that altitude anemia had not yet been demonstrated and that more research had to be done. This was a direct response to the common European notion that altitude had an effect on the inhabitants of Mexico City.[64]

Next, Orvañanos dealt with nutrition, following the studies by Samuel Morales Pereira,[65] which discussed the malnutrition of the majority of the population, whose basic diet consisted of maize, beans, and pulque. Then he analyzed various diseases.

Orvañanos's geographical and etiological study of diseases is emblematic of the way late-nineteenth-century Mexican hygienists interacted with the scientific methods of the international discipline. In fact, Orvañanos often quoted French, German, and U.S. studies, as well as reports sent from Mexico to other countries. For instance, in his treatment of leprosy, he first mapped the areas of concentration of the illness (mainly in Western Mexico)[66] and then discussed the etiology of the disease according to seven possible explanations that were addressed in detail. These seven explanations were a combination of old and new scientific ideas with traditional notions about disease origins. From the outset he accepted the idea of genetic causes. Regarding contagious transmission, he argued that there was neither a place nor a race on the face of the earth that had escaped leprosy; thus, he concluded, climatic and racial causes were less important than was transmission by contagion. Orvañanos supported the contagion thesis but nevertheless explained the counterargument. He believed that contagious transmission took place through sexual intercourse, and he argued that researchers who opposed the contagion thesis had been misled by leprosy's long incubation period. He identified the agent of the disease as the bacillus discovered by Hansen in Norway in 1874 and since internationally accepted.[67] Then he disqualified various possible causes that were collected in the questionnaires (such as obstruction of perspiration, use of salted water, overconsumption of pork). Regarding the treatment of leprosy, Orvañanos was cautious, and he proposed the undertaking of a real census of the districts in which the disease was epidemic.

As we can see from his analysis of this malady, Orvañanos not only was aware of the bacteriological advances in late-nineteenth-century hygiene but also shared the uncertainty and ambivalence about transmission and treatment.[68] Although he was prompt to point out the microbial origins of the disease, he could not come to a conclusion regarding the means of transmission, so he fell back on a combination of causes (genetic and social). Social causes were often called physiological misery, a polite way of saying poverty. Indeed, he explicitly located himself within the debate between contagionists and anticontagionists, and he clearly explained his position according to the data he had collected. Regarding the role that the state should play in hygiene, he called for more data before a final decision was made between more state interventions and more private care.[69]

Both the advanced methodology of Orvañanos and his uncertainty can also be observed in his examination of yellow fever. He located cases throughout the country and argued that what caused it was a microorganism: "an alga for Dr. Freire of Brazil; a fungus for Dr. Carmona y Valle of Mexico and for Dr. Finlay a micrococcus." But he wisely added that these explanations "contributed to affirming the ideas of the general medical world, that the essential cause of yellow fever is a microscopic being."[70] In effect, Mexican scientists were active participants in the study of this disease.[71]

As I have argued above, the scientific display mounted by Mexican hygienists in Paris also aimed to consolidate their technocratic role within the state. The role of Mexican experts in international exhibitions, as well as in the political and scientific life of Mexico as a whole, has to be understood through the development of the medical profession in Mexico. Physicians were the most important receptors and disseminators of idealist, positivist, hygienist, and to a large extent, liberal ideas in nineteenth-century Mexico. For them, the Porfirian peace brought about the continuation of their professional associations, which functioned as centers of scientific and political education.

Eduardo Liceaga, Porfirio Parra, Antonio Peñafiel, Domingo Orvañanos, Francisco Flores, José Ramírez, Angel Gaviño, Agustín Reyes, José L. Gómez, Jose D. Morales, Nicolás Ramírez de Arrellano, and Francisco Altamirano were all physicians and hygienists who occupied posts at the medical school in Mexico City, in various scientific institutes and societies, and in government agencies, especially in the sanitation council, which became their own source and space of power.[72] By the end of the 1880s they had gained recognition by the state, and once the Científicos group was consolidated in the 1890s they became one with the political and economic elite, a position they retained throughout the 1900s and 1910s.

However, the achievement of this role for the medical profession was far from harmonious. Within the profession there were scientific and ideological disputes, especially regarding the involvement of the state. Furthermore, the number of influential doctors and hygienists remained rather constant throughout the Porfirian regime, revealing that a small and closed elite controlled the profession's influential political role. By the 1890s the elite members of the medical profession had acquired such direct links with the government—in terms of control of the medical school, sanitary engineering contracts, and personal ties with politicians—that other doctors complained about the unhealthy centralization.[73]

There is good reason to believe that overall the Mexican elite hygienists were first-class scholars but most of them were also formidable politicians. Eduardo Liceaga, for example, was not only the director of the sanitation council during nearly the entire Porfirian period but also Mexico's envoy to important international conferences on sanitation, in addition to being the person in charge of the Mexican hygiene displays at various world's fairs. At the 1889 fair he was awarded a bronze medal, although he was not present in Paris. He had just left for Mexico to transport rabbits infected with Pasteur rabies vaccine in order to establish the Mexican antirabies institute.[74] By the 1900s Liceaga was the acknowledged master of hygiene in Mexico, allocating to his colleagues and friends work on sanitation projects (such as campaigns against tuberculosis and yellow fever) and participation in congresses and fairs around the world.[75] In 1900 the *Diario del Hogar* often criticized him for his servile attitude toward Díaz's reelection, for his ongoing leadership of the Superior Sanitation Council, and for having monopolized Mexico's international hygienic presence for himself.[76]

Hygiene had a different nationalist value in Mexico than it did, say, in France. In France, hygiene became an ingredient of nationalism as a matter of security and racial purity, whereas in Mexico hygiene became part of nationalism because it was crucial for two main developmental goals—foreign investment and immigration. Some people believed that if the image of Mexico were to change from that of an unsanitary nation to a healthy one, immigrants and capital would flood the country. Therefore, for Mexican hygienists, the bacteriological revolution, or the triumph of a particular version of conservative (that is, statist) liberalism, was important for their achievement of power within the state. Their command of the universal scientific language and their role as communicators and creators of the image of a sanitary country assured them of a significant role within the government. For instance, at the international hygiene congress in Paris, Angel Gaviño translated Mexico's sanitary reforms into the language of French sanitation measures by proclaiming Mexico's new sanitary code. He also furthered the Mexican government's desire to show that Mexico was a sanitary and hospitable place by maintaining that Mexico was up-to-date in its sanitary knowledge and that it was joining the modern nations thanks to French advancements, especially to Pasteur's work.[77]

Once hygienists had consolidated their role and power in the 1900s, they could scarcely distinguish between reasons of state and reasons of science. Accordingly, at the beginning of the twentieth century Liceaga wrote to his wife from an international sanitation congress in Costa Rica that "in sum, being healthy comes first; only then does one think of the rights of man, of freedoms, and moral improvement." In 1902 Liceaga was even more explicit in linking the interests of the state with those of Mexico and the hygienists when, in an international congress in Havana, he claimed that "to the state, man is priceless. The public wealth completely loses this valuable resource when a man dies. . . . The state has to spend money on assistance and in this way loses public wealth. . . . Those [illnesses] that cause his death are infinitely more costly than those that demand the greatest acts of reparation."[78]

Hygienists also had to lobby the government, both to further their scientific development and for their political and economic well-being. Contracts for sanitary engineering works were often disputed, and hygienists were always involved. By the 1900s many of the hygienists had interests in the development of Mexico's cities (in terms of transportation, sanitary services, and real estate), as well as in the new business of insurance.[79] For instance, in 1907 the governor of Guanajuato wrote to Liceaga about the celebration of a Pan-American medical congress in Mexico, primarily to let Liceaga know that he was about to send the data required; in passing he mentioned to Liceaga that "our" streetcar business was doing wonderfully. He explained to Liceaga that "in the course of one year, your stock will be worth twice as much."[80] Nonetheless, it is important to keep in mind that all of this was achieved only after political power based on scientific expertise was attained.

In Mexico hygiene indisputably became a state matter. In a country in which the construction of a nationalistic ideology, industrial promotion, and integrity were based on state sponsorship, statism in hygiene was not an issue. Since the Mexican hygienic congress of 1883, various participants had recommended that a centralized national agency be created, beyond private interests and beyond the various state jurisdictions, for the handling of hygiene and sanitation.[81] Along similar lines, in 1892 Liceaga, Manuel Septien, and Rafael Lucio argued that civilization and hygiene went together but that private initiative could go against the general well-being and should be controlled. In order that "the interests of capital are not to come before the rights of humanity,"[82] Liceaga believed that the state had to control and sponsor welfare policies. For Septien, the solution was the creation of a Ministry of Sanitation (something that was not instituted until after the Revolution of

1910).⁸³ In a word, in a nonwhite, backward country the issue of hygiene was a duty of the enlightened caudillos, and not even radical liberals were opposed to state intervention in this area.

The Porfirian hygienic image of Mexico was eventually held up to the mockery of public opinion in Mexico City (see chapter 10). In large part this was because even though knowledge of hygiene grew, the sanitary conditions of the city remained terrible. Despite the achievements of the Porfirian hygienists, in 1916 Alberto J. Pani called Mexico City the most unsanitary urban area in the world.⁸⁴ It must be conceded that Porfirian hygienists produced the proper scientific hygienic image of Mexico for both national and international consumption. The actual sanitary transformation was, of course, most visible in places like Mexico City, but the vast territory and the general indigence of most of the population made the Porfirian achievements look insignificant to a close observer. Only Mexico's hygienic image was comprehensive and cosmopolitan.

One issue undermined this image and frustrated the efforts of Mexican hygienists: race. Although this issue was properly the domain of experts in anthropology, archaeology, and the national epic, it had a direct impact on the hygienists' role in constructing the national image. How, in a nationalist and scientifically racist era, could a country of Indians be completely disinfected? The response of the Porfirian Científicos was to constantly look for, classify, reclassify, and adapt possible answers from international science, arts, and politics, but they found no final solution. How could they? The long-standing identification of the Indians with miasma and dirt was something that neither Western exoticism nor scientific hygienism could overcome. Nonetheless, hygienists knew that real modern nationalism needed modern hygiene, sanitation, and medicine. Whereas proof of Mexico's cleanliness could not be final because of its Indian and hybrid races, late-nineteenth-century hygienists knew that only through the constantly up-dated combinations of domestic uniqueness with international trends could they make their country look truly modern. That is precisely what, in 1889, the first issue of *El Estudio* maintained by making a call to create both a science of the nation and a national science: "A truly national medicine would be that which could boast facts discovered in this country, and possibly in some cases only applicable to this country. A Mexican pathology, a Mexican surgery, a Mexican therapeutics, a Mexican hygiene and obstetrics, these titles would give us the right to be respected in the scientific world beyond our seas and borders."⁸⁵

Detailed analysis of the construction of the scientific components of the national image has shown us the complex texture of the allegedly positivist and Frenchified Mexican elite. That is, on one hand the Mexican elite possessed dissimilar levels of expertise in the various sciences, depending on the particular history of the science in question in Mexico and on the specific economic interest of the Porfirian regime. On the other hand, after this brief excursion into the particularities of science in Mexico as exhibited in international fairs, we can recognize what some historians of science have rightly claimed;[86] that is, in certain areas Mexican scientists were as close as they had ever been—or would ever be—to the mainstream development of their respective disciplines. The scientific gap, albeit still wide, had never been as narrow for Mexico as it was in the late nineteenth century. This was because the technological revolution was just beginning to acquire its characteristic hyperaccelerated pace and because, in certain scientific fields, Mexican scientists, though often few, were working modestly but efficiently.

TEN

Irony

If the Eiffel Tower exhibition was a pocket picture of the modern world, then Mexico's exhibit was a reflection of that depiction. To conclude that the picture was false because it neither reflected the world as it actually was nor depicted the so-called real Mexico would be too simplistic. Of course, the harmony, well-being, and comfort on display at the exhibition were continually belied by the actuality of international conflicts, nationalism, urban poverty, and agrarian crisis. But the values and ideas that the fair mirrored were seldom rejected by most observers as the authentic and objective ideal of how the modern world ought to be if those values and ideas were pushed to realization. In effect, when it came to a belief in progress and the value of science, there was a general consensus that defied irony and contradiction. It was through such a consensus that irony was made possible, but as a denunciation of hypocrisy or distortion and not as a total negation. Nonetheless, there was a harsher sort of irony, one that indeed questioned progress, as was the case with Baudelaire's comments on the French exposition of 1855 or Henry Adams's insightful comments on the 1893 Chicago fair.[1]

For Mexico and its historical image, the main source of contradictions came not from Europe but from within Mexico itself. In France, for instance, the national image that Mexico was at such pains to project was received either with indifference or with an ostentatious paternalism that is so often the imitator's reward. It is more important to examine how the trappings that supposedly went with modern nationhood (that is, a cosmopolitan yet exotic appearance, hygiene and sanitation, good administration, and economic and social stability) squared with daily life in Mexico, especially that of Mexico City, where an urban, literate middle class had created a confined and small public sphere.

By the late 1880s the growth of a significant public opinion in the modern sense of the term was contradictorily both encouraged and censored by the Porfirian regime. The technological advancements in communications and publishing, as well as the growth of an urban, literate middle class, fostered the emergence of many national and local newspapers, journals, magazines, and pamphlets from all sorts of clubs and organizations.[2] However, political dissidence was constantly repressed, and media opposition, though functioning throughout the Porfirian regime, suffered continuous setbacks.[3]

Nonetheless, the possibilities for wording subtle political and social commentary before reaching the point of repression were ample. In literary, artistic, political, and scientific media, therefore, a certain free public opinion was restrained only by the writer's capacity for allegorical innovation. Ironic commentaries on Mexico's modern image were expressed essentially in humor.

Through humor, Mexico's modern national image, as depicted in Paris and other world's fairs, was used to make statements about Mexico's political and social problems. The irony was twofold: it was the confrontation of an ideal type with crude versions of Mexico's reality; and it was accomplished by sharing the values epitomized by Mexico's presence at world's fairs and by ridiculing the way in which the image of modern Mexico had been formed. Humor was not merely an escape but also a deliberate vehicle for a form of criticism that was rich, profound, and somewhat politically acceptable.

Diverse aspects of reality in Mexico were arranged and highlighted in various ways, according to various world views. This produced not one but many versions of what Mexico was actually like, just as, say, there were many versions of how real Paris diverged from the ideal account represented by the various world's fairs. At this level of contradiction many ironies emerged and formed an endless source of humor. However, only rarely did those who used versions of the real Mexico to satirize the Porfirian ideal go on to challenge the larger myth that inspired that ideal. That is, the critiques of the ideal Mexico were direct and obvious, but the critiques that were directed toward the larger ideal picture of the modern world aimed only to prove the fraudulence of Mexico's image, not to challenge that larger picture. Mexicans referred to the larger idealized picture of the modern world only to praise it more by showing that other versions of Mexico were more fitted for the cosmopolitan parameters. Rarely did they refer to the other critiques of the modern image of the world articulated by Europeans. When they did, as in literary circles, it was only marginally, as when the modernists were condemned for following the critiques of modernity when the country was not yet modern. The first goal, it was argued, was to be modern; then the country would worry about the *surmenages* (mental strains) of modern times (see chapter 11). In the last analysis, what most critiques attempted was to show that the image of modern Mexico was indeed modern but only partially Mexican: it had only the shape that the Porfirian regime gave it, without discussion and without considering the circumstances of the nation.

Humor and irony in Porfirian Mexico also derived from other sources: the critique of specific circumstances, the ephemeral, everyday jokes, and, overall, from the sense of humor that prevailed during the era—which the historian cannot fully recapture. That is, today's understanding of yesterday's irony is inevitably partial: time has erased from our understanding many aspects of yesterday's irony; and it has made other things more ironic for us than for those who experienced them firsthand.

The official and semiofficial press reported on the events surrounding Mexico's exhibitions at all world's fairs by paraphrasing the official despatches and intentions. As we have seen, this press coverage was part of the total desired effect.

Both the lack of democratic decision making and the presence of corruption in the creation of Mexico's modern image were aspects of Mexico's display at world's fairs to which the public was not privy, in exactly the same way as the working side of all exhibit paraphernalia was hidden underground. Accordingly, criticism of the official national image revolved around uncovering these seamier aspects and contrasting the idealized image of Mexico with what was seen as Mexican reality. The goal was to criticize the wizards of progress not so much for being wizards as for being charlatans: it was their illegitimate handling of the national image that made them open to criticism, not their attempts to perform magic in the name of progress.

The newspaper *El Hijo del Ahuizote,* a remarkable example of Mexico's nineteenth-century critical consciousness, sought to reveal the hidden aspects of Mexico's national image. It did this by making ironic allegories out of the official allegories, while often sharing the same basic abstract and pragmatic official goals (for example, progress as a doctrine, and immigrants and foreign investment as a development policy). These ironies were commonly constructed out of political opposition to specific policies of the Porfirian regime. For instance, if Mexico's goal was to attract immigration, for *El Hijo del Ahuizote* the national image presented at Paris in 1889 was both unsuccessful and—worse—only a way to cover up corruption:

> The colonization of the territory
> goes with these popes à la Juan Tenorio:
> I called settlers and they turned a deaf ear
> because they do not expect to grow fat here,
> for another voice and not mine responds
> to what Schnetz and Company do.[4]

Similarly, if the country were to show a true version of the great universal values of progress in industry, art, and sciences as practiced in Mexico, then the composition of the nation's exhibit would have been quite bizarre:

> From the industry go our delicacies
> (reelection, budget, contractors),
> from the arts priceless collections
> (contractors and land demarcations and elections),
> and from economic science and law
> (debts from the king and viceroys).[5]

With this mockery, *El Hijo del Ahuizote* criticized Porfirio Díaz's reelection, the land-demarcation policies, the recent loan signed with a German bank, and also the very pretentiousness of aiming to display progress in industry, arts, and sciences in Paris. The main lore of this poem was a real piece of caustic humor that strived to emphasize the usurpation of universal symbols by the Porfirian regime. The gracelessness of a dancing crab was chosen to insinuate the hopeless irony of Mexico's presence at Paris: "*De los cangrejos el son / marchemos contentos a la expocisión*" ("From the crabs comes the tune / Let us march happily to the exposition").[6]

The less jocose liberal criticism of *El Diario del Hogar* dealt equally harshly with the Porfirian ways of attracting colonization and immigration through an idealized picture of what they believed to be an unreal Mexico: "Wanting is not the same as portraying—the commission's list of accomplishments [at the 1889 Paris fair], recounted through the golden glow through which it sees Mexican exhibitors, will beyond doubt be unable to attract immigration, capital, and industry."[7] Moreover, with the typical anti-Americanism of nationalist liberals of late-nineteenth-century Mexico, *El Diario del Hogar* complained about the very exhibition of Mexican products at Paris: "What are we to exhibit when everything in Mexico is Yankee?"[8]

Critiques along these lines were best exemplified by a sarcastic article that ridiculed almost all of the elements and tools used by the Mexican government to create the national image, while commenting on the official call for products to be exhibited in Paris 1889:

> What shall we exhibit? The rapidly acquired wealth of certain individuals; an extensive library of concessions given to all sorts of foreigners; a map of the country with vast stretches of territory highlighted in blue, private property that could be called municipalities, districts, even states; a collection of memoirs from state and army dignitaries justifying their chunk of the budget . . . ; a photograph album of our deputies, senators, powerful generals (*generalotes*) . . . , several volumes from the officialist daily press that continually declare that Mexico, with the current government, is an earthly paradise where everybody lives happily. . . . The people will not positively respond to the official call.[9]

Political opposition based on the satirization of symbols and tactics of expositions, as well as the very irony of exhibiting, endured throughout the

Porfirian period. Land concentration, corruption, propagandism, and caudillism were often addressed in this ironic fashion. A shorter, more efficient, and often less censored—perhaps safer—style also appeared: the political cartoon. Visual, poetic, and humorous expressions communicated abundant irony and discontent in such an evasive and ambiguous way that repression was difficult. If the official style was a baroque, romantic, eloquent, and often tedious rhetoric, full of scientific metaphors, then the refuge of the opposition was the short, conceptually baroque, but rhetorically economical, instantaneousness of cartoons.

By the 1884 New Orleans exposition, the cartoons of the *Época Ilustrado* used the fair as a source of metaphorical ironies for not entirely political purposes. Both the authoritarianism of the Porfirian regime and its aristocratic tendencies were then criticized by utilizing the different meaning of the verb *exponer*.[10] So the wealthy aristocracy of Mexico City was portrayed on trips to New Orleans, playing with the irony of a widespread Catholic morality and with the Porfirian aristocracy's need to show off, as in the double entendre of a wealthy man with his aristocratic daughter who asked: "Dad, now that there is an exhibition, don't you want me to be exhibited [or to expose myself]?" Along similar lines, the czar of Porfirian letters, Ignacio M. Altamirano, was caricatured in the act of pompously saying to what seems to be a farmer ready to exhibit his products: "I do not expose my literature [or I do not put my literature at risk]," referring to his unwillingness both to exhibit his writings in New Orleans and to put at risk his literary position. In the same way, the famous band of Mexican musicians that was sent to New Orleans by train appeared in a cartoon that showed it crossing the Nochistongo canyon. The vicissitudes of the trip and the endeavors of the Porfirian regime to exhibit exotic Mexican *tipos populares* were summarized in the caption to this cartoon, in which the musicians observed: "Indeed, this time we were exposed," by being exhibited at New Orleans and by being put at risk at Nochistongo.[11]

Along similar lines, in its 1899 coverage of the national exposition that preceded and heralded Mexico's exhibit at the 1900 Paris fair, *El Hijo del Ahuizote* again used the cartoon as a form of effective criticism. On that occasion, its first page carried a cartoon of the statue *Doña Paz Trancazo*,[12] sculpted by "the caudillo from Tuxtepec, hero of La Noria" (see Fig. 23). The fat woman carrying a dagger, called *"La Matona,"* was a savage allegory of the Porfirian regime and of another allegory, for the free republic was represented as a woman in countless nineteenth-century sculptures.

The 1889 Paris exposition easily became an object of critiques and a source of metaphors for criticizing the policies and nature of the Porfirian regime. Parodying the allegorical obsession and cloying style of late-nineteenth-century European art, Díaz was held up as a symbol of dictatorship in an allegorical painting allegedly to be exhibited at the 1889 fair. In it, surrounded

IRONY   163

23. "Doña Paz Trancazo, Ice Sculpture, by the Distinguished Artist from Tuxtepec, Who Is Caudillo of *La Noria* and Palo Blanco [Porfirio Díaz]." Source: *El Hijo del Ahuizote*, 29 January 1899, 65.

by red roses, was the figure of Díaz as a female angel carrying the "*Oliva de la Paz*," a giant gun; the caption read "*la primavera tuxtepecana*" ("Springtime in Tuxtepec"; see Fig. 24).[13] And by the 1900 fair, a cartoon showed the wizards of progress carrying a huge sword called "the Tuxtepecano wonder."[14]

In the same way, paraphrasing the allegoric images of late-nineteenth-century France, a mythological painting entitled *Niobe and Her Sons* was published by *El Hijo del Ahuizote* (see Fig. 25).[15] The cartoon showed a woman who personified the Mexican Constitution of 1857 and her two sons (*sufragio libre* and *plan de Tuxtepec*), killed by the arrows of *abuso* (abuse) and *inconsistencia* (inconsistency), respectively. This metaphor incorporated a triple contextual reference that was well understood at the time: the Greek myth of Niobe, daughter of Tantalus, who turned into stone while bewailing the loss of her children; the late-nineteenth-century neoclassical Greco-Roman revival in which Europe found most of its metaphors; and Díaz as traitor to the Constitution of 1857. By addressing these three levels of reference, the ironic ef-

24. "Allegorical Painting: Springtime in Tuxtepec." Source: *El Hijo del Ahuizote*, 17 March 1889, 1.

fect was quite comprehensive, a parody both of modern cultural trends and of Mexican politics.

In another cartoon, the occasion of the Paris exposition was used to criticize both the constant threat that the United States represented to Mexico's industry and the government's failure to enact protective legislation. Once again, playing on the ambivalent meanings of the verb *exponer*, the cartoon argued that Mexican industry was already *expuesta* (put at risk) vis-à-vis the American industry (personified by a tiger in the cartoon), and this was in fact an *exposición permanente* (a constant risk).[16]

In the same way, the various foci of the fair were used to caricature Mexico's internal political life. *El Hijo del Ahuizote* observed that Mexico's great exhibit of machinery consisted of: "The loans machine; the debts machine;

IRONY 165

25. "Mythological Painting for the Paris Exposition: Niobe and Her Sons." Source: *El Hijo del Ahuizote*, 3 February 1900, 1.

the machine of personal contacts, the machines of suffrage and *tuxtepecanos;* the machine to scrape dignitaries; the engine of the legislative houses, the smasher of the free thinking, and the thrasher of the national territory trademark '*Deslinde,*' the reaper 'Reelection,' the perforator 'Dictatorship.'"[17] In such a way the undemocratic actions, the land policy, and the repression of the Porfirian regime were all satirized by utilizing the commonplaces of an era of world's fairs.

In view of Mexico's presence at Parisian exhibitions, Porfirio Díaz was often satirized as the Napoleon of Mexico. These satires were ironic in two senses—they suggested that Díaz was too mediocre to be like the great Napoleon and that Díaz was indeed aiming to become Mexico's eternal emperor. Ironically enough, Díaz asked Manuel Díaz Mimiaga, the Mexican commissioner for the 1889 Paris exhibition, to acquire for him a specific French biography of Napoleon. Díaz Mimiaga could not find the edition but sent instead a Belgian edition of Napoleon's life to serve as inspiration for Mexico's Napoleon *des tropiques*.[18]

Along similar lines, the status of science in Mexico, as revealed by the nation's exhibit at the 1889 Paris fair, was satirized by *El Hijo del Ahuizote* with the lines: "There is very little science. / Patience, to the contrary, / I believe, is more plentiful than it should be."[19] This sort of ironic comment was expressed even better in a poem published by the same newspaper:

> Haven't we Dubláns with doubloons
> and Pachecos with checks?
> Haven't we in the Ministry of Foreign Affairs
> Mariscals, Romeros, and Ramóns
> who can vociferously praise the contest
> and announce it, preach it, and claim it?
> Haven't we Peñafiels
> who can supplant the Eiffels,
> and the lighthouse of the Paseo de la Reforma,
> to which they can give more altitude and a different shape,
> so that as time goes by
> they embellish the exposition with their tower
> that colossally rises with arrogance
> and looks like that of Paris in France?[20]

The poem refers to Manuel Dublán, then minister of finance, and to Carlos Pacheco, minister of economic development and chief of Mexico's exhibit in Paris. In this satire, the lavish expenditures and personal opportunism of the two ministers were sarcastically treated, along with Mexico's pretensions about displaying itself in Paris. The modern image of Mexico was one that was controlled by the Porfirians to praise themselves. Moreover, Mexico's propaganda network was attacked with the reference to those who announced, preached, and claimed Mexico's image in Paris; that is, the officials of the Ministry of Foreign Affairs (Ignacio Mariscal, Matías Romero and the Mexican minister in Paris, Ramón Fernández).

By the same token, by making fun of the natural history concerns of the 1900 Paris fair, *El Hijo de Ahuizote* criticized the corruption and authoritarianism of the Porfirian regime in the form of animals that were to be sent to Paris. If Mexico's natural history collections were to be an important aspect of its presence at world's fairs, then these fictitious animals ought to be sent to represent the real Mexico: a *burra* (female donkey) that had carried Díaz for sixteen years (that is, the country), Ignacio Mariscal's parrot that spoke English (referring to his pro-American tendencies), Bernardo Reyes's eagle (that is, his recent appointment to the Ministry of Defense), and José Y. Limantour's raven (the Compañía de Fianzas).[21]

The very organization of the fair prompted criticism of the high cost and the corruption that surrounded the whole event. For *El Diario del Hogar,* the wizards of progress had no other merit than being "very close friends of the Minister of Economic Development,"[22] and the same newspaper complained about the astronomical expenses of Mexico vis-à-vis those of countries like the United States.[23] In 1888 *El Economista Mexicano* commented on the need for better organization of the Mexican presence at world's fairs. It argued that at the 1884 fair there had been many problems: "That avalanche of commissions that come and go, that contest among employees, causes the loss of objects and the delay in the distribution of prizes."[24] In June 1889 *El Diario del Hogar* was astonished by the sum already expended (2.5 million francs) and observed: "There is no doubt that Mexico has been splendid. However, in a few years we will starve to death."[25] The same complaints were made about Mexico's organization in 1900. For instance, Federico Gamboa recalled the disorganization and unreality of Mexico's presence at the 1900 exposition. He received a diploma for his books exhibited in Paris. "Oh, farces, farces, farces," he observed, "through Jesús Contreras I learned that all the boxes containing books were not even opened by the jury!!!"[26] Nonetheless, he himself had previously proclaimed that his "most beautiful literary chimera" was "to be read in Paris."[27] For him too, the problem was not with Paris but with those who were handling Mexico's image there.

Along similar lines, a cartoon in *El Hijo del Ahuizote* portrayed Díaz throwing away posts, commissions, and money for Mexico's presence at the 1889 Paris fair. Behind Díaz a group of friends carried signs that read "To Pacheco's Friends." A poem explained the cartoon:

> Don't think of this as a waste
> of what doesn't cost us anything. . . .
> This is an opportunity
> to travel a lot (*a trotemoche*)
> on ships, on trains, and on carriages.[28]

In such fashion were the lavish expenditures of the wizards of progress held up for criticism. In addition, the personalities of the wizards of progress were ridiculed as part of the general criticism of the Porfirian regime. For instance, various Mexican newspapers sent distinguished intellectuals and politicians as their representatives at world's fairs—among them, Amado Nervo, Ireneo Paz, Carlos Díaz Dufoo, and even Angel del Campo.[29] They became part of Mexico's propaganda network. By the 1900 Paris fair, Ireneo Paz was already a convinced reelectionist and the representative of *El Imparcial.* For his pains, he was caricatured as a Mexican Indian servant who, in the stereotypical Spanish language of Indian servants, said to French President Loubet: *"Quesque dice mi amo Don Porfirio que comostasté, que cómo le vasté y que si querusté religirse no más me diga pa' que li haga yo un clu"* ("Says my master Don Porfirio, how are you, how are you doing, and if you want to reelect yourself you only need to tell me and I'll organize a club for you)."³⁰

In the same way, Manuel Flores's well-known taste for alcohol was ridiculed in a cartoon that combined his alcoholism with a critique of the Mexican pavilion at the 1900 exposition. Amado Nervo's hyper-Catholic moralism was a perfect object of mocking contrast with Bohemian fin-de-siècle Paris, and so is the cartoon depicting Nervo with a cancan dancer to whom he is saying, "You should enter a convent." Alas, this may have paraphrased Hamlet's statement to Ophelia: "Get thee to a nunnery."³¹

For the purist liberal press, however, the values epitomized by France and its fairs were unquestionable. The problem for them was with the Porfirian handling of the Mexican display, but France itself was considered the leading nation of Europe. France was all the more respected in view of the threat that the United States posed for Mexico. Thus in July 1888 *El Diario del Hogar* observed: "In Europe, France is the heart of the Latin race, like Mexico in America; both nations have suffered wars brought on by the invading spirit of northern nations; both are the vanguard of reason."³²

This respect for French modernity was shared by conservative liberal statists in the Porfirian regime and by the more purist liberals of the opposition. Angel Pola in *El Diario del Hogar* was more explicit in the beginning of 1889 when he observed that Mexicans were both Mexican and French: "We make policy, feel, think, speak like the French and we are satisfied by France's beneficial influence, because it is a civilizing one that does not alter our nationality but perfects it."³³ In politics and in sciences, he went on, "What are we? / Mexicans. / Where do we come from? / From Spain. / Where are we going? / To France."³⁴

Other members of the liberal press shared the excitement for the great values epitomized by the exposition but made it a point not to attend owing to Mexico's circumstances. *El Diario del Hogar* observed in March 1888: "Despite the fraternity between France and Mexico, in all the republic there is a waning of enthusiasm that has no precedent in our history; the mistrust is general in every sense; no one responds with good will to the official calls." The newspaper concluded that "the people of Mexico are sensible; they will not take part in the great party of progress that the friendly people of France are celebrating."³⁵ Mexican criticisms of the idealized image of Mexico were especially harsh regarding the essential ethnic and philosophical nature of the nation under Porfirian rule. Here all political tendencies had their own views: Hispanism, indigenism, liberal indifference, cosmopolitanism, and so forth. For some, Mexico's image was too Indian; for others, not native enough; for still others, too cosmopolitan. Therefore, both Mexico's attempt to be innovative in architecture and its exotic displays were seriously criticized. Peñafiel, one of the designers of the Mexican pavilion for the 1889 fair, was sarcastically criticized for his attempt to make Mexico as unique as

France through the bizarre combination of pre-Hispanic motifs and modern architecture, as epitomized by the Aztec Palace. For some critics, Mexico could never be France, and attempts to try would only produce an ironic amalgamation:

> The plains of Narvarte
> can easily be Champ de Mars.
> And the square ditch, if it fills
> with rainwater, will be the Seine.
> From Paris will be brought the Caja de Agua,
> as they call our palace there.[36]

Of course, conditions in Mexico could hardly match Parisian standards, and the very contrast of Paris with Mexico City produced these ironic poems. Regarding those who would represent the country in an Aztec fashion, *El Hijo del Ahuizote* echoed the French criticism of the Mexican Aztec Palace as a Caja de Agua, to complement their mockery. In turn, *El Diario del Hogar* called the Mexican pavilion "a henhouse"[37] and referred to its design as the "Mexican architectural style of the Peñafielistic system."[38] With more democratic decisions, this newspaper argued, the Mexican pavilion would not have taken such a ridiculous form. Other newspapers defended the Mexican pavilion against this criticism, however. *La Crónica* observed that French criticism of the Mexican pavilion showed great ignorance: "[They do not] understand that if one were dealing with an artistic creation, there would have been numerous Mexican artists that could have sparkled their talent, but what the pavilion was about was historical accuracy."[39]

In fact, many harsh words were penned about the very unfitness of native things and people to be modern and universal. *El Diario del Hogar* sarcastically observed that in Paris the Mexican products would be most unfavorably contrasted with French counterparts: "sugar-cane liquors and tequila . . . to compete with those products from Lyon, Champagne, and Bordeaux."[40] Along the same ironic lines, the idea of an Aztec Mexico was severely satirized by the liberal opposition. Although by the 1880s indigenism was nothing new in Mexican intellectual and political discussions, some purist liberals criticized the prominence given to an official indigenism in Mexico's presence at the 1889 Paris fair. Moreover, they criticized the authoritarian form of this choice, observing that the Mexican pavilion had been decided on without even calling for a public contest.[41] Catholic opinion was, of course, opposed to anything pre-Hispanic and constantly criticized any attempt to give the nation any image save that of a Spanish Catholic country. The underlying irony resulted both from the bizarre idea of an Aztec Mexico in the Parisian belle epoque and from the authoritarian decision to give strong pre-Hispanic features to the national image. Therefore, not only did the Aztec Palace become an object of mockery, so did the display of exotic

Mexican people, foods, and art at Paris. In fact, if we were to judge this discussion by the indigenist standards of twentieth-century postrevolutionary Mexico, we would have to conclude that by the late 1880s the official Porfirian indigenism was much more progressive than were either the liberal or the Catholic critics.

Be that as it may, at the time the regime's critics had a field day with Porfirian indigenism. For example, *El Hijo del Ahuizote* ridiculed the idea of Mexican nativism in Paris: "President Carnota [*sic*] was very pleased last night upon seeing us eat with utensils and drink champagne as if it were water. Ramoncito presented us with some cans of *mole poblano*, hot *memelas* [oval corn tortillas] made right there and some jars of pulque." The sarcastic report concluded, "Carnot toasted the absent and present Aztecs."[42] Here, the irony not only skewered Mexican Francophilia combined with commercialized nativism (processed Mexican products) but also aimed a subtle insult—"present Aztecs"—at the Mexican wizards of progress for whom, we may be sure, any adjective having to do with Indians was no compliment. By 1899 a cartoon in *El Hijo del Ahuizote* showed Minister Gilberto Crespo appointing wizards of progress for the 1900 exhibition and other Científicos suggesting to him that Mexican envoys ought to be exotic but "[Europeans] shall see that we are indeed Indians, but refined ones."[43] Moreover, both Porfirian indigenism and Riva Palacio's new role as official historian—with his *México a través de los siglos*—were satirized by *El Hijo del Ahuizote* in a cartoon: an "Aztec picture for the history book *México a través de los yankees*." In such a way, orthodox liberals criticized the official histories, indigenism, and rapprochement of the Porfirian regime with the United States.[44]

The cartoon entitled "Our Facade in Paris: Sketches of the Universal Exposition" was even more revealing in this regard. It was a complete satire of the allegorical efforts of the Aztec Palace's facade (see Figs. 26 and 27). Instead of the original columns upholding the facade that represented Indian gods, in the cartoon two Indian-like figures of Díaz represent the Tuxtepec Plan and Díaz's reelection. These columns sustained the "palace" which, in the cartoon, is the Porfirian regime. At the right, instead of the original Indian burner, we see a burner with the face of Díaz Mimiaga, the director of the Mexican commission in France. At the left was a burner with the face of Minister of Economic Development Carlos Pacheco. In such fashion, the two main personalities behind Mexico's presence at the 1889 fair guarded the totemlike columns of Don Porfirio. On the architrave, six figures symbolized ironic motifs. One of these images, *plancarteo*, was the bust of the Catholic priest Antonio Plancarte, then controversial abbot of the Guadalupe temple who was lobbying for the Vatican crowning of the Image of Guadalupe. His image on the Aztec Palace symbolized the new rapprochement of the Porfirian regime with the church, which went against the Jacobinism of purist Mexican liberals. Ignacio Mariscal, minister of foreign affairs, was the figure

26. Facade of the Aztec Palace at the 1889 Paris Universal Exhibition. Source: José Francisco Godoy, *México en París* (Mexico City, 1891).

in *yancomanía*, which referred to his links with U.S. interests. The medal called *empréstitos* was a bust of Francisco Z. Mena, fellow general and friend of Díaz who, as Mexican minister to Germany, negotiated a German loan for Mexico in 1888. Minister of Finance Manuel Durán was portrayed in the medal entitled *niquel* because of his policies of circulating coins of nickel instead of silver or gold. Joaquín Baranda, minister of justice, was *psicología*, a sarcastic reference to the repression of the media in Mexico City. *Tío Pedro* represented Gen. Pedro Hinojosa, the war minister.

The six images were supported by the two columns personifying Díaz— an allegory of Porfirian power. On the right, in a pre-Hispanic outfit but imitating the dress of a matador, was a figure that seemed to be Gen. José Ceballos, then governor of Mexico City.[45] On the left, imitating Jesús Contreras's sculptures, was Interior Minister Romero Rubio in an Aztec-Roman outfit. Crowning the cartoon were two imitations of plumed serpents: a German lender and a Yankee businessman. In this way, the entire Aztec Palace was made a strong, oppositional, political statement.

The scientific aspects of the national image were also caricatured. Although science had become a public culture, its abuse at the hands of the Porfirian elite who monopolized it were criticized by liberals and conservatives, although the value of science was never questioned. What was especially an object of mockery were the efforts to portray Mexico as a hygienic

27. "Our Facade in Paris" (detail). Source: *El Hijo del Ahuizote*, 4 August 1889, 4–5.

and sanitary nation. Statistics and complaints about the lack of sanitation, insecurity, and high mortality in Mexico City were constantly published by the free media.

Newspapers reported on the need for annual killings of dogs and on public expenditures for monuments and fancy suburbs but not for sanitation.[46] In September 1888 *El Diario del Hogar* complained about Peñafiel's mortality statistics and argued that the mortality rate was in fact growing in Mexico City: "In 25 years the population would disappear if it weren't renovated by births."[47] The following May the same newspaper, in a wild exaggeration, argued that owing to the high mortality in Mexico and the low rate of population growth, in four years and three months Mexico City would be depopulated.[48] These complaints continued into the 1910s. The free media could not resist contrasting Mexico's hygienic display at the Paris fairs with the reality of conditions in Mexico City and the indifferent behavior of the Superior Sanitation Council. The irony of a hygienic image vis-à-vis an unsanitary city was joined with criticism of the political involvement and privileges of the members of the council, such as Eduardo Liceaga. In 1900 *El Diario del Hogar* observed that "the year 1900 began yesterday with the farce of ballots, an odd invention by Dr. Liceaga that has as its goal, according to what he explained in his last manifesto, to strengthen even more the unconditional adhesion to the reigning Caudillo."⁴⁹ In the same vein, while the wizards of progress prepared hygienic statistics to be sent to Paris in 1900, *El Hijo del Ahuizote* published a "dialogue" between two microbes, one from the miasmas of San Lázaro and the other from Peralvillo:

> Speaking in the serious style
> of all epidemics
> the stink here is that of corpse
> combined with cemetery.
> To no one is it a secret
> that this slovenly place is fertile ground
> for typhus that here acclimates itself
> for smallpox that hearths
> for cholera that is contagious
> and for measles that kill.⁵⁰

The role of Liceaga and the Sanitation Council was caricatured in a cartoon that depicted Liceaga as the owner of a funerary agency, saying that with the influenza epidemic of Mexico City, "my business is doing very well."⁵¹ Dr. Carmona y Valle was also ridiculed for his constant search for microbes: "so many microbes he found / that with microbes he constructed the support of his fame."⁵²

The much-publicized drainage system of Mexico City was ridiculed by *El Hijo del Ahuizote* as work begun "during the reign of the illustrious Chichimec Emperor Nezahualcoyotl" and "by mere chance completed under idem idem Zapoteca Porfioyotl."⁵³ By 1901, in view of yet another Mexican hygienic display at the Buffalo exposition, a cartoon satirized the usual street exhibits at world's fairs. The "Rue du Caire" in Paris 1889, and the "Streets of Mexico" in Buffalo 1901 were ridiculed, together with the customary exhibit of the drainage system in Mexico City. A clown, Díaz, is shown introducing Mexican "Drainage with All Its Odors," on "Escape-If-You-Can Street" (see Fig. 28).⁵⁴

The public character of science is worth noting. For the growing middle class, which was both literate and urban, science had become a common form of knowledge. Both the logic and rhetoric of science became a form of common sense for this group. The phenomenon was part of the modern image, but it also created contradictions. The critiques of the Porfirian regime often took a scientific shape, an indication that the presumed scientific nature of Mexico's national image was accompanied by public consumption of scientific ideas and language. But the popular consumption of science backfired against the official image in the form of parodies of science used for political opposition.

The public nature of science was present in the media and literature of the last part of the nineteenth century. World's fairs were important sources for popularization of the sciences, and news and commentaries about them

28. "Escape-If-You-Can Street." Source: *El Hijo del Ahuizote*, 2 June 1901, 308.

accelerated the public consumption of scientific ideas and rhetoric. In 1887 Emilio Rabasa parodied science in *La gran ciencia* as the corrupt maneuvers and violence required to stay in power, and he utilized biological, mechanical, and evolutionist metaphors to develop his plot. So did such famous writers as Angel del Campo, Manuel Acuña, and even Amado Nervo. In the same way, the news received about the scientific displays in world's fairs produced criticism and increased the interaction of scientific production and public opinion.

The science of geography, popularized in school and through political decisions that sought to form an accurate picture of the nation and its people, was identified with García Cubas. In fact, such geographical references as those represented by García Cubas were commonsensical in the era. Rabasa began his novel *La bola* by observing, "I do not know why this district capital does not appear either on the geographical maps of Mr. García Cubas, or in the numerous Mexican geographical treatises that have been published up to now."[55] In world's fairs, the geographical sciences were rapidly popularized, and García Cubas's books were translated and widely distributed. By 1891 a cartoon in *El México Gráfico* ridiculed the bureaucratization of García Cubas as the official geographer of the Porfirian regime. A poem observed:

> Without making any stops
> or even moving for a second

he knows the entire world
at least by map.

He happily spends his life
encrusted like a mollusk
into a grayish desk
in a section of [the Ministry of] Economic Development.[56]

Nonetheless, the overall faith in science was shared by the literary urban elites, and they showed an avid interest in news about great discoveries and new advancements, such as when the famous poet Manuel Gutiérrez Nájera wrote in his weekly chronicles of the "sad toys that the new wise man invents . . . the magician of Menlo Park [Edison]."[57] For them, the new technology promised comfort and a seemingly endless supply of therapeutic devices, from the "electric belt of Dr. McLaughlin" and the tonic "for impotence, the energizing San Germán wine," to "Dr. de Garay's spa."[58]

As we have seen, critiques of the Mexican presence at world's fairs, however sarcastic, nevertheless shared the same basic assumptions about the modern world and its future. This consensus was expressed in another realm: the private uses in Mexico of the prestige furnished by world's fairs.

Like the Mexican government, private Mexican companies transformed their success at world's fairs into domestic legitimacy. Once a cigarette factory, or an artist, or a scientific association was honored at an international fair, domestic credibility became indisputable. Within a consensus on the supremacy of modern values and production as epitomized by France and its fairs, the recognition granted by the ideal picture created tangible superiority within Mexico.

Mexican cigarette companies, along with those of Brazil, were especially well received at world's fairs, and it became a commonplace for them to list the honors received at fairs on their cigarette packets. In an emerging mass-consumption society, to display these recognitions through publicity became cashable legitimacy. For instance, El Valle Nacional earned a gold medal in the 1889 Paris exposition,[59] and by 1890 all its publicity mentioned the award, including a reproduction of the medal. Similarly, the company of Ernesto Pugibet—a Franco-Mexican entrepreneur who exhibited both machines to manufacture cigarettes and the cigarettes themselves—decorated its boxes of El Buen Tono, Mascota, Ideal, and Judic cigars with a woman dressed in Paris fashion with a French diploma in one hand and a cigarette in the other and with the legend "Universal Exhibition of Paris 1889. The highest prize for the manufacturing of cigars." The Noriega cigarette company advertisements contrasted the Eiffel Tower with the Mexican pavilion (see Fig. 29). After all, this was the company that had made an Eiffel Tower out of cigarettes in the halls of the Aztec Palace.

The media often questioned the official propaganda of the Mexican government. The numerous books and pamphlets sponsored by the Mexican government were nationally criticized for their lack of objectivity and their inadequacy. In 1900 *El Diario del Hogar* announced the publication of yet another propaganda book by Zayas Enríquez to be sent to the 1900 Paris exposition. It observed: "It is a pity that the basis on which such a beautiful monument of our progress rests is false and deplorable." It argued that books such as Zayas Enríquez's demonstrated "a shameful degree of backwardness in democratic practices, which make the Mexican people seem like a meeting of ignorant imbeciles."[60]

No one was more critical of this propaganda than Francisco Bulnes, the enfant terrible of the Porfirians. In *El porvenir de las naciones latinoamericanas* (1899) he devoted a section to what he called "*jauja y reverso*" (opulence and its other side), an analysis of the propaganda books published by Mexico and other Latin American countries. "After reading the books that explain our riches, Europeans are convinced that the wage laborers in Latin America are great gentlemen who plow the land with English *demi sang* horses, have a balcony at the opera, look eye to eye *a la Patti*, whose wives need but to shatter gravel in order to bejewel themselves, and that on filtering the water of our rivers enough gold dust remains for children to play with."[61]

Bulnes explained that Mexico was indeed promising for immigrants, but because of foreigners' competitive advantages, not the country's tropical wealth. Bulnes believed that Latin America offered no commercial and industrial competition for Europeans. However, Mexico had to compete with other countries to attract immigrants. In 1889 Ireneo Paz, in his articles for *El Diario del Hogar*, compared Mexico's performance with that of Brazil and of Argentina because, he believed, those, not the United States, were the countries with which Mexico was competing.[62] Paz's underlying assumption was that the United States, because of its industrial development and socioracial configuration, was unbeatable as a pole of attraction for European immigration. But in 1899 Bulnes did not hesitate to blame political chaos and hypocritical international propaganda for Mexico's failure to attract immigrants. His pragmatism and irony are worth quoting:

> The pure and respectable truth is that in Latin America nothing is given for free to any foreigner, no gold dust, no gravel full of diamonds, no rubies for the handles of hoes and pickaxes; among us, every foreigner has to work, and very hard if he is to make a fortune, but if he works hard, we neither want to nor can compete with him. To acquire real value, our resources need large capital investment, which in turn requires true government, whether democratic or dictatorial, it does not really matter, as long as they are governments

29. Tobacco advertisement depicting the Aztec Palace. Source: AGN, Centro de Información Gráfica, Teixidor Collection; reproduced courtesy of the Archivo General de la Nación, Mexico City. (Photograph by the Archivo General de la Nación)

in the full sense of the word, and not a hideous parade of petty politicians in the constant act of robbery and in the anarchic task of black beetles.[63]

He then compared the data presented in Mexican propaganda on immigrants with that of Switzerland, showing the immense advantages of Switzerland in terms of salaries, cost of living, security, sanitation, and general development. The Mexican wizards of progress in charge of writing the nation's propaganda (or employing others to write it) were dismissed by Bulnes as lay priests. Bulnes, a master of irony, painstakingly dissected the general format of those books and made fun of their different parts: "territory: double the real one," "customs: those of Arcadia," "rain: whenever the farmers ask for it," "public hygiene: that of a rock crystal," "administrative morality: that of a Druid virgin," "proletariat: opulent," while in regard to crime, cost of hospitality, abuses, judiciary deficiencies, people's vote, and so forth, there was "sepulchral silence."[64]

In sum, the irony of Mexico's modern public image vis-à-vis Mexico's actuality endured as part of the general criticism of the Porfirian regime. But the constant confrontation of the ideal and real visions of Mexico never weakened either the propaganda attempts of the Porfirian regime or the gradual generalization of relatively fixed features of a modern national identity. Those who criticized and mocked Mexico's modern image at world's fairs desolemnized that image by showing the way it was constructed, as well as its corrupt and undemocratic side. But they neither rejected the general ideal of that image nor the need for Mexico to create it. That was the greatest irony of all: the fact that at the receiving end, those who were supposedly included in the image did not recognize themselves, but this nonrecognition became the fuel (for official and nonofficial attempts) to restart the process; that is, in the last analysis, for Mexico this type of irony fed the impulse to begin again the "keep-trying" cycle—an imperative of a modern national image.

TWO

World's Fairs and Mexico after the Revolution of 1910

ELEVEN

Toward Revolutionary Mexico

The images of Mexico displayed in world's fairs after the Revolution of 1910 prolonged the Porfirian symbolic infrastructure, along with its contradictions. In this part of my analysis, however, historical continuities and breaks are seen within the specific limits of the creation of a homogeneous, dominant national image in the immediate postrevolutionary period. Nationalism is too much of a universal and long-in-the-making phenomenon to be explained solely, for example, by the Mexican Revolution. And the Mexican Revolution itself is too much of a many-sided happening to be reduced to the formation of a national image by various intellectuals and politicians in changing circumstances.

Before jumping to the 1922 Exposição Internacional do Centenario in Rio de Janeiro, it is necessary to briefly examine the development of Mexico's image at international fairs up to the 1900s in order to understand the changing nature of twentieth-century world's fairs in comparison with their nineteenth-century counterparts.[1]

THE FINALE OF THE AZTEC PALACE?

In January 1890 Parisian officials began to demolish the structures of the 1889 world's fair. The facades came down, and what once seemed to be a complete, universal, and harmonious cosmos vanished in a matter of weeks. Paris, however, maintained the great monument to industrial architecture, the Palace of Machines, until 1910, along with the Eiffel Tower, which endured to become the very symbol of Paris. While the French went about their demolition, the Mexican exhibition team was deliberating the destiny of the Mexican Aztec Palace and also planning the next performance, analyzing the best possible scenario: Glasgow? Madrid? Chicago?[2]

The Aztec Palace was dismantled and shipped to Mexico by the company of Furet and Rousseau.[3] At the same time, portions of the Mexican government's exhibit were sent to libraries, museums, and permanent exhibitions throughout Europe. The original plan had been to make the Aztec Palace into an archaeological museum, and, in fact, Antonio de Anza purchased heavy machinery to reconstruct the palace in Mexico.[4] But the palace, though shipped home, was never rebuilt, either in Mexico or anywhere else. It returned to its beginnings as assorted stage props for the drama of the Mexican image of a modern nation. All of its components were subjected to the vagaries of Mexico's political, social, economic, and cultural life, in addition to the corrosion of time.

Explaining why the Aztec Palace was never completely reassembled provides a clue to the dynamics of Mexico's modern nationalism. Many explanations can be posited. First, by the 1890s the discussion about a national architecture had moved toward a more radically cosmopolitan fashion, and it was simply impossible to keep alive the aesthetic experiment that was intrinsic to the Aztec Palace. Furthermore, even from a technical standpoint, reassembly of the Aztec Palace would have been difficult, for evidence indicates that major parts of the building suffered irreversible damage during the trip from Paris to Mexico.[5] Or possibly it was just because the pavilion was imprisoned in the cage of bureaucracy, left to corrode until it was impossible to reconstruct.[6]

The Aztec Palace was not destroyed, however; ostensibly it was only stored for a better use. By 1895 Contreras's sculptures were located in the main patio of the Museo Nacional de Artillería, where Cuauhtémoc, Itzcoatl, Netzahualcoyotl, Totoquihuatzin, and Cuitláhuac remained as the patrimony of Mexico's military strength during the Porfirian era.[7] But history is ongoing, never past. In 1940, during the heyday of postrevolutionary official indigenism, some of Contreras's sculptures that had graced the Aztec Palace were refurbished to crown Luis Lelo de Larrea's monument to La Raza in Mexico City—a postrevolutionary pyramid to honor Mexico's Indian origins, a symbolic break from the old regime's Francophilia and history of Indian exploitation (see Fig. 30.)[8] Ironically, the monument utilized both the symbolism and the actual material created by the Porfirian years of experimenting in modernity and nationalism.

In the same way as the indigenist anthropologists of the 1930s and 1940s obtained their training and basic research from the Porfirian anthropological infrastructure, a concrete pyramidal monument to La Raza adorned the intersection of the freeways of a hypermodern Mexico City. This time around the city claimed to have reached the final version of modernity and nationalism. The monument borrowed not only Contreras's sculptures but also the eagle originally designed to crown the Porfirian Opera House designed by the Italian architect Adamo Boari.[9] A replica of a pre-Hispanic pyramid

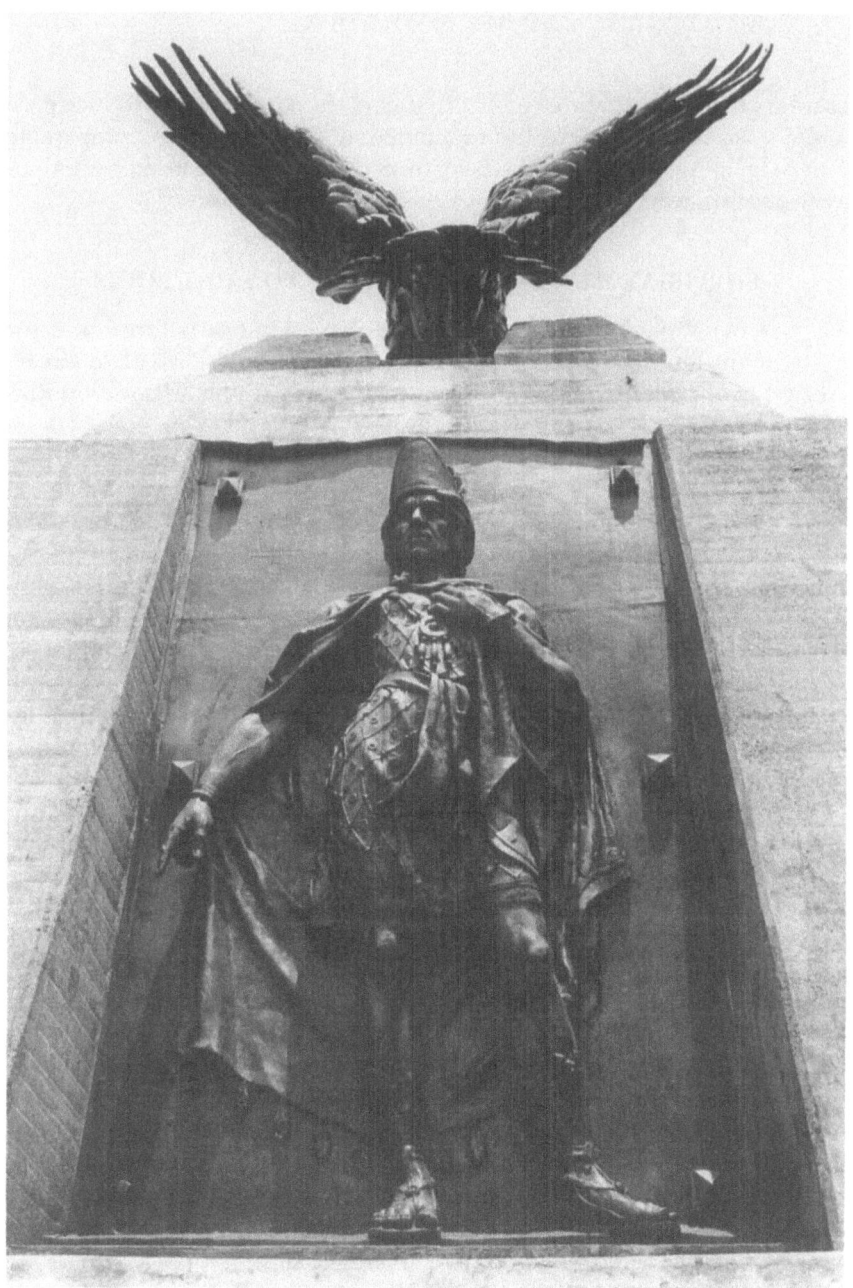

30. Jesús Contreras's sculpture *Totoquihuatzin* and the eagle designed for the Porfirian Opera House, now at the Monumento a la Raza (designed by Luis Lelo de Larrea, 1940). (Photograph by Carlos Contreras)

crowned by late-nineteenth-century figures of the Aztec rulers in Roman garb and a quasi-imperial eagle, the monument achieved an irony comparable only to imagining French kings rising from their graves and using guillotines as elegant shelves on which to store their crowns and capes.[10]

PORFIRIAN IMAGES FROM CHICAGO TO SAINT LOUIS

The type of nationalistic symbolism and ideological infrastructure found, for example, in Philadelphia 1876, New Orleans 1884, and Paris 1889 was re-created by the wizards of progress for many international expositions during the 1890s and 1900s. For Mexico, the most important exhibitions of these decades were Chicago 1893, Paris 1900, Buffalo 1901, and Saint Louis 1904. Although Mexico planned an extravagant exhibition for the monumental 1893 Chicago Columbian Exhibition, the economic crisis of the 1890s forced the wizards of progress to lower their sights (see Appendix 2). In contrast, both for the 1900 Paris universal exposition and the 1901 Buffalo pan-American fair, Mexico constructed important but makeshift buildings—the first in a neoclassical conservative style, the second in a Spanish mission style.

In Chicago, Mexico won 1,195 awards;[11] mining and agriculture were once again especially welcomed. The Mexican artists were not so successful, however; it was later argued that the poor locations in which Mexican paintings and sculptures were placed were the cause of such meager response. In addition, in Chicago, as in other American fairs, Mexico had some presence at the women's exhibit. In the same way that the American women's commission for Chicago exhibit was headed by the daughter-in-law of the president of the United States, the Mexican women's commission was headed by Carmen Romero Rubio, Porfirio Díaz's wife.[12] But of course the Mexican government was not truly interested in the modern social concerns with women. The aristocratic women's groups of Porfirian Mexico were part of the exhibition team, especially in the American fairs, where women had an important role to play. Generally Mexican women were represented only through their traditionally assigned domestic work. Nonetheless, one of the most significant aspects of the Mexican art exhibition in Chicago, according to the Mexican delegate M. Serrano, were the paintings by Gertrudis García Teruel.[13] In addition, José María Vigil prepared a collection of Mexican women's poetry, in order to show that Mexican women's poetic capacities were compatible with those of American and European women.[14]

The Mexican mining exhibit in Chicago was, as it had been throughout nineteenth-century exhibitions, very impressive and included an elaborate display of gold, silver, copper, steel, lead, opals, onyx, granites, and marbles. In addition, a *Carta estadística minera de la República Mexicana* was created and exhibited. Once again the Comisión Geográfico-Exploradora displayed natural history samples and scientific work; the Comisión Geológica Mexicana presented a collection of fossils and maps.[15] The newly created Ministry of Communication exhibited replicas, designs, and miniatures of monuments (Columbus and Cuauhtémoc), architectural plans, and improvements for the National Palace.

Mexico's presence in Chicago was especially notable for its ethnographic views. In the department of ethnology, numerous Mexican antiquities were exhibited, both by the Mexican government and by American anthropologists and ethnographers, together with pictures of ruins and models of *tipos populares*, Indian cloth, and Indian skulls (see Fig. 31).[16] In addition, reproductions of the architecture of exotic countries were constructed near the Dairy Building. These were replicas of the ruins of Uxmal, the House of Nuns, and the Labna group.[17] All of these replicas were made of papier-mâché and were the result of research conducted by the American archaeologist and diplomat E. H. Thompson, American consul in Yucatán, and of scientific studies by the American anthropologist F. W. Putnam.[18] This was part of the so-called Midway Exhibit that was, as historian James Gilbert has described, "a unitary exhibit of ethnic variations tied together by concepts of evolution and movement through stages of civilization."[19]

In terms of architecture, Chicago was destined to be an important point of departure. In general, the architecture of the Chicago exhibition was dominated by the aristocratic neoclassicist, Beaux Arts style of the Eastern architects. However, such innovative architects as Louis Sullivan constructed modernist buildings—the Transportation Building, for example—at the edges of the fair.[20] More importantly, the exhibits of exotic architectural styles nourished the emerging modernist architecture. Hence Frank Lloyd Wright, Sullivan's student, first saw Japanese and Mayan structures in Chicago, and from that inspiration he developed ingenious modern, functional buildings with Maya and Japanese influences (sometimes combined) in the modernist 1910s and 1920s.[21] That was the case, for example, with the Imperial Hotel he constructed in Tokyo in 1916 (a structure that combined traditional Japanese architecture with Maya motifs). In 1929, Mexico followed the same steps in its pavilion for the 1929 Ibero-American fair in Seville (see chapter 13).

After Chicago, and before 1900, Mexico participated in various American fairs, most of which were of regional importance and to which Mexico's private exhibitors and government sent the customary displays of raw materials, antiquities, and archaeological pieces. Two of these fairs were the 1895 Cotton States International Exposition in Atlanta and the 1898 Trans-Mississippi International Exposition in Omaha. Special envoys of the Atlanta exhibition traveled to Mexico to encourage participation in this rather modest fair,[22] and more than 160 Mexican exhibitors eventually attended. The Mexican commission for this fair was headed by Gregorio E. González, who eventually sent to the Ministry of Economic Development a list of American entrepreneurs interested in investing in Mexico. He also reported his diffi-

31. Maya ruins in Chicago. Source: Hubert Howe Bancroft, *The Book of the Fair: An Historical and Descriptive Presentation of the World's Science, Art, and Industry, as Viewed through the Columbian Exposition at Chicago 1893*, vol. 4 (Chicago, 1893), 633.

culties with the Mexican Village Company, which was negligent in paying the salaries and return tickets of the people from Tehuantepec who had been brought to the fair to make up the human circus of the "Mexican Village."[23] This exhibit was described as a village that "included many of the characteristic types of that country, with much of the local color for which Mexico is famous."[24] Ironically enough, although exhibiting people from Tehuantepec in what amounted to a human zoo (and not paying their salaries) caused no problems, the organizers of the "Mexican Village" were forced to cancel the originally planned "bloodless" bullfights after popular protest in which it was argued that "the terror of the horses would be cruelty in its worst form."[25]

The 1898 Omaha international fair was an echo of the 1893 Chicago fair for the states west of the Mississippi River. In it, Mexico occupied 3,000 square feet, exhibiting agricultural products and raw materials. In addition, "in one section historical articles were displayed showing articles and implements in use during Aztec days."[26] As in many other American fairs, Mexico's display in Omaha was directed by Albino R. Nuncio of the Ministry of Economic Development and the main member of what might be termed a second group of wizards of progress. This second group was often in charge of Mexico's displays at the many small American world's fairs, such as Atlanta 1895, Omaha 1898, Nashville 1897, Saint Louis 1904, Boston 1908, and San Antonio 1909.

32. The Mexican pavilion at the 1901 Buffalo world's fair. Source: México, Comisión de los Estados Unidos Mexicanos para la Exposición Pan-Americana de Buffalo, Nueva York, *A Few Facts about Mexico* (Mexico City, 1901), 57.

After Mexico's major performance at the 1900 Paris fair, its next relatively large-scale participation in international fairs took place at the 1901 Buffalo exhibition. Mexico sent a total of 860 exhibitors and was the most important foreign presence.[27] For this fair, Mexico constructed a Spanish colonial style pavilion to house its mining, artistic, and liberal arts exhibits (see Fig. 32).

Mexico's next appearance was at the 1904 Louisiana Purchase International Exposition in Saint Louis. Once again, Albino R. Nuncio headed the Mexican exhibit, together with Maximiliano M. Chabert and the engineer Luis Salazar.[28] For this exposition, Mexico constructed a modest building in the colonial style with a central patio, surrounded by gardens with native Mexican plants (see Fig. 33). Among the many Mexican exhibits, anthropological and archaeological studies had a significant presence. Alfredo

33. The Mexican pavilion at the 1904 Louisiana Purchase International Exposition in Saint Louis, Missouri. Source: J. W. Buel, *Louisiana and the Fair*, vol. 6 (Saint Louis, 1905), 2189.

Chavero and Antonio Peñafiel sent their respective studies.[29] The Ministry of Justice and Public Education exhibited a large collection of Mexican antiquities, not only Aztec objects but also artifacts from the Maya, Toltec, and other pre-Hispanic cultures. In the ethnography section Mexico displayed numerous collections of photographs of "pure" Indians. In addition, as in Atlanta 1895 and Buffalo 1901, there was an exhibit of Mexican *tipos populares* that was called "Aztecs and Their Industries," featuring live artisans who worked in Mexican brick, pottery, and copper (see chapter six and Fig. 9).[30] This exhibit was part of "The Pike" or, as a guidebook explained, a "storybook Land. All creeds and customs are there. Six thousand nondescript characters have stepped from the leaves of history, travel and adventure fiction to salute you in reality."[31] This display was complemented by a large exhibit of Philippine people (Igorrote Indians), which fascinated such distinguished visitors as the young T. S. Eliot.[32]

After the Saint Louis fair Mexico sent minor exhibits to such fairs as the 1908 food fair in Boston and the 1909 San Antonio fair.[33] But no new comprehensive performance was staged until 1922, and even then the extravaganzas of the nineteenth century were never repeated.

THE 1900 PARIS UNIVERSAL EXHIBITION

Mexico's presence at the 1900 Paris universal exhibition was almost equal to its participation at the 1889 Paris fair.[34] Sebastián B. de Mier, the director of Mexico's exhibition at the 1900 fair, estimated that whereas Mexico had spent nearly 1.3 million francs just in the construction of the Aztec Palace, the cost of the 1900 Mexican pavilion was around 600,000 francs.[35] The 1900 Paris Universal and International Exhibition was larger than that of 1889; in fact, it was the grandest of the entire nineteenth century. Accordingly, Mexico planned an enormous presence, but a monetary and agricultural crisis kept expenses under control.

From the outset the Paris exposition had neither a clear justification nor an implicit theme. The 1889 Paris world's fair had an unparalleled leitmotiv: to celebrate the centenary of the French Revolution. In contrast, the 1900 fair had as its only excuse the need to conclude the century with yet another universal exhibition, one that would "reflect the refulgent genius of France and show that, as in the past, we now stand at the vanguard of progress."[36]

The 1900 Paris exhibition was a diagnosis of the state of modern culture. Above all, it echoed three characteristics of fin-de-siècle modernity—overall grandiosity, cultural retrogression, and what we know as fin-de-siècle spirit. That is, the exhibition took place at almost the same site as the 1889 fair. It was larger, occupying all of Champ de Mars, Trocadero, the Esplanade des Invalides, the Cours de la Reine, and the banks of the Seine River between the Pont de l'Alma and the Place de la Concorde: nearly 5 million square feet of exhibition space. Over seven months, 39 million people visited the fair, three times the entire population of Mexico. Seventy-five foreign pavilions were constructed, mostly along the Quai d'Orsay, including those of the United States, Denmark, Austria, Portugal, Bosnia, Herzegovina, Peru, the United Kingdom, Spain, Bulgaria, Greece, and Mexico. Three traditional Latin American fair participants were absent—Argentina, Brazil, and Chile. As in the case of most nineteenth-century world's fairs, the 1900 Paris exhibition was an expression of the conviction that the ideals of modern times could be represented only through grandiosity.

The 1900 exhibition displayed a particularly retrograde tone: a return to conservative cultural features. Whereas the 1889 universal exhibition was characterized by the technologically innovative architecture, as epitomized by the Eiffel Tower, the 1900 exhibit had as its main attractions the massive use of electricity such as in the Chateau d'Eau palace and in a building known as "The Hall of Illusions."[37] In addition, two symbols of architectural innovation housed grandiose exhibitions of modern painting and sculpture (the Petit Palais) and French arts and crafts (the Grand Palais). Art nouveau has often been linked to this architectural innovation, but overall the fair was marked by neoclassical forms and canonic art. What also marked the 1900 fair was a pompous new bridge over the Seine that was inaugurated to honor the Russian Czar Alexander II, marking the rapprochement of Russia and France in the context of growing hostilities among European powers. The political arena was characterized by conservatism and retrograde nationalism after the Dreyfus affair.

Above all, the 1900 Paris fair, with its merging of retrograde art with art nouveau, of Bohemian Paris with the optimism of a modern ideal of city and world, was a prototypical fin-de-siècle event: a snapshot of ambivalence expressing both enchantment and disenchantment of modernism. The fair concluded not only the nineteenth century but also the "era of greater exhibitions."[38] The exhibition was, like the famed Rodin sculpture that was exhibited there, at the "Gates of Hell," at the entrance of total modern uncertainty. It enacted modernity at the "Gates of Hell," first, because it showed "the persistence of the old regime"; that is, despite progress and innovation, the fair showed that, as Arnold J. Mayer has maintained, "in form, content, and style the artifacts of high culture continued to be anchored and swathed in conventions that relayed and celebrated traditions supportive of the old order."[39] The 1900 fair showed that modernity was tradition tamed. Second, a posteriori we can acknowledge that the fair was indeed at the gates of the hell of radical uncertainty, violence, and destruction that swept Europe after 1914. It was the final edge of what George Steiner called the "imagined garden of liberal culture . . . the myth of the nineteenth century"—the fair was held at the brink of "a season in hell."[40] Third, it represented a sarcastic naming of the unnaming, as in Rodin's gates: cultural gates crowned by the Thinker-Poet "poised at the edge of the two worlds . . . the spectral no-man's-land where 'certainty dissolves into mystery.'"[41] That is, it was a conscious self-defeating, an awareness of progress, and a self-rumination about an ongoing cultural shift. These are the characteristics we assign to the notion of fin-de-siècle culture, and that is precisely why 1900 was the first and only fin de siècle in Western history.[42]

Mexico's presence at the 1900 Paris fair showed, on one hand, the increasing proficiency of the wizards of progress, who articulated a more selective and efficient modern image of Mexico, and, on the other hand, how Mexico adapted to the trendy nature of modernity: Mexico selectively echoed the grandiosity, retrogression, and, to some extent, the fin-de-siècle spirit of the fair.

Sebastián de Mier explained that, following a long process of learning about international fairs and owing to economic difficulties, Mexico's display in 1900 was bound to be less comprehensive than that of 1889 had been. In 1889 Mexico's display "was exhaustive and extended to all . . . human activity, in an attempt to demonstrate Mexico's potential. By contrast, Mexico's presence at the 1900 fair needed to be limited to assert what we have accomplished in practice."[43] Specific products and aspects were therefore emphasized: mining, tropical fruits, coffee, tobacco, cereals, fibers, wood, textiles, medical substances, paper, arts, liberal arts, and education.[44]

Overall, Mexico's presence at the 1900 fair was better organized and involved fewer people and less money. Instead of one director for each group of exhibits, individuals were in charge of three or more groups. The display included fewer exhibitors but earned more awards—51 percent of the 1,088 exhibitors won prizes.[45] One of the greatest moments in Mexican art was the grand prize awarded to Jesús Contreras's sculpture *Malgré-Tout*. Many exhibits, including those of the Comisión Geográfico-Exploradora, of tobacco, mining, and textiles, and of the Superior Sanitation Council, were essentially the same as those used during the previous twenty years.

What best exemplified Mexico's adaptation to the changing nature of modern times, to the fairs' renewed conservatism and spirit of fin de siècle, was the discussion about the pavilion to be placed along the Quai d'Orsay, near the palaces of War and Peace. Although no public contests were held for a construction design, throughout 1899 and 1900 two perspectives prevailed and conflicted: the officially supported project of engineer Antonio de Anza, and various projects supported by Jesús Contreras's artistic view. De Anza seemed to have the support of Minister Fernández Leal—who had substituted for Carlos Pacheco at the Ministry of Industrial Promotion—and Porfirio Díaz. Contreras was favored by the Mexican minister in Paris, by the French authorities, and, apparently, by de Mier. In coming to a final decision, Mexican artists, bureaucrats, and architects took into consideration— as usual—the internal balance of power of the wizards of progress, economic and technical limitations, and the maxims and tendencies of cosmopolitan nationalism, as these last were expressed in the 1900 Paris fair.

By 1900 Contreras had consolidated himself as the master of the statuary needs of Porfirian Mexico. He was an influential personality in both political and intellectual circles (see chapter 7). His lobbying to obtain the contract for the 1900 Mexican pavilion was overwhelming. Contreras hired French architects, and thus, once in Paris, de Anza proceeded to undo Contreras's contracts.[46] French organizers argued that de Anza's design was unharmonious with the nearby buildings, though in fact they were trying to put pressure on Mexican authorities to respect Contreras's French deals.[47] In response, de Anza's design was modified to match the standards of the nearby palaces of War and Peace (see Fig. 34).[48]

34. The Mexican pavilion at the 1900 Paris Universal Exhibition. Source: Gustave Gostkowski, *Au Mexique: Études, notes et renseignements utiles au capitalistes, a l'immigrant, e au touriste* (Paris, 1900), frontispiece. (Photograph by Carlos Contreras)

Two of Contreras's sketches of a Mexican pavilion were especially elaborate. The first was formed by two buildings linked by a modern, French romantic style, "the triumphant arch of peace."[49] The two structures merged various architectural styles in an attempt to depict the national history: the bottom part in pre-Hispanic Mitla style, the main corpus of the facade in Spanish colonial fashion, and the frieze in modern French romantic style. The second design added two allegorical compositions in the lateral facades of this intricate blueprint: on one facade, figures representing Mexican independence; on the other, La Reforma (Mexico's liberal reforms of the mid-nineteenth century). The second design also included a tower that encompassed what were, for Contreras, the priorities of modernity in natural order: "figures in the arts and industry that serve as bases for the symbol of science, which in turn ends in the tower of peace" (see Fig. 35).[50]

The collage of architectural styles comprising these designs aimed to depict the mature awareness of the evolution of the nation from pre-Hispanic times (the basement) to a Spanish colonial era, and finally to peace and cosmopolitanism (the frieze in romantic French fashion). This iconoclastic endeavor was a hazardous venture in such a retrograde fair as the 1900 Paris exposition. Instead, the wizards of progress decided to be cautious by con-

35. Jesús Contreras's model of the Mexican palace for the 1900 Paris Universal Exhibition. Source: Jesús Contreras's personal papers, reproduced courtesy of Carlos Contreras. (Photograph by Carlos Contreras)

structing a standard neoclassical pavilion, designed by the builder of the 1889 Aztec Palace, Antonio de Anza, whose know-how was used to serve modern trends.[51]

De Anza's project was the result of a conscious decision following a domestic discussion regarding the achievement of a national architectural style. As we saw in chapter 7, the main issues in this debate were the appropriateness of pre-Hispanic features as the essence of a national style and the lack of a real modern national architecture. The 1900 pavilion came to be an aesthetic and political statement in the debate: the national style could not be copied from pre-Hispanic forms, and a definitive Mexican architectural style was not yet attainable. Thus the 1900 pavilion seemed to claim that there was no option but to keep following cosmopolitan trends until a real national style emerged. De Anza explained that the pre-Hispanic forms were inadequate for modern standards and that the Spanish colonial style was already decadent when Spain conquered Mexico. Thus, "until today in Mexico we cannot point out a single building with an entirely national architecture. . . . It was impossible for a [national] school to emerge; we lacked the adequate environment and that set of circumstances that today are finally surfacing and that hopefully will become a favorable environment."[52]

In view of the conservative nature of the 1900 Paris fair, it seemed adequate for Mexicans to search for classicism in their own country. Thus the works of architect Ramón Rodríguez Arangoity, who had died in 1884, were rediscovered. Rodríguez Arangoity had taught various Porfirian architects and had traveled to Italy and France to study the classical forms of Rome and Pompeii. In fact, he had some experience in world's fairs, for he participated in the 1859 French imperial world's fair. In 1864 Emperor Maximilian appointed him as director of the works for the Chapultepec Castle. His works often combined modern iron structure with classicism.[53]

The classicist conservative architecture was revived by the 1900 world's fair, which prompted de Anza in Mexico also to rely on a classicist architect who had served Mexico's ephemeral, French-supported empire. Thus he resorted to Rodríguez Arangoity, the architect who, according to de Anza, had brought the "neo-Greek" style to Mexico (see Fig. 36). This style was canonized as the Napoleon III style and had already been represented at the 1889 Paris fair by such architects as Garnier and Formigé. It prevailed during the 1900 Paris fair, albeit with some innovative exceptions. Thus Mexico decided that because the country had no national architectural style that could represent its nationality—unlike Italy, Spain, or Norway—it needed to "adopt a serious style that could reveal the character of the government that rules Mexico's destiny. . . . The neo-Greek style, which fulfilled these conditions, was therefore adopted."[54] A truly modern national image had to be parsimoniously modern, as if modernity were a natural gift. Accordingly, Mexico's national image in Paris 1900 was epitomized in a building of "notable sobriety."[55] Mature modern nations used cosmopolitan forms and avoided lavish displays.

The neo-Greek pavilion included allegories of Mexico's historical eras (Independence, Reform, Peace). Fully illuminated with electric light,[56] it was built, as were all pavilions, of iron, plaster, and material that could easily be demolished.[57] During the fair, almost one million people visited the building.

Mexico's presence at the 1900 Paris fair also aimed at putting an end to the tortuous path of Mexico's nineteenth-century history. As a modern nation-state ruled by an enlightened authoritarian government, Mexico sought to participate in the spirit of fin de siècle in order both to prove Mexico's universalism and to end its uncivilized past. The nineteenth century was over, and so was Mexico's past chaos and instability. However, Mexican intellectuals and artists were ambivalent about what the spirit of fin de siècle actually symbolized. The debate that surrounded the construction of the 1900 Mexican pavilion was part of a wider debate of modernism as a suitable trend for Mexico. The decision to echo the return to classicism was a safe cultural

36. Construction of the Mexican pavilion in the Quai d'Orsay, Paris, 1900. Source: EXP, Box 31, Exp. 9; reproduced courtesy of the Archivo General de la Nación, Mexico City. (Photograph by the Archivo General de la Nación)

decision in an exhibition that was at the "gates of hell," but Mexican intellectuals and artists were nonetheless experimenting with the enchantments and disenchantments of modernity that the fair both displayed and tried to conceal.

With a neoclassical pavilion, in a fair organized in the "Remington" era,[58] Mexican intellectuals in Paris and Mexico debated all of the directions modernity could possibly take. Latin American intellectuals were experiencing their own modernism, which in a way echoed that of European intellectuals. The guru of such a movement, the Nicaraguan poet Rubén Darío, like Yeats in Europe ("Many ingenious things are gone . . ."),[59] expressed his awareness at the end of the century of the radical and sudden change that characterized modern times: "Yo soy aquel que ayer no más decía / el verso azul y la canción profana . . . y muy siglo diez y ocho y muy antiguo / y muy moderno; audaz, cosmopolita; / con Hugo fuerte y con Verlaine ambiguo, / y una sed de ilusiones infinita."[60]

The Mexican fin de siècle had to be as experimental and innovative as the European one, but less tragic. It was revolutionary and retrograde at the same time. It brought together the group of thinkers that was represented in *La Revista Moderna,* and it signified a return to Hispanism, spiritualism, antipopulism, and strong anti-Americanism in view of the 1898 Spanish-American war. In *La Revista Moderna*, where Nietzsche, Tolstoy, Kipling, Wilde, and Japanese poets were translated, the poet Jesús E. Valenzuela could claim: "La Ciencia ha hecho bancarrota! Un grito / del siglo moribundo lo proclama, / hay que empuñar de nuevo el oriflama / del ensueño en el término infinito."[61] But was Mexican modernism to reach the radical standards of European disenchantment? A Mexican literary critic and journalist, Victoriano Salado Álvarez, believed that modernism was a decadent literature which was at odds with a country that was not yet modern. The poet Amado Nervo, then in Paris reporting on the 1900 fair, rejected this idea, because in fact "all good things that we have in the nation are artificial and antithetical in relation to the environment, and thus everything has been accomplished without considering the people's criteria."[62] In effect, by 1900 the debate over Mexico's national image included even the modern reactions to modernity itself. And although the nation epitomized from the 1870s to the 1900s seemed to be consolidated, the idea of a Mexican nation was still an elite collective aspiration and had yet to be fully implemented.

THE PERSISTENCE OF THE WIZARDS OF PROGRESS

The 1915 San Francisco world's fair can be seen as a transition between the great nineteenth-century exhibitions and the new twentieth-century fairs. After 1910 the new revolutionary government attempted to take part at various international fairs, most notably at the 1915 San Francisco world's fair. Mexican preparations for San Francisco can be seen as evidence of postrevolutionary adjustments in handling the national image.[63]

Although the construction of the Panama-Pacific exposition started in 1911, the newly elected president, Woodrow Wilson, did not finally sanction celebration of the San Francisco world's fair until May 1913. Only then were invitations sent to foreign nations. The United States encouraged the participation of Latin American countries in part to smooth over its hitherto rather harsh relationships with that bloc. This effort, combined with the Mexican government's interest in obtaining official U.S. recognition, made Mexico's great effort to join the 1915 Panama-Pacific exposition inevitable.

At the beginning of 1913 Madero's government attempted to contact the Porfirian exhibition team in order to organize Mexico's participation at San Francisco. Madero's regime needed U.S. approval, and the Porfirian wizards of progress knew how to organize a performance that would demonstrate Mexican progress and stability. But the assault on the presidential palace by Felix Díaz and Bernardo Reyes and the consequent alliance with Victoriano Huerta, which ended in Madero's overthrow and assassination, ended the Maderistas' attempts to organize Mexico's presence in San Francisco.

During the first months of the Huerta regime the counterrevolutionary faction attempted a policy of reconciliation, especially toward Madero's followers. Thus Huerta not only endorsed Madero's intention to participate at the 1915 world's fair but also emphasized its importance even more with a view to finally securing official U.S. recognition. In June 1913 Albino R. Nuncio was appointed chief of the commission for Mexico's participation in the Panama-Pacific exposition. As we have seen, he had long been a member of the Porfirian exhibition team and had been in charge of Mexico's participation in Buffalo 1901 and Saint Louis 1904, among other fairs. He commissioned Carlos Velez as one of the San Francisco organizers. Velez wrote to his relative, Maximiliano M. Chabert, a long-time member of the Porfirian wizards of progress, saying that "it seems that in the government itself there are not many people experienced in this regard."[64]

By the end of 1913 a full commission was formed, with Albino R. Nuncio as chief. The commission for the 1915 fair followed to the letter the Porfirian manner of structuring and organizing a Mexican display. From mid-1913 to mid-1914 this organizational machinery worked despite all odds, and numerous reports and statistics reached the Ministry of Economic Development. Efforts to secure industrial exhibitors were accompanied by an attempt to utilize the traditional national symbols and descriptions. However, the Porfirian artistic, historiographical, and political infrastructure was dismantled, partly because of political and social unrest but mainly as a result of generational factors and an uncertain international intellectual environment. The long-time artistic producers of the national image and epic, such as the painter José María Velasco and the sculptor Jesús Contreras, had died, and it was uncertain whether their styles were still considered cosmopolitan enough to merit an international showing. The new generation of artists was considered too avant-garde for a world's fair in which, it was assumed, nineteenth-century modernism would still set the tone. Hence, neither Julio Ruelas nor Diego Rivera were appropriate for the exhibit that Mexico was planning. In contrast, photography was now more important as a means of reporting on the status of Mexico's politics, art, and culture. Such long-time photographers as Guillermo Kahlo, Melchert, and Waite were therefore requested to furnish samples of their work.[65]

Only two weeks after Madero was assassinated, on March 4, Woodrow Wilson was inaugurated, and the unfortunate diplomacy of Victoriano Huerta and American Ambassador Henry Lane Wilson suffered a change of direction. Attempts by Huerta's government to gain U.S. recognition now seemed doomed, and the strength of the constitutional alliance was growing. President Wilson's ambivalent position ended with the invasion of Veracruz in 1914 and, finally, with the debacle of the Huerta regime.[66] There is no official, documented explanation for Mexico's subsequent withdrawal from the San Francisco exposition, but there is no real need for one. By the end of 1914 Mexico's economy had touched the bottom of a serious depression.[67]

The various factions of the constitutionalist cause were about to enter Mexico City to start negotiations for a new balance of power, and U.S. troops were still in Veracruz. There was no way for Mexico to attend the festivities in San Francisco.

Mexico's aborted attendance at the Panama-Pacific exposition constitutes one of those untaken paths with which history is replete. However, the very attempt exemplifies the construction of the national image in troublesome times. It shows how, regarding Mexico's national images, there are deeper continuities in the past. An official historian of the San Francisco exhibition observed: "It was an ambition of the Panama-Pacific International Exposition management to produce in San Francisco a cosmos, so nearly complete that if all the world were destroyed except the 635 acres of land within the Exposition gates, the material basis of the life of today could have been reproduced from the exemplification of the arts, inventions, and industries there exhibited."[68] If the world had been destroyed, and if the only world and the only Mexico that could have been reconstructed had come from the ruins of the fair and from the records of Mexico's failed participation, what emerged would have been a picture of idealized progress and order, a world to which the whole fair belonged—as did the nineteenth century.

FROM THE EIFFEL TOWER TO DISNEYLAND

Between the 1890s and the 1930s world's fairs underwent a fundamental transformation in their very essence as comprehensive pocket pictures of the world. In 1893 Henry Adams visited the Chicago exhibition, where he "found matter of study to fill hundreds of years, and his education spread over chaos." For Adams, "The exposition itself defied philosophy.... As a scenic display, Paris had never approached it, but the inconceivable scenic display consisted in its being there at all.... No such Babel of loose and ill-joined, such vague and ill-defined and unrelated thoughts and half-thoughts and experimental outcries as the Exposition, had ever ruffled the surface of the lake."[69] Along similar lines, in 1900 the acclaimed Mexican poet Amado Nervo described the 1900 Paris exposition as the great ending of the nineteenth century. For him, to visit that fair was "like entering the country of miracles and of the ineffable." For Nervo, the Gallery of Machines was "large enough to contain two tempests."[70] Decades later the Russian-American novelist E. L. Doctorow related the experience of a first-generation New York Jewish boy at the 1939 New York world's fair. Commenting on one of the main parts of this Great Depression fair, the so-called Futurama, and on the whole fair as a perfect representation of an ideal world, Doctorow's main character observed: "In fact, this is what I realized and that no one had mentioned to me. [The fair] was a toy that any child in the world would want to own. You could play with it forever."[71] In effect, world's fairs had passed from absorbing universal amazement to conscious material amusement that could be possessed; from a symbolic and spatial, if ephemeral, universe that seemed to contain all visitors, to conscious, purchased entertainments; from the Crystal Palace and the Eiffel Tower to Disneyland; from pictures of a utopia to a "degenerated utopia"—an ideology clothed as a myth.[72]

I examined the nature of this global change in my introduction. The nineteenth-century type of world's fair changed because the essence of the nineteenth century had dissipated along with its chronological passing. By the 1920s the production of forms, values, tastes, and ways of life of a large portion of the population of European cities had changed radically. The change was both qualitative and quantitative, and it affected the forms of social organization, the action of governments, the poles of cultural development, and the fashions and tastes of the Western world. By the 1930s, efforts to organize a world's fair along nineteenth-century lines was supported by new economic and symbolic bases. On one hand, tourism, mass consumption, and corporate power had become the basic economic supports of world's fairs. On the other hand, the pragmatic goals of fostering recovery from economic depressions, or just imperial hangovers, resulted in nostalgic appeals to the ideal expressions of a mythical golden age of modern times: the nineteenth-century world's fairs.

For Mexico, the chronological, political, and cultural border between the nineteenth century and the twentieth century seems all too obvious: the Revolution of 1910. But Mexico's presence at sundry international fairs after the revolution was marked by this comprehensive historical mutation that included world's fairs, the Western world, and Mexico itself.

TWELVE

The 1922 Rio de Janeiro Fair

If only we were from the first generation of men, when even the most common and trivial places abounded with irresistible virginity.
JULIO TORRI, "DE LA NOBLE ESTERILIDAD DE LOS INGENIOS" (1917)

Mexico's attendance at the 1922 world's fair was the first Mexican participation in an international exhibit after the revolution that commenced in 1910. Throughout the nineteenth century, Brazil participated in most of the major world's fairs: London 1867, Vienna 1873, Philadelphia 1876, and Paris 1889 (although as a private Brazilian-French company). Emperor Dom Pedro II himself inaugurated the 1876 Philadelphia fair. Hence, in an era of centennial celebrations, it seemed a natural idea to commemorate the centenary of Brazil's declaration of independence from Portugal in 1822 with a world's fair. Despite Brazilian efforts made during the nineteenth-century world's fairs to look like a modern, progressive country, Brazil could not overcome European stereotypes.[1]

The 1922 Exposição Internacional do Centenario was held in Rio de Janeiro, then the nation's capital.[2] Originally planned to be a national exposition, the Rio fair, held from September 1922 through July 1923, gradually took on the structure and organization of the typical nineteenth-century-style universal exposition. In common with many nineteenth-century expositions, Rio's fair was tightly linked to the urban transformation of the city, which had passed from the artistic and monumental concerns of a belle-epoque urban center to the more modern preoccupations with sanitation and tourism. The fair had a strong emphasis on hygiene and included campaigns against tuberculosis and venereal diseases, and it represented an international effort to change the city's reputation as an unhealthy tropical port.[3] The sanitary focus was evident in the exhibits of countries like the United States and Portugal, but not that of Mexico, to which the fair was a matter of the spirit, not sanitation and industry.

Rio's world's fair included national and international sections. Argentina, Japan, Mexico, Great Britain, the United States, Italy, Denmark, Czechoslovakia, Norway, Belgium, France, and Portugal were among the countries with significant displays. The whole fair was characterized by the Portuguese colonial style in galleries and buildings, so the foreign pavilions followed rather conservative architectural styles. The United States constructed a large building in Portuguese colonial style, meant to be transformed into the American consulate in Rio de Janeiro after the exposition.[4] France built a replica of the 1766 Petit Trianon of Versailles, which was afterward donated to the Brazilian academy of letters.[5] Overall, the architecture of the Rio fair left a mark of neocolonialism in the city: foreign pavilions in neocolonial or traditional styles and new Brazilian buildings in neocolonial Portuguese style completed this exercise in nostalgia.

THE YEAR 1922

Rio's fair attracted national and international attention, and more than 3 million people visited the exposition. Yet it was a very expensive enterprise in both economic and political terms. The fair appeared to be an island of harmony and consensus surrounded by political turmoil, economic crisis, regional rebellions, social unrest, and intellectual controversies. For Brazil itself, 1922 was a year of radical changes, especially regarding the definition of the history and identity of a nation that was pompously commemorating a de facto independence by default.

It was an election year in the weak Brazilian republic, and the regime of President Epitácio Pessoa was threatened by strong regional conflicts and military rebellions. Historically, however, politics and universal expositions have found ways to be mutually complementary, and Pessoa's position vis-à-vis the exposition was similar to that of French President Sadi Carnot during the 1889 Paris world's fair in the no-less-fragile French Third Republic. Both found relief from their political troubles in the expositions, and a way to show political and economic vitality. For Pessoa, the fair was also a way to reinforce the centralization of power amid regional conflicts,[6] though the fair did not help in the regime's attempts to diminish the charges of corruption and waste leveled against it, of which the fair itself was a major example. This was evident even for Alonso Torre Díaz, Mexican minister in Brazil, who wrote home in 1922 about Brazil's precarious financial situation and the profligacy of Pessoa's government, which only exacerbated the already difficult political situation that had led to the declaration of a state of siege.[7]

The year also marked a watershed in Brazilian cultural life. The Modern Art Week was held in São Paulo, and Brazilian modernism was consolidating and acquiring recognition within the nation's intellectual life, with writers and artists such as Mario de Andrade, Oswald de Andrade, R. de Carvalho, Anita Malfatti, Tarsila do Amaral, and Heitor Villa-Lobos. They articulated an irreverent view of traditional Brazilian naturalist and conservative official culture, of which Rio and its exposition was the capital. In 1922 Brazilian modernist intellectuals were redefining the traditional language of national literature and culture, as was Mexico's intellectual group known as the Contemporáneos, albeit more profoundly and more nationalistically. They sought an "ideological and ironic modernity ... to face the cosmopolitan and the national."[8] For Brazil it was in 1922 that the Antropofagia came to stay.[9] In contrast, the centennial exposition of Rio exhibited the art of order and progress—the motto that appears on the Brazilian flag—the neocolonial architecture and an overall pro-Iberian environment very much fostered by a city already in the belle epoque style with a growing Spanish and Portuguese immigrant population. The exposition constituted a rather traditional civics lesson.[10] While the modernists were articulating the *Paulicea Desvairada*, Rio was organizing a neocolonial patriotic event. Industrial São Paulo was the center of rejection of the traditional Portuguese legacy, epitomized by the attempt to create a uniquely Brazilian language; it was the future of the nation. For the progressive cultural and economic sector of São Paulo, Rio was the antination.[11]

To this exposition, to this Brazil, President Álvaro Obregón sent not only a noteworthy Mexican exhibit but also a very special delegation headed by the then minister of education, José Vasconcelos, and by the influential Gen. Manuel Pérez Treviño. This constituted the first Mexican presence at an international exposition since the departure of Porfirio Díaz. The circumstances that had prevented Mexican attendance at the 1915 Panama-Pacific world's fair had changed radically, and Obregón's government had achieved a certain level of economic and political centralization among the revolutionary factions. With Carranza's assassination in 1920, the northern generals—basically Calles and Obregón—had achieved political and military victories over the numerous revolutionary groups. Mexico was still marked by the legacy of years of violence and political unpredictability, however, and in 1922 nothing seemed to signal the end of those years. Not only was a political balance still being negotiated with arms, money, and words, but also the concepts of nationalism, national culture, and education were in a state of flux. In this uncertain scenario the significance of random historical circumstances, as well as the virtu of the historical actors, stands out under the historian's scrutiny. When uncertainty reigns, and when the formation of a national image is at issue, the symbols and forms are likely to come about through decisive action on the part of one faction or another. This is what the Mexican Ulysses, José Vasconcelos, did in 1922.[12]

In that year, two of the fundamental preoccupations of Obregón's government were U.S. recognition of the new regime and rehabilitation of Mexico's international financial reputation, lost after years of violence and economic chaos. Adolfo de la Huerta, minister of finance, had tried to negotiate old and new loans with American banks, but he found it difficult to overcome the international image of Mexico as a violent and generally unstable country. Simultaneously, an international intellectual and artistic admiration for the achievements of Mexico's popular revolution was growing and was even shared by some financiers who were art connoisseurs.[13] In this context, for Obregón's regime the Brazilian fair of 1922 offered an opportunity to revitalize Mexico's international reputation by offering the works of a revolutionary Mexico, a nation that was economically and politically stable and secure, but now revolutionary and popular.

The 1922 Brazilian centennial exposition proved to be of importance to the United States and Europe as well. The image of Brazil as the land of the future, though as idealized as that of any other Latin American country, seemed to have great appeal for the world. The importance of this event for the United States was demonstrated both by U.S. expenditures for the fair and by the presence of Secretary of State Charles E. Hughes,[14] though it might be said that the United States was only returning the visit of Dom Pedro II to the 1876 centennial fair in Philadelphia. Still, the official American presence was very significant, and it also included an important private component.[15] Militarily, given the regional alliances already established by the United States in Latin America, the Brazilian exposition was an excellent occasion for consolidating the agreement with its most important ally in Latin America. What was sought in this instance was a treaty with the Brazilian government to reconstruct the Brazilian navy. The Mexican minister in Brazil related his private conversation with President Pessoa and explained the Brazilian president's strong pro-Americanism, which, he advised, ought to be considered with great suspicion.[16] In fact, the American interest in attending the Brazilian fair made the exhibition all the more appealing for the Mexican government.

Reciprocity was an additional and elegant diplomatic excuse: Brazil, it was officially argued, had had an important presence in both the centennial celebration of Mexico's independence in 1910 and in the commemoration of the conclusion of Mexico's independence in 1921.[17] Furthermore, Brazil had declared Mexico's official anniversary of the consummation of independence a national holiday and had even named one of Rio de Janeiro's main thoroughfares the Avenida Mexico.

MEXICO JOINS THE FAIR

In 1921 Obregón's government began to plan Mexico's presence in Brazil. Little is known about the budget assigned for this purpose, but it seems to have been administered in a disorganized fashion. Obregón himself decided to send a military battalion and an old navy boat, the *Nicolás Bravo*. As chief of this military delegation, he appointed the influential Gen. Manuel Pérez Treviño, chief of the president's general staff and eventually a prominent supporter of Plutarco Elías Calles.[18] A military delegation was customary at this kind of celebration, but for Mexico in 1922 this decision was rather surprising. It constituted an expensive gesture that contrasted with the economic difficulties the country was then experiencing.

President Obregón named Vasconcelos the special Mexican delegate to Rio de Janeiro to give the impression of stability and political unity, not, as Vasconcelos himself later wrote, to remove Vasconcelos from the political controversies surrounding the presidential succession of 1924. Indeed, Obregón was maneuvering with Calles over the military and political formulas to continue in power, but this he could do with or without Vasconcelos in Mexico. Although Vasconcelos was very helpful to Obregón in dealing with revolutionary intellectuals, in the final analysis he was quite dispensable. Mexico was a country of caudillos, and regardless of how indispensable the intellectuals considered themselves, they were largely irrelevant to the postrevolutionary political status quo.

Obregón's decision to appoint Vasconcelos was, in fact, influenced by Vasconcelos's own lobbying (within political circles, Vasconcelos clearly expressed his intentions of being appointed special delegate to Brazil) and also by Vasconcelos's intellectual prestige among the Latin American intellectual elites.[19] Vasconcelos had been in South America before 1922, and he wished to return to continue his thinking and writing about the emergence of Latin Americans as a leading race in the world. Indeed, from his 1922 trip to Brazil and Argentina came his most renowned book, *La raza cósmica* (*The Cosmic Race*), published in 1925—though for all its reputation, the book is merely the ruminations of a traveler in South America. Obregón was aware of Vasconcelos's fame and sent him not only to Brazil but also to Uruguay, Argentina, Chile, and Washington, D.C., as the intellectual voice of the new, revolutionary Mexico.

Unlike the Porfirian displays, the Mexican exhibit in Rio de Janeiro was not under the direction of a single group. The military delegation reported directly to the president.[20] The display of Mexican products and manufactures was supervised by a special agent assigned to the Commerce Department of the Ministry of Industry and Commerce.[21] And the special Mexican delegation was headed by Vasconcelos. It was Vasconcelos and his team who gave a coherent rhetorical and ideological shape to Mexico's display in Brazil. If there was an image of Mexico displayed in Rio, it was that constructed by Vasconcelos.

From the beginning, the diverse agents involved in Mexico's displays in Brazil suggested various ways of showing Mexico to the world. The bureaucracy had no experience in these matters, but it had its own idea of what Mexico was like. This idea was a complex combination of revolutionary popular discourses and patriotic elements rooted in the historical, anthropological, sociological, and artistic arguments synthesized by Porfirian intellectuals and politicians. For instance, Alonso Torre Díaz recommended at the end of 1921 that Mexico send to Brazil reproductions from the National Museum's collection of Mexican antiquities—the collection that had been doggedly copied and recopied by the Porfirian exhibition team. He also recommended the construction of a pavilion in the Aztec style.[22] He even spread word of this possibility to the Brazilian media, leading the *Jornal do Commercio* to announce in November 1921 that Mexico's pavilion was to be an Aztec building.[23] Obregón, with the same motivation, inquired about the cost of a bronze replica of the Cuauhtémoc monument on Mexico City's Paseo de la Reforma. As a result, the 1880s Roman-style Cuauhtémoc, the main relic of official Porfirian indigenism, was once again copied to be shipped to Rio, as it had previously been sent to Paris, Chicago, and countless other places. A contract was signed with the prestigious Tiffany Company of New York in July 1922 for the manufacture of this replica.[24] Ironically enough, Tiffany offered a discount to the revolutionary government because, after all, Porfirian Mexico had been a trustworthy old customer.[25] Tiffany had long been associated with Mexico's symbolic devices, and on this occasion it was employed to make not only the Cuauhtémoc replica but also the commemorative gold and bronze medals for Mexico's display at Rio's fair.[26]

Vasconcelos appointed his own team to accompany him on this trip. This team constituted a gathering of intellectuals, artists, and musicians who followed Vasconcelos throughout his tenure as minister of education and, later, as presidential candidate in 1929. Using the Porfirian model, Vasconcelos aimed to form a professional team able to produce the different effects involved in presenting a complete picture of a modern nation. His team comprised the professional diplomats Pablo Campos Ortiz and Alfonso de Rosenzweig, both as advisers; the painters Roberto Montenegro and Gabriel Fernández Ledesma; and the poets and writers Carlos Pellicer and Julio Torri.[27] In Brazil the team was joined by the Dominican writer, literary critic, and long-time resident of Mexico Pedro Henríquez Ureña.

Once Vasconcelos took control of Mexico's display, its ideological direction began to clarify. Vasconcelos could do nothing to nullify the reproduction of the Cuauhtémoc monument. He argued: "On the eve of my trip to Rio de Janeiro, Pansi [*sic*] informed me that a replica of the statue of Cuauhtémoc from the Paseo de la Reforma had been cast and that this would be Mexico's gift to its sister republic on her centennial anniversary. I had neither choice nor influence over his decision, and any protest on my part would have been useless."[28] He did not agree with the idea of reproducing the image of an Indian hero of a nation that was, he thought, fundamentally Hispanic. However, he assumed control of the rest of the Mexican exhibit, making the image of Mexico the expression par excellence of the cosmic race of which he dreamed.

Hence, owing to Vasconcelos's influence, a contest was held for the construction not of an Aztec building but of a colonial-style pavilion. In December 1921 the contest took place, with fifteen different plans entered.[29] Two young architects, Carlos Obregón Santacilia and Carlos Tarditti, won this contest, and for the former this was the beginning of a successful career as the architect for the needs of the postrevolutionary governments. (The Benito Juárez school—1923–1924—was his main neocolonial work à la Vasconcelos.)[30] Although Obregón Santacilia eventually converted to the functionalist modern Le Corbusier type of architecture, for the Mexican pavilion in Rio de Janeiro he designed a Mexican colonial baroque building that echoed the new building for the Ministry of Education, under construction at the time. It was a building of 600 square meters, located between the pavilions of Denmark and Czechoslovakia. In it, Vasconcelos sought to epitomize his whole conception of a new Mexico (see Fig. 37).

While Obregón Santacilia and Tarditti worked on the construction of the building, Montenegro and Fernández Ledesma designed the mural paintings that decorated the walls of its second floor. Whereas Vasconcelos criticized the mural paintings on the walls of the British pavilion in Rio for being classic examples of English imperialism,[31] an American art critic judged Montenegro's murals as rather colorful but traditional allegories and scenes of Mexico: "On one wall two women in natural dress stretch their arms toward a pile of natural products."[32] These were colonial scenes, panels from eighteenth-century Mexico. In fact, Montenegro had just returned from Europe and was being promoted, along with many other artists (including Diego Rivera and José Clemente Orozco), by Vasconcelos's cultural crusade. But Vasconcelos especially liked Montenegro's postacademic, modern, but not aesthetically or politically radical paintings.[33] As a whole, the building and its interior were presented as an example of the optimal synthesis of the essence of Mexico—the Spanish spiritual legacy—and the particular expression given it by the Indian influence, as exemplified in the Mexican baroque.

Obregón Santacilia was only a 26-year-old architect eager to obtain contracts, and his infatuation with the neocolonial style would not last long.[34] But in 1922 he was fulfilling the influential—in both architecture and political thought—pro-Hispanic understanding of Mexico. Not surprisingly, a U.S. visitor described his building as a "mingling of Spanish and native styles with polychromatic decoration."[35] The Brazilian press also thought that the Mexican pavilion was quite distinguished because it merged pre-Colombian and medieval Spanish architecture.

These characteristics were not random but, rather, a conscious allegorical exercise. As we have seen, since the 1890s architecture had been the crystallization of the intellectual and political debate about the nation and its modern future.[36] Vasconcelos himself had a great concern with architecture. For him it was a perfect art because it combined aesthetics and social functions. Buildings and monuments were the chief components of his cultural

37. The Mexican pavilion in the 1922 Centennial Exhibition of Rio de Janeiro. Source: Jornal do Commercio, *O Livro d'Ouro, Edição Comemorativa, 1822–1922* (Rio de Janeiro, 1922), 170.

campaign as minister of education.[37] He claimed that he sought to summarize his conception of Mexican nationhood in architecture, as he indeed attempted to do in the new Ministry of Education building, the construction of which he promoted. In this building, he explained, his goal was to demonstrate that "America will be the first continent on earth to witness the realization of a race of men derived from all of the superior aspects of previous races—this will be a final race, the cosmic race."[38]

Vasconcelos's conception of a hybrid but fundamentally neocolonial architecture epitomized the cultural synthesis he himself represented in Mexican cultural life. By the 1920s he had introduced the most influential synthesis of his time for conceiving what it meant to be Mexican and what Mexico ought to be like in the future. To find parallels to his position, one would have to go back to Lucas Alamán and his pro-Hispanic but complex and rich synthesis of Mexico's history.[39] If, as Manuel Gómez Morín has argued, a new Mexico was born out of the chaos of 1915,[40] it was in the early 1920s, with Vasconcelos at the Ministry of Education, that a group of intellectuals had the opportunity to give shape to that new nation.

A BUILDING FOR THE COSMIC RACE

The new shape of the nation did begin to be reflected in architecture, and so did the realization of how old Mexico was. In the Porfirian period the Cuauhtémoc monument had synthesized the proindigenist tendencies of some political and intellectual circles, just as these trends had been expressed architecturally in the Aztec Palace constructed for the 1889 Paris world's fair. However, the pro-Hispanic architectural tendencies began to acquire significance in Mexico after the turn of the century. As I explained in chapter 7, Jesús T. Acevedo, an architect trained in the last decade of the Porfirian period and a good friend of Vasconcelos, making use of a biological metaphor, claimed that it was colonial architecture, the main matrix of evolution, from which a real national architecture could emerge.[41] Also in 1913, Federico E. Mariscal criticized the attempts to re-create pre-Hispanic architecture and pointed out that it was in colonial times that the elements of Mexican nationhood were combined, and thus "this colonial architectural style is the one that has to suffer all the necessary aesthetic transformations to reveal through contemporary buildings the actual historical modifications that Mexican life itself has suffered throughout time."[42]

What was important about this postrevolutionary neocolonialism in architecture was not its pro-Hispanism per se—this had been present throughout Mexican history—but the conception of it as a democratic, popular, and natural direction for the country to follow. As such, it was maintained by both indigenists and Hispanists. The prominent postrevolutionary indigenist Manuel Gamio believed that in order to escape the vicious circle of European imitation, all too common during the Porfirian period, Mexican architecture ought to rediscover Spain.[43] Gamio disliked the American-style suburbs of Mexico City, such as the Colonia Juárez, and although he was willing to consider some architecture inspired by pre-Hispanic styles, he favored the Mexican colonial styles that seemed to include the hybrid synthesis for which he was looking.[44] In the same way, Vasconcelos favored the neocolonial style as the fortified merger of Indian hands and Spanish techniques and intelligence. Indeed, his pro-Hispanism in architecture echoed J. E. Rodó's type of pan–Latin American nationalism—and anti-Americanism.

In constructing a colonial building in Rio de Janeiro in 1922 Vasconcelos was not only fulfilling his ideas but also following a continental tendency. Since the 1890s Hispanism had emerged in Spain as a conservative, Catholic, anti-American ideology that maintained the belief in the uniqueness and superiority of the Hispanic race. This ideology was echoed throughout Latin America, often supporting a conservative, Catholic, nationalist populism.[45] In Spain, the consequences of Hispanism could be seen in the emergence of the Spanish Falange and in the official attempts to reestablish, at least spiritually, the Magnae Hispaniae—the great Hispanic empire. Shortly after the

1922 Brazilian fair, the 1929 Ibero-American exhibition would best epitomize this Hispanism. (See chapter 13.)

Consequently, whereas in São Paulo the Modern Art Week threatened the old aesthetic understandings of Brazil, Rio became the bastion of a new discourse based on the recovery of Brazil's colonial legacy as part of a continental ideology. The avant-garde nationalist Brazilian intellectuals of the 1920s eventually favored Le Corbusier functionalism, as Obregón Santacilia did in Mexico. But the no-less-nationalist official architects of Rio's exposition found in the neo-Portuguese colonial architecture a way to redefine the national personality of the capital city after the belle epoque. This tendency dated back to the works of Ricardo Severo, a Portuguese architect who lived in São Paulo and whose influence would enrich all of the major architects of modern Brazil, especially José M. Carneiro da Cunha Filho in Rio de Janeiro. As a reaction against the traditional neoclassical styles, and as a way to follow the international tendency of eclectic revival, Brazilian neocolonialism was best immortalized in Rio de Janeiro's centennial exposition.[46] Therefore, among the conservative Brazilian republican faction, Mexico's neocolonial building, together with the American neo-Portuguese pavilion, was the best liked of the foreign pavilions. Even President Pessoa expressed to Ambassador Torre Díaz his satisfaction that the two Latin American countries with distinctive colonial styles were Mexico and Brazil.[47]

The neocolonial styles that supposedly synthesized the various national tendencies with the basic Spanish matrix did indeed represent the real first beginning of the new cosmic race. Vasconcelos described the Brazilian buildings at the exhibition as "colonial-style Portuguese buildings . . . [reflecting] all of the splendor and luxury of the conquering nation of Portugal. . . . However, the Brazilian architects have enlarged the constructions, bestowing upon the buildings a spacious and attractive quality. This corresponds to the new Brazilian nation that has improved upon the older colonial traditions."[48] In truth, for thinkers like Vasconcelos, the neocolonial (Hispanic or Portuguese) style meant the renovation of the Iberian race, which, he believed, would come to lead Western civilization. Thus, in an interview with a Brazilian newspaper, he stated: "I regard European contributions to Latin America to be no longer important in the present. . . . I believe that in the next few decades Europe's role will be that of an observer of our development. They will describe the things we will have accomplished."[49]

The pro-Hispanic movement was as well established as the proindigenist trend in the discussion about nationalism in Mexico. By 1922, despite Vasconcelos's notoriety at the Ministry of Education, postrevolutionary indigenism had been redefined by the convergence of several phenomena: the popular mobilization of the Revolution of 1910; the metamorphosis of cosmopolitan aesthetics (more innovative and avant-garde, yet more socially en-

38. Indigenous motifs in tobacco advertising. Source: *Ethnos. Revista Mensual para la Divulgación de Estudios Antropológicos sobre México y Centro-América* 1, 3 (1920).

gaging); the movement of disciplines like anthropology and archaeology toward a more culturalist (Boasian) paradigm; and the official policies to delineate by all available means (education, media, murals) the meaning of the new revolutionary nation.[50] By the 1920s the combination of these factors had made Indian motifs into fashionable and acceptable cosmopolitan tokens. This trend can be seen in commercial advertisements that are always prompt to recognize and advance new tastes. Thus one brand of cigarettes—El Buen Tono—which in Porfirian times had depicted French-style women in its publicity, by 1922 advertised its products in Manuel Gamio's indigenist journal, *Ethnos*, with pre-Hispanic motifs (see Fig. 38). In the same way, foreign businesses, such as the oil company El Águila, also turned to pre-Hispanic themes in its advertising.[51] In fact, as a historian of Mexican archaeology observed, "Around 1920, for reasons that have little to do with archaeological research and more to do with changing aesthetic norms in Europe, ancient art forms came to be assigned a value and importance hitherto unknown."[52]

Furthermore, and although he would eventually harbor regrets about the choice, it was Vasconcelos himself who championed the artists who became the masters of Mexican postrevolutionary official indigenism.[53] He favored and sponsored the appreciation of popular arts, and he did not dismiss the significance of Indians in Mexico's history. In *Indología*, he maintained that the Latin American race contradicted Darwin's theory, because in Mexico and the rest of Latin America the races did not follow Darwinian natural selection, but rather lived in cooperation as expressed by theorists like Leclerc du Sablon in France and Georg Friedrich Nicolai in Germany.[54] But Vasconcelos, however messianic, discussed nationalism in the language furnished by the Porfirian era; that is, in terms of race.

Vasconcelos articulated his understanding of race most clearly in a series of lectures delivered at the University of Chicago in 1926.[55] There Vasconcelos aimed to overcome the legacy of nineteenth-century racist theorists that left no room for the Spanish American hybrid peoples. He attacked Herbert Spencer and the Latin American scientists who copied the evolutionist racist theories, and he defended miscegenation on two grounds: by vindicating Spanish spiritual superiority that permitted the overcoming of racial differences (that is, through miscegenation); and by contradicting racial theories on their own terms. He then tried to prove that miscegenation is both a messianic and a biological conclusion of history: "If we observe human nature closely we find that hybridism in man, as well as in plants, tends to produce better types and tends to rejuvenate those types that have become static."[56] He continued: "There is nothing left for us to do, but to follow the Spanish tradition of eliminating the prejudice of color, the prejudice of race.... No matter what our theoretical opinions might be, we have to start from the fact that the mestizo is the predominant element in Mexico."[57] This combination of pro-Hispanism (linked to criollo patriotism) and (so-to-speak) scientific racist antiracism allowed Vasconcelos to defend the universal task of the new mestizo nations (that is, "bringing together all the races of the earth ... with the purpose of creating a new type of civilization"). It also led him to expand the nineteenth-century racist theories into the twentieth-century postrevolutionary era. Thus he called for replacing Darwinism with Mendelism (in which "we might find more racial hope and more individual strength and faith"), as well as for collaboration of races, in order to avoid being "overwhelmed by the wave of the Negro, of the Indian, or of the Asiatic."[58]

Vasconcelos's understanding of race in the 1920s was, of course, different from the views articulated by nineteenth-century Mexican intellectuals such as Francisco Pimentel, Alfredo Chavero, or Vicente Riva Palacio. But it formed part of the same discussion, in the same terms, and it derived from the same basic assumptions. Furthermore, in common with the late Porfirian scientists, Vasconcelos in the 1920s was aware of the importance of science in this regard and of the ascientific strategies Mexicans and Latin Americans had to adopt in order to make science suit their special situation. He affirmed: "If all nations then build theories to justify their policies or to strengthen their deeds, let us develop in Mexico our own theories; or at least, let us be certain that we choose among the foreign theories of thought those that stimulate our growth instead of those that restrain it."[59] He could not imagine the radicalism into which indigenism would fall in the 1930s; he only conceived a sort of romantic assimilation of the Indian aspects of Mexico into its great Hispanic essence. Nonetheless, he seemed to have been aware that to achieve this fusion, negotiations had to take place among and within Mexico's elites according to their varied social and economic circumstances. His inauguration of a tropical Cuauhtémoc in Rio de Janeiro was a demonstration of this awareness.

A TROPICAL CUAUHTÉMOC

On 16 September 1922, at the intersection of the Avenidas Beira-Mar, Oswaldo Cruz, and Rui Barbosa, the four-meter-tall replica of Cuauhtémoc's monument was erected (see Fig. 39). As I mentioned before, Vasconcelos could not prevent this extravagant Mexican display, which he considered an unnecessary expenditure. President Obregón and Alberto J. Pani had been its promoters, and Vasconcelos had no choice but to comply. Hence he articulated a masterpiece of rhetorical ambivalence and inclusion that stated his idea of a Hispanic Mexico without denigrating the advocates of indigenism and their tropical Cuauhtémoc. And thus, through a combination of historical inaccuracies, classical metaphors, convincing allegorical images, and his well-known eloquence, Vasconcelos revived in splendid fashion Mexico's nineteenth-century rhetoric on the subject.[60] In front of President Pessoa, Vasconcelos claimed: "the bronzed Mexican Indian is re-created in this polished granite base. We provide the bronze, while you furnish the rock foundation for mounting it. Together, these elements represent the complete creation of a strong and glorious race." This having been said, he also described Hernán Cortés as "the greatest of all conquistadors, the unrivaled one [who] vanquished with his sword and persuaded through his words."

39. The Cuauhtémoc replica sent to the 1922 Rio de Janeiro exhibition. Source: SRE 7–16–67, II; reproduced courtesy of SRE.

He directed the flow of his ideas to the granite base, to which he constantly referred as the representation of the real new race, and to Cuauhtémoc, whom he depicted as the symbol of the end of Indian power, the hero "on whose behalf we request the hospitality of this city which is open to the ocean yet sustained by mountains. In other words, while at the open front there is the freedom to make any decision, there is at the base the granite through which the new Latin race will forge its destiny in this continent." Cuauhtémoc meant "the certainty of our own consciousness and the hope of a glorious future." He explained that in Mexico the veneration of this hero suggested neither the rejection of progress nor the ambition of going back to Aztec times. Neither, of course, did it mean the dismissal of Europe: "We have assimilated European influences, and now it is our duty to create." As always, he contrasted the emerging Latin America with the already successful civilization of the United States, and in such a contrast Cuauhtémoc's arrow appeared to be heading to the future. In the foreseeable future, he believed, Latin American civilization would overthrow North American power. Thus he ambivalently, if eloquently, concluded: "Full of faith, we brandish Cuauhtémoc as our flag and announce from our borders across the sea to the Iberian race that: Iberian race, be as faithful with your identity as the Indian was, be yourself." What ought to be copied from Indian peoples was not their particular identity but the fact that they did have an identity which allowed them to be just that—themselves.[61]

In Brazil, Vasconcelos's speech was welcomed for its eloquence but not really understood as a sample of how conflicting ideas about nationhood might be harmonized. After his discourse—Vasconcelos wrote to Obregón—President Pessoa "acted as you do when you are not content with official speeches: he talked and talked."[62] In Mexico, the speech was received with overall approval. Vasconcelos's ideas about miscegenation may, as some authors have suggested, have been imposed on him by the mestizo condition of the nation, and undoubtedly it later gradually changed toward a more pro-European Hispanist position.[63] But in 1922 Vasconcelos was minister of education and closer to power—that is, to the control of national symbols—than he had ever been before. At the time he believed that it was possible to build a universally accepted Hispanic, though mestizo, nation using a variety of political, representational, and rhetorical resources. Indeed, Vasconcelos was criticized for the numerous historical inaccuracies and errors that marked his Cuauhtémoc speech. Years later, he recalled the event as an irony of the times: he disliked very much the fact that the indigenist monument, interpreted by him as a flag for the new Hispanic cosmic race, was made by a Yankee company. More importantly, he dismissed those who criticized his historical imprecision and acknowledged that his speech was "a bit of a fantasy" because it was "symbolically embellished to convey our desire to be independent, not of Spain, but of Monroeism." Thus all his historical errors were irrelevant because, as he explained, "I don't intend to write history; I aim to create myth."[64]

The proindigenist tendency was also present in the congresses that took place around the Rio de Janeiro exposition. Especially significant in this regard was the 20th International Congress of Americanists, at which Manuel Gamio's works were presented, together with those of the venerable Mexican physician Nicolás León, a veteran measurer of Indian heads.[65] The official Mexican delegates to this congress were Alfonso del Toro and José Raygados Vetiz. Both very much shared Vasconcelos's pro-Hispanic nationalism. Alfonso del Toro wrote some articles from Brazil for Mexico City's periodical *Revista de Revistas*, in which he displayed a cruder version of Vasconcelos's anti-Americanism and old-fashioned aristocratic notions: "North American influence is nonexistent in Brazil. Rather, the refinement and good taste of the French are here apparent." For him, there were no *pelados*[66] in Rio de Janeiro, and there were fewer Blacks than in any American city.[67] Although expressed with less subtlety, Toro's impressions of Rio reflected those of Vasconcelos.

A VIEW OF MEXICO'S DISPLAY IN RIO

In addition to the neocolonial pavilion and the Cuauhtémoc monument, the Mexican display included a variety of products assembled by a commercial delegation headed by José Vázquez Schiaffiano and Luis G. Garfias.[68] The exhibit included a scale reproduction of Teotihuacán, furniture from Mexico City's department store El Palacio de Hierro, samples of mineral products, and food products. There was also a special book commissioned by the Mexican government to honor Brazil.[69] This book displayed Mexico's great ancient past, its recent material progress, and its natural beauty and wealth with statistics, paintings, and photographs. The images used in this book were exactly the same ones as those used by the Porfirian exhibition team in several world's fairs (paintings by Obregón and Velasco, photographs of railroads, and so forth). Two special exhibits were real innovations: a movie made during Vasconcelos's stay in Brazil,[70] and an important exhibit of popular art.

Popular art, both visual and vocal, became a significant aspect of Vasconcelos's educational campaign. Montenegro and Fernández Ledesma were prominent promoters of such art, as were the painter and writer Dr. Atl (Gerardo Murillo) and the anthropologist Miguel Othón de Mendizábal. As minister, Vasconcelos emphasized the production and promotion of popular art, and he had a pragmatic awareness of the international receptivity to this type of art.

Contrary to what scholar Claude Fell believes, with this international promotion Mexican popular art did not lose its exoticism but, quite the contrary, attained full international recognition—and market—for precisely this quality.[71] Mexican ceramics were especially appreciated in Brazil, as was a collection of photographs of Mexico by Guillermo Kahlo, the official photographer of the Porfiriato public works.[72]

However, the popularity of Mexico's exhibit with visitors to the exposition was not especially reflected in the number of awards received. Mexico won a total of 561 prizes (only 80 grand prizes and 68 gold medals)—a poor showing for an expensive exhibit that included not only a building and a four-meter-tall bronze monument but also 160 military men, 75 members of a military band, and 35 members of the Orquesta Típica Torreblanca.[73]

In addition to all this, Vasconcelos lectured in Rio de Janeiro, São Paulo, and, later, in Montevideo, Buenos Aires, and Santiago. Throughout South America, Vasconcelos's ideas were generally welcomed, in part because a pro-Hispanist stance was widespread in the criollo societies of Argentina, Brazil, Chile, and Uruguay. In Brazil his educational campaign was considered the core of the image of the new Mexico. In a conference at São Paulo's university, Victor Vianna compared Vasconcelos's work with that of Visher in England and Henriot in France. In turn, Vasconcelos praised the Brazilian educational system both in speeches and in his later writings (especially in *El desastre* and *La raza cósmica*). Only in Chile was he criticized by the conservative media for an overemphasis on race at the expense of nationhood and because he repudiated militarism.[74] In the Brazilian interior (Minas Gerais and São Paulo states) the Mexican delegation of poets, writers, singers, and artists was well received. However, at times the reality of Mexico seemed lost on the inhabitants of the Brazilian hinterlands, as when the *Folha do Norte*, a Belém newspaper, candidly declared that "two navy units from Porfirio Díaz's country visited Amazonia." Of course, historically, this was not an error but a lack of delicacy with Mexico's postrevolutionary and anti-Porfirist government.[75]

Brazil's centenary of independence had been celebrated in Mexico City with various artistic and political events,[76] and at the Rio de Janeiro exposition the favor was returned with a Mexican festival held on 14 September 1922. Once again, Vasconcelos organized the performance. The Orquesta Típica Torreblanca played traditional Mexican songs and some Mexican waltzes by Villanueva (which were notorious pieces of Porfirian nostalgia). Flora Islas, Abigael Bonilla, and Fanny Annitúa were the featured singers. Carlos Pellicer recited Mexican poems, though not those written by his generation, but the somewhat shopworn verses of Amado Nervo, Manuel Gutiérrez Najera, Salvador Díaz Mirón, and a relatively new poet, Enrique González Martínez.[77] In effect, at Rio, Mexico was represented by the same poems and music that had been performed at many other Mexican displays at world's fairs during the preceding century.

WITH THE NATION AT HAND AT GUANABARA BAY

Overall, the image that Mexico tried to convey at Rio de Janeiro was that of the spiritual leader of a continental push toward consummation of the cosmic race, an essentially Hispanic, anti-American, hybrid—and, above all, renewed—country. The industrial and touristic aspects of the nation were largely ignored, for it was a display of ideas and symbols based largely on Vasconcelos's thought. The ideal picture of the Mexico that Vasconcelos imagined existed, if only for ephemeral moments, beside Guanabara Bay. It was made possible by various historical factors for which the Revolution of 1910 had been the fundamental catalyst. First, Mexico's display in Rio revealed a generational change that was significant for the construction of the national symbols. Second, Mexico's presence in Brazil constituted in certain respects a dressed-up, somewhat more pragmatic, reflection of Mexico's old regime—especially evident in its focus on race and Hispanism and its obsession with style.[78] Finally, Mexico's exhibit showed a hitherto unknown—in Mexico's image at international fairs—single-minded character. The Mexico of Rio belonged to the unfolding of Vasconcelos's thought, and in Brazil he was not only exhibiting his conception of Mexico but also testing his own ideas. Rio in 1922 was an optimal scenario for doing this. It is not by chance that one of Vasconcelos's major books, *La raza cósmica*, is a report of travels in Brazil, Argentina, Uruguay, and Chile.

Obregón's regime could not rely on the Porfirian exhibition team. Regardless of the ideological and political discrepancies—which the postrevolutionary government proved to be very willing to overlook—by 1922 the Porfirian wizards of progress were either dead or too old to serve. In the 1920s, Mexico's culture and education were led by a young generation of intellectuals and artists, most of them followers of Madero's democratic movement or just part of—or direct beneficiaries of—what historian Luis González called "the blue generation," a modernist generation between the Porfiriato and the revolution. Vasconcelos, Gómez Morín, Vázquez del Mercado, Lombardo Toledano, Antonio Caso, and others occupied official posts.[79] They tasted power, and they liked it. Hence, in trying to create his utopia of a cosmic Mexico in Rio de Janeiro, Vasconcelos, as minister of education, incorporated members of the new generation that had been born in the era of great exhibitions, between 1880 and 1900. Vasconcelos (1881), the oldest, worked with artists and writers such as Julio Torri (1889), Fernández Ledesma (1900), and Carlos Pellicer (1896); architects and engineers such as Carlos Obregón Santacilia (1896) and José Vázquez Schiaffiano (1881); and professional diplomats such as Torre Díaz (1889) and Campos Ortiz (1898). They all belonged to a generation with no patriotic or technical training other than that of an urban middle class that came of age within and between the Porfirian era and the revolutionary years.

In Mexico's presence at Rio de Janeiro, the generational shift enlarged boundaries within which such concepts as nation, progress, cosmopolitanism, and modernity might be discussed on the political and cultural stage. New and old points of view that before were only marginally considered acquired the status of official positions. However, Vasconcelos's ephemeral command of the image of the nation constituted a continuity within the parameters of the old regime. At Rio the nation was defined by references to two fundamental dichotomies: race versus spirit, and universalism versus nativism. Vasconcelos had a solution for these dichotomies, which he tried to depict in all forms of expression—architecture, the plastic arts, rhetoric—in order to reiterate his proposal and make it simultaneously a statement for the world to read and a lesson for Mexico to learn. In effect, his solution was a messianic Hispanism. In it, racial imperatives acquired explanation and balance with the spiritual aspects he aimed to emphasize.[80] Also, Mexico's uniqueness was already included and formulated into a line of thought that was both a universal and a commanding course for the future.

Vasconcelos risked maneuvering Mexico's image in this single-handed fashion because he was a disenchanted positivist. "During the first century of national independence we were concerned with establishing the boundaries of the homeland.... The moment has arrived to strengthen the spirit of Mexico and provide her with a soul," Vasconcelos stated in a speech he delivered in Rio de Janeiro.[81] Indeed, he always sought to allude to this realm of souls, spirits, and symbols as domestic (Hispanist) realms versus a material outside. Small wonder, for he was a master of styles and forms. Although he studied the positivist foundation for Mexico's nationalism—that is, racial, economic, anthropological, and sociological ideas—he perceived that nationalism, as much as cosmopolitanism, was a matter of form. Through forms, symbols, and style he offered in Rio de Janeiro an idea of Mexico as a universal but unique nation. Oddly enough, this had been the dream of the Porfirian displays at world's fairs. Unlike the Porfirian efforts, however, Vasconcelos did not believe that prototypes of modernity and cosmopolitanism existed. Rather, they had to be created. The model for the cosmic race was Hispanic, but the race was still in the making. As with the Porfirian displays, Vasconcelos was aware of the contingency of his proposal, of its experimental character. However, and again along with the Porfirian Científicos, he imagined his idea of a cosmic Mexico to be a Comtian third and final stage. Nonetheless, his was not a scientific but a deliberately messianic end of history.

It has been exhaustively argued that Vasconcelos's ideas were a reaction to Porfirian positivism, but at the same time positivist thought had given Vasconcelos the basic language with which to speak about his beloved term: race. Thus his ideas ought to be seen in the continuum of the discussion of race.[82] In 1922 his image of Mexico constituted a continuation that did not deny previous empirical, scientific, and racist parameters but projected them toward a messianic spiritual goal. "Only through a spiritual leap, grounded in historical data, will we be able to achieve a clear perception of things which transcends the microideology of specialists," he argued in *La raza cósmica*.[83] Once he projected race, with its positivist imperatives, toward a spiritual messianism (that is, Hispanism), the concept found a deep and fertile national ideological ground. Throughout Mexican history criollo patriotism had been a solid intellectual and political tendency. This meant that positivist understandings of race adapted to and reflected the notions of long-established criollo patriotism (that is, of Francisco Xavier Clavijero or Carlos María de Bustamante) and nineteenth-century Mexican conservatism (that is, of Lucas Alamán).[84] Therefore, what Vasconcelos did in Rio de Janeiro was to bring to the national and international debate an image of Mexico that had been in the process of formation since colonial times, armed with Porfirian positivism, and projected into the future by his own messianic spiritualism.

The idea of a messianic Hispanic Mexico passed the test in Rio de Janeiro, because Vasconcelos found in Brazil the nutrients to feed the cosmic race.[85] His views on Brazil were merely the search for the utopian continent inhabited by the utopian race. But he was also betrayed by his nostalgia for order and progress, a counterrevolutionary yearning. Coming to the reconstructed Rio of the 1922 fair must have been idyllic for Vasconcelos: a city that had experienced a real architectural and urban belle epoque, that had reinforced its white ethnic look through an impressive Iberian immigration, and that had kept at least the facade of democracy. The Rio that Vasconcelos described never really existed, of course—he was carefully guided within the city, as he himself acknowledged. But the city he saw and invented to reinforce his ideas was a quasi-aristocratic, white, enlightened society that recalled the Mexico City of the Porfirian middle classes. Furthermore, his trip to São Paulo convinced him that industrial progress could be undertaken by Hispanic races. Four years later he again used São Paulo as the proof that "the fabulous rise of the American Middle West is being matched both agriculturally and industrially by the Latin Americans of Brazil."[86] In Minas Gerais (Belo Horizonte and Ouro Preto) he only saw the similarities with Mexico's great colonial mining towns: economic abandonment but bastions of marvelous architecture and national history. He saw political unrest but applauded the official government that maintained the impression of the order and progress he admired. In summation, Brazil became the perfect scenario for the performance of his image of Mexico. He never saw in São Paulo the *Paulicea Desvairada*.

Vasconcelos and his team acted as though they were starting from zero in Rio de Janeiro; from total chaos it was their honor and their right to create the cosmos they imagined. Yet they did not belong to the nonexistent first generation, to which Julio Torri aspired.[87] They were not creating new images for the nation but reproducing, reinventing, and overlapping old and new images. In essence, the image of Mexico in Rio de Janeiro borrowed from the revolution the circumstances that put Vasconcelos in the unforeseeable position of having control over the nation's symbols—and a ticket to Rio de Janeiro. But his destiny, his suicidal lover wrote in her diary, "was to awaken concerns without ever achieving control of the tiller of the boat that carried him off."[88]

THIRTEEN

The 1929 Seville Fair

One who follows blindly in a past generation's footsteps plunders that generation. One who creates a doctrine to be followed plunders future generations. Revolutionaries plunder the revolution. Nationalists plunder the nation. The avant-garde plunders its epoch. The exoticists, and the Mexicans among them, plunder what they find picturesque.

JORGE CUESTA, 1932

SEVILLE AND IMPERIAL NOSTALGIA

Between 1929 and 1930 a twofold Spanish exposition took place at the same time in Montjuic in Barcelona and in El Parque María Luisa in Seville. Whereas Barcelona's exhibit focused on industry, Seville's fair was fundamentally cultural and artistic. Only European nations sent significant industrial and technological displays to the Barcelona exposition. In common with the 1889 Paris world's fair, which displayed a "History of Habitation," Barcelona's fair also included a display called "The Spanish Town," a collection of exact replicas of traditional towns from all Spanish regions—a major exercise in modern autoethnography.[1]

In contrast, despite some controversies, Seville's fair was named *Exposición Ibero-Americana* and thus was joined by almost all Latin American countries, the United States, and Portugal.[2] On the inauguration day, José Cruz Conde, general commissary of Seville's exposition, said to King Alfonso XIII, "Certainly, Sir, since October 12, 1492, there has not yet been a single day in the history of America of more importance and spiritual significance than today, when the great Ibero-American Exhibition begins."[3] The fair was in fact the stage for the last act of the drama of imperial nostalgia and nationalism that characterized Primo de Rivera's era.

Plans to celebrate a world's fair in Seville had been in the making since 1905. In addition to interests of urban developers in Seville—who from the outset supported the idea of an exhibition in order to foster investment in urban transformation and sanitation—important ideological aspects favored the possibility of a world's fair in that city. This was an era of "decadent historical reality,"[4] and to commercially and spiritually reconquer America was one of the main goals of the exposition, especially after the war with the United States and its consequence, the loss of the last Spanish American colony, Cuba. Originally planned for 1911, and then for 1927, for numerous national and international causes the fair was deferred until 1928, and even then it was once again postponed to 1929. By then, the urbanistic needs of Seville had completely merged with the interests involved with the exposition. But "Ibero-Americanism was what motivated the central Spanish government itself to support the exposition in Seville."[5] In truth, Seville's exhibit was, as a Mexican observer argued in *Revista de las Españas,* "an objective expression of Spain's wish to reincorporate the Hispanic spirit into our ethnic family."[6]

La Plaza de España, designed in baroque Spanish style, was the center of the exhibit. In addition, there were galleries and pavilions from the various Spanish regions. Portugal, Brazil, Mexico, Argentina, Peru, Chile, Uruguay, Santo Domingo, Cuba, and the United States constructed original pavilions designed by their own architects. Colombia, Venezuela, and Guatemala hired Spanish architects to build their buildings.[7] Some maverick structures contrasted with the prevailing Spanish styles, and all shared a common goal: to honor the *Madre Patria* (motherland). In those days, the favorite metaphor was the image of the *madre piadosa* (clement mother) who was visited by her grown daughters; no hard feelings, no rancor, no guilt, but all warmly united in the arms of the Hispanic spirit.

Seville was organized in the fashion of the great fairs of the nineteenth century. Not only did its architecture follow the structure of the great French world's fairs of that period, but it also used a similar classification of exhibits. The exposition was divided into eleven sections: history, agriculture, mining, heavy industry, paper and graphic arts, light industry, communications and public works, education, sanitation, sociology, and statistics. As in the 1900 Paris fair, Seville's history exposition included anthropology (that is, skulls), archaeology, and ethnology. But the ethnology exhibit was subdivided into "Aboriginal Ethnology" (samples of the various primitive races, their habitation and crafts, and their daily life) and "Colonial Ethnology" (historical racial types, buildings, costumes, and arts). Within this ethnological classification various Mexican items were exhibited. In turn, what in 1889 the French fairs had started to call social economy was now laid out in the section of sociology, which included displays on social economy, workers' conditions, "*conflicto capital trabajo,*" and salaries.[8]

However, the aim of Seville's exhibit was not to portray the entire modern world but to modernize the idea of Hispanism, to give it a commercial and industrial connotation without losing its spiritual meaning. Therefore, in 1908 it had been proposed that the Americas' participation be limited to the "nations which were born into the world of civilization through the general collusion of *conquistadores.*"[9] Nonetheless, and in spite of serious resistance, the United States was finally invited, as was Cuba.[10] Indeed, Seville's exposition was a fiesta of Spain in every minute detail, from architecture to the official rhetoric, from the majestic Plaza de España to the organization of a contest for the best book to be read by Hispanic American children, a volume that would teach "love for Spain to the children of the newer Latin American republics."[11] Along these lines, in the interior of the neocolonial Peruvian pavilion were two sculptures, one depicting a Spanish conquistador and the other, a stylish Inca princess. In front of these two figures was a sculpture representing the Peruvian nation venerating both the Spanish warrior and the European-like Inca princess.[12] In the same vein, a Mexican book produced for distribution at the fair claimed that the conquistador was "the seed for our nationality."[13] A photographic collage depicted the rulers of Mexico as a natural line that went from Hernán Cortés to Emilio Portes Gil.[14] And on the walls of the Maya-style Mexican pavilion, Mexican officials had drafted a legend for all Spain to read: "Mother Spain: because you have illuminated American lands with the brilliance of your culture, and placed the devotional light of your spirit in my soul, now both in my land and soul those lights have blossomed. Méjico" (with a "j," the better to please Spain).[15]

Oddly enough, these were the Latin American homages to the Spain of Primo de Rivera, whose regime had organized the fair as part of a last-ditch effort to recover from an economic debacle—characterized by financial crisis, inflation, and unemployment—combined with political instability that included protests by workers, students, and intellectuals.[16] As we have seen, world's fairs had historically found a way to be mutually supporting with the politics of the host country. But not this time in Seville.

In addition, the Seville fair was to that date perhaps the most notorious modern expression of Spain's Hispanism, a tendency that was adopted by Primo de Rivera's regime as an official ideology. Diplomatic and commercial delegations were sent to Spanish American nations to strengthen the links of the Catholic "Hispanic family."[17] Hispanism consisted of a set of racial, psychological, historical, and strategic (geopolitical and commercial) explanations of the uniqueness and superiority of the Hispanic race. It was, incidentally, an ideology whose history was related to that of world's fairs. Since 1892 Spain had attempted to minimize the 1893 Chicago fair as the celebration of the "discovery" of America. The Spanish government commemorated the fourth centennial of the European presence in America with a historical exposition in Madrid that sought to show the greatness of Spain's civilizing historical role. In the same way, taking advantage of the 1900 Paris universal exhibition, the Spanish government requested the presence of all Spanish American envoys in Madrid to discuss the expansion of Hispanism in view of the recent Spanish-American War.[18] That same year, 1900, the Uruguayan José Enrique Rodó published *Ariel*—the emblem par excellence of Spanish American Hispanism.

But in 1929 neither the dictatorship of Primo de Rivera nor the international policy of Hispanism was especially supported in Mexico by Plutarco

Elías Calles, the *"jefe máximo"* of postrevolutionary Mexico. Of course, José Vasconcelos was a noted advocate of Hispanism, and in 1929 he included this ideology in his campaign for the presidency. But the strong Catholicism intrinsic to Hispanism, together with the uses of this ideology by Primo de Rivera's conservative and pseudomonarchist regime, made of Mexico's government an open, if soft, opponent of both. In 1929 Emilio Portes Gil's administration (1928–1931) finally gave official recognition to October 12 as the *"día de la raza":* the commemorative day not of mere Hispanism but of *mestizaje* (miscegenation), the day to honor both Columbus and Cuauhtémoc.[19] In turn, the crisis of the Spanish dictatorship was followed with great interest in Mexico. The poet Enrique González Martínez, then Mexican ambassador to Spain, eloquently described the situation: "I was blessed with the fortune of witnessing Spain still adorned with monarchic and traditional forms while republican sentiments spread among intellectuals and the Spanish community in general. These were moments of crisis which are convenient times for the awakening of popular feelings."[20] In 1930 Primo de Rivera resigned and left Spain, and the struggle to consolidate the Spanish republic began.[21] This turning point was saluted in Mexico even by a popular singer who composed a tune: "Spain! Spain! Your valor has crushed the monarchy / Spain! Spain! Your ancient history now has another glory thanks to your bravery."[22]

MEXICO AND SEVILLE, 1929

To this exposition and to this Spain, and despite its distaste, Portes Gil's administration dispatched a relatively large exhibit. Needless to say, the precarious political and economic environment that hampered Mexico's presence at the 1922 Rio de Janeiro exposition had scarcely improved in the intervening years, and, in fact, 1929 was a critical year in Mexico's postrevolutionary history. The more or less stable political status quo achieved by Obregón and Calles seemed to have been consolidated by Obregón's victory in the 1928 elections. But his assassination in the same year restarted the realignment of the revolutionary elites. During the provisional government of Portes Gil, Calles's growing power had to confront and negotiate, politically and militarily, with different factions. It was in this context that in 1929 Callistas and Obregonistas founded the Partido Nacional Revolucionario (PNR), direct antecedent of the long-lasting postrevolutionary Partido Revolucionario Institucional (PRI). However, when the rather obscure minister of Mexico in Brazil, Pascual Ortiz Rubio, and not Aarón Sáenz, who seemed to be Obregón's natural successor, was nominated as the PNR's candidate for the presidency, Calles's authority became all too evident. In 1929 the revolution made clear who was to be the caudillo who would form institutions.

But 1929 was also the year when the Cristero rebellion reached a critical point and forced the establishment of a new status quo between the Mexican government and the Catholic Church. Furthermore, it was the year of the Escobarista rebellion that put Calles back on the battlefield, while Vasconcelos began his quasi-messianic struggle for the presidency. All of this took place in an economy that had not yet recovered from the debacle of 1914 and 1915, aggravated by Mexico's recognition of its debt to American banks and by the international financial uncertainty that came to the surface in the black October of 1929. In such a context, it is rather amazing that the administration of Calles and, later, Portes Gil, joined Seville's fair, collecting Mexican products and manufactures, constructing a permanent building in Seville, and expending at least U.S.$125,000.[23]

Mexico's attendance at Seville's fair could, of course, be justified by the customary excuse of diplomatic reciprocity. Spain had sent delegations both in 1910, to the centenary of Mexico's independence, and in 1921, to the centennial celebration of the consummation of Mexico's independence. More importantly, in joining Seville's exposition Calles's government saw a chance to change the image of Mexico as a violent and chaotic country. It was also an opportunity to promote Mexico's products and art and to gain international prestige as an economically well organized and peaceful country.

Most of all, the fair was an occasion to exploit curiosity about, and to foster favorable international opinion of, the Mexican Revolution. In effect, among some activists and intellectuals in Europe and the United States, the Mexican Revolution had become an example to watch. To be sure, there also seemed to be what an official Mexican book at the fair called an attempt to "discredit ... the Revolution by the international press and capitalist propaganda" (for its violence and antipathy toward foreign capital).[24] But among some progressive international intellectuals and politicians the Mexican Revolution was seen as one of those rare moments when people seize control of their destiny. This was so in the arts, literature, and political militancy.[25] The Mexican government was willing to foster this body of opinion with new ideas and information. For instance, in 1929 González Martínez explained to the Spanish media: "While our sister countries in Latin America alternate periods of work with periods of rest, the Mexican people are obliged to designate half of their daily work to productive labor and the other half to the fight for liberty."[26] These were the ways (it was thought) to nourish the international romanticization of the Mexican Revolution that was beginning in the late 1920s. All in all, considering the size and ideological scope of Seville's fair, and considering especially Mexico's circumstances, one may wonder what it was about world's fairs that made them so appealing to the Mexico of Calles. Perhaps this decision was the result of historical inertia that makes things move the way they have always moved, or perhaps it was caused by a succession of ill-considered decisions that eventually made Mexico's presence in Seville inevitable.

In any event, from 1925 to 1927 there was a vigorous debate within the Mexican government about whether to take part in Seville's fair—and how. Among the participants were close advisers to President Calles, the Ministry of Foreign Relations, and the Ministry of Industry and Commerce. Finally, in 1926 the Mexican government accepted Spain's invitation, and the Ministry of Industry and Commerce, then headed by Luis N. Morones, was put in charge of all affairs related to Mexico's participation in the Seville exposition. Thus, at the beginning of 1926 the Mexican government made a call for design proposals for a Mexican pavilion in Seville. It was established that it had to be a provisional freestyle pavilion at a cost no greater than 90,000 pesos.[27] In April the winners were announced: first place went to Ignacio Marquina and Agustín García's design; the second, to the designer of the Mexican pavilion for Rio de Janeiro's world's fair, Carlos Obregón Santacilia; and the third to Alberto Mendoza. The fifth prize was awarded to a design made by a young Mexican architect from Yucatán, Manuel Amabilis, who eventually became the architect of the Mexican pavilion in Seville.[28] Marquina's design was for a pre-Hispanic style building that combined various parts of Uxmal's and Zayi's archaeological ruins.[29]

The Calles government soon realized that more money would have to be spent, and it was originally reluctant to assign new resources to Mexico's performance at Seville. However, once an affirmative response was given to Spanish authorities, Mexico had little choice, for it would be awkward to withdraw from participation or not to follow what other countries were doing. In this connection, González Martínez confidentially informed the Mexican government of the expenditures other countries were undertaking for their pavilions at Seville. He claimed that Argentina had assigned a budget of one million Argentine pesos[30] and that it was rather ridiculous for Mexico to spend only 90,000 pesos. Thus, by the end of 1926 the Ministry of Industry and Commerce had appointed three commissions in charge of Mexico's exhibit in Seville. The first commission was put in charge of the building and the exhibit itself; the second, of publicity and propaganda; and the third, of industrial promotion. In addition, a budget of 750,000 pesetas (U.S.$125,000) was approved,[31] and a new call for proposals for a building design was made in the beginning of 1927. The new building ought to be, it was established, a permanent, freestyle construction costing not more than 300,000 pesos. Amabilis's design of a Toltec-Maya building won this contest. The jury and the Mexican government decided to favor a pre-Hispanic building instead of, for example, the original neocolonial building proposed by Obregón Santacilia.[32] Hence, by the beginning of 1928 Amabilis was in Seville constructing his Maya-like building in El Parque María Luisa (see Fig. 40).[33]

Before examining Amabilis's building, let us consider how the officials in

40. The Mexican pavilion at the 1929 Seville exhibition. Source: SRE EMESP 523; reproduced courtesy of SRE.

charge of Mexico's display functioned. It is important to recall that, during the Porfirian period, world's fairs were considered important parts of industrial, commercial, and immigration promotion. By the 1920s, as we have seen, world's fairs had lost their nineteenth-century value as great showcases of the modern world. Therefore, a professional group of exhibition experts was not needed by the revolutionary governments. Nonetheless, in the early twentieth century, world's fairs were still an important way to promote a national image, something very much needed by the new revolutionary government to gain international acceptance. To produce this image at fairs for consumption abroad, the government did need in fact a small group of relatively professional bureaucrats, and the Callista governments sought to field such a team at Seville.

Originally the Mexican delegation was formed by Francisco A. Sáenz as president, Amabilis as chief architect (joined by the painter Victor Reyes and the sculptor Leopoldo Tomassi), and Rodolfo Ramírez, José M. Ramos, J. Montiel Olivera, and Luis R. Herrera as secretaries of the delegation.[34] In addition, the Mexican minister in Spain, González Martínez, was a fundamental part of this team. He was a modernist poet recycled in the revolutionary government, a bureaucrat who upheld, as the hypercritical Vasconcelos of the 1930s described him, "the diplomatic legation with modesty and grace," before he became "a militant *callista*, a revolutionary, and even a Bolshevik."[35] In mid-1929 Sáenz was removed from his post as president, and Rodolfo Ramírez provisionally headed the delegation until October 1929, when Francisco Orozco Ramírez assumed the presidency. The causes of these changes are unclear, but it is very likely that they reflected the harsh electoral processes which Mexico underwent beginning in March 1929, when Pascual Ortiz Rubio was nominated as the PNR's candidate for the presidency.[36]

This delegation had a rather inefficient and unorganized structure and functioning. They did not have a clear plan of action—how could they?— and hence they worked on a daily basis constantly consulting with the Mexican minister in Spain and directly with the various Ministers of Industry and Commerce—first Luis N. Morones, then Ramón P. Neri, and later in 1930, Luis L. León. Political and economic uncertainty prevailed throughout 1929 and 1930. Improvisations, overlapping of functions and changes of mind were all too common. There were constant communications with Amabilis asking him to take great care of the budget. In turn, Amabilis seriously complained many times of the economic restrictions he was living under: "I earn less than the most unskilled laborer," he complained in July 1928.[37]

In addition, serious internal problems made evident the existence of corruption and political frictions. This even caused some problems with Spain's legal authorities: at a country banquet organized by the Spanish contractor for the construction of the building (the Casso engineers) to celebrate the completion of the pavilion, Amabilis and Reyes resolved their disputes with alcohol and a brawl that concluded with the intervention of the police and the arrest of both.[38] Furthermore, in July 1930 a Mexican employee of the Mexican pavilion denounced to the Mexican government various irregularities apparently committed by the president of the delegation. These included robbery, fraud, and the hiring of a lover as an employee in the Mexican pavilion.[39] In effect, it seems that not only because of the officially indigenist pavilion but because of its administrative and political functioning, Mexico's presence in Seville was indeed a preview of the lasting postrevolutionary ideology and modus operandi.

THE MEXICAN PAVILION

In 1929 Manuel Amabilis (born in 1883) was an obscure architect from Yucatán trained at L'École Speciale d'Architecture, in Paris.[40] During the progressive administration of Salvador Alvarado in Yucatán, he was in charge of public works, and from this position he constructed the building La Casa del Pueblo in Mayan style. In addition, together with Colombian artist Rómulo Razo, he designed the Monumento a la Patria in Mérida. This was an indigenist monument that honored not only Mexican nationalism but especially Yucatecan nationalism. The monument summarized the entire history of Mexico, including pre-Hispanic times when, as Razo explained, "the land of the Mayans was a paradise."[41] For the Seville fair, Amabilis made a conscious effort to synthesize pre-Hispanic styles with modern construction techniques and uses of space. He wrote an explanatory book that was not only an architectural description but also, in fact, a historical, sociological, and artistic interpretation of what Mexico was and how it ought to be.[42] In it he aimed to explain, as he himself observed, why "Mexico presents itself to Europe through a shroud of ancient American tradition" and why this tradition "although scorned by the rich, bestowed worldwide recognition to the Mexican art scene. It is the Mexican Revolution that has had the honor of rescuing this tradition for the country."[43]

According to Amabilis, the triumph of the revolution had brought "an unknown national blossom, full of joy and well-being." The new Mexico needed a real Mexican art that could encompass its unique spirit. Although he realized that the search for the Mexican spirit had not ended, he observed that "while our philosophers may someday unravel the mystery of the spiritual ideal . . . we as artists are dedicated today to recording all aspects of this ideal, which has been revealing itself to our conscious minds." Thus he believed that his only role for the moment was "to achieve and recognize this communion of a native race, the love of an autonomous country."[44] Amabilis maintained that pre-Hispanic architecture could be adapted to modern standards of comfort and construction. Above all, to represent Mexico in pre-Hispanic native style, he asserted, was to express "in Mexican" feelings and thoughts that belonged to Western civilization: "This is our small contribution [*óbolo*] as Mexicans to the gestation and growth of the universal art that already influences contemporary European culture."[45]

The building was formed of two concentric squares. From each side of the smaller square a gallery was projected and crossed the sides of the larger square.[46] The two-storied structure had eight exhibition halls. The entire facade, surrounding fences, and a fountain in the outside gardens, were replete with sculpture in the same Maya-Toltec style (see Fig. 41). These were the work of Tomassi, a young sculptor and urbanist also from Yucatán. Among the pieces were two copies of Toltec stelae, placed to symbolize work and spirituality.[47] Both were conceived in materialistic terms: spirituality was understood not as ethereal but as the almost anatomical "synthesis of all positive functions of the human heart and mind." In addition, at the top of the building a sculpture of five figures expressed "the solidarity of all social classes for the progress of Mexico, which is one of the ideals of the Mexican Revolution."[48] These figures were represented not in pre-Hispanic fashion but in contemporary style. Thus, Amabilis argued, "the group symbolizes today's Mexico: emerging from a remote past that encompasses it, Mexico, a nation of Western civilization, actually arises to meet the modern day as in the symbolic sculpture; that is, surrounded by Toltec rhythms."[49] At the

41. Sculpture and fountain of the 1929 Mexican pavilion in Seville. Left to right: Victor Reyes, Leopoldo Tomassi, and Manuel Amabilis. Source: SRE EMESP 523; reproduced courtesy of SRE.

main entrance, two giant, plumed serpents served as columns. There Vasconcelos's dictum, "*Por mi Raza Hablará el Espíritu*" (For My Race the Spirit Shall Speak), was engraved in the frieze. Ironically, official indigenism was thus merged with Vasconcelos's Hispanism, and this in 1929, when the Mexican Ulysses was threatening the new revolutionary status quo with his presidential campaign.

In its interior, Amabilis's pavilion combined colorful decorative motifs, stained-glass windows, mural paintings, and bas-reliefs. The colorful decoration of murals and walls was part of the effort to make the pavilion look truly pre-Hispanic. The stained glass depicted Mexico's natural resources and tropical beauty with such titles as *El Papagayo, El Plátano,* and *La Palmera.* The bas-reliefs were four sets that the architect called *jambas:* allegorical representations of various historical topics. The most interesting of these *jambas* was that of the *Guerreros,* which portrayed both a Mexican and a Spaniard warrior because "our nationality is a product of their battles," and the *Jamba de la Fusión de las Razas,* which depicted Cortés, Malinche, and a child, "the first little mestizo."[50] Other bas-reliefs represented agriculture, sciences, traditions, and customs.

The most important mural paintings inside the building—all by Reyes—

42. Victor Reyes and his mural in the 1929 Mexican pavilion in Seville. Source: SRE EMESP 523; reproduced courtesy of SRE.

were located in the stairwell of the building (see Fig. 42).[51] There Reyes tried to do what Rivera was then doing in the National Palace. "Don Diego María Rivera," Amabilis explained, was the first to see "the profound sense of exile experienced by the Mexican people. Rivera awakens Mexico's joys and sorrows from this bitter indifference, in order to teach how to love this people so that through this love this nation can be directed toward an emancipation which is spiritual rather than material." By 1929 Rivera was becoming the prototype of the socially committed artist, the head of the Mexican revolutionary school, and although Amabilis shared Rivera's revolutionary populism, his argument was articulated in spiritual rather than in political and racial terms. Along these lines, Reyes painted a mural that covered the entire stairwell. The mural was in two parts. In one, out of the image of a Mexican woman, various motifs were depicted in a sequence of images, as Amabilis explained, like a film clip. In the other, the same effect was achieved with a male image. The female aspect of the Mexican race, one learns from Amabilis's description of the Reyes mural, represented opportunism; the masculine image stood above all for thinking and rationality: "from the representation of the masculinity of our race arise concepts and activities that attempt to implant ideals, create beauty, and perfect the human species. Conversely, from the female representation are derived practical, immediately obtainable concepts ... [because] those ideals of immense scope but difficult to secure are reserved for men."⁵² In sum, the Mexican pavilion condensed a relatively complete image of a revolutionary, more or less populist, modern, and virile Mexico.

In general, the pavilions of the rest of the Latin American countries at the exposition also seemed to be engaged in a conscious search for a "national style," so neocolonial hybridism prevailed. Peru, Argentina, Brazil, and the United States constructed neocolonial buildings with some type of local inspiration.⁵³ In contrast, the Mexican pavilion was exotic and eccentric, and during the exposition was known as the organ because its friezes bore a striking resemblance to the tubes of an organ.⁵⁴ Of course, the Catholic Spanish media criticized this Indian pagan building, as part of their campaign against the Mexican government for the expulsion of Spanish priests from Mexico during the Cristero rebellion.⁵⁵ These Catholic complaints not only emboldened others to criticize the Mexican building but also provoked King Alfonso XIII to reproach González Martínez for the expulsion of priests during the monarch's visit to the Mexican Pavilion.⁵⁶

In addition, some art critics complained less about the indigenist style than about the general anachronism of the art of Mexico and other Latin American countries. Pedro de Repide, in *La Libertad* (Madrid), not only complained that the art of most Latin American countries did no more than copy French aesthetics of the 1900s but also claimed that the indigenist tendency simply did not "come together" in the new circumstances.⁵⁷ On the other hand, pro-Hispanic Mexicans approved of the building, with some reservations. For instance, Rodolfo Reyes, the well-known son of Gen. Bernardo Reyes, who was then residing in Spain, stated that the Mexican pavilion was acceptable only as an evolution of the "matrix civilization" (that is, Spain). He claimed that "[in art] our people are imaginative apprentices with good intentions who rely on a few of our own indigenous traditions, such as the Maya and the Inca," and, he added, "the Asian exoticism [*primorismo*] of our indigenous races could be an important element to develop. However, the naturalist and instinctive qualities that we Mexicans boldly proclaim in our carvings and paintings are outlines to consider, rather than definitive directions to follow."⁵⁸

The architecture of the Mexican pavilion was only part of the total image of Mexico at Seville. The building's amalgamation of pre-Hispanic architecture with all sorts of representational techniques contrasted with the strong pro-Hispanic rhetoric to be seen in its interior. For example, engraved on the interior walls of the building was the above-mentioned legend "Mother Spain: because you have illuminated American lands with the brilliance of your culture . . . Méjico." Along these lines, in a propaganda article that was published in various Mexican and Spanish periodicals, Francisco A. Sáenz, president of the Mexican delegation in Seville, claimed that the Latin American countries were in Seville because "one single call from Spain to her daughters, now mature women, was sufficient" for them to come.[59] The general tone of Mexico's exhibit was that of veneration for Spain, but in a supposedly "mature" relationship. "Spain, upon inviting and receiving us, demonstrates a generosity beyond rancor. In attending her noble exhibition, we affirm our Spanish ancestry and take pride in our spirit and blood line," González Martínez maintained.[60]

In fact, Reyes had drafted more legends to accompany the various allegories throughout the interior of the building—allegories of the national culture, the male and female races of the nation, and the legislators' instruments (that is, the constitution, land reform, and labor laws). One of them read: "Three beacons illuminate the culture that Mexico imparts to her children—three foundations nourish it: European civilization, Christianity, and Mexican traditions." These legends were never actually used in the building, but they epitomized the ideological aspects that Mexico wished to emphasize. Reyes's inelegant prose was not considered appropriate, however, and the idea was dropped.[61]

Nonetheless, the Spanish government was pleased with this Mexican Hispanism—so much so that the mayor of Seville wrote a letter of gratitude to the Mexican delegation that expressed not only Spain's gratitude but also Andalucía's pride, in an even more pompous rhetoric: "Certainly: Spain illuminated American lands with the brilliance of her culture. However, the creative vigor emerged from the fertile lands of Andalucía and from the no less fertile lands of Extremadura. . . . Indeed, Spain has also illuminated Mexico's soul with the lamp of her devotional spirit, but this lamp was nourished by Seville's holy oil."[62] Oddly enough, as late as the 1992 Seville world's fair, the phrase was still recalled with great pride by a local historian of Seville.[63]

EXHIBITING REVOLUTIONARY MEXICO

Framed in indigenist architecture, with an overlay of Hispanist rhetoric, Mexico displayed exactly the same agricultural products, pictures, books, and crafts that had graced the preceding fifty years of its presence at world's fairs—tropical fruits, coffee, cocoa, cactus, hats, and gaudy ornaments, together with the same seemingly eternal products of industry: beer (Cervecería Cuauhtémoc), cigarettes (El Buen Tono), and canned food (Clemente Jacques). All of these industries had been part of Mexico's displays since the 1880s. What was new about the industrial exhibit were the displays of petroleum companies (Huasteca Petroleum, El Águila, and so forth) and the bas-relief of Plutarco Elías Calles, made by Julio Sosa, which replaced the bust of Porfirio Díaz that was always displayed in nineteenth-century world's fairs.[64]

However, as discussed above, the Mexican display in Seville appealed not only to the imperial Hispanism of the fair but also to the international fascination with the Mexican popular revolution. As such, it was extremely well received by republican Spanish intellectuals. This reception—and Mexico's use of this favorable opinion—was especially visible during the week of the exposition that honored Mexico in June 1930. By then the Mexican exhibit was directed by Orozco Ramírez, who organized a set of events that featured Mexican and Spanish intellectuals and artists who were favorable to the Mexican Revolution.[65] The Mexican musical folklorist Ignacio Fernández and the poet Luis G. Urbina were the only official Mexican participants during this week (although it was also attended by the poet Jaime Torres Bodet). Thus a radio session of poetry reading (once again with verses by Nervo, Díaz Mirón, and González Martínez) was combined with talks by the Spanish intellectuals and activists Luis Araquistáin and Fernando de los Ríos. Araquistáin spoke about Mexico's social evolution and was extremely favorable to the social transformation produced by the Mexican Revolution. He characterized it as the first real Hispanic social revolution, and he added, "Politically, Spain has never been truly European, but Asian or African." Thus, in the Mexican Revolution "not only is the historical credibility of a nation pledged, but also the credibility of an entire race."[66] For his part, de los Ríos delivered a paper titled "En Torno a la Tierra y el Alma Mejicana, Impresiones y Recuerdos." Both were socialists in the struggle against Primo de Rivera's regime, and both used the Mexican Revolution as a cosmopolitan symbol of modern social politics and development.[67] Mexico promoted those ideas with its exhibition in Seville, without damaging its pro-Hispanic conservative tone. Thus began Mexico's official policy of making the revolution its passport to the modern cosmopolitan world.

As always, Mexico organized a good propaganda network that consisted of national and international journalists and writers paid by the Mexican government.[68] What was new about this network was the massive use of cinema for propaganda purposes. The United States impressed the Spanish public with its film *Hoover in Spanish America*, among many others,[69] but the Mexican exhibit showed at least ten movies with titles such as *El Museo Nacional, Yucatán: La tierra del afamado henequén, Industria de la plata, La industria del petróleo en México, San Juan Teotihuacán,* and *Ruinas de Yucatán*.[70] A specially produced movie about the economic and industrial development of Mexico was also shown,[71] and numerous photographs that portrayed Mexico's beauty and progress as well as its exoticism were exhibited. Old and new masters of those images were present: Hugo Brehme, Guillermo Kahlo, Tina Modotti, and Manuel Álvarez Bravo.

Some people opposed the exhibition of the same exoticism that had been featured in the past. For instance, the Mexican consul in Berlin, F. R. Serrano, wrote in 1925 to Aarón Sáenz, then minister of foreign affairs, that Mexico ought not to send "pranks," by which he meant huaraches, tequila, pulque, and Indian textiles: "I find it contradictory that on the one hand we try to expunge the white cotton trousers and leather sandals [*guaraches*] of the Indians from our nation, while on the other hand we make an effort to exhibit these articles in foreign countries."[72] Nonetheless, the pictures and figures of *tipos populares*, Indian cloth, huaraches, furniture in Aztec and Maya styles, and traditions were displayed just as they had been in the nineteenth century.[73]

Despite this opposition, Mexico's efforts were rewarded. The nation won a total of 137 grand prizes, 23 honor diplomas, 368 gold medals, 462 silver medals, and 286 bronze medals.[74] In general, the winners were those items that reflected Spanish expectations of Mexico. Mexican authors such as Vasconcelos, Federico Gamboa, Urbina, José Juan Tablada, González Martínez, Jesús Galindo y Villa, and Antonio Caso were granted grand prizes and honor diplomas for their books. A collection of *tipos populares* made in wax by Juan Lechuga was also awarded a grand prize, as were the architect, the painter, and the sculptor of the Mexican pavilion. But books dealing with colonial Mexican art were especially welcomed: Dr. Atl's book on Mexican churches, Manuel Toussaint's on the Mexican cathedral, and Manuel Gómez Morin's *España Fiel*. The new Mexican literature earned some acknowledgments but no grand prizes. José Gorostiza won a silver medal with his *Canciones para cantar en los barcos,* Ortiz de Montellano won gold with *El trompo de siete colores,* and gold was also given to Julio Jiménez Rueda, Salvador Novo, and Xavier Villaurrutia. But best received was the romantic popular music of Mexico, which was already acquiring a nostalgic nature: Alfonso Esparza Otero, María Greaver, and Manuel M. Ponce were awarded grand prizes and honor diplomas. They represented Porfirian high culture transformed into a popular romantic sensibility.

WELCOME TO TWENTIETH-CENTURY MEXICO

Mexico's presence at the 1929 Ibero-American Exposition in Seville was a debut for the postrevolutionary official notions of the Mexican modern nation. Although the Mexican display was not essentially different from those Mexican exhibits at nineteenth-century world's fairs, it highlighted some aspects and included some new elements of the nation's image. There was neither the liberal-positivist consensus nor the loyalty to the supreme caudillo that had given coherence and order to Porfirian displays. Neither was there the prevalence of a single point of view shaped by the virtu of a personality that intrudes into history, as was the case with Mexico's attendance at the Rio de Janeiro world's fair. Undoubtedly the idea of Mexico depicted in 1929 was intellectually contradictory and ambivalent about its own identity, as well as unclear in political and administrative terms. Notwithstanding, culturally one could see it—of course from the historian's advantageous point of view— as displaying the basic milieu in which notions such as nation, progress, and modernization would be discussed throughout the twentieth century. This is a realm constituted by a set of old and new ingredients, combined with old and new tactics.

In brief, I would argue that Mexico's presence at Seville can be seen from two perspectives: from the continuity of intellectual and cultural tendencies that, though long-established, had acquired special cohesion during the Porfirian peace; and from the view of the emergence of new languages, strategies, and elements that both reinforced and changed the traditional continuities. After all, I am dealing with snapshots of modern Mexico, and hence whatever fluctuation I notice may be irrelevant before the full sweep of Mexico's history. Yet in these flashing instants (that is, world's fairs) change—when present—is nicely perceivable.

The continuities were noticeable in the focus on the nation's natural wealth and beauty, as well as in the glorification of the Indian past of Mexico. They were also in the artifices used to achieve both the impression of natural wealth and the historical glorifications; that is, in the use of artistic, scientific, and rhetorical devices that were as cosmopolitan and modern as possible. Thus Mexico's tropical fertility and beauty were represented in stained-glass windows, in statistics, in samples of exotic fruits, or in photographs and murals. The overall aim was to highlight the possibilities for commerce and investment and to appeal to the twentieth century's new industry: tourism. In contrast, Mexican industrial exhibits changed scarcely at all in composition from those of the 1890s.[75] All in all, Mexico's presence at Seville did not put particular accent on this issue. In this regard, and from what it is possible to perceive, Mexico's exhibit in Seville was carried on as a rather old-fashioned policy of commercial and industrial development.

Continuities were especially evident in the cultural aspects Mexico highlighted in an exposition that dealt above all with ideology and culture. In addressing issues such as race, national spirit, and modernization, Mexico's presence at Seville made use of a warehouse of the nation's basics, and it included scientific, symbolic, artistic, and intellectual *utilería* (assorted stage material). As I have maintained throughout this study, when considering nations, nationalism, and modernism, what is essential are forms, styles, and experiments; in these regards, history is our main instructor.

To illustrate these continuities, Amabilis's pavilion was a curious amalgamation of Indian styles with modern construction techniques and requirements. On the one hand, it was inspired by the expanding anthropological and archaeological studies that were heavily promoted during the administrations of Obregón and Calles. Miguel Othón de Mendizábal, Moisés Sáenz, and even Manuel Gamio—though he had a profound disagreement with Calles—were fundamental in this advancement of anthropology and archaeology, which eventually fed the artistic and populist official indigenism. Most of these archaeologists and anthropologists believed in the need to incorporate Indians into modern national development. Their works and research were a continuation of the aim to reach an autoethnology acceptable and useful both for the nationalistic needs of the Mexican elites and for the demands of the modern scientific perspective of the Western world. This aim had a long history in Mexico, but it was especially developed within a modern scientific framework during the Porfirian peace.[76] In Seville, for Mexican officials there was no other language in which to talk about such topics as race, acceptable evolutionary paths that proved Mexico's adequate racial shape, and potential for the future of a hybrid race, than that furnished by the long-established processes of trial and error and discussion of the last part of the nineteenth century. In this sense, the very fact that the Mexican pavilion was above all about race underlines the deep-rooted continuities.

These tendencies were expressed in Amabilis's pavilion. But in so doing he was only, as he argued, trying to propose a tentative combination of styles that could eventually form the national style.[77] Just as the Mexican colonial building in Rio de Janeiro favored one of the various profound cultural and intellectual historical tendencies, Amabilis's building favored another kind of deep-rooted national trend. For its tentative character, for its indigenism, as well as for the official decision to introduce it as a symbolic summary of the nation, the Mexico display at Seville was a continuation of how modernity and nationalism had been culturally constructed in Mexico since the 1880s. Features of this continuity were, first, constant and conscious internal negotiations and disputes regarding symbols and epic; second, constant reading and rereading of prototypical recent Western conceptions of modernity and nationalism (from Europe or from the United States), searching both for arms to fight the national discussion and for an edge as to where to insert the national debate into the course of modern cosmopolitanism; and finally, by means of all the above, an endless trial-and-error process led by elites, who adjusted and maneuvered the image of the nation according to new domestic and international circumstances in favor of their own interests.

What best illustrates this continuity are the other pre-Hispanic building planned for Mexico's presence in the 1889 Paris fair—the Aztec Palace, another attempt, another set of goals, another world, but essentially the same recipe and identical ingredients, so to speak—and the building constructed by Lázaro Cárdenas's government for the 1937 Paris international exhibition. If in 1889 the Porfirian government opted for Peñafiel's building, it was because of the coherence with which it epitomized the official historiography. But in the very feat of erecting an Aztec Palace at the 1889 Paris world's fair, the Porfirian elite showed its decision to favor pro-indigenist national tendencies in view of the European cosmopolitan demands for the exotic. They thought such a building would give them the best opportunity to acquire presence and visibility at Paris, "capital of the nineteenth century."

It was a trial they rejected afterward. In the same way, Calles's decision to construct Amabilis's building favored the indigenist national tendencies, but it was based also on the perception of the potential effect it would have on both European exoticism (important for tourism) and on the international artistic and political rediscovery of Mexico after the revolution.[78] Furthermore, it was combined with a pro-Hispanic rhetoric that made the exotic building both attractive and acceptable.

In sharp contrast, for the 1937 Paris international exhibition of "arts and techniques of modern life," Mexico constructed a Functionalist-style pavilion. That fair would be remembered for its avant-garde architecture and massive, fascist, and socialist arts, as well as for the display of Picasso's *Guernica*. Among Mexican officials and intellectuals, a long debate took place regarding whether to join the 1937 fair, and how. Finally, Lázaro Cárdenas's government decided to attend. Of course, a regime with a socialist rhetoric, with indigenist and nationalist policies, and, more importantly, with severe economic difficulties did not aim to present a Porfirian-like display in Paris. However, money was expended in constructing a pavilion, and despite the fact that the exhibit emphasized arts, the Mexican government sent the repeatedly exhibited official propaganda of statistics, maps, exotic products, and proofs of Mexico's beauty. In 1937, once again, Mexican officials and intellectuals debated about whether to build an indigenist structure (as in Paris 1889 or in Seville 1929) or a colonial structure (as in Buffalo 1901 or in Rio de Janeiro 1922). Manuel Chacón, engineer in charge of the construction, argued that archaeology should not be confused with architecture. Although it seemed natural for Cárdenas's government to favor an indigenist style, Chacón explained that a pre-Hispanic national architectural style was impossible because it was hopeless to try to reconstruct the old structures and their utility, which were understood only by their original creators. For him, a colonial style was also an "archaeological style."[79] Nonetheless, as in 1889, in 1900, or in 1929, the Cardenista government used the old rules of trial and error and showed that it had learned its lesson. That is, in 1937, using the tired and long-in-the-making artistic infrastructure, Mexico constructed a building in the most avant-garde cosmopolitan style in order to publicize new and old pragmatic goals (tourism and foreign investment) (see Fig. 43). In addition, Mexican officials clothed in an international fashion what they had made into Mexico's most cosmopolitan product: the Mexican Revolution and its social and cultural surroundings. Therefore, they constructed a cosmopolitan, if small, Functionalist-style building at the Trocadero, with a giant sculpture of a campesino with a sickle and a worker with a hammer. Conceptually and architecturally, the building was far from the Aztec Palace of 1889, from the neoclassical building of 1900, or from the Maya pavilion of 1929, but it was close, physically and conceptually, to the giant

43. The Mexican pavilion at the 1937 Paris world's fair. Source: AGN, Centro de Información Gráfica, colección presidentes, Cárdenas; reproduced courtesy of the Archivo General de la Nación, Mexico City. (Photograph by the Archivo General de la Nación)

Nazi building of Germany and the no less enormous and modernist building of the Soviet Union. It also appealed to international concerns with the Mexican Revolution.

To return to 1929, Mexico's presence at Seville can also be seen as depicting the transformation experienced by Mexico and the world in the 1910s and 1920s. In brief, by 1929 the revolutionary governments of Mexico had not yet radically transformed the social and economic shape of the country. What the popular movements of the Mexican Revolution had done to the image of the nation was, on one hand, to radically change the balance of political and economic power and thus of the nation's symbols and metaphors. On the other hand, these movements had fostered the emergence of a new language to describe new situations but also to rephrase old circumstances.

In terms of cultural and intellectual creation, the decade of the 1920s represented a creative looseness of authority: fertile creative ground to take advantages of disorder, to abuse alliances, and to merge ideas.[80] In Mexico's presence at Seville, therefore, former leading intellectuals of the last part of the Porfirian modernist movement—such as González Martínez and Urbina —were working together with technocrats trained in the best fashion of the

Porfirian era—that is, Amabilis—with new iconoclast artists—Reyes and Tomassi—and with the revolutionary bureaucracy, particularly sensitive to the political movements in Mexico—that is, Francisco A. Sáenz and Orozco Muñoz. From the beginning, the entire exhibit was organized by the more radical faction of Obreristas through the Ministry of Industry, Commerce and Work—that is, first Morones and later Neri. This combination—in the last analysis inevitable for any revolutionary government wishing to establish a stable regime—facilitated the amalgamation of various tactics and views of the image of the nation.

It was possible, thus, to portray the country as experimentally indigenist, with great concern for the solidarity of all classes in the national reconstruction but also universally Hispanic. This Mexico was above all inclusionist: it merged Porfirian symbols of order and progress and Porfirian indigenism with Vasconcelos's focus on race and spirit and with Gamio's type of indigenism, all combined with a more or less radical populist rhetoric.

The new language forged for the revolution was a synthesis of the many revolutionary demands by the various groups during the violent struggle. It was also made of the striking experience of the urban intellectuals and political elites: the city taken by Indians and mestizos, all poor, threatening the Mexican belle epoque. Now it was possible to refer to the history of the nation as preparing the real great event: the revolution. Everything else became antecedent. Now it was possible to name them with pride: our Indians, our popular classes. It was also possible to talk about class struggle, but not without mentioning the existence of solidarity of classes in the common will of national reconstruction. And all that acquired an acceptable aesthetic representation in the 1920s and 1930s. This was Amabilis's building.

In 1929 it was impossible to control all of the various aspects involved in this new language and to see where it might go. Thus some sort of socialist radicalism, Catholic philanthropism, social realism, and romantic idealism had to flow freely in what seemed to have an unclear structure. In Seville, Mexico's symbolism acted like a shotgun: it was a rain of bullets aiming to hit all perspectives in order to miss no opportunity. Yet it already included what eventually became a centralized, officially imposed image of Mexico: a selective anthropological, archaeological, and political indigenism, a rewriting of the national history to change the moment of emergence of the country's golden age, a strong tendency toward both homogenizing and mythologizing revolutionary symbols, and reconstructing the understanding of the nation by decree. Mexico was tropical, fertile, beautiful, fundamentally virile, statist, and populist. This was not so much a new image of Mexico as a redefined one, fabricated with long-established ingredients and tactics.

This redefinition would not have been possible without yet another revolution: the crisis of Western politics and thought during the 1910s and 1920s. A new aesthetic and political language was created with the avant-garde movements in Paris, with the Russian Revolution of 1917, and with World War I. In fact, the Spanish fair sought to be for Europe the proof that there was a not fully European option to revitalize Europe: Spain. The Russian Revolution and the international socialist movement, as well as workers' general discontent, had made socialism appear to be the twentieth century's greatest hope—and Mexico's redefinition of its image appealed to these transformations. Of course, Mexico's presence at Seville's exposition did not display its avant-garde facade, not because there were no Mexican innovative intellectuals who could have helped to modernize the image of the nation in this direction but because Seville's fair was already anachronistic. Eventually, world's fairs would be held in which Mexico would be able to camouflage the same nationalism in avant-garde art and architecture (for instance, Paris 1937). But Mexico did display its new social concerns at Seville, which was, after all, a rather imperialist and conservative exposition. It seems to be that for the image of the nation, Mexico's social revolution had to be exploited as Mexico's best chance to be accepted in twentieth-century modern terms. In effect, the Mexican Revolution was being transformed not only into a national unifying myth but also into a patrimony of the truly modern world. In the last analysis, during the 1920s and 1930s very few minds foresaw the powerful ideology that was in the making. But how can anyone ever interpret the hints of history when the past is present?

Epilogue

From the 1880s to the 1920s an enduring nationalistic infrastructure was created in Mexico, one whose development has been examined here through a study of the traces left in world's fairs. The development of a Mexican national image in modern times included a historical cornerstone (the Indian past and an epic-mythical foundational structure), racial definition (either criollo or mestizo), natural appropriation (the beauty of land and its productivity), economic position (protection of a national bourgeoisie, search for foreign investment, immigration, and economic recognition), and the pursuit of cosmopolitan culture. These aspects were only specific expressions of the global phenomenon of modern nationalism. Some final remarks are needed, both to clarify my approach and to offer some general propositions.

THE LIMITS OF THE APPROACH

In modern times nationalism became both anational and unavoidable. In essence, nationalism was neither a purely domestic output nor a culturally productive force. It constituted an intricate global phenomenon, a molding power that, rather than giving rise to new and original cultural phenomena, reoriented, revitalized, and rearranged existing cultural features and tailored a comprehensive ideology that was assumed to be a unique and natural historical production. That is, modern nationalism emerged as a sculptural will that recast its appropriated raw materials: traditions, customs, social and scientific ideas, and history. As a result, we live in a world of nationalistic nations, in which each appears to be an exceptional and inimitable product of the same sculptor.

But I have examined only a small, though emblematic, part of the complex issue of modern nationalism and its particular unfolding in Mexico (see the introduction), namely, national images. Accordingly, I have considered modern nationalism in this book essentially as cultural and political centralization, homogenization, and constant adaptation to new ideas, technologies, and circumstances. Once developed, nationalism became a quasi-ontological requirement of modernity. This homogenization generally occurred within (or aimed to create) the physical and historical boundaries of modern nation-states, so nationalism is linked to state formation.

I am fully aware of the limitations of my approach and also conscious of the areas I have left untreated. Therefore, one way to clarify what I hope to be the significance of my project is to lay out a clear picture of this book's explored as well as unexplored terrains.

Although the picture of a modern nation is always presented as a homogeneous, natural, dominant, civilized, and genuinely historical outcome, in fact it is a particular expression of the continuum of interactions of modern nationalism's main components: the interplay between tradition and modernity, non-Western and Western trends, popular and elitist expressions and interests. Thus modern nationalism can be seen as the arena, historically constituted, in which each new and old nation-state tries to develop a synthesis of history, culture, and traditions that can be presented as unique yet universal. By the late nineteenth century the universal parameters were dictated by the predominant model of a modern nation that has been in ascendance in Western history since the Enlightenment. Nonetheless, modern nationalism is far from a homogeneous and stable dominant ideology. It is the complex arena in which all nations define each other by affirmations or negations and in which modernity and tradition, popular and elitist interests, inside and outside, lose their clear distinctions.

I study that arena through a very delimited analytical window: national images created for world's fairs from the 1880s to the 1920s. But although my analysis is narrow, it is also, I believe, revealing because it has moved freely in the very manufacturing arena of modern nationalism. Accordingly, my approach has centered on the elite's making of nationalism, on the interaction of the global model of nationalism and its particular transformation, adaptation, and rejection by the builders of a new nation.

One vast terrain I have left unexplored is the realm of the fragmented, domestic, traditional, and popular; the zone in which local senses of belonging interact with central notions of nations; in which alternative cultural views enter into conflicts and negotiations, most of the time in relation to universal parameters set by modern nationalism as a global phenomenon,[1] but also at times rejecting and/or influencing the particular definition of the nation. This crucial aspect deserves to be studied in depth. It deserves another book.

The fact that I have left this terrain unexplored should not be considered as either a political or a theoretical disdain for alternative approaches. As this study has shown, the dissection of the making of a modern nation involves an elaborate tissue of histories. I have not, nor could I have, treated them all. On the other hand, I have shown where and how national images have been debated in modern times, and I have thereby exposed the fragility, artificiality, and contingency of modern nationalism. But in doing so I have not sought to disclose the route toward a solid, genuine, and real nation. The "real" nation, whatever that might be, is neither at the central arena where modern nationalism is debated nor at the local popular level in which various ideas of the nation may interact (very often sharing references to the central arena). Power for inclusion, exclusion, and centralization has been at play in the historical composition of nationalism. But I am unable to arm myself with absolute truths about the essential principles related to nationalism; I cannot aim to kill the "dragon" of power with the sword of the "real nation." My aim has been more modest: to expose the "dragon's" entrails.

CLARIFYING THE SOURCES OF MODERN NATIONALISM IN MEXICO

What or who made the global idea of modern nationalism possible? I have addressed this complicated question only briefly. Scholars debate the origins of nationalism, but its final genealogy is unattainable. Elucidation of the issue is beyond the scope of this book, but I have dealt with a special sort of nationalism: postcolonial nineteenth-century nationalism. For this kind of nationalism, to talk about pristine origins is misleading because this type of nationalism is a product of imperialism and globalization. What is generally accepted is that nationalism is an inherent part of modernity and that by the nineteenth century it was a comprehensive phenomenon whose real center and original focus were diffuse and obscure.[2]

As a modern product, I have contended that a nationalistic ideology, especially in its depiction of a national image, is engineered primarily within the web of power. In each country the creation of a national image was undertaken by those with power in reference to other national images, because only through this globalization did these images make sense. A relatively clear "standard" of nationalism thus emerged.

In the late twentieth century, to be French, German, Mexican, or American has profoundly popular connotations, but the ways in which the symbolic, lexical, and scientific bases of nationalism were created were only marginally popular. This is not to say that popular customs, beliefs, and claims were not included in nationalist ideologies; but a national image is inclusive and linked to often centralized (socially and/or geographically) particular interests and can interact or oppose localized, popular senses of belonging. Alternatives to the established national image were and are present throughout history, and they influence the creation of a national image depending on their economic or military strength as well as on their coherent articulation and social and political resonance. But modern nationalism is fundamentally not about authenticity but about efficiency, defined as two mutually dependent goals: the maximization of domestic economic and political gains (always historically defined) and the achievement of and contribution to nationalism as an international, global phenomenon.

ON IDENTITY AND THE LEVIATHAN'S LIMITS

Local, regional, or even, to some extent, today's national identities are as undeniable as they are difficult to define.[3] For us, late-twentieth-century citizens of nation-states, to fully dissect the components of our nationalism would be like trying to remove from our bodies the clothing bequeathed to us by our modern nationalistic education. The difficulty arises because it seems that when this kind of garment leaves our bodies, it takes our skin with it; to be without a national image is to be naked, identity-less, which is to be either insane or a traitor. This should be clear: this book is not about identity; at no point have I tried to scrutinize the sense of belonging of the people.

Nationalism is only partially related to the overly discussed issue of identity.[4] On one hand, inasmuch as homogenized, centralized, and powerful notions of a nation are presented as official and exclusive syntheses, various identities are affected. On the other hand, nationalism requires the constant influence, transformation, destruction, and reinvention of local traditions and identities. The destinies of the various identities within a nation are constantly being negotiated in the framework of modern nationalism. But until the emergence of comprehensive hypermodern mass production and industrialization, national identity remained an oxymoron: if the identity of a people was to be reflected by a nationalist ideology, the idea of a single nationwide identity was itself the negation of almost all identities included in what we now understand as a nation-state.

Power is needed not only to create the national image but also, as the psychoanalyzed Marxists of the 1970s used to say, to introject this image in the people. Before the appearance of the printed media, education, and electronic media, the main lessons of civic religion were epitomized by capital cities, monuments, and national histories. In Mexico these methods were only effective for the urban middle classes. As in nineteenth-century France or Spain, in Porfirian Mexico the model of citizenship applied only to those who rejected social anonymity. In the Middle Ages theocentric morality, though inclusive and rigid, could not contain everything. It left various geographical and cultural spaces untouched and free for the rich and sinful popular culture of the era. Modern nationalistic ideologies reached their impressive comprehensiveness in recent times, and the late-nineteenth-century ideologues of nationalism could have not imaged the proportions their ideological offspring would eventually acquire in a mass industrial society.

Nonetheless, because of its particular approach, this study may seem to insinuate that a national image is merely a Leviathan's matter. The focus of the book has been on the specificities of the creation of the national image, and that is why the power of Mexico's Leviathan might have appeared distorted.[5] Indeed, in regard to the creation of a nationalist ideology, the power of the Mexican Leviathan was both absolute and insignificant. That is, the Porfirian state's source of strength was in its role as the administrator of wealth and power and as the custodian of peace. Precisely because of its success as arbitrator of peace and wealth, the Porfirian state won exclusivity in the management of Mexico's modern national image. But there its power ended. In other countries the nation was made essentially to be taught, to be learned by the majority of the people. Instead, in Mexico the nation created in the nineteenth century was made primarily to be exhibited, and only then did it become—restrictively—teachable.

In the nineteenth century Mexico was a set of largely rural, illiterate, dispersed, and heterogeneous societies. In such a context, the Leviathan's power to impose a nationalist ideology was not only limited but also self-consciously confined. Therefore, the nationalist power of Mexico's Leviathan resided in its control over the national image to be exhibited, in its narrow capacity to teach the nation to a small but influential urban middle class, and in its very self-awareness of the impossibility of spreading the idea of the nation to the whole country.

In making the nation by exhibiting it, the agents of the Mexican state made possible that, domestically, the nation was understood as a show, as a uncommon occurrence. The nation was not an individual feeling but a collective, if ephemeral and exceptional, celebration. Gradually Mexican cities and towns began to create a nation by acting it out in countless local and regional exhibitions, parades, and gatherings. In doing so they showed an essence that did not actually exist: the nation. Industrial homogenization of the population, educational and technological transformations, and social conflicts and confrontations eventually made those performances a commonsensical world view. The nation was then made possible because it was a shared and comprehensive drama, not because it stopped being a performance.

It would be difficult, on the other hand, to claim that the articulation of modern national images by elites possessed a class character in the strict sense of the word. Doubtless nationalism was maneuvered and reformulated according to the particular interests of those with political and economic power. But more than being the pure reflection of the character of a single class, nationalism was marked by the conditions of negotiations among and within the classes that articulated it. That is to say, modern national images required diverse domestic mediations among competing economic interests, political aspirations, intellectual views, cultural perspectives, and local social circumstances. Furthermore, these bargains always remained part of a larger discussion with international circumstances, pressures, intellectual influences, and cultural implications. The results of this process were both intricate (as was the whole negotiation) and provisional. Nations were always in the process of being created, consciously aiming to extend themselves beyond particular interests.

Other aspects of the conditions of negotiation of the national image are stamped in the image, particularly the regional identity of the articulators and their unquestioned assumptions that are rarely negotiated. Therefore, the national image of Mexico was dictated by the collage of victorious economic and military elites that had Mexico City as their final destination. As Paris became France, or New England the United States, Mexico City gave shape to the nation by ignoring or selectively appropriating features of other regional and social identities. In addition, the images of each nation included various issues that were taken for granted: gender, racial, political, and cultural features that were rarely negotiated.

In the case of Mexico, thus, from the 1880s to the 1920s nationalism as a global, coherent, comprehensive reshaping of the country's image was managed by elites. As David Brading has so lucidly been pointing out since the 1970s, the criollo nationalism of the late colonial period and early nineteenth century could rely on a truly inclusive and popular worldview to articulate a patriotic explanation of the existence of their nation. This was a real lingua franca among criollos, mestizos, and Indians, and it was made possible only after centuries of one of the most successful conquests of souls in the history of humankind—an ideological triumph that encompassed cities, towns, and the most remote sites—that is, Catholicism. Doubtless the Virgin of Guadalupe became a syncretic popular symbol of a nationalistic ideology during the independence period. But this unifying myth was created in the place of popular myths and through the conscious will—as don Edmundo O'Gorman showed—of both clerical authorities and intellectuals.[6] In the same way, although Abraham Lincoln became a popular national hero in the United States for northerners and southerners after the Civil War, the cult and justification of his heroism were calculated by a political and intellectual elite that, for example, discussed down to the last detail the characteristics of a monument to the slain president in Washington during Reconstruction.[7]

Modern Mexican nationalism nonetheless gave rise to a civic religion that was (had to be) not only secular but also laden with some Jacobin hints donated from a history of popular-religious rebellions and of conservative-versus-liberal encounters marked by foreign interventions. The constitution of this civic religion could not encompass overnight the geographical and social map of the country. And it need not have done so. The makers of the new nationalist doctrine were urban elites whose common socialization was not a product merely of secret societies. They were a restricted, close-knit group that ruled the country as if it were their patrimony; they did business together, married each other, and were buried together. In fact, the civic religion required not that all persons in Mexican territory be Mexicans but that they become so only when they were incorporated into the real environment of late-nineteenth-century national citizenship: the cities and the market.

Throughout the nineteenth century, foreign interventions and wars of liberation, together with local cultures and senses of belonging, gave rise to various popular patriotisms.[8] In wars and in discourses, the articulators of nationalist ideologies used and abused those popular patriotisms. People opposed, adapted, readapted, and learned to cope with the national image. The real Mexico has never existed: the national image officially created was indeed fake, but neither could popular patriotisms conform to the real nation. However, we late-twentieth-century historians tend to talk in these terms because we have assigned ethical value to the idea of nation, and we may never finish doing so. It might already be past the time, as the German writer Robert Musil suggested back in the 1920s, to come out with a new moral that would not consider either the nation or the state "as ideals, but simply as objects that have to correspond to their ends."[9]

NATIONALISM AND PERIPHERAL MODERNIZATION

In countries like Mexico, which came out of a process of decolonization and arrived late at modern industrial development, nationalism acquired a specific feature epitomized by the inseparable link between nationalism and modernization. For Mexico, nationalism is especially anational because it has been historically linked to modernization. That is, for an economically peripheral country, nationalism was above all an economic dictum, both a requirement for and the main consequence of modernization; this is a historical formula grounded in the idea that modernization came from the outside. To be a modern nation meant to follow, ambivalently but constantly, the paradigmatic model of Europe or the United States. Modern values, capital, and technology were not inside but outside the country. Therefore, nationalism and modernization became interchangeable terms, and whenever one or the other had to be negotiated, there materialized the dichotomy of a traditional, backward, and obstructing inside versus a progressive, modern outside. The notion of a modern nation is introduced as a cosmopolitan model to which all modern nations adapt their own uniqueness. That uniqueness is itself a fundamental requirement of global nationalism, but it is not the only requirement. What I have sought to show is that even those who arrived late participated in and contributed to a gathering that in fact had no clear hostess, a party that was randomly organized and in which no one knew what it was about and when it was to conclude.

Certainly, there were dominant cultural trends monopolized by certain regions, but nationalistic and modern ideas were never complete, static, harmonious historical entities; instead, they were dynamic, ambiguous, and in the making. All modern elites wished to share those ideas, so the gathering of modernity, rather than being a by-invitation-only cocktail party controlled by a few selected ones, was a bacchanalian feast, a promiscuous orgy of ideas and trends of all sorts, which nonetheless was dominated by the nouveaux riches who were anxious to procure all sources of economic and cultural capital.

However, the dichotomy between a traditional inside versus a modernizing outside has been expressed differently in the various postcolonial nation-states. These differences derived, first, from each country's particular history and, second, from the moment of independence—in the case of colonial countries—or from the moment of acceleration of a nation's drive to the "West." Mexico's or Latin America's nationalisms are nineteenth-century phenomena of colonies that were dominated by "peripheral" Western countries. Their nationalist elites articulated a view of the inside-versus-outside dichotomy that was different from, say, that held by the elites of twentieth-century India, for whom the nationalisms of the Americas were an inherent part of modern Western nationalism. To twentieth-century anticolonial Indian nationalists, it was clear that "the greater one's success in imitating the Western skills in the material domain . . . the greater the need to preserve the distinctness of one's spiritual culture."[10] For late-nineteenth- and early-twentieth-century Mexican nationalists, the goal seemed to be what a 1940s Brazilian poet expressed in a line: to be "submerged in the past, every day even more modern and more antique."[11] They aimed to modernize both the present and the interpretations of the past in order to acquire not just a national epic but a modern national epic.

Mexico, like the rest of Latin America and the United States, was an intrinsic ingredient in the making of modern Western nationalism.[12] The independences of the Americas were historical experiments of liberalism, nationalism, and republicanism. Europe and the Americas mutually shaped modern nationalism. But the new countries of Latin America were not sufficiently Western to duplicate the West and not sufficiently non-Western to be taken as the West's radical other. They were the forgotten side of the West.

Therefore, Mexico vis-à-vis the West appeared to be traditional, backward, and not fully Westernized. Mexican and Latin American elites have seen nationalism, democracy, and modernity as a whole as mirror images. Modernity is outside, so the country needs to reflect the large image reflected by Western modernity. But that large image is already made up of various mirror reflections of Europe's own historical playing of tradition-modernity, progress-backwardness, self-other. The mirror effects do not end there: what is considered Western modernity, reproduced by the elites of countries like

Mexico, is in turn superimposed in the colonized country on many domestic mirrors that reflect both local images and also their own versions of the large image of modernity. These diverse interactions of mirrors shape the nationalism of a country like Mexico, so this type of nationalism is simultaneously cosmopolitan, parochial, modern, traditional, and, especially, illusory.

Nationalism in Mexico has been, thus, a process of trial and error aimed simultaneously at modernization and at nationalism, all within the inescapable global scope of modern nationalism. The inside and outside became increasingly illusory. From the historian's point of view, it appears to be that at some point in history all national images began to be forged and experienced together.

MEXICO: THE PERSISTENCE OF THE "OLD REGIME"

I have aspired to show how, in the specific context of the creation of Mexico's national image, the maze of continuities and breaks between the prerevolutionary and postrevolutionary periods is much more labyrinthine than often thought. There exists the widespread belief that the ideology of the postrevolutionary government was above all nationalist and that if there is a term that best defines Porfirian ideology, it would be modernization. To say that the Porfirians were also nationalists and that the postrevolutionary elites were indeed modernizers is to say very little. As explained above, nationalism and modernization in countries like Mexico are linked in a historically established union, within which both prerevolutionary and postrevolutionary thinkers functioned. Each of their nationalist statements related to modernization; and all modernization efforts brought about discussions of nationalism.

We can conclude from this study that, at least for the specific phenomenon of the creation of a national image, there are different levels of goals.[13] At the epochal-teleological level, so to speak, there is indeed great continuity between the goal sought by the prerevolutionary and the postrevolutionary elites, inasmuch as there is continuity in the global beliefs in progress, modernity, and nationalism. Both the Porfirian and the revolutionary elites aimed to create a workable balance between domestic particularities geared to fulfill universal patterns of economic and cultural nationalism and general modernization. Hence, to say that the corporatist system established by the revolution was neo-Porfirian in the sense that it meant authoritarian modernization is to argue at a high teleological level in which we all can agree.

At a second level of goals, there are significant differences in the creation of national images. This is the level of historical specificity. First, to put it simply, the late-Porfirian model was gradually leading toward a modern, cosmopolitan, urban nationalism in the style of French universalism. In this sense, the nation was presumed to be a homogeneous Westernized construct, oriented toward the international market and scientifically ruled and organized. White immigration and foreign investment were key components of this concept. Despite the fact that American institutions were considered models for national development, the image of the nation was created following the example of French universalism. The United States likewise looked to the French. However, the United States found in the idea of frontier, nature, and rampant industrialism a source of uniqueness that made the American nation both original and universal. Mexican elites, in contrast, appealed to the raw material from which all nationalisms are made: history. Reorganizing, inventing, and reinventing the past epic—especially through a peculiar recapitulation of what Brading calls criollo patriotism—the Porfirian elite rearranged the national graphic representations and rhetoric that had been in the making since colonial times. One might liken modern nations to giant warehouses that store the paraphernalia demanded by modernity and nationalism. There one could find, in overlapping piles, the various understandings, sundry experiments, and constructing side of today's nationalistic common sense, all awaiting possible new uses. Indeed, as long as modern nationalism continues to prevail, whatever lies in those warehouses may find new uses again and again.

Porfirians used and abused their pre-Hispanic past, and this reinforced a Porfirian indigenism. To consider such indigenism as merely an insignificant trend of purely aesthetic consequences would be like contending that Lázaro Cárdenas's land reform had only geological and botanical implications. Porfirian indigenism was fundamental in the construction of the national image not only because there is no way to understand the culture of Mexico's fin de siècle without it but also because it was not a domestic but a cosmopolitan component of nationalism as a whole. Porfirian indigenism was located at the junction of aesthetic, anthropological, archeological, sociological, and medical universal discussions. Never before was the national epic so much a part of Western civilization. It was therefore as scientific as it was racist; it was as laden with social and philanthropic concerns as with exoticism and orientalism; it was as much an ethnography as an autoethnography.

At this second level of objectives, the Porfirian national image differed from the postrevolutionary image in its directly pragmatic aims. The nation imagined by Mexican elites in the late nineteenth century was reminiscent of a family patrimony. An internationally acceptable image (which included the recognition of Mexico as a secure, sanitary, free, sovereign, liberal, republican, and democratic country) translated into internal legitimacy and economic benefits (investment, migration, and commerce). The main concerns were internal negotiation between national elite and foreign interests and the administration of peace and order. Beyond their internal—and important—conflicts, elites had no interest in political and social forces. A democratic facade was kept in order to maintain the image of the modern nation intact, but there was little interest in making that image available and acceptable to the vast majority of the population.

At this level of specificity, the image gradually assembled by the postrevolutionary government drastically altered the Porfirian goals. It was claimed that Mexico was indeed national for the first time: it was popular, mestizo, and Indian. It was considered a Mexico for all Mexicans and for the world to see as a modern mestizo nation. Instead of white immigration and foreign investment, the new national image had equally practical goals: industrialization, national and foreign investment, tourism. Moreover, due to the chaos produced by the revolution and by widespread popular mobilization, the goals of the new image of the nation were even more pragmatic: to obtain not only international recognition but also internal cohesion, concentration, and consolidation for the new revolutionary elite. But Mexican masses made their debut in an international era of mass politics, and thereafter they have had to be more clearly considered in the articulation of national images. In essence, the new revolutionary image of the nation was not more popular but more populist.

The pragmatic goals of modernization and nationalism were forced simultaneously by internal circumstances and by international transformations. The postrevolutionary national image was indeed new and original, not because of its authenticity but, rather, its efficiency: the revolutionary governments soon realized that it was the very symbol of the revolution that could make the image of the nation radically national and at the same time more universal than ever before. This represented a profound break with the previous image of the nation that had always been on the border of disqualifying parochialism or crass, mimetic universalism. Just as Michelet found in the French Revolution the key to making France the epitome of modernity and universalism, so Mexican historians, artists, and diplomats with official backing made the Mexican Revolution Mexico's greatest passport to universal modernity.

The revolution, it seemed, had made Mexico more Mexican. Accordingly, in the early 1920s the perceptive Mexican poet Ramón López Velarde believed that "the country's material relaxation, in thirty years of peace, nourished the notion of a pretentious and multimillionaire *patria* which was honorable in its present and epic in its past. These years of suffering have been necessary to conceive a less external, more modest, and perhaps more beautiful *patria*."[14] However, by 1940 a canny Mexican intellectual, Jorge Cuesta, wrote to the Mexican president: "When all is said and done, the Revolution is a *national political truth,* but now it seems almost totally a *lie,* a *maneuver.*"[15] This duality indicated—as some years later the Mexican historian Daniel Cosío Villegas would point out—both the political and social failures of the revolution and its great accomplishment. For Mexico's nationalism, the revolution had become a "national political truth" (though some, like Cuesta, realized that it was a "maneuver"). If, as some believe, the revolution was a national war of liberation, its new and lasting effect on Mexican nationalism did not derive from its presumed anti-imperialist character —which could be seen as a reformulation of the old criollo anti-Hispanism—but from its universalist potential as a mass popular movement in an era of mass politics and social revolutions. In fact, the revolution became the patrimony of the nation, as much as its territory or its indigenous past did, and as such it was manipulated and maneuvered. The revolution became one with the nation, and all Mexicans were required to recognize themselves in it. In terms of the national image, this was the revolution's greatest achievement.

The visible break at this second level of goals can be understood only by analyzing the various means by which the image of the nation was constructed. It can be said that it is in the realm of means that continuity is both most prevailing and most astonishing. The images of the nation had been created through a trial-and-error process of maneuvering domestic phenomena, interpreting what were believed to be universal trends, and adjusting and readjusting. Such a process was carried out by means of an overall authoritarian negotiation that often resulted in a forced centralization and homogenization. Regardless of the specific content of the image of the nation, in Mexico that image has always been officially created, promoted, and canceled by a central (in political and geographical terms) authority. Therefore, the formalities of modern nationalism and the requirements of changing ideas of modernization have been fulfilled in a drama in which, though the characters and lines may have changed, the plot, costumes, and stages have remained the same.

It could be said that the Porfirians were right: Mexicans gradually became Mexicans and came to identify themselves with a modern national image. Mexico underwent an impressive socioeconomic transformation during the 1940s and 1950s. Just when the country was becoming more urban, industrial, consumerist, and relatively literate than ever before, the popular heroes comprised a bizarre mosaic of urban life and Bohemia, together with bucolic nostalgia, a combination that almost all Mexicans shared and that only Mexicans of the time fully understood. If, as the late-nineteenth-century liberals imagined, to be Mexican meant to share one language, one race, and one spirit, then by the 1950s Mexican nationality had never been so concrete an entelechy.

Within this twentieth-century cultural transformation, the long-in-the-making nationalistic ideology was adopted and thus transformed. The nationalistic infrastructure continued to be propagated and re-created by a rather authoritarian revolutionary family, according to sundry and changing interests and circumstances. But just as Indians had learned the catechism in their own way, so twentieth-century Mexicans adopted the nationalistic symbols as their own, but in unimagined ways. By the 1950s we find Guadalupe, Juárez, and Zapata as much in evidence at soccer matches where flags and chauvinism reached unbelievable levels, as we do on the streets of East Los Angeles as symbols on the tattooed skin of brown bodies. The symbols went back and forth from San Francisco to Tijuana, from Chicago to Monterrey, from Mexico City to Mérida. And the central control and monitoring of that symbolism became increasingly dispersed. Nonetheless, the care and organization of the official national image remained in the hands of centralized power holders.

By the 1950s, however, there was both a pride and a price in the historical act of being Mexican. As the Porfirians dreamed, large portions of the population were finally incorporated and formatted as Mexicans. Patriotic lessons were both acted and learned through a multiplicity of means—schools, monuments, discourses, media, patriotic celebrations. But together with the pride and festivity of flags and sombreros, there was great woe in the inevitability of being Mexican. By the 1940s Mexicans sensed both the anguish and the pride of reciting *"México creo en ti"* (Mexico, I believe in you), knowing that this faith was always counteracted by the certainty that the nation "laughs a lot, perhaps because [it] knows that laughter is a silent woe." Of course, the revolutionary return to nationality was something to be proud of, but also something inevitable: "To our nationality we return because of love, and because of poverty,"[16] observed Mexico's national poet, Ramón López Velarde. By the 1950s the radios of the rapidly growing Mexico City were broadcasting countless official speeches, commercials, and popular romantic songs that unveiled the ways of being sensually and proudly Mexican—a sentimental milieu that was also a legacy of Porfirian times. One popular tune was sung by a mulatto woman, in whose metaphoric and sensual mouth trembled "the painful groan / of a race full of bitterness." The song made Mexicans dance for their own "bronze race," a race that had been born valiant, but solely "To suffer all of its misfortunes / To suffer all of its misfortunes."

Appendix 1

The Porfirian Wizards of Progress

Name	Dates	Profession	Fair Experience	Expertise
Altamirano, Francisco	1848–1907	Physician	Paris 1889, Chicago 1893	Medicine, hygiene, natural history
Anza, Antonio M. de	1847–1925	Engineer, architect	Paris 1889, Chicago 1893, Paris 1900	Chief architect of Mexican pavilions
Bablot, Alfredo	?–1892 (born in France)	Singer, musician, journalist, bureaucrat	Philadelphia 1876, Paris 1889	Fair organization, music
Bárcena, Mariano	1842–1899	Engineer	Philadelphia 1876, New Orleans 1884, Chicago 1893, Paris 1900	Statistics, education, agriculture
Baz, Gustavo	1852–1904	Diplomat, writer	Philadelphia 1876, Paris 1889	Railroads, propaganda, general organization
Best, Alberto	—	—	Paris 1889, Chicago 1893	Electricity
Busto, Emiliano	1844–1897	Economist	Paris 1889	Public administration
Caballero, Manuel	1849–1926	Journalist	Chicago 1893	Propaganda

255

APPENDIX 1

Name	Dates	Profession	Fair Experience	Expertise
Camacho, Sebastián	—	Engineer (mining)	Philadelphia 1876, New Orleans 1884, Paris 1889, Paris 1900	Industry, mining
Casasus, Joaquín	1858–1916	Lawyer, statistician, writer	Paris 1889, Paris 1900	Political economy
Chabert, Maximiliano M.	1868–1964	—	Chicago 1893, Paris 1900, Buffalo 1901, Saint Louis 1904, Boston 1908	Education, liberal arts, general organization
Chavero, Alfredo	1841–1906	Lawyer, writer, historian	Philadelphia 1876, New Orleans 1884, Paris 1889, Saint Louis 1904	Arts, history, propaganda
Chávez, Agustín	—	—	Chicago 1893	Machinery
Cházaro, Esteban	—	—	Chicago 1893	Natural products
Contreras, Jesús	1866–1902	Sculptor	Paris 1889, Paris 1900	Sculpture
Crespo Martínez, Gilberto	1853–1916	Engineer	New Orleans 1884, Paris 1889, Chicago 1893	Mining
Cuoto y Cuoto, Manuel	—	—	Chicago 1893	Transportation
Díaz, Porfirio	1830–1915	Military officer, president	New Orleans 1884	Director of the Mexican Central Committee[a]
Díaz Dufoo, Carlos	1861–1941	Economist, journalist, writer	Chicago 1893, Paris 1900	Propaganda
Díaz Mimiaga, Manuel	—	Diplomat	Paris 1889	Chief commissioner of Mexico's presence

[a] Also indirectly involved at all international exhibitions as the supreme authority of Mexican presence.

Name	Dates	Profession	Fair Experience	Expertise
Donde, Rafael	1834–1911	Lawyer, writer	Philadelphia 1876	Organization
Escandón, Pedro	1824–1877	Entrepreneur	Philadelphia 1876	General organization
Fernández, Leandro	1851–1921	Engineer (geodesy)	Paris 1889	Industry, public works
Fernández, Ramón	—	Diplomat	Paris 1889	General organization
Fernández Leal, Manuel	1831–1909	Engineer	Chicago 1893, Paris 1900	Ministry of Economic Development, 1892–1909
Ferrari Pérez, Fernando	?–1927	Teacher, naturalist, biologist	Paris 1889, Chicago 1893	Liberal arts, Comisión Geográfico-Exploradora
Fleury, Juan de D.	—	—	Buffalo 1901	General organization
Flores, Manuel	1853–1924	Teacher, educator	Paris 1889, Paris 1900	Industry
García Cubas, Antonio	1832–1912	Engineer, geographer	Philadelphia 1876, New Orleans 1884, Paris 1889, Chicago 1893, Paris 1900	Geography, statistics, progaganda
Garibay, Enrique H.	—	—	Buffalo 1901	General organization
Genin, Auguste	1862–1931	Entrepreneur, ethnographer, writer, poet	Paris 1889, Paris 1900	Propaganda, industry, ethnography
Godoy, José Francisco	1851–1930	Diplomat, writer, journalist, publicist	Philadelphia 1876, New Orleans 1884, Paris 1889, San Antonio 1890, Chicago 1893, Paris 1900, Buffalo 1901, Seville 1929	Propaganda

APPENDIX 1

Name	Dates	Profession	Fair Experience	Expertise
González, Gregorio E.	—	—	Atlanta 1895	General organization
Gostkowski, Gustave	—	—	Paris 1889, Paris 1900	Propaganda
Lancaster Jones, Alfonso	1842–1903	Lawyer, diplomat, writer, publicist	Philadelphia 1876, New Orleans 1884 (and other American fairs)	Propaganda
Lascurain, Ramón	—	—	Chicago 1893	General organization
Liceaga, Eduardo	1839–1920	Physician	Paris 1889, Chicago 1893, Paris 1900 (and others)	Hygiene and sanitation
Mancera, Gabriel	1839–1925	Engineer	Philadelphia 1876	General organization
Maria y Campos, Ricardo de	—	Lawyer	Paris 1889 Chicago 1893, Paris 1900	Commerce, financial organization of fairs, propaganda
Martínez Baca, Francisco	—	—	San Diego 1899, Buffalo 1901, Saint Louis 1904	General organization
Mier, Sebastián B. de	—	—	Paris 1889, Paris 1900	General organization; Mexican commissioner for Paris 1900
Mier y Celis, Antonio	1834–1904	Entrepreneur, diplomat	Paris 1889, Paris 1900	Industry, general organization
Mondragón, Enrique	—	—	Buffalo 1901	General organization

Name	Dates	Profession	Fair Experience	Expertise
Nuncio, Albino R.	—	Engineer	Atlanta 1894, Omaha 1898, San Antonio 1899, Buffalo 1901, Saint Louis 1904, Boston 1908	Chief organizer
Obregón, José	1832–1902	Painter	New Orleans 1884, Paris 1889, Chicago 1893	Canvases with pre-Hispanic motifs
Pacheco, Carlos	1839–1891	Military officer	New Orleans 1884, Paris 1889	Minister of Economic Development, in charge of exhibitions
Paso y Troncoso, Francisco del	1842–1916	Historian, writer	Paris 1889 (and others)	Pre-Hispanic history
Paz, Ireneo	1836–1924	Lawyer, journalist, writer	Paris 1889, Paris 1900	Propaganda
Peñafiel, Antonio	1839–1922	Physician, archeologist, historian, statistician	Paris 1889, Chicago 1893, Paris 1900	Ethnology, anthropology, statistics
Ramírez, José	1852–1904	Physician, naturalist	New Orleans 1884, Paris 1889, Chicago 1893, Paris 1900	Natural history, bacteriology
Ramos, José	1859–1909	Physician	Paris 1889	Medicine
Ramos Arizpe, Rafael	—	—	Paris 1889, Paris 1900	General organization, electricity
Rincón Gallardo, Pedro	1836–1891	Military officer	New Orleans 1884	Agriculture

Name	Dates	Profession	Fair Experience	Expertise
Río de la Loza, Maximino	1830–?	Inventor, chemist	Paris 1889 (and others)	Inventions
Romero Rubio, Manuel	1828–1895	Politician	Philadelphia 1876	Organization
Salazar, Luis	1849–?	Engineer	Paris 1889, Saint Petersburg 1892 (Congress of Railroads), Paris 1900, Saint Louis 1904	Electricity, transportation, pavilion construction
Segura, José C.	1845–?	Engineer	Philadelphia 1876, New Orleans 1884, Paris 1889, Chicago 1893, Paris 1900	Agriculture
Sellerier, Carlos	—	Engineer	Paris 1900, Buffalo 1901	Mining
Senties, Pedro J.	—	—	Paris 1889, Chicago 1893	Agriculture
Serrano, Miguel	1842–1916	—	Paris 1889, Paris 1900	Education, chief organizer
Valdés, Rodrigo	1851–1930	Military officer	Paris 1889, Paris 1900	Military exhibitions, mechanics
Velasco, José María	1840–1912	Painter	Philadelphia 1876, Paris 1889, Chicago 1893, Paris 1900	Landscape painting
Viadas, Lauro	—	Engineer	Buffalo 1901, Saint Louis 1904	Agriculture
Vigil, José María	1829–1909	Historian, educator, writer, librarian	Philadelphia 1876, New Orleans 1884	Education

Name	Dates	Profession	Fair Experience	Expertise
Zamacona, Manuel María de	1826–1904	Lawyer	Philadelphia 1876	General organization, political negotiations
Zárate, Eduardo E.	1853–1913	Lawyer, writer	Philadelphia 1876, New Orleans 1884, Paris 1889, Chicago 1893, Paris 1900	Manufacturing
Zayas Enríquez, Rafael de	1848–1932	Lawyer, writer, poet, sociologist	Paris 1889, Paris 1900	Propaganda

Appendix 2

The Economic Cost of World's Fairs

Considering the size of Mexico's economy during the last part of the nineteenth century and bearing in mind that world's fairs were only ephemeral events, Mexico's expenses for late-nineteenth-century Parisian world's fairs were impressively high. The cultural value given to world's fairs and their significance for Porfirian development policies seemed to justify these expenditures. By the twentieth century, Mexico's expenditures in world's fairs had dropped drastically, for two reasons: world's fairs lost their cultural and developmentalist importance, and Mexico had political difficulties and a new revolutionary regime.

The table that follows summarizes the available information about the costs of fairs for Mexico. Although the total cost of Mexico's presence at Paris 1889 constituted only 11 percent of the expenditures of the Ministry of Economic Development for the year 1889 (compared with 31 percent for Chicago 1893 and with 46 percent for Paris 1900),[1] it was the highest sum ever paid by Mexico in a world's fair. What explains the variations in the percentage for the Ministry of Economic Development is the reduction in resources it suffered after the creation of the Ministry of Public Works in 1891. In addition, in 1893 the silver crisis reduced the Mexican government's total expenditures for 1893 and 1900.

Both Yeager and Riguzzi argue that Mexico's expenditures in Chicago were the highest (a total of U.S.$700,000), and they estimate expenditures of Mexico in Paris 1899 as only U.S.$400,000. I believe these figures reflect only the original budget assigned to each event. Indeed, Mexico's original budget for Chicago was planned to be the highest, but the silver crisis nullified the plans. In fact, the construction of a Mexican pavilion in Chicago was also canceled, and the cost of transportation could not have been as high as that of transportation to Paris. In addition, although originally Mexico planned to spend around U.S.$400,000 (approximately 400,000 pesos) in Paris 1889 (as reported by the *Anales* of Economic Development and by the *Cuenta Pública* of the *Contaduría de la Federación*), the detailed information found in the archival material—which in part was collected by Sebastián B. de Mier for his report on Mexico's participation at the 1900 Paris fair—shows that Paris 1889, first, and Paris 1900, second, were the most expensive exhibitions staged by Porfirian Mexico. Even in a preliminary summary account made in May 1891, total expenses were 500,442.63 pesos (1,976,748.40 francs), without including the cost for the rest of 1891 and 1892 (especially the cost of disassembling the Mexican pavilion and transporting the pavilion, products, and personnel back to Mexico).[2]

1. For the fiscal year 1888–1889, and 8 percent for the year 1889–1890. Between these two years, the budget assigned to the Ministry of Economic Development was significantly increased (from 5.3 million pesos to 7.5 million pesos). This increase was in part due to the expenses for the 1889 exposition. See México, El Colegio de México, *Estadísticas económicas del porfiriato: Fuerza de trabajo y actividad económica por sectores* (Mexico, n.d.), 250.

2. See Yeager, "Porfirian Commercial Propaganda," 234–35; Riguzzi, "La imagen nacional en el porfiriato," 148–50; and Mier, *México en la Exposición Internacional*.

Exhibition	Pavilion	Estimated Cost of Exhibition				
		in pesos of the time	in constant (1889) pesos	as percentage of total expenditures for that year	as percentage of Ministry of Economic Development expenditures	as percentage of Ministry of Justice and Education expenditures
London 1851	none	—	—	—	—	—
Paris 1855	none	—	—	—	—	—
Paris 1867	none (private participation)	—	—	—	—	—
Philadelphia 1876	none	—	300,000[a]	—	—	—
Paris 1884	none (private participation)	—	—	—	—	—
New Orleans 1884	The Mexican Alhambra	200,000	198,020	0.4	1.7	24.7
Paris 1889	The Aztec Palace	605,318	605,318	1.7	11.3 (1888–89) 8.0 (1889–90)	45.4
Madrid (Historical Exhibition) 1893	none	—	—	—	—	—
Chicago 1893	none	183,391–200,000	131,936–143,885	0.4–0.47	31.0–34.0	7.3–7.9
Atlanta 1895	none	—	—	—	—	—
Nashville 1897	none	—	—	—	—	—
Omaha 1898	none	—	—	—	—	—
Paris 1900	Neoclassical building	523,972	436,644	0.9	46.8	19.7
Buffalo 1901	Spanish-colonial building	61,780	47,523	0.1	5.5	—

Saint Louis 1904	Spanish-renaissance building	—	—	—	
Boston 1908	none	4,137	2,586	0.1
San Antonio 1909	none	—	—	—
Rio de Janeiro 1922	Colonial building	—	—	—
Seville 1929	Pre-Hispanic building	322,500[b]	179,166[c]	0.8
Paris 1937	Modern crystal building	—	—	—
New York 1939	Modern building	—	—	—

SOURCES: EXP; México, El Colegio de México, *Estadísticas económicas del porfiriato: Fuerza de trabajo y actividad económica por sectores* (Mexico City, n.d.); México, Secretaría de Fomento, *Anales de la Secretaría de Fomento*, various volumes (Mexico City, 1877–1910); México, Secretaría de Hacienda, *Boletín*, 1915–1932; México, Tesorería General de la Federación, *Contaduría de la Federación: Cuenta pública*, various volumes (Mexico City, 1877–1909); Sebastián B. de Mier, *México en la Exposición Internacional de París—1900* (Mexico City, 1901); SRE; see texts.

[a] Based on limited information.
[b] This figure represents only the cost of the buildings. No more precise information is available.
[c] Constant prices for 1929 are calculated according to price index for Mexico City only, as presented in México, Secretaría de Programación y Presupuesto, *Estadísticas históricas de México*, vol. 2 (Mexico City, 1985).

NOTES

Abbreviations used in the notes are listed on page 331.

PREFACE

1. "For all things proof is found / and also a reason to support everything / and there is no explanation at all because there is so much explanation" (Sor Juana Inés de la Cruz, "Acusa la hidropesía de mucha ciencia, que teme inútil aun para saber y nociva para vivir," in her *Obras completas*, vol. 1 (Mexico City, 1951), 5–8.

INTRODUCTION

1. For the historical emergence of the concepts of modern and modernity that I use here, see Hans Ulrich Gumbrecht, "A History of the Concept 'Modern,'" in *Making Sense in Life and Literature*, ed. H. U. Gumbrecht (Minneapolis, 1992), 79–110.
2. Alan Trachtenberg, *The Incorporation of America* (New York, 1982), 209.
3. José Ortega y Gasset, *La rebelión de las masas* (Madrid, 1930), 22.
4. RUP 1:338.
5. For notions of commerce within world's fairs, see Paul Greenhalgh, *Ephemeral Vistas* (Manchester, 1988), 22–23.
6. Helix, "The Industrial Exhibition of 1851," *Westminster and Foreign Quarterly Review* (April 1850), quoted in ibid., 27.
7. "Exposition Universelle Internationale de 1900 à Paris," quoted in *Le Livre des expositions universelles, 1851–1889* (Paris, 1983), 105.
8. John Brisben Walker, "What the Louisiana Purchase Exposition Is," *The Cosmopolitan*, September 1904, 405.
9. Gumbrecht, "History," 94.
10. Charles Baudelaire, "Exposition Universelle 1855: Beaux-Arts," in *Oeuvres complètes* (Paris, 1968), 361–70.
11. See Tatsushi Narita, "Eliot and the World's Fair of St. Louis: Collateral Evidence of His Fairoutings," *Nagoya City University Studies in Social Sciences and Humanities* 38 (1984):1–23; and Tatsushi Narita, "Eliot and the World's Fair of St. Louis: His 'Stockholder's Coupon Ticket,'" *Nagoya City University Studies in Social Sciences and Hu-*

manities 36 (1982):1–24. Both articles were originally written in Japanese, with English abstracts. See Narita's note, "Fiction and Fact in T. S. Eliot's 'The Man Who Was King,'" in *Notes and Queries* 39 (June 1992):191–92. I thank Peter Stansky for having called my attention to Eliot's relationship with world's fairs.

12. See Fyodor Dostoyevsky, *Notes from Underground*, trans. Michael R. Katz (New York, 1989), 18.

13. Henry Adams, *The Education of Henry Adams* (Boston, 1915), 345.

14. J. R. Hawley, "The Value of International Exhibitions," *North American Review* 149 (September 1889):317.

15. *La Typographie Française*, 1 July 1889, quoted by M. Reberioux, "Au tournement des expos: 1889," *Le Mouvement Social*, no. 149 (1989):6.

16. G. Flaubert, *Dictionnaire des idées reçues*, ed. Lea Caminite (Paris, 1966), 78.

17. Various studies of nationalism have influenced my historical approach, most especially Eric Hobsbawm, *Nation and Nationalism* (Cambridge, 1990); Benedict Anderson, *Imagined Communities* (London, 1983); Roger Bartra, *La jaula de la melancolía* (Mexico City, 1987); E. Gellner, *Nations and Nationalism* (Oxford, 1983); Liah Greenfeld, *Nationalism* (Cambridge, 1992); José Murilo de Carvalho, *A formação das almas* (São Paulo, 1990); Pierre Nora, ed., *Les Lieux de mémoire*, 2 vols. (Paris, 1984); David Brading, *The Origins of Mexican Nationalism* (Cambridge, 1985); Partha Chatterjee, *Nationalist Thought and the Colonial World* (Tokyo, 1986); Kenneth Cmiel, *Democratic Eloquence* (New York, 1990); and Hans Kohn, *The Idea of Nationalism* (New York, 1944).

18. For modes of expressions of universal exhibitions, see Pascal Ory, "Étude comparée du centenaire et du cent-cinquantenaire de la Révolution Française," in *Les Images de la Révolution Française*, ed. M. Vovelle (New York, 1990), 2177–83.

19. Paul Groussac, *Del Plata al Niágara* (Buenos Aires, 1925), 324, 346.

20. Virginia Woolf, "Mr. Bennet and Mrs. Brown," in *Collected Essays*, vol. 1 (London, 1966), 320.

21. Eric Hobsbawm, *The Age of Empire, 1875–1914* (New York, 1987).

22. William McKinley, *President McKinley's Last Speech, Delivered September 5, 1901, President's Day at the Pan-American Exposition, Buffalo* (New York, 1901), 5.

23. The 1992 Seville Universal Exposition followed the path of the last universal fair of the twentieth century (Brussels 1958). For the 1992 Seville Universal Exposition seen along the lines proposed by this book, see M. Tenorio, "Sevilla 1992: De la Torre Eiffel al gran nopal," *La Jornada Semanal*, 27 September 1992, 16–23; and John E. Findling, "Fair Legacies: Expo '92 and Cartuja '93," in *Fair Representations*, ed. Robert Rydell and Nancy E. Gwinn (Amsterdam, 1994), 180–96. For the year 2000, there are plans for world's fairs in Hannover, Toronto, and Venice. See J. E. Findling, ed., *Historical Dictionary of World's Fairs and Expositions, 1851–1988* (New York, 1990), 403–10.

24. See Louis Marin's commentary on Disneyland, in his *Utopiques* (Paris, 1973), 297–324.

25. *El Correo Español*, 1 September 1891.

26. J. Michelet, *Extraits historiques de J. Michelet*, prepared by Ch. Seignobos (Paris, 1907), 7.

27. See the remarkable anarchist geography of the world by Elisée Reclus, *L'Homme et la terre*, vol. 2 (reprint, Paris, 1990), 403–6.

28. As explained in the preface, the epilogue includes a summary of how historiographical and conceptual notions are used in the book.

1. FRANCE AND HER FOLLOWERS

1. *Bulletin de l'Exposition Universelle de Paris 1889,* 15 October 1888, 3.
2. For an explanation of the different confrontations, see Blenda Nelms, *The Third Republic and the Centennial of 1789* (New York, 1987), 13–17.
3. See Richard D. Mandell, *Paris 1900* (Toronto, 1967), ix.
4. The nine groups were: Group 1, the arts; Group 2, education; Group 3, furniture; Group 4, textiles; Group 5, raw and manufactured products (the extractive arts); Group 6, mechanical industries and electricity; Group 7, food products; Group 8, agriculture; and Group 9, horticulture. The groups were subdivided into a total of 83 classes. See RUP 1.
5. See Walter Benjamin, "Paris, Capital of the 19th Century," in *Reflections,* ed. Peter Demetz, trans. E. Jephcott (New York, 1986), 146–58. In interpreting the significance of nineteenth-century world's fairs, three authors have elaborated on Benjamin's concept of "pilgrimage of the commodity fetish." See the translation of the German study by Werner Plum, *Exposiciones mundiales en el siglo XIX* (Bonn, 1977), 3–9; the Brazilian work by Francisco Foot Hardman, *Trem fantasma* (São Paulo, 1988), 49–66; and the French study by Philippe Hamon, *Expositions* (Berkeley, 1992).
6. See Nelms, *Third Republic,* 11–64.
7. The 1889 Paris fair officially ended on November 6.
8. See François Furet and Mona Ozouf, eds., *A Critical Dictionary of the French Revolution* (Cambridge, 1989), 882–90.
9. See Greenhalgh, *Ephemeral Vistas,* 27–41.
10. See, for example, Fernando Rosenzweig, "La industria," in HMM, *El porfiriato: Vida económica,* 465–94; and Stephen Haber, *Industry and Underdevelopment* (Stanford, 1989).
11. For an example of this encouragement of private exhibitors, see EXP, Box 30, Exp. 23.
12. *Tout-d'Union,* 1 September 1891.
13. See Nelms, *Third Republic,* 30–31.
14. For an explanation of the diplomatic causes and consequences of the boycott, see Brigitte Schroeder-Gudehus, "Les Grandes Puissances devant l'Exposition Universelle de 1889," *Le Mouvement Social,* no. 149 (1989):15–24.
15. Émile Durer, "Edison," *Revue Illustrée* 8 (June-December, 1889): 174–78.
16. In this regard, see Burton Benedict, "International Exhibitions and National Identity," *Anthropology Today* 6 (June 1991):7–9; and the analysis by Greenhalgh, *Ephemeral Vistas,* 82–111.
17. *La Revue Diplomatique,* August 1886, 5. Meulemans published various articles on Mexico and other Latin American countries in *La Revue Diplomatique;* he included some of these articles in a volume published in order to be distributed during the 1889 Paris fair. See Auguste Meulemans, *Revue Diplomatique: Chefs d'état, ministres et diplomates* (Paris, 1889).
18. See Greenhalgh, *Ephemeral Vistas,* 3–26, 52–81; and R. Rydell's examination of American imperialism in American world's fairs, *All the World's a Fair* (Chicago, 1984).
19. See J. L. Phelan, "Pan-Latinism, French Intervention in Mexico (1861–1867) and the Genesis of the Idea of Latin America," in *Conciencia y autenticidad históricas,*

Escritos en homenaje a Edmundo O'Gorman, ed. J. Ortega y Medina (Mexico City, 1968), 279–98.

20. In this regard, see the transformation of the concept of modern after 1850, in Gumbrecht, "History," 92–101.

21. RUP 7:359–68.

22. Émile Monod, *L'Exposition Universelle de 1889*, 4 vols. (Paris, 1890), 591–97, quoted by Hélène Trocmé, "Les États-Unis et l'Exposition Universelle de 1889," *Revue d'Histoire Moderne et Contemporaine* 37 (April-June 1990):288.

23. Merle Curti, "America at the World Fairs, 1851–1893," *American Historical Review* 55, 4 (1950):856.

24. Opinion of a traveler in Mexico, Mary Blake, *Mexico Picturesque, Political, Progressive* (Boston, 1888), 8.

25. Francisco Inacio de Carvalho Moreira, *Relatório sobre a Exposição International de 1862* (London, 1863), xv, quoted in French by Marcus Olender, "Le Premier Centenaire de la révolution et la participation brésilienne à l'Exposition Universelle de 1889 à Paris: espaces et mentalités," in *L'Image de la Revolution Française*, ed. M. Vovelle, vol. 3 (New York, 1990), 2167. See also the collection of photographs that were exhibited by Brazil at international expositions, by Maria Inez Turazzi, "Poses e trejeitos na era do espectáculo: a fotografia e as exposições universais (1839–1889)," reported in *Domingo: Jornal do Brasil*, 12 July 1992; in particular, for Brazil's presence at the 1976 Philadelphia exhibition, see Sandra Jatahy Pesavento, "Exposições universais: Palcos de exibição do mundo burgues: Em cena, Brasil e Estados Unidos," *Siglo XIX*, no. 12 (1992):63–87. For the Brazilian presence at the 1889 Paris fair, see "L'Exposition du Brésil au Champ de Mars à Paris," *La Nature* 17 (1889):342–43. For an analysis of this presence, see Olender, *Les Images*; José Luiz Foresti Werneck da Silva, "La Participation de l'Empire du Brésil à l'Exposition Universelle Internationale de 1889 à Paris: La Section brésilienne aux Champ-de-Mars," *Revista do Instituto Histórico e Geográfico Brasileiro*, no. 364 (1989):417–20; and Foot Hardman, *Trem fantasma*, 67–96.

26. See Olga Vitali, "1889: La Argentina en la Exposición Mundial de Paris," *Todo es Historia*, no. 243 (1987):29–37; on Argentina's building, see Marta Dujoune, "La plástica: El realismo y el impresionismo," in J. L. Romero, *Buenos Aires: Historia de cuatro siglos*, vol. 2 (Buenos Aires, 1983), 131–39.

27. Eugen Weber, *Peasants into Frenchmen* (Stanford, 1976), 3.

28. For Mexican views on the French Third Republic, see Charles Hale, *The Transformation of Liberalism in Late Nineteenth-Century Mexico* (Princeton, 1989), 38–40. See also Charles Hale, "Fundación de la Modernidad Mexicana," *Nexos*, no. 170 (1992): 45–54.

29. See Hale, *Transformation of Liberalism*, 39.

30. *El Imparcial*, 1 May 1899.

31. *El Siglo XIX*, 31 August 1891.

32. F. Bulnes, *El porvenir de las naciones latinoamericanas ante las recientes conquistas de Europa y Norteamérica (estructura y evolución de un continente)* (Mexico City, 1899), 110–14.

33. O France! c'est de toi que m'est venu le Livre,
    C'est de ton esprit clair que mon esprit s'enivre,
    Ma voix de ta voix est l'écho;

> Mes fils aiment tes fils; tes fêtes sont mes fêtes
> Et c'est pour te chanter qu'aujourd'hui mes poètes
> Prennent leur lyre à Mexique.
> Leurs accents toucheront ton coeur, car leur génie
> Est né sous le soleil de ta glorie infinie
> D'un éclair que ton front jeta:
> Alarcon et Corneille ont pu marcher ensemble,
> Ignace Ramirez à Voltaire ressemble
> Comme Juarez à Gambetta.
> France, j'ai Jean Peza, mon doux François Coppée;
> Guillermo Prieto chante mon épopée
> En Béranger de mon drapeau;
> Gorostiza, pour moi, c'est Collin d'Harleville;
> Sierra c'est Sainte-Beuve et Casasus, Delille,
> Altamirano, Mirabeau!

Auguste Genin, *France-Mexique* (Mexico City, 1910), 3.

34. See, for example, the coverage of Mexico's awards ceremony in *Tout-d'Union*, 1 September 1891.

35. For an explanation of the mystification of the French Republic in monuments, see Mona Ozouf, "Le Panthéon: L'École normale des morts," in Nora, *Les Lieux de mémoire*, vol. 1, 139–66; and Charles Rearik, "Festivals in Modern France: The Experience of the Third Republic," *Journal of Contemporary History* 12 (1977):435–60. On the debate over the commemorative monument for the centennial celebration of the French Revolution, see Nelms, *Third Republic*, 65–105.

36. See Nelms, *Third Republic*, 249.

37. See Jean Marie Mayeur and Madeleine Reberioux, *The Third Republic from Its Origins to the Great War, 1871–1914*, trans. J. R. Foster (Cambridge, 1984), 42–65. See also Jean-Luc Pinol, *Le Monde des villes au XIXe siècle* (Paris, 1991), 29–31.

38. Pascal Ory, *Les Expositions Universelles de Paris* (Paris, 1982).

39. RUP 9:25. It was not until the Paris Universal Exhibition of 1900, for which Picard served as general commissioner, that his concept of social economy was developed through the establishment of a tenth group, on social economy. See André Gueslin, *L'Invention de l'économie sociale* (Paris, 1987), especially his explanation of the role played by Charles Gide in social economic thought (pp. 157–60). See also Charles Gide, *Économie sociale: Rapports du jury international, Exposition Universelle de 1900* (Paris, 1901).

40. For the growth of the so-called Professors' Republic, see Christophe Charle, *La République des universitaires, 1870–1940* (Paris, 1994), especially his discussion of the emergence of a "social model of intellectuals" and the role of intellectuals in politics (pp. 291–307).

41. See Gueslin, *L'Invention*, 4.

42. Letter from Manuel Flores to Carlos Pacheco, March 1888, reproduced in José Francisco Godoy, *México en París* (Mexico City, 1891), 216–18. In the 1880s there were indeed various *asociaciones mutualistas* in Mexico, most of them linked to artisan and crafts organizations. In this regard, see David W. Walker, "Porfirian Labor Politics: Working Class Organization in Mexico City and Porfirio Díaz, 1876–1902," *The Amer-

icas 37 (1981):257–89; and John M. Hart, *Anarchism and the Mexican Working Class, 1860–1931* (Austin, 1987), 43–59.

43. Porfirio Díaz's letter to Vicente Riva Palacio, 25 May 1891, Vicente Riva Palacio's letters, Genaro García Collection, University of Texas at Austin.

44. See RUP 3:337–38.

45. See, for example, Report Serrano-Davis, EXP, Box 84, Exp. 18; reproduced by José Francisco Godoy, *La ciudad de Chicago y la Exposición Universal de 1893* (Chicago, 1892), 94–95.

46. See Claude Nicolet, *L'Idée républicaine en France (1789–1924)* (Paris, 1982), 251–67.

47. William Henry Bishop, "A Paris Exposition in Dishabille," in *Atlantic Monthly*, May 1889, 621. For a similar opinion of the fair as an "electoral device," see William Henry Hulbert, *France and the Republic* (London, 1890), lxxxix–xcvi.

48. See Mayeur and Reberioux, *Third Republic*, 55–65.

49. See F. Crouzet, "Essai de construction d'un indice annuel de la production industrielle française au XIXe siècle," *Annales* 25 (January-February 1970):56–99.

50. Harry W. Paul, "The Debate over the Bankruptcy of Science in 1895," *French Historical Studies* 5, 3 (1968):300.

51. In 1889 P. Bourget published *Le Disciple*, challenging the general belief of the second part of the nineteenth century in *l'idée scientifique du déterminisme universel*. See Antoine Compagnon, *La Troisième République des lettres: De Flaubert à Proust* (Paris, 1983), 174–90.

52. See Zeev Sternhell, "The Political Culture of Nationalism," in *Nationhood and Nationalism in France: From Boulangism to the Great War, 1889–1918*, ed. R. Tombs (London, 1991), 22–24.

53. See Avner Ben-Amos, "Les Funérailles de Victor Hugo: Apothéose de l'événement spectacle," in Nora, *Les Lieux de mémoire*, vol. 1, 473–522.

54. See Arnold Hauser, *The Social History of Art: Naturalism, Impressionism, the Film Age*, vol. 4 (New York, 1985), 60–106, 166–225; Jerrold Seigel, *Bohemian Paris: Culture, Politics, and the Boundaries of Bourgeois Life, 1830–1930* (New York, 1987), 215–365; and Joshua Taylor, ed., *Nineteenth-Century Theories of Art* (Berkeley, 1987), 370–83, 415–30.

55. The English translation is quoted in Philippe Jullian, *The Triumph of Art Nouveau* (London, 1974), 33, and in Greenhalgh, *Ephemeral Vistas*, 116, and Findling, *Historical Dictionary*, 33–34.

56. See Stephen Kern, *The Culture of Time and Space, 1880–1918* (Cambridge, 1983), 65–88, 314–18. See the discussion of the so-called reactionary modernism in Jeffrey Herf, *Reactionary Modernism* (Cambridge, 1984).

57. Émile Goudeau, "Une journée d'esposition," *Revue Illustrée*, no. 92 (1889):244.

2. THE IMPERATIVES OF MEXICAN PROGRESS

1. For a general view of the political and social environment of early-nineteenth-century Mexico, see Michael Costeloe, *The Central Republic in Mexico, 1835–1846: Hombres de Bien in the Age of Santa Ana* (Cambridge, 1993); and Josefina Vázquez, "El federalismo mexicano, 1823–1847," in *Federalismos latinoamericanos: México, Brasil, Argentina*, ed. Marcelo Carmagnani (Mexico City, 1993), 15–50.

2. Justo Sierra, *Evolución política del pueblo mexicano* (Caracas, 1980), 287.

3. Regarding the regional and professional origins of this elite, as well as its political and economic unfolding, see François X. Guerra, *México del antíguo régimen a la revolución*, trans. Sergio Fernández Bravo, vol. 1 (Mexico City, 1988), 59–181; José C. Valadés, *El porfirismo: Historia de un régimen*, vol. 1 (Mexico City, 1987), 70–89; A. de Maria y Campos, "Porfirianos prominentes: Orígenes y años de juventud de ocho intelectuales del grupo de los científicos, 1846–1876," *Historia Mexicana* 34 (1985): 610–51.

4. For insights on the notion of aristocratic culture, see William H. Beezley, *Judas at the Jockey Club and Other Episodes of Porfirian Mexico* (Lincoln, Nebraska, 1987). See also the account of the nostalgia of the Porfirian belle époque in Carlos Tello Díaz, *El exilio: Un relato de familia* (Mexico City, 1993).

5. German Foreign Office papers, quoted by Friedrich Katz, "Mexico: Restored Republic and Porfiriato, 1867–1910," in *The Cambridge History of Latin America*, ed. L. Bethell, vol. 5 (Cambridge, 1986), 57.

6. By 1900, Guerra argues, 82 percent of the Porfirian elite were professionals: 57 percent, lawyers; 15 percent, medical doctors; and 10 percent, engineers. See Guerra, *México*, vol. 1, 65.

7. See Esther Acevedo, *Catálogo del retrato del siglo XIX en el Museo Nacional de Historia* (Mexico City, 1982); Enrique Krauze, *Místico de la autoridad: Porfirio Díaz* (Mexico City, 1987); and Alan Knight's comments on Díaz seen by foreigners as "probably all white" (Alan Knight, *The Mexican Revolution*, vol. 1 [Cambridge, 1986], 3–4).

8. For the emergence and significance of this group within the Mexican liberal tradition, see Hale, *Transformation of Liberalism*, 3–13, 20–24, and chap. 2.

9. Justo Sierra, *Evolución política del pueblo mexicano* (Caracas, 1980), 265.

10. See Hale, *Transformation of Liberalism*, 3–8, 25–36.

11. Knight, *Mexican Revolution*, vol. 1, 15.

12. DO, 15 May 1889, 1.

13. On the concept of atomization, see Guerra, *México*, vol. 1, 46.

14. Compare Guerra's characterization of social actors in the Porfirian regime and the two types of solidarities—modern and traditional (ibid., 127–80).

15. Regarding the belief in Mexico's beauty and natural wealth, see Moisés González Navarro, HMM, *El porfiriato: Vida social*, 135–48. See also Cosío Villegas's explanation of the liberal consensus in the prosperity of Mexican lands: Daniel Cosío Villegas, "La riqueza legendaria de México," in *Extremos de América*, ed. Daniel Cosío Villegas (Mexico City, 1949), 82–111. For an analysis of the influence of this belief on the creation of a national literature, see Jorge Rueda de la Serna, *Los orígenes de la visión paradisiáca de la naturaleza mexicana* (Mexico City, 1987), 65–89.

16. See Leopoldo Zea's classic account of Mexican positivism: *El positivismo en México* (Mexico City, 1968), originally published in 1943. A different perspective is in William D. Raat, *El positivismo durante el porfiriato, 1876–1910* (Mexico City, 1975). For a deeper understanding of positivism vis-à-vis Darwinism and sciences in Mexico, see Hale, *Transformation of Liberalism*, chap. 7; Roberto Moreno, *La polémica del darwinismo en México, siglo XIX* (Mexico City, 1989); and M. González Navarro, *Historia y sociología* (Mexico City, 1970).

17. David Brading has examined lucidly the notion of criollo patriotism. See David

Brading, *The Origins of Mexican Nationalism* (Cambridge, 1985); and David Brading, *Prophecy and Myth in Mexican History* (Cambridge, 1984), esp. 37–53.

18. This is an important point that is often overlooked. For Mexico, see Hale's discussion of the influence of Emilio Castelar and the concept of an "age of eloquence" in *Transformation of Liberalism*, 40–43; and Hale, "Political and Social Ideas in Latin America, 1870–1930," in *The Cambridge History of Latin America*, ed. L. Bethell, vol. 4 (Cambridge, 1986), 367–441, 637–643. For analyses of these aspects in other Latin American historiographical traditions, see A. Woll, *Functional Past: The Uses of History in Nineteenth-Century Chile* (Baton Rouge, 1982); and Germán Colmenares, *Las convenciones contra la cultura* (Bogotá, 1987). See also Hugh Cunningham, "The Language of Patriotism, 1750–1914," *History Workshop*, no. 12 (1981):1–32; and Josep M. Fradera, *Cultura nacional en una societat dividida* (Barcelona, 1992), 127–234.

19. Luis González, *La ronda de las generaciones* (Mexico City, 1984), 32.

20. Lucas Ayarragaray, "Porfirio Díaz," *Revista de Derecho, Historia y Letras* 10 (1901):428.

21. See Eugène-Melchior de Vogüé's passionate discussion of the pavilions of war and social economy in "À travers l'Exposition. VII. La Guerre.–La Paix sociale," *Revue des Deux Mondes* 95 (October 1889):677–93.

22. As in many other realms, the history of the Mexican economy has put a strong emphasis on the Revolution of 1910 as a watershed. New histories are beginning to break this historiographic-political belief. In this regard, see John Womack, "The Mexican Economy during the Revolution, 1910–1920: Historiography and Analysis," *Marxist Perspective* 1 (1978):80–123; and Stephen Haber, "The Industrialization of Mexico: Historiography and Analysis" (1992), manuscript.

23. See Stephen Haber, "Assessing the Obstacles to Industrialization: The Mexican Economy, 1830–1940" (1991), manuscript, 1–2.

24. For an account of the economic difficulties and of the political consequences of these difficulties in the aftermath of the González era, see Don M. Coerver, *The Porfirian Interregnum: The Presidency of Manuel González of Mexico, 1880–1884* (Fort Worth, 1979), 187–230, 243–70.

25. In this regard, see the interesting analysis of the Porfirian elite management of both American and British interests (in economic, financial, and diplomatic terms) in Paolo Riguzzi, "México, Estados Unidos y Gran Bretaña, 1867–1910: Una difícil relación triangular," *Historia Mexicana* 41 (1992):365–436.

26. See Hilda Sánchez Martínez, "El sistema monetario y financiero mexicano bajo una perspectiva histórica: el porfiriato," in *La banca, pasado y presente: Problemas financieros mexicanos*, ed. José Miguel Quijano (Mexico City, 1983), 21. The growth of the textile industry in the 1890s was especially impressive, as Stephen Haber observed in "Industrialization of Mexico," 18, and in "Industrial Concentration and the Capital Markets: A Comparative Study of Brazil, Mexico, and the United States, 1830–1930," *Journal of Economic History* 51 (1991):575.

27. For the generational, professional, and political structure of the Porfirian elite, see Guerra, *México*, vol. 1, 58–125, appendix.

28. Rafael de Zayas Enríquez, *Les États-Unis Mexicains* (Mexico City, 1891), 231.

29. See, for instance, the *Annuaire de l'Économie Politique et de la Statistique* (Paris, 1889–1901); the American almanac *Appletons' Annual Cyclopaedia and Register of Im-*

portant Events . . . 1889 (New York, 1890), 556–57; and the British one *The Annual Register: A Review of Public Events at Home and Abroad, 1888* (London, 1889), 546.

30. See Riguzzi, "México, Estados Unidos y Gran Bretaña," 385–97, 420–27.

31. Archibald Dunn, *Mexico and Her Resources* (London, 1890), 3–4. For another example, see E. J. Howell, *Mexico: Its Progress and Commercial Possibilities* (London, 1892). For Howell's recommendations to British investors, see pp. 163–68.

32. HMM, *El porfiriato: Vida política interior* 1:690. See also José Luis Ceceña, *México en la órbita imperial* (Mexico City, 1970), 49–101.

33. It was also influential in the agricultural sector, especially on sugar and rubber in Veracruz. See Sánchez Martínez, "El sistema monetario y financiero mexicano," 16–17. In 1938 Chávez Orozco estimated French investment in the oil and mining industries at 10,000 pesos for 1910, far below the 499,000 pesos invested by the United States and the 87,200,000 pesos invested by Great Britain. See Luis Chávez Orozco, *Historia económica y social de México* (Mexico City, 1938), 168.

34. L. N. D'Olwer, "X. Las inversiones extranjeras," in HMM, *El porfiriato: Vida económica*, 1018–23. See also J. Lejeune, *Au Mexique* (Paris, 1892). The author describes the significance of French people and investment in Mexico's urban life. The so-called *almacenes de novedades* were monopolized by French merchants: in 1891 they owned 70. French investment and imports, as well as Mexico's exports to France, presented a decreasing tendency throughout the Porfirian period. See A. Genin, *Les Français au Mexique* (Mexico City, 1910); and Rosenzweig, in HMM, *El porfiriato: Vida económica*, 635–720.

35. F. Bianconi, *Le Mexique a la portée des industriels, des capitalistes, des négotiants, importateurs et exportateurs et des travailleurs avec une carte du Mexique commerciale, boutière, minière et agricole* (Paris, 1989), 7–10.

36. See Haber, "Industrialization of Mexico," 10–11.

37. See Ricardo de Maria y Campos, *Datos Mercantiles, compilados por Ricardo de Maria y Campos* (Mexico City, 1889). De Maria y Campos revised this study for the 1900 Paris fair as *Renseignements commerciaux sur les États-Unis Mexicains* (Mexico City, 1899). The revision was better organized and more comprehensive (see pp. 51–214).

38. See chapter 10; and González Navarro, HMM, 102–33.

39. México, Secretaría de Fomento, *Memoria, 1877–1882*, vol. 1; Coerver, *Porfirian Interregnum*, 210–16; and González Navarro, HMM 4:134–52. For a recent account of the complex role played by land-survey companies, see Robert Holden, *Mexico and the Survey of Public Lands: The Management of Modernization, 1876–1911* (DeKalb, Illinois, 1994).

40. In his book for Mexico's display at Paris 1889, García Cubas gave examples of successful *colonias*. See Antonio García Cubas, *Étude géographique statistique descriptive et historique des États-Unis Mexicains* (Mexico City, 1889).

41. González Navarro estimated that 48,000 foreigners resided in Mexico in 1895; by 1910 there were 116,527, of which only 9 percent were in the agricultural sector. Hence immigration was never as expected, and it was especially insignificant in Mexico's agricultural development. See González Navarro, HMM 4:184.

42. See, as an example, Zayas Enríquez, *Les États-Unis Mexicains*.

43. García Cubas, *Étude géographique*, 650, an updated version in French of Antonio García Cubas, *Cuadro geográfico y estadístico, descriptivo e histórico de los Estados Unidos Mexicanos* (Mexico City, 1884), which was prepared for the 1884 New Orleans

fair. See also the favorable opinion of Mexico's condition for investment in Dreyfus's article on Mexico and Chile in Paris 1889 in *L'Économiste Français*, 23 August 1890.

44. Clement Bertier-Marriot, *Un parisien au Mexique* (Paris, 1886), 59–61. The author was the envoy of *Le Figaro* at the inauguration of the railroad line between Mexico City and New York City. The book included some presumed salaries offered in Mexico for workers: for example, 7 francs for a carpenter, and 2.50 francs for a female dressmaker.

45. Dunn, *Mexico and Her Resources*.

46. See, for example, Eugenio Martuscelli, *Apunti sul Messico* (Naples, 1892). See also E. Chabrand, *De Barcelonette au Mexique* (Paris, 1892), in which the author glorifies Mexico's progress in only a few years; and A Gringo, *Through the Land of the Aztecs or Life and Travel in Mexico* (n.p., 1892).

47. See Justo Sierra's commentary on the proposal made by Zayas Enríquez for a *Memoria*, EXP, Box 18, Exp. 8. In it, Sierra stated that Mexico's display ought to show that Mexico had come to *"el fin de nuestra primera gran etapa en el camino del progreso positivo."*

48. See González Navarro, HMM 4:134–84.

49. Francisco Pimentel, "La colonización negra," in *Obras completas*, vol. 5 (Mexico City, 1904), 511, 513.

50. See Moisés González Navarro, "Las ideas raciales de los científicos, 1890–1910," *Historia Mexicana* 37, 4 (1988):575.

51. See the study by José María Romero, *Dictamen del vocal ingeniero . . . encargado de estudiar la influencia social y económica de la inmigración asiática en México* (Mexico City, 1911). In 1889 a *Tratado de amistad, navegación y comercio* was signed with China, and more immigration was allowed. Chinese immigration increased, and in 1904 a commission assigned to study it, headed by José Covarrubias, concluded that Chinese immigrants would never assimilate into the Mexican nationality. Overall, there was a consensus on the inferiority of the Chinese race. See González Navarro, HMM 4:166–68; and González Navarro, "Las ideas raciales," 576.

52. See the pamphlet, Argentina, *République Argentine: La Vie sociale et la vie légale des étrangers* (Paris, 1889). This book was for sale in the Argentine pavilion.

53. For Vasconcelos, Argentina and the United States were more successful than Mexico was in attracting immigrants, largely because of their more democratic regimes. See José Vasconcelos, *Breve historia de México* (Mexico City, 1937), 501–19.

3. MEXICO AND THE WORLD AT LARGE

1. This motto was inscribed on the medals awarded at the 1851 London exhibition.

2. México, Secretaría de Fomento, *Anales de la Secretaría de Fomento* 1 (1877–1882):413–14.

3. See Paolo Riguzzi, "México próspero: Las dimensiones de la imagen nacional en el porfiriato," *Historias*, no. 20 (1988):137–60; G. Yeager, "Porfirian Commercial Propaganda: Mexico in the World Industrial Expositions," *The Americas* 34 (October 1977):230–43; and María de la Concepción de la Fuente Salceda, "La participación de México en la Exposición Universal de Filadelfia 1876" (Tesis de Licenciatura, Universidad Iberoamericana, 1984).

4. These two long letters can be found in manuscript form (annotated and in

full) in EXP, Box 79, Exp. 1, 10–100. Also, they were published, with several corrections, as Gabriel Mancera, *Informes que el C. Gabriel Mancera comisionado especial de la junta de exposiciones en los Estados Unidos de Norte-América y miembro de ella rinde sobre el desempeño de su cargo* (Mexico City, 1875).

5. *El Siglo XIX*, 1 January 1875.

6. Translated from *The Athenian* of New York, published by *El Proteccionista*, 13 July 1876, and reproduced in de la Fuente Salceda, "La participación de México," 298 (my translation).

7. Translated from *The Standard* of London by *El Federalista*, 25 August 1876 and reproduced in ibid., 302 (my translation).

8. For a description of the particular space occupied by Mexico, see ibid., 37–38, 56–58. In addition to the Mexican exhibit in the main building of the Philadelphia fair, Mexico displayed some photographs—attributed to the Mexican photographers Cruces and Campa at the Art Gallery (ibid., 61).

9. According to de la Fuente Salceda (ibid., 92), 90,000 pesos had been spent on the building that had been constructed for the National Exposition of 1875. These figures are not reliable, for 300,000 pesos seems to be an inflated figure vis-à-vis the dimensions and size of Mexico's display at Philadelphia.

10. *El Eco de Ambos Mundos*, 14 January 1875, quoted in ibid., 77.

11. "Mexico at the Centennial," NYT, 1 April 1876, quoted in Paul A. Tenkotte, "Kaleidoscopes of the World: International Exhibitions and the Concept of Cultural Space, 1851–1915," *American Studies* 28, 1 (1987):5.

12. In 1885 another fair, in which Mexico also participated, took place in New Orleans, organized by railroad companies. It was known as the North, Central, and South American Exposition.

13. John Allwood, *The Great Exhibitions* (London, 1977), 74. See also Findling, *Historical Dictionary*, 86–90.

14. Sebastián B. de Mier, *México en la Exposición Universal Internacional de París—1900* (Mexico City, 1901), 6.

15. Godoy (1851–1930) wrote semiofficial laudatory books on Mexico for several universal exhibitions, as well as biographies and directories of great men. He was a writer for the *Two Republics* and *La Patria*. He participated in various world's fairs as part of Mexican commissions and wrote several books for the Mexican government in both Spanish and English, including a Spanish and English biography of Porfirio Díaz: José Francisco Godoy, *Porfirio Díaz, President of Mexico* (San Francisco, 1910). Among his books on fairs are *México en París; México en Sevilla* (Mexico City, 1928); and *La ciudad de Chicago y la Exposición Universal de 1893*. In addition, he participated in the preparation of Mexico, Comisión de los Estados Unidos Mexicanos para la Exposición Pan-Americana de Buffalo, Nueva York, *A Few Facts about Mexico* (Mexico City, 1901). See also José Francisco Godoy, *Enciclopedia biográfica de contemporáneos* (Washington, 1898). In 1929 Godoy was still an active journalist, writing *efemérides* in Mexico City's newspaper *Excélsior*.

16. Santiago Ramírez, *Noticia histórica de la riqueza minera de México y de su actual estado de explotación* . . . (Mexico City, 1884). The first pages stated that it was a "special report on the occasion of the New Orleans Industrial and Cotton Exhibition, 1884–1885."

17. Rydell, *All the World's a Fair*, 90–94.

18. BEMP 2 (1888):149. For Mexican expenditures at the New Orleans fair, see EXP, Box 78, Exp. 3, 9; Box 71, Exp. 1–11, 17–24, 25–33, 34–41; Box 72, Exp. 1–23, 24, 25–28, 29–30 (*cuentas*); Box 73 (*cuentas*), Exp. 5–7, 1–4.

19. See, for example, how the French-speaking media praised Mexico for its state-sponsored policies of industrial development: *L'Abbeille*, March 1885, included in a report sent by Lancaster, EXP, Box 79, Exp. 1, 139–142.

20. This building was later dismantled and reerected on the central Alameda of Mexico City. Later, the monument to Benito Juárez was put on the same site. There were plans to locate the Juárez monument facing the Palacio Nacional. Thanks to Limantour's influential opposition, it was finally placed on Avenida Juárez. Ibarrola's building was moved to the Alameda of the suburb of Santa María la Ribera, where it is still visible today. See Fausto Ramírez, "Vertientes nacionalistas en el modernismo," in *El nacionalismo en el arte mexicano (IX Coloquio de Historia del Arte)* (Mexico City, 1986), 111–67; see also EXP, Box 79, Exp. 1, 152–53.

21. For the influence of the Philadelphia architectural style in Latin American countries, especially Brazil, see Pesavento, "Exposições universais," 63–87.

22. A copy of the contract is in EXP, Box 78, Exp. 2.

23. Findling, *Historical Dictionary*, 89.

24. This was a steamship, owned by the Compañía Mexicana de Navegación (EXP, Box 71, Exp. 11).

25. For the Mexican exhibitors in New Orleans, see EXP, Box 74, Exp. 1–13, 14–33, 34–54; Box 75, Exp. 36–41, 1–20, 21–35, 43–59 (*envíos*), 60 (*contingente* from Chihuahua).

26. For the works and organization of the New Orleans fair, see the minutes of the commission's meetings in *Libro de Juntas Exposición Universal de Nueva Orleans 1884–1885*, meetings from 15 March 1884 to 18 November 1884, EXP, Box 73, Exp. 8–9. For a complete list of prizes, see DO, 25 November 1886, 2–4. The awards were distributed by Porfirio Díaz on 5 February 1887, in Mexico City, together with the prizes obtained by Mexicans at the Buenos Aires Continental Exhibition (EXP, Box 78, Exp. 10).

27. According to Escandón, Mexico had 50 square meters at the 1851 London fair (Pedro de Escandón, *La industria y las bellas artes en la Exposición Universal de 1855* [Paris, 1856], 12).

28. Bullock had established the famous Egyptian Hall of London, in which numerous exhibitions, panoramas, and exotic products were presented to the European public. He traveled to Mexico in 1822 and brought a cast of the Calendar Stone, carvings, models of tombs, manuscripts, codices, life-size reproductions of Mexican fruits and vegetables, thousands of specimens of birds and fishes, and minerals. See William Bullock, *A Description of the Unique Exhibition, Called Ancient Mexico* (London, 1824); and William Bullock, *Six Months' Residence and Travels in Mexico* (London, 1824). For some data and pictures of these exhibitions, see Hugh Honour, *The New Golden Land* (New York, 1975), 183–85; and Richard D. Altick, *The Shows of London* (Cambridge, 1978), 246–48.

29. Escandón, *La industria y las bellas artes*, 12.

30. Ibid., 8–11.

31. Escandón, *La industria y las bellas artes*, 14. Adorno managed to publish in Paris

a pamphlet related to his musical machine: *Melagraphie, ou nouvelle notation musicale par Juan N. Adorno* (Paris, 1855).

32. See the various entries for Adorno in the Patentes y Marcas; his *Resumen ordenado de las discusiones pronunciadas por el ciudadano Juan Nepomuceno Adorno ante los ciudadanos redactores y editores de la prensa periódica* (Mexico City, 1873); and his *Acerca de la hidrografía, meteorología, seguridad hidrogénica y salubridad higiénica del valle y en especial de la Capital de México* (Mexico City, 1865). See also Ramón Sánchez Flores, *Historia de la tecnología y la invención en México* (Mexico City, 1980), 259 ff.; Pablo González Casanova, *Una utopía de América* (Mexico City, 1953), 31–59; and the comments on and catalogue of Patentes y Marcas by Jorge A. Sobernis, "Catálogo de patentes de invención en México durante el siglo XIX (1840–1900)" (Tesis de Licenciatura, Universidad Nacional Autónoma de México, 1989), 109–12.

33. Escandón, *La industria y las bellas artes*, 11–25.

34. EXP, Box 102, Exp. 9 contains an inventory that must have been prepared some time after Mexico's attendance at the 1900 Paris fair and was very likely ordered by Sebastián B. de Mier in the course of writing his own report on Mexico's participation. (Hereafter I refer to this document as Inventario.) The Inventario includes some evidence of Mexico's participation in various European and American fairs, but the actual documents are lost.

35. See Honour, *New Golden Land*, 183–85; and Daniel Schálvelzon, "El pabellón Xochicalco en la exposición internacional de París de 1867," in *La polémica del arte nacional en México, 1850–1910*, ed. Daniel Schálvelzon (Mexico City, 1988), 165–70. Schálvelzon considers the 1867 Xochicalco replica as the direct precursor of the Mexican Aztec palace in Paris 1889. But in fact the French models of the Xochicalco building (made by the French engineer Leon Mehédin) were not even considered to picture Mexico at the 1889 world's fair, though they were proposed by Ramón Fernández (SRE leg. 1103). In this regard, see minutes of 2 June 1888, reproduced in Godoy, *México en París*, 75. For Leon Mehédin's models of Xochicalco, see BEMP 1 (1888): 228–32.

36. F. Ducuing, "Exposition Universelle de 1867 Illustrée" (Paris, n.d.), 46; quoted in *Le Livre des expositions universelles, 1851–1989*, 46.

37. HMM 2:639.

38. According to Yeager, Mexico did take part in the 1878 Paris fair. However, there is no evidence that Mexico had an official presence there. UIA-Díaz 29:132 contains some evidence regarding an article in the *New York Herald* which argued that in 1876 Mexico had been informed of but not officially invited to the Paris fair of 1878. Nevertheless, some Mexican private exhibitors may have attended the fair (Yeager, "Porfirian Commercial Propaganda," 230–43).

39. See Yeager, "Porfirian Commercial Propaganda," 234–35. Mexico also joined the International Electricity Congress in Paris in 1881. See *Anales de la Secretaría de Fomento* 1 (1877–1882):416–17. For the Berlin fair, see also SRE 19-22-14.

40. Evidence of temporary and permanent fairs can be found in SRE, as follows: permanent exhibition of Mexican products in Austria-Hungary, 187?, 19-20-72; Museo de Productos Mexicanos en el Consulado de México en 1900, 19-22-53; Museo de Productos Mexicanos en Guatemala, 1902, 19-22-66; project to establish various Mexican exhibits in numerous European cities, 1882, 19-22-48; project to

celebrate the fourth centennial of Columbus's arrival with an International Exhibition in Mexico, 1892, 15–2–18; permanent coffee exhibit in New York, 1882, 19–22–16; and report on the exhibition of Mexican products in Liverpool, 1902–1903, 20–23–31.

41. EXP, Box 11, Exp. 12.

42. SRE 19–22–58.

43. See Zamacona, *Carta reservada,* 29 May 1879, SRE 19–22–58. In this regard, see Cosío Villegas's consideration of Zamacona's "lobbying" for the Díaz regime in the United States in Daniel Cosío Villegas, *Estados Unidos contra Porfirio Díaz* (Mexico City, 1956), 211.

44. EXP, Box 99, Exp. 1, p. 5 and charts.

45. *El Faro,* 19 March 1889. Reprinted as Antonio de Medina y Ormaechea, *Iniciativa para celebrar el Primer Centenario de la Independencia de México con una Exposición Universal* (Mexico City, 1893), 15–19, 25–51. Medina y Ormaechea continued to push for the celebration of such a world's fair in Mexico City and printed the pamphlet *La Exposición Universal del Primer Centenario Mexicano* (Mexico City, 1894).

46. Medina y Ormaechea, Iniciativa, 16. By 1900 *El Diario del Hogar* was advocating Medina's idea, but on 5 May it announced his death.

47. *Gran Exposición Internacional de México que se abrirá el día 15 de septiembre de 1895 y que se clausurará el día 3 de abril de 1896* (Mexico City, 1894), 3–10. See also *Agreement Made between Mr. John R. Dos Passos, as Legal Representative of the Mexican National Exposition and Land Company, and Vicomte R. de Cornely, in San Francisco, México,* 22 April 1896, in EXP, Box 99, Exp. 1; and México, Secretaría de Fomento, *Anales de la Secretaría de Fomento, 1897–1900* (Mexico City, 1908).

48. In fact, Bolivia was promoting the creation of such a union for the 1889 event. See the Guatemalan communication: *Carta confidencial sobre la próxima Exposición Internacional de París,* Legación de Guatemala en París, *El Guatemalteco. Diario Oficial,* no. 56 (1889):445.

49. *Le Temps,* 29 January 1887, reproduced France's official invitation to Mexico.

50. For responses to invitations by various Mexican states, see BEMP 1 (1888): 27–41.

51. Lucia Robina, *Reconciliación de México y Francia (1870–1880)* (Mexico City, 1963); HMM 2:639–714.

52. *Acuerdo Presidencial,* 20 January 1888.

53. From 1887 to the beginning of 1889, the various states responded to the Secretaría de Fomento. For an account of products promised by the states, see Godoy, *México en París,* 39–41.

4. THE WIZARDS OF PROGRESS: PARIS 1889

1. For an analysis of the confrontation of modern and traditional solidarities and links, see Guerra, *México,* vol. 1, 58–245; and Fernando Escalante, *Ciudadanos imaginarios* (Mexico City, 1993), 21–53.

2. In January 1888 a commission, consisting of Carlos R. Ruiz, Luis Salazar, and José Ramírez, was appointed to prepare a budget (EXP, Box 4, Exp. 1). For the analysis of the personnel of the Mexican exhibit at the 1889 Paris fair, I am depending on archival evidence. However, both Godoy (*México en París*) and the BEMP reproduced

various documents. I compared the BEMP's and Godoy's evidence with my own findings in order to present the best possible information.

3. EXP, Box 1, Exp. 7.
4. EXP, Box 2, Exp. 12.
5. DO, 9 February 1888.
6. EXP, Box 4, Exp. 1, pp. 1–5.
7. This is close to the figures reproduced in México, Tesorería General de la Federación, *Contaduría de la Federación: Cuenta Pública* (Mexico City, 1889–1890), under the name *Cuenta de egresos Número 102, Gastos para la exposición de París*. According to this *cuenta*, the expenses were 328,024.74 pesos and the budget approved was 450,000.00 pesos.
8. The intermediary agent between Mexico and the Mexican Commission in France was Eduardo Santos y Cía. For *cuentas* and expenses see EXP, Box 13, Exps. 1, 2; Box 14, Exps. 1, 4; Box 17, Exp. 3; Box 18, Exps. 1, 3, 6; Box 12, Exp. 1; Box 16, Exp. 3.
9. Argentina was second, with 3.2 million francs, and the United States was third, with 1.125 million francs (RUP 9:360).
10. EXP, Box 2, Exp. 6.
11. Among them, Francisco Díaz Covarrubias (Mexican consul in Paris), Gustavo Baz (first secretary of the Mexican embassy in Paris), Antonio Mier y Celis, José Yves Limantour, Julio Limantour (attaché of the Mexican diplomatic mission in Paris), and Rafael de Zayas Enríquez. See Díaz Mimiaga's report, EXP, Box 12, Exp. 6, pp. 15a–16.
12. In fact, Santiago Rebull, a distinguished painter of classical subjects during the second half of the nineteenth century, was originally appointed chief in 1888, but he declined the offer, claiming bad health. See BEMP 1 (1888):282. See also *Carta a Fomento*, 21 January 1889, EXP, Box 2, Exp. 7.
13. EXP, Box 7, Exp. 9.
14. EXP, Box 5, Exp. 20.
15. EXP, Box 4, Exp. 26.
16. For instance, see C. Romero Rubio's lobbying in favor of publicist Salvador Quevedo y Zubieta in EXP, Box 3, Exp. 6.
17. EXP, Box 5, Exp. 19.
18. Others personalities that were part of the team were Dr. José D. Morales and inventor Maximino Río de la Loza (EXP, Box 6, Exp. 12).
19. His family ran a well-known candy business in Mexico. He published books, such as *Estudio sobre las razas mexicanas* (1885), *Poèmes aztèques* (1890), and *Notes sur le Mexique* (1910); he translated the works of Antonio Peñafiel and Rafael de Zayas Enríquez for the 1889 exposition; and he was the editor of the *Boletín de la Exposición Mexicana en París* (1888–1891). In addition, he was a wealthy entrepreneur and a merchant, involved in the Cámara Francesa de Comercio de México, the Bank of London and Mexico, the Compañía Cigarrera Mexicana, the Cervecería Moctezuma, the Compañía de las Fábricas de Papel San Rafael y Anexas, and, as agent, El Palacio de Hierro. See Alberto María Carreño, "Augusto Genin: In Memoriam," in *Semblanzas*, vol. 2 (Mexico City, n.d.), 252–69; and Luis Everaert Dubernard, *México 1900* (Mexico City, 1994), which includes some data taken from Genin's personal papers.

20. EXP, Box 6, Exp. 12.
21. México, Secretaría de Fomento, *Reglamento económico* (Mexico City, 1989), 4.
22. EXP, Box 5, Exp. 24.
23. DO, 27 June 1888, Jalisco's exhibition. See also Presidential Address to the 14th Congress, DO, 17 September 1888; and DO, 25 October 1888, Morelos's exhibition.
24. DO, 13 September 1888.
25. Article 12 of the Mexican *Reglamento económico*. Originally, it was also established that each group had to write a report on its activities.
26. The principal receivers of Mexican material were the Bibliothèque Nationale of Paris and the British Library of the British Museum in London. Special collections of medical, chemical, biological, and ethnographic material were sent to the Pasteur Institute, the University of London, the Austrian Museum, and the Trocadero Museum in Paris. The University of Texas at Austin and the University of California at Berkeley (especially the Bancroft Library) also contain numerous examples of these materials.
27. See the annotated circular signed by Gilberto Crespo, Ferrari Pérez, and Manuel Flores in March 1888. In the notes at the margins, it is possible to observe the way in which the work of producing the image of the modern nation was divided (EXP, Box 1, Exp. 18, pp. 8–9).
28. DO, 21 September 1888.
29. See, for instance, the letter to Pacheco by the community of Cuautempan, Puebla in EXP, Box 8, Exp. 17.
30. García Cubas, *Étude*, v.
31. Annotated circular in EXP, Box 1, Exp. 18, pp. 8–9.
32. Annotated circular in ibid.
33. Ibid.
34. Bodo von Glümer, *Cuadro estadístico de los Estados Unidos Mexicanos: Formado con datos oficiales y por disposición de la Secretaría de Estado y del Despacho de Hacienda y Crédito Público* (Mexico City, 1882).
35. EXP, Box 1, Exp. 18, pp. 68–81.
36. See DO, 21 March 1889; documents reproduced in Godoy, *México en París*, 184–90.
37. For instance, there is evidence of the shipment of at least 744 samples of Maria y Campos's book in the steamship *Ville Marseille* (EXP, Box 8, Exp. 29).
38. Mexico published its own catalogue in French and Spanish. See France, Ministère du Commerce et de l'Industrie, *Exposition Universelle Internationale de 1889. Direction Générale de l'Exposition. Adjudication du Catalogue Général* (Paris, 1888); and México, Exposition Universelle International de Paris 1889, *Catalogue officiel de l'Exposition de la République Mexicaine* (Paris, 1889).
39. Velasco won a prize at the 1876 Philadelphia exhibit. At the 1878 Paris exposition he also displayed his paintings (at the Spanish section, since Mexico did not join that fair). See Fausto Ramírez, "Acotaciones iconográficas a la evolución de episodios y localidades en los paisajes de José María Velasco," in *José María Velasco: Homenaje*, ed. Fausto Ramírez (Mexico City, 1989), 43. See also chapter 7.
40. Notwithstanding, Pedro Calvo, Johann Moritz Rugendas, and Daniel Thomas Egerton preceded Velasco in landscape painting in Mexico. See Xavier Moyssén, "El dibujo de José María Velasco," in ibid., 8.

41. See Luis Islas García, *Velasco: Pintor Cristiano* (Mexico City, 1932); and the various essays on Velasco in Ramírez, *José María Velasco: Homenaje*. While I was revising this manuscript, Mexico City's Museo Nacional de Arte published a handsome two-volume catalogue of a national homage to Velasco. These volumes include important data on Velasco's life and significance in Mexican art. See México, Museo Nacional de Arte, *Homenaje nacional a José María Velasco (1840–1912)*, 2 vols. (Mexico City, 1993).

42. EXP, Box 2, Exp. 14.

43. EXP, Box 6, Exp. 12.

44. See *Acta de sesión*, 18 May 1889, EXP, Box 12, Exp. 3.

45. Velasco exhibited paintings in both the railroad section and the industry section. See México, *Catalogue officiel de l'Exposition de la République Mexicaine*. See also two long reports on the Mexican exhibition: one by Léon Cahun in *Le Phare de la Loire*, "L'Exposition Universelle. Le Mexique" (20 June 1889); and the article in *La Presse Industrielle*, 4 July 1889, reproduced in Godoy, *México en París*, 270–75. In January 1889 the DO announced that Mexico City's delegation sent Alberto Herrera's canvas of the Cuauhtémoc monument (DO, 25 January 1889); Gabriel Guerra proposed to send a replica of Cuauhtémoc. See BEMP 1 (1888):154–55; and, for the contract to make this replica for 950 pesos in January 1888, see BEMP 1 (1888):212–14. Another sculptor, Gabriel Guerra, also exhibited a bust of Porfirio Díaz.

46. DO, 17 April 1888.

47. DO, 17 April 1888.

48. See Sierra's allusion to his 1900 visit to the world's fair, in his 1910 welcome speech for the participants in the Congress of Americanists, held in Mexico City (Sierra, *Obras completas* [Mexico City, 1948], vol. 5, 253–56). For a description of Sierra's fascination with the 1900 Paris fair, see Claude Dumas, *Justo Sierra y el México de su tiempo, 1848–1912*, vol. 2 (Mexico City, 1986), 20, 34–35.

49. See, for example, "Chronique de l'Exposition," *Le Temps*, 24 August 1889.

50. DO, 17 April 1888.

51. Zárate, in a document reproduced in Godoy, *México en París*, 104.

52. For an analysis of the role played by statistics in the general modern image, see chapter 8.

53. Reproduced in Godoy, *México en París*, 103–6.

54. See RUP 6 (Groups 5 and 7).

55. See UIA-Díaz 842, Box 18, L. 40, *Catálogo de la colección mineral del General Porfirio Díaz*.

56. According to Argentine reports of mining exhibits, Mexico's mining display was especially impressive and included gold, copper, silver, and onyx. See Argentina, Exposition Universelle, 1889, *Argentine Republic: Colección de informes reunidos*, vol. 1 (Paris, 1890), 130–31. This report also included Mexican companies per state, with value of production (p. 131).

57. Ignacio Mariscal's letter to the Ministry of Foreign Affairs, reproduced in México, Secretaría de Fomento, *Documentos relativos a la venta de tabacos mexicanos en la Exposición Internacional de París, en 1889* (Mexico City, 1889), 14.

58. DO, 4 February 1890.

59. Mexico was second only to France in the total of products exhibited: France had 27,201; Mexico, 3,206.

60. See Gibbs's study of Porfirian propaganda in the United States between 1877 and 1878: William E. Gibbs, "Díaz' Executive Agents and United States Foreign Policy," *Journal of Interamerican Studies and World Affairs* 20, 2 (1978):165–89.

61. In this regard, see Paolo Riguzzi, "México próspero: Las dimensiones de la imagen nacional en el porfiriato," *Historias*, no. 20 (1988):137–57.

62. EXP, Box 8, Exp. 19. About Godoy's propaganda books on Mexico's presence at world's fairs, see chapter 3.

63. About this book, see also EXP, Box 11, Exp. 7, in which Godoy requested economic support for its project. See Godoy, *México en París*.

64. EXP, Box 8, Exp. 19; Ireneo Paz, *Los hombres prominentes de México*, 4 vols. (Mexico City, 1888). A French journalist, J. L. Regagnón, was paid to write the French part, and José Francisco Godoy prepared the English part.

65. Paz invited Riva Palacio to add his name by paying a "subscription" of 50 pesos. See Paz's letter to Vicente Riva Palacio, 1 September 1887, Vicente Riva Palacio's letters, Genaro García Collection, University of Texas at Austin. For data about Paz's book, see Juan Bautista Iguiniz, *Bibliografía biográfica mexicana* (Mexico City, 1969). For the prize awarded to Paz's book, see México, Secretaría de Fomento, *Lista de los premios y recompensas obtenidos por México en la Exposición de París de 1889* (Mexico City, 1891).

66. EXP, Box 8, Exp. 19. See Manuel de Olaguibel, *Memoria para una bibliografía científica de México en el siglo XIX* (Mexico City, 1889).

67. Some 10,000 copies of each issue were published, at a cost of 600 francs per issue. See *Actas de sesión*, 15 July 1889, EXP, Box 12, Exp. 3.

68. The book, which appeared in 1889, was published in Paris by Imprimerie et Librairie Centrales. Bianconi was financed by the Mexican government, though I have not been able to determine the total amount of money he received. For specific payments to Bianconi, see *Sesión*, 11 May 1889, EXP, Box 12, Exp. 3; BEMP 3 (1889):794–96; and BEMP 5 (1889):476.

69. BEMP 1 (1888):182–85.

70. E. Levasseur, ed., *Le Mexique au début du XXe siècle*, 2 vols. (Paris, 1904).

71. See Reclus, *L'Homme et la terre*.

72. There are few bibliographical data about this character, who played a role in various Mexican international displays. He seems to have been extremely well connected in international propaganda circles. Justo Sierra refers to him as *El Barón* and as *"enfant du pavé flâneur,"* who authored humorous texts. He argued that Gostkowski went from bohemian to entrepreneur. See the article in *El Federalista*, 20 June 1874, reproduced in Justo Sierra, *Obras completas*, vol. 3, ed. Agustín Yáñez (Mexico City, 1948), 177–80.

73. EXP, Box 12, Exp. 2.

74. See EXP, Box 15, Exp. 2, for various clippings. He received 1,561 francs.

75. Gustave Gostkowski, *Au Mexique* (Paris, 1900).

76. Ramón Fernández wrote to Porfirio Díaz that Díaz Mimiaga did not handle the propaganda well. He believed that the money disbursed in this regard was *"malgastado."* See UIA-Díaz, L. 14, C. 25, 12492–505.

77. See Díaz Mimiaga's report in EXP, Box 12, Exp. 6.

78. Ibid.

79. EXP, Box 9, Exp. 10.

80. See Paz, *Los hombres prominentes de México*. It has not been easy to find bibliographical data on Díaz Mimiaga. See José C. Valadés, *El Porfirismo*, vol. 2 (Mexico City, 1987), 157; and Luis G. Zorrilla, *Relaciones de México con la República de Centro América y con Guatemala* (Mexico City, 1984), 495. All of these authors point out Díaz Mimiaga's difficult personality.

81. Díaz Mimiaga, 1849–1891, according to Manuel Mestre Ghigliazza, *Efemérides biográficas* (Mexico City, 1945).

82. EXP, Box 6, Exp. 8.

83. See *Acta de sesión*, 8 May 1889. Díaz Mimiaga complained that Bablot sent the minutes without his signature and censorship (EXP, Box 12, Exp. 3). See also *Acta de sesión*, 3 June 1889, EXP, Box 12, Exp. 3.

84. See Bablot's full report, copy to the Minister of Foreign Affairs, in which he explained his motivations for arranging a scientific meeting with Latin American specialists: Letter, 19 August 1889, SRE Le. 1104, pp. 276–88.

85. See *Informe detallado por orden de fechas, relativo a diversas trabajos, principalmente de escultura y fundición artística, y que rinde el que subscribe . . . ,*" Ramón Fernández, 21 November 1889, IPBA, Box 5, Exp. 18. In this regard, see also Fausto Ramírez, "Dioses, héroes y reyes mexicanos en París 1889," in *Historia, leyendas y mitos de México* (Mexico City, 1988), 215.

86. For Contreras's plans with French engineer Colibert, and his petition for 220,000 francs, see BEMP 1 (1888):188–94.

87. EXP, Box 13, Exp. 4, pp. 8–101. All of the quotations concerning the conflict were taken from this document.

88. Manuel Gutiérrez Najera, "Alfredo Bablot," in *Obras críticas y literarias*, vol. 1 (Mexico City, 1959), 468–69. This was a panegyric for Bablot, who died in 1894.

89. See Justo Sierra's account of his travels, *Viajes en Tierra Yankee, en la Europa Latina*, in Justo Sierra, *Obras completas*, vol. 6, ed. José Luis Martínez (Mexico City, 1948), 15–61.

5. THE AZTEC PALACE AND THE HISTORY OF MEXICO

1. José Martí, *La edad de oro* (Río Piedras, 1971), 111–12. In 1889 José Martí wrote a children's magazine, *La Edad de Oro*, which used the 1889 Paris fair as a way to explain the modern world to Latin American children. It is not clear whether Martí learned about the Paris fair through books and periodicals or visited the fair. His descriptions are rich in detail. I thank José Prieto for having referred me to Martí.

2. DO, 15 June 1888. About this building, and from a knowledgeable, artistic point of view, Fausto Ramírez has written two indispensable essays: "Vertientes nacionalistas en el modernismo"; and "Dioses, héroes y reyes mexicanos en París, 1889." Daniel Schávelzon reprinted some of the documents that dealt directly with the debate about the Mexican Aztec Palace in Paris. See "La polémica de la 'Arquitectura nacional' y el Pabellón de México en París," in *La polémica del arte nacional*, ed. Daniel Schávelzon (Mexico City, 1988), 137–64. In addition, Díaz y de Ovando's article contains some interesting reprints of the media coverage of the Mexican exhibit in Paris: Clementina Díaz y de Ovando, "México en la Exposición Universal de 1889," *Anales del Instituto de Investigaciones Estéticas*, no. 61 (1990): 109–71. As I was revising this man-

uscript, I gained access to María Auxiliadora Fernández, "The Representation of National Identity in Mexican Architecture: Two Case Studies (1680 and 1889)" (Ph.D. diss., Columbia University, 1993), which deals with the Aztec Palace and with Carlos de Sigüenza y Góngora's Triumphal Arch—"Teatro de Virtudes Políticas." Fernández's insightful analysis incorporates postcolonial and representational theory into art history. Unfortunately, although she devotes more than 200 pages to an examination of Góngora's arch, she gives fewer than 30 pages to the Aztec Palace.

3. For orientalism at universal expositions, see Timothy Mitchell, "The World as Exhibition," *Comparative Studies of Society and History* 31, 2 (1989):217–37; Timothy Mitchell, *Colonising Egypt* (Cambridge, 1988), 1–33; Sylviane Leprun, *Le Théâtre des colonies* (Paris, 1986), 130–48; Zeynep Çelik, *Displaying the Orient* (Berkeley, 1992); and Raymond Corbey, "Ethnographic Showcases, 1870–1930," *Cultural Anthropology*, 8 (1993):338–69.

4. Regarding the characteristics of nineteenth-century Latin American patriotic history, see Colmenares, *Las convenciones contra la cultura*.

5. I use the term as explained by David Brading, "Creole Patriotism," in his *The Origins of Mexican Nationalism* (Cambridge, 1985), 3–23. The main aspects of this patriotism were the "exaltation of the Aztec past, the denigration of the Conquest, the xenophobic resentment against the *gachupines*, and the devotion to Our Lady Guadalupe" (p. 3). See also Enrique Florescano, *Memoria mexicana* (Mexico City, 1987), 300–308.

6. For this radical indigenism, see David Brading, *The First America* (Cambridge, 1991), 583–602; Brading, *Origins of Mexican Nationalism*, 81–88; and Luis Villoro, *Los grandes momentos del indigenismo en México* (Mexico City, 1950, 1984), 137–44.

7. See Lucas Alamán, *Historia de Méjico desde los primeros movimientos que prepararon su independencia en el año de 1808 hasta la época presente*, 5 vols. (Mexico City, 1849–1852).

8. For instance, consider José Vasconcelos's hispanism that recalls that of don Lucas. See chapter 12.

9. Quoted in Çelik, *Displaying the Orient*, 11.

10. See Manuel Payno, *Compendio de la historia de México para uso de los establecimientos de instrucción pública en la República Mexicana* (Mexico City, 1870); and Josefina Vázquez, "La historiografía romántica en México," *Historia Mexicana* 10, 1 (1960): 1–13.

11. Compare Valadés's argument. He believed that it was during the Porfiriato that official history started (Valadés, *El porfirismo*, vol. 2, xxv).

12. Concern that the lack of an objective national history was an obstacle in the consolidation of the nation was shared by conservatives and even by monarchists. In this regard, see Josefina Vázquez, *Nacionalismo y educación en México* (Mexico City, 1970), 66–67.

13. Because, as Josefina Vázquez has shown, the first two textbooks about independent Mexico had not assimilated the Mexican past, leaving aside or misrepresenting such events as the war with the United States. See Josefina Vázquez, "Síntesis de la historia de México de historiadores mexicanos," in *Investigaciones contemporáneas sobre historia de México* (Mexico City, 1971), 213–27; and Vázquez, *Nacionalismo y Educación*, 44–132.

14. In addition to Riva Palacio's book, Ballesca published the next general and major history of Mexico, Justo Sierra's *México, su evolución social*, 2 vols. (Barcelona, 1900–1902). On Ballesca's relationship with Riva Palacio, see Victoriano Salado

Álvarez, *Memorias de Victoriano Salado Álvarez*, vol. 1, *Tiempo Viejo* (Mexico City, 1946), 324–27; and Ballesca's correspondence with Riva Palacio, 1 September 1887, Vicente Riva Palacio's letters, Genaro García Collection, University of Texas at Austin.

15. Justo Sierra argued that he was invited by Riva Palacio to participate and that the idea for the book emerged within the intellectual discussions of the Altamirano group. See Justo Sierra, "México a través de los siglos," *Revista nacional de letras y ciencias*, no. 2 (1889):120–21. In turn, historian Daniel Cosío Villegas argued that the book had originated as a study of the war of intervention which was requested of Riva Palacio by President González (HMM 8:660–66). Valadés observed that *México a través de los siglos* had begun as a reaction to José María Roa Bárcena's "Recuerdos de la invasión norteamericana," published in *El Siglo XIX*. See Valadés, *El porfirismo*, vol. 1, 413–14. Gargallo di Castel Lentini believes that after Juárez's reforms, a small group of intellectuals realized that it was necessary to create a national literature based on the reinterpretation of national history. *México a través de los siglos* was part of this reinterpretation. See Francesca Gargallo di Castel Lentini, "Vicente Riva Palacio: Uno storico liberale," *Revista di Storia della Storiografia* 3, 2–3 (1982):123–30. See also Clementina Díaz y de Ovando, *Vicente Riva Palacio y la identidad nacional* (Mexico City, 1985).

16. "Proyecto de historia general de México," 3, preserved in Vicente Riva Palacio's papers, Genaro García Collection, University of Texas at Austin.

17. His novels and short stories were often inspired by colonial times. In fact, he held the records of the Inquisition and wrote novels about this topic, such as *Monja casada, vírgen y mártir*, and *Martín Garatuza*. See González Navarro, HMM, 689.

18. Riva Palacio, *México a través de los siglos*, vol. 2, 471.

19. See Brading, *The Origins of Mexican Nationalism* (Cambridge, 1985).

20. As both Moreno and Hale observe, late-nineteenth-century liberals read Darwin in French and thus absorbed the French interpretation of evolutionism as *transgresisme*. Riva Palacio's footnotes referred to French translations of Darwin's works, especially to Ch. Darwin, *La Descendance de l'homme*, 2d ed., 2 vols. (Paris, 1873–1874). See Riva Palacio, *México a través de los siglos*, vol. 2, 474–81; Hale, *Transformation of Liberalism*, 206–10; Moreno, *La polémica del darwinismo*; and Roberto Moreno, "Mexico," in *The Comparative Reception of Darwinism*, ed. Thomas F. Glick (Chicago, 1988), 346–74.

21. See Riva Palacio, *México a través de los siglos*, vol. 2, 472–73.

22. For examples of the contemporary endurance of this view, see Díaz y de Ovando, *Vicente Riva Palacio*, 38; and Agustín F. Basave Benítez, *México mestizo: Análisis del nacionalismo mexicano en torno a la mestizofilia de Andrés Molina Enríquez* (Mexico City, 1992), 13–41, 121–24.

23. In this regard, see Victor Rico González, *Hacia un concepto de la conquista de México* (Mexico City, 1953), 205.

24. Compare Chavero, *Xochitl* and *Quetzalcóatl*, and the criticisms by Vicente Riva Palacio, which were made under the pseudonym of Cero: *Los Ceros* (Mexico City, 1882). Chavero, as mentioned in previous chapters, participated in the 1904 Saint Louis Fair. See Chavero, *Discurso pronunciado el 24 de septiembre de 1904 en el Congreso de artes y ciencias de la Exposición Universal de San Luis Missouri* (Mexico City, 1905).

25. Riva Palacio satirized Chavero's archaeological concerns and his private interests in public positions (Cero, *Los Ceros*, 156–57).

26. Ibid., 154.
27. For an explanation of the origins of the neoclassical discourse in Mexico, see David Brading, "Héroes republicanos y tiranos populares," *Cuadernos Americanos,* Nueva Época 5, 11 (1988):9–26. See also Hale's concept of the era of eloquence, in "Political and Social Ideas in Latin America," 367–441.
28. Chavero, *México a través de los siglos,* vol. 1, 67.
29. Ibid., 80.
30. Santiago Ballesca's letter to Riva Palacio, 23 April 1889, Vicente Riva Palacio's letters, Genaro García Collection, University of Texas at Austin.
31. "Proyecto de historia general de México," 4.
32. R. Canto was a Catalan designer of theater stages and a devoted admirer of representational capabilities of expositions. See Justino Fernández, *El arte del siglo XIX en México* (Mexico City, 1967), 396. In 1888, for Barcelona's universal exposition, Canto published his *Dedicatoria d'un pagés de montanya à la Universal Exposició de Barcelona* (Barcelona, 1888). See Elías A. de Molins, *Diccionario biográfico y bibliográfico de escritores y artistas catalanes del siglo XIX,* 2 vols. (New York, 1972); and Canto's letter to Riva Palacio (in which Canto seems to have been a sort of benevolent critic of Riva Palacio's amateur paintings), Vicente Riva Palacio's letters, Genaro García Collection, University of Texas at Austin.
33. Especially the descriptions by Desiré de Charnay, who was given permission in 1880 to do archaeological research and to keep a good portion of what he discovered (to be shipped to France). See Justo Sierra's support of this permission in México, Cámara de Diputados, *Diario de los Debates* 1 (1880):532, 536. The various volumes of *México a través de los siglos* also included paintings by José María Velasco, among others.
34. By the late 1880s technology not only had made books more accessible but also had produced new ways of enriching the expressive capabilities of books. In this regard, the study of the relationship between romanticism and technology is linked to the analysis of media, nationalism, and modes of representation. Compare Walter J. Ong, *Rhetoric, Romance, and Technology* (Ithaca, 1971); and Lee Fontanella, *La imprenta y las letras en la España romántica* (Frankfurt, 1982).
35. Ch. Baudelaire, "L'Exposition Universelle de 1855: Beaux-Arts," in his *Oeuvres complètes,* préface, présentation et notes de Marcel A. Ruff (Paris, 1968), 345.
36. Edward King Kingsborough, *Antiquities of Mexico,* 9 vols. (London, 1831–1848), reprinted as *Antigüedades de México, basado en la recopilación de Lord Kingsborough,* study and interpretation by José Corona Nuñez (Mexico City, 1964–1967).
37. See Jean Fréderic de Waldeck, *Voyages pittoresque et archéologique dans la province d'Yucatan (Amérique Central), pendant les années 1834 et 1836* (Paris, 1838) and Jean Fréderic de Waldeck and E. Brasseur de Bourbourg, *Monuments anciens du Mexique: Palenque et autres ruines* (Paris, 1866).
38. See Guillerme Dupaix, *Antiquitiés mexicaines: Relation des trois expeditions du Capitaine Dupaix,* 3 vols. (Paris, 1824); and Desiré de Charnay, *Les Anciennes Villes du Nouveau Monde: Voyages d'explorations au Mexique et dans l'Amérique Centrale* (Paris, 1885).
39. Alfredo Chavero, *Historia antigua y de la conquista,* in Riva Palacio, *México a través de los siglos,* vol. 1 (Barcelona, 1888).

40. Ramírez, "Dioses," 220.
41. Letter from Salazar to Pacheco, 26 May 1988, EXP, Box 1, Exp. 7. Lithographs and plans of the building are missing from the archive. They can be found, together with a partial reproduction of Salazar's letter to Pacheco, in Godoy, *México en París*, 69–73.
42. *El Monitor Republicano*, 9 June 1888, reproduced in Godoy, *México en París*, 65–68. For a final version, see the official description of the Mexican pavilion by Antonio Peñafiel, *Explication de l'édifice mexicaine à l'Exposition Internationale de Paris en 1889* (Barcelona, 1889).
43. Antonio Peñafiel, *Monumentos del arte mexicano antiguo: Ornamentación, mitología, tributos y monumentos* (Berlin, 1890). Peñafiel acknowledged that several mythological characters for the Mexican pavilion were based on Sahagún's designs which in turn were included in the original of Sahagún's *Historia de la Nueva España*, a book that was furnished to Peñafiel by Eduard Seler, who had found it in Florence (Letter to Pacheco, 12 May 1988), reproduced in Godoy, *México en París*, 65–68. Fausto Ramírez adds that Peñafiel also used Diego Durán's *Historia de las indias de la Nueva España e islas de tierra firme*, published in 1867 by José Fernández and in 1880 by Gumersindo Mendoza. In the second volume of this last book, Peñafiel found the useful description and depiction of Indian rites and gods (*Libro de los ritos y ceremonias en las fiestas de los dioses y celebración de ellas*). He also utilized Manuel Orozco y Berra, *Historia antigua de la conquista de México* (Mexico City, 1880). See Ramírez, "Dioses," 221.
44. Peñafiel, *Explication de l'édifice mexicaine*.
45. Ibid., 1. See also Peñafiel, *Monumentos del arte mexicano antiguo*. This book was written at the specific request of the Mexican Ministry of Economic Development and contained texts in Spanish, French, and English.
46. Peñafiel, *Explication de l'édifice mexicaine*, 1.
47. Ibid., 10.
48. Ibid., 3.
49. Ibid., 4.
50. Ibid., 56.
51. Ibid., 66.
52. Ibid., 72.
53. *Acta de la sesión del 12 de mayo de 1888*, in part reproduced in Godoy, *México en París*, 73–75. Chavero headed the commission in charge of evaluating Salazar's design. See BEMP 1 (1888):787.
54. Bablot, declaring himself unable to judge either project, did not vote.
55. In this regard, see "Instrucciones a las que deben sujetarse la comisión encargada de contratar las obras para el edificio de la exposición mexicana en París," signed by Pacheco, 7 June 1888, EXP, Box 1, Exp. 7, 10–11. About the contract with Santos y Cía., see BEMP 2 (1888):239.
56. See Díaz Mimiaga's request for a new location in EXP, Box 1, Exp. 8.
57. Mexican engineers had to deal with an old railroad track that crossed the Mexican lot in Paris. Salazar requested that the rails be removed by French authorities. See EXP, Box 1, Exp. 7. See also Díaz Mimiaga's final report, EXP, Box 12, Exp. 6, p. 4; Letter, Díaz Mimiaga to Fomento, EXP, Box 8, Exp. 14; and BEMP 1 (1888):48–51.
58. EXP, Box 8, Exp. 14, Spanish version of the contract "Antiguo Establecimiento

Cail. Pabellón de México en la Exposición Universal Internacional de 1889 en París. Contrato."

59. Díaz Mimiaga's final report—and Fausto Ramírez following it—claimed that the works of Zinc were produced by the house of Gillardin and designed by Julio Miltgen. The bronze works were done in the workshop of Thiebault Brothers (see Ramírez, "Dioses").

60. For copies of the contract, see EXP, Box 8, Exp. 14, pp. 2–15, and partial reproduction (without the specific prices of each part) in Godoy, *México en París,* 235–42. See also DO, 26 November 1888.

61. For all the works of cement, carpentry, plumbing, zinc, and so forth, see the description of each realm, in EXP, Box 8, Exp. 13.

62. Godoy reproduced some views of the interior of the building. Other images can be found in *Bulletin de l'Exposition Universelle de Paris 1889,* no. 52 (1889):92; and no. 32 (1889):252.

63. *La Lanteinier,* 24 June 1889. See also *Exposition Universelle. 1889. Pavillon du Mexique. Musique militaire-orchestre. Programmé du 22 juin,* SRE Le. 1104. Mexico spent more than 10,000 francs on the inauguration (Díaz Mimiaga's estimate, EXP, Box 12, Exp. 6, p. 24a).

64. *Le Petit Journal,* 24 June 1889.

65. *L'Événement,* 24 June 1889.

66. Emilia Pardo Bazán, "Al pie de la torre Eiffel," in her *Obras Completas,* vol. 19 (Madrid, n.d.), 246–47.

67. Vicente Riva Palacio, *Mis versos* (Madrid, 1893), 61.

6. MEXICAN ANTHROPOLOGY AND ETHNOGRAPHY

1. Eugène-Melchior de Vogüé, "À travers l'Exposition. VI. Les Exotiques.–Les Colonies," *Revue des Deux Mondes* 95 (September 1889):65.

2. See Martí's explanation of the 1889 fair in *Ismaelillo,* 81–91.

3. See France, Paris, Exposition Universelle de 1889, *Congrès International des Traditions Populaires. Première session. Compte rendu* (Paris, 1891). Although nothing Mexican was discussed in this congress, Mexico was represented by Eduardo Zárate and Rafael de Zayas Enríquez.

4. Stocking elaborates on Thomas Hardy's idea of universal exhibitions as precipices of time. See George Stocking, *Victorian Anthropology* (New York, 1987), 3–5.

5. World's fairs as a whole were main events for European and American orientalism. However, colonial expositions—within and outside universal exhibitions—were more emblematic examples of this orientalism. See Leprun, *Le Théâtre des colonies,* 17–23; for English fairs, Altick, *Shows of London,* 268–301; for American fairs, Rydell, *All the World's a Fair;* Corbey, "Ethnographic Showcases"; and Tankotte, "Kaleidoscopes of the World," 5–29.

6. Quoted in Mandell, *Paris 1900,* 21–22.

7. See Mitchell, *Colonising Egypt,* 1–33. See also Vogüé's account of the exhibit of the history of labor and anthropology: Eugène-Melchior de Vogüé, "À travers l'Exposition. IV. Les Arts libéraux.-L'Histoire du travail," *Revue des Deux Mondes* 94 (August 1889):929–44.

8. For further elaboration on the concepts of inside and outside, see Mary Louise Pratt, *Imperial Eyes: Travel and Transculturation* (New York, 1992), 6–9.

9. C. de Varigny, "L'Amérique à l'Exposition Universelle," *Revue des Deux Mondes* 95 (September-October 1889):837.

10. A copy of this pamphlet can be found at the Paris National Library, and in EXP, Box 12, Exp. 2, Ch. Possonnier, *L'Exposition mexicaine* (n.p., n.d.).

11. *La Presse Industrielle*, 4 July 1889, translated in Godoy, *México en París*, 271.

12. Leopoldo Batres, *Monografías de arqueología mexicana: Teotihuacán; o, la ciudad sagrada de los toltecas* (Mexico City, 1889).

13. See Peñafiel, *Monumentos del arte mexicano*; and Peñafiel, *Explication de l'édifice mexicaine*.

14. Çelik, *Displaying the Orient*, 2.

15. Charles Garnier and A. Ammann, *L'Habitation humaine* (Paris, 1892), iii–iv, quoted in ibid., 71–73.

16. Martí, *La edad de oro*, 63.

17. EXP, Box 8, Exp. 12.

18. See the lively descriptions and designs in Eugène-Emmanuel Viollet-le-Duc, "Les Nahuas, les toltèques," in his *Histoire de l'habitation* (Paris, 1875), 278–92; and his long prologue in Desiré de Charnay, *Cités et ruines americaines* (Paris, 1863), 10–103. Here he suggested that pre-Hispanic architecture resembled that of the Aryan people.

19. See Garnier and Ammann, *L'Habitation humaine;* and Argentina's report made by the French architect Alberto Ballu, "La arquitectura en la Exposición Universal de París 1889." Informe argentino, found in the world's fairs collection of the Smithsonian Institution.

20. In this regard, see Burton Benedict, "The Anthropology of World's Fairs," in *The Anthropology of World's Fairs: San Francisco Panama Pacific International Exposition of 1915* (Berkeley, 1984), 43–52; and Corbey, "Ethnographic Showcases," 341–45.

21. This exhibition was organized by the private McGrave Company. See Alfredo Barrón's report in SRE 19–22–25. The American photographer C. B. Waite, hired by the Mexican government, attended this fair and took photographs of the "street of Mexico" and its native people. See F. Ballesteros Montellano, "C. B. Waite, profesional fotógrafo" (Tesis de Licenciatura, Universidad Nacional Autónoma de México, 1989).

22. Rydell, *All the World's a Fair*, 94, 147–48. Regarding Mexico's presence at the 1894 Atlanta fair, see *Anales de la Secretaría de Fomento* (1897), 59–60, 282–89. See also Justo Sierra's commentaries in Justo Sierra, *Viajes en tierra yankee*, in his *Obras completas*, vol. 6, 46–49.

23. The Aztec Lilliputians were a male three feet four inches tall, and a female two inches shorter. See Altick, *Shows of London*, 284–87.

24. See the report of the Mexican commissioner at the 1895 Atlanta fair, Gregorio E. González, in México, Secretaría de Comercio, *Memoria de la Secretaría de Comercio, 1892–1896* (Mexico City, 1898), 59, 282–89. See also chapter 11.

25. See the account of this exhibit by Alfred Charles Collineau, *L'Anthropologie à l'Exposition Universelle de 1889* (Paris, 1890); and France, Paris, Exposition Universelle de 1889, *La Société, l'école et le laboratoire d'anthropologie de Paris à l'Exposition Universelle de 1889* (Paris, 1889).

26. France, Ministère du Commerce et de l'Industrie, *Exposition Universelle Inter-*

nationale de 1889 à Paris: Monographie, palais-jardins-constructions diverses-installations générales (Paris, 1892–1895).

27. France, Exposition Universelle Internationale de 1889 à Paris, *Catalogue général officiel: Exposition Rétrospective du travail et des sciences anthropologiques, Section 1, anthropologie, ethnographie* (Lille, 1889), 26, 28–29.

28. Ibid., 10.

29. See ibid., 655; and Stephen Jay Gould, *The Mismeasure of Man* (New York, 1981), 75–77.

30. García Cubas, *Étude*, 17–20.

31. Nicolás León argued that the origins of Mexico's scientific anthropology date back to 1864, when the French Scientific Commission of Mexico, sent by Napoleon III, arrived. See *Memorias de la Sociedad Antonio Alzate* 14 (1899–1900):63. See also his later history of Mexican physical anthropology, Nicolás León, "Historia de la antropología física en México," *American Journal of Physical Anthropology* 2, 3 (1919):229–49.

32. According to José María Velasco, this agency gained great recognition in the 1889 International Congress of Conservation and Protection of Artistic Works (*Memoria grupo primero*, December 1889, EXP, Box 18, Exp. 12). See also Salomón Nahmad, "Las ideas sociales del positivismo en el indigenismo de la época pre-revolucionaria en México," *América Indígena* 33, 4 (1973):1172.

33. See Jesús Galindo y Villa, "Discurso de sesión solemne conmemorativa del primer centenario de la muerte de Antonio de Alzate," *Memorias de la Sociedad Antonio Alzate* 13 (1899):15.

34. See León, "Historia de la antropología física," 235.

35. "La antropología actual y el estado de las razas," *La Naturaleza* 6 (1882–1884):126.

36. This is argued by M. S. Stabb, "Indigenism and Racism in Mexican Thought: 1857–1911," *Journal of Inter-American Studies* 1 (1959):406.

37. On degeneration, see J. Edward Chamberlain and Sander L. Gilman, eds., *Degeneration: The Dark Side of Progress* (New York, 1985). For some insights on the growth of these ideas in Latin America (Mexico, Argentina, and Brazil), see Nancy Leys Stepan, *The Hour of Eugenics* (Ithaca, 1991), 21–26.

38. For a lucid and complete discussion of this process in French anthropology, see Yvette Conry, *L'Introduction du darwinisme en France au XIXe siècle* (Paris, 1974), 51–89. See also Angèle Kremer-Marietti, "L'Anthropologie physique et morale en France et ses implications idéologiques," in *Histoire de l'anthropologie (XVIe-XIXe siècles)*, ed. Britta Rupp-Eisenreich (Paris, 1984), 319–51.

39. Stocking, *Victorian Anthropology*, 76.

40. Daniel Brinton, "The Nation as an Element in Anthropology," in *Memoirs of the International Congress of Anthropology*, ed. C. Staniland Wake (Chicago, 1894), 20; and Daniel Brinton, *Races and Peoples: Lectures on the Science of Ethnography* (New York, 1890), 40.

41. E. T. Hamy, "La Science française au Mexique," reprinted in his *Décades Américanae: Mémoires d'archéologie et d'ethnographie américaines* (Paris, 1884), 116. Hamy refers to various travel accounts published by Baradère. See also Anne-Christine Taylor, "L'Américanisme tropical: Une frontière fossile de l'ethnologie," in *Histoire de l'anthropologie (XVIe-XIXe siècles)*, ed. Britta Rupp-Eisenreich (Paris, 1984), 213–32; and Raoul d'Harcourt, *L'Américanisme et la France* (Paris, 1928).

42. G. d'Eichthal, *Études sur les origines bouddhiques de la civilization américaine*, extract from *Revue Archéologique* (Paris, 1864).

43. See France, Ministère de l'Instruction Publique, *Archives de la Commission Scientifique du Mexique* (Paris, 1865). In "La Science française au Mexique" Hamy mentioned various other French studies on Mexico.

44. Congreso Internacional de Americanistas, *Actas de la 11 reunión. Mexico 1895* (Mexico City, 1897), 29.

45. In this regard, see Stocking's explanation of the difference between the English (that is, "not a major center of physical anthropology") and French (that is, anatomical) anthropological traditions in the 1860s (Stocking, *Victorian Anthropology*, 67).

46. For a brief but lucid account of this debate, see Claude Blanckaert, "Monogénisme et polygénisme en France de Buffon à Paul Broca (1749–1880)" (Ph.D. diss., University of Paris, 1981); and Claude Blanckaert, "On the Origins of French Ethnology: William Edward and the Doctrine of Race," in *Bones, Bodies, Behavior: Essays on Biological Anthropology*, ed. George W. Stocking (Madison, 1988), 18–55.

47. Nahmad found in García Granados and his essay of 1910 a transitional position between pure positivism and culturalism, within the Porfirian regime. See Ricardo García Granados, *El concepto científico de la historia* (Mexico City, 1910), also published in the *Revista Positiva*; and Nahmad, "Las ideas sociales."

48. In fact, in this regard the Anglo-Saxon tradition was more appealing to Mexican intellectuals. Hence, in Spencer and Darwin, both studied in French, Mexicans found, as historian Charles Hale has argued, a version of social Darwinism that allowed them to "put attention on the peculiarities of their society within the universal scheme of evolution" (Hale, *Transformation of Liberalism*, 213–20). See also Ricardo Godoy, "Franz Boas and His Plans for an International School of American Archaeology and Ethnology in Mexico," *Journal of the History of the Behavioral Sciences* 14 (1977):228–42; and Luis Vázquez, "Historia y constitución profesional de la arqueología mexicana (1884–1940)," in *II Coloquio Pedro Bosch Gimpera* (Mexico City, 1993), 30–77.

49. Nicolás León, "Anomalías y mutilaciones étnicas del sistema dentario entre los tarascos pre-colombinos," *Anales del Museo Michoacano* 3 (1890):168–73, reprinted in Moreno, *La polémica del darwinismo*, 257–61. For biographical and bibliographical data about Nicolás León, see the essay "Nicolás León" by Germán Somolinos D'Ardois in his *Historia y medicina: Figuras y hechos de la historiografía médica mexicana* (Mexico City, 1957), 129–60. In this regard, see also Alfonso Herrera's rejection of Riva Palacio's conclusion, in Alfonso L. Herrera, "Nota relativa a las causas que producen atrofia de los pelos. Refutación a un argumento de M. de Quatrefages," *Anales del Museo Nacional de México*, 1st series, 4–5 (1891):216–24, reprinted in Moreno, *La polémica del darwinismo*, 262–72.

50. This was published in *Diario del Hogar*, 13 January 1889, as a result of a request to Batres for the Mexican anthropological exhibition at the 1889 Paris fair.

51. Leopoldo Batres, "Antropología mexicana: Clasificación del tipo antropológico de las principales tribus aborígenes de México," *Revista Nacional de Letras y Ciencias* 1 (1889):191–96.

52. Peñafiel published an article about his *Monumentos mexicanos* in the 8th ses-

sion of the International Congress of Americanists, "Archéologie mexicaine," in Congrès International des Américanistes, *Compte Rendu de la Huitième Session* (Paris, 1890), 519–21. See also his description of the Mexican pavilion in "L'Edifice mexicaine," *Revue d'Ethnologie* 8 (1889):192–200.

53. This is argued by Herzfeld in his analysis of ancient Greek archaeology: M. Herzfeld, *Anthropology through the Looking-Glass: Critical Ethnography in the Margins of Europe* (Cambridge, 1987), 7.

7. MEXICAN ART AND ARCHITECTURE IN PARIS

1. See Ramírez, "Dioses," 201–53; Ramírez, "Acotaciones iconográficas," 15–85; and Ramírez, "Vertientes nacionalistas." See also Fernández, *El arte del siglo XIX.*

2. José María Velasco, "Memoria grupo primero," manuscript, 28 December 1889, EXP, Box 18, Exp. 12.

3. For an example of parallel phenomena in India, see Tapati Guha-Thakurta, *The Making of a New "Indian" Art: Artists, Aesthetics and Nationalism in Bengal 1850–1920* (Cambridge, 1992).

4. For a description of the interior of the Argentine building, see RUP 2:213–14. See also Vitali, "1889," 29–37.

5. RUP 2:213–32.

6. Mier, *México en la Exposición Universal,* 220. For the 1900 Paris fair, see chapter 11.

7. For shifts in European taste, see Raymond Rudorff, *Belle Epoque: Paris in the Nineties* (London, 1972), chap. 3; and Debora L. Silverman, *Art Nouveau in Fin-de-Siècle France: Politics, Psychology, and Style* (Berkeley, 1989), 1–11.

8. Ignacio Manuel Altamirano, "La pintura histórica en México," *El Artista* 1 (1874):8, reprinted in Ida Rodríguez Prampolini, *La crítica de arte en el siglo XIX,* vol. 2 (Mexico City, 1964).

9. Luis Miguel Aguilar, *La democracia de los muertos* (Mexico City, 1988), 106.

10. For an itemized description of the various styles, see Israel Katzman, *Arquitectura del siglo XIX en México* (Mexico City, 1973), 63–219.

11. In this regard, see Çelik's analysis of Oriental pavilions at world's fairs: Çelik, *Displaying the Orient,* 135–37. See also chapter 11.

12. For an analysis of the *arquitectura de la ingeniería,* see Renato de Fusco, *Historia de la arquitectura contemporánea* (Madrid, 1992), 30–63.

13. Çelik, *Displaying the Orient,* 136.

14. Garnier's dislike is referred to by Katzman (*Arquitectura del siglo XIX en México,* 256) and by Tepozcaconetzin Calquetzani, the pseudonym used by the opponent of Luis Salazar's pro–pre-Hispanic article, "Bellas Artes: Arquitectura, arqueología y arquitectura mexicana," *El Arte y La Ciencia* 1 (December 1899), reprinted in Rodríguez Prampolini, *La crítica,* vol. 2, 379–80.

15. See Ballu, "La arquitectura en la Exposición Universal," 370–71 on Mexico, 377 on Argentina.

16. Minutes, session of the Mexican commission, 1 June 1889, EXP, Box 12, Exp. 3.

17. *El Nacional,* 11 September 1890, 7 November 1890, reprinted in Rodríguez Prampolini, *La crítica,* vol. 3, 254.

18. Manuel Francisco Álvarez, *Las ruinas de Mitla y la arquitectura* (Mexico City, 1900), 258.
19. See Fusco, *Historia de la arquitectura contemporánea*, 59–63.
20. In this regard, see F. Seitz, "Architects et engénieurs: L'Exposition de 1889," *Revue d'Histoire Moderne et Contemporaine* 39 (July-September 1992):483–92.
21. *Encyclopaedia Britannica*, 11th ed., vol. 2, 441.
22. César Daly, "Discours prononcé au nom des anciens élèves de Félix Duban" (1871)," quoted in Çelik, *Displaying the Orient*, 136.
23. Eugène-Melchior de Vogüé, "À travers l'Exposition. II. L'Architecture.–Les Feux et les eaux.–Le Globe," *Revue des Deux Mondes* 94 (July-August 1889):441.
24. See Çelik, *Displaying the Orient*, 115–16.
25. For a discussion of this appeal, see Álvarez, *Las ruinas de Mitla*, 257–59. Álvarez was for many years the director of the Escuela de Artes y Oficios, and as such he traveled to the 1900 Paris fair to attend the congresses related to architecture. For information about him, see the introductory study to a re-edition of some of his articles, Elisa García Barragán, "Manuel F. Álvarez," in *Manuel F. Álvarez: Algunos escritos*, selection by Elisa García Barragán (Mexico City, 1981–1982), 8–16.
26. For typical view in this regard, see E. Barberot, *Histoire des styles d'architecture dans tous les pays despuis les temps anciens jusqu'à nos jours*, 2 vols. (Paris, 1891).
27. See Eugène-Emmanuel Viollet-le-Duc, "Les Nahuas, les Toltèques," in his *Histoire de l'habitation*, 278–92. See also his long prologue in Desiré de Charnay's *Cités e ruines americaines* (Paris, 1863), 10–103. On Viollet-le-Duc in Mexico, see Vicente Martín Hernández, *Arquitectura doméstica de la ciudad de México* (Mexico City, 1981), 256–57.
28. See the entry "Style," in Eugène-Emmanuel Viollet-le-Duc's *Dictionnaire raisonné*, as reprinted in *The Foundations of Architecture: Selections from the Dictionnaire raisonné*, introduction by Barry Bergdoll, trans. K. D. Whitehead (New York, 1990), 231–63.
29. See Jesús T. Acevedo, "Apariencias arquitectónicas," a lecture delivered in the last years of the Porfirian period at the Sociedad de Conferencias, included in Jesús T. Acevedo, *Disertaciones de un arquitecto* (Mexico City, 1967), 35–54.
30. See Jaime Genaro Francisco Javier Cuadriello Aguilar, "La arquitectura en México (ca. 1857–1920): Ensayo para el estudio de sus tipos y programas" (Tesis de Licenciatura, Universidad Iberoamericana, 1983); and Katzman's explanation for the decline of classicism in Mexico (*Arquitectura del siglo XIX en México*, 69).
31. See Katzman, *Arquitectura del siglo XIX en México*, 313; and Nicolás Mariscal, *La enseñanza de la arquitectura en México* (Mexico City, 1902), 13–16. See also M. Bazant, "La enseñanza y la práctica de la ingeniería durante el porfiriato," in *La educación en la historia de México: Lecturas de historia mexicana* (Mexico City, 1992), 167–210.
32. See letter from E. Bonaffe to Jean-Camille Formigé, *Gazette des Beaux-Arts* 2 (1889):167–73. See also Seitz, "Architects et engénieurs."
33. He constructed the Mexican pavilions for both the 1889 and the 1900 Paris fairs. In addition, he finished the penitentiary in Mexico City. See Katzman, *Arquitectura del siglo XIX en México*, 266.
34. See J. F. Godoy, *Enciclopedia de contemporáneos* (Washington, 1898), 48–49. Two other architects, Vicente Reyes and José María Alva, participated in the design of Salazar's project. See Katzman, *Arquitectura del siglo XIX en México*, 291.

35. On the relationship between technology and style, see Cuadriello Aguilar, "La arquitectura en México," 24; regarding construction, see Katzman, *Arquitectura del siglo XIX en México*, 63–220.

36. See Robert Goldwater, *Primitivism in Modern Art* (Cambridge, 1986); and Jullian, *Triumph of Art Nouveau*.

37. Fausto Ramírez also points out the generational aspect as an important role in the consolidation of a new aesthetic vision that eventually concluded in modernism. See Ramírez, "Vertientes nacionalistas," 114–15.

38. Nicolás Mariscal, "Bellas Artes: Arquitectura," *El Arte y la Ciencia* 1 (April 1899):49.

39. See Luis Salazar, "La arqueología y la arquitectura," in *Actas del XI Congreso Internacional de Americanistas* (Mexico City, 1895), 137–49. In 1898 he published the same essay as a pamphlet, and in 1899 he presented the last version of the paper in *El Arte y la Ciencia* 1 (1899):1–3; 2 (1899):113–14; 3(1899):129–30.

40. Salazar, "La arqueología y la arquitectura," *El Arte y la Ciencia* 1 (1899): 130. The three parts of this article are reprinted in Rodríguez Prampolini, *La crítica*, vol. 3, 367–77, quotation on p. 376.

41. Of course, the revival of the past in architecture was only a part of the general construction of a nationalistic ideology. In Mexico, Salazar's attempts were paralleled by various efforts to reconstruct Hispanic architecture. See Tepoztecaconetzin Calquetzani, "Bellas artes, arquitectura, arqueología, y arquitectura mexicana," *El Arte y la Ciencia* 1, 11–12 (1899), reprinted in Rodríguez Prampolini, *La crítica*, vol. 3, 377–80. Fausto Ramírez has interpreted this debate in his lucid essay on nationalism (Ramírez, "Vertientes nacionalistas," 111–67).

42. Fausto Ramírez has pointed this out, although he supports the idea of a clear and definite distinction between nationalists and cosmopolitans. See Ramírez, "Vertientes nacionalistas," 114–15.

43. See Simmel's concept of architecture as a battle between spirit and nature, always won by nature in George Simmel, "Las ruinas," *Revista de Occidente* 2 (June 1924):304–7.

44. For an example of this consciousness, see Nicolás Mariscal, *El desarrollo de la arquitectura en México* (Mexico City, 1901); Álvarez, *Las ruinas de Mitla*, 257–59; and *El Nacional*, 11 September–7 November 1890, reprinted in Rodríguez Prampolini, *La crítica*, vol. 3, 252–75.

45. Lecture delivered in the 1910s and included in Acevedo, *Disertaciones de un arquitecto*, 53.

46. Federico E. Mariscal, *La patria y la arquitectura nacional* (Mexico City, 1915), 10.

47. I have benefited from Fausto Ramírez's lucid analysis of the inherent problems that originated in Peñafiel's historic-nationalist project and in Contreras's aesthetically cosmopolitan concepts. See Ramírez, "Dioses."

48. See Cecilio A. Robelo, *Diccionario de mitología nahuatl* (Mexico City, 1951), 344–45.

49. Robelo argues that in the *Códice Telleriano*, Centeotl is pictured as a man married to Xochiquetzalli; in the Vatican Codice, this deity is represented as a woman. See Robelo, *Diccionario*, 54.

50. Clendinnen believes that Chalchiutlicue was represented as a woman at the lake, as a sort of natural "visible presence personified for easy intelligibility": Inga

Clendinnen, *Aztecs: An Interpretation* (Cambridge, 1991), 251. According to Ramírez, these images were taken by Peñafiel from Durán's book. See Fray Diego Durán, *Historia de las Indias de la Nueva España*, vol. 2 (Mexico City, 1951), which includes, as an appendix, Alfredo Chavero, *Explicación del Códice geroglífico de M. Aubin* (Mexico City, 1951).

51. Peñafiel, *Explication de l'édifice*, 7.
52. Robelo, *Diccionario*, 474.
53. Ibid., 47.
54. Clendinnen, *Aztecs*, 164, 168.
55. Ramírez, "Dioses," 227.
56. Peñafiel, *Explication de l'édifice*, 9.
57. Orozco y Berra, *Historia antigua*.
58. For a detailed description of the aesthetic aspects of this combination, see Ramírez, "Dioses," 233–41.
59. EXP, Box 1, Exp. 7. In his report to Gustavo Baz, Minister of Justice, Contreras told of his studies in Spain and France in the workshops of Gagbot and the House of Allard Hodot, in which he obtained his Placa de Obrero de Primera. See also DO, November 1889, 1–2; Justino Fernández, *El arte moderno en México: Breve Historia—Siglo XIX* (Mexico City, 1937), 192–98; and Patricia Pérez Walters, "Jesús Contreras (1866–1902): Imágenes escultóricas y personalidad artística" (Tesis de Licenciatura, Universidad Iberoamericana, 1989); and the summary of this thesis in the text prepared for an exhibit of Contreras's works (México, Consejo Nacional para la Cultura y las Artes, *Jesús Contreras, 1866–1902: Escultor finisecular* [Mexico City, 1990].
60. This was true for all nations. For instance, leading American sculptors, such as Augustus Saint-Gaudens and Daniel Chester French, were in France in the 1880s. See Kathryn Greenthal, "Late Nineteenth Century American Sculpture in Its International Context," in *La scultura nel XIX secolo*, edited by Horst W. Janson (Bologna, 1981), 241–47.
61. See BEMP 1 (1888):188–94.
62. In the UIA-Díaz are letters from Díaz Mimiaga to Porfirio Díaz and from Contreras to Porfirio Díaz. Despite differences with Porfirio Díaz (in the beginning of 1889), Contreras was personally recommended by Díaz Mimiaga to Díaz. Contreras visited Díaz in January 1890 with a letter of introduction by Díaz Mimiaga. See UIA-Díaz, Leg. 15, Box 6, Doc. 2501; Leg. 15, Box 3, Doc. 1278; and Leg. 15, Box 6, Docs. 2610–12.
63. *El Diario del Hogar*, 3 January 1892, quoted in Pérez Walters, *Jesús F. Contreras*, 23. Contreras also was involved in real estate and in the urban transformation of Mexico City.
64. Contreras did not break completely with classicism, although he introduced romantic and eclectic tendencies. For analyses of the French sculpture of the era, see William Hauptman, "'La Mélancolie' in French Romantic Sculpture," in *Saloni, gallerie, musei e loro influenza sullo sviluppo dell'arte dei secoli XIX e XX*, ed. F. Haskell (Bologna, 1981), 111–15; Ruth Butler, "Nationalism, a New Seriousness, and Rodin: Some Thoughts about French Sculpture in the 1870s," in Haskell, *Saloni*, 67.
65. See the discussion of liberal aesthetics and the explanation of romanticism in Mexican sculpture in Mario Monteforte Toledo, *Las piedras vivas: Escultura y sociedad en México* (Mexico City, 1965). See also Fernández, *El arte del siglo XIX*, 196–97;

and Salvador Moreno, "Un siglo perdido de la escultura mexicana: El siglo XIX," *Artes de México*, no. 133 (1970):5–93.

66. Léon Cahun, "L'Exposition Universelle. VII. Le Mexique (1er article)," *La Phare de la Loire*, 20 June 1889. Part of this article was reproduced in *El Mundo* of Mexico City (15 August 1889), but the name of the author was changed to León Satin. A portion of the article was reproduced in Rodríguez Prampolini, *La crítica*, vol. 3, 235–36.

67. See Ramírez, "Acotaciones iconográficas."

68. For an elaboration of Velasco's type of realism, see Juan de la Encina, *El paisajista José María Velasco (1840–1912)* (Mexico City, 1943), 87–97.

69. See ibid., 97. On landscape painting as naturalistic exercise, see Yi-Fu Tuan, *Topophilia: A Study of Environmental Perception, Attitudes, and Values* (Englewood Cliffs, 1974); and Ann Bermingham, *Landscape and Ideology: The English Rustic Tradition, 1740–1850* (Berkeley, 1986).

70. See Angela Miller, "Everywhere and Nowhere: The Making of the National Landscape," *American Literary History* 4 (1992):208.

71. Cahun, "L'Exposition Universelle."

72. For Velasco's archeological paintings, see Carlos Martínez Marín, "Jesús Velasco y el dibujo arqueológico," in Ramírez, *José María Velasco*, 203–32. For Velasco's scientific paintings, see Elías Trabulse, "Aspectos de la obra científica de José María Velasco," in Ramírez, *José María Velasco*, 123–80; and Elías Trabulse, *José María Velasco: Un paisaje de la ciencia en México* (Toluca, 1992).

73. See Ramírez, "Acotaciones iconográficas."

74. México, *Catalogue officiel de l'Exposition de la République Mexicaine*.

75. Claude Debroise, "José María Velasco y el paisaje fotográfico decimonónico (apuntes para un paralelismo)," in Ramírez, *José María Velasco*, 103–21.

76. Peter Hales, *William Henry Jackson and the Transformation of the American Landscape* (Philadelphia, 1988), 173–75. According to Hales, these pictures are in the U.S. Library of Congress, in the Detroit Company Collection. José Antonio Rodríguez argues that 600 of these pictures were published in the *Album of Documentary Views of México*, 4 vols., 1884–1885. See José Antonio Rodríguez, "Vues mexicaines, el libro perdido de A. Briquet," *Dominical: El Nacional* (17 November 1991):4–8; and W. Jones, "William Henry Jackson in México," *American West* 14, 4 (1977):10–21.

77. See Debroise, "José María Velasco," 115. See also Claude Debroise, "Plein soleil: Le Cas mexicain," *Photographies*, no. 6 (1984):32–38.

78. Alan Trachtenberg, *Reading American Photography: Images as History: Mathew Brady to Walker Evans* (New York, 1989), 288.

79. See Rosa Casanova and Olivier Debroise, *Sobre la superficie bruñida de un espejo: La fotografía en México en el siglo XIX* (Mexico City, 1989), 12. See also Michel Poivert, "La Photographie artistique à l'Exposition Universelle de 1900," *Histoire de l'Art*, no. 13–14 (1991):60–66.

80. Velasco seems to have been fascinated by photography. During his sojourn in Paris in 1889, he became very interested in the development of photography. See Debroise, "José María Velasco," 120; and Islas García, *Velasco*.

81. See Patricia Massé, "Ilusiones compartidas entre la albúmina y el óleo: Las tarjetas de visita de Cruces y Campa," *Anales del Instituto de Investigaciones Estéticas*, no. 63 (1992):125–36. On Romualdo García and Valleto, see Enrique Fernández

Ledesma, *La gracia de los retratos antiguos* (Mexico City, 1950), which includes a catalogue of nineteenth-century photographers.

82. See Casanova and Debroise, *Sobre la superficie;* Claudia Canales, *Romualdo García: Un fotógrafo, una ciudad, una época* (Guanajuato, 1980); and Olivier Debroise, *Fuga Mexicana* (Mexico City, 1994), 54–76. See also Olivier Debroise, "Plein Soleil."

83. See Ian Jeffrey, *Photography—A Concise History* (London, 1981). He observes that this phrase was the title of the first photography book ever published.

84. Fernández, *El arte del siglo XIX*, 137.

85. In New Orleans, he exhibited "Ariadna abandonada." See *El Siglo XIX*, 5 November 1884. See also Fernández, *El arte del siglo XIX*, 109–10.

86. For the discussion of pre-Hispanic motifs in painting, see Stacie G. Widdifield, "National Art and Identity in Mexico, 1869–1881" (Ph.D. diss., University of California, Los Angeles, 1986); Stacie G. Widdifield, "Dispossession, Assimilation, and the Image of the Indian in Late-Nineteenth-Century Mexican Painting," *Art Journal* 49 (Summer 1990):125–32; Eloísa Uribe, "Más allá de lo que el ojo ve: Sobre el relieve de Fray Bartolomé de las Casas (1864) por Miguel Noreña," *Memoria*, Museo Nacional de Arte, no. 3 (1991):5–25; Ramírez, "Vertientes nacionalistas."

87. *El Siglo XIX*, 21 October 1895. Other paintings with pre-Hispanic themes at the Academia de San Carlos were: *El tormento de Cuauhtémoc*, by Leandro Izaguirre; *La prisión de Cuauhtémoc*, by Joaquín Ramírez; *Visita de Cortés a Moctezuma*, by Juan Ortega; and *Fray Bartolomé de las Casas, protector de los indios* and *Episodios de la conquista*, both by Felix Parra (included in Rodríguez Prampolini, *La crítica*, vol. 3, 330).

88. See Robelo, *Diccionario*, 467.

89. See Ignacio Manuel Altamirano's section on arts in *Primer almanaque histórico, artístico y monumental de la República Mexicana*, ed. Manuel Caballero (New York, 1883–1884). The full text is included in Rodríguez Prampolini, *La crítica*, vol. 3, 156.

90. See the following examples, which I have located in the medical press: Ernesto Ulrich, "Consideraciones respecto a la acción del pulque sobre la economía," *Gaceta Médica de México*, 3d ser., 4 (1909):614–27; "Dictamen del Jurado calificador de la Academia sobre la memoria 'El hígado reasumiendo la historia del alcoholismo en la economía, constituye también respecto del pulque el punto objetivo de sus efectos patológicos,'" *Gaceta Médica de México* 20 (1885):410–51; and the study by a member of the exhibition team, José Segura, *Dictamen sobre el pulque* (Mexico City, 1901). There were also some studies that, based on the economic advantages of the maguey industry, defended pulque. See, for example, *El maguey y sus productos* (Mexico City, 1901); and Antonio Carbajal, *Estudio sobre el pulque considerado principalmente desde el punto de vista zinotécnico* (Mexico City, 1901).

91. See José G. Lobato, *Estudio químico-industrial de los varios productos del maguey mexicano* (Mexico City, 1884).

92. On the issue of gender in this painting, see Widdifield, "National Art and Identity"; and "Dispossession."

93. See México, *Catalogue officiel de l'Exposition de la République Mexicaine;* and Islas García, *Velasco*.

94. See México, *Catalogue officiel de l'Exposition de la République Mexicaine*.

95. See Goldwater, *Primitivism in Modern Art*, xv–xviii.

96. Velasco, "Memoria grupo primero."

97. Ibid.

98. See France, Paris, Exposition Universelle de 1889, *Catalogue officiel illustré de l'Exposition Centennale de l'Arte Français, 1800 à 1889*, ed. Ludovic Bachet, reprinted by Garland (Paris, 1981).

99. On Velasco's dislike of impressionism, see Encina, *El paisajista*.

100. Among them, works by Puvis de Chavannes, Léon Bonnat, Carolus-Duran, William A. Bouguereau, Jules Lefebre, J. Felix Barrias, Benjamin Constant, Gaston Saintpierre, Aime Morot, and Alfred Roll.

101. In this regard, see the interesting opinion of the English critic Alfred Haddon, *Evolution in Art* (London, 1895).

102. Sala was a well-known British critic who wrote extensively on art in the late nineteenth century; he was also an illustrator for Dickens's writings. Pierre Fritel was a French painter known for his historical canvases, such as *L'Enfance de Jeanne d'Arc*. Guillon was a distinguished late-nineteenth-century French landscape painter.

103. Velasco, "Memoria grupo primero."

104. It seems that he disliked traveling, as shown by his impressions of his trip to Paris and, later, of his trip to the 1893 Chicago world's fair. Only two canvases resulted from his trip to Paris: one of Havana Bay; the other a view of the sea (see Islas García, *Velasco*; and Velasco, "Memoria grupo primero"). See also M. Payno's letter to Riva Palacio, 5 November 1889, Vicente Riva Palacio's letters, Genaro García Collection, University of Texas at Austin.

105. Velasco, "Memoria grupo primero."

8. STATISTICS, MAPS, PATENTS, AND GOVERNANCE

1. Condorcet, *Fragment on the New Atlantis, or Combined Efforts of the Human Species for the Advancement of Science*, reprinted in *Condorcet: Selected Writings*, ed. K. M. Baker (Indianapolis, 1976), 300.

2. In this regard, see Kuhn's use of what he calls the Merton thesis to explain the "geographical patterns" in science: Thomas Kuhn, "Mathematical versus Experimental Traditions in the Development of Physical Science," in his *The Essential Tension* (Chicago, 1977), 58–59.

3. Claude Nicolet, *L'Idée républicaine*, 310.

4. Gabino Barreda's educational reform in 1867 was the bedrock on which the scientific turn of the late nineteenth century was based. See Hale, *Transformation of Liberalism*, 141.

5. José Yves Limantour, *Discurso pronunciado por el Sr. Lic. José Ives Limantour* (Mexico City, 1901), 1.

6. México, Secretaría de Fomento, *Reglamento económico de la Junta y personas auxiliares de la Comisión Mexicana en la Exposición Universal de París*, EXP, Box 18, Exp. 8, p. 10.

7. Annotated circular, EXP, Box 1, Exp. 18, p. 8. See also article 25 of *Reglamento*, EXP, Box 18, Exp. 8, p. 10. The article asked the directors of each of the nine groups of products to keep themselves up-to-date in their respective areas of production, scientific expertise, or artistic concerns.

8. I examined the symbolic aspects in chapters 5, 6, and 7.

9. In this regard, see K. Rose's review essay, "Governing by Numbers: Figuring out Democracy," *Accounting, Organizations and Society* 16 (1991):673-92; and Ian Hacking's books on the history of statistics and probability: *The Emergence of Probability* (Cambridge, 1975) and *The Taming of Chance* (Cambridge, 1990).

10. For instance, in 1851 the comparative tables on moral statistics of the French statistician A. M. Guerry won recognition during the Crystal Palace meeting of the British Association for the Advancement of Science: A. M. Guerry, *Essai sur la statistique morale de la France* (Paris, 1833). See Hacking, *Taming of Chance*, 77.

11. See RUP 9.

12. See Stuart Woolf, "Contribution à l'histoire des origines de la statistique: France, 1789-1815," in École des Hautes Études en Sciences Sociales, *La Statistique en France à l'époque napoléonienne* (Brussels, 1980), 45-126; and Hacking, *Taming of Chance*, 28-34.

13. See the detailed account of the technical development of statistics in Stephen M. Stigler, *The History of Statistics* (Cambridge, 1986), 159-220. For the opposition to Quetelet's use of statistics in the 1830s and 1840s, see Gerd Gigerenzer et al., *The Empire of Chance* (Cambridge, 1989), 45-48.

14. See *La Grande Encyclopédie* (Paris, 1886-1902), vol. 30, 448.

15. Jesús Hermosa, *Manual de geografía y estadística de la República Mejicana* (Paris, 1857), vi. See also one of the first Mexican manuals for the making of statistics, José María Pérez Hernández, *Curso elemental de estadística* (Mexico City, 1874). Also in this regard, see Ramón Manterola, *Ensayo sobre una clasificación de las ciencias* (Mexico City, 1884), which developed the concept of probability in science.

16. Emiliano Busto, *Estadística de la República Mexicana* (Mexico City, 1880), iii.

17. Agustín Aragón, "La estadística," *Revista Positiva*, no. 23 (1902):484-93.

18. Antonio Peñafiel, "La estadística en la República Mexicana," *Boletín de la Sociedad Mexicana de Geografía y Estadística*, 4th epoch, 4 (1897):512-13.

19. Regarding this institution, see Enrique de Olivarría y Ferrari, *La Sociedad Mexicana de Geografía y Estadística* (Mexico City, 1901).

20. See Carlos Díaz Dufoo, *México, 1876-1892* (Mexico City, 1893).

21. Quetelet established the concept of the "average man" in society and thus the idea of deviation. For my analysis of the creation of a modern nation, it is important to bear in mind that Quetelet was not only a great statistician but also, as Hacking characterizes him, "the greatest of international propagandists for the value of statistics." Small wonder that, as many did in England and Germany, in Mexico Peñafiel referred to him to justify the importance of statistics. See Hacking, *Taming of Chance*, 74; and Peñafiel, "La estadística."

22. See Antonio García Cubas, *Importancia de la estadística* (Mexico City, 1871).

23. Juan de D. Bojorquez, *Orientaciones de la estadística en México: Conferencia sustentada en la Sociedad Mexicana de Geografía y Estadística, el 14 de Mayo de 1929* (Mexico City, 1929); and Francisco Barrera Lavalle, *Apuntes para la historia de la estadística en México, 1821-1910: Concurso Científico y Artístico del Centenario* (Mexico City, 1911).

24. See annotated circular, EXP, Box 1, Exp. 18, pp. 8-9.

25. See Godoy, *México en París*, 214-16, 221-22; and for the tables described here, see EXP, Box 51, Exp. 8-15; Box 52, Exp. 1-10; and Box 53, Exp. 1-11.

26. For instance, in 1888 the president of the Sociedad Agrícola Mexicana was asked about data on haciendas in Mexico City. He replied that such information was

completely unavailable (EXP, Box 8, Exp. 20). The general agricultural statistics prepared for the 1900 Paris fair included Mexico City (EXP, Box 52, Exp. 2).

27. Argentina, Comisión, Exposición de París 1889, *L'Agriculture et l'élevage dans la République Argentine d'après le recensement de la première quinzaine d'octobre de 1888 . . . ouvrage publié sous la direction de F. Latzina* (Paris, 1889). The province of Buenos Aires produced Comisión Auxiliar Provincial, Exposición Universal de París 1889, *Censo agrícola-pecuario de la provincia de Buenos Aires . . . para contribuir a la representación de la República Argentina en la Exposición Universal de París* (Buenos Aires, 1889), which included information on the nationalities of people working on ranches. Previously, Argentina had prepared a statistical study for the 1867 Paris fair: Argentina, La Confederation Argentine a l'Exposition Universelle de 1867 à Paris, *Notice statistique générale et catalogue* (Paris, 1867).

28. See E. Levasseur, *Le Brésil*, 2d ed. (Paris, 1889). This collection of statistical and geographical data was also published as part of the Brazil entry in the *Grande Encyclopédie*.

29. See Rafael Reyes, *Apuntamientos estadísticos sobre la república del Salvador* (San Salvador, 1888).

30. Before the mathematical development of probability, the rule of large numbers was constantly invoked. See Gigerenzer et al., *Empire of Chance*, 39–40.

31. Hacking, *Taming of Chance*, 77.

32. F. Galton, *Natural Inheritance* (London, 1889).

33. Manuel Orozco y Berra, *Apuntes para la historia de la geografía en México* (Mexico City, 1881), 428. See also Bernardo García Martínez, "La Comisión Geográfico-Exploradora," *Historia Mexicana* 24, 4 (1975):485–555.

34. Document reproduced in Godoy, *México en París*, 220–21. See the particular catalogue of this commission by Díaz: Agustín Díaz, *Catalogue des objets composant le contigent de la Commission, précédé de quelques notes sur son organisation et ses travaux* (Paris, 1889).

35. DO, 28 March 1888.

36. See the report on the 1889 map: México, Secretaría de Fomento, *Memoria para la carta general geográfica de la República Mexicana: Año de 1889* (Mexico City, 1890); and García Martínez, "La Comisión Geográfico-Exploradora," 492–93.

37. Indeed, before any lobbying of the wizards of progress, this display was awarded two grand prizes by the French jury. See México, Commission Géographique Exploratrice de la République Mexicaine, *Catalogue* (Mexico City, 1889), 26 and 52; and México, Secretaría de Fomento, *Lista de los premios y recompensas obtenidos por México en la Exposición Internacional de París de 1889* (Mexico City, 1891), 7.

38. About him, see Miguel A. Sánchez Lamego, "Agustín Díaz, ilustre cartógrafo mexicano," *Historia Mexicana* 24 (1975):556–65.

39. Díaz, *Catalogue des objets*, 4–5. See also Sánchez Lamego, "Agustín Díaz," 563; and Orozco y Berra, *Apuntes*, 429.

40. See EXP, Box 4, Exp. 28. Here García Cubas was appointed to write a geographical and statistical study of the country.

41. Based on this book, Antonio García Cubas wrote *Mexico: Its Trade, Industries and Resources* (Mexico City, 1893) for Mexico's display in Chicago. For a history of García Cubas's original maps and the development of his works until 1880, see Orozco y Berra, *Apuntes*, 421–34. See also García Cubas's archive at the Sociedad Mexicana de Geografía y Estadística.

42. Castillo and Aguilera created the Instituto Geológico. As a result of Aguilera's initiative the institute was granted the building it possessed in Santa María, Mexico City. See Alberto María Carreño, "Un insigne geólogo mexicano: Ing. José G. Aguilera," in his *Semblanzas*, vol. 2 (Mexico City, n.d.), 5–22. See also Mexico, Secretaría de Fomento, *Bosquejo de una carta geológica de la República Mexicana*, 1:300,000,000 (Mexico City, 1889).

43. In this regard, see Gabriel Gohau, *A History of Geology*, trans. Albert and Marguerite Carozzi (New Brunswick, 1990), 99–110, 125–37.

44. See *Catálogo de los trabajos de la comisión especial para la formación del Bosquejo de una Carta Geológica de la República*, 22 April 1889, signed by Antonio del Castillo, EXP, Box 1, Exp. 16, pp. 114–114bis.

45. EXP, Box 3, Exp. 12.

46. Ibid.; and EXP, Box 1, Exp. 16, p. 71. See also Teodoro Flores, "Panorama de la geología en México (1551–1951)," in *Memoria del Congreso Científico Mexicano* 3 (1953), 23–61.

47. Castillo's report in EXP, Box 1, Exp. 16. See also Antonio del Castillo's study: *Catalogue descriptif des météorites* (Paris, 1889).

48. EXP, Box 1, Exp. 15. See also the "Catálogo descriptivo de los meteoritos de México," *La Naturaleza*, 2d series, 1 (1887–1890):328.

49. Regarding this unification of science and technology, see Thomas Kuhn, "The Relation between History and the History of Science," in his *Essential Tension*, 127–61.

50. See Alfred Chandler, *Scale and Scope: The Dynamics of Industrial Capitalism* (Cambridge, 1990), 47–89; and David S. Landes, *The Unbound Prometheus: Technological Change and Industrial Development in Western Europe from 1750 to the Present* (Cambridge, 1969), 196–201.

51. To Juan Andrés Velarde, for a new way to amalgamate metals. From the AGN Gobernación Leg. 132, quoted in Sánchez Flores, *Historia de la tecnología y la invención*, 291. According to Mexican patent laws, the president had to sign the patent and a fee of 50 to 150 pesos had to be paid. See *Patent and Trade-Mark Laws of America*, Bulletin 3 (Washington, 1891).

52. Previously, there were other regulations (the law of 7 May 1832 and the *reglamento* of 12 July 1852). See Juan de la Torre, *Legislación de patentes y marcas* (Mexico City, 1903); and Elías Trabulse, *Las patentes de invención durante el siglo XIX en México*, Boletín del Archivo General de la Nación, 3d series, no. 34 (Mexico City, 1988). See also the catalogue and research by Soberanis, "Catálogo de patentes de invención en México."

53. For instance, for the 1901 Buffalo world's fair, Mexican officials produced the following pamphlets (in English): *Patent Law of the United States of Mexico; Law for the Promotion of New Industries in the United States of Mexico; and Trade Mark Law of the United States of Mexico*, both mentioned in Albino R. Nuncio, "Informe relativo a la participación de México y a los trabajos de la Comisión Mexicana, en la Exposición Pan-Americana celebrada en Buffalo N.Y. en 1901," in México, Secretaría de Fomento, *Memoria presentada al Congreso de la Unión por el Secretario de Estado y del Despacho de Fomento, Ing. Leandro Fernández, 1 de enero 1901–31 de diciembre de 1904* (Mexico City, 1909), 181–203. See also México, Comisión Nacional de los Estados Unidos Mexicanos para la Exposición Pan-Americana de Buffalo, Nueva York, *Official Catalogue of the Mexican Exhibit at the Pan-American Exposition at Buffalo* (Buffalo, 1901).

54. In the Patentes y Marcas I have been able to find the registration of only three inventions: Maximino Río de la Loza's device to avoid railroad accidents, Pugibet's machine to fabricate cigarettes, and a machine to process vegetable fibers (henequen).

55. See French requirements and rules for exhibitors in RUP 1.

56. EXP, Box 8, Exp. 24.

57. The products exhibited in the industry group are listed in México, *Catalogue officiel de l'Exposition de la République Mexicaine*.

58. These machines were important to the economy of Yucatán. In fact, during the 1860s a dispute took place regarding the patent of the first scraping machines. By the 1880s the debate was over and new technology was imported from the United States. In this regard, see Narcisa Trujillo, "Las primeras máquinas desfibradoras de henequén," in *Enciclopedia Yucatanense*, ed. C. Echánove Trujillo, vol. 3 (Mérida, Mexico, 1946), 627–56; and Cámara Zavala, "Historia de la industria henequenera hasta 1919," in *Enciclopedia Yucatanense*, vol. 3, 657–725.

59. Inventory of boxes in the steamship *Chateau Margaux*, EXP, Box 8, Exp. 27.

60. EXP, Box 3, Exp. 11.

61. EXP, Box 8, Exp. 26.

62. See the numerous entries of his name in Patentes y Marcas.

63. Jules Verne, "Five Weeks in a Balloon," translation quoted in René Dubos, *Reason Awake: Science for Man* (New York, 1970), 56.

64. See Jochen Hoock, "Économie politique, statistique et réforme administrative en France et en Allemagne dans la deuxième moitié du 18e siècle," in *Formation et transformation du savoir administratif en France et en Allemagne (18e/19e s.)*, ed. Guido Melis et al. (Baden-Baden, 1989), 34–35.

65. For an insightful analysis of the origins of rational politics in France during the attempt to reconstruct a "government culture" after the revolution and during the first decade of the nineteenth century, see Pierre Rosanvallon, *Le Moment Guizot* (Paris, 1985), 21–25.

66. As such, administration acquired a certain independence from politicians, but not from government. In this regard, and to explain the different traditions of administrative knowledge (that is, French, English, and American), see Rosamund Thomas, *The British Philosophy of Administration* (London, 1978).

67. Regarding public administration in France, see Guy Thuillier, *Bureaucratie et bureaucrates en France au XIXe siècle* (Geneva, 1980), 220–42, 479–98; and Guy Thuillier, *La Bureaucratie en France aux XIXe e XXe siècles* (Paris, 1987), 663–88. For the way in which scientific politics supported the origins of the French Third Republic, see Rosanvallon, *Le Moment Guizot*, 58–71.

68. See Nicolet, *L'Idée républicaine*, 287.

69. See Pierre Legendre, *Histoire de l'administration de 1750 à nos jours* (Paris, 1968) 87–90.

70. Box 1, Exp. 18.

71. About him and his work, see C. Javier Guillén, "Emiliano Busto y su aportación a la investigación social en México" (Tesis Licenciatura, Universidad Nacional Autónoma de México, 1977).

72. A contract was signed with the French editor R. Dupont for 10,453 francs for the publication of 2,000 copies of the book. See EXP, Box 1, Exp. 19.

73. Emiliano Busto, *La administración pública en Méjico* (Paris, 1889).
74. See Busto's reports to Díaz in UIA-Díaz, L. 14, c. 23, d. 11382, 11383; L. 14, c. 26, d. 12911, 12913; and L. 14, c. 14, d. 6700, 6701.
75. EXP, Box 1, Exp. 18.
76. News of this study was published in such media as *Le Temps* and *Le Figaro*. See EXP, Box 1, Exp. 18.
77. Jules Josat, *Le Ministère de Finances* (Paris, 1883). This is exactly the same definition that Josat presented on p. 1.
78. Busto, *La administración pública en Méjico*, 117–18.
79. The book that Busto followed was Josat, *Le Ministère de Finances*. In 1894 Josat published *Recueil de rédactions sur des sujets d'économie politique et sur des questions financières et administratives* (Paris 1894). In 1883 he lamented the general lack of scientific manuals of administration in France, as did Busto in Mexico. But, as historian Omar Guerrero observed, Busto did not include Mexico's history of administrative thought, which included such authors as de la Rosa, Madrazo, Castillo Velasco, and Alamán. See Omar Guerrero, Introducción a la administración pública (Mexico City, 1985), 230–31.
80. Josat, *Le Ministère de Finances*, 1.
81. Busto transcribed Josat's *tableau récapitulatif* (graphic summary) for each French ministry and used the same format to develop the *cuadros sinópticos* for the Mexican ministries.
82. Busto, *La administración pública en Méjico*, 119.
83. For a list of previous studies on public administration in Mexico, see Guerrero, *Introducción a la administración pública*, 209–11.
84. Hale, *Transformation of Liberalism*, 21.
85. Studies by bureaucrats pointed out the need to control corruption, clientelism, and favoritism. Lorenzo de Zavala (1820s), Lucas Alamán (1830s), José María Luis Mora (1830s), Luis de la Rosa (1850s), Julio Jiménez (1880s), and others pointed out the problem of *empleomanía* (large bureaucracy) and corruption. See Guerrero, *Introducción a la administración pública*, 218–40.
86. See Gilles J. Guglielmi, *La Notion d'administration publique dans la théorie juridique française* (Paris, 1991); and Thomas, *British Philosophy of Administration*.

9. NATURAL HISTORY AND SANITATION

1. See Francisco de Asís Flores y Troncoso, *Historia de la medicina en México*, vol. 3 (Mexico City, 1888). See also Alamán's description of work in natural history and its effect on the concept of a wealthy Mexico: Alamán, *Historia de Méjico*, vol. 1, 114–16, 120–23.
2. See José María Velasco's explanation of the development of natural history in relation to the "new" peace, in *La Naturaleza* 6 (1882–1884):4–5.
3. EXP, Box 4, Exp. 27. He also wrote a study on pulque that was displayed in Paris.
4. EXP, Box 4, Exp. 27, pp. 6–7, *Informe que tiene la honra de rendir el que suscribe al jefe del 5to. Grupo de Exposición*. Mexico's exhibits at world's fairs disclosed the existence of a quiet but fecund and serious dedication of Mexican scientists to natural

history. Altamirano's botanical studies became an indispensable part of Mexico's presence at various world's fairs. See, for example, the English version of his study prepared for the 1904 Saint Louis fair: Francisco Altamirano, *Materia Médica Mexicana* (Saint Louis, 1904).

5. Among the material that was lost were: 28,625 samples of dried vegetables, 14,604 samples of insects, 908 birds, 165 reptiles, 47 mammals, 1,580 mollusks, 2,000 mineral rocks, 12,000 fossils, 293 kinds of wood, and 230 fruits. See Carlos Pacheco, *Memoria presentada al Congreso de la Unión por el Secretario de Estado y del Despacho de Fomento, Colonización, Industria y Comercio, corresponde a los años transcurridos de enero de 1883 a junio de 1885*, vol. 1 (Mexico City, 1887), 108.

6. The exhibition comprised 2,000 samples of fossils, 5,500 samples of plants, 30,445 samples of diverse insects, 15 samples of stuffed reptiles, 50 samples of reptiles in alcohol, 1,254 samples of stuffed birds, 6,631 of birds in skin, 50 samples of stuffed mammals, 112 samples of mammals in skin, and 3 skeletons. See México, Commission Géographique Exploratrice de la République Mexicaine, *Catalogue*, 59.

7. This was argued by Agustín Díaz, director of the commission, in the catalogue of the commission's exhibit in Paris. See ibid., 41.

8. This was the case with other countries; see, for example, the Chilean study by Adolfo Murillo, *Plantes médicinales du Chile* (Paris, 1889).

9. See Eli de Gortari, *La ciencia en la historia México* (Mexico City, 1965), 189–95; and Elías Trabulse, *La ciencia en México* (Mexico City, 1983), vol. 1, 46–49.

10. Mexico, Commission Géographique Exploratrice, *Catalogue*, 25. The collections exhibited were: Distrito Federal, *Collection de mille plantes* . . . , a French edition of Alfonso Herrera's *Nouvelle pharmacopée mexicaine;* state of Morelos, 100 samples of indigenous medicinal plants; state of Puebla, 216 samples of indigenous medicinal plants; state of Michoacán, 29 samples of indigenous medicinal plants; and state of Veracruz, 3 samples of indigenous medicinal plants. Previously, these types of collections had been sent to Philadelphia and New Orleans (see "Catálogo de la colección de productos naturales indígenas remitidos por la Sociedad de Historia Natural," *La Naturaleza* 3 [1876], 382).

11. See Godoy, *Enciclopedia biográfica de contemporáneos*, 107–8.

12. See Mexico, Commission Géographique Exploratrice, *Catalogue*, 30 and 123.

13. EXP, Box 6, Exp. 9. He was also appointed the Mexican representative at the International Congress of Chemistry in Paris.

14. EXP, Box 6, Exp. 9.

15. DO, 16–18 October 1890. He analyzed the teaching and research qualities of laboratories, their architecture, and their location (EXP, Box 6, Exp. 9). Regarding the history of this first modern laboratory in Mexico, see José Joaquín Izquierdo, *Balance cuatricentenario de la fisiología en México* (Mexico City, 1934), 245–46.

16. See *El Estudio*, no. 2 (1889).

17. "A L'Exposition. Le Palais Mexicain. L'Édifice et ses dimensions.–Une des plus curieuses expositions du Nouveau-Monde.–Le Pays des Aztéques.–Textiles et oiseauxmouches," *La Lanteinier*, n.d.

18. See Ory, *Les Expositions Universelles de Paris*, 9–27; and Ann-Louise Shapiro, *Housing the Poor of Paris, 1850–1902* (Madison, 1985), 87. Regarding social economy at the 1889 exhibition, see X. Ryckelynck, "L'Économie sociale dans le rapport d'Alfred Picard sur l'Exposition Universelle de 1889," *Le Revue de l'Économie Sociale* (1990):97–

107; and Laure Godineau, "L'Économie sociale à l'Exposition Universelle de 1889," *Le Mouvement Social*, no. 149 (1989):71–87. For the 1900 exposition, see Marc Pénin, "L'Économie sociale à travers le rapport de Charles Gide sur l'Exposition Universelle de 1900," *Le Revue de l'Économie Sociale* (1990):137–157; and France, Paris, Exposition Universelle de 1889, *Congrès International d'Assistance, tenu du 28 juillet au 4 août 1889*, 2 vols. (Paris, 1889). For an analysis of the transformation of the concept of public assistance, see Jean-Baptiste Martin, *Le Fin des mauvais pauvres: De l'assistance à l'assurance* (Seyssel, 1985).

19. See Gide, *Économie sociale*. For the origins of the concern with public assistance, see William Coleman, *Death Is a Social Disease* (Madison, 1982), 24–33; Catherine Jean Kudlick, "Disease, Public Health and Urban Social Relations: Perceptions of Cholera and the Paris Environment, 1830–1850" (Ph.D. diss., University of California, Berkeley, 1988), 18–97; and Gueslin, *L'Invention de l'économie sociale*, 151–60.

20. See Ann F. Le Berge, *Mission and Method: The Early Nineteenth-Century French Public Health Movement* (Cambridge, 1992). For public health in the French Third Republic, see Martha L. Hildreth, *Doctors, Bureaucrats, and Public Health in France, 1888–1902* (New York, 1987); the controversial interpretation by Bruno Latour, *The Pasteurization of France* (Cambridge, 1987); Jacques Léonard, *La Médicine entre les savoirs et les pouvoirs* (Paris, 1981), 149–85, 241–327; and Kudlick, "Disease," 18–34.

21. Regarding this issue, see Hildreth, *Doctors*, 1–35, 107–63; and Kudlick, "Disease," 62–84.

22. See Léonard, *La Médicine*, 317.

23. See Jules Rochard, "L'Hygiène en 1889," *Le Revue des Deux Mondes* 96 (November-December, 1889):54–85.

24. RUP 2:139–41.

25. See, for example, the opinions of three historians of French hygiene. Le Berge (*Mission and Method*, 2) argues that within scientism, "public hygiene was one of those areas that had to be transformed into a scientific discipline.... If the hygienists' method was scientific, their mission was hygienism, a kind of medical imperialism incorporating both the medicalization and moralization of society." Shapiro (*Housing the Poor*, 134) believes that during the second half of the century "hygienists abandoned their earlier romanticist aspirations to become therapeutic clergy administering to a regenerated population. Instead they were more likely to address problems of sanitary engineering and the control of contagious diseases." Finally, the controversial historian Bruno Latour maintains that not until the Pasteurian revolution, and not before 1895, did hygiene acquire a clear scientific and political status (Bruno Latour, "Le Théâtre de la preuve," in *Pasteur et la révolution pastorienne*, ed. Claire Salomon-Bayet, [Paris, 1986]), 341).

26. See Kudlick, "Disease," 79–81.

27. For a short analysis of the different forms of professionalization, see Jan Goldstein, *Console and Classify: The French Psychiatric Profession in the Nineteenth Century* (Cambridge, 1987), 8–40; and Charle, *La République des universitaires*, 168–85. See also Hildreth, *Doctors*, 107.

28. Especially after the 1883–1884 cholera epidemic.

29. In this regard, see Andrew Aisenberg, "The *enquête*," in his "Contagious Disease and the Government of Paris in the Age of Pasteur" (Ph.D. diss., Yale University, 1993).

30. By 1889, however, Pasteur was already a national hero. He was received at the Congress of Hygiene in the Hotel de Ville of Paris with "Le Marseillaise." France, Paris, Exposition Universelle de 1889, *Congrès International d'Higiène et de Démographie, 1889. Compte rendu* (Paris, 1890). In this regard see also J. Léonard, "Comment peut-on être pasteurien?," in Salomon-Bayet, *Pasteur*, 151–52.

31. The literature on this topic is vast. See the classical study by Erwin Ackerknecht, "Anticontagionism between 1821–1867," *Bulletin of the History of Medicine* 22 (1948): 562–93; and Le Berge, *Mission and Method*, 1–6.

32. It could be argued that the legacy of the early health movements was not completely overcome by the 1880s. See Le Berge, *Mission and Method*, 96.

33. This is argued in Shapiro, *Housing the Poor*, 154. Hildreth (*Doctors*, 19) observed that "the anxieties over population resulted [in the 1880s] from the comparison of France, Germany, and Britain."

34. See Rochard, "L'Hygiène en 1889"; and Latour, "Le Thèâtre," 353.

35. Among the duties of this council was to certify doctors' diplomas. See México, Secretaría de Gobernación, *La salubridad e higiene pública en los Estados Unidos Mexicanos*, lxxvii.

36. From 1877 to 1879 the role of the council was briefly devaluated when it was incorporated into the Junta Directiva de la Beneficencia Pública (ibid., lxxvii–lxix).

37. México, Consejo Central de Salubridad, *Memoria leída por el Secretario del Consejo Central de Salubridad el día 17 de enero de 1867* (Mexico City, 1867), 1.

38. See France, *Congrès International d'Higiène et de Démographie, 1889*. Dr. Gaviño presented this code at the congress.

39. See "Proyecto de Código Sanitario de los Estados Unidos Mexicanos, sometido a la Secretaría de Gobernación, 30 de Junio 1889," reprinted in Gutiérrez et al., *Historia de la salubridad y la asistencia en México*, vol. 3 (Mexico City, 1960), 327–29.

40. Gayol was named general engineer of Mexico City in 1884, and he traveled abroad to study sanitary systems. See Eduardo Liceaga, "Progresos alcanzados por la higiene de 1810 a la fecha," in SSA, Box 9, Exp. 9.

41. See Miguel Angel de Quevedo, *Memoria sobre el Valle de México* (Mexico City, 1889).

42. See México, *Catalogue officiel de l'Exposition de la République Mexicaine*, 141–42.

43. For a detailed account of the pamphlets and books published by the institute for the year 1889, see Francisco Fernández del Castillo, *Historia bibliográfica del Instituto Médico Nacional de México (1888–1915)* (Mexico City, 1961), 32–33.

44. As Mexican envoys to the Public Assistance Congress, the archival material only mentions Alfredo Bablot, but the reports of the congress mentioned Pedro García and Angel Gaviño and reproduced Gaviño's speech. See France, Paris, Exposition Universelle de 1889, *Congrès International d'Assistance, tenu du 28 juillet au 4 août 1889*, vol. 1 (Paris, 1889), xxi–xxii. Regarding Angel Gaviño, see Rafael Heliodoro Valle, *La cirugía mexicana del siglo XIX* (Mexico City, 1942), 250. See also France, Paris, Exposition Universelle de 1889, *Congrès International de Dermatologie et de Syphiligraphie, 1889* (Paris, 1890). According to Mexican sources, Pedro García, Manuel Flores, and José Ramírez attended the second congress, but no official Mexican envoy is mentioned in the French report of it.

45. They were joined by Angel Treviño. See France, Paris, Exposition Universelle de 1889, *Congrès International de Medicine Mentale tenu à Paris 2–20 août 1889* (Paris, 1890); and France, *Congrès International d'Higiène et de Démographie, 1889*.

46. See SSA, Box 7, f. 37, report by Alvarado that included the translation of sanitary codes from the states of Maine, Pennsylvania, Indiana, and New York.

47. See Manuel María Carmona y Valle, *Leçons sur l'étiologie et la prophylaxie de la fièvre jaune* (Mexico City, 1885). For the history of the disease, see Folke Henschen, *The History and Geography of Diseases*, trans. Joan Tate (New York, 1966), 36–39.

48. In this regard, see the analysis of Carmona y Valle's role in the international fight against yellow fever in François Delaporte, *The History of Yellow Fever*, trans. Arthur Goldhammer (Cambridge, 1991), 68–74. See Porfirio Parra, "Discurso pronunciado en la solemne inauguración del IV Congreso Médico Nacional Mexicano, por su presidente, Dr. Porfirio Parra," in México, Secretaría de Instrucción Pública, *Fiestas del centenario de la independencia, organizadas por la Secretaría de Instrucción Pública* (Mexico City, 1910), 154–60.

49. See Rafael Lucio, *Opúsculo sobre el mal de San Lázaro o elefantiásis de los griegos* (Mexico City, 1889).

50. See *El Estudio* 1 (1889); and the translation of articles collected in one volume after the exhibition, México, Ministerio de Agricultura de México, Instituto Médico Nacional, *Travaux publiés par El Estudio* (Paris, 1892). Distinguished physicians and hygienists, among them José Ramírez, Francisco Altamirano, Francisco Río de la Loza, Eduardo Armendariz, Domingo Orvañanos, and Secundino Sosa, were involved in *El Estudio*.

51. Francisco de Asís Flores y Troncoso, *El himen en México* (Mexico City, 1885), 22.

52. See Florencio Flores, *Ligeros apuntes de pelvimetría comparada* (Cuernavaca, 1881), 9–11, 55–56.

53. See Alain Corbin, *Women for Hire*, trans. Alan Sheridan (Cambridge, 1990), 3–29.

54. See *Gaceta Médica de México* 25 (1890):8–15; 25, 2 (1890):27–39; 25, 3 (1890): 47–58; 25, 4 (1890):76–77; 25, 5 (1890):90; 25, 6 (1890):108; 25, 8 (1890):148–60; and 25, 9 (1890):173–79. See also Manuel Acuña, *Obras: Poesías, teatro, artículos y cartas*, ed. José Luis Martínez (Mexico City, 1965), 20.

55. Regarding this congress and the interesting debate, see SSA, Box 1, Exp. 2, 4.

56. In this regard, the story of Matilde Montoya is revealing. After many attempts and difficulties (which included having to work alone with corpses because it was improper for a woman to see naked bodies in the presence of a man), Montoya obtained her degree in 1887. She was the first woman doctor in Mexico, and for a long time the only one. See Laureana Wright de Kleinhans, *Biografías de mujeres notables mexicanas de la época prehispánica, la colonia y el siglo XIX* (Mexico City, 1910), 541.

57. EXP, Box 6, Exp. 15.

58. See Domingo Ovañanos, *Ensayo de geografía médica y climatología de la República Mexicana*, 2 vols. (Mexico City, 1889).

59. *El Estudio* 1 (1889), 398.

60. Some of these letters and questionnaires were published by the BEMP. See, for example, BEMP 3:34–38, 72–75, 198–204, 271–76, 289–304, 432–51.

61. The treatment of climates was based on Orvañanos's previous work, "Apuntes para el estudio del clima en México," *Gaceta Médica de México* 14, 3 (1879):302.

62. Liceaga did not agree with this figure. He believed that it was actually higher than that, but he did not furnish an estimate. See Alberto Correa, *Geografía de México: Obra adoptada como texto en los escuelas públicas del Distrito y territorios federales* (Mexico City, 1889).

63. The population comprised 5 million mestizos, 4 million Indians, 2 million Europeans, and 250,000 Blacks (*Geografía Médica*, 14).

64. See, for example, D. Jourdanet, *Du Mexique au point de vue de son influence sur la vie de l'homme* (Paris, 1861), which deals with the relationship between altitude and diseases.

65. As quoted in *Puebla: Su higiene, sus enfermedades* (Mexico City, 1888).

66. Indeed, the results of this study were first presented to the Academia Nacional de Medicina de México (*Gaceta Médica de México* 24, 8 [1889]:281–87).

67. The microbe *Mycibacterium Leprae* causes leprosy, but the disease is transmitted by vermin, fleas, and lice. See Henschen, *History and Geography of Diseases*, 117–18.

68. His data were supported by the analysis of the Massachusetts State Board of Health and by Émile Poincaré's *Prophilaxie et géographie médicale des principales maladies tributaires de l'hygiène* (Paris, 1884).

69. Ibid., 60.

70. Ibid., 83.

71. See Delaporte, *History of Yellow Fever*, 83–101.

72. For a complete list of hygienists in Mexico, see the list prepared for the Fourth Panamerican Medical Congress, Panama, 1904, in SSA, Box 6, Exp. 7.

73. See, for instance, Fernando Malanco, "Intereses profesionales, males y remedios," *Gaceta Médica de México* 24, 12 (December 15, 1889):465–80.

74. See Liceaga's memoirs *Mis recuerdos de otros tiempos*, ed. Francisco Fernández del Castillo (Mexico City, 1949); his speech in the Hygienic Exposition during the centennial celebration of Mexico's independence in 1910, "Progresos alcanzados por la higiene de 1810 a la fecha," in SSA, Box 9, Exp. 9; and the speech he delivered at the Sociedad Pedro Escobedo in 1911, "Algunas consideraciones acerca de la higiene social en México," SSA, Box 10, Exp. 3, also published with the same title (Mexico City, 1911). On how the vaccine against rabies was brought to Mexico, see *Congreso Médico Panamericano*, vol. 2 (Mexico City, 1896), 899–905. On the way in which the vaccine was developed in Mexico, see N. Ramírez de Arrellano, "Higiene. Profilaxis de la rabia," *Gaceta Médica de México* 24, 6 (1889):206–9.

75. See, for example, Liceaga's command of the situation in SSA, Box 4, Exp. 21. Liceaga sent José Ramírez to the International Sanitary Conference in Washington in 1902, then to work on controlling bubonic plague in Mazatlán, and then, in 1903, to Brussels to the International Sanitary and Demographic Congress, where he fell ill and died. For Liceaga's success in fighting yellow fever, see SSA, Box 8, Exp. 4 (1907).

76. See, for example, *Diario del Hogar*, 2 January 1900 (editorial). Liceaga was active in the Porfirian reelectionist campaigns.

77. France, *Congrès International d'Higiène et de Démographie, 1889*, 336.

78. SSA, Box 4, Exp. 24.

79. Liceaga, as a doctor, appeared on the board of directors of various insurance companies and also lobbied on behalf of insurance companies with President Díaz (see UIA-Díaz, L. 14, Box 13, 6035–36, in which Liceaga requests appointments for the directors of the insurance company La Mutua). Liceaga was the personal physician of Porfirio Díaz's wife.

80. SSA, Box 8, Exp. 1.

81. México, *Dictámenes y resultados del Congreso Nacional de Higiene* (Mexico City, 1884), 3.

82. SSA, Box 4, Exp. 24.
83. SSA, vol. 18, Edición especial documentos e informes presentados en la 20 reunión anual de la Asociación Americana de Salubridad Pública, Ciudad de México, November 29–December 2, 1892, Concord, N.H., Republican Press Association, 1894.
84. Alberto J. Pani, *La higiene en México* (Mexico City, 1916).
85. *El Estudio* 1, 1 (1889):2.
86. See, for example, Perla Chinchilla Pawling, "Introduction," in Trabulse, *La ciencia en México*, vol. 4, 9–25. She argues that between 1870 and 1914 Mexican science had its best chance to catch up with international modern science.

10. IRONY

1. For Baudelaire's views, see Charles Baudelaire, "Exposition Universelle 1855: Beaux-Arts," in his *Oeuvres complètes: Préface, présentation et notes de Marcel A. Ruff* (Paris, 1968), 361–70. For Henry Adams's, see his beautiful account of the Chicago Columbian exhibition in his *The Education of Henry Adams* (New York, 1918), 331–45.
2. In this regard, see Hale, *Transformation of Liberalism*; Guerra, *México*, vol. 1 (Mexico City, 1988); and Alicia Perales Ojeda, *Asociaciones literarias mexicanas: Siglo XIX* (Mexico City, 1957). For an insightful parallel regarding the mutual creation of a particular polity and a public opinion, see Keith Baker, "Public Opinion as Political Invention," in his *The Invention of the French Revolution* (Cambridge, 1990), 167–99.
3. The Porfirian regime was active in repressing the press, but it was even more successful in "sponsoring" newspapers and journalists. According to Bulnes, by the end of the Porfirian period 70 percent of the intellectuals and journalists were on the government's payroll. Nonetheless, between 1889 and 1900 active opposition could be found in newspapers such as *El Hijo del Ahuizote, El Diario del Hogar, El Monitor del Pueblo* (1885–1893), *El Popular* (beginning in 1897), to a certain extent *The Mexican Herald* (beginning in 1895), and *El Siglo XIX* (until 1896). See González Navarro, HMM, 388; José Bravo Ugarte, *Periodistas y periódicos mexicanos hasta 1935* (Mexico City, 1966); Florence Toussaint Alcaraz, *Escenario de la prensa en el porfiriato* (Mexico City, 1989); Henry Lepidus, *The History of Mexican Journalism* (Columbia, 1928), 47–80; and María del Carmen Ruiz Castañeda, "La prensa durante el porfiriato," in *El periodismo en México: 450 años de historia*, ed. María del Carmen Ruiz Castañeda (Mexico City, 1974), 209–64.
4. *El Hijo del Ahuizote*, 15 February 1989, 6. "Schnetz and Company" is a reference to E. Schnetz, a former member of the French tobacco company in Paris and Havana and an entrepreneur in Mexico who promoted French investment in manufacturing and in land-demarcation companies.
5. Ibid.
6. Ibid., 6.
7. *El Diario del Hogar*, 13 April 1888. For criticism of Pacheco's colonization policies, see *El Diario del Hogar*, 25 September 1889; 6, 8, 11, 12, and 26 October 1889; and 13 November 1889. In those editorials *El Diario del Hogar* analyzed the failure of colonization and the problems with Americans, French, Dutch, Germans, Italians, Chinese, Spaniards, and Blacks from Africa.

8. Ibid., 14 April 1888.

9. Ibid. The same newspaper complained on 15 February 1889 that Pacheco was negligent in his colonizing polices.

10. In Spanish, *exponer* can mean to exhibit, but it can also mean to expose, to show, to disclose, to put at risk, to uncover. Curiously, the French art and literary critic Philippe Hamon has written a book, *Expositions*, about literature and architecture in nineteenth-century France, taking as his point of departure the ambivalence of the word *exposition* and of the verb *exposer* in French.

11. *Época Ilustrado*, 23 November 1884.

12. *El Hijo del Ahuizote*, 29 January 1899, 65.

13. Ibid., 17 March 1889, 1.

14. Ibid., 4 June 1899, 160–61.

15. Ibid., 3 February 1889, 1.

16. Ibid., 20 January 1889, 1.

17. Ibid., 7 July 1889, 3.

18. Letters between Díaz Mimiaga and Porfirio Díaz, UIA-Díaz, Box 5, Leg. 15, Doc. 2497–2499.

19. *El Hijo del Ahuizote*, 8 September 1889, 3.

20. Ibid., 11 August 1889, 3.

21. Ibid., 18 February 1900, 101. I cannot fully dissect the irony of this satire because it refers to the specific humorous phrases and places of the time.

22. *El Diario del Hogar*, 15 March 1888.

23. Ibid., 13 April 1888. The official figure of 450,000 pesos was compared with the 200,000-peso budget of the United States.

24. *El Economista Mexicano*, reprinted and discussed in *El Diario del Hogar*, 17 February 1888.

25. *El Diario del Hogar*, 16 June 1889.

26. Federico Gamboa, *Mi diario: Mucho de mi vida y algo de los otros*, 1st series, vol. 3 (Mexico City, 1920), 352–53.

27. Ibid., 1st series, vol. 1, 51. This is what he commented after receiving an offer to translate his novel *Apariencias*: see ibid., 51.

28. *El Hijo del Ahuizote*, 20 January 1889, 4–5.

29. For Amado Nervo's effort to be named envoy to the 1900 Paris fair, see Salado Álvarez, *Memorias*, 280–82. Nervo sought to be appointed an envoy of *El Imparcial*, but an article he published in the *Revista Moderna* irritated the director of *El Imparcial*, and he had to survive in Paris writing for many small papers. Ireneo Paz was an envoy of *El Diario del Hogar* and his own newspaper, *La Patria*, in 1889 and of *El Imparcial* in 1900. Díaz Dufoo was the envoy of *El Imparcial* in 1900. There is some evidence of Angel del Campo's work as an envoy of Associated Press of Mexico at the 1893 Chicago exposition.

30. *El Hijo del Ahuizote*, 29 April 1900, 297.

31. Ibid., 29 April 1900, 267. This is Charles Hale's suggestion. I thank him for the reference.

32. *El Diario del Hogar*, 14 July 1888, editorial.

33. Ibid., 20 January 1889.

34. Ibid.

35. Ibid., 8 March 1888.
36. *El Hijo del Ahuizote*, 11 August 1889, 3.
37. *El Diario del Hogar*, 23 August 1888.
38. Ibid., 25 September 1889.
39. *La Crónica*, 16 June 1889.
40. *El Diario del Hogar*, 14 April 1888.
41. See the complaints in ibid., 15 March 1888.
42. *El Hijo del Ahuizote*, 7 July 1889, 3. "Ramoncito" is a reference to Ramón Fernández, Mexican minister in France.
43. Ibid., 9 April 1889, 232–33.
44. *El México Gráfico*, 29 July 1888, 4–5.
45. The matador outfit might refer to his problems with antibullfight campaigns in 1888: he was so fond of these spectacles that he himself inaugurated the Plaza Bucareli in 1888 and the Plaza México in 1889. See González Navarro, HMM, 729–33.
46. See, for example, *El Diario del Hogar*, 8 March, 24 July, and 22 August, 1888 (complaints about expenditures and need for sanitary reforms). About tenant houses and hygiene, see *El Diario del Hogar*, 7 September 1888.
47. Ibid., 14 September 1888.
48. Ibid., 8 May 1889.
49. Ibid., 2 January 1900.
50. *El Hijo del Ahuizote*, 8 January 1899, 3.
51. *México Gráfico*, 9 February 1890, 1.
52. Ibid., 11 May 1890, 1.
53. *El Hijo del Ahuizote*, 8 April 1900.
54. Ibid., 2 June 1901, 308.
55. Emilio Rabasa, *La bola y la gran ciencia* (Mexico City, 1948), 9.
56. *El México Gráfico*, 11 January 1891, 1.
57. *El Universal*, 7 January 1894.
58. These announcements were among the thousands of commercial "therapeutical" announcements in the media during the 1880s and 1890s.
59. See *El Diario del Hogar*, 6 September 1889.
60. Ibid., 23 January 1900.
61. Bulnes, *El porvenir*, 249.
62. *El Diario del Hogar*, 29 October 1889.
63. Bulnes, *El porvenir*, 70.
64. Ibid., 270–71.

11. TOWARD REVOLUTIONARY MEXICO

1. In this regard, see my introduction.
2. During the first months of 1890, various communications dealt with the possibility of sending part of Mexico's exhibit at Paris to the 1890 Glasgow world's fair. Finally, the Mexican government announced its decision not to join the Glasgow fair. Therefore, the Mexican exhibition team began to prepare what was planned to be Mexico's greatest presence—at the Chicago fair of 1893—and the historical exhibit for Madrid in 1892.

3. The total cost of disassembling was 111,600 francs (Díaz Mimiaga, EXP, Box 12, Exp. 6, p. 46).

4. See de Anza's recommendations for disassembling the Aztec Palace in BEMP 5 (1889):743–47, 781–800.

5. The old inventory of expositions shows several signs of the serious damage suffered by one of the main steel columns of the building. Those documents are lost. See Inventario, EXP, Box 102, Exp. 9.

6. In 1891 there were rumors that the Aztec Palace was to be reassembled on a site belonging to the School of Agriculture, in Tacuba and Popotla (see Pérez Walters, "Jesús Contreras"; and Ramírez, "Dioses," 253). Later, the sculptures of the palace were stored at the Artillery Museum in the Ciudadela in Mexico City. There were also rumors that the Aztec palace was going to be reerected for the 1893 Chicago fair (see IPBA, Box 236, Exp. 6, f. 1; and letter by Ramón Fernández, SRE 44-6-13, II).

7. Gustavo Casasola's collection includes pictures of the patio of the National Museum of Artillery and of Contreras's sculptures. See Gustavo Casasola, *Seis siglos de historia gráfica de México, 1325–1900*, vol. 2 (Mexico City, 1967), 1082–83.

8. See México, Distrito Federal, *Catálogo de monumentos escultóricos y conmemorativos del Distrito Federal* (Mexico City, 1976).

9. Itzcoatl, Nezahualcoyotl, and Totoquihuatzin.

10. By the 1990s Contreras's sculptures had once again been relocated. Another sign of the epoch was that at the same time that Contreras was reappreciated and honored with an exhibition in the National Museum of Mexico City, the Mexican army reopened a museum in downtown Mexico City and located copies of Contreras's works at the side of the colonial building designed by Manuel Tolsa—the Palacio de Minería.

11. Report, M. Caballero to George R. Davis, EXP, Box 83, Exp. 18.

12. See Report, Serrano to Davis, EXP, Box 84, Exp. 18; and Godoy, *La ciudad de Chicago*, 94–95.

13. Report, Serrano to Davis, EXP, Box 84, Exp. 18.

14. See José María Vigil, *Poetisas mexicanas, siglos XVI, XVII, XVIII y XIX* (Mexico City, 1893).

15. See Mexico, Comisión Geográfico-Exploradora, Exposición Internacional Colombina de Chicago en 1893, *Catálogo de los objetos que componen el contingente de la comisión* (Jalapa, 1893). This catalogue was also prepared by Agustín Díaz.

16. See the report sent by M. Serrano to George R. Davis, general director of the Chicago fair, EXP, Box 83, Exp. 12, pp. 5–12.

17. The old Inventario (EXP, Box 102, Exp. 9) also contains some evidence of the request for financial support made by Othón Tello from Chihuahua to exhibit an Indian or Aztec town in Chicago (see the old Inventario's classification, Exp. 2564, which is lost in the new organization of EXP).

18. Photographs of these replicas are found in *The Columbian Exposition Album* (New York, 1893). See also E. H. Thompson, *The Chultunes of Labná, Yucatán*, Peabody Museum Memoirs, vol. 1, no. 3 (Cambridge, 1897); Thompson's memoirs, *Peoples of the Serpent: Life and Adventure among the Mayas* (Boston, 1932); and Don D. Fowler and Nancy J. Parezo, "Mayans in Chicago, Mound Builders in Buffalo: Archaeology at World's Fairs, 1876–1915" (paper presented at the History of Archaeology Sympo-

sium, Society for American Archaeology Annual Meeting, Saint Louis, Mo., April 16, 1993). Regarding the exhibits of "exotic" peoples in Chicago, see R. Rydell, *All the World's a Fair;* and Rydell, "A Cultural Frankenstein? The Chicago World's Columbian Exposition of 1893," in *Grand Illusions: Chicago's World's Fair of 1893*, ed. Neil Harris et al. (Chicago, 1993), 143–70.

19. James Gilbert, *Perfect Cities: Chicago's Utopias of 1893* (Chicago, 1991), 109. The Midway Exhibit was based on Putnam's anthropological conception of evolution.

20. See Edward C. Relph, *The Modern Urban Landscape* (Baltimore, 1987); and Peter Blake, *Frank Lloyd Wright: Architectural Space* (Baltimore, 1965), 22–24.

21. The most remarkable example of Wright's Mayan influence was depicted in the Hollyhock House, constructed in 1928 in California. On Wright's Mayan inspiration derived from the 1893 Chicago fair, see Jack Quinan, "Frank Lloyd Wright in 1893: The Chicago Context," in *Frank Lloyd Wright in the Realm of Ideas*, ed. Bruce Brooks (Carbondale, 1988), 119–32; and, especially, D. Tselos, "Exotic Influences in the Architecture of Frank Lloyd Wright," *Magazine of Art*, April 1953, 163.

22. See Walter G. Cooper, *The Cotton States and International Exposition and South, Illustrated* (Atlanta, 1896), 49–50. Col. Isaac W. Avery was sent to South America and Mexico. For Mexico, Charles H. Redding was the special agent.

23. See the report by Gregorio G. González in Mexico, Secretaría de Fomento, *Anales de la Secretaría de Fomento, 1892–96* (Mexico City, 1898), 59, 282–89.

24. Cooper, *Cotton States*, 90.

25. Ibid.

26. James B. Haynes, *History of the Trans-Mississippi and International Exposition of 1898* (Omaha, 1910), 90–91.

27. Mexico earned a total of 611 awards. To put it in perspective, see the table presented in Nuncio's report of Mexico's presence at the 1901 Buffalo fair. According to this table, the largest numbers of prizes won by Mexico were at the 1893 Chicago fair (1,177) and the 1900 Paris fair (1,088). But in terms of number of Mexican exhibitors who won awards, Buffalo was the most successful presence: 71 percent of exhibitors received prizes, in contrast to 51 percent at the 1900 Paris fair and 32 percent at the 1893 Chicago fair. See Albino R. Nuncio's report, in México, Secretaría de Fomento, *Anales de la Secretaría de Fomento, 1901–1904* (Mexico City, 1909), 191. See also México, *Official Catalogue of the Mexican Exhibit at the Pan-American Exposition at Buffalo*.

28. For a detailed list of the personnel involved in this fair, see México, Comisión Nacional Mexicana, *Catálogo oficial de las exhibiciones de los Estados Unidos Mexicanos, Exposición Internacional de St. Louis Mo., 1904* (Mexico City, 1904).

29. Chavero exhibited *Apuntes viejos de bibliografía mexicana* (1903); *La piedra del sol. Estudio arqueológico* (1886); *Pinturas jeroglíficas, primera parte* (1901); and *Calendario o rueda del año de los antiguos mexicanos: Estudio cronológico* (1901). Peñafiel displayed, among other studies, *Teotihuacán: Estudio arqueológico e histórico, texto y láminas*, 2 vols. (1901–1902), *Indumentaria antigua: Manera de vestir de los antiguos mexicanos, guerreros y civiles* (1903), *Colección de documentos para la historia mexicana*, and his 1890 study, *Monumentos del arte mexicano antiguo*. See México, Comisión Nacional Mexicana, *Catálogo oficial de las exhibiciones de los Estados Unidos Mexicanos*, 291–92.

30. See pictures and explanation in David R. Francis, *The Universal Exposition of 1904*, 2 vols. (Saint Louis, 1913).

31. M. J. Lowenstein, ed., *Official Guide to the Louisiana Purchase Exposition* (Saint Louis, 1904), 134.

32. See the analysis of the importance of this exhibit for Eliot's fascination with "primitivism," as he saw it in the 1904 Saint Louis fair, in Narita, "Eliot and the World's Fair of St. Louis: Collateral Evidence of His Fairoutings"; and Narita, "Eliot and the World's Fair of St. Louis: His 'Stockholder's Coupon Ticket.'"

33. For detailed descriptions of Mexico's presence at the New England fair, see the report by Albino R. Nuncio in México, Secretaría de Fomento, *Anales de la Secretaría de Fomento, 1908–1909* (Mexico City, 1910), 74–87. According to Nuncio, for Mexico the total cost of this fair was U.S.$8,274. For the 1909 San Antonio fair, see México, Secretaría de Fomento, *Anales de la Secretaría de Fomento, 1909–1910* (Mexico City, 1910), 101–9. No cost was reported.

34. I develop the analysis of this exhibition more fully in M. Tenorio, "1900: At the Gates of Hell: Mexico and the 1900 Paris Fair" (manuscript).

35. See EXP, Box 64, Exp. 9, pp. 265–268; and Mier, *México*.

36. Rudorff, *Belle Epoque*, 322. Regarding the 1900 Paris universal exhibition, I relied on the following primary and secondary sources: Mandell, *Paris 1900*; the report France, Paris, Exposition Universelle de 1900, *Exposition Universelle Internationale de 1900 à Paris: Rapport du jury international* (Paris, 1904); Charles Rearick, *Pleasures of the Belle Epoque: Entertainment and Festivity in Turn-of-the-Century France* (New Haven, 1985); Madeleine Raberioux, "Approaches de l'histoire des expositions universelles à Paris du Second Empire a 1900," *Bulletin du Centre D'Histoire Économique et Sociale de la Region Lyonnaise* 1 (1979):1–20; Jullian, *Triumph of Art Nouveau*; Frédéric Moret, "Images de Paris dans les guides touristiques en 1900," *Le Mouvement Social*, no. 160 (1992):79–98; Pénin, "L'Économie sociale; Poivert, "La Photographie artistique; Findling, *Historical Dictionary*; X. Ryckelynck, "Les Hommes de l'Exposition Universelle de 1889: Le Cas Alfred Picard," *Le Mouvement Social*, no. 149 (1989):25–42; and, for data and memorabilia, Smithsonian Institution, *The Books of the Fairs: Materials about World's Fairs, 1834–1916, in the Smithsonian Institution Libraries* (Chicago, 1992).

37. Inspired by the emphasis on electric light, Mexican authorities commissioned Rafael R. Arizpe to undertake a study of Mexico City's electrification. As a result, Arizpe produced the book *El alumbrado público en la ciudad de México: Estudio histórico* (Mexico City, 1900).

38. Rearick, *Pleasures of the Belle Epoque*, 144. See also Mandell, *Paris 1900*, ix. Mandell maintains that the 1900 Paris fair "was the last time any one tried to include all of man's activity in one display" (p. xi).

39. Arnold J. Mayer, *The Persistence of the Old Regime: Europe to the Great War* (New York, 1981), 189.

40. George Steiner, *In Bluebeard's Castle: Some Notes towards the Redefinition of Culture* (New Haven, 1971), 5, 27.

41. Silverman, *Art Nouveau*, 266. The author quotes the French poet Maurice Rollinat.

42. For the idea of fin de siècle, see Carl E. Schorske, *Fin-de-Siècle Vienna: Politics and Culture* (New York, 1980), xvii–xxvii.

43. Mier, *México*, 28.

44. See Circular 9, by Minister Fernández Leal, reproduced in ibid., 195–97. Regarding mining, see Carlos Sellerier, *Data Referring to Mexican Mining, Prepared in View*

of the Participation of Mexico in the Universal Exposition of Paris in 1900 (Mexico City, 1901).

45. The second most successful Mexican display, in terms of percentage of exhibitors winning awards, was that staged for the 1893 Chicago fair (32 percent). See Nuncio's report in Mexico, *Anales de la Secretaría de Fomento, 1901–1904*, 191. For a detailed list of exhibitors winning awards, see EXP, Box 55, Exp. 10, pp. 83–114.

46. See Mier's letter (25 April 1899), in which he writes about Contreras's petition to hire a French architect for the construction of the Mexican pavilion, in EXP, Box 69, Exp. 5.

47. See Mier's letter to Fernández Leal, 7 May 1889. He describes this conflict and acknowledges having received "three or four" projects by Contreras based on "*la capilla del posto en Guadalupe*" and in "*la casa de los azulejos*" in Mexico City. See EXP, Box 58, Exp. 2.

48. See Mier, *México*, 83 ff.

49. EXP, Box 31, Exp. 9, p. 65.

50. EXP, Box 31, Exp. 9, pp. 66–68.

51. For a description of the building, see Mier, *México*, 220–29; and for a detailed report of the construction, see de Anza's report to Minister Fernández Leal, in EXP, Box, 31, Exp. 9, pp. 85–104.

52. Reproduced in Mier, *México*, 227.

53. See Mariscal, *El desarrollo de la arquitectura*, 19. According to the author, Rodríguez Arangoity received a prize from Napoleon III at the imperial exhibition of 1859 for his plan for a port and naval school in Tehuantepec. See also Katzman, *Arquitectura del siglo XIX en México* (Mexico City, 1973), 375–76.

54. Reproduced in Mier, *México*, 229.

55. This was the description found in the anonymous, long manuscript report titled "La participación de las potencias extranjeras en la exposición de París. México," in EXP, Box 59, Exp. 12, pp. 158–204.

56. On the illumination of the building, see EXP, Box 32, Exp. 6, pp. 34–46.

57. See "Contrato para la ejecución de los modelos en yeso de la decoración del pabellón mexicano en la Exposición Universal de París de 1900," in EXP, Box 32, Exp. 2, pp. 52–54.

58. Certificado, 31 July 1900, EXP, Box 58, Exp. 3.

59. See Yeats's poem "Nineteen Hundred and Nineteen," in W. B. Yeats, *Símbolos*, bilingual ed. (Mexico City, 1977), 150–57.

60. "I am the one who yesterday used to say no more than / the blue verse and the profane song . . . / and being very eighteenth century and very antique / and very modern; bold, cosmopolitan / with strong Hugo and with ambiguous Verlaine, / and with an endless thirst of hopes" (Rubén Darío, "Yo soy aquel que ayer decía," in his *Cantos de vida y esperanza* [Buenos Aires, 1940 (first published in 1905)], 25–30).

61. "Science is in bankruptcy! So proclaims / A cry of the moribund century, / once again this is the time to grab the oriflamme / of illusion in its infinite term" (Jesús E. Valenzuela, "Poesía pronunciada por su autor en la velada organizada en honor del eminente filósofo don Gabino Barreda . . . ," *La Revista Moderna*, no. 7 [1900]:102–5).

62. Amado Nervo, letter to Salado Álvarez, December 1897, in his *Obras Completas* (Madrid, 1973), 340.

63. About the 1915 San Francisco world's fair, see Allwood, *Great Exhibitions,* 117–122. For an analysis of the ethnographic and anthropological aspects of San Francisco's exposition, see the essays collected in Benedict, *Anthropology of World's Fairs;* and the insightful study by Rydell, *All the World's a Fair.* After San Francisco's world's fair, a comprehensive five-volume work was published which includes data and pictures on all aspects of the fair: Frank Morton Tood, *The Story of the Panama-Pacific Exposition,* 5 vols. (New York, 1921). For pictorial records, see Donna Ewald and Peter Clute, *San Francisco Invites the World: The Panama-Pacific International Exposition of 1915* (San Francisco, 1991).

64. EXP, Box 94, Exp. 1. For Mexico's plans to participate in San Francisco's world's fair, see EXP, Box 94, all Exp.; Box 95, all Exp.; and Box 98, Exp. 1–16, 96, 97.

65. "Lista de expositores, *FOTOGRAFIA* (Photographers)," EXP, Box 94, Exp 5. It is not clear whether they agreed to participate.

66. For detailed data on U.S.–Mexican relations in the troubling years of 1913, 1914, and 1915, see Mark T. Gilderhus, *Diplomacy and Revolution* (Tucson, 1977); Berta Ulloa, *La revolución intervenida: Relaciones diplomáticas entre México y Estados Unidos (1910–1914)* (Mexico City, 1971); and the short but detailed work by James L. Tigner, "The Relation of the U.S. and Mexico, 1909–1914" (M.A. thesis, Stanford University, 1949). For a profound analysis of the real effectiveness of American intervention in times of tumult in Mexico—and of Mexico's nationalism in this context—see Alan Knight, *U.S.–Mexican Relations, 1910–1940* (San Diego, 1987), 103–42.

67. In this regard, see the important explanations of 1914 as the year zero in economic terms in Womack, "Mexican Economy during the Revolution."

68. Tood, *Story of the Exposition,* vol. 1, 9–10.

69. Adams, *Education of Henry Adams,* 331–32.

70. Amado Nervo, "Discurso pronunciado en una distribución de premios," Teatro Abreu, Mexico, in his *Obras Completas,* 494–96. The phrase, he said, was inspired by an Argentine poet whose name he did not mention.

71. E. L. Doctorow, *World's Fair* (New York, 1985), 253.

72. See Louis Marin's views on Disneyland in *Utopiques,* 297–324.

12. THE 1922 RIO DE JANEIRO FAIR

1. See Pesavento, "Exposições universais," 63–85.

2. On the 1922 Rio exposition, see Jornal do Commercio, *O Livro d'Ouro, Edição Comemorativa, 1822–1922* (Rio de Janeiro, 1922); Annie S. Peck, "The International Exposition of Brazil," *Current History* 15, 5 (1923):1042–49; Findling, *Historical Dictionary;* Marly Silva da Motta, *A nação faz 100 anos* (Rio de Janeiro, 1992); and Lúcia Lippi Oliveira, "As festas que a República manda guardar," *Estudos Históricos* 2, 4 (1989):172–89.

3. In 1903 this sanitary reform began in Rio de Janeiro. See Jaime Larr Benchimol, *Pereira Passos: um Haussmann tropical: a renovação urbana da cidade do Rio de Janeiro no início do século XX* (Rio de Janeiro, 1990); and Jeffrey D. Needell, *A Tropical Belle Epoque: Elite Culture and Society in Turn-of-the-Century Rio de Janeiro* (Cambridge, 1987).

4. The U.S. government authorized $1 million to be spent in Brazil, of which $350,000 was for the construction of the building (NYT, 28 May 1922).

5. According to the Mexican reports, France authorized an expenditure of 5,136,000 francs (SRE 18–5–72, I). See J. P. Curtis, "Architecture of the Brazil Centennial Exposition," *Art and Architecture* 5 (September 1923):95–104.

6. For a summary account of the Brazilian First Republic, see Boris Fausto, "Brazil: The Social and Political Structure of the First Republic (1889–1930)," in *The Cambridge History of Latin America*, ed. L. Bethell, vol. 5 (Cambridge, 1987), 779–830.

7. See Torre Díaz's economic and political reports to the Mexican Ministry of Foreign Affairs for 1922 and 1923, SRE 41–7–23.

8. Daniel Pécaut, *Entre le peuple et la nation* (Paris, 1988), 18. See also pp. 11–46.

9. For a short review of the development of Brazilian intellectual life in this period, see Alfredo Bosi, "As letras na Primeira República," in *História Geral da Civilização Brasileira*, ed. Sérgio Buarque de Holanda, vol. 8 (São Paulo, 1977), 295–319; and Martins Wilson, *História da Inteligência Brasileira*, vol. 6 (São Paulo, 1915–1933), 272–376; Aracy Amaral, *Artes plásticas na Semana de 22* (São Paulo, 1970); Pécaut, *Entre le peuple et la nation;* and Sergio Miceli, *Intelectuais e classe dirigente no Brasil (1920–1945)* (São Paulo, 1979).

10. So argued the organizers of the exhibition, according to Silva da Motta, *A nação faz 100 anos*, 71.

11. An explanation of this dichotomy can be found in ibid., 94–102; also in Nicolau Sevcenko, *Literatura como missão* (São Paulo, 1983).

12. "Mexican Ulysses" is the title of José Vasconcelos's autobiography (*Ulises criollo*, 3d ed. [Mexico City, 1935]).

13. See Helen Delpar, *The Enormous Vogue of Things Mexican: Cultural Relations between the United States and Mexico, 1920–1935* (Tuscaloosa, 1992).

14. In *La raza cósmica* (Paris, 1925), Vasconcelos writes about a diplomatic encounter with Hughes in a tense environment (see pp. 115–16).

15. The Westinghouse Corporation displays were especially remarkable. See Peck, "International Exposition of Brazil."

16. Torre Díaz sent classified letters to the Mexican Ministry of Foreign Affairs reporting on his talk with Pessoa, who, he argued, was promoting a Society of Nations, which he believed was too pro-American (SRE 7–16–67, II).

17. Ibid. For insights into how this excuse was constructed within the government, see the account of one of the actors in the drama, Alberto J. Pani, *Mi contribución al nuevo régimen (1910–1933)* (Mexico City, 1936), 292–98.

18. For this official appointment, see SRE 5–20–524.

19. In *El desastre* (Mexico City, 1951), Vasconcelos argued that Obregón aimed to put him far from Mexico in order to be free to maneuver politically and also to limit his growing prestige as minister of education (see pp. 145–48). Alberto J. Pani, then minister of foreign affairs, argued that he himself had suggested Vasconcelos's name to Obregón, bearing in mind that Vasconcelos had expressed his desire to be appointed. See Pani, *Mi contribución,* 292–98. In addition, there is evidence that Vasconcelos lobbied to be appointed to this position, both in the AGN Obregón-Calles and in SRE 18–5–72, I–III.

20. See Gen. Manuel Pérez Treviño's long report on this delegation's activities:

Informe del comandante del cañonero Nicolás Bravo en su viaje por América del Sur, SRE 18-5-72, II; and the letter to Obregón in AGN Calles-Obregón 104-b-30 (20, 21).
  21. See SRE 18-5-72, II.
  22. SRE 18-5-72, I, letters of November and December.
  23. *Jornal do Commercio,* 21 November 1921.
  24. SRE 7-16-67, II.
  25. Ibid., I. Tiffany was hired even though Williams Inc. offered a better deal (May 1922). Porfirio Díaz's regime hired Tiffany, among other things, for the crystal curtain of the National Theater (Palacio de Bellas Artes).
  26. There is no record of these medals in SRE, but Vasconcelos (*El desastre,* 149) mentioned that they were distributed (both to the Mexican and Brazilian presidents as well as to Pani).
  27. Regarding Torri's trip to Brazil see Julio Torri, *Diálogos de los libros* (Mexico City, 1980), 240–43.
  28. Vasconcelos, *El desastre,* 149.
  29. SRE 18-5-72, I, II.
  30. Obregón Santacilia grew up in the Porfirian aristocracy and was educated at the School of Fine Arts of San Carlos. He was, first, a great promoter of a colonialist revival in Mexico, inspired by a member of the Ateneo de la Juventud, Jesús T. Acevedo; and he followed the teachings of Federico E. Mariscal. Later he experimented with art deco and, finally, with functionalist mechanist architecture. With his building for the 1922 Brazilian exhibition, and with his friendship with Pani, he began his successful career as one of the architects of the postrevolutionary regimes. Among his main works are the transformation of the Porfirian Legislative Palace into the Monument of the Revolution, the building for the Ministry of Sanitation, the Reforma and del Prado hotels, and the offices of the Bank of Mexico in the former Guardiola plaza. See Carlos Obregón Santacilia, *Cincuenta años de arquitectura mexicana* (Mexico City, 1925); and Carlos Obregón Santacilia, *El maquinismo, la vida y la arquitectura* (Mexico City, 1939). About him, see María Luisa Adame, "Arquitecto Carlos Obregón Santacilia," cultural supplement to *Novedades,* 16 October 1955; Israel Katzman, *Arquitectura contemporánea mexicana: Precedentes y desarrollo* (Mexico City, 1963); Mexico, Partido Revolucionario Institucional, *Tradición de la cultura: Nacionalismo cultural: Carlos Obregón Santacilia* (Mexico City, 1988); Ramón Vargas Salguero, "La arquitectura de la revolución," in *México: 75 años de revolución, Educación, Cultura y Comunicaciones,* vol. 2 (Mexico City, 1988), 437–77; and Enrique X. de Anda, *La arquitectura de la revolución mexicana: Corrientes y estilo en la década de los veinte* (Mexico City, 1990).
  31. In the interior of the British pavilion, Vasconcelos argued, "[there] were represented the four parts of the world, in the customary way in which the British depict the world, only to remind us that they are the masters of the world" (Vasconcelos, *La raza cósmica,* 82).
  32. Margaret Hutton Abels, "Painting at the Brazil Centennial Exposition," *Art and Archaeology* 16 (Summer 1923):108.
  33. In this regard, see Justino Fernández, *Roberto Montenegro* (Mexico City, 1962); and Ramírez's analysis of the artistic and cultural debate between 1914 and 1921 (an examination of journals and newspapers published during that period): Fausto Ramírez, *Crónica de las artes plásticas en los años de López Velarde, 1914–1921* (Mexico

City, 1990). See also Montenegro's autobiographical notes, Roberto Montenegro, *Planos en el tiempo* (Mexico City, 1962).

34. In this regard, see Carlos Obregón Santacilia, *México como eje* (Mexico City, 1947), 103.

35. Peck, "International Exposition of Brazil," 1044.

36. See Katzman, *Arquitectura contemporánea mexicana; Arquitectura del siglo XIX;* Carlos Lira Vásquez, *Para una historia de la arquitectura mexicana* (Mexico City, 1990); Xavier Moyssén, "El nacionalismo y la arquitectura," *Anales del Instituto de Investigaciones Estéticas,* no. 55 (1986):111–31; Rafael López Rangel, *La modernidad arquitectónica mexicana* (Mexico City, 1989); and Anda, *La arquitectura.*

37. In this regard, see Claude Fell, *José Vasconcelos: Los años del águila (1920–1925)* (Mexico City, 1989), 456–62. For an analysis of Vasconcelos's own self-construction of his spiritual ideas in education around 1922, see the lucid, if short, essay by Enrique Krauze, "José Vasconcelos en 1921: Arquitecto del espíritu," in *Cultura urbana latinoamericana,* ed. Jorge Enrique Hardoy (Buenos Aires, 1985), 95–102.

38. Vasconcelos, *La raza cósmica,* 40.

39. For the early intellectual influences on Vasconcelos, see John Skirius, *José Vasconcelos y la cruzada de 1929* (Mexico City, 1978), 13–43.

40. "In 1915, when the Revolution's failure seemed more imminent than ever . . . changes began to appear providing evidence of a new direction. . . . The Mexican Revolution was born out of that year's chaos. A new Mexico was born out of that year's chaos" (quoted in Carlos Monsiváis, "Notas sobre cultura mexicana en el siglo XX," in El Colegio de México, *Historia general de México,* vol. 2 (Mexico City, 1985), 1406.

41. Lecture delivered in the 1910s, reprinted in Acevedo, *Disertaciones,* 53.

42. Mariscal, *La patria y la arquitectura nacional,* 10. Other names associated with colonial revival in architecture were Manuel G. Revilla in the 1890s and Manuel Romero de Terreros, José Juan Tablada, Manuel Toussaint, and Gerardo Murillo in the 1910s and 1920s. See José Juan Tablada, *Historia del arte en México* (Mexico City, 1927); Manuel Toussaint, *Arte colonial en México* (Mexico City, 1948); and Gerardo Murillo, *Iglesias de México,* 6 vols. (Mexico City, 1924–1927). In this regard, see also Manuel González Galván, "La revaloración de la arquitectura colonial en el primer cuarto del siglo XX: teoría y práctica," in *Saturnino Herrán: Jornadas de homenaje,* ed. Juan Castañeda (Mexico City, 1989), 95–106.

43. See Manuel Gamio, "El actual renacimiento arquitectónico de México," *Ethnos* 1 (1921):248–50. On Gamio's architectural conception, see Angeles González Gamio, *Manuel Gamio: Una lucha sin final* (Mexico City, 1987), 67–74; and on neocolonial architecture, see López Rangel, *La modernidad arquitectónica,* 39–45.

44. The construction of his own house in neocolonial Mexican style, in the Colonia Juárez, shows this. See González Gamio, *Manuel Gamio,* 74.

45. Regarding the ideology of Hispanism, see the uneven but useful study by Frederick B. Pike: *Hispanism, 1898–1936: Spanish Conservatives and Liberals and Their Relations with Spanish America* (Notre Dame, 1971). On the origins of this tendency, see Mark Jay Van Aken, *Pan-Hispanism: Its Origins and Development to 1866* (Berkeley, 1959). On the influence of falangism in Hispanism, see Ricardo Pérez Montfort, *Hispanismo y Falange* (Mexico City, 1992), 19–73.

46. See Carlos A. C. Lemus, "Architectura contemporânea," in *Histórica geral da*

arte no Brasil, ed. Walter Zanini, vol. 2 (São Paulo, 1983), 825–32; and Octaviano C. De Fiore, *Architecture and Sculpture in Brazil* (Albuquerque, n.d.), 20–23.

47. May 1922, meeting of Torre Díaz and Pessoa, SRE 18–5–72, I.

48. Vasconcelos, *La raza cósmica*, 83.

49. *Jornal do Brasil*, newspaper clipping in SRE, no exact date.

50. Regarding the aesthetic transformation that favored the consolidation of indigenism, see chapters 6 and 7.

51. See, for example, *Ethnos* 1, 3 (1920).

52. Ignacio Bernal, *Historia de la arqueología en México* (Mexico City, 1962), translation presented in an English edition (1980), 183.

53. See José Clemente Orozco, *Apuntes autobiográficos* (Mexico City, 1966). For a discussion of Vasconcelos's official support of mural paintings, see Fell, *José Vasconcelos*, 401. In a letter to Gómez Morín, Vasconcelos confessed his regret at having supported the *"pintor plebeyo de la revolución"*—Rivera (from Gómez Morín's archive, quoted in Skirius, *José Vasconcelos*, 35).

54. José Vasconcelos, *Indología* (Paris, n.d.), 200–229. G. F. Nicolai seems to have been well known in Argentina, especially by intellectuals like José Ingenieros. Some of Nicolai's works were translated in Argentina; Vasconcelos's knowledge of Nicolai's works very likely derives from these translations. M. Leclerc du Sablon was a well-known biologist in the last part of the nineteenth century. See G. F. Nicolai, *La base biológica del relativismo científico* (Córdoba, 1925); and Mathieu Leclerc du Sablon, *Les Incertitudes de la biologie* (Paris, 1912).

55. He and Manuel Gamio were lecturing together. See José Vasconcelos and Manuel Gamio, *Aspects of Mexican Civilization: Lectures on the Harris Foundation 1926* (Chicago, 1926).

56. Ibid., 85.

57. Ibid., 89.

58. Ibid., 100–102.

59. Ibid., 96.

60. This rhetorical piece was reproduced in *Livro d'Ouro*, 358–59 and was published in Mexico by Julio Jiménez Rueda, "El discurso de Vasconcelos a Cuauhtémoc," in his *Bajo la cruz del sur* (Mexico City, 1922), 112–21. Blanco both refers to and briefly interprets Vasconcelos's speech in Brazil: see José Joaquín Blanco, *Se llamaba Vasconcelos: Una evocación crítica* (Mexico City, 1977), 117–22.

61. José Vasconcelos's speech on Cuauhtémoc, in Jiménez Rueda, "El discurso de Vasconcelos," 112–21.

62. Letter to Obregón, AGN Obregón-Calles, 104-b-30 (21), 17 September 1922.

63. In fact, official indigenism was not very different from Vasconcelos's type of indigenism. The official indigenism of Manuel Gamio (both positivist—anthropologically and archaeologically—and liberal) exemplified by *Forjando Patria* (1916) was indeed, as David Brading has shown, as integrationist as Vasconcelos's position, although less Catholic and more liberal. See Basave Benítez, *México Mestizo*, 130–36; and Alberto Guaraldo, "Indigenismo e investigación etno-antropológica en México," in *America Latina: Dallo Stato Coloniale allo stato nazione*, ed. Antonio Annino, vol. 2 (Turin, 1987), 822–37. See also David Brading, "Manuel Gamio and Official Indigenism in Mexico," *Bulletin of Latin American Research* 7, 1 (1988):75–89.

64. Vasconcelos, *El desastre*, 150.

65. See Congreso Internacional de Americanistas, *Anais do XX Congreso Internacional de Americanistas*, 3 vols. (Rio de Janeiro, 1922); and "Notes on the Brazil Centenary Exposition," *Hispanic American Historical Review*, 2 (1922):506-12.

66. According to Christopher J. Hall's translation of Bartra's *La jaula de la melancolía*, the literal meaning of *pelado* is "shorn one." It refers to "a Mexican social type from the working class noted for his coarse, uneducated, uncouth language and behavior" (*The Cage of Melancholy: Identity and Metamorphosis in the Mexican Character*, trans. Christopher J. Hall [New Brunswick, N.J., 1992], 33).

67. Alfonso del Toro, "La bella ciudad carioca," *Revista de Revistas*, 20 October 1922, 11–13. In *La raza cósmica* (pp. 52–60), Vasconcelos suggested that the official Brazilian personnel tried to guide him in order to avoid black and poor sections in the various cities he visited.

68. For data on Vázquez Schiaffiano, a petroleum engineer, see SRE Le. 1006.

69. México, Secretaría de Industria, Comercio y Trabajo, *México, sus recursos naturales, su situación actual* (Mexico City, 1922).

70. Documentary, México, Secretaría de Relaciones Exteriores, *México en las fiestas del centenario de Brasil* (Mexico City, 1922).

71. Fell (*José Vasconcelos*, 449–56) believes that because it was internationally recognized, Mexican popular art acquired "credibility in aesthetic, economic, social, and most of all, cultural aspects." But its international credibility was only because of its exoticism. For an illustrative analysis of the discovery of popular art in Mexico, see John F. Scott, "La evolución de la teoría de la historia del arte por escritores del siglo XX sobre el arte mexicano del siglo XIX," *Anales del Instituto de Investigaciones Estéticas*, no. 37 (1968):71–104. Scott deals with the national and international recognition of the artistic works of the lithographer José Guadalupe Posada.

72. See the report by Vázquez Schiaffiano in SRE 18–5–72, III. On Guillermo Kahlo, a German photographer and father of famous Frida, see the catalogue and study by the Museo Nacional de Arte, *Guillermo Kahlo: Vida y obra: Fotógrafo 1872–1941* (Mexico City, 1994).

73. It is extremely difficult to estimate the cost of Mexico's presence at the Rio de Janeiro fair. Expenditures seemed to have been made with no clear budget approval but through direct request to President Obregón. At times the Mexican delegation in Rio de Janeiro exhausted its resources. According to Vasconcelos, what was especially expensive was maintenance of the military delegation. Vasconcelos himself directly and urgently requested U.S.$16,000 from Obregón in September 1922 (AGN Calles-Obregón, 104-b-30 [21]). See also Vasconcelos, *El desastre*, 151–52.

74. See the article in the Chilean newspaper *El Diario Ilustrado*, 4 November 1922. This incident resulted in an apology by the Mexican minister in Chile, Carlos Trejo Lerdo de Tejada, that was published in *El Mercurio* (Santiago, Chile), 6 November 1922.

75. *Folha do Norte*, 19 November 1922.

76. See *Revistas de Revistas*, no. 2 (1922), an issue devoted to Brazil.

77. See Jiménez Rueda's account of this trip in *Bajo la cruz del sur*.

78. Regarding race, Knight has lucidly shown the continuity of racism in prerevolutionary and postrevolutionary indigenism: Alan Knight, "Racism, Revolution, and Indigenismo: Mexico, 1910–1940," in *The Idea of Race in Latin America, 1870–1940*, ed. R. Graham (Austin, 1990), 71–113.

79. See Enrique Krauze, *Caudillos culturales de la revolución mexicana* (Mexico City, 1985), 104–10. See also Luis González's analysis of this generation in *La ronda de las generaciones* (Mexico City, 1984), 66–80; and Carlos Monsiváis, "Notas sobre cultura mexicana en el siglo XX," in El Colegio de México, *Historia General de México*, vol. 2, 1417–21; and, for the specific case of artists vis-à-vis generational change, Ramírez, "Vertientes nacionalistas," 111–67.

80. See Vasconcelos's discussions of racial theory in his *Raza cósmica* and in Vasconcelos and Gamio, *Aspects of Mexican Civilization*. In addition, see Mariátegui's review of Vasconcelos's *Indología*: José Carlos Mariátegui, *Temas de nuestra América* (Lima, 1960), 78–84. Mariátegui supported Vasconcelos's utopianism but opposed its almost mystic faith in the future without action in the present.

81. "Los problemas de México," reprinted in *Boletín de la Secretaría de Educación Pública*, 28 August 1922.

82. In this regard, see Knight, "Racism, Revolution, and *Indigenismo*," 78–98.

83. Vasconcelos, *La raza cósmica*, 3.

84. On this point, as on many others in this chapter, I have benefited from David Brading, "Social Darwinism and Romantic Idealism: Andrés Molina Enríquez and José Vasconcelos in the Mexican Revolution," in his *Prophecy and Myth in Mexican History* (Cambridge, 1984), 63–83, 92–95.

85. The issue of Vasconcelos's self-deceit during his trip to South America is also briefly noticed by José Joaquín Blanco, who argues that Vasconcelos "let himself be deceived" by the democratic regimes of Argentina, Brazil, and Chile (in sharp contrast to Mexico's antidemocratic government). See Blanco, *Se llamaba Vasconcelos*, 117–22.

86. Vasconcelos and Gamio, *Aspects of Mexican Civilization*, 12.

87. See the opening quotation in this chapter.

88. The last entry in the diary of Antonieta Rivas Mercado, quoted in Martha Robles, *Entre el poder y las letras* (Mexico City, 1989), 103.

13. THE 1929 SEVILLE FAIR

1. See Alfredo Serrano, "La originalidad en las grandes exposiciones internacionales: Un comentario a la maravilla del pueblo español," *Revista de las Españas*, no. 36–37 (1929):340–44.

2. Originally it was called Exposición Hispanoamericana, but it was renamed in order to include Brazil, Portugal, and the United States. See Blanca Ríos de Lampérez et al., *Nuestra raza es española* (Seville, 1926). On the fairs in Barcelona and Seville, see Allwood, *Great Exhibitions*, 135–36; Findling, *Historical Dictionary*, 254–57; Seville, *El libro de oro iberoamericano*, vol. 1 (Seville, 1929); Arthur Stanley Riggs, "The Spanish Exposition," *Art and Archaeology*, no. 27 (1929):156–64; Fernando Real Balbuena, *La Exposición Ibero-Americana: Origen y gestación de la magna empresa* (Seville, 1961); Encarnación Lemus López, *La Exposición Ibero-Americana a través de la prensa local (1923–1929)* (Seville, 1987); and the chronology of events included in Manuel Trillo de Leyva, *La Exposición Iberoamericana: La transformación urbana de Sevilla*

(Seville, 1980), 183–204. For the origins and problems confronted by the Seville fair since 1905, see Narciso Ciaurriz, *Origen y primeros trabajos de la Exposición Iberoamericana* (Seville, 1929); Eduardo Rodríguez Bernal, *La Exposición Ibero-Americana de Sevilla de 1929 a través de la prensa local* (Seville, 1981). For an analysis of the fair in view of Seville's urban transformation, see Alberto Villar Movellán, *Arquitectura del regionalismo en Sevilla, 1900–1935* (Seville, 1979), 412–75.

3. "Inauguración de la Exposición Iberoamericana de Seville," *Revista de las Españas*, no. 33 (1929):157.

4. Rodríguez Bernal, *La Exposición Ibero-Americana de Sevilla*, 269.

5. Trillo de Leyva, *La Exposición Iberoamericana*, 35.

6. Rodolfo Reyes, "Una interpretación de la Exposición Iberoamericana," *Revista de las Españas*, no. 42 (1930):129–30.

7. Villar Movellán, *Arquitectura del regionalismo*, 452–53.

8. See *El libro de oro iberoamericano*, vol. 1. For the transformation of the notion of social economy, see Gueslin, *L'Invention de l'économie sociale*.

9. Informe General, Consul Mexicano, Barcelona, SRE IV–294–I.

10. NYT, 25 January 1929, announced that the United States was going to build a pavilion "which will later be used for the consulate." In addition, Archer M. Huntington, president of the Hispanic Society of America, donated a statue of El Cid Campeador.

11. SRE, letter of invitation to the competition [the prize for which was 20,000 pesetas], SRE EMESP, 531.

12. Reported by the Mexican consul in Barcelona (SRE IV–294–1).

13. México, Comité Organizador de la Participación de México en la Exposición Ibero-Americana de Sevilla, *México* (Mexico City, 1929), iii.

14. Ibid.

15. In Spanish the legend is "Madre España: porque en mi campo encendiste el sol de tu cultura, y en mi alma la lámpara devocional de tu espíritu, ahora en mi campo y en mi corazón han florecido. Méjico" (SRE IV–295–I).

16. For the context of social unrest and the exhibition, see Shlomo Ben-Ami, *Fascism from Above: The Dictatorship of Primo de Rivera in Spain, 1923–1930* (Oxford, 1983), 353–56.

17. Ibid., 202–5; and Leandro Álvarez Rey, *Sevilla durante la dictadura de Primo de Rivera* (Seville, 1987), 235–38.

18. See Pike, *Hispanism*, 35–47, 178–84; and Pérez Montfort, *Hispanismo y Falange*.

19. See Miguel Rodríguez, "El 12 de octubre: Entre el IV y el V centenario," in *Cultura e identidad nacional*, ed. Roberto Blancarte (Mexico City, 1994), 145–51. I thank Victor Arriaga for access to this material.

20. Enrique González Martínez, *La apacible locura* (1951), included in his *Obras Completas* (Mexico City, 1977), 780. This work is the second part of González Martínez's autobiography. The first part, *El hombre buho: Misterio de una vocación*, was first published in 1944. About his days in Spain during the Seville fair, see *Obras completas*, pp. 775–80.

21. For a brief review of the socioeconomic history of this period, see Raymond Carr, *Oxford History of Modern Europe: Spain, 1808–1939* (Oxford, 1966), 581–602.

22. This tune was composed by Guty Cárdenas, who was then a popular singer

and composer from the Yucatán and one of the first radio stars of Mexico City's urban culture.

23. The figure of 750,000 pesetas was announced by the Ministry of Industry and Commerce in October 1927 and published in *Excélsior*, 2 November 1927. It should be considered a minimum figure, and though the final total is unclear, it is very likely that it was significantly larger than this sum. See Appendix 2.

24. México, Comité Organizador, *México*, 2.

25. For instance, in 1930 Ortiz de Montellano published an article in *Los Contemporáneos* in which he explained the growing American and European interest in Mexico's literature: Bernardo Ortiz de Montellano, "Literatura de revolución y literatura revolucionaria," *Los Contemporáneos* 7, 23 (1930):77–81.

26. *La Libertad* (Madrid), 17 May 1929.

27. SRE IV-295-I.

28. SRE IV-295-I, II. See also *Boletín de la Secretaría de Industria, Comercio y Trabajo...*, 22 April 1926. The projects were exhibited at the National Academy of Fine Arts.

29. See the explanation and illustrations of this building in *Excélsior*, 8 May 1926. As a "Porfirian" architect, Marquina designed two aristocratic mansions along the Paseo de la Reforma and in the Colonia Juárez of Mexico City. Later he became a great advocate of pre-Hispanic–style architecture.

30. Confidential letter, 6 May 1926.

31. SRE IV-295-I, II.

32. Regarding Obregón Santacilia's proposal, see Ramón Vargas Salguero, "La arquitectura de la revolución," in *México: 75 años de revolución, educación, cultura y comunicaciones*, vol. 2 (Mexico City, 1988), 437–77; and Partido Revolucionario Institucional, *Tradición de la cultura*.

33. The total cost of the building was 300,000 pesos, 10 percent of which went to Amabilis (SRE EMESP 525).

34. Godoy, *México en Sevilla*. I have dealt with Godoy in previous chapters. By 1929 he was a veteran member of the Porfirian exhibition team, and in that year he was still an active writer for *Excélsior* in Mexico City. He died in 1930. See also Francisco Sáenz, *Comité Organizador de la Participación de México en la Exposición Ibero-Americana de Sevilla* (Mexico City, 1929); and México, Secretaría de Industria, Comercio y Trabajo, *Exposición iberoamericana de Sevilla 1929: La participación de México* (Mexico City, 1928).

35. Vasconcelos, *El desastre*, 378.

36. SRE EMESP 539. These changes may have been caused by the defeat of Aarón Sáenz as a presidential candidate and by the conflict between Portes Gil and Luis N. Morones.

37. Amabilis's letter to the Ministry of Industry and Commerce, 15 July 1928 (SRE EMESP 532). See also letter to Amabilis, 3 February 1928, from Emilio Narváez asking him to take great care of the budget (SRE EMESP 528). For a detailed explanation of expenditures between 1927 and 1930, see *"Libro Mayor,"* SRE EMESP 530 (which included calls not to repeat the mistakes of Mexico's presence at the Rio de Janeiro fair, which caused considerable economic troubles); SRE EMESP 752.

38. The Mexican consul in Seville paid the fine and freed Amabilis. The incident took place in July 1929 (SRE EMESP 534).

39. Some replies by Orozco Ramírez affirm these accusations. Enrique González

Martínez promised an investigation. There are no more records or final results about this incident. See SRE EMESP 539.

40. See Katzman, *Arquitectura del siglo XIX*, 267.

41. For this monument, and for Amabilis's works in Mérida city, see Carlos Echánove Trujillo, ed., *Enciclopedia Yucatanense* (Mexico City, 1946), vol. 4, 445–48, and vol. 6, 553–62, quotation on p. 554.

42. Manuel Amabilis, *El pabellón de México en la Exposición Ibero-Americana de Sevilla* (Mexico City, 1929). This book was proposed by Amabilis in April 1928 (SRE EMESP 529) and approved and paid for by the Mexican government in June (SRE EMESP 531).

43. Amabilis's "Propuesta para una monografía sobre el edificio mexicano en la exposición de Seville," April 1928, SRE EMESP 529. For his ideas on the revolution, see Manuel Amabilis, *Mística de la revolución mexicana* (Mexico City, 1937).

44. Amabilis, *El pabellón*, 23–24.

45. Ibid., 27.

46. Amabilis acknowledged that he took the general idea of the concentric squares from the notion of *Sección Aurea* articulated by Macody Lund in his *Teoría Real de la Arquitectura* and in his studies of the geometric structures of the ancient and medieval religious architectural forms found in the Nodarós Cathedral (see Amabilis, *El pabellón*, 32).

47. Ibid., 38.

48. Ibid., 50.

49. Ibid., 50–51.

50. Ibid., 55–56. The other two *jambas* were *La Jamba de los Sacerdotes* and *La Jamba de los Constructores*.

51. In addition, Reyes painted three murals which represented miners, farmers, and people from Yucatán.

52. Amabilis, *El pabellón*, 76–77.

53. Argentina constructed a neocolonial type of building, designed by Martín S. Noel, which combined baroque aspects with Inca and Calchaquís motifs. Manuel Piquerons Cotolí constructed the Peruvian pavilion in what he called neo-Peruvian style: extravagant but rational. See Cherif-El-Maldini, "El pabellón peruano en la Exposición Ibero-Americana: Una interesante charla con el arquitecto autor del proyecto...," *El Liberal* (Seville) 6 September 1927, quoted by Villar Morellán, *Arquitectura del regionalismo*, 457. The United States constructed its main pavilion in neocolonial California style. It was designed by William Templeton Johnson, a follower of Bertram G. Goodhue, who built the 1915 San Diego world's fair—the zenith of colonial California style. Chile constructed a building which imitated the majesty of the Andes. See Villar Morellán, *Arquitectura del regionalismo*, 453–65.

54. *La Unión*, 2 September 1928.

55. Reported to the Ministry of Foreign Affairs, SRE EMESP 533.

56. See González Martínez's account of his troublesome meeting with the Spanish king, in González Martínez, *La apacible locura*, in *Obras Completas*, 775–80.

57. *La Libertad*, 22 May 1929.

58. Reyes, "Una interpretación de la Exposición Iberoamericana," 129–30.

59. In *El Liberal* (Seville), in *El Noticiero Sevillano*, originally published in *Industria y Comercio*, Mexico.

60. *El Liberal* (Madrid), 17 May 1929.
61. The legends were written by Reyes without the permission of either Amabilis or González Martínez. In fact, it seems that even the legend *"Madre España"* was put there without their permission. Both González Martínez and Amabilis disliked the legends, not for their connotations but because of their tacky prose. Thus all of those *letreritos* (little signs), as Amabilis called them, were removed by order of González Martínez in 1928, except *"Madre Patria"* that had already been read by Spanish authorities, who were very pleased with it. For the legends, see SRE IV-295-I, II; for the debate about them, see SRE EMESP 533.
62. Letter to González Martínez, 2 January 1929, SRE EMESP 537.
63. See M. Alfonso Rivera, *Sevilla y su exposición, 1929* (Seville, 1992), 64.
64. Godoy, *México en Sevilla*.
65. About this week, see González Martínez's report, 26 June 1930, SRE EMESP 539. He, of course, did not like the spirit of the Mexican week because of its radicalism and because of its lack of Mexican presence.
66. See Luis Araquistáin, *La revolución mejicana: Sus orígenes, sus hombres, su obra* (Madrid, 1929), 353.
67. See the reprints of Fernando de los Ríos, *El sentido humanista del socialismo* (Madrid, 1976); and Fernando de los Ríos, *Escritos sobre democracia y socialismo* (Madrid, 1974). For the role of these intellectuals in Spain during the late 1920s and their fascination with Mexico, see Genoveva García Queipo, *Los intelectuales y la dictadura de Primo de Rivera* (Madrid, 1988), 181–84, 525–30.
68. For instance, the book *México* was the counterpart of the many propaganda books published during the nineteenth century. It was published by the Comité Organizador de la Participación de México en la Exposición Ibero-Americana de Sevilla in 1929. Of the 3,000 copies printed, 80 were dedicated to Spanish and international authorities: it had been prepared by Luis A. Herrera with the collaboration of distinguished intellectuals, such as Salvador Novo, director of the Propaganda Section in the Ministry of Industry.
69. See "Inauguración de la Exposición Iberoamericana de Sevilla." The American pavilion was indeed three buildings: one in Spanish colonial style—to be made into the American consulate following the fair—another industrial gallery, and a movie theater.
70. These films were requested by the Mexican Embassy in Belgium in January 1928. They seem to have been exhibited throughout Europe. SRE EMESP 528.
71. See SRE EMESP 523.
72. Ibid.
73. For the exhibit, see the list of products and objects awarded in SRE EMESP 539; and Sáenz, *Comité Organizador*.
74. Report, 4 April 1930, SRE EMESP 539. The highest Spanish award was the grand prize (followed by honor diploma, gold, silver, bronze, and finally honorable mention).
75. Regarding the continuity of business in prerevolutionary and postrevolutionary Mexico, see Haber, *Industry and Underdevelopment*.
76. See Jaime Noyola Rocha, "La visión integral de la sociedad nacional (1920–1934)," in *La antropología en México: Panorama histórico*, vol. 2, *Los hechos y los dichos (1880–1986)*, ed. Carlos García Mora (Mexico City, 1987), 133–222; Guaraldo,

"Indigenismo e investigación etno-antropológica"; Juan Comas, "Historia del indigenismo en México," *América Indígena* 8 (1948):182–86; and, for Gamio's conflict with Calles, González Gamio, *Manuel Gamio*, 79–92.

77. In this respect, see Moyssén, "El nacionalismo y la arquitectura."

78. In the late 1920s international interest in Mexican archaeological ruins was widespread, especially among American institutions. Thus a Maya building in a world's fair helped to popularize this interest. However, architecturally there were already some examples of European or American uses of pre-Hispanic motifs—the California buildings of Frank Lloyd Wright, for example. In addition, interestingly enough, between 1927 and 1934 the American architect Robert B. Stacy-Judd promoted the use of Maya architecture in order for American architecture to come out with a real "all-American" style. This bizarre American architect—who believed that "Christ's last words were pure Maya"—constructed various buildings with Maya inspiration in California, including, in about 1927, the Aztec Hotel in Moraga and the First Baptist Church in Ventura. For instance, see articles by Robert B. Stacy-Judd in the journal of *The Architect and the Engineer* from October 1933 to November 1934, and the summary of his impressions on Maya architecture in his *The Ancient Mayas: Adventures in the Jungles of Yucatan* (Los Angeles, 1934). See also the recently published interpretation of Stacy-Judd's Mayism: David Gebhard, *Robert B. Stacy-Judd: Maya Architecture and the Creation of a New Style* (Santa Barbara, 1993).

79. See SRE III–236–3, especially the opinions of Jaime Torres Bodet and Marte R. Gómez regarding the advantages of Mexico's presence at the 1937 Paris fair. Compare Mexico's presence at the 1939 New York world's fair, at which Mexico exhibited a "graphic synthesis" of President Lázaro Cárdenas's six-year plan as well as traditional clothing on models that represented "the most typical characteristics of the autochthonous races of Mexico" (México, Secretaría de la Economía Nacional, *Memoria de la Secretaría de Economía Nacional, 1939–1940* [Mexico City, 1940], 17).

80. In this regard, see the analysis of the vivid intellectual discussion that took place in 1925 in Victor Díaz Arciniega, *Querella por la cultura "revolucionaria" (1925)* (Mexico City, 1989).

EPILOGUE

1. Examples of this alternative approach are: for Mexico and from an anthropological synchronic perspective, Claudio Lomnitz, *Exits from the Labyrinth* (Berkeley, 1992), esp. chap. 1, and Guy P. C. Thomson, "Bulwarks of Patriotic Liberalism: The National Guard, Philharmonic Corps and Patriotic Juntas in Mexico, 1847–1888," *Journal of Latin American Studies* 22 (February 1990):31–68; for Bengal India, Partha Chatterjee, *The Nation and Its Fragments* (Princeton, N.J., 1993), 3–12, 158–99; and for France, the classic study by E. Weber, *Peasants into Frenchmen* (Stanford, 1976).

2. Of course, there are authors who disagree in this assertion. For an example, see John Breuilly, *Nationalism and the State* (Chicago, 1982).

3. Too much has been written about identity. By identity I refer solely to the abstract notion of a people's own sense of attachment and belonging, be it an ethnic, cultural, geographical, or religious sense of communal existence.

4. See Étienne Tassin, "Identités nationales et citoyenneté politique," *Esprit*, no. 198 (1994):97–111.

5. I thank Paolo Riguzzi for his comments on this point.

6. See Edmundo O'Gorman's *Destierro de sombras: Luz en el origen de la imagen y culto de Nuestra Señora de Guadalupe del Tepeyac* (Mexico City, 1986).

7. See William Tobin, "'A Shrine to Which All May Worship': The Making of the Lincoln Memorial and the Representation of the Modern American Nation-State" (manuscript, 1992).

8. There are various studies on the emergence of these popular patriotisms. For an excellent synthesis of these patriotisms, see Knight, *U.S.–Mexico Relations;* Thomson, "Bulwarks of Patriotic Liberalism"; and Guy P. C. Thomson, "Movilización conservadora, insurrección liberal y rebeliones indígenas, 1854–1876," in *America Latina: Dallo Stato Coloniale allo Stato Nazione,* ed. Antonio Annino, vol. 2 (Turin, 1987), 592–614.

9. See Musil's collection of essays published in German as *Gesammelte Werke,* ed. Adolf Frise (Hamburg, 1978). I used the Spanish translation of the collection, published as *Ensayos y conferencias,* trans. José L. Arántegui (Madrid, 1992), 95–108, quotation on p. 107.

10. Chatterjee, *The Nation,* 6.

11. Lêdo Ivo, "Acontecimento do sonêto" (1949), from *Acontecimento do sonêto* (Rio de Janeiro, 1965), 10.

12. François Xavier Guerra argues that Spanish American countries "belong in their own right—at least in terms of their elites' origins and culture—within a European cultural area. Countries which were among the first within this cultural area to set up modern political regimes." F. X. Guerra, "The Spanish-American Tradition of Representation and Its European Roots," *Journal of Latin American Studies* 26 (1994):1.

13. Knight distinguishes goals and means in nationalist social actors; I follow this distinction. See Alan Knight, "Revolutionary Project, Recalcitrant People: Mexico, 1910–1940," in *Revolutionary Process in Mexico,* ed. J. E. Rodríguez (Los Angeles, 1990), 227–64.

14. Ramón López Velarde, *Obras* (Mexico City, 1971), 232.

15. Jorge Cuesta, "Carta a Portes Gil" (1940), in Cuesta, *Poesía y crítica* (Mexico City, 1991), 233.

16. López Velarde, *Obras,* 232.

BIBLIOGRAPHY

ARCHIVES AND ABBREVIATIONS

AGN Cárdenas. Archivo General de la Nación, México, Ramo Presidentes, Lázaro Cárdenas.
AGN Obregón-Calles. Archivo General de la Nación, México, Ramo Presidentes, Álvaro Obregón y Plutarco Elías Calles.
BEMP. *Boletín de la Exposición Mexicana en París, 1889.*
DO. *Diario Oficial de la Federación,* México.
EXP. Archivo General de la Nación, México, Ramo Fomento, Exposiciones Internacionales.
HMM. Cosío Villegas, Daniel, ed. *Historia Moderna de México.* 9 vols. Mexico City: Editorial Hermes, 1955–1964.
Industrias Nuevas. Archivo General de la Nación, México, Ramo Fomento, Industrias Nuevas.
IPBA. Archivo General de la Nación, México, Ramo Instrucción Pública y Bellas Artes.
NYT. *The New York Times.*
Patentes y Marcas. Archivo General de la Nación, México, Ramo Fomento, Patentes y Marcas.
RUP. Picard, A., ed. *Exposition Universelle Internationale de 1889 à Paris.* 10 vols. Paris, 1891–1892.
SRE. Secretaría de Relaciones Exteriores, México, Archivo Histórico Genaro Estrada.
SRE EMESP. Secretaría de Relaciones Exteriores, México, Archivo Histórico Genaro Estrada, Embajada de México en España.
SSA. Secretaría de Salubridad y Asistencia, México, Archivo Histórico.
UIA-Díaz. Archivo Porfirio Díaz, Universidad Iberoamericana, México.

PERIODICALS

Anales del Museo Nacional
El Arte y la Ciencia
Boletín de la Exposición Mexicana en Chicago

Bulletin de l'Exposition Universelle de Paris 1889
La Crónica. Periódico político mercantil de noticias y avisos, regalo a los subscriptores del Álbum de la Mujer
El Diario del Hogar
El Economista Mexicano
Época Ilustrado. Semanario de literatura, humorística y caricaturas
El Estudio. Semanario de Ciencias Médicas
Ethnos. Revista Mensual de Divulgación de Estudios Antropológicos sobre México y Centro-América
Excélsior
Gaceta Médica de México
El Hijo del Ahuizote
El Imparcial
Memorias de la Sociedad Antonio Alzate
El México Gráfico
Le Moniteur de l'Exposition de 1889
El Monitor Republicano
El Mundo Ilustrado
La Naturaleza. Sociedad Mexicana de Historia Natural
La Nature. Revue des Sciences et de leurs Applications aux Arts et à l'Industrie
The New York Times
Revista de las Españas
Revista de Revistas
Revista Moderna
Revista Nacional de Letras y Ciencias
Revista Positiva
Revue des Arts Decoratifs
Revue des Deux Mondes
Revue Illustrée
El Siglo XIX
El Universal

SELECTED BIBLIOGRAPHY

This bibliography does not include all of the works cited in this book. Additional citations to works on the various topics covered in this book can be found in the endnotes.

Abels, Margaret Hutton. "Painting at the Brazil Centennial Exposition." *Art and Archaeology* 16 (Summer 1923):105–14.

Acevedo, Jesús T. *Disertaciones de un arquitecto.* Prologue by Justino Fernández. Mexico City: Instituto Nacional de Bellas Artes, 1967.

Adorno, Juan Nepomuceno, *Acerca de la hidrografía, meteorología, seguridad hidrogénica y salubridad higiénica del valle y en especial de la Capital de México.* Mexico City: Mariano Villanueva, 1865.

———. *Melagraphie, ou nouvelle notation musicale par Juan N. Adorno.* Paris: F. Didot, 1855.

———. *Resumen ordenado de las discusiones pronunciadas por el ciudadano Juan Nepo-*

muceno Adorno ante los ciudadanos redactores y editores de la prensa periódica. Mexico City: Ignacio Cumplido, 1873.
Aimone, Linda, and Carlo Olmo. *Le Esposizioni Universali, 1851–1900: Il progresso in scena.* Torino: U. Allemandi, 1990.
Alamán, Lucas. *Historia de Méjico desde los primeros movimientos que prepararon su independencia en el año de 1808 hasta la época presente.* 5 vols. Mexico City: Imprenta de J. M. Lara, 1849.
Allwood, John. *The Great Exhibitions.* London: Studio Vista, 1977.
Altamirano, Francisco. *Materia Médica Mexicana. A Manual of Mexican Medical Herbs.* Saint Louis, Mo.: Mexican National Commission, 1904.
Altick, Richard D. *The Shows of London.* Cambridge, Mass.: Belknap Press, 1978.
Álvarez, Manuel Francisco. *Manuel F. Álvarez: Algunos escritos.* Selection by Elisa García Barragán. Mexico City: Cuadernos de Arquitectura y Conservación del Patrimonio Artístico, 1981–1982.
———. *Las ruinas de Mitla y la arquitectura, por el arquitecto e ingeniero director de la Escuela Nacional de Artes y Oficios de México.* Mexico City: Talleres de la Escuela Nacional de Artes y Oficios, 1900.
Álvarez Rey, Leandro. *Sevilla durante la dictadura de Primo de Rivera.* Seville: Diputación Provincial de Sevilla, 1987.
Amabilis, Manuel. *Mística de la revolución mexicana.* Mexico City, 1937.
———. *El pabellón de México en la Exposición Ibero-Americana de Sevilla.* Prologue by Enrique González Martínez. Mexico City: Talleres Gráficos de la Nación, 1929.
Amaral, Aracy. *Artes plásticas na Semana de 22.* São Paulo: Perspectiva, 1970.
Anderson, Benedict. *Imagined Communities: Reflections on the Origins and Spread of Nationalism.* London: Verso, 1983.
Annuaire de l'Économie Politique et de la Statistique, fondé por MM. Guillaumin et Joseph Garnier continué depuis 1856 par M. Maurice Block. Paris: Guillaumin et Cie., 1889–1901.
The Annual Register: A Review of Public Events at Home and Abroad. London, 1887–1900.
Appletons' Annual Cyclopaedia and Register of Important Events . . . 1889. New York, 1890.
L'Architecture à l'Exposition Universelle de 1900. Paris: Librairies-Imprimeries Réunies, 1902.
L'Architecture & la sculpture a l'Exposition de 1900. Paris: A. Guerinet, 1904.
Argentina. *République Argentine: La Vie sociale et la vie légale des étrangers.* Paris: n.p., 1889.
Argentina. Comisión, Exposición de París 1889. *L'Agriculture et l'élevage dans la République Argentine d'après le recensement de la première quinzaine d'octobre de 1888 . . . ouvrage publié sous la direction de F. Latzina.* Paris: P. Muillot, 1889.
Arnason, Johann P. "Nationalism, Globalization and Modernity." In *Global Culture: Nationalism, Globalization and Modernity,* edited by Mike Featherstone, 207–36. London: Sage Publications, 1990.
Badger, R. *The Great American Fair: The World's Columbian Exposition and American Culture.* Chicago: N. Hall, 1979.
Ballu, Alberto. "La arquitectura en la Exposición Universal de París 1889." Informe argentino, 1889–1890.
Bárcena, Mariano. *Ensayo estadístico del Estado de Jalisco: Referente a los datos necesarios para promover el adelanto de la agricultura y la aclimatación de nuestras plantas industriales.* Mexico City: Secretaría de Fomento, 1888.

———. *Los ferrocarriles mexicanos*. Mexico City: Filomeno Mata, 1881.
Bartra, Roger. *La jaula de la melancolía*. Mexico City: Grijalbo, 1987.
Batres, Leopoldo. *Monografías de arqueología mexicana: Teotihuacán; o la ciudad sagrada de los toltecas*. Mexico City: Talleres de la Escuela de Artes y Oficios, 1889.
Baz, Gustavo, and E. L. Gallo. *History of the Mexican Railway: Wealth of Mexico, in the Region Extending from the Gulf to the Capital of the Republic, Considered in Its Geological, Agricultural, Manufacturing and Commercial Aspects, with Scientific, Historical and Statistical Notes*. Translated by George F. Henderson. Mexico City: Gallo and Co., 1876.
Beezley, William H. *Judas at the Jockey Club and Other Episodes of Porfirian Mexico*. Lincoln: University of Nebraska Press, 1987.
Ben-Ami, Shlomo. *Fascism from Above: The Dictatorship of Primo de Rivera in Spain, 1923–1930*. Oxford: Clarendon Press, 1983.
Benedict, Burton. *The Anthropology of World's Fairs: San Francisco's Panama Pacific International Exposition of 1915*. Berkeley: University of California Press, 1983.
———. "International Exhibitions and National Identity." *Anthropology Today* 6 (June 1991):5–9.
Benjamin, Walter. "Paris, Capital of the 19th Century." In *Illuminations*, edited by Peter Demetz, translated by E. Jephcott, 146–58. New York: Harcourt, Brace and World, 1986.
Bernal, Ignacio. *Historia de la arqueología en México*. Mexico City: Porrúa, 1979.
Bertier-Marriot, Clement. *Un parisien au Mexique*. Paris: E. Déntu, 1886.
Best, Alberto. *Notice sur les applications de l'electricité dans la République mexicaine*. Paris: Secretaría de Fomento, 1889.
Bianconi, F. *Le Mexique à la portée des industriels, des capitalistes, des négociants, importateurs et exportateurs et des travailleurs avec une carte du Mexique commerciale, boutière, minière et agricole*. Paris: Imprimerie Chaix, 1889.
———. *Texte et carte commerciale des États-Unis du Mexique*. Paris: Imprimerie Chaix, 1889.
Blanco, José Joaquín. *Se llamaba Vasconcelos: Una evocación crítica*. Mexico City: Fondo de Cultura Económica, 1977.
Brading, David. "Héroes republicanos y tiranos populares." *Cuadernos Americanos*, nueva época, 11 (1988):9–28.
———. "Manuel Gamio and Official Indigenism in Mexico." *Bulletin of Latin American Research* 7, 1 (1988):75–89.
———. *The Origins of Mexican Nationalism*. Cambridge, England: Cambridge University Press, 1985.
———. *Prophecy and Myth in Mexican History*. Cambridge, England: Cambridge University Press, 1984.
Breckenridge, Carol A. "The Aesthetics and Politics of Colonial Collecting: India at World Fairs." *Comparative Studies in Society and History* 31, 2 (1989):195–216.
Breuilly, John. *Nationalism and the State*. Chicago: University of Chicago Press, 1982.
Brinton, Daniel. *Races and Peoples: Lectures on the Science of Ethnography*. New York, 1890.
Bueno Fidel, María José. *Arquitectura y nacionalismo: Los pabellones españoles en las exposiciones universales del siglo XIX*. Málaga: Universidad de Málaga, Colegio de Arquitectos, 1987.
Bullock, William. *A Description of the Unique Exhibition, Called Ancient Mexico: Collected*

on the Spot in 1823 by the Assistance of the Mexican Government, and Now Open for Public Inspection at the Egyptian Hall, Piccadilly. London: J. Bullock, 1824.
Bulnes, Francisco. *El porvenir de las naciones latinoamericanas ante las recientes conquistas de Europa y Norteamérica (estructura y evolución de un continente).* Mexico City: Imprenta de M. Nava, 1899.
Burg, D. F. *Chicago's White City of 1893.* Lexington: University Press of Kentucky, 1976.
Busto, Emiliano. *La administración pública en Méjico: Breve estudio comparativo entre el sistema de administración de hacienda en Francia y el establecido en Méjico.* Spanish and French bilingual ed. Paris: P. Dupont, 1889.
———. *Estadística de la República Mexicana: Resumen y análisis de los informes remitidos a la Secretaría de Hacienda.* Mexico City: Imprenta de I. Cumplido, 1880.
Caballero, Manuel. *México en Chicago.* Chicago: Knight Leonard, 1893.
———, ed. *Primer almanaque histórico, artístico y monumental de la República Mexicana.* New York: Chas. M. Green Printing Co., 1883–1884.
Carbajal, Antonio. *Estudio sobre el pulque considerado principalmente desde el punto de vista zinotécnico.* Mexico City: Tip. de la Secretaría de Fomento, 1901.
Carmona y Valle, Manuel María. *Leçons sur l'étiologie et la prophylaxie de la fièvre jaune.* Preface by Eduardo Liceaga. Mexico City: Imprimerie Ministère des Travaux Publics, 1885.
Carr, Raymond. *Oxford History of Modern Europe: Spain, 1808–1939.* Oxford: Oxford University Press, 1966.
Carreño, Alberto María. *Semblanzas.* 2 vols. Mexico City: Edición privada, Ediciones Victoria, n.d.
Carvalho, José Murilo de. *A formação das almas: O imaginário da república no Brasil.* São Paulo: Companhia das Letras, 1990.
Castillo, Antonio del. *Catalogue descriptif des météorites (fers et pierres météoriques) du Mexique: avec l'indication des localités dans lesquelles ces météorites sont tombés ou ont été decouverts.* Paris: Imprimerie L. Ouin, 1889.
Castillo Negrete, Emiliano del. *México en el siglo XIX, o sea su historia desde 1800 hasta la época presente.* 7 vols. Mexico City: Imprenta del Universal e Imprenta del Castillo, 1875–1883.
Çelik, Zeynep. *Displaying the Orient: Architecture of Islam at Nineteenth-Century World's Fairs.* Berkeley: University of California Press, 1992.
Cero [Vicente Riva Palacio]. *Los Ceros.* Mexico City: Francisco Díaz de León, 1882.
Chamberlain, J. Edward, and Sander L. Gilman, eds. *Degeneration: The Dark Side of Progress.* New York: Columbia University Press, 1985.
Charle, Christophe. *La République des universitaires, 1870–1940.* Paris: Seuil, 1994.
Charlot, Jean. *Mexican Art at the Academy of San Carlos, 1785–1915.* Austin: University of Texas Press, 1962.
Charnay, Desiré de. *Les Anciennes Villes du Nouveau Monde: Voyages d'explorations au Mexique et dans l'Amérique Centrale.* Paris: L. Hachette et Cie., 1885.
———. *Cités e ruines americaines.* Paris: Gide, 1863.
Chatterjee, Partha. *Nationalist Thought and the Colonial World: A Derivative Discourse?* Tokyo: Zed Books, for the United Nations University, 1986.
Chavero, Alfredo. *Discurso pronunciado el 24 de septiembre de 1904 en el Congreso de artes y ciencias de la Exposición Universal de San Luis Missouri.* Mexico City: Imprenta del Museo Nacional, 1905.

———. *Historia antigua y de la conquista.* Vol. 1 of *México a través de los siglos.* Edited by Vicente Riva Palacio. Barcelona: Espasa y Cía., 1888.
———. *Obras del Licenciado Alfredo Chavero. Biblioteca de autores mexicanos.* Vol. 1, *Teatro: Xochitl, La Enamorada de Santa Fe, El Valle de Lágrimas, Sin Esperanza, Quetzalcóatl.* Prologue by Nicolás León. Mexico City: Tipografía de Victoriano Agüeros, 1904.
Ciaurriz, Narciso. *Origen y primeros trabajos de la Exposición Iberoamericana.* Seville: Tipografía Española, 1929.
Cmiel, Kenneth. *Democratic Eloquence: The Fight over Popular Speech in Nineteenth-Century America.* New York: William Morrow, 1990.
Coerver, Don M. "The Perils of Progress: The Mexican Department of Fomento during the Boom Years, 1880–1884." *Inter-American Economic Affairs* 31, 2 (1977):41–62.
———. *The Porfirian Interregnum: The Presidency of Manuel González of Mexico, 1880–1884.* Fort Worth: Texas Christian University Press, 1979.
Coleman, William. *Death Is a Social Disease: Public Health and Political Economy in Early Industrial France.* Madison: University of Wisconsin Press, 1982.
Collineau, Alfred Charles. *L'Anthropologie à l'Exposition Universelle de 1889.* Paris: Imprimerie Wattier et Cie., 1890.
Colmenares, Germán. *Las convenciones contra la cultura: Ensayo sobre historiografía hispanoamericana del siglo XIX.* Bogotá, Colombia: Tercer Mundo Editores, 1987.
The Columbian Exposition Album, Containing Views of the Grounds, Main and State Buildings, Statuary, Architectural Details, Interiors, Midway Plaisance Scenes, and Other Interesting Objects at the World's Columbian Exposition. New York: Rand McNally, 1893.
Comas, Juan. "Un precursor de la antropología física mexicana: E. Domenech, 1825–1904." *Anales de Antropología* 7 (1970):9–24.
Comte, Jules Abel. *L'Art a l'Exposition Universelle de 1900: Texte de Ernest Babelon . . . gravures et litographies de Boilivin . . . sous la direction de Jules Comte.* Paris: Librairie de l'Art Ancien et Moderne, 1900.
Congrès International des Américanistes. *Compte Rendu de la Huitième Session.* Paris: Congrès International des Américanistes, 1890.
Congreso Internacional de Americanistas. *Actas de la XI reunión. México 1895.* Mexico City: Agencia Tipográfica de F. Díaz de León, 1897.
———. *Annaes do XX Congresso Internacional de Americanistas, realizado no Rio de Janeiro de 20 a 30 de agosto 1922.* 3 vols. Rio de Janeiro, 1922.
Cooper, Walter G. *The Cotton States and International Exposition and South, Illustrated.* Atlanta, Ga.: Illustrator Co., 1896.
Corbey, Raymond. "Ethnographic Showcases, 1870–1930." *Cultural Anthropology* 8 (1993):338–69.
Corbin, Alain. *Women for Hire: Prostitution and Sexuality in France after 1850.* Translated by Alan Sheridan. Cambridge, Mass.: Harvard University Press, 1990.
Corre, A. *Le Crime en pays créoles (esquisse d'ethnographie criminelle).* Paris: G. Masson, 1889.
Cosío Villegas, Daniel. "La riqueza legendaria de México." In *Extremos de América*, edited by Daniel Cosío Villegas, 82–111. Mexico City: Fondo de Cultura Económica, 1949.
———, ed. *Historia Moderna de México.* 9 vols. Mexico City: Editorial Hermes, 1955–1972.
Cronon, William. *Nature's Metropolis: Chicago and the Great West.* New York: W. W. Norton, 1991.

Cuadriello Aguilar, Jaime Genaro Francisco Javier. "La arquitectura en México (ca. 1857–1920): Ensayo para el estudio de sus tipos y programas." Tesis de Licenciatura, Universidad Iberoamericana, 1983.
Curti, Merle. "America at the World Fairs, 1851–1893." *American Historical Review* 55, 4 (1950):833–56.
Curtis, J. P. "Architecture of the Brazil Centennial Exposition." *Art and Architecture* 16 (September 1923):95–104.
Delannoi, Gil. "La Théorie de la nation et ses ambivalences." In *Théories du nationalisme: Nation, Nationalité, Ethnicité*, edited by G. Delannoi and P. A. Tagguieff, 9–14. Paris: Editions Kime, 1991.
Delaporte, François. *The History of Yellow Fever: An Essay on the Birth of Tropical Medicine*. Translated by Arthur Goldhammer. Cambridge, Mass.: MIT Press, 1991.
Demy, Adolphe. *Essai historique sur les expositions universelles de Paris*. Paris: Librairie A. Picard, Libraires des Archives Nationales et de la Société de l'École de Chartes, 1907.
Deniker, J., and L. Laloy. "Les Races exotiques à l'Exposition Universelle de 1889." In *L'Anthropologie: Matériaux pour l'histoire de l'homme. Revue d'Anthropologie–Revue d'Ethnographie*, edited by E. Cartailhac, E. Hamy, and P. Topinard, vol. 1, 257–94, 513–46. Paris: G. Masson Editeur, 1890.
Díaz y de Ovando, Clementina. "Justo Sierra en la mira de Vicente Riva Palacio." *Anales del Instituto de Investigaciones Estéticas*, no. 52 (1983):151–66.
———. "México en la Exposición Universal de 1889." *Anales del Instituto de Investigaciones Estéticas*, no. 61 (1990):109–71.
———. "Vicente Riva Palacio y la arqueología, 1878–1880." *Anales del Instituto de Investigaciones Estéticas*, no. 58 (1987):179–86.
———. *Vicente Riva Palacio y la identidad nacional*. Mexico City: Universidad Nacional Autónoma de México, 1985.
Dubos, René. *Reason Awake: Science for Man*. New York: Columbia University Press, 1970.
Dunbar, Gary. "The Compass Follows the Flag: The French Scientific Mission to Mexico, 1864–67." *Annals of the Association of American Geographers* 78, 2 (1988):229–40.
Dunn, Archibald. *Mexico and Her Resources*. London: A. Boot & Son Printers, 1890.
Dupin de Saint-André, A. *Le Mexique aujourd'hui: Impressions et souvenirs de voyage*. Paris: Librairie Plan, 1884.
École des Hautes Études en Sciences Sociales. *La Statistique en France à l'époque napoléonienne*. Brussels: Centre Guillaume Jacquemyns, 1980.
Encina, Juan de la. *El paisajista José María Velasco (1840–1912)*. Mexico City: El Colegio de México, 1943.
Escalante, Fernando. *Ciudadanos imaginarios*. Mexico City: El Colegio de México, 1993.
Escandón, Pedro de. *La industria y las bellas artes en la Exposición Universal de 1855*. Paris: Centrale de Napoléon Chaix et Cie., 1856.
Everaert Dubernard, Luis. *México 1900*. Mexico City: Salvat, 1994.
Ewald, Donna, and Peter Clute. *San Francisco Invites the World: The Panama-Pacific International Exposition of 1915*. San Francisco: Chronicle Books, 1991.
Fell, Claude. *José Vasconcelos: Los años del águila (1920–1925)*. Mexico City: Universidad Nacional Autónoma de México, 1989.

Fernández, Justino. *El arte del siglo XIX en México.* Mexico City: Universidad Nacional Autónoma de México, 1967.

———. *El arte moderno en México: Breve historia—Siglo XIX y XX.* Mexico City: Porrúa, 1937.

———. *Roberto Montenegro.* Mexico City: Universidad Nacional Autónoma de México, 1962.

Fernández, María Auxiliadora. "The Representation of National Identity in Mexican Architecture: Two Case Studies (1680 and 1889)." Ph.D. diss., Columbia University, 1993.

Fernández del Castillo, Francisco. *Historia bibliográfica del Instituto Médico Nacional de México (1888–1915).* Mexico City: Universidad Nacional Autónoma de México, 1961.

Figaro-Exposition 1889: La Mode de Demain. Prologue by Émile Blavet. Paris, 1889.

Findling, John E., ed. *Historical Dictionary of World's Fairs and Expositions, 1851–1988.* New York: Greenwood Press, 1990.

Flores, Teodoro. "Panorama de la geología en México (1551–1951)." *Memoria del Congreso Científico Mexicano* 3 (1953):23–61.

Flores y Troncoso, Francisco de Asis. *El himen en México.* Mexico City: Oficina de la Secretaría de Fomento, 1885.

———. *Historia de la medicina en México desde la época de los indios hasta la presente.* 4 vols. Mexico City: Oficina Tip. de la Secretaría de Fomento, 1886–1888.

Florescano, Enrique. *Memoria mexicana.* Mexico City: Joaquín Mortiz, 1987.

Foot Harman, Francisco. *Trem fantasma: A modernidade na selva.* São Paulo: Companhia das Letras, 1988.

France. *Annuaire statistique de la France.* Nancy, 1889.

———. Ministère de l'Instruction Publique. *Archives de la Commission Scientifique du Mexique, publiées sous les auspices du Ministère de l'Instruction Publique.* Paris, 1865.

France. Paris. Exposition Universelle de 1889. *Actes du Deuxième Congrès International d'Anthropologie Criminale.* Paris, 1889.

———. *Catalogue général officiel: Exposition retrospective du travail et des sciences anthropologiques. Section 1, anthropologie, ethnographie.* Lille: Imprimerie L. Danel, 1889.

———. *Catalogue officiel illustré de l'Exposition Centennale de l'Arte Français, 1800 à 1889.* Edited by Ludovic Bachet. Paris: Modern Art in Paris, 1981.

———. *Conférences de l'Exposition Universelle de 1889.* 2 vols. Paris: Imprimerie Nationale, 1890.

———. *Congrès International d'Assistance, tenu du 28 juillet au 4 août 1889.* 2 vols. Paris: G. Rongier & Cie., 1889.

———. *Congrès International de Dermatologie et de Syphiligraphie, 1889. Comptes rendus publiés pour Dr. Henri Ifeulard.* Paris: G. Masson Editeur, 1890.

———. *Congrès International de Medicine Mentale tenu à Paris 2–20 août 1889.* Paris: G. Masson Editeur, 1890.

———. *Congrès International des Oeuvres et Institutions Féminines.* Paris: Bibliothèque des Annales Économiques, 1890.

———. *Congrès International des Sciences Ethnographiques.* Paris: Imprimerie Nationale, 1889.

———. *Congrès International des Traditions Populaires. Première session. Compte rendu.* Paris: Bibliothèque des Annales Économiques, 1891.

———. *Congrès International d'Higiène et de Démographie, 1889. Compte rendu.* Paris: Bibliothèque des Annales Économiques, 1890.
———. *Exposition Universelle Internationale de 1889. Direction Générale de l'Exposition. Adjudication du Catalogue Général.* Paris: Imprimerie Nationale, 1888.
———. *Exposition Universelle Internationale de 1889 à Paris. Monographie, palais-jardins-constructions diverses-installations générales.* Paris: A. Alphard, J. Rothschild Editeur, 1892–1895.
———. *Exposition Universelle Internationale de 1889 à Paris. Rapport général.* Edited by A. Picard. 10 vols. Paris: Imprimerie Nationale, 1891–1892.
———. *Projects pour l'Exposition Universelle de 1989 à Paris.* Paris: Livre Blanc Flamarion, 1985.
———. *La Société, l'école et le laboratoire d'anthropologie de Paris à l'Exposition Universelle de 1889.* Paris, 1889.
France. Paris. Exposition Universelle Internationale de 1900. *L'Économie sociale à l'Exposition Universelle de 1900: Livre d'or des exposants du groupe XVI, pub. sous le patronage du Jury international et du Musée social.* Paris: A. Rousseau, 1903.
———. *Exposition Universelle Internationale de 1900 à Paris: Rapport du jury international.* Paris: Impr. Nationale, 1904.
Francis, David R. *The Universal Exposition of 1904.* 2 vols. Saint Louis, Mo.: Louisiana Purchase Exposition Co., 1913.
Fuente Salceda, María de la Concepción de la. "La participación de México en la Exposición Universal de Filadelfia, 1876." Tesis de Licenciatura, Universidad Iberoamericana, 1984.
Galindo y Villa, Jesús. *Breve noticia histórico-descriptiva del Museo Nacional de México.* Mexico City: Imprenta del Museo Nacional, 1896.
Gamboa, Federico. *Mi Diario: Mucho de mi vida y algo de la de los otros.* 1st series. Guadalajara, Mexico: Imprenta de La Gaceta de Guadalajara, 1907.
———. *Mi Diario: Mucho de mi vida y algo de la de los otros.* 2d series, 2. Mexico City: Ediciones Botas, 1938.
García Cubas, Antonio. *Album del ferrocarril mexicano: Colección de vistas . . . por Casimiro Castro.* Mexico City: V. Debray, 1877.
———. *Cuadro geográfico y estadístico, descriptivo e histórico de los Estados Unidos Mexicanos.* Mexico City: Secretaría de Fomento, 1884.
———. *Étude géographique statistique descriptive et historique des États Unis Mexicains.* Mexico City: Imprimerie du Ministère des Travaux Publics, 1889.
———. *Importancia de la estadística.* Mexico City: Imprenta del Gobierno, 1871.
———. *Mexico: Its Trade, Industries and Resources.* Mexico City: Secretaría de Fomento, 1893.
García Granados, Ricardo. *El concepto científico de la historia.* Mexico City: Tipografía Económica, 1910.
García Martínez, Bernardo. "La Comisión Geográfico-Exploradora." *Historia Mexicana* 24, 4 (1975):485–555.
García Quintana, Josefina. *Cuauhtémoc en el siglo XIX.* Mexico City: Universidad Nacional Autónoma de México, 1977.
Gargallo di Castel Lentini, Francesca. "Vicente Riva Palacio: Uno storico liberale." *Revista di Storia della Storiografia* 3, 2–3 (1982):123–30.

Gargollo y Prida, Manuel. *La necesidad de un estilo moderno de arquitectura.* Mexico City: Asociación de Ingenieros Civiles y Arquitectos, 1869.
Garnier, Charles, and A. Ammann. *L'Habitation humaine.* Paris: Libr. Hachette, 1892.
Gautier, Albert Hippolyte. *Les Curiosités de l'Exposition Universelle, 1867.* Paris: Ch. Delagrave et Cie., 1867.
Gellner, E. *Nations and Nationalism.* Oxford: Oxford University Press, 1983.
Genin, Auguste. *France-Mexique: vers dit par l'auteur.* Mexico City: Imprimerie du Courrier du Mexique, 1910.
Gerste, S. J. A. *Notes sur la médicine et la botanique des anciens mexicains.* Rome: Imprimerie Polyglotte Vaticanne, 1910.
Gibbs, William E. "Diaz' Executive Agents and United States Foreign Policy." *Journal of Interamerican Studies and World Affairs* 20, 2 (1878):165–89.
Gide, Charles. *Économie sociale: Rapports du jury international, Exposition Universelle de 1900.* Paris: Exposition Universelle de 1900, 1901.
Gigerenzer, Gerd, et al. *The Empire of Chance.* Cambridge, England: Cambridge University Press, 1989.
Gilbert, James. *Perfect Cities: Chicago's Utopias of 1893.* Chicago: University of Chicago Press, 1991.
Glümer, Bodo von. *Cuadro estadístico de los Estados Unidos Mexicanos: Formado con datos oficiales y por disposición de la Secretaría de Estado y del Despacho de Hacienda y Crédito Público.* Mexico City: Secretaría de Hacienda, 1882.
Godineau, Laure. "L'Économie sociale à l'Exposition Universelle de 1889." *Le Mouvement Social,* no. 149 (1989):71–87.
Godoy, José Francisco. *La ciudad de Chicago y la Exposición Universal de 1893.* Chicago: Cía. Panamericana, 1892.
———. *Enciclopedia biográfica de contemporáneos.* Washington, D.C.: Thos. W. Cadick, 1898.
———. *México en París: Reseña de la participación de la República Mexicana en la Exposición de París en 1889.* Mexico City: Tipografía de Alfonso E. López, 1890.
———. *México en Sevilla: Breves apuntes acerca de la Feria o Exposición Ibero-Americana que se verificará en el año de 1929 en la ciudad de Sevilla, y de lo que se está haciendo para que nuestro país sea dignamente representado.* Mexico City: Papelería Nacional, 1928.
———. *Porfirio Diaz, President of Mexico: The Master Builder of a Great Commonwealth.* New York: G. P. Putnam's Sons, 1910.
Goldwater, Robert. *Primitivism in Modern Art.* Cambridge, Mass.: Belknap Press, 1986.
González, Luis. *La ronda de las generaciones.* Mexico City: Secretaría de Educación Pública, 1984.
González Galván, Manuel. "La revaloración de la arquitectura colonial en el primer cuarto del siglo XX: Teoría y práctica." In *Saturnino Herrán: Jornadas de homenaje,* edited by Juan Castañeda, 95–106. Mexico City: Universidad Nacional Autónoma de México, 1989.
González Martínez, Enrique. *Obras Completas.* Mexico City: El Colegio Nacional, 1977.
González Navarro, Moisés. *La colonización en México, 1877–1910.* Mexico City: Talleres de Impresión de Estampilla y Valores, 1960.
———. "Las ideas raciales de los científicos, 1890–1910." *Historia Mexicana* 37, 4 (1988):565–83.

———. *Sociología e historia en México (Barreda, Sierra, Parra, Molina Enríquez, Gamio)*. Mexico City: El Colegio de México, 1970.
Gostkowski, Gustave. *Au Mexique: Études, notes et renseignements utiles au capitalistes, a l'immigrant, e au touriste*. Paris: Maurice de Brunoff, 1900.
Goubert, Jean-Pierre. *La Conquête de l'eau: L'Avènement de la santé à l'âge industriel*. Introduction by E. Le Roy Ladurie. Paris: Editions Robert Laffont, 1986.
Goudeau, Émile. "Une journée d'exposition." *Revue Illustrée*, no. 92 (1889):240–44.
Gould, Stephen Jay. *The Mismeasure of Man*. New York: W. W. Norton and Co., 1981.
La Grande Encyclopédie. Paris, 1886–1902.
Greenblatt, Stephen. "Towards a Poetics of Culture." In *The New Historicism*, edited by H. Aram Veeser, 1–14. New York: Routledge, 1989.
Greenfeld, Liah. *Nationalism: Five Roads to Modernity*, Cambridge, Mass.: Harvard University Press, 1992.
Greenhalgh, Paul. *Ephemeral Vistas: The Expositions Universelles, Great Exhibitions and World's Fairs, 1851–1939*. Manchester, England: Manchester University Press, 1988.
Guerra, François Xavier. *México: Del antiguo régimen a la revolución*. Translated by Sergio Fernández Bravo. 2 vols. Mexico City: Fondo de Cultura Económica, 1988.
Guerrero, Julio. *La génesis del crímen en México: Estudio de psiquiatría social*. Paris: Ch. Bouret, 1901.
Guerrero, Omar. *Introducción a la administración pública*. Mexico City: Trillas, 1985.
Gueslin, André. *L'Invention de l'économie sociale: Le XIXe siècle français*. Paris: Economica, 1987.
Guglielmi, Gilles J. *La Notion d'administration publique dans la théorie juridique française: De la révolution à l'arrêt Cadot (1789–1889)*. Paris: Librairie Générale de Droit et de Jurisprudence, 1991.
Guha-Thakurta, Tapati. *The Making of a New "Indian" Art: Artists, Aesthetics and Nationalism in Bengal, 1850–1920*. Cambridge, England: Cambridge University Press, 1992.
Guide bleu du Figaro et du petit Journal Paris. Paris, 1889.
Gumbrecht, Hans Ulrich. "A History of the Concept 'Modern.'" In *Making Sense in Life and Literature*, edited by H. U. Gumbrecht, 79–110. Minneapolis: University of Minnesota Press, 1992.
Gutiérrez, Alonso, et al. *Historia de la salubridad y la asistencia en México*. 4 vols. Mexico City: Secretaría de Salubridad y Asistencia, 1960.
Guzmán, David J. *Catalogue des objects exposés par la République du Salvador, rédirigé par M. le Dr. David J. Guzmán*. Paris, 1878.
Haber, Stephen H. "Assessing the Obstacles to Industrialization: The Mexican Economy, 1830–1940." 1991. Manuscript.
———. *Industry and Underdevelopment: The Industrialization of Mexico, 1890–1940*. Stanford, Calif.: Stanford University Press, 1989.
Hacking, Ian. *The Taming of Chance*. Cambridge, England: Cambridge University Press, 1990.
Haddon, Alfred. *Evolution in Art*. London: W. Scott, 1895.
Hale, Charles. *Mexican Liberalism in the Age of Mora, 1821–1853*. New Haven, Conn.: Yale University Press, 1968.
———. "Political and Social Ideas in Latin America, 1870–1930." In *The Cambridge History of Latin America*, edited by L. Bethell, vol. 4, 367–441. Cambridge, England: Cambridge University Press, 1986.

———. *The Transformation of Liberalism in Late Nineteenth-Century Mexico.* Princeton, N.J.: Princeton University Press, 1989.
Hall, Joy H. "Sheetiron, Syphilis, and the Second International: The Paris International Exposition of 1889." *Proceedings of the Western Society for French History,* no. 11 (1984):244–54.
Hamon, Philippe. *Expositions: Literature and Architecture in Nineteenth-Century France.* Translated by Katia Sainson-Frank and Lisa Maguire. Berkeley: University of California Press, 1992.
Hamy, E. T. *Décades américanae: Mémoires d'archéologie et d'etnographie américaines.* Paris: E. Leroux Editeur, 1884.
Harcourt, Raoul d'. *L'Américanisme et la France.* Paris: Librairie Larousse, 1928.
Harriss, Joseph. *The Tallest Tower: Eiffel and the Belle Époque.* Boston: Houghton Mifflin, 1975.
Harris, Neil, et al., eds. *Grand Illusions: Chicago's World's Fair of 1893.* Chicago: Chicago Historical Society, 1993.
Havard, Louis. *Maison salubre et la maison insalubre a l'Exposition Universelle de 1889: Étude sur l'exposition du service de l'assainissement.* Paris: Imprimerie de C. Noblet et fils, 1890.
Hawley, J. R. "The Value of International Exhibitions." *North American Review* 149 (September 1889):313–20.
Heidegger, Martin. *The Question Concerning Technology and Other Essays.* Translated by William Lovitt. New York: Harper & Row, 1977.
Henschen, Folke. *The History and Geography of Diseases.* Translated by Joan Tate. New York: Seymour Lawrence Book, 1966.
Hermosa, Jesús. *Manual de geografía y estadística de la República Mejicana.* Paris: Librería de Rosa, Bouret y Cía., 1857.
Hernández Martín, Vicente. *Arquitectura doméstica de la ciudad de México.* Mexico City: Escuela Nacional de Arquitectos, Universidad Nacional Autónoma de México, 1981.
Herzfeld, M. *Anthropology through the Looking-Glass: Critical Ethnography in the Margins of Europe.* Cambridge, England: Cambridge University Press, 1987.
Hidalgo. Junta Correspondiente de la Exposición Universal de Nueva Orleans. *Reseña relativa al Estado de Hidalgo que la junta correspondiente remite a la Exposición Universal de Nueva Orleans.* Pachuca, Mexico, 1884–1885.
Hildreth, Martha L. *Doctors, Bureaucrats, and Public Health in France, 1888–1902.* New York: Garland Publishing, 1987.
Hobsbawm, Eric. *The Age of Empire, 1875–1914.* New York: Pantheon Books, 1987.
———. *Nation and Nationalism.* Cambridge, England: Cambridge University Press, 1990.
Hodeir, Catherine. "L'Expo des expos." *Histoire* 60 (1983):96–100.
Honour, Hugh. *The New Golden Land: European Images of America from the Discoveries to the Present Time.* New York: Pantheon Books, 1975.
Hulbert, William Henry. *France and the Republic: A Record of Things Seen and Learned in the French Provinces during the "Centennial" Year 1889.* London: Longman, Green, and Co., 1890.
Iguiniz, Juan Bautista. *Bibliografía biográfica mexicana.* Mexico City: Instituto de Investigaciones Históricas, Universidad Nacional Autónoma de México, 1969.

Islas García, Luis. *Velasco: Pintor cristiano.* Mexico City: Proa, 1932.
Izquierdo, José Joaquín. *Balance cuatricentenario de la fisiología en México.* Mexico City: Ciencia, 1934.
Jiménez Rueda, Julio. *Bajo la cruz del sur: Impresiones de Sudamérica.* Mexico City: Librería Editorial de M. Manón, 1922.
Jones, W. "William Henry Jackson in Mexico." *American West* 14, 4 (1977):10–21.
Jornal do Commercio. *O Livro d'Ouro, Edição Comemorativa, 1822–1922.* Rio de Janeiro, 1922.
Josat, Jules. *Le Ministère de Finances: Son fonctionnement; suivi d'une étude sur l'organization générale des autres ministères.* Paris: Berger Levrault, 1883.
———. *Recueil de rédactions sur des sujets d'économie politique et sur des questions financières et administratives, subjets et questions données aux différents concours, tratés avec tous les développements qu'ils compartent et groupés dans un ordre méthodique et raisonné.* Paris: Berger Levrault, 1894.
Jourdaner, D. *Du Mexique au point de vue de son influence sur la vie de l'homme.* Paris: J. B. Ballière et fils, 1861.
Jullian, Philippe. *The Triumph of Art Nouveau: Paris Exhibition, 1900.* Translated by Stephen Hardman. London: Pahidon, 1974.
Katz, Friedrich. "Mexico: Restored Republic and Porfiriato, 1867–1910." In *The Cambridge History of Latin America,* edited by L. Bethell, vol. 5, 3–79. Cambridge, England: Cambridge University Press, 1986.
Katzman, Israel. *Arquitectura contemporánea mexicana: Precedentes y desarrollo.* Mexico City: Instituto Nacional de Antropología e Historia, 1963.
———. *Arquitectura del siglo XIX en México.* Mexico City: Universidad Nacional Autónoma de México, 1973.
Keen, Benjamin. *The Aztec Image in Western Thought.* New Brunswick, N.J.: Rutgers University Press, 1971.
Knight, Alan. *The Mexican Revolution.* 2 vols. Cambridge, England: Cambridge University Press, 1986.
———. "Revolutionary Project, Recalcitrant People: Mexico, 1910–1940." In *The Revolutionary Process in Mexico: Essays on Political and Social Change, 1880–1940,* edited by Jaime Rodríguez, 227–64. Los Angeles: University of California Press, 1990.
———. *U.S.–Mexican Relations, 1910–1940: An Interpretation.* San Diego, Calif.: Center for U.S.–Mexican Studies, University of California, San Diego, 1987.
Kohn, Hans. *The Idea of Nationalism: A Study in Its Origins and Background.* New York: Macmillan Co., 1944.
Koselleck, Reinhart. *Future Past: On the Semantics of Historical Time.* Translated by K. Tribe. Cambridge, Mass.: MIT Press, 1985.
Kremer-Marietti, Angèle. "L'Anthropologie physique et morale en France et ses implications idéologiques." In *Histoires de l'anthropologie (XVIe-XIXe siècles),* edited by Britta Rupp-Eisenreich, 319–51. Paris: Klincksieck, 1984.
Kuhn, Thomas. *The Essential Tension: Selected Studies in Scientific Tradition and Change.* Chicago: University of Chicago Press, 1977.
Larousse, P., ed. *Grand dictionnaire universel du XIXe siècle.* Paris: Administration du Grand Dictionnaire Universel, 190?.

Larrainzar, Manuel. *Algunas ideas sobre la historia y la manera de escribir la de México, especialmente la contemporánea, desde la declaración de independencia en 1821, hasta nuestros días*. Mexico City: Imprenta de Ignacio Cumplido, 1865.

Larsen, M. T. "Orientalism and the Ancient Near East." In *The Humanities between Art and Science: Intellectual Developments, 1880–1924*, edited by M. Harbsmeier and M. Larsen. Copenhagen: Akademisk Forlag, University of Copenhagen, Center for Research in the Humanities, 1989.

Legendre, Pierre. *Histoire de l'administration de 1750 à nos jours*. Paris: Press Universitaire de France, 1968.

Lemus López, Encarnación. *La Exposición Ibero-Americana a través de la prensa local (1923–1929)*. Seville: Excma. Diputación Provincial de Sevilla, 1987.

León, Nicolás. "Anomalías y mutilaciones étnicas del sistema dentario entre los tarascos pre-colombinos." *Anales del Museo Michoacano* 3 (1890):168–73.

———. "Historia de la antropología física en México." *American Journal of Physical Anthropology* 2, 3 (1919):229–49.

Léonard, Jacques. *La Médicine entre les savoirs et les pouvoirs*. Paris: Aubier-Montaigne, 1981.

Lepidus, Henry. *The History of Mexican Journalism*. Columbia: University of Missouri, 1928.

Leprun, Sylviane. *Le Théâtre des colonies: Scénographie, acteurs et discours de l'imaginaire dans les expositions, 1855–1937*. Paris: Editions L'Harmattan, 1986.

Levasseur, E. *Le Brésil . . . avec la collaboration de m.m. de Rio Branco, Eduardo Prado . . . d'Ovrem Henri Gorceix, Paul Maury, E. Trouessart et Zaborowski*. 2d ed. Paris: Le Syndicat Franco-Brésilien pour l'Exposition Universelle de Paris en 1889, A. Lamirail et Cie., 1889.

———, ed. *Le Mexique au début du XXe siècle*. 2 vols. Paris: Librairie C. Delagrave, 1904.

Liceaga, Eduardo. *Algunas consideraciones acerca de la higiene social en México: Estudio presentado en la Sociedad Médica Pedro Escobedo*. Mexico City: Tipografía Viuda de F. Díaz de León, 1911.

———. *Mis recuerdos de otros tiempos*. Edited by Francisco Fernández del Castillo. Mexico City, 1949.

Limantour, José Yves. *Discurso pronunciado por el Sr. Lic. José Yves Limantour, Secretario de Hacienda, en la reunión de clausura del concurso científico nacional*. Mexico City: Talleres de Tipografía, Encuadernación y Rayado de M. Gabucio, 1901.

Le Livre des expositions universelles, 1851–1989. Paris: Union Centrale des Arts Décoratifs, 1983.

Lobato, José G. *Estudio químico-industrial de los varios productos del maguey mexicano y análisis químico del aguamiel y el pulque*. Mexico City: Secretaría de Fomento, 1884.

Lomnitz, Claudio. *Exits from the Labyrinth*. Berkeley: University of California Press, 1992.

López Rangel, Rafael. *La modernidad arquitectónica mexicana: Antecedentes y vanguardias, 1900–1940*. Mexico City: Universidad Autónoma Metropolitana, Azcapotzalco, 1989.

Lowenstein, M. J., ed. *Official Guide to the Louisiana Purchase Exposition, at the city of St. Louis State of Missouri, April 30th to December 1st, 1904*. Saint Louis, Mo.: Official Guide Co., 1904.

Lucio, Rafael. *Opúsculo sobre el mal de San Lázaro o elefantiásis de los griegos*. Mexico City: Secretaría de Fomento, 1889.

El maguey y sus productos: Su importancia social como fuente de riqueza pública. Exposición dirigida al presidente de la Sociedad Agrícola Mexicana, con motivo de los ataques dirigidos al pulque. Mexico City: Tipografía Filomeno Mata, 1901.
Mallen, Bernardo. *Mexico Yesterday and Today, 1876–1904.* Mexico City: Müller Hermanos, 1904.
Mancera, Gabriel. *Informes que el C. Gabriel Mancera comisionado especial de la junta de exposiciones en los Estados Unidos de Norte-América y miembro de ella rinde sobre el desempeño de su cargo.* Mexico City: Imprenta del Comercio, de Dublán y Compañía, 1875.
Mandell, Richard D. *Paris 1900: The Great World's Fair.* Toronto: University of Toronto Press, 1967.
Manterola, Ramón. *Ensayo sobre una clasificación de las ciencias.* Mexico City, 1884.
Maria y Campos, Ricardo de. *Datos mercantiles, compilados por Ricardo de Maria y Campos.* Mexico City: Oficina Tipográfica de la Secretaría de Fomento, 1889.
———. *Renseignements commerciaux sur les États-Unis Mexicains.* Mexico City: Imprimerie du Ministère de Fomento, 1899.
Marin, Louis. *Utopiques: Jeux d'espaces.* Paris: Les Editions de Minuit, 1973.
Mariscal, Federico E. *La patria y la arquitectura nacional: Resúmenes de las conferencias dadas en la casa de la Universidad Popular Mexicana del 21 de octubre de 1913 al 29 de julio de 1914.* Mexico City: Imprenta Stephan y Torres, 1915.
Mariscal, Nicolás. *El desarrollo de la arquitectura en México.* Mexico City: Oficina Tipográfica de la Secretaría de Fomento, 1901.
———. *La enseñanza de la arquitectura en México: Observaciones relativas al proyecto de plan de estudios formado por los señores Nicolás Mariscal. . . .* Mexico City: Tipografía Artística Primera Revillagigedo, 1902.
Martí, José. *La edad de oro.* Río Piedras, Puerto Rico: Editorial San Juan, 1971.
Martínez Baca, Fernando. *Estudios de antropología criminal: Memoria que por disposición del supremo gobierno del estado de Puebla, presentan para concursar en la Exposición Internacional de Chicago, los doctores Francisco Martínez Baca. . . .* Puebla: B. Lara, 1892.
Martínez de la Torre, Rafael. *La salubridad del Valle y de la Ciudad de México.* Mexico City: Imprenta de la Escuela Nacional de Artes y Oficios, 1877.
Martuscelli, Eugenio. *Apunti sul Messico.* Naples: Tipografia Angelo T., 1892.
Mason, Otis T. "Anthropology in Paris during the Exposition of 1889." *American Anthropologist* 3 (January 1890):27–36.
———. "Progress of Anthropology in 1889." In *Annual Report of the Board of Regents of the Smithsonian Institution, Showing the Operations, Expenditures, and Condition of the Institution to July 1889,* 591–668. Washington, D.C.: Government Printing Office, 1890.
Masuoka, Susan N. "Architecture of the Turn of the Century: Mexico Enters the Modern World." *Journal of the West* 27 (1988):33–40.
Mathieu, C., and F. Cachin. *1889: La Tour Eiffel et l'Exposition Universelle.* Paris: Editions de la Réunion des Musées Nationaux, 1989.
Mayeur, Jean Marie, and Madeleine Reberioux. *The Third Republic from Its Origins to the Great War, 1871–1914.* Translated by J. R. Foster. Cambridge, England: Cambridge University Press, 1984.
Medina y Ormaechea, Antonio de. *Las colonias de rateros.* Mexico City: Imprenta del gobierno en el ex-Arzobispado, 1895.

———. *La Exposición Universal del Primer Centenario Mexicano*. Mexico City: Secretaría de Fomento, 1894.

———. *Iniciativa para celebrar el Primer Centenario de la Independencia de México con una exposición universal*. Mexico City: Oficina de la Secretaría de Fomento, 1893.

———. *México ante los congresos internacionales penitenciarios por el Lic. Antonio de Medina y Ormaechea: Edición especial destinada a la Exposición de Chicago*. Mexico City: Tipografía de Fomento, 1892.

Mestre Ghigliazza, Manuel. *Efemérides biográficas: Defunciones–nacimientos*. Mexico City: Antigua Librería Robledo, 1945.

Meulemans, Auguste. *Revue diplomatique: Chefs d'état, ministres et diplomates*. Paris: E. Déntu, 1889.

México. *Acta y documentos para la distribución de premios obtenidos en la Exposición Internacional de Filadelfia por los expositores de México*. Mexico City: Imprenta de Francisco Díaz de León, 1877.

———. Cámara de Senadores. 2ndo Año. Primer Período. *Dictamen de la Comisión de Industria que consulta no es de aprobarse el contrato celebrado entre el Ministerio de Fomento y el apoderado de la Compañía del Ferro-Carril de Tehuantepec, para revalidar la concesión de diciembre de 1874*. Mexico City: Cámara de Senadores, 1876.

México. El Colegio de México. *Estadísticas económicos del porfiriato: Fuerza de trabajo y actividad económica por sectores*. Mexico City: El Colegio de México, 1964.

———. *Historia general de México*. 2 vols. Mexico City: El Colegio de México, 1985.

México. Comisión de los Estados Unidos Mexicanos para la Exposición Pan-Americana de Buffalo, Nueva York. *A Few Facts about Mexico*. Mexico City, 1901.

———. *Official Catalogue of the Mexican Exhibit at the Pan-American Exposition at Buffalo*. Buffalo: White-Evans-Penfold, 1901.

México. Comisión Geográfico-Exploradora. Exposición Internacional Colombina de Chicago en 1893. *Catálogo de los objetos que componen el contingente de la comisión*. Jalapa, Mexico: Tip. de la Comisión Geográfico-Exploradora, 1893.

México. Comisión Nacional Mexicana. *Catálogo oficial de las exhibiciones de los Estados Unidos Mexicanos, Exposición Internacional de St. Louis Mo., 1904*. Mexico City: Tip. Secretaría de Fomento, 1904.

México. Comité Organizador de la Participación de México en la Exposición Ibero-Americana de Sevilla. *México*. Mexico City, 1929.

México. Commission Géographique Exploratrice de la République Mexicaine. *Catalogue*. Mexico City: Imprimerie F. Pichon, 1889.

México. Consejo Central de Salubridad. *Memoria leída por el Secretario del Consejo Central de Salubridad el día 17 de enero de 1867*. Mexico City: Imprenta Imperial, 1867.

México. Consejo Nacional para la Cultura y las Artes. *Jesús Contreras, 1866–1902: Escultor finisecular*. Text by Patricia Pérez Walters. Mexico City: Consejo Nacional para la Cultura y las Artes, 1990.

México. Departamento de la Estadística Nacional. *La estadística moderna y sus revelaciones: Edición publicada en español y francés*. Mexico City: Talleres Gráficos de la Nación, 1926.

México. *Dictámenes y resultados del Congreso Nacional de Higiene*. Mexico City: Imprenta del Gobierno en Palacio, 1884.

———. Distrito Federal. *Catálogo de monumentos escultóricos y conmemorativos del Dis-

trito Federal. Mexico City: Oficina de Conservación de Edificios Públicos y Monumentos, 1976.
México. Exposition Universelle Internationale de Paris 1889. *Catalogue officiel de l'Exposition de la République Mexicaine.* Paris: Générale Lahure, 1889.
México. Ministerio de Agricultura de México. Instituto Médico Nacional. *Travaux publiés par El Estudio . . . sous la direction de M. Secondino Sosa, edition française publiée por M Henri Bocaullon-Limousin.* Paris: Typographie A. Hennuter, 1892.
México. Museo Nacional de Arte. *Homenaje nacional a José María Velasco (1840-1912).* 2 vols. Mexico City: Museo Nacional de Arte, 1993.
México. Partido Revolucionario Institucional. *Tradición de la cultura: Nacionalismo Cultural: Carlos Obregón Santacilia.* Mexico City: Colección Forjadores de México, PRI, 1988.
México. Secretaría de Fomento. *Anales de la Secretaría de Fomento, 1857-1910.*
———. *Boletín de la exposición mexicana en la internacional de París,* 1887-1890.
———. *Bosquejo de una carta geológica de la República Mexicana formada por disposición del Secretario de Fomento, General Carlos Pachedo por Antonio del Castillo.* Mexico City, 1889.
———. *Documentos relativos a la venta de tabacos mexicanos en la Exposición Internacional de París, en 1889.* Mexico City: Tipografía de la Secretaría de Fomento, 1889.
———. *Exposición Universal Internacional de 1900, en París. Actas de organización.* Mexico City: Oficina Tipográfica de la Secretaría de Fomento, 1897.
———. *Lista de los premios y recompensas obtenidos por México en la Exposición de París de 1889.* Mexico City: Tip. de la Secretaría de Fomento, 1891.
———. *Memoria para la carta general geográfica de la República Mexicana: Año de 1889.* Mexico City: Oficina Tipográfica de la Secretaría de Fomento, 1890.
———. *Proyectos de edificio para la Exposición Internacional de París 1889.* Mexico City: Tip. de la Secretaría de Fomento, 1888.
———. *Reglamento económico de la Junta y personas auxiliares de la Comisión Mexicana en la Exposición Universal de París, aprobado por la Junta Directiva de México, en sesión extraordinaria de 7 del presente mes de marzo 1889.* Mexico City: Secretaría de Fomento, 1889.
México. Secretaría de Gobernación. *La salubridad e higiene pública en los Estados Unidos Mexicanos: Brevísima reseña de los progresos alcanzados desde 1810 hasta 1910.* Mexico City: Casa Metodista de Publicaciones, 1910.
México. Secretaría de Industria, Comercio y Trabajo. *Exposición iberoamericana de Sevilla 1929: La participación de México.* Mexico City: Talleres Gráficos Galas, 1928.
———. *México, sus recursos naturales, su situación actual: Homenaje al Brasil en ocasión del primer centenario de su independencia.* Mexico City: Edición de la Secretaría de Industria, Comercio y Trabajo, 1922.
México. Secretaría de Industria y Comercio. *Boletín de la Secretaría de Industria, Comercio y Trabajo,* 1922-1930.
México. Secretaría de Instrucción Pública. *Fiestas del centenario de la independencia, organizadas por la Secretaría de Instrucción Pública.* Mexico City, 1910.
México. Secretaría de la Economía Nacional. *Memoria de la Secretaría de Economía Nacional, 1939-1940.* Mexico City, 1940.
México. Tesorería General de la Federación. *Contaduría de la Federación: Cuenta pública.* Mexico City, 1889-1909.

Michelet, J. *Extraits historiques de J. Michelet.* Prepared by Ch. Seignobos. Paris: Librairie Armand Colin, 1907.
Mier, Sebastián B. de. *México en la Exposición Universal Internacional de París—1900.* Mexico City: Secretaría de Fomento, 1901.
Mitchell, Timothy. *Colonising Egypt.* Cambridge, England: Cambridge University Press, 1988.
———. "The World as Exhibition." *Comparative Studies of Society and History* 31, 2 (1989):217-37.
Monod, Émile. *L'Exposition Universelle de 1889.* 4 vols. Paris: E. Dentu, 1890.
Monteforte Toledo, Mario. *Las piedras vivas: Escultura y sociedad en México.* Mexico City: Universidad Nacional Autónoma de México, 1965.
Montenegro, Roberto. *Planos en el tiempo.* Mexico City: Imprenta Arana, 1962.
Moreno, Roberto. "Mexico." In *The Comparative Reception of Darwinism,* edited by Thomas F. Glick, 346-74. Chicago: University of Chicago Press, 1988.
———. *La polémica del darwinismo en México, siglo XIX.* Mexico City: Universidad Nacional Autónoma de México, 1989.
Motta, Marly Silva da. *A nação faz 100 anos: A questão nacional no centenário da independência.* Rio de Janeiro: Fundação Getulio Vargas, 1992.
Moyssén, Xavier. "El nacionalismo y la arquitectura." *Anales del Instituto de Investigaciones Estéticas,* no. 55 (1986):111-31.
Musil, R. *Ensayos y Conferencias.* Translated by José L. Arántegui. Madrid: Visor, 1992.
Nahmad, Salomón. "Las ideas sociales del positivismo en el indigenismo de la época pre-revolucionaria en México." *América Indígena* 33, 4 (1973):1169-82.
Nelms, Blenda F. *The Third Republic and the Centennial of 1789.* New York: Garland Publishing, 1987.
Niçaise, Auguste. *L'Archéologie à l'Exposition Universelle de 1889.* Paris: Martin Frères, 1890.
Nicolet, Claude. *L'Idée républicaine en France (1789-1924): Essai d'histoire critique.* Paris: Gallimard, 1982.
Nora, Pierre, ed. *Les Lieux de mémoire.* 2 vols. Paris: Gallimard, 1984.
Noriega Elio, Celia, ed. *El nacionalismo mexicano.* Zamora, Mexico: El Colegio de Michoacán, 1992.
"Notes on the Brazil Centenary Exposition." *Hispanic American Historical Review* 2 (1922):506-12.
Noyola Rocha, Jaime. "La visión integral de la sociedad nacional (1920-1934)." In *La antropología en México,* edited by Carlos García Mora, vol. 2, 133-222. Mexico City: Instituto Nacional de Antropología e Historia, 1987.
Obregón Santacilia, Carlos. *Cincuenta años de arquitectura mexicana.* Mexico City: Editorial Patria, 1925.
———. *El maquinismo, la vida y la arquitectura.* Mexico City: Editorial Letras de México, 1939.
Ocaranza, Fernando. *La novela de un médico.* Mexico City: Talleres Gráficos de la Nación, 1940.
O'Gorman, Edmundo. *México: El trauma de su historia.* Mexico City: Universidad Nacional Autónoma de México, 1977.
Olaguíbel, Manuel de. *Memoria para una bibliografía científica de México en el siglo XIX.* Mexico City: Secretaría de Fomento, 1889.

Olavarría y Ferrari, Enrique de. *La Sociedad Mexicana de Geografía y Estadística: Reseña histórica escrita por Enrique de Olavarría y Ferrari.* Mexico City: Oficina de Tipografía de la Secretaría de Fomento, 1901.

Olender, Marcos. "Le Premier Centenaire de la révolution et la participation brésilienne à l'Exposition Universelle de 1889 à Paris: espaces et mentalités." In *Les Images de la Révolution Française: Communications presentées lors du Congrès Mondial pour le bicentenaire de la Révolution,* edited by M. Vovelle, vol. 3, 2165–72. New York: Pergamon Press, 1990.

Oliveira, Lúcia Lippi. "As festas que a República manda guardar." *Estudos Históricos* 2, 4 (1989):172–89.

Orozco y Berra, Manuel. *Apuntes para la historia de la geografía en México.* Mexico City: Imprenta de F. Díaz de León, 1881.

———. *Historia antigua de la conquista de México.* Mexico City: Tipografía de G. A. Esteva, 1880.

Ortiz de Montellano, Bernardo. "Literatura de revolución y literatura revolucionaria." *Los Contemporáneos* 7, 23 (1930):77–81.

Orvañanos, Domingo. *Ensayo de geografía médica y climatología de la República Mexicana.* Prologue by Eduardo Liceaga. 2 vols. Mexico City: Oficina Tipográfica de la Secretaría de Fomento, 1889.

Ory, Pascal. "Étude comparée du centenaire et du cent-cinquantenaire de la Révolution Française." In *Les Images de la Révolution Française: Communications presentées lors du Congrès Mondial pour le bicentenaire de la Révolution,* edited by M. Vovelle, vol. 3, 2177–83. New York: Pergamon Press, 1990.

———. *Les Expositions universelles de Paris: Panorama raisonné, avec des aperçus nouveaux et des illustrations par les meilleurs auteurs.* Paris: Ramsay, 1982.

Ozouf, Mona. "Célébrer, savoir et fêter." *Le Debat,* no. 57 (1989):17–33.

Pani, Alberto J. *Mi contribución al nuevo régimen (1910–1933).* Mexico City: Editorial Cultura, 1936.

———. *La higiene en México.* Mexico City: Ballesca, 1916.

Pardo Bazán, Emilia. *Al pie de la torre Eiffel.* In her *Obras Completas,* vol. 19. Madrid: Edit. Administracíon, n. d.

Patent and Trade-Mark Laws of America. Bulletin no. 3. Washington, D.C.: U.S. Department of State, Bureau of the American Republics, 1891.

Paul, Harry W. "The Debate over the Bankruptcy of Science in 1895." *French Historical Studies* 5, 3 (1968):299–327.

Paz, Ireneo. *Los hombres prominentes de México. Les Hommes eminents du Mexique. The prominent men of Mexico.* Mexico City: Imprenta y Litografía de la Patria, 1888.

Pécaut, Daniel. *Entre le peuple et la nation: Les Intellectuels et la politique au Brésil.* Paris: Editions de la Maison des Sciences de l'Homme, 1988.

Peck, Annie S. "The International Exposition of Brazil." *Current History* 15, 5 (1923):1042–49.

Peñafiel, Antonio. *Explication de l'édifice mexicaine à l'Exposition Internationale de Paris en 1889.* Barcelona: d'Espase et Cía., 1889.

———. *Monumentos del arte mexicano antiguo: Ornamentación, mitología, tributos y monumentos.* Berlin: A. Asher & Co., 1890.

Pénin, Marc. "L'Économie sociale à travers le rapport de Charles Gide sur l'Exposition Universelle de 1900." *Le Revue de L'Économie Sociale* (1990):137–57.

Pérez Montfort, Ricardo. *Hispanismo y Falange: Los sueños imperiales de la derecha española*. Mexico City: Fondo de Cultura Económica, 1992.
Pérez Walters, Patricia. "Jesús Contreras (1866–1902): Imágenes escultóricas y personalidad artística." Tesis de Licenciatura, Universidad Iberoamericana, 1989.
Pesavento, Sandra Jatahy. "Exposições universais: Palcos de exibição do mundo burgues: Em cena, Brasil e Estados Unidos." *Siglo XIX*, no. 12 (1992):63–87.
Picard, Alfred. *Exposition Universelle Internationale de 1900 à Paris: Rapport général, administratif, et technique*. 3 vols. Paris: Imprimerie Nationale, 1903.
———. *Rapports du Jury International, publiés sous la direction de M. A. Picard*. 16 vols. Paris: Imprimerie Nationale, 1890–1892.
Pike, Frederick B. *Hispanism, 1898–1936: Spanish Conservatives and Liberals and Their Relations with Spanish America*. Notre Dame, Ind.: University of Notre Dame Press, 1971.
Pimentel, Francisco. *Obras completas publicadas para hacer la memoria del autor, sus hijos Jacinto y Fernando Pimentel y Fagoga*. Prologue by Francisco Sosa. 5 vols. Mexico City, 1903.
Plum, Werner. *Exposiciones mundiales en el siglo XIX*. Bonn: Instituto de Investigaciones de la Fundación F. Ebert, Instituto Latinoamericano de Investigaciones Sociales, 1977.
Pombo, Luis. *México, 1876–1892 [Estudio estadístico]*. Mexico City: Impr. de "El siglo diecinueve," 1893.
Pomian, Krzysztof. "Musée archéologique: Art, nature, histoire." *Le Debat*, no. 49 (1988):57–68.
———. "Musée, nation, musée national." *Le Debat*, no. 65 (1991):166–75.
Possonnier, Charles. *L'Exposition mexicaine*. N.p., n.d.
Pratt, Mary Louise. *Imperial Eyes: Traveling and Transculturation*. New York: Routledge, 1992.
Prevost, M., and Roman D'Amant, eds. *Dictionnaire de biographie française*. Paris: Librairie Letourey et Ané, 1954.
Prospectus of the Mexican International Exposition of Industries and Fine Arts to Be Opened in the City of Mexico, September 15, 1886. N.p., n.d.
Quevedo, Miguel Angel de. *Memoria sobre el valle de México, su desagüe y saneamiento, presentada a la Junta Directiva del Desagüe y mandada imprimir por la Secretaría de Fomento para la Exposición Internacional de París*. Mexico City: Oficina Tipográfica de la Secretaría de Fomento, 1889.
Ramírez, Fausto. *Crónica de las artes plásticas en los años de López Velarde, 1914–1921*. Mexico City: Universidad Nacional Autónoma de México, 1990.
———. "Dioses, héroes y reyes mexicanos en París 1889." In *Historia, leyendas y mitos de México: Su expresión en el arte*, 201–53. Mexico City: Universidad Nacional Autónoma de México, 1988.
———. *Saturnino Herrán (1887–1918)*. Mexico City: Universidad Nacional Autónoma de México, 1976.
———. "Vertientes nacionalistas en el modernismo." In *El nacionalismo y el arte mexicano (IX Coloquio de Historia del Arte)*, 111–67. Mexico City: Universidad Nacional Autónoma de México, 1986.
———, ed. *José María Velasco: Homenaje*. Mexico City: Universidad Nacional Autónoma de México, 1989.

Ramírez, Santiago. *Noticia histórica de la riqueza minera de México y de su actual estado de explotación*. . . . Mexico City: Secretaría de Fomento, 1884.
Rasmussen, A. "Les Congrès internationaux lies aux expositions universelles de Paris (1867–1900)." *Mil Neuf Cent. Revue d'Histoire Intellectual*, no. 7 (1989):23–44.
Rearik, Charles. "Festivals in Modern France: The Experience of the Third Republic." *Journal of Contemporary History* 12 (1977):435–60.
Reclus, Elisée. *L'Homme et la terre: Histoire contemporaine*. Paris: Fayard Edition, 1990. Originally published in 1906–1908.
Relph, Edward C. *The Modern Urban Landscape*. Baltimore, Md.: John Hopkins University Press, 1987.
Renan, Ernest. *Qu'est-ce qu'une nation?* Paris: Calnann Lévy, 1882.
Reyes, Rafael. *Apuntamientos estadísticos sobre la República del Salvador, escrita por Rafael Reyes, director general de estadística: Trabajo destinado a dar una idea del país en la Exposición Universal de París 1889*. San Salvador, El Salvador: Imprenta Nacional, 1888.
Rico González, Victor. *Hacia un concepto de la conquista de México*. Mexico City: Universidad Nacional Autónoma de México, 1953.
Riggs, Arthur Stanley. "The Spanish Exposition." *Art and Archaeology*, no. 27 (1929): 156–64.
Riguzzi, Paolo. "Mexico, Estados Unidos y Gran Bretaña, 1867–1910: Una difícil relación triangular." *Historia Mexicana* 41 (1992):365–436.
———. "México próspero: Las dimensiones de la imagen nacional en el porfiriato." *Historias*, no. 20 (1988):137–57.
Ríos de Lampérez, Blanca de los, et al. *Nuestra raza es española, ni latina ni ibérica. La Exposición Hispanoamericana de Sevilla y el problema de la raza. Artículos de Doña Blanca de los Ríos de Lampérez, de Don Adolfo Bonilla y Dan Martín, del profesor norteamericano Don A. M. Espinosa, y de Don Juan C. Cebrián, aparecidos en Raza Española y otras*. Seville, 1926.
Riva Palacio, Vicente. *Mis versos*. Madrid: Sucesores de Rivadeneyra, 1893.
———, ed. *México a través de los siglos: Historia general y completa del desenvolvimiento social, político, religioso, militar, artístico, científico y literario de México desde la antigüedad más remota hasta la época actual*. Barcelona: Espasa y Cia., 1887–1889.
Rivera y Cambas, Manuel. *México pintoresco, artístico y monumental*. Mexico City: Litografía Luis Garcés y M. Restori, 1880–1883.
Robelo, Cecilio A. *Diccionario de mitología nahuatl*. Mexico City: Ediciones Fuente Cultural, 1951.
Robina, Lucía. *Reconciliación de México y Francia (1870–1880)*. Mexico City: Secretaría de Relaciones Exteriores, 1963.
Robles, Martha. *Entre el poder y las letras: Vasconcelos en sus memorias*. Mexico City: Fondo de Cultura Económica, 1989.
Rodríguez Bernal, Eduardo. *La Exposición Ibero-Americana de Sevilla de 1929 a través de la prensa local: Su génesis y primeras manifestaciones (1905–1914)*. Seville: Excma. Diputación Provincial de Sevilla, 1981.
Rodríguez Prampolini, Ida. *La crítica de arte en el siglo XIX*. 3 vols. Mexico City: Universidad Nacional Autónoma de México, 1964.
Romero, José María. *Dictamen del vocal ingeniero . . . encargado de estudiar la influencia social y económica de la inmigración asiática en México*. Mexico City: Imprenta A. Carranza e Hijos, 1911.

Romero, Matías. *The Tehuantepec Isthmus Railway*. Washington, D.C., 1894.
Roumagnac, C. *Crímenes sexuales y pasionales: Estudio de psicología morbosa*. Mexico City: Librería Ch. Bouret, 1906.
———. *Por los mundos del delito: Los criminales en México: Ensayo de psicología criminal*. Mexico City: Editorial El Fenix, 1904.
Rousselet, Louis. *L'Exposition universelle de 1900*. Paris: Librairie Hachette, 1901.
Rovirosa, José N. *Tabasco en la Exposición de París: Opúsculo escrito por José N. Rovirosa por orden del Ciudadano Gobernador del Estado Dr. Simón Sarlat*. San Juan Bautista, Mexico: Tipografía del Gobierno de Tabasco, 1889.
Ruiz Castañeda, María del Carmen. *El periodismo en México: 450 años de historia*. Mexico City: Editorial Tradición, 1974.
Ruiz y Sandoval, Gustavo. *Estadística de mortalidad y sus relaciones con la higiene y la patología de la capital: Tesis para el examen profesional de medicina y cirujía*. Mexico City: Imprenta del Gobierno, 1872.
———. *Trabajos del Segundo Congreso Médico Mexicano*. Mexico City: Imprenta Francisco Díaz de León, 1881.
Ryckelynck, Xavier. "L'Économie sociale dans le rapport d'Alfred Picard sur l'Exposition Universelle de 1889." *Le Revue de L'Économie Sociale* (1990):97–107.
———. "Les Hommes de l'Exposition Universelle de 1889: Le Cas Alfred Picard." *Le Mouvement Social*, no. 149 (1989):25–42.
Rydell, R. *All the World's a Fair: Visions of Empire. International Expositions 1876–1916*. Chicago: University of Chicago Press, 1984.
———. "A Cultural Frankenstein? The Chicago World's Columbian Exposition of 1893." In *Grand Illusions: Chicago's World's Fair of 1893*, edited by Neil Harris et al., 143–70. Chicago: Chicago Historical Society, 1993.
Sáenz, Francisco. *Comité Organizador de la Participación en la Exposición Ibero-Americana de Sevilla*. Mexico City: Talleres Gráficos de la Nación, 1929.
Said, Edward W. "Third World Intellectuals and Metropolitan Culture." *Raritan* 9, 3 (1990):27–50.
Salado Álvarez, Victoriano. *Memorias de Victoriano Salado Álvarez*. Vol. 1, *Tiempo Viejo*. Mexico City: Edición y Distribución Ibero Americana de Publicaciones, S.A., 1946.
Salazar, Luis. "La arqueología y la arquitectura." In *Actas del XI Congreso Internacional de Americanistas*, 137–49. Mexico City, 1895.
Salmon, Philippe. *L'Age de la pierre a l'Exposition Universelle de 1889: L'Industrie, l'art et les races humaines prehistoriques*. Paris: Imprimeries Réunies, Établissement A, 1889.
Sánchez Flores, Ramón. *Historia de la tecnología y la invención en México: Introducción a su estudio y documentos para los anales de la técnica*. Mexico City: Fomento Cultural Banamex, 1980.
Sánchez Lamego, Miguel A. "Agustín Díaz, ilustre cartógrafo mexicano." *Historia Mexicana* 24 (April-June 1975):556–565.
Sánchez Santos, Trinidad. *El alcoholismo en la República Mexicana: Discurso pronunciado en la sesión solemne que celebraron las Sociedades Científica y Literarias de la nación el día 5 de junio de 1896, y en el salón de sesiones de la Cámara de Diputados*. Mexico City: Imprenta del Sagrado Corazón de Jesús, 1896.
Santa-Anna Néry, Frederico José de. *Le Brésil en 1889 avec una carte de l'empire en chromolithographie, des tableaux statistiques, des graphiques et des cartes: Ouvrage publié par*

les soins du syndicat du Comité Francobrésilien pour l'Exposition Universelle. . . . Paris: C. Delagrave, 1889.
Schávelzon, Daniel, ed. *La polémica del arte nacional en México, 1850–1910.* Mexico City: Fondo de Cultura Económica, 1988.
Schiller, Francis. *Paul Broca: Founder of French Anthropology, Explorer of the Brain.* Berkeley: University of California Press, 1979.
Schroeder-Gudehus, Brigitte. "Les Grandes Puissances devant l'Exposition Universelle de 1889." *Le Mouvement Social,* no. 149 (1989):15–24.
Seigel, Jerrold. *Bohemian Paris: Culture, Politics, and the Boundaries of Bourgeois Life, 1830–1930.* New York: Penguin Books, 1987.
Seitz, F. "Architects et engénieurs: L'Exposition de 1889." *Revue d'Histoire Moderne et Contemporaine* 39 (July-September 1992):483–92.
Sellerier, Carlos. *Data Referring to Mexican Mining, Prepared in View of the Participation of Mexico in the Universal Exposition of Paris in 1900.* Mexico City: F. P. Hoeck, 1901.
Sevcenko, Nicolau. *Literatura como missão: Tensões sociais e criação cultural na Primeira República.* São Paulo: Brasiliense, 1983.
———. *Orfeu extático na metrópole. São Paulo: Sociedade e cultura nos frementes anos 20.* São Paulo: Companhia das Letras, 1992.
Seville. *El libro de oro iberoamericano.* Seville: n. p., 1929.
Shapiro, Ann-Louise. *Housing the Poor of Paris, 1850–1902.* Madison: University of Wisconsin Press, 1985.
Sierra, Justo. *Compendio de historia de la antigüedad.* Mexico City, 1877.
———. *Evolución política del pueblo mexicano.* Caracas: Biblioteca Ayacucho, 1980. Originally published in 1900.
———. *México, su evolución social: Síntesis de la organización administrativa y militar y del estado económico de la federación mexicana.* . . . 2 vols. Barcelona: J. Ballesca y compañía, sucesor, 1900–1902.
———. *Obras completas.* 6 vols. Mexico City: Universidad Nacional Autónoma de México, 1948.
———. "México a través de los siglos." *Revista nacional de letras y ciencias,* no. 2 (1889):113–22.
———, ed. *Mexico: Its Social Evolution.* Translated by G. Sentiñón. 4 vols. Mexico City: Ballesca, 1900–1904.
Silva, José Luiz Foresti Werneck da. "La Participation de l'Empire du Brésil à l'Exposition Universelle Internationale de 1889 à Paris: La Section brésilienne aux Champ-de-Mars." *Revista do Instituto Histórico e Geografico Brasileiro,* no. 364 (1989): 417–20.
Silva Herzog, Jesús. *El pensamiento económico, social y político de México, 1810–1964.* Mexico City: Instituto Mexicano de Investigaciones Económicas, 1967.
Silverman, Debora L. *Art Nouveau in Fin-de-Siècle France: Politics, Psychology, and Style.* Berkeley: University of California Press, 1989.
Simmel, George. "Las ruinas." *Revista de Occidente* 2 (June 1924):304–17.
Skirius, John. *José Vasconcelos y la cruzada de 1929.* Mexico City: Siglo XXI, 1978.
Smithsonian Institution. *The Books of the Fairs: Materials about World's Fairs, 1834–1916, in the Smithsonian Institution Libraries.* Chicago: American Library Association, 1992.
Soberanis, Jorge A. "Catálogo de patentes de invención en México durante el siglo

XIX (1840–1900): Ensayo de interpretación sobre el proceso de industrialización del México decimonónico." Tesis de Licenciatura, Universidad Nacional Autónoma de México, 1989.
Somolinos D'Ardois, Germán. *Historia y medicina: Figuras y hechos de la historiografía médica mexicana.* Mexico City: Imprenta Universitaria, 1957.
Sosa, Francisco. *Apuntamientos para la historia del Monumento de Cuauhtémoc.* Mexico City: Oficina Tipográfica de la Secretaría de Fomento, 1887.
Stabb, M. S. "Indigenism and Racism in Mexican Thought: 1857–1911." *Journal of Inter-American Studies* 1 (1959):405–23.
Stamper, John W. "The Galerie des Machines of the 1889 Paris World's Fair." *Technology and Culture* 30, 2 (1989):330–53.
Stepan, Nancy Leys. *The Hour of Eugenics: Race, Gender, and Nation in Latin America.* Ithaca, N.Y.: Cornell University Press, 1991.
Sternhell, Zeev. "The Political Culture of Nationalism." In *Nationhood and Nationalism in France: From Boulangism to the Great War, 1889–1918,* edited by R. Tombs, 22–37. London and New York: HarperCollins Academic, 1991.
Stigler, Stephen M. *The History of Statistics: The Measurement of Uncertainty before 1900.* Cambridge, Mass.: Harvard University Press, 1986.
Stocking, George W. *Victorian Anthropology.* New York: Free Press, 1987.
———, ed. *Bones, Bodies, Behavior: Essays on Biological Anthropology.* Madison: University of Wisconsin Press, 1988.
Tablada, José Juan. *La feria de la vida (memorias).* Mexico City: Ediciones Botas, 1937.
Tassin, Étienne. "Identités nationales et citoyenneté politique." *Esprit,* no. 198 (1994):97–111.
Taylor, Anne-Christine. "L'Américanisme tropical: Une frontière fossile de l'ethnologie." In *Histoires de l'anthropologie (XVIe-XIXe siècles),* edited by Britta Rupp-Eisenreich, 213–32. Paris: Klincksieck, 1984.
Tello Díaz, Carlos. *El exilio: Un relato de familia.* Mexico City: Cal y Arena, 1993.
Tenkotte, Paul A. "Kaleidoscopes of the World: International Exhibitions and the Concept of Cultural Space, 1851–1915." *American Studies* 28, 1 (1987):5–30.
Thomas, Rosamund. *The British Philosophy of Administration: A Comparison of British and American Ideas.* London: Longman, 1978.
Thompson, J. Marie. "The Art and Architecture of the Pan-American Exposition, Buffalo, New York, 1901." 2 vols. Ph.D. diss., State University of New Jersey, 1980.
Thuillier, Guy. *Bureaucratie et bureaucrates en France au XIXe siècle.* Preface by Jean Tulard. Geneva: Librairie Droz, Centre de Recherches d'Histoire et de Philologie, 1980.
Tood, Frank Morton. *The Story of the Panama-Pacific Exposition.* 5 vols. New York: G. P. Putnam's Sons, 1921.
Torre, Juan de la. *Historia y descripción del Ferrocarril Central Mexicano: Reseña histórica de esa vía férrea, noticias sobre sus principales obras de arte, datos históricos, estadísticos, descriptivos, referentes a los estados, ciudades, pueblos, estaciones y en general todos los lugares notables de la línea.* Mexico City: Imprenta de I. Cumplido, 1888.
———. *Legislación de patentes y marcas.* Mexico City: Antigua Imprenta de Murguía, 1903.
Torri, Julio. *Diálogos de los libros.* Mexico City: Fondo de Cultura Económica, 1980.
Toussaint, Manuel. *La litografía en México en el siglo XIX: sesenta y ocho reproducciones en facsímil.* Mexico City: Estudios Neolitho, 1934.

Toussaint Alcaraz, Florence. *Escenario de la prensa en el porfiriato*. Mexico City: Universidad de Colima, Fundación Manuel Buendía, 1989.
Trabulse, Elías. *La ciencia en México*. 4 vols. Mexico City: Fondo de Cultura Económica, 1984.
——. *Las patentes de invención durante el siglo XIX en México*. Boletín del Archivo General de la Nación, 3d ser., no. 34. Mexico City: Archivo General de la Nación, 1988.
Trachtenberg, Alan. *The Incorporation of America: Culture and Society in the Gilded Age*. New York: Hill and Wang, 1982.
Trigger, Bruce G. *A History of Archeological Thought*. Cambridge, England: Cambridge University Press, 1989.
Trillo de Leyva, Manuel. *La Exposición Iberoamericana: La transformación urbana de Sevilla*. Seville: Servicio de Publicaciones del Excmo. Ayuntamiento de Sevilla, 1980.
Trocmé, Hélène. "Les États-Unis et l'Exposition Universelle de 1889." *Revue d'Histoire Moderne et Contemporaine* 37 (April-June 1990):283–96.
Valadés, José C. *El porfirismo: Historia de un régimen*. 3 vols. Mexico City: Universidad Nacional Autónoma de México, 1987.
Varigny, C. de. "L'Amérique à l'Exposition Universelle." *Revue des Deux Mondes* 95 (September-October 1889):836–66.
Vasconcelos, José. *Breve historia de México*. Mexico City: Ediciones Botas, 1938.
——. *El desastre*. Mexico City: Ediciones Botas, 1951.
——. *Indología: Una interpretación de la cultura ibero-americana*. Paris: Agencia Mundial de Librería, n.d.
——. *La raza cósmica: Misión de la raza iberoamericana. Notas de viajes a la América del Sur*. Paris: Agencia Mundial de Librería, 1925.
——. *Ulises criollo*. 3d ed. Mexico City: Ediciones Botas, 1935.
Vázquez, Josefina. "La historiografía romántica en México." *Historia Mexicana* 10, 1 (1960):1–13.
——. *Nacionalismo y educación en México*. Mexico City: El Colegio de México, 1970.
——. "Síntesis de la historia de México de historiadores mexicanos." In *Investigaciones contemporáneas sobre historia de México. Memorias de la tercera reunión de historiadores mexicanos y norteamericanos, Oaxtepec, Morelos, noviembre de 1969*, 213–27. Mexico City: Universidad Nacional Autónoma de México, University of Texas at Austin, 1971.
Vázquez, Luis. "Historia y constitución profesional de la arqueología mexicana (1884–1940)." In *II Coloquio Pedro Bosch Gimpera*, 30–77. Mexico City: Universidad Nacional Autónoma de México, 1993.
Vigil, José María. *Poetisas mexicanas, siglos XVI, XVII, XVIII y XIX*. Mexico City: Tip. de la Secretaría de Fomento, 1893.
Villar Movellán, Alberto. *Arquitectura del regionalismo en Sevilla, 1900–1935*. Seville: Excma. Diputación Provincial de Sevilla, 1979.
Villoro, Luis. *Los grandes momentos del indigenismo en México*. Mexico City: Ediciones de la Casa Chata, 1979.
Viollet-le-Duc, Eugène-Emmanuel. *Histoire de l'habitation*. Paris: Bibliothèque d'Education et Récréation, 1875.
Vitali, Olga. "1889: La Argentina en la Exposición Mundial de París." *Todo es Historia*, no. 243 (1987):29–37.

Vogüé, Eugène-Melchior de. *Remarques sur l'Exposition du Centenaire.* Paris, 1889.
Vovelle, Michel, ed. *Les Images de la Révolution Française: Communications presentées lors du Congrès Mondial pour le bicentenaire de la Révolution.* 4 vols. New York: Pergamon Press, 1990.
Wake, C. Staniland, ed. *Memoirs of the International Congress of Anthropology.* Chicago, 1894.
Walton, William. *Chefs-d'oeuvre de l'Exposition Universelle de Paris, 1889.* Philadelphia: G. Barrie; Paris: Barrie frères, 1889.
Weber, Eugen. "Of Stereotypes and of the French." *Journal of Contemporary History* 25 (1990):169–203.
———. *Peasants into Frenchmen: The Modernization of Rural France, 1870–1914.* Stanford, Calif.: Stanford University Press, 1976.
Widdifield, Stacie G. "Dispossession, Assimilation, and the Image of the Indian in Late-Nineteenth-Century Mexican Painting." *Art Journal* 49, 2 (1990):125–32.
———. "National Art and Identity in Mexico, 1869–1881." Ph.D. diss., University of California, Los Angeles, 1986.
Williams, Rosalind. *Notes on the Underground.* Cambridge, Mass.: MIT Press, 1990.
Womack, John. "The Mexican Economy during the Revolution, 1910–1920: Historiography and Analysis." *Marxist Perspectives* 1 (1978):80–123.
Wright de Kleinhans, Laureana. *Biografías de mujeres notables mexicanas de la época prehispánica, la colonia y el siglo XIX.* Mexico City: Secretaría de Instrucción Pública y Bellas Artes, 1910.
Yeager, G. "Porfirian Commercial Propaganda: Mexico in the World Industrial Expositions." *The Americas* 34 (October 1977):230–43.
Yengoyan, Aram A. "Culture, Ideology and World's Fair: Colonizer and Colonized in Comparative Perspective." 1993. Manuscript.
Zárate, Julio. *Compendio de historia general de Méjico para uso de las escuelas.* Mexico City: Tipografía La Providencia, 1892.
Zayas Enríquez, Rafael de. *Les États-Unis Mexicains, leur resources naturelles, leur progrès, leur situation actuelle.* Mexico City: Imprenta del Ministerio de Fomento, 1891.
———. *La rendición de una raza: Estudio sociológico.* Veracruz, Mexico: Tipografía de R. de Zayas, 1887.
Zelinsky, Wilbur. *Nation into State.* Chapel Hill: University of North Carolina Press, 1988.

INDEX

Academia de Letrán, 98
Academia de San Carlos, 55
Acedo, Angel, 134
Acevedo, Jesús T., 104, 208, 320n30
Acuña, Manuel, 150, 174
Adams, Henry, 7, 158, 198
Adorno, Juan Nepomuceno, 43, 134, 278–79n31
Afrancesamiento (Francophilia), 12, 20–22. *See also* France
Agriculture: French investment in, 275n33; use of statistics in, 129, 301–2n26
Aguilera, José G., 132, 303n42
Ahuhuétes (Velasco), 115
Aizpurul, Alberto, 151
Alamán, Lucas, 67, 69, 133, 207
Albert, Prince of England, 43
Alexander II (czar of Russia), 190
Alfonso XIII (king of Spain), 220, 231
Almanza, Cleofas, 55
Alt, Dr. (Geraldo Murillo), 215, 234
Altamirano, Francisco, 120–21, 142, 153, 305–6n4
Altamirano, Ignacio Manuel, 53, 97, 162
El alumbrado público en la ciudad de México: Estudio histórico (Arizpe), 316n37
Alva, José María, 66, 73
Alva Ixtlilxochitl, Fernando de, 120
Alvarado, Ignacio, 149
Alvarado, Salvador, 227
Álvarez, Manuel Francisco, 99, 295n25
Álvarez Bravo, Manuel, 233
Amabilis, Manuel: pre-Hispanic/modern synthesis of, 225, 228–31, 235–37; public buildings of, 227–28; on Victor Reyes's legends, 328n61; on Diego Rivera, 230; as Seville delegate, 226, 227, 326nn37,38
Amaral, Tarsila do, 201
Americanism: and European nationalism, 91–92
Anales del Instituto Médico Nacional (formerly *El Estudio*), 142, 149
Andrade, Mario de, 201
Andrade, Oswald de, 201
Annitúa, Fanny, 216
Anthropology: Chicago exhibits on, 185, 314n17; classificatory structure of, 88–89, 94; Mexican promotion of, 89, 95, 235–36, 292n31, 293n48; physical vs. ethnographic approaches of, 91–92; race issues of, 89–92, 93–94, 132; world fairs' focus on, 85, 87
Anti-Americanism: of postrevolutionary pro-Hispanics, 208, 214–15
Antiquities of México (Lord Kingsborough), 73
Anza, Antonio M. de: Aztec Palace of, 66, 73, 100, 182; Científicos peers of, 23; and Contreras, 61, 111; as engineer, 102, 295n33; Paris pavilion design of, 191, 193–94
Anzorena y Agreda, Luis, 55
"Apuntes para el estudio del clima en México" (Orvañanos), 309n61
Aragón, Agustín, 128
Araquistáin, Luis, 233

357

358 INDEX

Architecture: avant-garde cosmopolitan, 237–38; engineering and, 100–102; Latin American exhibits of, 97; Mexican professionalization of, 102, 296n37; modernist innovations in, 185, 315n21; national style uncertainty in, 97–100, 102–4, 193–94, 208, 321n44; postrevolutionary neocolonial, 201, 206–7, 208–9; pre-Hispanic form of, 100–101, 103–4; pre-Hispanic/modern synthesis in, 228–29, 231–32, 327n53; revived classicism in, 194–95
Argentina, 18, 43; architectural presentations of, 97, 327n53; as immigrant destination, 37, 176, 276n53; national image of, 19; statistical studies from, 129–30, 302n27; world's fair budgets of, 225, 281n9
Arias, Juan de Dios, 68
Ariel (Rodó), 222
Arista, Mariano, 43
Arizpe, Rafael R., 316n37
El Ateneo de la Juventud, 21
Atlanta Cotton States International Exhibition (1895), 85, 185–86
Aubin, J. M. A., 91
Au Mexique: Études, notes et renseignements utiles au capitalistes, a l'immigrant, e au touriste (Gostkowski), 59
Austria-Hungary, 17
Austrian Museum, 282n26
Avant-garde movements, 239–40
Avery, Isaac W., 40
Awards: Buffalo fair, 315n27; Chicago fair, 184, 315n27, 317n45; Paris 1889 fair, 21, 58, 59–60, 64, 121, 122, 131, 191, 302n37; Paris 1900 fair, 110, 191, 315n27; Rio fair, 215–16; Seville fair, 234, 328n74
Aztec Lilliputians, 85, 291n23
Aztec Palace: architects' criticism of, 98–99; commissions assigned to, 66; cost of, 189; disassembly/storage of, 181–82, 184, 313n2, 314nn3,5,6,7; as engineering/architectural exhibition, 101–2; as exotic/modern synthesis, 64–65, 67, 71, 73, 75, 77, 82–84, 123–24; facade of, 82, 94, 99, 105, 108, 110; inauguration coverage of, 79–80; interior designs of, 78–79, 82–83, 99; landscape paintings of, 112, 114–16, 121–22; media satirization of, 99, 169, 170–71; Peñafiel's design of, 66, 73, 75, 94–95, 289n43; photography exhibits of, 117–18; precursor to, 279n35; pre-Hispanic style of, 70, 97, 101, 103–4, 118–21; racial ambivalence of, 88; Salazar's proposal on, 66, 73, 103–4, 289n41, 296n42; scientific works in, 125–26; site and construction of, 78, 289n57, 290n59. *See also* Sculptures (Aztec Palace)
Aztecs: Contreras's eclectic sculptures of, 108, 110, 112, 297n64; cultural preeminence of, 70; mythology of, 105; Obregón's paintings of, 118, 119–21. *See also* Indians
"Aztecs and Their Industries" (Saint Louis exhibit), 85, 188
Aztec stand (Philadelphia exhibit), 39, 277n9

Bablot, Alfredo, 49, 61–62, 99, 285n88, 289n54, 308n44
Balbuena, Bernardo de, 31
Ballesca, Santiago, 68, 70–71, 286–87n14
Ballu, Albert, 97, 98–99
Baranda, Joaquín, 171
Barcelona exhibition, 220
Bárcena, Mariano, 40, 44, 50
Barreda, Gabino, 29
Batres, Leopoldo, 84, 88, 89, 93–94
Baudelaire, Charles-Pierre, 6, 71, 158
Baz, Gustavo, 79, 281n11, 297n59
Belgium, 17
Belmont, Andrés, 121
Beltrán, Joaquín, 49
BEMP (*Boletín de la Exposición Mexicana en París, 1889*), 280–81n2
Benjamin, Walter, 269n5
Berger, George, 23
Berlin fair (1883), 44
Bertier-Marriot, Clement, 276n44
Bianconi, F., 34, 58, 284n68
Bibliothéque Nationale (Paris), 282n26
Bibriesca, Alberto, 55
Bibriesca, Antonio, 121
Biographical dictionaries, 58, 284n65
Bishop, William Henry, 25
Black immigration, 36–37
Blanco, José Joaquín, 322n60, 324n85
Blumenbach, Johann Friedrich, 92
Boari, Adamo, 182

Boas, Franz, 93
La bola (Rabasa), 174
Boletín de la Exposición Mexicana en París, 1889 (BEMP), 280–81n2
Boletín de la Sociedad Mexicana de Geografía y Estadística, 143
Bolivia, 18, 19, 97, 280n48
Bonaparte, Prince Roland, 59
Bonilla, Abigael, 216
The Book of Thousand and One Nights, xi
Boston food fair (1908), 189
Botanical studies, 142, 143–44, 305–6nn4,10
Boulanger, Ernest Jean Marie, 25
Bourbourg, Brasseur de, 91
Bourgeoisie, Louis, 59
Bourget, P., 272n51
Brading, David, 246, 250, 286n5, 322n63
Brazil: Mexican delegation to, 203–4, 216; national image of, 19; neocolonialist renovation in, 202, 209; regional conflicts in, 201; statistical exhibits from, 130; as Vasconcelos's utopia, 219, 323n67, 324n85; at world's fairs, 43, 200
Brehme, Hugo, 233
British Library of the British Museum (London), 282n26
British Royal Commission, 17
Broca, Paul, 92, 93
Budgets: Chicago fair, 17, 262; media on, 167, 312n23; of Mexico, 262–65; New Orleans fair, 17, 40–41; Paris 1889 fair, 16, 17, 43, 49–50, 189, 262, 263, 281nn7,9; Paris 1900 fair, 49–50, 189; Philadelphia fair, 17, 39, 277n9; Rio fair, 319nn4, 5, 323n73; Seville fair, 224, 225, 326n23; state responsibility for, 17, 39, 40–41, 277n9
El Buen Tono (cigarette brand), 211
Buffalo world's fair (1901), 8, 11, 184, 187, 303n53, 315n27
Bulletin de l'Exposition Universelle de Paris 1889, 15
Bullock, William, 43, 278n28
Bulnes, Francisco, 21, 176–77, 311n3
Bustamante, Carlos María de, 67
Busto, Emiliano, 56; public administration study by, 137–41, 304n72, 305nn79,81; statistical focus of, 54, 128, 129; technocratic peers of, 23, 49

Cacama (Aztec hero), 77, 105, 108

Cahun, Léon, 112, 114, 115
Calles, Plutarco Elías, 202, 204, 222–23, 224, 232, 237
Calvo, Pedro, 282n40
Camaxtli (god), 77, 105, 108
Campa (photographer), 277n8
Campo, Angel del, 167, 174, 312n29
Campos Ortiz, Pablo, 205, 217
Cañada de Metlac (Velasco), 115
Canciones para cantar en los barcos (Gorostiza), 234
Canto, R., 71, 288n32
Carbajal, Antonio, 134–35, 148
Cárdenas, Guty, 325–26n22
Cárdenas, Lázaro, 236, 237
Carmona y Valle, Manuel María, 149, 173
Carneiro da Cunha Filho, José M., 209
Carnot, Sadi, 22, 25, 79, 201
Carrasco, Gonzalo, 41
Carta estadística minera de la República Mexicana (Chicago exhibit), 184
Carta general geográfica (Paris 1889 exhibit), 131
Carta general geológica (Paris 1889 exhibit), 132–33
Carta general minera de la República Mexicana (Paris 1889 exhibit), 132–33
La Carte générale de la République à la cent-millionèsime partie, par le système horizontal, 131
Cartographic exhibits (Paris 1889), 130–32, 302n37
Cartoons: as ironic critiques, 162–64, 312n10
Carvalho, R. de, 201
Casasola, Gustavo, 314n7
Casasus, Joaquín, 23
Caso, Antonio, 217, 234
Castillo, Antonio del, 132, 133, 303n42
Catholic church, 99, 169, 224, 231
Cazeneuve, Felipe, 58
Ceballos, José, 171, 313n45
Çelik, Z., 84, 98
Census, 54
Centeotl (goddess), 77, 105, 296n49
César, José María, 134
Chabert, Maximiliano M., 187, 197
Chacón, Manuel, 237
Chalchiutlicue (goddess), 77, 105, 296–97n50
Charcot, Jean-Martin, 138
Charnay, Desiré de, 67, 73, 85, 91, 288n34

Chavero, Alfredo: on Aztec Palace proposals, 77; on Camaxtli god, 108; exhibition team peers of, 55; Lerdo de Tejada panegyric by, 30–31; *México a través de los siglos*, 68, 70, 73, 84; Saint Louis fair exhibits of, 187, 315n29
Chávez Orozco, Luis, 275n33
Chicago Columbian Exposition (1893): Henry Adams on, 7, 198; antagonistic views of, 8–9; awards at, 184, 315n27, 317n45; exhibits at, 25, 56, 127, 131, 184–85, 314n17; Hispanism and, 222; Mexico's financing of, 17; U.S. national image and, 19, 41, 43
Chile, 18, 97, 216, 323n74, 327n53
Chinese immigration, 35, 36, 37, 276n51
Científicos, 23, 24, 29, 126, 128, 153. *See also* Porfirian elites
Cigarette companies, 175–76
Class: indigenist/Hispanic synthesis and, 239; modernity's construction of, 22–23, 88–89, 124, 292n31
Clavijero, Francisco Xavier, 31, 67
Clendinnen, Inga, 296–97n50
Climate: and disease transmission, 151, 152, 309n61
Colegio de Minería, 101
Colibert, E., 110–11
Colonia Juárez (Mexico City), 208, 321n44
Columna de la Independencia (Mexico City), 55
Comisión de Límites, 131
Comisión Geográfico-Exploradora, 131, 142–43, 184, 302n37
Comisión Geológica Mexicana, 184–85
Comtian positivism. *See* Positivism
Condorcet, Marquis de, 125
Congreso Internacional de Americanistas (1895), 91
Congreso Pedagógico Higiénico (1882), 150–51
Consejo Superior de Salubridad (Superior Sanitation Council), 147, 172, 173, 308nn35,36
Conservative liberalism: and state intervention, 137–40, 305n85
Contaduría de la Federación: Cuenta Pública (Mexico City, 1889–1890), 281n7
Contemporáneos group, 202
Contreras, Jesús, 55; awards to, 110, 191; bronze focus of, 78, 110, 297n59; Díaz Mimiaga and, 111, 297n62; in exhibition conflicts, 61; Paris pavilion design of, 191–92, 317nn46,47; relocated sculptures of, 182, 314nn6,7,10; sculptural style of, 105, 108, 112, 297n64; statuary corporation of, 112
Corbin, Alain, 150
Cornely, René de, 45–46
Correa, Alberto, 152
Cortés, Hernán, 212
Cosío Villegas, Daniel, 251, 287n15
Cosmes, Francisco, 20
The Cosmic Race (Vasconcelos). *See La raza cósmica*
Cosmopolitanism: controlled portrayals of, 2; exoticist reconciliation with, 81–82, 83–84, 114–15; nationalism and, 8, 9, 71, 96–97; of proindigenist trends, 209–11. *See also* Modern nation
Costa Rica, 18
Cotton States International Exhibition (1895, Atlanta), 85, 185–86
Covarrubias, José, 276n51
Crespo, Gilberto, 23, 50, 57, 170, 282n27
Criollo patriotism, 67, 69–70, 246, 250, 286n5. *See also* Indigenism
Cristero rebellion, 224, 231
La Crónica, 169
Cruces (photographer), 277n8
Cruces y Compañía, 118
Cruz, Juana Inés de la, 267n1
Cruz Conde, José, 220
Crystal Palace fair (1851). *See* London Crystal Palace fair
Crystal Palace (London exhibit), 100
Cuadro estadístico (Glümer), 54
Cuauhtémoc (emperor of the Aztecs), 66, 77
Cuauhtémoc monument: Herrera's design of, 55, 283n45; Rio fair's replica of, 205; sculptural style of, 77, 105, 108, 208; Vasconcelos on, 212–14, 322n60
Cuesta, Jorge, 251
Cuitlahuac (Aztec hero), 77, 105, 108
Cuvier, Georges, 92

Darío, Rubén, 195, 317n60
Darwinism: anthropological use of, 92–93, 293n48; geological links to, 132; mestizo fusion vs., 211–12; of Riva Palacio, 69, 93, 287n20

De historia plantarum Novae Hispanae (Hernández), 143
Democracy: as changing concept, 5
El descubrimiento del pulque (Obregón), 118, 119–21
De Vogüe, Eugène-Melchior, 81, 82, 100
El Diario del Hogar: on Aztec Palace, 169; on idealized national image, 161, 168, 172–73, 312n9; on Liceaga, 154; on Mexican world's fair, 45, 280n46; on propaganda, 176; on world's fair budget, 167, 312n23
Díaz, Agustín, 131, 306n7
Díaz, Felix, 196
Díaz, Porfirio: anthropology support from, 93; awards distribution by, 278n26; bust exhibits of, 55, 121, 283n45; Contreras and, 111, 297n62; exhibit interests of, 57, 85, 131, 138; exhibition team and, 49, 50, 60, 61, 62, 77; media satires of, 162–63, 165–66, 167, 170, 173; on social issues, 24; transformed regime of, 29; wife of, 25, 50, 184
Díaz Covarrubias, Francisco, 50, 281n11
Díaz Dufoo, Carlos, 129, 167, 312n29
Díaz Mimiaga, Manuel: appointment of, 47; in Aztec Palace negotiations, 78, 289nn57,59; Contreras and, 55, 111, 297n62; Porfirio Díaz and, 50, 165–66; difficult personality of, 61, 285n80; exhibition team role of, 47, 49, 59; media on, 170
Dirección General de Estadística, 129
Le Disciple (Bourget), 272n51
Disease: international debates on, 149; transmission of, 145, 148, 151–52, 153
Doctorow, E. L., 198
Dominican Republic, 18
Dostoyevsky, Fyodor, 6–7
Drainage systems, 148, 173, 308n40
Dreyfus affair (1894), 25
Dublán, Manuel, 166
Dunn, Archibald, 36
Dupaix, Guillerme, 67, 73
Dupont, R., 304n72
Durán, Diego, 289n43
Durán, Manuel, 171

El Economista Mexicano, 167
Ecuador, 18, 97
La Edad de Oro (Martí), 285n1

Edge Moor Iron Company (United States), 45
Edison, Thomas, 18, 135
Education: Paris 1889 exhibits on, 55–56; and racial fusion, 89–90
Egerton, Daniel Thomas, 282n40
Eiffel Tower (Paris 1889 exhibit), 27, 84, 98, 100, 101
Electricity exhibits (Paris 1900), 102, 189–90, 316n37
Eliot, T. S., 6, 188
El Salvador, 18, 130
Encina, Juan de la, 114
Engineering: architecture and, 101–2
England, 16–17, 34, 206, 275n33, 320n31
English Ethnological Society, 85
Ensayo de geografía Médica y climatología de la República Mexicana (Orvañanos), 151
Época Ilustrado, 162
Escandón, Pedro de, 43, 278n27
Escobarista rebellion, 224
España Fiel (Gómez Morin), 234
Esparza, Isaac, 134
Esparza Otero, Alfonso, 234
El Estudio (later *Anales del Instituto Médico Nacional*), 142, 149
Estudio sobre las razas mexicanas (Genin), 281n19
Ethnography: race issues of, 91–92. *See also* Anthropology
Ethnos, 211
Europe: exotic interests of, 7–8, 18, 97, 236–37, 329n78; Mexican anthropology interest of, 91, 292n41; public hygiene in, 145–46, 307n25, 308n32
Evolutionism. *See* Darwinism
Exoticism: cosmopolitanism's reconciliation with, 81–82, 83–84, 114–15; 1890s decline of, 102, 296n37; European demands for, 18, 97, 236–37, 329n78; and European nationalism, 91–92; Mexican exhibitions of, 7–8; of modernist architecture, 185, 315n21; of popular art, 215, 323n71
Explication de l'edifice mexicaine (Peñafiel), 84
Exponer (to exhibit, to expose), 162, 164, 312n10
Exposição Internacional do Centenario (1922). *See* Rio de Janeiro world's fair
Exposición Ibero-Americana (1929). *See* Seville world's fair

Expositions (Hamon), 312n10
Extractive arts exhibits: at Chicago fair, 184–85; at Paris 1889 fair, 57, 132–33, 283n56, 303n42

Fell, Claude, 215, 323n71
Fernández, Ignacio, 233
Fernández, Justino, 118, 120
Fernández, Leandro, 50
Fernández, Ramón, 47, 61, 79, 279n35
Fernández Leal, Manuel, 12, 51, 191, 317n47
Fernández Ledesma, Gabriel, 205, 206, 215, 217
Ferrari Pérez, Fernando, 50, 55, 282n27
Ferrocarril Nacional Mexicano, 116
Ferry, Jules, 16
Financing. *See* Budgets
Finlay, Carlos, 149
Flameng, Leopold, 122
Flaubert, Gustave, 8
Flores, Francisco, 149–50, 153
Flores, Manuel: media satirization of, 168; Paris 1889 exhibition role of, 24, 50, 77, 148, 271–72n42, 282n27, 308n44
Foreign investment: competition for, 19, 37; by France, 34, 275nn33,34; hygiene's importance to, 154–55; media satirization of, 161; patents registration and, 133–34, 303n53; Porfirian goal of, 33, 34, 126; statistical basis of, 129
France: anthropological approach of, 91–92; antipositivist reaction in, 26, 272n51; architectural trends in, 99–101, 102; Aztec Palace negotiations in, 78; classicist art of, 122; exoticist displays from, 7, 18; foreign investment interests of, 18, 34, 275nn33,34; freedom concept of, 5; hygiene concerns in, 144, 145, 307n25; Mexican diplomatic relations with, 47–48; Mexican media on, 168; Porfirian idealization of, xii, 12, 20–22; public administration study of, 137–38, 139, 304n72, 305nn79,81; revolution commemorative of, 15–16; social economy issues of, 22–24, 271n39; technocracy image of, 23, 125; transformed nationalism of, 25–26; universalism model of, 16, 17–18, 26–27, 249–50; world's fair budgets of, 16, 319n5
Freedom: fairs' celebration of, 4–5; Porfirian conception of, 31

French, Daniel Chester, 297n60
French Ministry of Finance, 138
French Revolution (1789), 15, 16
French Second Empire, 5
French Third Republic. *See* France
Fritel, Pierre, 123, 300n102
Fuente Salceda, María de la Concepción, 277n9
Fundición Artística Mexicana, 112
Funerales de un Indígena (Jara), 118
Furet and Rousseau (shipping company), 182, 314n3
Fuste, F., 71

Gabarrot, E., 57
La Gaceta Médica de México, 134, 150
Galindo y Villa, Jesús, 234
Galton, Francis, 87, 130
Gamboa, Federico, 150, 167, 234
Gamio, Manuel, 93, 208, 211, 214–15, 235, 321n44, 322n63
García, Augustín, 225
García, Pedro, 308n44
García Chávez, Antonio, 134
García Cubas, Antonio, 35–36, 55, 89, 129, 132, 174, 275n41
García Granados, Ricardo, 293n47
García Teruel, Gertrudis, 184
Garfias, Luis G., 215
Gargallo di Castel Lentini, Francesca, 287n15
Garnier, Charles, 84, 85, 98, 100, 103
Garza, Abraham P. de la, 50
Gaviño, Angel, 148–49, 153, 154–55, 308n44
Gayol, Roberto, 308n40
Genin, Auguste, 21–22, 50–51, 57, 59, 88, 281n19
Geographical sciences, 130–32, 174–75
Geologische Reichsanstalt (Vienna), 133
Geology exhibits. *See* Extractive arts exhibits
Germany, 17, 34
Gibson, W. Hamilton, 8
Gide, Charles, 144
Gilbert, James, 185
Glasgow world's fair (1890), 181, 313n2
Glümer, Bodo von, 54
Godoy, José Francisco, 40, 58, 277n15, 280–81n2, 326n34
Gómez, José L., 153
Gómez Morín, Manuel, 207, 217, 234, 321n40

Gomot, Hippolyte, 59
González, Gregorio E., 185–86
González, Luis, 32, 217
González, Manuel, 29, 40
González Martínez, Enrique, 216; awards to, 234; Mexican pavilion activities and, 321, 326–27n39; on Mexican revolutionaries, 224; on Victor Reyes's legends, 328n61; on Spanish republic, 223; Vasconcelos on, 226–27
González Navarro, Moisés, 275n41
Goodhue, Bertram G., 327n53
Gorostiza, José, 234
Gostkowski, Gustave, 59, 284n72
Goudeau, Émile, 27
La gran ciencia (Rabasa), 174
Greaver, María, 234
Grevy, Jules, 25
Gros Caillou (tobacco factory), 57
Groussac, Paul, 8–9
Guatemala, 18, 43
Guernica (Picasso), 237
Guerra, François Xavier, 273n6, 330n12
Guerra, Gabriel, 55, 121, 283n45
Guerrero, Omar, 305n79
Guerreros (Seville exhibit), 229
Guerry, A. M., 301n10
Guillon, François Pierre, 123, 300n102
Gutiérrez, Rodrigo, 118
Gutiérrez Najera, Manuel, 62, 175, 216, 285n88

Haber, Stephen, 33, 274n26
Hacking, Ian, 130, 301n21
Haiti, 18
Hale, Charles, 20, 93, 287n20, 293n48
Hall, Christopher J., 323n66
Hamon, Philippe, 312n10
Hamy, E. T., 91, 93, 97, 292n41
Hausen, Gerhard, 152
Henríquez Ureña, Pedro, 205
Hermosa, Jesús, 128
Hernández, Francisco, 142, 143
Herrera, Alberto, 55, 283n45
Herrera, Alfonso, 93, 306n10
Herrera, Luis R., 226, 328n68
Hidalgo, Miguel, 66
Hidgreth, Martha L., 308n33
El Hijo del Ahuizote: hygiene caricatures in, 173; ironic cartoon critiques in, 162–64; on Mexican exhibits, 166, 169, 312n21;

on national image presentation, 99, 160–61, 167, 170, 311n4; on Porfirian political machine, 164–65
El himen en México (Flores), 149–50
Hinojosa, Pedro, 171
Hispanic fair (1883, Buenos Aires), 44
Hispanism: emergence of, 208–9; indigenist synthesis with, 206–7, 209, 212, 214–15, 231, 239; Seville's modern expression of, 221–23; Vasconcelos's messianic, 218–19, 324n80
Histoire de l'habitation (Garnier), 100
Historia antigua de la conquista de México (Orozco y Berra), 289n43
Historia de la Nueva España (Sahagún), 289n43
Historia de las indias de la Nueva España e islas de tierra firme (Durán), 289n43
Historia de Méjico (Alamán), 67
History: as accessible narrative, xi, 267n1; Alamán's account of, 67; Aztec Palace's reconstruction of, 65–66; as development of reason, 4; modern view of, 1; Porfirian presentation of, 68–71, 95, 286nn11,12,13, 287n15
"History of Habitation" (Paris 1889 exhibit), 82, 84
Hobsbawm, Eric, 10
Hollyhock House (California), 315n21
Los hombres prominentes de México (Paz), 58, 61, 284n65
Honduras, 18
Hoover in Spanish America (film), 233
Huerta, Adolfo de la, 202–3
Huerta, Victoriano, 196–97
Hugo, Victor, 26, 27
Humboldt, Alexander von, 31, 67, 129
Hygiene: disease transmission and, 146, 151–53, 308n32; media satirization of, 171–73; medical profession and, 147–48; as national image element, 154–55, 156; Rio fair's emphasis on, 200, 318n3; sanitary engineering and, 148, 308n40; as scientific enterprise, 145–46, 307n25; state intervention in, 155–56; women's issues and, 149–51
Hymen studies, 149–50

Ibarrola, Ramón, 41
Ibero-American Exhibition (1929). *See* Seville world's fair

Identity, 244, 329n3. *See also* National image
Iglesias, José María, 29
Immigration: Chinese and black, 35, 36–37, 276n51; competition for, 19–20, 176–77, 276nn44,53; hygiene's importance to, 154–55; media on policy of, 160–61; patents registration and, 133–34; Porfirian goals on, 126, 300n7; from United States, 35, 39
Imperial Hotel (Tokyo), 185
Imperialism: exoticist displays of, 7, 18; French nationalism and, 25–26
Import-substitution policy, 35
Indians: educability of, 45, 89–90; evolutionary superiority of, 93–94; hygiene issues and, 156; in national image portrayal, 53; Porfirian ambivalence on, 88, 121; reconstructed past of, 66–67, 69–70, 73, 75, 77, 119–21. *See also* Aztecs
Indigenism: anthropology's advancement of, 235–36; cosmopolitan aesthetics and, 209–11; of criollo patriots, 67; Hispanism's synthesis with, 206–7, 209, 212, 214–15, 231, 239, 322n63; media on, 169–70; postrevolutionary monument to, 182, 184. *See also* Indians
Indología (Vasconcelos), 211
Industria de la plata (film), 233
La industria del petróleo en México (film), 233
Industrialization, 3, 17, 33, 53, 274n26
Inspección y Conservación de Monumentos Arqueológicos de la República, 84, 89, 292n32
Instituto Geográfico, 129
Instituto Geológico, 303n42
Instituto Médico Nacional, 127
International Congress of Conservation and Protection of Artistic Works (1889), 292n32
International corporations: world's fairs and, 45–46, 203, 319n15
International School of Anthropology (Mexico City), 93
Inventions, 134–35, 304n58
Islas, Flora, 216
Italy, 17, 35
Itzcoatl (Aztec hero), 77, 105, 108

Jackson, William Henry, 116–17
Jamba de la Fusión de las Razas (Seville exhibit), 229

Jambas (allegorical representations), 229
Japan, 41
Jara, José, 118
Jiménez Rueda, Julio, 234, 322n60
Johnson, William Templeton, 327n53
Jones, Owen, 100
Jornal do Commercio (Brazil), 205
Josat, Jules, 138, 139, 305nn77,79,81
Juan Antonio (Mexican Indian), 8, 54
Juárez, Benito, 66, 278n20

Kahlo, Guillermo, 215, 233
Keystone Bridge Company (Pittsburgh), 41
Kingsborough, viscount of, 67, 73
Knight, Alan, 30, 323n78, 330n13
Krantz, Jean-Baptiste, 23

Landesio, Eugenio, 114
Landscape painting, 112, 114–16; photography vs., 117
La Laterne journal, 144
Latin America: architectural presentations from, 96–97; collective exhibitions of, 47, 280n48; foreign interests in, 18, 34, 275nn33,34; idealization of France, xii–xiii, 22, 27; immigration competition within, 19–20, 176–77, 276n53; neocolonial hybridism of, 231, 327n53; Vasconcelos's ideas in, 204, 216, 323n74; Western-dominated nationalism of, 248, 330n12; world's fair participation by, 18–19, 40
Latour, Bruno, 307n25
Lavista, Rafael, 149
Le Berge (scientist), 307n25
Lechuga, Juan, 234
Leclerc du Sablon, Mathieu, 211, 322n54
Leçons sur l'étiologie et la prophylaxie de la fièvre jaune (Carmona y Valle), 149
Le Corbusier, 206, 209
Lelo de Larrea, Luis, 182
León, Luis L., 227
León, Nicolás, 89, 93, 215, 292n31
Le Play, Frédéric, 23, 144
Leprosy, 149, 152–53, 310n67
Lerdista group, 30–31
Lerdo de Tejada, Sebastián, 17, 29, 30–31, 39–40
Levasseur, E., 59, 130
La Libertad group, 29, 36, 98
La Libertad (Madrid), 231

INDEX   365

La Libertad (Porfirian newspaper), 20
Libraries: data distribution to, 51, 282n26
Liceaga, Eduardo, 151, 309n62; Científicos peers of, 23, 153; hygiene role of, 147, 154, 155, 310nn75,79; media criticism of, 172–73
Limantour, José Yves, 23, 49, 50, 126, 278n20, 281n11
Limantour, Julio, 50, 281n11
Lombardo Toledano, Vincente, 217
London Crystal Palace fair (1851), 4–5, 6–7, 43, 127, 278nn27,28, 301n10
López Velarde, Ramón, 251, 253
Louisiana Purchase International Exposition (1904, Saint Louis), 6, 85, 187–88, 315n29
Low Countries, 17
Lucio, Rafael, 149, 155
Lund, Macody, 327n46

Machines Gallery (Paris 1889 exhibit), 98, 100, 101
McKinley, William, 11
Madero, Evaristo, 51
Madero, Francisco I., 51, 196–97
Madrid historical exhibition (1892), 97
Malfatti, Anita, 201
Malgré-tout (Contreras), 110, 191
Mallarmé, Stéphane, 26
Malo, Salvador, 46
Mancera, Gabriel, 39
Mandell, Richard D., 316n38
"The Man Who Was King" (Eliot), 6
Mariátegui, José Carlos, 324n80
Maria y Campos, Ricardo de, 35, 54, 282n37
Mariscal, Federico E., 104, 208, 320n30
Mariscal, Ignacio, 57, 170–71
Mariscal, Nicolás, 102–3, 104
Marquina, Ignacio, 225, 326n29
Martí, José, 64, 81, 84, 285n1
Massachusetts State Board of Health, 310n68
Maximilian (emperor of Mexico), 20, 47, 68, 194
Maya architecture, 185, 315n21, 329n78
Mayer, Arnold J., 190
Media: on Aztec Palace, 99, 169, 170–71; on Porfirio Díaz, 162–63, 165–66, 167; fair envoys from, 167–68; on idealized national image, 159–62, 167, 168–69, 171–73, 176–78, 311n4, 312n9; on official indigenism, 169–70; on Porfirian political machine, 164–65; science caricatures in, 166, 171–75, 312n21; state's relationship with, 59, 159, 167–68, 311n3; on world's fair budget, 167, 312n23
Medical profession: hygiene contributions by, 147–48; as political elites, 153–54, 155–56, 310n79; women's exclusion from, 151, 309n56
Medina y Ormaechea, Antonia A., 45, 280n46
Mehédin, Leon, 279n35
Meissonier, J. L. Ernest, 122, 123
Melagraphie, ou nouvelle notation musicale par Juan Adorno (Adorno), 278–79n31
Melchert (photographer), 197
Mena, Francisco A., 171
Mendieta y Nuñez, Lucio, 235
Mendizábal, Miguel Othón de, 215, 235
Mendoza, Alberto, 225
Mestizos, 69–70, 89
Meteorites (Paris 1889 exhibit), 133
Meulemans, Auguste, 18, 269n17
Mexican Alhambra (New Orleans exhibit), 41, 278n20
Mexican-American War, 39
Mexican exhibits (Paris 1889): awards for, 131, 302n37; budget for, 49–50, 281n7; cartographic, 130–32, 302n37; commercial commission on, 54, 282n37; ethnographic focus of, 84–85, 291n21; extractive arts, 57, 132–33, 283n56, 303n42; group directors of, 50; hygiene and sanitation, 148–51; local fairs' collection for, 51, 282n26; media satirization of, 160–64, 166, 171–72, 312n21; national image goals of, xii–xiii, 34, 52–54; natural history, 142, 143–44, 306n6; patent protection for, 133–34, 304n54; product categories of, 55–58; proposed inventions for, 134–35, 304n58; public administration study, 137–41, 304n72, 350nn79,81; societies contributing to, 125–26; statistical, 127–28, 130. *See also* Aztec Palace; Sculptures (Aztec Palace)
Mexican Pavilion (Seville 1929): corruption and, 227, 326–27n39; cost of, 326n33; cultural continuities of, 235–37; design proposal for, 225; explanatory book on, 228, 327n42; legends for, 232, 328n61;

Mexican Pavilion (Seville 1929) (*continued*)
    pre-Hispanic/modern synthesis of, 228–31, 327n46
Mexican Revolution (1910): and national image transformation, 224, 228, 238–39, 240, 251–52, 326n25; reevaluation of, xii, 274n22
Mexican Society for Consumption (Sociedad Mexicana de Consumo), 45
"Mexican Village" (Atlanta exhibit), 85, 186
Mexico: ambivalent modernism of, 190–91, 194–96; anthropological developments in, 89, 92–94, 95, 292n31, 293n48; architectural expertise in, 101–2, 296n37; centenary independence festival of, 216; class structure of, 88–89; delegation to Brazil from, 202, 203–4; democracy's connotation in, 5; exoticist exhibits from, 7–8; financing of fairs in, 17, 39, 40–41, 49–50, 262–65, 277n9; foreign investment interests in, 34, 37, 275nn33,34; French idealization by, 12, 20–22, 123; under Huerta regime, 196–98; hygiene issues in, 144–45, 146–49, 155–56; Ibero-Hispanism and, 222–23; immigration to, 35–37, 176–77, 275n41; industrial transformation in, 33, 274nn22,26; landscape painting in, 112, 114–15; local collection fairs in, 51, 282n26; national image creation in, 158–60, 249–53; nationalism-modernization linkage in, 247–49; natural history tradition in, 142–44; under Obregón, 202–3; patents registration in, 133–34, 303n53, 304n54; population statistics, 152, 309n62, 310n63; postrevolutionary national image of, 223–24, 234, 238–39; public administration study of, 137–41, 304n72, 305nn79,81; Reform era of, 68; scientific developments in, 126–27; social-economy issues in, 24–25, 250–51, 271–72n42; technocratic bureaucracy in, 23, 29–30, 48; as world's fair location, 44–46. *See also* Porfirian elites
México: su evolución social (Sierra), 80, 286–87n14
México a través de los siglos, 66, 68–69, 70–71, 73, 170, 287n15, 288nn33,34; replacement of, 80
Mexico City: Paris vs., 169–70; as proposed fair location, 44–46; sanitation conditions in, 156, 172–73
México en París (Godoy), 58, 280–81n2
El México Gráfico, 174
"Le Mexique, a la France" (Genin), 21–22
Le Mexique a la portée des industriels, des capitalistes, des négociants importateurs et exportatuers et des travailleurs avec une carte du Mexique commerciale, boutière, minière et agricole (Bianconi), 58, 284n68
Le Mexique au début du XXe siècle (Levasseur, ed.), 59
Le Mexique, son passé, son présent, son avenir (Cazeneuve), 58
Michelet, Jules de, 12, 27, 251
Mier, Sebastián B. de, 49, 97, 189, 190–91, 263, 317nn46,47
Mier, Teresa de, 108
Mier y Celis, Antonia, 281n11
Miltgen, Julio, 290n59
Minas Gerais, 219
Mining École Supérieur (Paris), 133
Mining exhibits. *See* Extractive arts exhibits
Le Ministère de Finances (Josat), 305n79
Ministry of Communication, 185
Ministry of Economic Development, 38, 47, 49, 52, 116, 134, 138, 262
Ministry of Education, 207
Ministry of Finance, 54
Ministry of Justice and Public Education, 187–88
Ministry of Public Works, 262
Ministry of Sanitation, 155
Ministry of War, 54
Miscegenation, 211–12, 214. *See also* Race
Modern Art Week (São Paulo), 201, 209
Modernity: ambivalent view of, 10–11, 189–91, 194–96, 316n38; of Brazilian intellectuals, 201–2; contradictory connotations of, 6–7; exotic/cosmopolitan element of, 81–82, 83–84, 114–15; fairs' representation of, 1–3, 9; nationalism's link to, xii–xiii, 82, 247–49; style's construction of, 32, 98, 118, 123–24. *See also* National image; Nationalism
Modern nation: classificatory structure of, 88–89, 124; continuities in construction of, 235–37; hygiene/sanitation issues of, 144, 145–46, 156, 308n33; Indian past's synthesis with, 65–67, 71, 73, 75, 77;

Mexico's debut as, 234–35; peace component of, 32; Porfirian ideal of, xiii–xiv, 30–32; postrevolutionary versions of, 182, 184; public administration role of, 136–37, 139–41, 305n85; state's representation of, 40–41, 51–53, 282n27; statistical component of, 130, 136. *See also* National image; Nationalism
Modotti, Tina, 233
Molina, Luis G., 55
Monografías de arquelogía mexicana: Teotihuacán; o, la ciudad sagrada de los Toltecas (Batres), 84
Montenegro, Roberto, 205, 206, 215
Montiel Olivera, J., 226
Montoya, Matilde, 309n56
Monumento a la Patria (Mérida), 227–28
Monumentos del arte mexicano antiguo (Peñafiel), 75, 84, 289n45
Morales, José D., 153
Morales Pereira, Samuel, 152
Moreno, Roberto, 93, 287n20
Moreno Carbonero, José, 122
Moritz Rugendas, Johann, 282n40
Morones, Luis N., 225, 227, 239
Murillo, Gerardo (pseud. Dr. Atl), 215, 234
Musée National d'Histoire Naturelle (Paris), 133
Museo del Hospital Militar (Mexico City), 54
Museo Nacional de Arte (Mexico City), 283n41
Museo Nacional de Artillería, 182, 314nn6,7
El Museo Nacional (film), 233
Musical machine (Paris 1855 exhibit), 43, 278–79n31
Musil, Robert, 247
Mythological representation: in Aztec Palace, 75, 77, 105, 108

El Nacional, 99
Nahmad, Salomón, 293n47
Nahuatl mythology, 105
Napoleon III, 18, 44, 47, 165–66
Nashville world's fair (1896), 85
National image: architectural ambivalence on, 97–100, 102–4, 193–94, 208, 321n44; Aztec Palace's presentation of, 64–67, 71, 73, 75, 77; bronze sculpture and, 110, 297n60; centralized articulation of, 82–83, 243–44, 246–47, 252–53; domestic negotiation of, 245–46; goals in creation of, 249–53, 330n13; hygiene's contribution to, 154–55, 156; as ideal/reality contradiction, 159–60; media's critique of idealized, 160–62, 167, 168–69, 176–78, 311n4, 312n9; in *México a través de los siglos*, 70–71; Porfirian elites' production of, xii–xiii, 19, 33–34, 38, 52–54, 236, 244–45, 249–50; propaganda promotion of, 19, 35–36, 58–59, 276n44, 328n68; revolutionary movement's transformation of, 234, 238–40, 251–52; scientific character of, 125–26, 130–32, 173–75; Vasconcelos's conveyance of, 214–15, 216–19. *See also* Modernity; Modern nation
Nationalism: as an anational phenomenon, 241, 247; anthropology's ties to, 90–91; continuities in construction of, 235–37; cosmopolitanism and, 8, 9, 71, 96–97; French transformation of, 25–26; and identity, 244, 329n3; modernity's link to, xii–xiii, 82, 247–49; tradition-modernity dichotomy of, 248–49; universalist component of, 26–27, 249–50, 252. *See also* Modernity; Modern nation
National Medical Institute (Mexico), 142, 144, 148
La Naturaleza, 89, 115, 143
Natural history exhibits, 142–44, 305–6n4, 306nn5,6,10; media satirization of, 166, 312n21
Natural History Museum (Mexico), 143, 306n7
Natural Inheritance (Galton), 130
Naturalism, 26, 115
Naturhistorisches Museum (Vienna), 133
Neocolonialism: as indigenist/Hispanic synthesis, 206–7, 208, 209, 231; national architecture and, 104, 208, 321n44; of Rio fair exhibits, 201, 202. *See also* Hispanism
Nepaltzin, 128
Neri, Ramón P., 227, 239
Nervo, Amado, 167, 168, 174, 196, 198, 216, 312n29
New Orleans fair (1884), 38; awards at, 278n26; financing for, 17, 40–41; Mexican exhibits at, 25, 52, 142–43, 306n5

New Orleans fair (1885), 277n12
Newspapers. *See* Media
New York Herald, 279n38
New York Times, 39
New York world's fair (1939), 198
Nezahualcoyotl (Aztec hero), 77, 105, 108
Nicaragua, 18
Nicaraguan Canal project, 40
Nicolai, Georg Friedrich, 211, 322n54
Nicolet, Claude, 125
Noel, Martín S., 327n53
Noriega cigarette company, 175–76
North, Central, and South American Exposition (1885, New Orleans), 277n12
Notes sur le Mexique (Genin), 281n19
Noticias climatológicas de la República, recopiladas por la Secretaría de Fomento, para la formación de la Geografía Médica Mexicana (Ramírez and Rodríguez Rivera), 151–52
Nouvelle pharmacopée mexicaine (Herrera), 306n10
Novo, Salvador, 234, 328n68
Nuncio, Albino R., 186, 187, 197, 315n27

Obregón, Álvaro, 202, 203–4, 205, 212, 223, 319n19, 323n73
Obregón, José, 41, 55, 118–19
Obregonistas, 223
Obregón Santacilia, Carlos, 206, 209, 217, 225, 320n30
Obreristas group, 239
Ocampo, Cayetano, 55
O'Gorman, Edmundo, 246
Olaguíbel, Manuel de, 58
Olaguíbel y Aristas, Carlos de, 151
Olavarría y Ferrari, Enrique de, 68
Omaha world's fair (1898), 186
On the Origin of Species by Means of Natural Selection (Darwin), 92
Opúsculo sobre el mal de San Lázaro o elefantiásis de los griegos (Lucio), 149
Orientalism. *See* Exoticism
The Origins of Mexican Nationalism (Brading), 286n5
Orozco Ramírez, Francisco, 227, 233, 326–27n39
Orozco y Berra, Manuel, 67, 77, 108, 130, 293n44
Orquesta Típica Torreblanca, 216
Ortega, Juan, 55

Ortega y Gasset, José, 3
Ortiz de Montellano, Bernardo, 234, 326n25
Ortiz Rubio, Pascual, 223, 227
Orvañanos, Domingo, 23, 148; disease study of, 151, 152–53, 309n61, 310n68; on prostitution regulations, 150
Ory, Pascal, 23
Otero, Mariano, 29
Ottoman reformers, 67–68
"Our Facade in Paris: Sketches of the Universal Exposition" (cartoon), 170

El pabellón de México en la Exposición Ibero-Americana de Sevilla (Amabilis), 327n42
Pacheco, Carlos: exhibition team and, 50, 51, 60, 62, 77, 271–72n42; media criticism of, 166, 312n9; Río de la Loza and, 143–44; on small producers, 52; statistical department of, 129
Paez, F., 134
Paintings: accuracy-effectiveness paradox and, 120–21; European impressions of Mexican, 112, 121, 122–23, 300n102; French classicist, 122; landscape, 112, 114–16; neocolonial, 206; photography vs., 117; populist theme of, 230–31, 327n51; pre-Hispanic motifs of, 118–21
Palace of Electricity (Paris 1900 exhibit), 102, 189–90
Panama Canal, 18, 25
Panama-Pacific International Exposition (1915, San Francisco), 63, 196–98
Pan American Exhibition (1901). *See* Buffalo world's fair
Pani, Alberto J., 156, 212, 319n19
Paraguay, 18
Paris, 12, 169–70
Paris Universal Exhibition (1867), 44, 100, 144, 279n35
Paris Universal Exhibition (1889): anthropological research focus of, 85, 87; awards at, 21, 58, 59–60, 64, 121, 122, 131, 191, 302n37; budgets for, 16, 17, 43, 49–50, 189, 262, 263, 281nn7,9; catalogue of, 54, 282n38; classicist French painting at, 122; demolition of, 181; European boycott of, 17; exhibit categories at, 55–58, 283n56; exoticist aspects of, 7, 18, 81–82, 83–85, 290nn3,5; immigration goals of, 35–36, 37; inventions at, 134–35, 304n58; Latin American participants at, 18–19; media

critiques of, 161–64; as modernity model, 16, 269n5; national image production at, xii–xiii, 34, 52–54; patent protections at, 134, 304n54; product classification at, 15, 269n4; propaganda network for, 35–36, 37, 58–59, 276n44, 284n72; social concerns of, 22–23, 24. *See also* Aztec Palace; Mexican exhibits (Paris 1889); Porfirian exhibition team; Sculptures (Aztec Palace)
Paris Universal Exhibition (1900): ambivalent modernity of, 189–91, 194–96, 316n38; awards at, 110, 191, 315n27; budget for, 17, 189; Contreras's proposal for, 191–92; economy's impact on, 184; exhibits at, 23, 127, 144, 271n39; media agent for, 59; media critiques of, 162, 166; neoclassical pavillion of, 97, 193–94; Amado Nervo on, 198
Paris world's fair (1855), 6, 23, 27, 71
Paris world's fair (1878), 44, 47, 279n38, 280n48, 282n39
Paris world's fair (1937), 236, 237–38
Parra, Porfirio, 153
Partido Nacional Revolucionario (PNR), 223
Partido Revolucionario Institucional (PRI), 223
Paso y Troncoso, Francisco del, 85, 105
Pasteur, Louis, 138, 145, 146
Pasteur Institute, 282n26
Patents, 133–34, 135, 303nn51,53, 304n54
Payno, Manuel, 50, 68, 123
Paz, Ireneo, 58, 61, 167–68, 176, 284n65, 312n29
Peace, significance of, 32
Pedro II (emperor of Brazil), 200
Pelados (shorn ones), 215, 323n66
Pellicer, Carlos, 205, 216, 217
Peñafiel, Antonio: architectural synthesis of, 100; Aztec Palace design of, 66, 73, 75, 94–95, 289n43; book exhibits of, 84, 187, 315n29; exhibition team peers of, 50; on history of statistics, 128–29; hygiene role of, 148–49, 153, 308n45; media criticism of, 168–69, 172; sculptural representations of, 105, 108
Pérez Treviño, Manuel, 202, 203–4
Peru, 327n53
Pessoa, Epitácio, 201, 203, 209, 214, 319n16
Petit Trianon of Versailles (Rio fair replica), 201

Philadelphia fair (1876), 38; awards at, 282n39; financing for, 17, 39, 277n9; Mexican exhibits at, 25, 39–40, 115, 277n8; Pedro II and, 200
Photography, 116, 117–18
Physicians. *See* Medical profession
Picard, Alfred, 4, 23, 49–50, 59, 144, 271n39, 281n9
Picasso, Pablo, 237
Picq (architect), 97
Pimentel, Francisco, 36, 212
Piquerons Cotolí, Manuel, 327n53
Plancarte, Antonio, 170
Plano geológico del Peñón de los Baños donde se encontró el hombre fósil prehistórico (Paris 1889 exhibit), 132
PNR (Partido Nacional Revolucionario), 223
Poèmes aztèques (Genin), 281n19
Poincaré, Émile, 310n68
Pola, Angel, 168
Ponce, Manuel M., 234
Popular art, 215, 323n71
Popular patriotisms, 247
Porfirian elites: ambivalence toward Indian past, 88, 121; class structure of, 88–89; exhibition team of, 62–63; foreign investment goals of, 33, 34, 126; French idealization by, xii, 12, 20–22; homogeneity of, 29, 246–47; hygienists as, 153–54, 155–56; immigration policy of, 35–37, 126, 300n7; industrial development by, 33, 274n26; as masters of form/style, 4, 32, 60–61; media criticism of, 99, 160–62, 164–68, 173, 174–75, 312n10; Mexico City fair project of, 44–46; modern nation formula of, xiii, xiv, 30–32; national history enterprise of, 68–71, 95, 286nn11,12,13, 287n15; national image production by, xii–xiv, 19, 33–34, 52–54, 236, 244–45, 249–50; occupational makeup of, 273n6; postrevolutionary national image vs., 249–52; propaganda network of, 58–59; social economy indifference of, 24–25, 250–51; technocratic governance of, 23, 29–30
Porfirian exhibition team: budget commission of, 280–81n2, 281n8; budget submission by, 49–50, 281nn7,8; Huerta regime and, 196–97; internal conflicts of, 60–62, 77–78; lobbying for awards,

Porfirian exhibition team (*continued*)
59–60; members of, 50–51, 255–60, 281n11; product display directors of, 50, 281n12; recruitment/development of, 48–49; as Rio fair model, 205
Portes Gil, Emilio, 223, 224
Portugal, 17
El porvenir de las naciones latinoamericanas (Bulnes), 176
Positivism, 20–21, 26, 31, 115, 128, 218–19
Possonnier, Charles, 84
Pradilla, Francisco, 122
Prescott, William H., 67
PRI (Partido Revolucionario Institucional), 223
Primo de Rivera, Miguel, 220, 222
Product groups (Paris 1889), 15, 50, 51, 269n4, 281n12
Progress: contemporaneity and, 5–6; scientific/industrial foundations of, 2, 116, 126; selective manifestation of, 6–7, 9–10; and transformation of fairs, 10–11. *See also* Modern nation
Propaganda: films, 233, 328nn69,70; media on, 166, 176–77; newspaper contribution to, 51, 59, 167–68; Paris 1889 costs of, 58; to promote immigration, 19, 35–36, 37, 176–77, 276n44; on public administration, 137–41, 304n72; published works of, 58–59, 284nn68,72, 328n68
Prostitution regulation, 150
Prussia, 22
Public administration: Busto's study of, 137–40, 305nn79,81; corruption issues in, 140–41, 305n85; as scientific endeavor, 23, 29–30, 54, 136, 304n66; state intervention in, 137, 138, 140, 305n77
Public works, 53
Puente curvo del Ferrocarril Mexicano en la Cañada de Metlac (Velasco), 115
Pugibet, Ernesto, 57, 134, 175, 304n54
Pulque beverage, 118, 121
Putnam, F. W., 185

Quatrefages, Armand de, 92
Quetelet, Adolphe, 129, 301n21
Quevedo, Miguel Angel de, 148

Rabasa, Emilio, 174
Race: anthropological approaches to, 89–92, 93–94, 132, 292n31; class structure presentation of, 88–89; nationalistic concerns over, 82–83, 91, 156; population breakdown by, 152, 310n63; Vasconcelos's theories of, 211–12, 214, 218–19. *See also* Indians; Indigenism
Railroad construction, 33
Railroad paintings, 115–16
La Ramera (Acuña), 150
Ramírez, Fausto, 73, 96, 115, 289n43, 296nn37,42
Ramírez, José, 23, 88, 148–49, 151, 153, 280–81n2, 308n44, 310n75
Ramírez, Leandro, 134
Ramírez, Rodolfo, 226
Ramírez, Santiago, 40
Ramírez de Arrellano, Nicolás, 153
Ramos, José M., 226
Raygados Vetiz, José, 215
La Raza, 182, 184
La raza cósmica (*The Cosmic Race*, Vasconcelos), 204, 217, 323n67
Razo, Rómulo, 227, 228
Rebull, Santiago, 41, 55, 281n12
Reclus, Elisée, 12, 59
La Régie (tobacco company), 57
Reglamento económico (Bablot), 61–62
Renacimiento group, 98
Renan, Ernest, 69
Repide, Pedro de, 231
Republicanism, 5, 25
Revista de las Españas, 221
Revista de Revistas, 215
La Revista Moderna, 195–96
La Revue Diplomatique, 18, 269n17
Reyes, Agustín, 153
Reyes, Bernardo, 50, 196
Reyes, Rodolfo, 231
Reyes, Victor, 226, 229–31, 232, 327n51, 328n61
Reyes, Vincente, 66, 73
Rhetoric: of Porfirian political culture, 4, 32, 60–62
Riguzzi, Paolo, 262
Rio de Janeiro, 203–4, 219, 318n3, 323n67
Rio de Janeiro world's fair (1922): awards at, 215–16; budgets for, 319nn4,5, 323n73; Cuauhtémoc monument replica at, 205, 212–14, 322n60; exhibit supervision at, 204–5; Mexico's national image at, 216–19; neocolonial style of, 201, 202, 206–7, 208, 209; popular art at, 215,

323n71; sanitation focus of, 200, 318n3; U.S. interest in, 203
Río de la Loza, Francisco, 143–44, 306n15
Río de la Loza, Leopoldo, 143–44
Río de la Loza, Maximino, 134, 143, 304n54
Ríos, E. M. de los, 37
Ríos, Fernando de los, 233
Riva Palacio, Vicente, 80; Darwinism of, 93, 287n20; Porfirio Díaz and, 24; history texts of, 68–69, 287nn15,17; media satirization of, 170; mestizo nation of, 69–70; Ireneo Paz and, 284n65
Rivas Mercado, Antonio, 55, 101
Rivera, Diego, 197, 230
Rivera (exhibitor), 134
Rivero, M., 57
Robelo, Cecilio A., 296n49
Rochard, Jules, 145
Rodin, Auguste, 190
Rodó, José Enrique, 208, 222
Rodríguez, Francisco, 103
Rodríguez Rivera, Ramón, 49, 151
Rodríguez y Arangoity, Ramón, 45, 194, 317n53
Romero Rubio, Carmen (Mrs. Porfirio Díaz), 25, 50, 184
Romero Rubio, Manuel, 29
Rosenzweig, Alfonso de, 205
Rousseau, E., 78–79
Rousseau, Jean-Jacques, 4
Rubio, Romero, 33, 171
"Rue du Caire" (Paris 1889 exhibit), 82, 173
Ruelas, Julio, 197
Ruinas de Yucatán (film), 233
Ruiz, Carlos R., 280–81n2
Ruiz, Luis E., 150
Ruiz y Sandoval, Gustavo, 151
Russia, 17
Russian Revolution (1917), 240

Sáenz, Aarón, 223, 233
Sáenz, Francisco, 226, 227, 231–32
Sáenz, Moisés, 235
Sahagún, Bernardino de, 67, 108, 289n43
Saint-Gaudens, Augustus, 297n60
Saint Louis world's fair (1904). *See* Louisiana Purchase International Exposition
Saint-Simonianism, 10, 23
Sala, George A. H., 123, 300n102
Salado Álvarez, Victoriano, 196
Salazar, Luis, 187; Aztec Palace proposal of, 66, 73, 103–4, 289n41, 296n42; Contreras and, 61; Paris 1889 role of, 23, 280–81n2; pre-Hispanic style and, 100, 103, 296n41; professional background of, 102
San Antonio fair (1909), 189
Sánchez Solis, Felipe, 118
San Francisco world's fair (1915), 63, 196–98
Sanitation. *See* Hygiene
San Juan Teotihuacán (film), 233
Santa (Gamboa), 150
Santos y Cía, Eduardo, 281n8
São Paulo, 201–2, 219
Schálvelzon, Daniel, 279n35
Schnetz, E., 160, 311n4
Science: Mexican developments in, 125–27; Mexican envoys of, 148–49, 308nn44,45; modernity's foundation on, 2, 3, 126; Porfirian conception of, 31; propaganda books on, 58; public character of, 173–75; social economy applications of, 144–46, 307n25; of statistics, 127–30, 136, 301nn10,21,26, 302nn27,30; women's exclusion from, 150–51, 309n56. *See also* Hygiene; Public administration
Scientific Commission of Mexico, 91
Scraping machines, 134, 304n58
Sculptures (Aztec Palace): as national identity renderings, 75, 77, 105, 108, 110; storage/relocation of, 182, 314nn6,7,10; use of bronze in, 110, 297n60
Seler, Edward, 75, 289n43
El Senado de Tlaxcala (Gutiérrez), 55, 84, 118, 119
Sentíes, Pedro, 50, 129
Septien, Manuel, 155–56
Serrano, F. R., 233–34
Serrano, M., 184
Severo, Ricardo, 209
Seville Universal Exposition (1992), 268n23
Seville world's fair (1929), 324–25n2; awards at, 234, 328n74; budgets for, 224, 225, 326n23; cultural continuities of, 235–37, 238–39; Ibero-Americanism goal of, 220–21; Latin American exhibits at, 222, 231, 327n53; Mexican delegation to, 226–27; modernized Hispanism of, 221–23; propaganda on, 233, 328nn68,70; romanticized Revolution at, 224, 232–33, 326n25; Toltec-Maya exhibit at, 225, 326n33. *See also* Mexican Pavilion (Seville 1929)

Shapiro, Ann-Louise, 307n25
Sierra, Justo, 20, 21, 29, 55, 284n72, 286–87n14, 287n15
Sierra, Santiago, 20, 29
Social economy: French focus on, 22–23, 271n39; Porfirian indifference to, 24–25, 250–51; state intervention in, 144–45. *See also* Hygiene
Sociedad Mexicana de Consumo, 45
Sociedad Mexicana de Geografía y Estadística, 129, 131
Sociedad Mexicana de Historia Natural, 143
Société Cali, 78
Société d'Anthropologie de Paris, 92
Société des Études Pratiques d'Économie Sociale, 144
Soriano, Manuel S., 150
Sosa, Julio, 232
Spain, 17, 35, 208–9, 223, 325–26n22
Spanish-American War (1898), 220–21, 222
Spanish Conquest, 67, 68, 69, 77
"The Spanish Town" (Barcelona exhibit), 220
Spencer, Herbert, 211, 293n48
Stacy-Judd, Robert B., 329n78
Statistics, 127–30, 136, 301nn10,21,26, 302nn27,30
"Statistics and History of the Mexican Republic" (García Cubas), 132
Steiner, George, 190
"Streets of Mexico" (Buffalo exhibit), 85, 173, 291n21
Sullivan, Louis, 185
Superior Sanitation Council. *See* Consejo Superior de Salubridad
Sweden, 17
Switzerland, 177

Tablada, José Juan, 234
Taine, Hippolyte, 20–21
Tarascan Indians, 93
Tarditti, Carlos, 206
Technocracy: governmental role of, 23, 29–30. *See also* Porfirian elites
Tello, Othón, 314n17
Tenorio, Adolfo, 55
Tepoztecaconetzin Calquetzani (pseud.), 103
Textile fabrics exhibits (Paris 1889), 56–57
Textile industry, 33, 274n26
Thompson, E. H., 185
Tiffany Company (New York), 205, 320nn25,26

Tlaloc (god), 77, 105
Tolsa, Manuel, 314n10
Tomassi, Leopoldo, 226, 228
Toro, Alfonso del, 215
Torre Díaz, Alonso, 201, 205, 209, 217, 319n16
Torres Bodet, Jaime, 233
Torri, Julio, 205, 217
Totoquihuatzin (Aztec hero), 77, 105, 108
Toussaint, Manuel, 234
Tout-d'Union, 17
Traité d'hygiène sociale (Rochard), 145
Trans-Mississippi International Exposition (1898, Omaha), 186
Trejo Lerdo de Tejada, Carlos, 323n74
Treviño, Angel, 308n45
Trocadero Museum (Paris), 78, 282n26
El trompo de siete colores (Ortiz de Montellano), 234
Tuxtepec rebellion, 39
20th International Congress of Americanists, 214–15

United States: architectural style of, 201, 327n53; emigration from, 35, 39; fair participation goals of, 19, 40, 196; as immigrant destination, 37, 176, 276n53; Mexican investment by, 34, 275n33; national image of, 135, 250; propaganda from, 233, 328n69; San Francisco fair in, 196–97; world's fair budgets of, 17, 281n9, 312n23, 319n4; world's fair participation by, 43, 203, 221, 319n15, 325n10
Universalism: fairs' expression of, 1–4, 15, 269n4; French tradition of, 16, 17–18; of national image model, 26–27, 249–50, 252
University of California (Berkeley), 282n26
University of London, 282n26
University of Texas (Austin), 282n26
Urbina, Luis G., 233, 234
Uruguay, 18

Valadés, José C., 286n11, 287n15
Valdés, Rodrigo, 49, 50, 54, 148
Valenzuela, Jesús E., 196, 317n61
Vallarta, Ignacio L., 44
El Valle Nacional (tobacco factory), 57, 175
Varigny, C. de, 83–84
Vasconcelos, José: awards to, 234; on British

pavilion, 206, 320n31; budget requests by, 323n73; on Cuauhtémoc monument, 205, 212–14, 322n60; on immigration, 37, 276n53; Latin America prestige of, 204, 216, 323n74; messianic Hispanism of, 214–15, 218–19, 324n80; neocolonial synthesis of, 206–7, 208, 209; on popular art, 215; presidential campaign of, 223, 224, 229; race theories of, 211–12, 214, 218–19; as Rio delegate, 202, 204, 217, 319n19; utopian Brazil of, 219, 323n67, 324n85
Vázquez, Josefina, 286n13
Vázquez del Mercado, Alejandro, 217
Vázquez Schiaffiano, José, 215, 217
Velarde, Juan Andrés, 303n51
Velasco, Emilio, 47
Velasco, Idelfonso, 147
Velasco, José María, 41, 50; awards to, 121, 122; Léon Cahun on, 112, 114, 115; on French art, 96, 122–23, 300n104; interest in photography, 298n80; paintings of, 114–16, 117, 118, 144; prominence of, 55, 282nn39,40, 283nn41,45, 288n33
Velázquez, José María, 50
Velez, Carlos, 197
Venezuela, 19
Veracruz invasion, 197
Verlaine, Paul, 26
Verne, Jules, 135
Vianna, Victor, 216
Vigil, José María, 68, 184
Villa-Lobos, Heitor, 201
Villaurrutia, Xavier, 234
Viollet-le-Duc, Eugène, 85, 100–101
El virreinato (volume II of *México a través de los siglos*), 69

Waite, C. B., 197, 291n21
Waldeck, Jean Fréderic, 73
Weber, Max, 137
Wilson, Henry Lane, 197
Wilson, Woodrow, 196, 197
Wizards of progress. *See* Porfirian elites; Porfirian exhibition team
Women: exhibits on, 24–25, 41, 184; forums' exclusion of, 150–51, 309n56; scientific studies of, 149–50
Woolf, Virginia, 10

Working class: modernist emphasis on, 22–23
World's fairs: capitalist use of, 84–85, 175–76; as celebration of freedom, 4–5; ethnographic focus of, 84–85, 291nn21,23; exoticism aspects of, 7–8, 81–82, 290n5; Hispanism's ties to, 222; historical vantage point of, 1; immigration/investment goals of, 19, 126; late-twentieth-century, 11–12, 268n23; Latin American participation in, 18–19, 40; Mexico City location for, 44–46; Mexico's budgets for, 262–65; Mexico's participation in early, 43–44, 278nn27,28,31, 279nn34,35, 279nn38,40; as modernity representations, xi–xii, 1–3, 6–10, 16, 269n5; national image production at, xii–xiii, 33–34; natural history displays at, 142–44, 305–6n4, 306nn5,6, 306nn7,10; radical transformation of, xiii, 10–12, 198–99, 268n23; scientific developments and, 125–27; social issues at, 22–23, 24–25; state financing of, 16–17, 39, 40–41, 277n9. *See also* Awards; Budgets; *individual fairs*
World's Industrial and Cotton Centennial Exposition (1884). *See* New Orleans fair (1884)
Wright, Frank Lloyd, 185, 315n21, 329n78

Xochicalco temple (Paris 1867 replica), 44, 279n35
Xochiquetzal (god), 77, 105, 108
Xochitl presenta al rey Tépancalzin el pulque (Obregón), 118

Yacatecuhtli (god), 77, 105, 108
Yeager, G., 262
Yellow fever, 149, 153
Yucatán, 304n58
Yucatán: La tierra del afamado henequén (film), 233

Zamacona, Manuel María de, 45
Zárate, Eduardo, 50, 56, 61–62, 77, 290n3
Zárate, Julio, 68
Zayas Enríquez, Rafael de, 21, 34, 88, 176, 281nn11,19, 290n3
Zola, Émile, 26

Compositor: Integrated Composition Systems
Text: 10/12 Baskerville
Display: Baskerville

www.ingramcontent.com/pod-product-compliance
Lightning Source LLC
Chambersburg PA
CBHW031416230426
43668CB00007B/323